seventh edition

The Theory and Practice of International Relations

160201

Edited by

William Clinton Olson
The American University
Visiting Research Fellow,
Royal Institute of International Affairs
Chatham House, London

PRENTICE-HALL, INC., *Englewood Cliffs, New Jersey 07632*

Library of Congress Cataloging-in-Publication Data

The Theory and practice of international relations.

1. International relations.   I. Olson, William C.
JX1395.T49 1987   327   86–25459
ISBN 0–13–914573–7

Editorial/production supervision and
   interior design: **Susan E. Rowan**
Cover design: **John Olson**
Manufacturing buyer: **Barbara Kelly Kittle**

Printed in the United States of America

10 9 8 7 6 5 4 3 2 1

ISBN 0-13-914573-7 01

PRENTICE-HALL INTERNATIONAL (UK) LIMITED, *London*
PRENTICE-HALL OF AUSTRALIA PTY. LIMITED, *Sydney*
PRENTICE-HALL CANADA INC., *Toronto*
PRENTICE-HALL HISPANOAMERICAN, S.A., *Mexico*
PRENTICE-HALL OF INDIA PRIVATE LIMITED, *New Delhi*
PRENTICE-HALL OF JAPAN, INC., *Tokyo*
PRENTICE-HALL OF SOUTHEAST ASIA PTE. LTD., *Singapore*
EDITORA PRENTICE-HALL DO BRASIL, LTDA., *Rio de Janeiro*

DEDICATION

To the students whose excellence
in scholarship in International Relations
has earned them election to *Sigma Iota Rho,*
the national honorary recognition society in this field.

CONTENTS

PREFACE   xiii

PART I
THE INTERNATIONAL SYSTEM
AND ITS PARTICIPANTS

chapter 1
THE BASIC UNIT IN A COMPLEX SYSTEM   *1*
   Introductory Text and Discussion Questions

1. Nation-State and Nationalism   7
      Theodore A. Couloumbis and James H. Wolfe

2. The Actors in International Politics   13
      Arnold Wolfers

3. Powers: A Philosophical and Historical Perspective   17
      Martin Wight

chapter 2
THE INTERNATIONAL POLITICAL ECONOMY   *22*
   Introductory Text and Discussion Questions

4. I.P.E.—What Is It?   29
      Roger Tooze

5. The Structure of World Economic Cooperation   36
    Richard T. McCormack

6. Mastering the 'Worldeconomy'   38
    Albert Bressand

7. Positive Adjustment in an Increasingly Interdependent World   43
    Paolo Guerrieri

chapter 3
POWER AND THE BALANCING PROCESS   49
Introductory Text and Discussion Questions

8. Nine Variations of The Balance of Power   55
    Martin Wight

9. The Balance of Power and its Present Relevance   66
    Hedley Bull

chapter 4
*RULES AND ORDER
IN THE RELATIONS OF STATES   74*
Introductory Text and Discussion Questions

10. International Law: Myth or Reality?   81
    A. V. Lowe

11. The Utility of the United Nations   86
    Louis Henkin

12. Islamic Law and International Law   93
    Majid Khadduri

chapter 5
CHANGE IN THE INTERNATIONAL SYSTEM   96
Introductory Text and Discussion Questions

13. The Rise and Fall of the Modern System   101
    F. H. Hinsley

14. The International System: Unequal and Revolutionary   108
    David S. McLellan

15. The Passing of Remoteness   115
    Harlan Cleveland

PART II
PATTERNS AND OPTIONS IN STATECRAFT

chapter 6
NATIONAL BEHAVIOR IN CRISIS   122
Introductory Text and Discussion Questions

16. The Concept of the National Interest   128
    Fred A. Sondermann

17. Crisis and Superpower Behavior   136
    E. Raymond Platig

18. Lessons from the Falklands   144
    Andrew Burns

chapter 7
DIPLOMACY OLD AND NEW   148
Introductory Text and Discussion Questions

19. Diplomacy as Communication   155
    Alan James

20. The Future of Diplomats   157
    Charles Maechling, Jr.

21. The Twilight of Diplomacy   164
    George C. McGhee

22. Cultural Relations   169
    Frank A. Ninkovich

chapter 8
THE MANAGEMENT OF ALLIANCES   173
Introductory Text and Discussion Questions

23. The Dumbbell Won't Do   179
    John W. Holmes

24. The ANZUS Relationship   190
    Paul D. Wolfowitz

25. A New Piece in an Old Puzzle   194
    Charles Kegley and Gregory Raymond

chapter 9
FORCE: THE ULTIMATE OPTION   *199*
Introductory Text and Discussion Questions

26. Perception and Misperception:
    The Spiral of International Insecurity   207
    Robert Jervis

27. On the Use of Military Force
    in the Contemporary World   213
    Klaus Knorr

28. The Causes of Wars   219
    Michael Howard

chapter 10
ENDS AND MEANS IN FOREIGN POLICY   227
Introductory Text and Discussion Questions

29. The Moral Dimension of Diplomacy   234
    Kenneth Thompson

30. Ethics and Power in International Politics   247
    Michael Howard

31. Let's Sink the Lifeboat Ethics   252
    James W. Howe and John W. Sewell

PART III
SOME ISSUES IN CONTEMPORARY WORLD SOCIETY

chapter 11
HUNGER   256
Introductory Text and Discussion Questions

32. Ending Hunger   262
    The Hunger Project

33. Agricultural and Food Policy:
    The Conceptual Issues   268
    Bryan G. Norton

34. The Politics of Famine   277
    David A. Korn

chapter 12
HUMAN DIGNITY AND OPPORTUNITY   *285*
Introductory Text and Discussion Questions

35. What Terrorism Is and Isn't   291
    Charles Maechling

36. Terrorism and International Relations   292
    Irwin Wall

37. The Global System and the Realization
    of Human Dignity and Justice   294
    Harold K. Jacobson

38. The Inequities of the Old Economic Order   297
    Mahbub ul Haq

chapter 13
THE NEW HAVE-NOTS AND THE DEBT CRISIS   *304*
Introductory Text and Discussion Questions

39. What the Third World Wants and Why   309
    Stephen D. Krasner

40. LDC Debt: Beyond Crisis Management   319
    William H. Bolin and Jorge Del Canto

41. East-South Economic Relations   328
    Emilio Gasparini

chapter 14
CONFRONTATION AND THE NON-ALIGNED   *332*
Introductory Text and Discussion Questions

42. The New Challenge in Superpower Relations   337
    Claiborne Pell

43. The U.S. and the Revolution in Nicaragua   340
    James H. Wolfe

44. The Paradox of Non-Alignment   342
    Nicholas G. Onuf

45. The Future of Détente   347
    John Lewis Gaddis

Epilogue
THE STATE OF THE FIELD *352*

46. Observations on the State of the World 353
Charles Burton Marshall

47. The Study of "I.R.": How It Developed 354
William C. Olson and Nicholas G. Onuf

48. Joining Theory and Reality 364
Michael Banks

49. The Responsibilities of Competence in the Global Village 367
J. David Singer

PREFACE

First of all, both the title and the cover design reflect a desire to relate the practical and theoretical dimensions of contemporary thinking about the international system and some of its problems. The sections draw upon those who *do,* those who *think,* and especially those who think about what they do. Here I salute the insight of my former coeditors David McLellan and the late Fred Sondermann.

Second, you should not regard *The Theory and Practice of International Relations* as a textbook. While a well-organized professor presenting comprehensive, basic lectures may well use it as such, it is designed as a *second* book, a supplement to shed different light on basic knowledge which the good student will already have at his or her command before reading these almost fifty carefully chosen selections.

In the third place, there has been an effort to locate some of the most interesting recent pieces from sources not readily available elsewhere. To make the book more useful as a basis for discussion, either within or beyond the regular classroom teaching plan, you will find several questions ending each chapter's text. These are meant to be challenging, even provocative, and (like the selections themselves) avoid any "line" or doctrinaire approach.

In keeping with our previous practice, only a few of the selections have been utilized before, and the textual material has been carefully edited and up-dated. There is a new chapter on the international political economy and a change in the emphasis in several others, including the final series on the field of international relations itself.

Finally, the textual material opening each of the chapters should prove illuminating. These sections profit from the thoughts and exchanged views of the late Fred Sonderman, Dave McLellan, and myself, as we have seen all of the categories of I.R. develop since we were graduate students together in the Yale Institute of International Studies after World War II.

Not all textbooks divide the subject in exactly the same manner, but one is encouraged by the high degree of consensus which characterizes the literature of international relations today, both in this country and abroad, as a *field of study.* Not so questions of policy and polemics; and yet as members of a free society, we cherish our *differences of opinion.* Long may we all enjoy the privilege of disagreement.

It is customary at this point to acknowledge the assistance of those without whose help and patience this seventh edition would never have seen the light of midnight oil. I want to express my special gratitude to staff, colleagues, and friends who did a lot of dirty work of typing, proofing, editing, checking, searching, and sometimes even questioning what we were up to; especially Mary Eager, Professors Ted Couloumbis and Nick Onuf, John Luhman, Veronica Weht, and Tina Taylor of the School of International Service; Elizabeth O'Brien and Susan E. Rowan of Prentice-Hall. Special gratitude is felt and hereby expressed to two of my doctoral students, Farhat Hussein and Matthew Mallet, and to my long-suffering and wise spouse, Betsy.

WILLIAM CLINTON OLSON
Chatham House, London

The Theory
and Practice
of International
Relations

chapter 1

THE BASIC UNIT IN A COMPLEX SYSTEM

Nations dwell in perpetual anarchy, for no central authority imposes limits on the pursuit of sovereign interests. This common condition gives rise to diverse outcomes. Relations among states are marked by war and concert, arms races and arms control, trade wars and tariff truces, financial panics and rescues, competitive devaluation and monetary stabilization. At times, the absence of centralized international authority precludes attainment of common goals. Because as states, they cannot cede ultimate control over their conduct to a supranational sovereign, they cannot guarantee that they will adhere to their promises. The possibility of a breach of promise can impede cooperation even when cooperation would leave all better off. Yet, at other times, states do realize common goals through cooperation under anarchy.

Kenneth A. Oye,
"Explaining Cooperation Under Anarchy: Hypotheses and Strategies" p. 1
World Politics Vol. 38, No. 1 October 1985.

At least four great periods can be discerned in the development of the <u>fundamental feature of modern world politics, the nation-state</u>. The first involved the birth pangs of the new system which emerged from the Thirty Years' War in 1648, when the nation-state began to dominate. Prior to that the expression "international relations" was not even appropriate. The second brought twenty or so Central and South American countries, formerly colonies of Spain and Portugal, onto the stage as separate actors early in the nineteenth century. The third great moment followed in the wake of the First World War, mainly because of the breakup of the Austro-Hungarian Empire into its smaller national elements in the center of Europe but also because of the appearance of states throughout the world which wanted a voice in the new League of Nations. The fourth is still going on, heralded by what British Prime Minister Harold Macmillan called "the winds of change" sweeping across old colonial territories, so that today there are over 150 of these legalistically equal but politically and economically very unequal states whose spokesmen regularly address that beleaguered forum of international relations, the United Nations in New York.

The basic unit in international relations still remains the national state, despite spectacular shifts as well as routine adjustments in the configuration of world politics in recent years. Its designation as the most fundamental entity in contemporary world politics does not imply, however, that this is the only factor to be observed by anyone seriously endeavoring to make sense out of the politically confusing global environment in which we live. One could, for example, focus upon organizations within states such as powerful political movements and interest groups—inside and outside the formal governmental structure—which comprise the political entity to which we attach the shorthand label "nation-state." Or one could focus on individuals, some of whom exert considerable influence upon the course of events, both for good (Mother Teresa) and for evil (the random terrorist).

On the other hand, one might concentrate upon certain international supranational or other-than-national bodies such as world organizations (both public and private) which have made and continue to make an impact upon world affairs. Movements such as Zionism and institutions such as the Catholic Church, international labor unions, multilateral corporations, professional organizations—and literally hundreds of others—all participate in and to some degree alter the character of international relations. The selection in this chapter by the late Arnold Wolfers[1] takes many of these transnational forces into account. Concentrating upon the state and its government does not render the others irrelevant, as the remainder of this book will make quite apparent. The state is the central entity simply because, at this stage of human history, it lies at the core of power and human loyalty. It has not always been so.

To understand the nation-state, one must make some important distinctions. The first of these is the difference between the two elements "nation" and "state."

The term *nation* is essentially an ethnic one. It is, as the late Martin Wight shows in this chapter, based upon a common heritage, language, culture, and sense of identity among the people who make up a nation. *State* is a legal and territorial expression involving a population politically organized under one government with sovereign rights. Sovereignty refers to the exclusive jurisdiction that a state possesses within its territory and to its freedom to act in international affairs without being subject to the legal control of *any* other state. From a number of perspectives, a state may encompass more or less than one nation, just as a nation may or may not possess statehood; but taken together, nations and states form the units or bases of power whose interrelationships dominate the international system in which we live. It is the organization of human activities and loyalties into national communities that gives international relations in our time its distinctive character. This may not always have been so, nor is it always likely to remain so, but for present purposes this is the heart of the matter.

A second distinction is between the state and the government. This can perhaps be explained most easily by observing that while governments come and

---

[1]Tradition and nostalgia, as well as continuing relevance, determined this choice. It has appeared in every edition of *Theory and Practice* and was written by the editor's professor at Yale University.

go frequently, states come and go very infrequently. Normally, analysts of international affairs can depend upon the continued existence of a given state as a politically viable entity with infinitely more assurance than they can depend upon the continued existence of a given regime or administration of that state. The old saying "The King is dead; long live the King" emphasized the idea of the continuity of the state, despite a change in its leader. Today most monarchies are gone, but the states which they controlled (France, for example) still exist. In the United States, the term *the Administration* is used to describe the changing of the guard every four or eight years.

Third, it is most important to distinguish between states as they are organized for purposes of domestic government and internal politics, and states as they are organized for purposes of external relations or foreign policy. Among states, there are nearly as many varieties of internal organization as there are states themselves. There are federal states and unitary ones, dynastic states and republican ones, democratic states and authoritarian states, totalitarian states and those in which the government performs only a very limited function. It is the outward focus of a state—its ability to organize itself for purposes of conducting external relations, to formulate and pursue national goals abroad, and to enter into engagements with other states—that concerns those who would understand world politics, though they must increasingly take domestic influences into account.

As Couloumbis and Wolfe emphasize, the ethnic quality of the nation-state is a fundamental fact which is too often overlooked. Many of the new states were based upon artificial entities created in the last century by colonial governments in their rivalry to carve up Africa. They often contain within their boundaries as many as three, four, or more tribes or linguistic-cultural entities. Borders were drawn in such a way as to divide a people, putting part in one European country's colony and part in another's. In Asian societies, several different ethnic or religious groups have coexisted for many centuries (for example, in India or Indonesia); but as central governments attempt to exert their control, they make ethnically and regionally different people conscious of each other as rivals, thereby stimulating severe tensions and even civil wars. Minority nationalism has led to the breakup of Pakistan (Bangladesh) and the attempted breakup of Nigeria (Biafra). The border wars that have broken out between India and Pakistan, between Ethiopia and Somalia, and between Cambodia and Vietnam are all examples of the unsettled relationship between nationalism and government in many Third World countries.

These conditions markedly contribute to the tension and instability of the modern era, not only because of the breakdown of peace and order, but also because the superpowers are often drawn into choosing sides in these contests, with dangerous and costly implications for world peace and security. It is one of the great dilemmas of the modern world that many governments still lack the means of establishing their authority peacefully, either because their legitimacy is not recognized by part of the population, or because they cannot meet economic needs fast enough to allay the fear and suspicion that exists between different groups. But minority nationalism exists outside of Third World; the examples of Quebec, Ulster, and the Basque Provinces show that minority nationalism is a powerful force in developed countries as well. As a senior member of the Senate Foreign Relations Committee has pointed out in a widely-read article, the ethnic factor is of growing significance in the determination of United States foreign policy.[2]

Most students of the state use four widely recognized attributes to characterize this particular form of human organization. First of all, a state must possess *a territorial base.* It must be somewhere on the map. The dimensions of that base are irrelevant: Luxembourg is just as much a state as is the People's Republic of China. There are certain units, however, such as Liechtenstein, Andorra, and the Maldive Islands, whose status remains uncertain; they are sometimes grouped under the label of "ministates." The physical quality of any state, regardless of size, implies that its territory is defined, that it is circumscribed, and that within it, the government of the state has complete jurisdiction.

Another attribute of a state is that it must have a *government*—one that is capable of governing its people and meeting their basic needs, capable of entering into international commitments, and capable of abiding by its obligations. The specific form of government is less important to the analyst of international relations than is the effect that form may have on the government's conduct of its foreign relations. What is primarily important is that the government must have the loyalty and support of significant portions of the population, whether maintained by democratic or authoritarian means, in order to govern effectively.

A third characteristic of a state is that it has a *population.* Again, as in the case of territory, there is no clearly defined limit to the size of a state's population. Populations range from a few thousand people such as Tonga or Malta to perhaps a billion in China.

The final aspect of statehood is *sovereignty.* To understand this complex concept, one must first note that the contemporary state system dates roughly from the end of the Thirty Years' War, which ended with the Peace of Westphalia in 1648. The temporal rulers of England, France, and the German Reformation states, as well as the lesser princes and potentates of Europe, took advantage of the anarchy produced by the religious wars and assumed and kept authority within their respective territorial domains. Earlier, they not only had to bow to the authority of the pope in religious affairs and to the emperor of the defunct Holy Roman Empire in secular matters, but they also had to tolerate the challenge of powerful feudal lords within their own kingdoms. Now, supreme authority (or sovereignty) came to be identified with the state, whose rights, independence, and power derived from its "territoriality."

Once established, sovereignty connoted the right of each state to utilize the strength of its people and its resources in whatever way it wished, without regard for any political superior, either inside or outside the national territory. This transformation created a world of sovereign, independent states theoretically equal but varying widely in real power. Each depended for its survival upon balancing is own resources and ingenuity with the constellation of forces existing outside its own boundaries. We deal with this "process" in Chapter Three.

---

[2]Senator Charles M.C. Mathias, Jr., "Ethnic Groups and Foreign Policy," *Foreign Affairs,* 59, no. 5 (Summer 1980), 975–98.

From the middle of the seventeenth century on, then, individual security, diplomacy, international law, war, commerce, the development of culture and indeed of civilization itself would be influenced in their form and content by the nation-state, as the highest sovereign political entity. In its fundamentals, that system of nation-states, now extended around the globe, prevails to the present day.

Just before World War I, there were only about sixty-three independent countries in the world; on the eve of World War II the number had increased to seventy. Subnational movements may produce even more states as large states break up, as in the case of Bangladesh's separation from Pakistan. At the same time, new states may result from the union of smaller ones, as with the amalgamation of Tanganyika and Zanzibar into Tanzania. More than 100 states lie completely in the Northern Hemisphere; eleven lie athwart the equator, and the remainder lie completely in the Southern Hemisphere. Just under sixty countries lie completely in the tropics and nearly fifty in temperate zones, with the remainder straddling these geographic/climatic zones. About twenty states are insular. While almost thirty are landlocked, more than eighty face one or more bodies of water leading to the open ocean.

It would be a mistake, however, for the student of international relations to conclude from all this that the world is made up of completely independent political bodies, moving about, so to speak, on the table of world action like so many billiard balls, changing direction as they bounce off each other but remaining internally unchanged.[3] If there is a fundamental new trend in world politics, it is that the clear distinction between nation-states is breaking down, so far without destroying the integrity of the system. There are two primary indicators of this breakdown. One is the increasing ability of groups and even individuals within states to influence and even change the policies of governments toward one another, often apparently against the will of their leaders. The other is the fact that transnational forces (those which operate across national boundaries) are becoming more powerful, even though they do not yet threaten the existence or continuation of the independent-state system.

During the long period in which the international system afforded at least the dominant states an opportunity to develop in comparative peace and prosperity, the nation-state performed a timely and generally constructive function. With the coming of the twentieth century, however, certain trends which had already begun to undermine the principle of territorial impenetrability (the ability of each country to exist alongside similar states), became more pronounced, particularly after the Second World War. These trends reflect the difficulties inherent in the application of the principle of self-determination, in the intensified development of techniques and instruments of ideological-political interpenetration, in growing economic interdependence, and in the accelerated development of weapons of mass destruction.

---

[3]Hans Morgenthau, a leading authority on politics among nations, argued that the nation-state is already obsolete, citing the absence of many of its characteristics in the new states which have emerged in the past half century. See *Truth and Power: Essays of a Decade, 1960–70* (New York: Holt, Rinehart & Winston, 1970), p. 274.

It remains to be seen whether these trends portend an end of the nation-state system as the world has known it in its various transmutations over the past 300 or more years. For the moment, however, the system based upon the interrelationships of nation-states continues, in its often frightening way, to prevail if not to flourish. Hence, before turning to the nature of that complicated system, we must first give our attention to the entities whose interplay makes the system what it is today.

DISCUSSION QUESTIONS

1. What does Wight mean by "powers"?

2. Do you agree with Wolfers that it is the "state-as-actor" that still best serves as the foundation for a theory of international politics?

3. Couloumbis and Wolfe emphasize the distinction between the nation (nationalism) and the state (government). Why have most newly emergent or Third World governments had to engage in a conscious effort to develop a sense of nationhood and nationalism among their people?

4. How do the dangers and problems posed by multiethnic societies help us to understand the stresses and violence many countries are experiencing?

5. Many say that nationalism is a menace to peace. Yet patriotism is usually greatly admired. How do you account for this apparent contradiction?

6. From what the several writers say, do you expect an early end to the nation-state system? If so, do you see any prospect of an alternative? If not, do you think "wars and rumors of wars" will continue to plague the human race indefinitely?

1. Nation-State and Nationalism

Theodore A. Couloumbis/James H. Wolfe

A specialist on the element of ethnicity in international politics, Dr. Couloumbis is a Professor on the Faculty of Law at the University of Thessaloniki, Greece. James Wolfe is a Professor of International Relations and Political Science at the University of Southern Mississippi.

Nations and States

The terms "nation" and "state" are quite distinct conceptually, yet unfortunately they are often used interchangeably. The nation is an historical concept founded on a cultural identity shared by a single people; the state is a political unit defined in terms of population, territory, and an autonomous government. The state provides a basis for political loyalty in the form of citizenship, whereas the nation promotes an effective relationship through which the individual gains a sense of identity. Nations and states do not always have the same cultural and territorial boundaries. Therefore, the term nation-state has been used by social scientists to denote the gradual fusion that may occur between cultural and political boundaries after prolonged maintenance of political control of a population by a centralized governmental authority.

Nationalism can be defined as a perceived identity of oneself with a territorially organized political collectivity, such as the United States, the USSR, and other countries. The psychological need to define oneself in terms of membership in a given political community is at the root of nationalist sentiment. The hallmarks of nationalism are a sense of territoriality manifested in a love of one's

This selection is excerpted from Theodore A. Couloumbis and James H. Wolfe, *Introduction to International Relations: Power and Justice,* 3rd edition, © 1986, pp. 64–83. Reprinted by permission of Prentice-Hall, Inc., Englewood Cliffs, New Jersey. (Most footnotes have been removed; those remaining have been renumbered.)

homeland, a written and spoken language, a tradition of achievement in the arts and literature, a narrative history (as opposed to legends or folktales), and, frequently, the perpetuation from generation to generation of the fear of the "enemy" whose real or imagined hostility threatens the security of the nation. . . .

The first large national entities in the West developed in Spain, England, and France between the middle of the thirteenth century and the middle of the sixteenth century. These nation-states were initially loose and pluralist agglomerations of people held together primarily by the absolute authority of monarchs. Spain, for example, emerged as a single country as a result of the fusion of Aragon and Castile following the marriage of Ferdinand and Isabella.

Dynastic legitimacy rather than national cohesiveness provided the cement that kept countries such as Spain, France, and Britain together. The rising merchant and professional middle classes found that the absolute power of the king was a convenient device for eroding the power of corrupt and decadent traditional aristocracies and distant imperial bonds. But for the process of modern nationalist development to be completed, supreme authority had to be transferred from kings and queens to the people.

Seventeenth-century England is usually presented as the first modern nation-state in which nationalism became coequal with the idea of individual liberties and popular participation in public affairs. The American Revolution (1776) and the French Revolution (1789) are landmarks in the development of heterogeneous nationalism (in the United States) and homogeneous nationalism (in France). The United States was the result of the unification of former British colonies that had fought against their metropolis to obtain political rights, tolerance of religious diversity, and individual liberties. The Declaration of Independence proclaimed a brand of nationalism based on the perpetuation of a system of liberal ideas and a pluralist and secular way of lie. Certain "truths" were held to be self-evident, "that all men are created equal that they are endowed by their Creator with certain inalienable rights, that among these are life, liberty, and the pursuit of happiness." Given the subsequent ethnic and religious diversity of Americans, the coining of the patriotic slogan *e pluribus unum* is not surprising.

French nationalism was more vigorous, romantic, and culturally homogeneous than the verbally restrained Anglo-Saxon versions, but equally expansionist. Maximilien Robespierre (1758–1794), one of the masterminds of the French Revolution, exemplified the French spirit with these words of self-sacrifice: "I am French, I am one of thy [France's] representatives. . . . Oh sublime people! Accept the sacrifices of my whole being. Happy is the man who is born in your midst; happier is he who can die for your happiness."[1] Napoleon Bonaparte transformed nationalist sentiments such as these into an expansionist ideology. The institution of mass conscription called for deep and tangible involvement of citizens in the life of the nation. Napoleon's "citizen armies" carried him to victory after victory throughout Europe and the Middle East. Eventually, he was defeated by the very forces of nationalism he had helped awaken.

A third variation of nationalism is associated with the North American frontier of the eighteenth and nineteenth centuries and with the political unification of Germany (1864–1871). Some of the proponents of this brand of nationalism likened the state to a living organism passing through the phases of birth, adolescence, maturity, and finally old age. Often, they claimed a dominant role for their nation because of its presumed superior biological heritage. Others saw the nation-state as inspired by a divine idea and charged it with a unique historical mission. Whatever the nuances of interpretation, a central idea unites what came to be known as the organic school: the state must expand or die; the conquest of living space (*Lebensraum*) is therefore vital. Benito Mussolini (1883–1945), the *Duce* of Fascist Italy, epitomized the organic view of the nation-state:

> Fascism is an historical conception, in which man is what he is only insofar as he works with the spiritual process in which he finds himself, in the family or social group, in the nation and in the history in which all nations collaborate. . . . Outside history man is nothing. Consequently Fascism is opposed to all the individualistic abstractions of a materialistic nature like those of the eighteenth century; . . . Against individualism, the Fascist conception is for the State; and it is for the individual insofar as he coincides with the State, which is the conscience and universal will of man in his historical existence. . . . The nation as the State is an ethical reality which exists and lives insofar as it develops. To arrest its development is to kill it. . . . Thus [the State] can be likened to the human will which knows no limits to its development and realizes itself in testing its own limitlessness.[2]

The organic and mystical conception of the nation-state was built substantially on the philosophical foundations provided by Georg Wilhelm Friedrich Hegel (1770–1831), the German philosopher. Hegel viewed the history of human civilization as a succession of national cultures. For him, the national state was the highest form of political unit, the embodiment of political power. The *Volksgeist*, the genius and the spirit of a nation, imbued the nation with the qualities of a huge, collective, living, and growing organism. The parts of this organism (such as individuals, groups, regions, and political parties) were to be subordinated to the whole. A lack of such subordination would result in anarchy and chaos. True freedom could be found only within the strict disciplinary lines of the nation-state. The state (as a government) thus emerged as the embodiment of a nation's will and destiny. Finally, the state was seen as having no higher duty than to preserve and strengthen itself.

According to his conception, individuals are best understood as "means" of the state, their value to be measured in terms of their contribution to the survival of the state organism. History is seen as proceeding according to organic laws that are beyond the control of individuals. Thus, concluded Hegel, true political genius could be found among those persons who knew how to identify with higher principles such as the survival, growth, and prosperity of their nation-states. . . .

National Sovereignty

A major characteristic of the nation-state is sovereignty. In the literature of international relations, sovereignty has been defined as supreme state authority subject to no external limitations. The French philosopher Jean Bodin (1530–1596) is associated with the earliest clear definition of this concept. Bodin was concerned with the fragmentation and sectionalism that had led to frequent civil wars and chaos in France. His main object, therefore, was to strengthen the position of the monarch as the source of order and unity throughout France. Writing in 1586, Bodin defined the state as "a lawful government of several households, and their uncommon possessions, with sovereign power."[3] Citizenship became the subjection of an individual to the sovereign. Sovereignty was defined as "supreme power over citizens and subjects unrestrained by law."[4] Thus, the king was given the right to *make, interpret, and execute law unrestrained by all human authority.* He was subject only to the laws of God and to fundamental natural laws such

as those requiring the keeping of agreements and respect for private property.

Thomas Hobbes (1588–1679), the famous British political philosopher, elaborated on the concept of sovereignty, subtly shifting its emphasis from the person of the king to the abstraction called government or state. During the turbulent years from 1640 to 1651 in England, which were marked by factionalism and bloodshed, Hobbes wrote with the purpose of strengthening the authority of the king and of absolute government. Hobbes felt that if humans remained in a state of nature (i.e., prior to being organized politically), leading a "solitary, poor, nasty, brutish, and short" life, bloody and uncontrollable conflict would be inevitable. Thus, in order to limit conflict and to preserve the collectivity, it was necessary to concentrate all social authority in the sovereign. The sovereign, a "moral God" on earth, was equated with the state, which in turn was equated with the government. For sovereignty to shift to its third and contemporary phase, ultimate authority had to be transferred symbolically from the government to the people inhabiting the nation-state.

The French Revolution (1789) epitomizes the symbolic transfer of sovereignty from the king and the government to the people. Since it has proved difficult, however, for the people as a totality to rule in other than small-town settings, sovereignty has remained substantially in the hands of governments who rule in the name of their people. In such states, there is an implicit understanding that the people will scrutinize governmental actions and as a last resort will revolt should their government betray its implicit contract with [them].

A helpful distinction should be made between internal and external sovereignty. Internal sovereignty concerns the supreme and lawful authority of the state over its citizens. External sovereignty, on the other hand, refers to the recognition by all states of the independence, territorial integrity, and inviolability of each state as represented by its government. The Dutch jurist Hugo Grotius

(1583–1645), reputed to be the father of international law, defined sovereignty as "that power whose acts are not subject to the control of another." For Grotius, sovereignty was manifested when a state, in dealing with its internal affairs, remained free from the control of all other states. Thus defined, sovereignty has become the cornerstone of the modern international system, where power and authority remain consciously divided and decentralized.

In the final analysis, sovereignty is the ability of a nation-state, through its government, to be master in its house, to have control over its domestic affairs, and in its foreign affairs to have the options of entering or leaving alliances, of going to war or remaining neutral so as to best defend its interests. In practice, however, we find that certain countries have been "more sovereign" than others: some of the great powers enjoy the substance as well as the letter of sovereignty, whereas smaller countries, especially if they are strategically located, are penetrated quite often by the great powers and can be called "sovereign" only in a relatively inauthentic sense of the word. . . .

In international as well as in domestic affairs, governments have tried to endow their actions with an aura of legitimacy. Consequently, by adhering to treaties and to customary international law, different ruling elites found that they could benefit mutually. Over time, the development of a nation-state system founded upon an acceptable balance of power gave impetus to the renaissance of the international law of which Grotius was a leading spokesman. The formalization of diplomatic procedure, the establishment of collective defense systems through alliances, and the acceptance of the principle of sovereignty and its corollary of nonintervention in the domestic affairs of other states—all of these were developments that strengthened the hand of nation builders. But in the case of ideologically or ethnically fragmented societies, coercive means such as subversion and war were often employed to overthrow legitimate governments. Without a firm basis in a stable political community, sovereignty often proved to be an illusion.

The modern doctrine of popular sovereignty has transferred the source of absolute power from the monarch to the "people." But this transfer of power does not necessarily mean that individual citizens become more able to check the transgressions of expanding administrative states. Indeed, the popularization of sovereignty gave rise to the ideology of mass nationalism, which equates the fate of the citizenry with that of its political leadership. Mass conscription for either military or industrial service, government control of the mass media for the purpose of propagandizing foreign-policy objectives, and the centralization of educational systems to insure an uninterrupted process of political socialization combined to spread the fever of nationalism that produced the major conflicts of the twentieth century.

Challenges to Nationalism and Nation-States

. . . . Nationalism grew steadily in the last two hundred years to encompass an identification of the individual with the state. The process of political socialization, carried out by the family, schools, and peer groups, taught the citizen the inescapable lesson that loyalty to the state fulfills not only an ideological but also a pragmatic purpose. For it is the state that, in return for obedience to its laws, provides innumerable concrete services. Thus, citizen allegiance and government efficiency in the performance of its functions are mutually supportive.

The rise of modern states that were based on a strong nationalistic sentiment was a logical historical response to the industrial revolution. But in the present-day postindustrial international setting, the idealized notion of the nation-state is coming under increasing attack from three quarters: the advance of military technology, the rise of supranational organizations, and the growing role of transnational ideological, religious, functional, and political movements. In the 1950s, many analysts pointed out the increasing military vulnerability of the state. Principal among these was John Herz, who wrote of the "demise" of the state, arguing that it was no longer capable of protecting its citizens in the event of a three-dimensional modern war involving nuclear, psychological and economic weapons. Herz foresaw the transformation of the international system into a system dominated by conflicting regional alliances. Under the impact of decolonization, however, Herz gradually abandoned his notion of the demise of the state. Yet, as long as the economic and military viability of many of the new states remains in question, the image of a bi- or tripolar international system retains some validity. In a future time, George Orwell's dreary *1984* scenario may indeed materialize, and our earth may be dominated by the three superpowers of Oceania, Eurasia, and Eastasia.

Assuming that the hallmark of national sovereignty is the rigorous application of the doctrine of nonintervention in the affairs of one state by another, the development of supranational organizations poses the second problem for the future of presumably impermeable nation-states. Among the democracies of the West, notably those of Europe, supranational collaboration to achieve shared goals in the fields of economic development, health, and education is proceeding swiftly. Member states of supranational organizations with policy-making and policy-implementing powers, such as the European Common Market and Nordic Council, employ the argument (or perhaps the rationalization) that their sovereignty remains unaffected because they have delegated governmental authority to the international civil servants who staff the executive bodies of these organizations. In a legal sense this argument merits respect, but the politics of interdependence have eroded the absolutist quality of the concept of sovereignty and are likely to create rivals for the nation-state as the sole focus of political loyalty.

Transnational ideological/political movements of the twentieth century, such as fas-

cism and communism, present a third formidable challenge to nationalism. The "New Order" of the German National Socialists led by Adolf Hitler (1889–1945) castigated the liberal nineteenth-century version of the nation-state and called for the formation of a hierarchical European system dominated by what Hitler considered a biologically select race committed to an ideology of purity and power. In accordance with this objective, the Elite Guard (SS) of the Nazi movement organized non-German units throughout occupied Europe and sought to use them as a basis for a new Praetorian state whose military despotism would sound the death knell of the conventional European national communities. The outcome of the Nazi assault on the traditional European nation-states was a cataclysmic war from which humankind has yet to recover materially, and from which it may never completely recover spiritually.

Marxism—from a very different angle—also sought to challenge the nation-state and nationalism. In the *Communist Manifesto* (1847) Karl Marx and Freidrich Engels rejected nationalism, viewing it as a perversion of the historical mission of the proletariat. Although Joseph Stalin (1879–1953) modified this ideological doctrine by making Soviet policy in 1928 a policy of "socialism in one country" and also by appealing to the historic force of Russian nationalism during the great war with Germany, orthodox Marxists continue to this day to treat the nation-state as a "category of history" that is designed to serve the interests of capitalism and that is doomed to disappearance once working classes everywhere rise to power.

On the tactical level, however, revolutionary communist movements have readily espoused the cause of nationalism and have sought to align themselves with anticolonial forces in the Third World. For instance, the support of a coalition of nationalist forces such as the Popular Movement for the Liberation of Angola (MPLA) had been an integral part of Soviet policy. Demands for political self-determination in Eastern Europe, on the other hand, tend to receive a markedly different response. Ruling East European Communist parties subscribe, rather, to the doctrine of "proletarian solidarity" and accept an obligation to combat presumed counterrevolutionary tendencies within their bloc. Under the leadership of the Soviet Union, the members of the Warsaw Pact (with the exception of Rumania) occupied Czechoslovakia in 1968 in order to limit revisionist Czech liberalism and by extension Czech nationalism.

The Polish events of 1980–81 reflected yet another powerful example of the gradual fusion between nationalism and communism. The attempt of Polish workers, peasants, and students (supported by the powerful Catholic Church of Poland) was obviously aimed toward the objective of attaining communism with a "Polish Face. . . .'

Contemporary research indicates that international wars waged to regain lost territory and revolutions undertaken by an ethnic minority in the interest of national self-determination have accounted for 70 percent of all international conflicts. Given the strong relationship between nationalism and violence, a difficult question arises: Are nationalism and its corollary, the nation-state, useful or harmful forces in world affairs? The answer must be carefully qualified.

Nationalism can be a useful force when it provides the individual with a sense of identity and belonging. It allows the individual to unite with others in the pursuit of the common good—a behavior pattern that may well reduce individualism and alienation. This pattern may also engender competitive and even mildly conflicting behavior in the form of national assertiveness in the face of obstacles. This type of competition and conflict is a key element in the process of social evolution. However, national self-actualization in this sense should not be synonymous with violence and expansionism. Only to the extent that social systems compete peacefully to overtake one another by improving their own quality of life do people in general benefit.

Nationalism can be a destructive force when it postulates a hierarchy of peoples and seeks to impose this world view by force. Whenever a nation-state ascribes to itself a superior role that can be fulfilled only at the expense of the territory and welfare of others, armed conflict becomes unavoidable. The history of the twentieth century is filled with the tragedy wrought by such nationalist-expansionist movements. . . .

The processes of international politics are dynamic. The phenomena of national integration and disintegration can and often do occur simultaneously. Nationalism can be a force for either the unification or the fragmentation of a state. On the international level as well, the satisfaction of nationalist demands can have either stabilizing or destabilizing effects. In order to understand and cope with this most powerful force, social scientists representing various disciplines and approaches have employed their techniques and findings in an effort to synthesize nationalism and internationalism in such a way that humankind will not have to sacrifice cultural pluralism in the name of world order and at the same time will not have to subordinate its general welfare to the wishes of a few powerful and acquisitive nation-states.

NOTES

[1] Hans Kohn, *Nationalism: Its Meaning in History*, rev. ed. (New York: Van Nostrand, Reinhold, 1965), p. 27.

[2] Quoted in Michael Oakeshott, *The Social and Political Doctrines of Contemporary Europe* (London: Cambridge University Press, 1939), pp. 165–68.

[3] George H. Sabine, *A History of Political Theory*, 3rd ed., rev. (New York: Holt, Rinehart & Winston, 1961), p. 402.

[4] Ibid., p.405.

2. The Actors in International Politics

Arnold Wolfers

The late Arnold Wolfers was for many years Sterling Professor of International Relations at Yale University before establishing the Washington Center for Foreign Policy Studies at the School for Advanced International Studies of the Johns Hopkins University.

Theorizing about almost any feature of international politics soon becomes entangled in a web of controversy. Even the identity of the "actors"—those who properly can be said to perform on the international stage—is a matter of dispute which raises not unimportant problems for the analyst, for the practitioner of foreign policy, and for the public. If the nation-states are seen as the sole actors, moving or moved like a set of chess figures in a highly abstract game, one may lose sight of the human beings for whom and by whom the game is supposed to be played. If, on the other hand, one sees only the mass of individual human beings of whom mankind is composed, the power game of states tends to appear as an inhuman interference with the lives of ordinary people. . . .

Until quite recently, the states-as-the-sole-actors approach to international politics was so firmly entrenched that it may be called the traditional approach. After the Napoleonic wars, nation-states, particularly the European "great powers," as they were called, replaced the image of the princes or kings of former centuries as the sovereign, independent, single-minded actors, the movers of world events. To nation-states were ascribed the acts that accounted for changes in the distribution of power, for alignments and counter-alignments, for expansion and colonial conquest, for war and peace—the

This selection is excerpted by permission of the publisher from William T.R. Fox, ed., *Theoretical Aspects of International Relations* (Notre Dame: University of Notre Dame Press, 1959). (Footnotes have been deleted.)

chief events in international affairs whenever a multitude of sovereigns have been in contact with one another. The concept of a multistate system composed of entities of strikingly similar character and behavior appeared realistic to observers and analysts.

Starting in the period between the two world wars and gaining momentum after World War II, a reaction set in against the traditional states-as-actors approach. This reaction has taken two distinct forms: one new theory has placed individual human beings in the center of the scene that had been reserved previously to the nation-states; the second theory emphasized the existence, side by side with the state, of other corporate actors, especially international organizations. Both reactions have led to valuable new insights and deeper understanding of the dynamics of world politics, but they are in fact supplements to the traditional theory rather than substitutes for it.

The individuals-as-actors approach first appeared in the minds-of-men theory of international politics. It was soon to be followed by the decision-making approach which was a reaction against tradition from another angle. Both demanded that attention be focused on individual human beings as actors. Together, the new schools of thought represent a swing of the pendulum from an extreme "state" emphasis to an equally extreme emphasis on the men who act for states. These new approaches must be credited with humanizing international politics by attracting attention to the human element minimized in the traditional approach. It was the aim of the new theories to replace the abstract notion of the state with the living realities of human minds, wills, and hearts. But the result, on the whole, was to substitute one set of abstractions for another because, in politics, it is also an abstraction to examine the individual apart from the corporate bodies by means of which he acts politically. . . .

The new approach's criticism of the states-as-actors theory turns mainly on the distinction between genuine human needs and what appear to be the a-human interests of the state. There are those who claim that too great an emphasis on the role of states and their interests in power, prestige, territory, and the like, will divert political action from the satisfaction of the common man's real needs and desires to the service of the few who can parade their interests as those of the nation. Is it credible, they ask, that Egyptian fellaheen and Pakistani peasants, desperately in need of food, shelter, and improved conditions of health, should, as their governments contend, yearn for the satisfaction of such "state interests" as the liquidation of Israel or the unification of Kashmir under Pakistani rule, when the pursuit of such interests requires great sacrifices of the masses? Does the state not take on the character of an a-human monster to whom dignity is given gratuitously, if it is regarded as an actor in its own right, at liberty to place its interests above those of the human beings who compose it?

Still, one may question whether the quest for national security and power, for national independence, aggrandizement, or unification is any less "human"—and therefore necessarily less appealing to the masses—than the quest for food, shelter, comfort, and happiness. Actually, the minds-of-men theory and its humanization of international politics must be carried several steps further than its exponents have gone. Any analysis of the dynamics of international politics must take into account the fact that man is more than a private individual concerned only with his personal welfare or with the welfare of his family. Often enough he is ready to compromise his own well-being for the benefit of the groups and organizations with which

he identifies himself. Psychologically, nothing is more striking today than the way in which men in almost every part of the globe have come to value those possessions upon which independent national statehood depends, with the result that men, in their public capacity as citizens of a state, are willing to make the most sweeping sacrifices of their own well-being as private individuals in the interest of their nation. Therefore, state interests are indeed human interests—in fact, the chief source of political motivation today.

One can argue that a nationalistic age has distorted men's pattern of values or that the manipulators of public opinion are chiefly responsible for this distortion. Nevertheless, the fact remains that a sufficient number of men identify themselves with their state or nation to justify and render possible governmental action in the name of state interests. . . .

One wonders today, for instance, whether the bulk of the population in countries facing the risks of nuclear war will long continue to regard as vital, and thus worthy of defense in war, all the state interests they were once ready to place in this category. Signs point to the likelihood that the masses, who have gained greater influence as behind-the-scenes actors, will push for greater restraints upon the pursuit of those state interests such as national security or prestige—that are seen to conflict with private welfare needs. Such a development will indicate not that individuals are suddenly taking over the function formerly performed by states, but rather that larger bodies of individuals are sharing the role once reserved to the members of small elites who formerly decided what the "national interest" demanded or justified. It always would have been possible to interpret international politics through an examination of the individuals responsible for state action: the "humanizing" approach. But it must be recognized that in the course of the present century the number of these individuals has been greatly enlarged.

The failure to see man in his double capacity, as a private individual and as a political being, accounts for an illusion common among the more idealistic exponents of the minds-of-men approach. They assume that better understanding between peoples opens the safest path to peace, while Dunn[1] has pointed out that peoples who know and understand each other perfectly may nevertheless become involved in war. The explanation for this apparent paradox is not hard to find, provided one thinks in terms of the whole man rather than solely in terms of his private aims and desires. If one were in contact with the people of the Soviet Union today, one probably would find them preoccupied with the tasks of furthering their personal welfare, happiness, and social advancement in much the same way as any similar group of people in the United States. The discovery of such similarities of interest and aspiration tends to arouse a sense of sympathetic understanding; it certainly does not provoke fear or serve to justify policies based on the expectation of international conflict. As a result, people who think exclusively in terms of private individuals and who experience harmonious relationships with citizens of "hostile" countries are inclined to see nothing but unhappy misunderstanding, if not evil, in the way governments act toward one another.

Yet, the fact that Americans and Russians, in much the same fashion, pursue the same goals when acting as private individuals, gives no indication of their aims as citizens who are concerned with the national interests of their respective countries. Here there is far less chance that their aims will be found to be in harmony. Better understanding may in fact reveal the incompatibility of their respective objectives. . . .

It is therefore clear that an exclusive minds-of-men approach with its concentration on the motives and activities of individual actors is inadequate and misleading. It is undeniable that men alone, and not states, are capable of desires and intentions, preferences and feelings of friendship or hatred; men, not states, can be tempted or provoked, can overestimate or underestimate their own country's power relative to the power of other states, and can establish the goals of national policy and sacrifices consistent with national security. However, although nothing can happen in the world arena unless something happens inside the minds and hearts of scores of men, psychological events are not the whole stuff out of which international politics is formed. If they were, the political scientist would have to leave the field to the psychologist.

The minds-of-men approach, while able to render important and indispensable services to a comprehensive theory of international politics, cannot do justice to all the essential events that fill the international arena. There can be no "state behavior" except as the term is used to describe the combined behavior of individual human beings organized into a state. Not only do men act differently when engaged in pursuing what they consider the goals of their "national selves," but they are able to act as they do only because of the power and influence generated by their nations organized as corporate bodies. Therefore, only when attention is focused on states, rather than on individuals, can light be thrown on the goals pursued and means employed in the name of nations and on the relationships of conflict or co-operation, of power competition or alignment that characterize international politics. . . .

The decision-making approach naturally appeals to the historian who is interested in identifying the unique aspects of past events, which necessitates consideration of all conceivable variables, including the personal traits of particular human actors. But it poses a serious problem for the theorist whose task is not to establish the uniqueness of events but rather to gain a generalized knowledge of behavior in international politics, which means knowledge on a relatively high level of abstraction. Should he not, therefore, abstract from the personal predispositions of those who are instrumental in the making of decisions? If his use of the deductive method, as described earlier, permits him to formulate expectations of probable state behavior that prove relatively accurate, why should he take a long, effort-consuming "detour" of the kind required by the decision-making approach and conduct an extensive empirical investigation into the motivations of a Stimson or a Truman? Could it be that use of the A-bomb against Japan was predictable on the ground that "states tend to use their most powerful weapons," or American intervention in Korea by the proposition that "no great power, if it can help it, will permit its chief opponent to change the distribution of power by the unilateral use of military force?"

At first glance, it would seem as if the actual performance of a particular state could conform only by sheer coincidence with expectations based on extremely crude generalizations about the way states tend to act under given circumstances. Why should the particular individuals responsible for United States policy in 1945 or 1950, men differing from others by a multitude of psychological features—motivations, idiosyncrasies, preferences, temperament—reach decisions of the kind the state-as-actors theory deduces from its abstract model? Yet the correlation in many instances between the predictions of theory and actual behavior is not accidental. Such correlation may be expected if two assumptions on which the theory rests are justified by the circumstances prevailing in the real world.

There is, first, the assumption that all men acting for states share the same universal traits of human nature. Specifically, these men are expected to place exceedingly high value on the so-called possessions of the nation—above all, on national survival, national independence, and territorial integrity—and to react in fear against any threats to these possessions. It is also assumed that they share a strong inclination to profit from opportunities for acquisition or reacquisition of cherished national possessions, with national power as the chief means of preserving or acquiring national values. To the extent to which these traits are shared and have a decisive effect on the actions or reactions of statesmen and peoples, they create conformity as if by a kind of inner compulsion.

The second assumption concerns the environment in which governments are required to act. If it is true that the anarchical multistate system creates a condition of constant danger to national core possessions—specifically, to national survival—and, at the same time, provides frequent opportunity for new acquisitions, the actors can be said to act under external compulsion rather than in accordance with their preferences.

It is easy to see that both these sweeping assumptions are not the products of unrealistic fantasies. Attachment to possessions, fear, and ambition—although they vary in degree from man to man and from people to people—can properly be called "general traits of human nature," which are likely to operate with particular strength in men who hold positions of authority and national responsibility. That the condition of multiple sovereignty is one in which states "live dangerously" is also a matter of common experience and knowledge. The real question is whether internal and external pressures are strong enough everywhere and at all times to transform the actors into something like automatons lacking all freedom of choice. Certainly, to the degree that these compulsions exist in the real world, the psychological peculiarities of the actors are deprived of the opportunity to express themselves and therefore can be discounted as irrelevant to an analysis of international politics.

NOTE

[1] Ed. note: Frederick Sherwood Dunn was director of the Yale Institute of International Studies until 1951.

3. Powers: A Philosophical and Historical Perspective

Martin Wight

The late Martin Wight taught at the London School of Economics and later as a Professor of History at Sussex University.

"Power politics" has the merit of pointing to a central truth about international relations, even if it gets certain other things out of focus. For, whatever else it may suggest, "power politics" suggests the relationship between independent powers, and we take such a state of affairs for granted. It implies two conditions. First, there are independent political units acknowledging no political superior, and claiming to be 'sovereign'; and secondly, there are continuous and organized relations between them. This is the modern states-system. We have the independent units, which we call states, nations, countries or *powers,* and we have a highly organized system of continuous relationships between them, political and economic, diplomacy and commerce, now peace, now war.

It will help us to understand this state of affairs if we recall that it is by no means the rule in history. The present states-system has existed roughly since the early sixteenth century, and we have the illusion that it is normal. But looking further back, we can see it was preceded by something different. In the eleventh or twelfth centuries there were no sovereign states repudiating any political superior, for the conception of sovereignty was

unknown. There was instead, in theory, a single juridical unit, known as Christendom, and presided over in ecclesiastical affairs (which included much of what today passes as 'politics') by the successor of St. Peter at Rome. The innumerable kingdoms, fiefs and cities which composed medieval Christendom did not assert (perhaps because they were too imperfectly organized to assert) their political independence in the absolute terms of the modern sovereign state. Again, Christendom had external relationships of trade and war with the Mohammedan powers across the Mediterranean and the Byzantine Empire across the Ionian Sea; and these relationships showed much the same principles as those of the modern states-system; but they were not in the same degree continuous and organized. If we look still further back, across an interval of confusion and migrations, we see something different again: another single juridical unit, occupying a rather different geographical position from Christendom—the Roman Empire. This was a centralized state with a single, absolute, divine ruler instead of a loose confederation, with limited authorities. It too had diplomatic relations and wars with the Parthian and Persian Empires across the Euphrates, and it even traded with distant China; but these contacts were still more intermittent and irregular than those of Christendom with the Byzantines and the Moslems.

But looking back once more beyond the Roman Empire, we see the familiar sight of a warring family of independent states, brilliant cities and broad kingdoms, each jealous of its freedom and ambitious to expand,

This selection is excerpted by permission from "Powers," Hedley Bull and Carsten Holbraad, eds. © Royal Institute of International Affairs from *Power Politics* (London: Penguin, 1978), pp. 23–29. The essay was apparently written in the late 1960s. (Some footnotes have been removed; those remaining have been renumbered.)

17

fighting and intriguing, making alliances and holding conferences, and all of them at last conquered, pacified and swallowed up by the strongest among them, the Roman Republic. This political kaleidoscope of the Greek and Hellenistic ages looks modern to our eyes, while the immense majesty of the Roman peace, and the Christian unity of the medieval world, seem remote and alien. The political writings of the Greek period of antiquity have remained classical because their relevance and topicality have been experienced afresh by each succeeding generation. One of the supreme books on power politics is the history by Thucydides of the great war between Athens and Sparta, commonly called the Peloponnesian War. It was this that General Marshall had in mind when he spoke at Princeton University in 1947:

> It has been said that one should be interested in the past only as a guide to the future. I do not fully concur with this. One usually emerges from an intimate understanding of the past, with its lessons and its wisdom, with convictions which put fire in the soul. I doubt seriously whether a man can think with full wisdom and with deep convictions regarding certain of the basic international issues of today who has not at least reviewed in his mind the period of the Peloponnesian War and the fall of Athens.[1]

Power politics in the sense of international politics, then, came into existence when medieval Christendom dissolved and the modern sovereign state was born. In the medieval world there were growing up tribal and national authorities which shaped the modern nations of Europe, and they fought constantly among themselves. At the zenith of the Middle Ages the two highest potentates, the Pope and the Emperor, waged a two hundred years' war for supremacy (1076–1268). This conflict itself destroyed the balance of medieval society, and led to

a revolution in politics that culminated in the Reformation.

Most obviously, it was a revolution in loyalties. Medieval man had a customary loyalty to his immediate feudal superior, with whose authority he was in regular contact, and a customary religious obedience to the Church under the Pope, which governed every aspect of his life; but his loyalty to the King, whom he probably never saw and was seldom aware of, was weaker than either. In due course the King suppressed the feudal barons and challenged the Pope, becoming the protector and champion against oppression and disorder at home and against a corrupt and exacting ecclesiastical system whose headquarters was abroad. The common man's inner circle of loyalty expanded, his outer circle of loyalty shrank, and the two met and coincided in a doubly definite circle between, where loyalty before had been vague. Thus the modern state came into existence; a narrower and at the same time a stronger unit of loyalty than medieval Christendom. Modern man in general has shown a stronger loyalty to the state than to church or class or any other international bond. A power is a modern sovereign state in its external aspect, and it might also be defined as the ultimate loyalty for which men today will fight.

More fundamentally, there was a change in the moral framework of politics. Medieval politics were grounded in a deep sense of religious and social unity, which emphasized the whole rather than the part: they were mainly concerned with defining or interpreting a hierarchy where everyone in theory had his place, from the Pope and the Emperor down to the meanest feudal baron. 'Medieval history', said the historian Stubbs, 'is a history of rights and wrongs; modern history as contrasted with medieval is a history of powers, forces, dynasties and ideas . . . Medieval wars are, as a rule, wars of rights; they are seldom wars of unprovoked, never wars of absolutely unjustifiable aggression; they are not wars of ideas, or liberation, or of glory, or of nationality, or of propagandism.[2] In the modern states-system the sense of unity has become rarefied as a multitude of powers have developed their independence of one another, and agreement on moral standards has been weakened by doctrinal strife within Europe and the expansion of the states-system beyond Europe. It seems that 'international society' is only the tally of sovereign states, that the whole is nothing but the sum of parts. The medieval political outlook saw the gulf between ideals and facts as a condemnation of the facts, not of the ideals. The modern political attitude is expressed rather in the saying of Bacon: 'So that we are much beholden to Machiavel and others, that write what men do and not what they ought to do.'[3]

The power that makes a 'power' is composed of many elements. Its basic components are size of population, strategic position and geographical extent, and economic resources and industrial production. To these must be added less tangible elements like administrative and financial efficiency, education and technological skill, and above all moral cohesion. Powers which have declined from former greatness, like Britain or France, or which have not attained great power, like India, naturally emphasize the value of political maturity and moral leadership, though these phrases are more likely to carry weight within their own frontiers than beyond. In times of international tranquility these imponderables can have great influence. Nevertheless, just as in domestic politics influence is not government, so in international politics influence is not power. It is concrete power in the end that settles great international issues.

> When men dislike Bismarck for his realism, what they really dislike is reality. Take his most famous sentence: 'The great questions of our time will not be settled by resolutions and majority votes—that was the mistake of the men of 1848 and 1849—but by blood and iron.' Who can deny that this is true as a statement of fact? What settled the question of Nazi domination of Europe—resolutions or the allied armies? What will settle the question of Korea—majority votes at Lake Success or American strength? This is a very different matter from saying that principles and beliefs are ineffective. They can be extremely effective if translated into blood and iron and not simply into resolutions and majority votes.[4]

The moral cohesion of powers is often spoken of in terms of nationality or nationalism. But this can cause confusion, since these words have several meanings. First, in its oldest sense, a nation means a people supposed to have a common descent and organized under a common government. Here the word nation is almost interchangeable with the words state or power; it was formerly possible to speak of the republic of Venice or the kingdom of Prussia as nations. The sense is illustrated by the phrase 'the law of nations', and survives in the adjective 'international'. Secondly, after the French Revolution the word nation came to mean in Europe a *nationality*, a people with a consciousness of historic identity expressed in a distinct language. Italy or Germany or Poland were nations in this sense, though each was divided among many states, and the Habsburg and Russian Empires were 'multinational' powers. The principle of national self-determination asserts the right of every nationality to form a state and become a power, and the peace settlement of 1919 attempted to reorganize Europe in accordance with it. Thirdly, in Asia and Africa, since the First World War, the word nation has come to mean a political unit asserting its right of independent statehood against European domination. Some of these units are ancient civilizations, like India and China; some are historic kingdoms, like Ethiopia and Persia; some, like the Arab states, are fragments of a wider linguistic group and most perhaps have been created by European colonial administrators, like Indonesia and Ghana. But in terms of nationality more of them resemble the Habsburg Empire than Ireland or

Denmark. They combine the passions of the second kind of nation with the social diversity of the first kind. Of the five surviving nominal great powers today, France alone comes near to being a homogeneous nationality. The Soviet Union and China are multinational states; the United Kingdom is the political union of the English, Welsh, Scottish and Northern Irish nations; and the United States is a unique attempt to create a new nation from immigrants of all European nationalities.

The word 'nationalism' describes the collective self-assertion of a nation in any of these three senses, but especially in the second and third. This compels us to speak of conflicting nationalisms within a single state: there is both a Scottish nationalism and a British, a Sikh nationalism and an Indian, a Ukrainian and a Soviet nationalism. (The word 'patriotism' is generally reserved by the ruling class for the larger and inclusive loyalty.) The student of power politics will not be misled by nationalist claims, and will remember that in most cases the freedom or rights of one nation or nationality have been purchased only by the oppression of another nation or nationality. Every power that is a going concern will in course of time generate loyalties which it will be proper to call nationalist, but powers are less the embodiment of national right than the product of historical accident.

It is a consequence of nineteenth-century nationalism that we personify a power, calling it 'she', and saying that *Britain* does this, *America* demands that, and the *Soviet Union*'s policy is something else. This is mythological language, as much as if we speak of John Bull, Uncle Sam or the Russian Bear. 'Britain' in such a context is a symbol for an immensely complex political agent, formed by the permanent officials of the Foreign Office, the Foreign Service, the Foreign Secretary, the Prime Minister, the Cabinet, the House of Commons, the living electorate, and the dead generations who have made the national tradition, combining and inter-

acting in an infinitude of variations of mutual influence. These shorthand terms are of course unavoidable in political writing, but they are dangerous if they lead us into thinking that powers are inscrutable and awesome monsters following predestined laws of their own. A power is simply a collection of human beings following certain traditional ways of action, and it is possible that if enough of them chose to alter their collective behaviour they might succeed in doing so. There is reason to suppose, however, that the deeper changes in political behaviour can only be produced by a concern for non-political ends.

We must note in conclusion that the phrase 'power politics' in common usage means, not only the relations between independent powers, but something more sinister. Indeed, it is a translation of the German word *Machtpolitik,* which means the politics of force—the conduct of international relations by force or the threat of force, without consideration of right and justice. (About the time of the First World War, 'power politics' in this sense superseded an older and more elegant phrase, *raison d'état,* which implied that statesmen cannot be bound in public affairs by the morality they would respect in private life, that there is a 'reason of state' justifying unscrupulous action in defence of the public interest.) As Franklin Roosevelt said in his last Annual Message to Congress, 'In the future world the misuse of power as implied in the term "power politics" must not be the controlling factor in international relations.'[5] It would be foolish to suppose that statesmen are not moved by considerations of right and justice, and that international relations are governed exclusively by force. But it is wisest to start from the recognition that power politics as we defined them at the outset are always inexorably approximating to 'power politics' in the immoral sense, and to analyse them in this light. When we have done this we can more usefully assess the moral problem.

NOTES

[1]Speech of 22 February 1947 in *Department of State Bulletin,* Vol. 16, p. 391.

[2]W. Stubbs, *Seventeen Lectures on the Study of Medieval and Modern History,* (Oxford: Clarendon Press, 1886) pp. 209, 217.

[3]Francis Bacon, *Advancement of Learning,* Book II, XXI, p. 9.

[4]A. J. P. Taylor, *Rumours of War* (London: Hamish Hamilton, 1952), p. 44.

[5] 6 January 1945 in S. I. Rosenman, ed., *The Public Papers and Addresses of Franklin D. Roosevelt,* Vol. IV (New York: Harper & Row, Pub., 1950), pp. 483–507.

chapter 2

THE INTERNATIONAL POLITICAL ECONOMY

Given the scale and complexity of these problems, the remainder of the twentieth century will be at best a traumatic period for mankind, even with a frontal attack on the principal threats to human well-being. At worst it will be catastrophic. At issue is whether we can grasp the nature and dimensions of the emerging threats to our well-being, whether we can create an integrated global economy and a workable world order, and whether we can reorder global priorities so that the quality of life will improve rather than deteriorate.

Lester Brown,
former policy adviser to the Secretary of Agriculture,
World Without Borders (1973), pp. 11–12.

Like history, the study of international relations must always take into account the economic as well as the political dimension. In recent years, an old term, "political economy" has increasingly come into vogue in an international context. A fundamental dilemma of the sovereign-state system has been the fact that states divide people into self-enclosed *political* entities, whereas *economic* life prospers from the greatest possible exchange of goods and investments among people. During much of the nineteenth century, under the influence of British laissez-faire and free-trade principles, it appeared that the two realms—the political realm of the state and the world realm of economic capitalism—might be made to coexist successfully. Few of the advanced capitalist states adhered completely to free trade, however. Like the United States, France, and even Germany, many pursued protectionist policies such as high tariffs and subsidies for agriculture and industry in order to develop their domestic economies before venturing to compete with England. Richard Cooper has put this in stark comtemporary terms in defining what he terms *the central problem*, which is keeping the benefits of world trade free of restrictions without undermining the freedom of each country to try to meet its own valid aims.[1] From time to time, other terms rise to the surface and can be very useful, for example macroeconomics, macrosociology, and macropolitics.[2]

Lenin and other neo-Marxists developed their theories of war and imperialism upon the adduced contradictions between the needs of a capitalist economy and the limitations imposed upon it by the artificial compartmentalization of the world into political entities called states. The capitalist owners of the means of production, unable to squeeze profits out of domestic production, were theoretically driven to expand overseas into Latin America, Africa, and Asia. In order to do this, they had to use the apparatus of the state to conquer and govern colonies. But sooner or later, it was argued, even these outlets would prove insufficient and the great European powers would be driven into wars against each other for control of the globe. It was against this background of global imperialism that World War I occurred, giving apparent support to Leninist and other neo-Marxist theories. The facts are, however, that the war began in the Balkans over the assassination of an Austrian archduke, that it was prompted by the German government's fear that if it did not help to crush the Serbian challenge, the Austro-Hungarian Empire would crumble and Germany would be at the mercy of its Russian and French enemies; capitalist and colonial rivalries were not the precipitating cause of World War I.

The theory that capitalist competition causes imperialism and war has also been challenged by findings on the part of historians that frequently it is governments in the pursuit of political and strategic advantages that support financial interests in their penetration of other countries and areas so that the governments will then have a pretext for becoming politically involved. Inasmuch as states employ economic policies in various ways and for various purposes, a distinction needs to be made between policies pursued for essentially economic ends and policies pursued primarily for political or strategic ends—a point we will return to in Part II on policy options open to nation-states.

What is clear is that after World World I, the capitalist world economy had become increasingly interdependent, and a breakdown anywhere would produce convulsive results throughout the system. Unfortunately, the inability of governments to appreciate this new condition during the interwar period was one factor leading to a series of economic catastrophes—the German inflation of the early 1920s, the uncontrolled banking and stock-market speculation of the 1920s, the Great Depression, and mass unemployment—all of which contributed to the victory of Nazism in Germany and of militarism in Japan. By adopting protectionism and cutthroat competition to protect their own economies, modern states destroyed the basis for peaceful management of the global economy, thereby helping to bring on World War II.

---

[1]William C. Olson and David S. McLellan, eds., The Theory and Practice of International Relations, 6th ed., (Englewood Cliffs, N.J.: Prentice-Hall, Inc., 1983), pp. 156–59.

[2]In one of the better of many "I.R." textbooks, Professor Richard Sterling of Dartmouth actually used the latter in his title: Macropolitics: International Relations in a Global Society (New York: Alfred A Knopf, Inc., 1974).

As a result of this interwar folly, and out of an implicit belief that American capitalism could only flourish in a stable and well-regulated world economy, the United States government took the initiative after World War II to establish a set of institutions and policies designed to avoid a repetition of these events. Because the two most important institutions of this American design—the International Monetary Fund and the World Bank—were brought into existence at a meeting of the allied nations at Bretton Woods, New Hampshire, in 1944, the system is sometimes called the Bretton Woods system discussed by Richard McCormack below. This system consisted of a set of arrangements designed to cushion shocks to the international economy and to avoid the need for states to resort to cutthroat economic practices to protect their citizens against unemployment. The Monetary Fund provided a pool or reserve of funds available to help any country going through a period of economic dislocation to surmount the crisis without, if possible, devaluation of its currency. The World Bank was designed to facilitate loans by the industrially advanced countries to the underdeveloped Third World countries. There were also agreements among the advanced countries to reduce tariffs and increase trade among them. Above all, the United States provided an economic shot in the arm to the international economy by granting Europe $18 billion in Marshall Plan assistance after 1947 and in providing upwards of $100 billion in economic grants and aid to other countries (principally in the Third World) in the quarter-century that followed.

The result of these measures was an era of unprecedented economic growth and prosperity for the advanced capitalist world and for some fortunate parts of the Third World. Real income increased by four and five times between 1945 and 1965, especially that of the Europeans and Japanese; trade quadrupled and then quadrupled again; the European Common Market came into existence; multinationals led by the Americans undertook overseas operations that sought our profitable new investment and production. There has never been an era in world history in which the material wealth of so many people increased so markedly and so rapidly.

Unfortunately, this boom was marked by unhealthy traits and developments that have once again put the stability of the international economy in doubt and given rise to national rivalries and cutthroat competition. First and foremost, the United States government tried for too long to use the strength of the dollar to sustain a global strategy of containment of communism and of nation building. On the one hand, it incurred an annual military expenditure of $75 billion, climaxed by the Vietnam War in which labor and resources were consumed in an unproductive and non-income-earning activity. Second, other billions were expended each year in economic- and military-aid programs to a dozen or so selected countries—principally to America's anti-Communist allies like South Korea and Taiwan. Other billions were transferred overseas by American multinationals to purchase or establish businesses abroad. Meanwhile, America's former wartime enemies, Germany and Japan, having concentrated on modernizing their economies, were increasingly America's competitors as well as partners. As a result, more dollars went out than came in, and the dollar became overvalued in relation to the German, Swiss, and Japanese currencies, a process which was later reversed by joint government action.

The weakness of the American economy and of the dollar were covered from 1968 until 1971 by the willingness of other governments to hold onto their surplus United States dollars, but this entailed increasing nationalist resentment of America's privileged position. Moreover, the deficit in the American balance of payments and the adverse effect of an overvalued dollar on the American economy could not be postponed indefinitely. Finally, in August 1971, then President Richard Nixon abandoned the American attempt to sustain and exploit the overvalued dollar by devaluing it cumulatively by almost 30 percent, by ending the right of countries to exchange their surplus dollars for United States gold, and by putting a 10 percent surtax on all United States imports. In a sense, the Nixon economic shock of the summer of 1971 brought an end to Bretton Woods system, though as McCormack brings out in his statement below, it has continuing relevance in the international political economy.

Devaluation was followed two years later by a fourfold increase in the price of oil. Cheap oil had fueled the world economic miracle of 1950–1973. The additional $100 billion in annual oil charges meant that much less would be available for investment and profits to Western capitalist economies, placing an almost unmanageable burden on Third World economies. The oil-price increase was followed almost immediately by recession in 1974 and 1975. The Organization of Petroleum Exporting Countries (OPEC) doubled the price of oil again in 1978 and 1979, depressing still further the international economy. After a century of cheap resources, the capitalist economies had to face the fact that the world would have to pay more for increasingly scarce minerals. The "oil glut" of the mid-eighties could be temporary.

The cumulative impact of these changes has had a dramatic effect upon the economic context of world politics. Instead of national economies exchanging goods and services, we have a highly interdependent world economy in which the economic benefits to each country depend on smooth functioning of the economy on a global basis. But it is a global economy in which governments are increasingly driven to protectionism—that is, to raising tariffs and employing other means to keep foreign goods out and subsidize one's own producers. But once again as in the thirties, protectionism is an issue in U.S. politics in the eighties.

As a consequence of these conditions, there has been a marked upsurge in protectionism, and the advanced capitalist states no longer find it as easy to manage the world economy as they did a decade ago. Already the movement toward European economic integration has slowed down and America and its allies are increasingly at odds over economic matters. Should the international order that fosters trade, investment, and access to vital materials break down, we would once again face a situation in which resort to war becomes acceptable. The warning by former U.S. Secretary of State Henry Kissinger that the United States might have to resort to force should another OPEC oil embargo or price hike threaten the economic life of the advanced industrial countries may have been a bluff, but it was also an intimation of what might really occur.

As Albert Bressand brings in his article in this chapter, international economics is not only a process; it is also a form of political power.[3] Economically advanced nations have always exploited their economic power to gain advantages at the expense of weaker societies. This sometimes takes the form of outright imperialism, but it also takes more indirect forms such as in setting terms for the right of access to investment capital, terms that are more advantageous to the lender than to the borrower. Of the many types of economic pressures which an advanced state may employ, the following have been among those used for several decades now:

(1) financial manipulations to diminish the value of an opponent's currency and enhance that of one's own country;

(2) economic penetration of weaker countries, with the eventual objective of exerting pressure on the government of the penetrated society;

(3) exploitation of a strategic economic position through such policies as price fixing, dumping, the imposition of quotas, exchange controls, and so forth;

(4) boycotting or a refusal to buy from another country;

(5) the use of economic subsidies;

(6) preemptive buying of goods produced in other countries in order to withhold them from other purchasers; and

(7) the stockpiling of important goods[4]

Another form of economic power is that of economic bribes and military subventions, by which a more powerful state ties lesser states to it in a form of dependence. For decades, Great Britain subvened Prussia and other allies on the continent as a means of keeping them actively opposed to the hegemonic ambitions of the Hapsburg and Napoleonic empires.

As the Cold War developed and the United States found itself engaged in a struggle with the Soviet Union for influence in the Third World, a far more elaborate use of economic assistance as a weapon of foreign policy began to be deployed. On the premise that unless the newly emergent nations were helped to develop they would either fall into anarchy, go Communist, or both, the United States began a massive program of economic and military aid to the Third World. An elaborate ideology dubbed "nation building" was concocted to justify to the American people the transfer of billions in foreign aid. It probably is wrong to say that the ideology was "concocted," because the American leadership and the American people were equally convinced that the United States had a duty and a self-interest in tiding the newly emergent countries over their period of economic growth until they were sufficiently developed to take their place as dem-

---

[3]For another formulation of this concept, see Joan Edelman Spero, *The Politics of International Economic Relations* 2nd ed., (New York: St. Martin's Press, 1981), especially the "Introduction: The Link Between Economics and Politics," pp. 1–20.

[4]Charles C. Abbott, "Economic Penetration and Power Politics," *Harvard Business Review,* 26 (1948), pp. 410–24.

ocratic, independent, and, naturally, anti-Communist societies. The plausibility of the United States being able to guide and subsidize the transformation and development of societies as culturally diverse and impoverished as India, Indonesia, Ethiopia, and Peru was never really questioned by the idealists and ideologues of foreign aid. Perhaps the American government found it convenient to maintain the assumption that economic development could actually be promoted through such transfers of money, investment, and services because it helped to sweeten other purposes of such aid programs—which were to bribe governments to align themselves with the United States in the Cold War, and, more concretely, to provide the United States military with bases and American business and banks with investment opportunities.

Much economic aid, of course, has taken a multilateral form. That is to say, the United States and other countries have made annual contributions to international organizations such as the World Bank and the United Nations to finance humanitarian and development purposes. But the fact that America's contribution was sufficiently large gave it a veto power over grants or loans to countries whose regimes were offensive to the United States—such as Allende's Chile—thereby enabling it to punish and weaken them.

In effect, the foreign aid and military programs, like American policy generally (as those of our European allies), were increasingly directed toward maintaining the status quo; while a similar Communist economic and military aid program was aimed at supporting countries opposed to the United States. As a result, economic and military assistance (and sales) has become one of the most significant methods used in contemporary world politics. As the United States has experienced deception with the results of foreign aid and economic stringency in its own position, however, economic aid has formed a smaller and smaller percentage of America's gross national product, and aid has either been increasingly tied to narrow American interests or has taken the form of loans and investments by private banks and multinationals. There has also been a rising nationalist resistance on the part of Third World countries against subordinating their foreign policies to any form of foreign-aid control and toward demanding aid as an obligation that the rich countries owe to the poor. The opposite side of the coin, so to speak, is the debt the poor countries owe to the rich in the form of loan repayments to Western banking institutions. This North-South "debt crisis" (discussed in Chapter 41) of the last fifteen years of this century threatens the international political economy to a degree which many fear may exceed the consequences of the West-West debt crisis which followed World War I.

DISCUSSION QUESTIONS

1. Why has Bressand introduced a new word, "worldeconomy"?

2. What is the conflict between the way the international economy works and the way the international system is organized into sovereign states?

3. What changes have occurred and are occurring in the global economy that are reducing not only America's competitive position but also its ability to perform the role of global leader?

4. Can you see how Western Europe's reluctance to support U.S. boycotts of the Soviet Union at the time of the Afghan and Polish crises is tied to the economic stake Europe has in trade with the Soviet bloc?

5. Can you think of ways to improve the U.S. economic performance rather than resorting to protectionism? Is Bretton Woods still relevant, as McCormack argues, or have events overtaken it?

6. From your own exposure to "the media" show how protectionism has become an issue in American politics, including the arguments on *both* sides of the fence.

4. I.P.E.—What is it?

Roger Tooze

Organizer of the International Political Economy Group of the British International Studies Association, Roger Tooze is a lecturer at North Staffordshire Polytechnic in England and has lectured at the University of Southern California in the United States.

International political economy (IPE) is very much in vogue. Over the past few years we have seen a deluge of literature—theory, general analyses, issue analyses, reports and recommendations—on, or purporting to be on, the subject. Joan Spero's popular introductory textbook which uses a very narrow conception of IPE contains a bibliography stretching over twenty-five closely printed pages. Those who wish to understand the issues and problems of IPE, or even find out what it is all about, are confronted with a galaxy of writings, each of which views IPE from a particular perspective and each of which embodies a particular interpretation of how the world 'works'. As each one of us reading this literature also views the world from our own perspective, how can we make sense of it all and take advantage of the insights IPE offers without falling foul of its many pitfalls? This chapter provides a 'consumers' guide' to the literature through a focus on its basic perspectives and central theory.

Every guide, however, contains its own assumptions about how the field of knowledge has developed and how it is currently organised. In the nature of social production of knowledge this chapter cannot be any different. But it will, it is hoped, provide a set of explicit criteria by which one should be able to identify and utilise the IPE literature and perspectives that are relevant to the questions we are asking.

International Political Economy: What Is It?

The nature and content of the study of IPE is itself contentious. Hence the present discussion reflects a particular perception of IPE: one that is drawn from within the perspective of international relations, rather than directly from economics or politics. As such it reflects an initial emphasis on the international (or world) level, if only because both economics and politics, and their respective forays into 'political economy', have been bounded by the state as the unit-of-analysis. They have in the past taken little account of the international context of state activity. At a time when states are characterised by degrees of penetration by other social, economic and political entities, the lack of attention to international factors is misleading.

International political economy is here a focus of inquiry. It denotes an area of investigation, a particular range of questions, and a series of assumptions about the nature of the international 'system' and how we understand this 'system'. These three criteria clearly overlap, but taken together they define the field.

'An Area of Investigation'

In a contemporary sense the focus is initially defined by the areas, issues, and problems under investigation. In general, we are con-

Excerpted from Susan Strange, ed., "Perspectives and Theory: A Consumers' Guide," *Paths to International Political Economy* (London: George Allen and Unwin, 1984). Reprinted with the permission of the publisher. Copyright © 1984 George Allen and Unwin, Ltd., (Footnotes have been deleted.)

cerned with that area formed by the merger of the previously separated areas of 'international' economics, 'international' politics, domestic (that is, national) economics and domestic policies. Specifically this produces a concern with problems and issues such as international trade, international monetary relations, North-South relationships, transnational corporations, global economic problems, the foreign economic policies of states and a whole host of other specific topics. The general domain created constitutes the focus of IPE, where economics and politics at international and domestic levels are integrated and cannot be understood independently of each other.

However, the extent to which each of these conventionally separate areas is, in fact, separate, and can be understood as such, is a moot point, and forms part of the intellectual and political debate within IPE at the moment. Much of the international politics literature focuses solely on questions of international security and military affairs, and relegates both domestic and international issues and concerns to the 'non-political' and unimportant. And economics too has conventionally, and conveniently, ignored E. H. Carr's warning that 'The science of economics presupposes a given political order and cannot be profitably studied in isolation to it' and has developed a whole literature which is sadly deficient when the 'given political order', whether it is international or national, undergoes change. So the very use of the term 'international political economy' or 'political economy', and the adoption of an IPE focus, is a mark of dissatisfaction with the conventional definition of the issues and boundaries of international relations, political science and economics. This dissatisfaction comes from a growing realisation that many of the world's problems—poverty, inflation, the nuclear arms race—and conflicts—over trade and services, in international money, in industrial bargaining and within conventional governments—cannot be understood within the conventional framework of knowledge whereby histori-

cally defined academic disciplines each have their own exclusive area of inquiry. We need better intellectual tools not only to cope with more complex questions, but to direct us towards different questions.

The definition of a subject area of inquiry—*what* is considered legitimate within a field of study and *how* it is best studied—is never fortuitous. The boundaries and methodology of a subject are set by the wider assumptions that form the social and political context of that subject area. Hence Marxist scholars have always used the term 'political economy' in line with their perspective and latterly to differentiate their understanding from 'conventional economics', which early on separated out the politics from 'political economy'. Perhaps the important question is, therefore, how and why economics and politics became separated in the first place and how, in a similar process, the field of international relations came to be defined in a particular way.

. . . The separation of economics and politics can be traced to the particular historic period which produced a conceptual separation between the state (or political society) and civil society: the eighteenth and early nineteenth centuries. The separation broadly corresponds to two distinct spheres of human activity, 'to an emergent society of individuals based on contract and market relations which replaced a status based society, on the one hand, and a state with functions limited to maintaining internal peace, external defence and the requisite conditions for markets, on the other'. This conception reflects a particular historical distribution of power, as did the notions of mercantilism before it, in which the interests of an emergent middle class are served by the separation and legitimation of an economics free from political (state) intervention. The interests of this group are further served by the institutionalisation of the separation, in the form of a dominant ideology (liberalism), as well as in state political processes and norms of behavior. Liberalism became the defining perspective, the mainstream of Anglo-Saxon society, that shaped our conceptions, to the extent of setting the parameters for the establishment, maintenance and understanding of the postwar international economic order. The incorporation of a particular notion of economics and politics into a prevailing ideology subsumes this notion as a given or fixed aspect of the social definition of reality. In this way it becomes the only legitimate way to define the field.

In a similar process the content and 'proper' concern of international relations also reflected the distinction between state and civil society. As political society is defined by the state, then 'politics' is state action, particularly to ensure internal peace and the maintenance of the 'requisite conditions for markets'. Only one major political outcome, the achievement of security from external attack, required the state to engage in foreign intercourse, and depended on how successfully it did so. Hence a special mode of thinking was developed in order to understand the processes and outcomes of the 'anarchic' international society. Given the presumption of separability from politics, the resultant study of international relations developed a separate set of theories, requiring particular knowledge, which explained and clarified the outcomes of state external action, principally in the context of war.

However, much like the separation of economics and politics, the separation of international relations from politics only makes sense within the context of this distinction. If conditions change or if we can demonstrate that the original presumption of separability is historically and ideologically determined (as we have seen it is), then it becomes much harder to argue that the study of international relations is separate from the study of politics and that each can be pursued independently of the other. And if international relations is not in general separate from politics, then the area of inquiry of international political economy must necessarily include domestic politics and economics.

This theoretical conclusion is easily sup-

ported by our experience of international reality. Here the 'boundary-crossing character of political processes challenges the assumptions of the autonomy of political processes within their own sphere of competence'. The permeability of state authority is clear. Whether we understand this as 'the domestication of international politics' or the internationalisation of domestic politics, as implied by Katzenstein, is for the moment secondary to its theoretical impact. If we have, as it seems, 'penetrated systems whose boundaries do not conform to the divisions between national and international systems', the study of international relations in general, and international political economy in particular, must encompass this reality. Moreover, as Hans Schmitt points out in one of the few analyses of this problem, 'The boundaries of the modern nation-state reflect the interaction of three separately bound phenomena: the nation, the state, and the economy'. Any change in the nature and extent of these phenomena or in the nature of their interaction will affect the area of inquiry.

The original definition of international relations produced an emphasis on international *politics* with war and the diplomacy of war (its avoidance and/or successful conclusion) as the principal processes and issue, and the state as the key political entity. Later characterised by Robert Keohane and Joseph Nye as 'state-centric realism', the core assumptions of this definition successfully resisted the intellectual attacks of Marxism, from the late nineteenth century onwards, idealism in the 1920s and, in a different sense, behaviouralism in the 1960s. But even though 'state-centric realism' came under increasing criticism from academics in the 1970s, it remained then, and is still today, very attractive to government policy-makers.

Over time the basic assumptions of conventional international relations have been added to or modified. Reacting to and encouraging the forces of nationalism, the state expanded its economic role nationally and internationally through the late nineteenth century, and this modifies the conception of state embodied in the literature. 'State' increasingly becomes equated with 'government', with important implications both for the implicit conception of politics utilised and the notions of political economy absorbed into the assumptions.

The study of international relations also takes on national characteristics and reflects particular aspects of national concern and perception. We see the academic dominance of the subject by American scholars not just by their production of more books than anyone else, but in the way the field is defined by American writings and policies. Some of the major assumptions and concepts of these American scholars are not shared by others just as 'liberal'. The existence of an independent and traditional 'English school' of thought in the subject is illustrative. Yet as with the so-called 'great debate' between behaviouralism and traditionalism these national differences were initially perceived as differences in method, in line with the 'social science' thinking of the time, rather than political challenges to the prevailing definitions. The gradual change from the post-1945 'state-centric realism' to a 'world politics' perspective introduced concepts and frameworks such as interdependence, issue analysis and regime and enlarged the area of inquiry to include new actors, processes and issues, particularly economic ones. Such developments largely reflected changing American perceptions of the world role and capabilities of the United States. But they also sensitised us to the importance of non-state entities and transnational processes and, importantly, prepared the way for a ree-mergence of IPE itself.

'Mainstream' work in international relations now confronts and contains much that is economic, albeit in a particular way. Kenneth Waltz's *Theory of International Politics* represents a 'state of the art' discussion of the field. His explicit concerns for the nature of thinking and explanations, the problems of encompassing a totality of relationships and his desire to integrate economic rela-

tionships all demonstrate that, to a certain extent, the 'conventional' study has taken on board the challenges of the IPE critique. However, much of the dissatisfaction with mainstream definitions of the field still remains. The dissatisfaction is expressed by those who work within a completely different perspective and those who remain broadly within the mainstream but who urge redefinition of the field. One of the first, and best, of such redefinitions was Robert Gilpin's *US Power and the Multinational Corporation* in which he discusses the need for a political economy approach and subsequently develops a 'mercantilist' type of explanation. More important, he develops an integrating conception of international political economy that is still relevant and widely used, as 'the reciprocal and dynamic interaction in international relations of the pursuit of wealth and the pursuit of power'. As you might expect, even this conception can be criticised for its assumptions—that behaviour is rational; that politics imply action; and that international political economy is limited to the international level. The perceived collapse of the postwar economic order produced other analyses that attempted to redefine the area of concern, but the majority of these still incorporated the basic assumptions of mainstream international relations.

The Range of Questions

We have seen how the perspective inherent in theory defines the area of investigation, although we have not as yet considered the full range of perspectives on international political economy that have evolved. Perspective also sets what some call the 'approach', and this term can normally be used instead of 'perspective'. Each reflects the overall social and political context of inquiry—the what and the how. Perspectives also contain a range of questions about the field. The range of questions implicit in a perspective is sometimes called (after the French *problematique*) its 'problematic': every perspective contains value judgements as to what is important in the world, what processes are critical and what outcomes are preferable. Its problematic translates these into an analytical framework, which describes and explains, and more important, into a rationalisation of the perspective. Rationalisation gives direction and meaning to the perspective and also enables those who work within it to understand the perspective on its own terms. Each perspective can only be judged on the basis of whether or not the individual accepts its problematic. Does one see the world in terms of the 'liberal', 'Marxist', 'mercantilist', or any other problematic? The choice eventually comes down to the individual's own values because there cannot be any logical *a priori* reasons for selecting one perspective over another, or indeed for developing your own.

International political economy as a focus of inquiry extends beyond the problematic of conventional international relations, although we have seen that this itself has changed. Questions of war and security are clearly of fundamental importance, but these questions are part of an international political economy and are meaningful in as much as they relate to both politics and economics. An IPE problematic will initially ask questions about assumptions and values. IPE developed as a critique of existing orthodoxy through exposing the implicit assumptions and values in accepted perspectives. Consequently most of the perspectives of IPE are consciously critical approaches which link empirical study much more explicitly into an analysis of basic assumptions and values. IPE *starts* from an awareness of the centrality of perspective in setting the problematic: what you ask is often more important than the answers you get. Because what you ask and how you go about getting the answer nearly always determine the answer for you. If your problematic identifies, say, questions of regime and regime change as important, you might be tempted to assume that contemporary IPE consists of myriad and complex processes of regime construction and change.

Yet, another problematic may see regimes as peripheral to the major concerns of IPE, as particular and limited instances of the attempt by a declining hegemonic power to maintain control. What one problematic categorises as a central question needing urgent resolution, another ignores.

An IPE problematic also asks questions about the relationship between politics and economics at the international level and about the link between domestic policies and processes. Concepts such as hegemony and imperialism link politics and economics and require an examination of the precise nature of the relationship. Individual policies and events are questioned for their implications for other areas, for example, the impact of the Vietnam War upon the unchallenged supremacy of the dollar as an international currency, or the effect of today's rapidly changing international monetary situation upon general world political and economic stability. No process, policy, or event is unquestioningly accepted as either purely economic or political or, for that matter, as purely international or domestic. We have seen that the traditional definition of international relations (IR) precludes international political economy from inquiring into domestic processes, but now the problematic reflects the superfluous character of the IR/politics distinction for most issues and problems. For many processes of IPE, the distinction is simply irrelevant.

Finally, the problematic also directs attention to preferable outcomes and ways of attaining these outcomes. Perspectives of IPE embody a theory of change, however implicit, and in some cases, however simplistic, which prevents a past, present and future image. Analysis of the present is sustained by historical understanding of change, and action is directed towards achieving the future according to the particular image presented by the problematic. In the prevailing conventional problematic change, action and the future are reflections of the present distribution of power and wealth. The operations of the International Monetary Fund

(IMF), for example, clearly reflect a 'liberal' problematic; economic problems in countries are defined as those of increasing efficiency, pushing up levels of production, increasing capital investment, and so on. They are problems of 'technical' change within the existing framework.

Other non-conventional problematics focus on questions which challenge the basis of the existing system of world economy—questions of justice, questions of the distribution of wealth, education and technology, and questions about food. These basic questions are linked to further analyses of how the present situation arose and what can be done to move out of it towards some preferred alternative goal. The various 'structural' perspectives of IPE, particularly those concerned directly with the creation of a New International Economic Order (NIEO), contain an imperative for change based on historical analysis and a critique of existing structures and processes. In this respect the crucial part of the problematic is that which links analysis to action, that part which produces specific questions, particular political policies and bargaining positions from generalised statements. The link between theory and practice, and in some perspectives the *unity* of theory and practice in the concept of praxis, transforms an intellectual position into a political force—whether it be for a continuance of the existing state of affairs or for a fundamental change in those affairs. . . .

. . . A 'world' economy has been defined by Charles-Albert Michalet in terms of production and service structures which extend beyond national territorial boundaries, in contrast with the international economy based on flows of goods, payments and capital. Michalet's thesis is that both structural models coexist in the world today: 'international' (old and of declining importance); and 'world' (new and of growing importance). Hence the term 'world political economy' is often used instead of 'international political economy' to denote a much broader concept of political economy, one not necessarily defined and limited by the state. A perspective that focuses on the state, such as the mercantilist, or a liberal transnational perspective would not identify such a development. . . .

The key concept in IPE is the nature of political-economic relations, which is derived from notions of the nature of politics itself. In most non-Marxist perspectives politics is conceptualised in a particular way: politics is concerned with the state—but not just the state in general, but the state as defined by Max Weber. Weber defines the state as an organisation—government—which claims a monopoly on the legitimate use of force. This conception, as David Sylvan so ably shows in his analysis of the 'newest mercantilism', gives rise to a particular notion of political-economic relations. 'From a theoretical standpoint economic activities are linked to politics insofar as they involve the government as actor or object of action. From a methodological standpoint, then, the way to study political-economic relations is by looking at actions'. The first implication is that politics is defined narrowly with the result that political economy is defined as government economic activities and international political economy as the attempts by governments to regulate and manage international economic relations.

Alternative conceptions see political economy as much wider—economics is never above or below politics   economics *is* politics. A narrow conception of political economy precludes understanding of many new situations and skews the overall description of the world political economy itself towards government activity and policy, rather than at the totality of political-economic relationships.

The conception of politics as action is inherent in liberal, transnational, mercantilist and some other non-structural perspectives. Politics as 'actions' takes no account of the broader framework within which action takes place. This framework is rarely institutionalised, particularly at the international level, but encompasses a wide range of social relationships which set the parameters for action and inaction. Again Robert Cox puts this very succinctly: 'action is never absolutely free but takes place within a framework' which has the form of an historical structure,

> a particular combination of thought patterns, material conditions and human institutions which has a certain coherence among its elements. These structures do not determine people's actions in any mechanical sense but constitute the context of habits, pressures, expectations and constraints within which action takes place.

Clearly, a conception of political economy which fails to take account of this broader framework is essentially limited in its explanatory potential. It can only describe and, perhaps, explain actions and issues within the terms of the actions and issues themselves. It can never explain why some actions are never taken or how some issues never achieve even discussion. The major weaknesses of such important analytical concepts as 'issue analysis' and 'regime analysis' is precisely that they fail to take account of the historical structure of the world political economy. And, in so doing, they incorporate certain values, which in the main reflect the present American position in and attitudes to the world economy, which makes them 'problem-solving' analyses rather than critical concepts.

The extent of analytical and conceptual openness is critical in assessing the worth of a perspective. We have seen that just in respect of two basic areas—the definition of the units of analysis and the concept of political economy—many problems arise because of the values contained within the concepts themselves. The third element of openness, the 'substantive', is even more of a problem. Substantive openness as suggested by Reuveny, is 'the capacity of the framework to explain situations which essentially differ from those which shaped the original premises of the [perspective], accounting for both similarities and differences'.

The origins of 'conventional' economics, politics and international relations were all within the similar general social and political context of the late eighteenth and nineteenth centuries. All three have had to face new situations and problems which were essentially different from and could not be explained in terms of the conditions prevailing in those times. The enormous differences between then and now just, say, in the growth of the world economy or in the power of the state, confront these historically located perspectives with great difficulties. A particular difficulty for 'radical' as well as 'conventional' perspectives has been the emergence of the Third World, and the problem of explaining the Third World with a single set of concepts based on Western experience and values. The cultural values implicit in most perspectives quickly reveal their limitations in explaining other Western and especially non-Western experiences.

The combination of historical change and geographical, non-Western expansion of the world political economy produced problems for existing perspectives and generated a whole new range of perspectives at the same time. Dissatisfaction with the apparent inability of perspectives based on the previous historical experience to describe and explain brings with it a desire for alternative approaches as it brings about a new problematic. These new problematics focus on a different range of questions than established perspectives, and suggest different descriptions, explanations and policies. Typical of the non-traditional perspectives is the 'structuralist' approach to international relations (which will be briefly discussed later), which does not suffer from the assumption of the ideological separation of economics and politics and is generally concerned with specifying and describing world structures of dominance and dependency, rather than focusing on interstate relations.

If the necessity of coming to terms with new situations has led to the growth of new perspectives, we are still left with the question of how well these perspectives, old and new, explain situations. No one perspective at this moment provides an adequate description and explanation of contemporary world political economy. And no body of empirical research is sufficient to sustain or falsify any one perspective. Some perspectives highlight certain areas, some others.

Much good and useful work has been done on a wide variety of important problems, areas and issues, including monetary problems, trade relations and, increasingly, the service structure. But as yet we do not know enough of the actual workings and processes of change in the structure as a whole to support any one coherent description, let alone a single explanation of the world political economy. Specific questions related to particular structures of the world economy, such as security, production, trade and transport, credit and money, and the communication and knowledge structure, can be analysed in a problem-solving sense that, if done with an explicit awareness of assumptions and values, can be very useful. But we cannot assume that such studies necessarily add to our overall understanding unless they are conducted in a critical way, in the sense we have discussed. Better than producing value-laden and culture-bound studies would be a move towards such a critical perspective that is explicitly aware of its own cultural and value assumptions.

The moral for the student of international political economy, as we are all aware, is to be truly sceptical of all claims and analyses in the entire literature. Only then is one in a position to begin to evaluate what is useful, and what is not, along the lines suggested here.

----

5.   The Structure of World Economic Cooperation

Richard T. McCormack

Richard McCormack serves in the U.S. Department of State as Assistant Secretary for Economic and Business Affairs.

Forty years ago, a group of distinguished and farsighted men erected what has be-

Excerpted from "The Bretton Woods Legacy: Its Contemporary Relevance," an address by Richard T. McCormack, Assistant Secretary for Economic and Business Affairs, at a conference commemorating the 40th anniversary of the signing of the Bretton Woods agreements, Bretton Woods, New Hampshire, July 13, 1984. United States Department of State, *Bureau of Public Affairs*, Washington, D.C.

come a living historical landmark of international economic cooperation. The structure they erected enabled the world economy to achieve an unprecedented four decades of reconstruction, growth, and change. Today, the Bretton Woods institutions, having proven both resilient and flexible, are in the forefront of our efforts to resolve current international economic problems. . . .

Developing a Stable Monetary Order

What did the Bretton Woods founders believe they had accomplished? How successful were they? What elements of their design are most relevant to our concerns today? Let me begin with the quote from U.S. Treasury Secretary Morgenthau reproduced in our program: "What we have done here in Bretton Woods," Morgenthau said, "is to devise machinery by which men and women everywhere can freely exchange, on a fair and stable basis, the goods which they produce with their labor." A commonplace observation? Perhaps it seems so today. But compare the ideal to the then-existing reality.

The interwar period had left international economic intercourse in virtual anarchy, with countries attempting to defend themselves against external shocks (and, indeed, to export their unemployment to others) through all kinds of devices—exchange rate manipulation, multiple rates and exchange controls of various kinds, import barriers, and restrictive bilateral agreements. In this context, Morgenthau's simple claim must have seemed visionary indeed.

The first order of business, then, was to bring countries together in a structure that would substitute stability, cooperation, and open markets for the existing chaos. At the same time the founders wanted to leave individual countries scope to pursue their legitimate individual economic objectives. Balancing these two goals—discipline and cooperation versus freedom of action—was one of the most fundamental and difficult problems facing the negotiators 40 years ago.

The Bretton Woods founders believed that these goals could best be reconciled within a system of fixed but adjustable exchange rates. They had very much in mind the experience of the interwar period with its turbulent spells of flexible exchange rates and "beggar-thy-neighbor" devaluations. Therefore, in their system, countries were committed to the maintenance of exchange rates within narrow margins around agreed parities, and the International Monetary Fund (IMF) was to exercise discipline over changes in these parities.

Did Bretton Woods Fail?

Although this exchange rate structure provided the foundation for the world's monetary system for almost 30 years, it is now generally believed to have had fatal defects which caused it to be abandoned by the major countries a little more than a decade ago—in practice, in 1973; in law, with the second amendment to the IMF articles in 1976.

Many learned writers have written countless pages on the reasons why this happened. The consensus, as I understand it, is that the system proved in practice to be too rigid in the face of changing conditions. Currency convertibility, fixed exchange rates, and independent national macroeconomic policies become increasingly inconsistent with growing economic interdependence. The Bretton Woods escape hatch—adjustment through major exchange rate realignments only after fundamental disequilibrium had clearly emerged—proved unworkable in a world economy where vast amounts of capital can move relatively freely across the exchange markets to hedge or speculate on an anticipated realignment.

Of course, the Bretton Woods founders did not foresee—they could not reasonably have foreseen—the vast increase in funds free to cross and recross national borders over the postwar decades. And it is clear at least some of them gave far less weight to the benefits of free capital movement than to those of free trade. To their credit, the founders viewed their arrangements as experimental, not immutable. If anything, those who followed ought probably to have modified the system at an earlier stage, before it collapsed.

Did the collapse of the Bretton Woods exchange rate system signify that the founders failed in their efforts to construct an international monetary system? In terms of their most fundamental objectives, the answer is no, they did not fail.

After all, the original exchange rate system provided sufficient stability and confidence over a quarter century so that nations could move from the chaotic, restrictive, prewar system to successively greater currency convertibility, vastly reduced barriers to the flow of goods and services, and freer capital movements. Largely under the aegis of the IMF, the major trading countries of the world have adopted a regime of free financial flows among nations. These developments together provided the foundation for a rapid expansion of trade and interdependence, in turn helping to produce an astonishing recovery from war and a sustained increase in production and material well-being. The removal of exchange controls in accord with the Fund's articles has been instrumental in achieving the six-fold increase in world trade (in real terms) that has occurred since the end of European reconstruction in 1953. Economists, of course, complain about the misallocation of resources which occurred with the growing exchange rate misalignments of the latter part of the period; these misalignments reflected

our failure to introduce more flexibility into the operation of the system as conditions changed.

Even more important, gains from that earlier period—convertibility and open markets—were not lost as the system was transformed by the *force majeure* of the marketplace to a more flexible exchange rate system. Compare the evolution with the monetary disintegration of the interwar period, and you will see clearly the lasting benefits of Bretton Woods. The fundamental principles of international monetary cooperation survived and are still operating as we work to improve our economic performance with the present exchange rate arrangements. The principles that 1. exchange rates and other international monetary issues are a matter for mutual concern, not unilateral decisions; 2. stable domestic policies are fundamental to international monetary stability; and 3. the repercussions of one country's policies on another country's well-being cannot be ignored are still the core of our present system. This is one lasting legacy—more important than the details of any exchange rate system—that the Bretton Woods founders left us.

---

6. Mastering The "Worldeconomy"

Albert Bressand

Deputy Director of the Institut Français des Relations Internationales (IFRI). Albert Bressand is also the director of their annual RAMSES report, *The State of the World Economy*.

Does a global economy still exist? If one were to base one's judgment solely on the recent

Excerpted from *Foreign Affairs*, vol. 61, no. 4 (Spring 1983). Copyright © 1983, Council on Foreign Relations, Inc. Reprinted by permission of the publisher.

meetings of the world's most powerful decision-makers—whether at Geneva, Versailles or Cancun—the answer might well be "no." Conflicting perceptions, diverging priorities, and lack of any sense of direction suggest, indeed, that the concept of world interdependence has been lost in a policy and intellectual vacuum. Seldom have so many common interests run into so many common problems to produce so little common action.

Let us hope that the period extending from the July 1981 Ottawa summit to the Versailles summit of June 1982 and to the Geneva GATT [General Agreement on Tariffs and Trade] ministerial meeting in November 1982 will be seen in retrospect as the nadir of international economic cooperation. The story of the 1960s had been that of a prosperous blossoming of the trees planted at Bretton Woods. With a few noticeable exceptions, the story of the 1970s and early 1980s was one of missed opportunities and growing intellectual disarray. We failed to plant the seeds of organization and reform that the emergence of a truly global economic system was beginning to call for.

It simply has not sunk in how rapidly the world has changed, not only during the fast-growth period of the 1960s but also during the lower-growth decade of the 1970s. We confuse stagnant growth with "no change" scenarios, when in fact the level of interdependence between countries may never have increased faster and the underlying structure of power changed more deeply than in the latter period.

Thus, we are still striving to overcome an international economic crisis through national economic policies. Models of closed national economies still govern much of our thinking, and we wonder with incredulity at their failure—be it on the Keynesian or on the monetarist side. Modest coordination proposals aimed at promoting a much needed world recovery still arouse controversy and skepticism—when in fact national policy-makers have obviously lost control over their much cherished spheres of economic autonomy.

The time has come to realize that the international economy can no longer be defined as, and limited to, the intersection of national economies. Rather, it is now the national economies which must be looked upon as the extension of a global and integrated system with a logic of its own. To make the point clear, let me call the global system the "worldeconomy."

Once we accept this notion of a world-economy which is qualitatively different from simple national interactions, much of what is said and done today appears remarkably narrow and limited in scope. National decision-makers are revealed as sailors on an open sea, taking the utmost care to adhere to the course of their choosing when in fact the currents, winds and swirls are often carrying them in the opposite direction.

Acknowledging the existence and influence of a worldeconomy implies much more than castigating economic nationalism. Indeed, a major part of today's problem is to understand how the "free trade" and "free market forces" we think of as the opposite of economic nationalism are actually operating. As I try to make clear in the following pages, the "free trade" approach still widely identified with international-mindedness is also an inheritance from days of lesser complexity and interdependence. A good rule for trade relations considered in isolation, it still has to take into account the complex relationships which now make for unexpected feedbacks between trade, money, finance and the changing industrial standing of countries.

The experience of a global economic system in which the free market approach prevails, albeit imperfectly, not only for trade but also for the monetary system and financial flows, is much more recent than we often realize. We have in fact been living in such a system for only half a dozen years. And yet, it is striking to see how often we have already had to revise our assumptions of what free trade *cum* floating exchange rates *cum* free capital flows would look like.

The 1976 Jamaica agreements on exchange rates, for example, did little but formally bury the Bretton Woods monetary system. The absence of a new set of rules to replace the old ones was assumed to clear the way for a self-stabilizing monetary and financial system. These hopes have now been proven wrong, beyond any reasonable doubt,

by repeated and prolonged incoherent exchange rate situations (as well as by the poisoned fruits of the flowers of recycling). That
not all free floaters are ready, as yet, to open
their eyes only illustrates again the well-known
power of cognitive inertia.

The trade machine took longer to grind
to a standstill. Buoyant markets and the early
launching of the Tokyo Round negotiations
preserved the momentum well into the late
1970s. But theory and new realities were
moving further and further apart, and by
the GATT meeting in Geneva, calls for more
liberalization as a buffer to exploding restrictions—or "freeze" and "standstill" proposals in the face of a tide of protection—
suddenly appeared as a well-meaning, well-
tried but narrow and obsolete strategy. Strategic mistakes were compounded by clumsy
tactics, as the American delegation called for
initiatives—in services and technology—
without specific proposals. The only tour de
force achieved was that American attacks did
succeed in getting even the British to speak
in defense of the European Economic Community (EEC) common agricultural policy.
In all other respects, Geneva was the Wa-
terloo of the GATT—unlike 1815, for some
peculiar reason, the French thought this was
good news.

Lack of collective control over events, now
threatening in finance, money and trade, has
been with us in energy for ten years. After
two oil shocks and two episodes of taking
comfort in OPEC's change of fortune, we
are still projecting the future in the light of
the last three months in the market. The
present extension of the pure market approach to oil must be questioned when one
remembers that trade in oil (to the tune of
$450 billion) is 20 times larger than in any
other commodity and has profound impact
on trade and financial flow patterns. It is
hardly surprising, therefore, that the present drops in price are being greeted with
some of the same apprehension as upward
oil shocks. The markets are not and cannot
be perfect.

Strong fluctuations of a key parameter—
whether upward or downward—are a threat
to the survival of the system. They exact tremendous adjustment costs. In particular,
much of the recent steady decline of capacity
utilization has reflected accelerated obsoles-
cence of industrial equipment resulting from
the major relative price changes of the 1970s,
above all in energy and energy-dominated
factors of production. In the mid-1980s, we
may see the reverse—premature obsoles-
cence of the major investments that were
supposed to "adjust" to this situation. Either
way, we experience an unprecedented was-
tage of scarce resources.

Failure to acknowledge the existence of
this type of threat illustrates a gap in our
intellectual apparatus, already visible, in a
more complex setting, with respect to the
wild swings of the major currencies. Confusing perfect or quasi-perfect market models
with the reality of world economic competition, the present American economic decision-makers look at a 30-percent change in
the external value of the world's central currency in the same casual manner they would
treat a weather report. Warner stock can
plummet when videogames fare badly, co-
coa can lose half its value when demand for
chocolate softens, so why could not the price
of the dollar, the price of oil, the price of
money or the cost of servicing international
debt undergo 20- to 50-percent changes if
"market forces" warrant? Such was the sophisticated view of the world on which the
most powerful nation tried to build its non-
policy.

As for those who oppose this less and less
benign neglect, they have still to come up
with something better than the proposal to
put the worldeconomy in H.G. Wells' time
machine—to bring it back to the good old
Bretton Woods days, if not to the gold-ex-
change standard.

The absence of an international analytical
framework for today that could capture the
difference between the role of exchange rates
and that of Chicago pork bellies futures has
left the door wide open for each country to
follow the downhill road of economic nationalism.

Politicians were on the front line, but

economists also deserve their fair share of blame for the present state of policy disarray. Rather than intermediary investigation tools, economic models have become ends in themselves. Nobel prize winners spend their lectures teaching second-class mathematics. A modicum of calculus gives the right to look elsewhere when the world gets untidy. Like would-be bodhisattvas, our great thinkers have devised various methods of cutting the link between the nirvana of pure thought and the world of pains, emotions and problems. It takes the eyes and health of a Wassily Leontief to shout—but who listens?—that the king is naked, and the model dumb.

To no small extent, the difficulties we are presently going through and the vulnerabilities we have developed reflect a crisis of ignorance. We called for a worldeconomy. Now we have it. The time has come to learn how to make productive use of it, lest we become the victims of our own creation. Our first duty is to acknowledge how little we know. Our second is to close the widening gap between growing interdependence and declining collective capacity to deal with the perils it brings with it.

II

Whereas only three years ago energy seemed to have become, far into the future, the weak point of the world economic system, financial vulnerability now appears as its Achilles' heel.

Yet, it is worth taking note of the many threads that run from the energy crisis of the 1970s to the financial crisis of the 1980s. It is also useful to recall that financial issues as such had already arisen intermittently: at the outset of the two bursts of petro-recycling (in 1973–74 and 1979–80) and in the Brazilian debt problem of 1980. One may also wonder at the striking inclination displayed over the last few years by the financial community for moving in a few months from doomsday scenarios to self-congratulation.

There is no need here to recall in detail the recent convulsions of the world financial system. Poland is in undeclared default. Romania and Argentina did not even gather their bankers before telexing a rescheduling. Mexico is on the brink of disaster, and may be further hurt by plummeting oil prices. Countries of lesser weight have been queueing at the door of the "Club of Paris" in the dozens instead of in the handfuls.[1] Overall, it can now be estimated that almost half of all Third World and East European debt is located in countries which have had, in one way or another, to renege on their official obligations.

There is a way to look at these figures and find some source of comfort: after all, half of what could go wrong has done so and we are still here. Furthermore, the minefield has now been largely walked through—witness the noise and smoke. Falling oil prices may add Nigeria, Venezuela and Algeria to the *Who's Who* of international default, but they would also mitigate the plight of a large number of oil-importing countries, both in the South and North. Thus, to the superficial observer, the worst is over.

True, one can agree with the optimists' school that our short-term capacity to weather well-identified crises has been quite remarkable indeed. But our capacity to move from crisis management to problem solving is far less impressive. In several cases, our short-term successes can even be shown to have been at the expense of increased long-term tensions and vulnerabilities.

On the first point, our crisis management capacity has been clearly illustrated by the rapid Western reaction to the Mexican debt crisis. One could learn, almost in the same newspaper article, that Mexican debt (widely assumed to be on the order of $40–$50 billion) had come to rest on a mountain of short-term credits and was closer to $80 billion— *and* that central bankers, meeting at the Bank for International Settlements, had put together an impressive rescue package. This package included several billion dollars of immediate bilateral support, the setting up of a jumbo International Monetary Fund loan, and a three-month moratorium on short-term debt involving no less than 1,400 different banks. Not only did every element of the package quickly materialize, but the Managing Director of the IMF, Jacques de Larosière, was even able to arm-twist all banks involved into further increasing their exposure by seven percent. The "crash of 1982" will never make it into history textbooks, and the key actors in that story deserve our admiration.

The most reassuring thing we learned was that the half-dozen or so top officials who should consult regularly, actually do so whatever their ideological pronouncements. Averting the crisis implied, for example, that Paul Volcker print some money, and he rightly did so. The world economy was not sacrificed—at least not in a single stroke—to some ill-defined monetary aggregate.

In the medium and long term, however, reasons for self-congratulation are less obvious. True, some strengthening of the safety nets is taking place. The accelerated 47.5-percent increase in IMF quotas and the extension of the General Agreements to Borrow must be applauded and are probably sufficient. But present policies are not conducive, to say the least, to the elimination of the "country risks" hanging over international finance. Most problems are simply postponed. Worse, as real interest rates remain at usurious levels, the "adjustment policies" that are the counterpart of the financial first-aid package are becoming a powerful deflationary force: between the two of them, Mexico and Brazil are committed to reducing their annual imports by a dozen billion dollars. As for the wider "system risks" that stem from the operation of the system itself—such as the danger of fragmentation of the interbank market—they are hardly, if at all, on the agenda.[2]

In the next few years, one can think in terms of two broad scenarios, depending on what relationship will prevail between the "real" economic sphere and the financial one. In the first, the optimistic one, the real economy will be able to grow faster than the size of the financial "deadweight" with which it is now burdened. If that were to happen,

specific country or corporate situations could still be sources of difficulty but, on the whole, the debt overhang would gradually dissolve itself. Nothing more drastic than heavy rescheduling might be needed.

The second broad scenario, however, looks more likely, at least in the absence of concerted recovery policies of the type described below—that policies of financial "adjustment" would converge toward deflation on a global scale and would increase rather than reduce the fundamental economic, social and political vulnerabilities. At some point, the weight of accumulated debt would be such that repudiation could not be avoided, and might even be the only way out of an implosion trap. In the best cases, it would be organized, for example, through the purchase by some international institution, one hopes at a discount, of doubtful debt. It would be the bankers' pot of the century, to be divided out on principles yet unborn. In the worst cases, of course, ayatollahs of one type or another would deprive the banking community of the bitter pleasure of masterminding the dividing up of such a pot.

The first scenario is not totally beyond reach. Whereas the successful liquidation of debts is usually associated with high inflation, this need not necessarily be the case. Success depends on our capacity to promote, simultaneously, higher economic growth rates and lower real interest rates so that the real economy again starts moving faster than the debt burden. The present situation—no growth and excessively high real interest rates—is such that substantial room for maneuver does exist on both sides of the equation.

The role of interest rates in shaping our medium-term economic environment is crucial: their decline would both slow down the growth of existing debt and facilitate a stronger economic recovery. And because of their leading role in the international interest rate structure, American interest rates are really what matter. Hence, like it or not, U.S. monetary—and to some extent budgetary—policies do not belong simply to

America. If we are to preserve an integrated worldeconomy, their critical impact on the system has to be both recognized and acted on. Within a framework still to be spelled out, they have to become a matter for international discussion—negotiations would be too strong a word; "consensus building" would probably better describe the type of process to foster.

One can of course reject this view, provided that one is also ready to do away with the central role assigned to the dollar in the international monetary system. Indeed, the time for greater consistency has come. Either the United States wants to preserve the role of the dollar and the special role and privileges associated with it—and must then manage its currency as the *international* currency, which means in close cooperation with others, notably Japanese and Europeans. Or the United States gives priority to preserving the autonomy of its domestic economic policy—notably monetary—and must then work with others to greatly reduce the impact of that policy on the rest of the world.

A "leader" who is *neither* all-powerful *nor* international-minded cannot hope to retain the type of legitimacy which the pax americana had entailed. Without political legitimacy, the worldeconomy cannot operate. Policies built on the assumption that the dollar is both the central world currency and a commodity of the most trivial kind are leading us to a world of irresponsibility, conflict and, eventually, fragmentation. . . .

NOTES

[1]The Club of Paris brings together the treasury officials of the lending countries, together with those of any debtor country needing to adjust its official obligations.

[2]For a detailed analysis of "system risks" and the broader issues of financial and economic security, see the annual report of IFRI (Institut Français des Relations Internationales), *RAMSES 1982: The State of the World Economy* (Cambridge: Ballinger, 1982; and London: Macmillan, 1982) hereafter cited as *The State of the World Economy, 1982*.

---

7. Positive Adjustment in an Increasingly Interdependent World

Paolo Guerrieri

Associate Professor of Economics at the University of Camerino, Italy, Paolo Guerrieri collaborates with the Istituto Affari Internazionale of Rome on research translation.

The performance of the international economic system in the 1970s was very disappointing, in sharp contrast with the brilliant

Reprinted by permission from *Lo Spettatore Internazionale*,17, no. 2 (April–June 1982), 105–112. Copyright © 1982 Istituto Affari Internazionale. Footnotes have been deleted.

results achieved in the first twenty years after World War II. The negative records of economic trends at the national and global level in this period are well known and need not be recalled here. This period has aptly been called the "crisis of the seventies" to underline the deep changes, for the most part irreversible, in the growth mechanism on which the post-war experience had been based, and the breakdown of the balance of international economic relations that had been developed and consolidated in that period.

The failure of the rules of the game which regulated the former system has led to growing uncertainty and instability at the international level, to a multiplication of destabilizing actions on the part of the major industrial countries, to increasing conflicts between different economic areas and within each of them. Examples of such trends abound: currency crises have become a recurrent fact; protectionism, in new and old forms, is growing in the industrial area; conflicts between blocs and countries over international trade are intensifying; the increased average size of current account surpluses and deficits is generating enormous problems with regards to how to transfer and redistribute huge real and financial resources.

A series of developments and changes in relations among the various countries underscores above all the international dimension and origins of the crisis of the seventies. Over the past decade interdependence among countries and groups of countries has increased enormously, not only through a deepening of the pre-existing economic ties of the leading industrial nations, but also through an extension of the area of mutual dependence to include a growing number of less developed countries (LDCs). This network of ties (interdependence) took on decisive importance for all the major countries precisely because of the economic events of the seventies, and heavily conditioned each country's national economic policy.

In this sense we can say that both the sensitivity and vulnerability of each country to external factors have been increased. Sensitivity involves the degree to which the conditions in one country are affected by events occurring elsewhere. Vulnerability involves the degree to which a country is capable of overriding the effects of events occurring elsewhere. Therefore in recent years each

major country has been unable to avoid being influenced by outside occurrences and has been unable to reverse the effects of external events except at very high cost to itself.

Moreover, as the importance of the forces of global interdependence grew, there was no parallel development of institutions, rules and agreements to ensure the manageability of the system. Developments over the past decade, which I will deal with in detail later, confirm that the initiatives taken have indeed produced an exactly opposite effect. In fact, it would not be exaggerated to say that the international economic conditions prevailing at the beginning of the 1980s are in a state of quasi-anarchy. The disarray in international economic relations highlights the fact that the national governments' ability to manage global international factors has decreased in inverse ratio to the increase in importance of such factors.

The major countries economic policies in the '70s have to a great extent aggravated or been responsible for the current crisis in management at the international level. Governments have generally adopted policies serving exclusively national interests and have acted in accordance with traditional codes of conduct which are for the most part inadequate to solve the problems posed by the forces of global interdependence.

A good example to illustrate this inadequacy is represented by the macroeconomic policies adopted by all major countries after the first oil crisis.

The redistribution of resources at the international level as a result of the increases in the price of oil and the stagnation of domestic demand has accentuated the role played by foreign markets and international demand in influencing the nature and the intensity of the major nations' domestic growth paths. In response all countries have adopted a policy of maximizing net exports, tending toward a neo-mercantilist behavior. If all countries act in the same way, pursuing an aggressive commercial policy, attempting to relaunch domestic activity by increasing exports and decreasing imports to the detriment of their trading partners, at the macroaggregate level these policies will almost certainly be inconsistent and the end result self-defeating, as has been proved in recent years. Without forms of coordination and concertation of international effective demand the vast majority ends up as losers. This stems from the fact that the abandonment of fixed exchange rates in favor of a flexible system not only has not eliminated, as many expected, the transmission mechanism of demand impulses from country to country, but has instead, as proved by recent events, made it in many ways more effective. Differences in domestic demand from country to country, amplified by the transmission mechanism, have thus influenced the process of readjustment of current account imbalances in a much more significant way than variations of real exchange rates. The degree of interdependence of domestic demand trends has thus increased and with it the degree of interdependence of national economic policies. In the past years many proposals to neutralize the oil deficits without resorting to beggar-my-neighbor policies have been put forward in order to find a way of effectively managing this interdependence. As is well-known, these proposals have remained a dead letter. Economic nationalism has prevailed making it impossible to agree on forms of concertation and coordination of the major countries' economic policies at the international level, and even at more restricted levels, such as the European Community.

The conflict within the industrialized world to corner a bigger share of a stagnant international market—what all this means in terms of more markedly neo-protectionist policies, a widening of the area of "managed trade," intensification of the struggle to secure primary resources—is bound to worsen as the medium-term growth prospects of world income decline. And this is the result of the economic policies pursued by almost all the major industrial countries, with only rare exceptions, since the second oil crisis and the more recent "dollar shock."

The fixing of rigid targets for monetary aggregates, the return to the rules of financial orthodoxy in terms of balanced public budgets, reliance on the allocative capacities of the domestic and international market based on the conviction that redistribution of resources is favored by a relative stagnation of effective demand—these are the basic elements of a common line of economic policy that has taken hold in the major industrial countries, notably in the USA, albeit with significant differentiations from country to country. Restraint of medium-term growth by means of a restrictive monetary policy, based on the monetarist prescription of controlling the expansion of the stock of money, is seen as a panacea for contrasting inflation and reducing the oil deficit. But it is a shortsighted strategy based on national solutions, inconsistent with each other, therefore inadequate to the new international context, and will probably not bring the hoped for results. With regards to the first goal, the fight against inflation, the equilibrium of the international system which is most likely to evolve is an ex-post deflationary adjustment of quantities, while inflationary pressure stemming from external cost pushes will persist. At the same time, a slowdown in growth certainly does not favor positive adjustment to the new relative prices. It penalizes industrial investment for this purpose and the accumulation process in general. Moreover, because of the aforementioned transmission mechanism, if the monetarist recipe is followed by all the major countries, the cumulative effects will be even more disastrous.

With regards to the second goal, that of neutralizing the negative effects of the oil deficit and the energy constraint, growth in the major industrial countries would have to settle at such low levels that strongly destabilizing internal and international tensions would inevitably arise. In the 1970s energy consumption as a proportion of total domestic spending declined thanks mainly to the forms of energy saving encouraged by high oil prices and the relative stagnation of investments in energy-intensive sectors. But this is not enough to justify the optimism now in vogue of those who take for granted that the balance of power has now turned in favor of the consuming countries and that the oil constraint can be eliminated by slowing down the rate of growth. It is still true that faster expansion of world income in the medium term will be possible only if more rapid progress is made in developing energy-saving techniques and new sources of supply of energy. But this can be achieved only through greater accumulation and industrial restructuring. Therefore, an alternative economic policy at the international level will have to be found which penalizes the single areas and the world economy less in terms of growth. The major countries will have to evolve a policy aimed at avoiding drastic confrontations with the oil-producing countries, at favoring greater participation of the latter in the management of the international monetary system and at developing new forms of cooperation in the exchange of manufactured goods and raw materials. This means that in the short term the major problem for policy at the international level will continue to be that of how to deal with the importing countries' current account deficits. The magnitude of the current account imbalances of the 1970s accentuated the role of financial mechanisms in the process of real adjustment. Access to international sources of credit greatly influenced the way in which a country attempted to adjust its economy in response to the external shocks.

After the first oil crisis the industrialized countries managed a quick return to surplus positions, thus shifting the major burden of the oil deficit onto the non-oil developing countries. The oil surplus was recycled through the international private credit markets, with private banks playing a preeminent role while the part played by the official international agencies was only marginal. Credit was distributed according to the allocative criteria of the private banks and this meant limiting the circle of potential

borrowers to a small number of newly industrialized countries (NICs) which because of the favorable dynamics of their exports could offer the greatest guarantees of financial solvency. The NICs were able to finance their growth by increasing their indebtedness to dangerously high levels. Instead, the middle and low income LDCs were obliged to drastically cut back their imports and consequently their growth rates in order to reduce their external deficits. These countries were excluded from the international credit markets managed by the private banks and could resort to official loans only to a very limited extent. Their indebtedness has in fact changed very little with respect to the '60s.

The second oil crisis made it clear that new solutions would have to be found to the problems posed by the structural surpluses of the OPEC countries, since the deep division at world level between saving and investment centers has been consolidated. The most important goal is of course real adjustment on the part of the consuming countries. But in the short term it is just as important to find solutions to the problem of financing and sharing the burden of the oil deficit of the importing countries. The way in which this is done will be decisive in determining the nature and the forms of medium-term adjustment of these countries' productive structures. Important changes in the present system of international financing are needed. There are a number of factors which seem to indicate that it can no longer continue in its present form: today the possibilities of recycling the oil surpluses through the private international credit markets are more limited. The major banks operating in the Euromarkets are heavily in debt. The oil countries are less willing to deposit their surpluses in such markets. The risks of insolvency of certain debtor countries have increased with the enormous accumulation of indebtedness over the past few years. If the difficulties in managing international financial flows increase, the worst repercussions will undoubtedly be felt by the LDCs in terms of a strong penalization of their growth potential. But the negative effects would eventually be felt by the industrialized countries too because in recent years the LDCs have become important purchasers of the industrial countries' exports. Many aspects of the situation are alarming. But the solution does not lie, as many have recently suggested, in a simple return to a more rigid adherence to the rules of financial orthodoxy. In other words, a drastic reduction in the flow of credits to the LDCs is not the answer. Again to preserve monetary and financial stability, some means must be found to ensure consistency among national policies. This means minimizing conflicts over the distribution of the economic costs of real adjustment processes. In order to attenuate the above-mentioned risks certain changes, possibly very deep ones, are certainly needed in the workings of financial intermediation at the international level. It is necessary to ensure greater balance and diversification of the sources of international credit, with a bigger role for the official organizations, favoring certain trends already underway. But this is not enough to guarantee greater stability to the credit markets and to pursue the consistency objective. The financial aspects and the problems of real adjustment are closely interrelated. In order to avoid the risks of insolvency of single countries or entire areas something must be done to help the LDCs continue to expand their industrialization since their financial solidity depends largely on their development prospects over the next few years. The industrial countries could do much in this direction by incurring deficits on an appropriate scale, foregoing excessively rapid adjustments, thus offering the LDCs better opportunities in terms of aid and export credit on the one hand and markets for their exports on the other. This would open the way for growth capable of guaranteeing noteworthy advantages to the industrial world too.

Just as decisive from the point of view of real adjustment to the external oil shock is a redistribution at the international level of industrial activities by major countries. In

the 1970s both the volume and the composition of fixed industrial investment changed in all the major industrial countries. On the one hand, fixed industrial investment as a percentage of GNP has declined. On the other, the pattern of investment has changed. The share of investments to increase mechanization in various sectors has increased, with a strong acceleration of the process of intensification of plant stock, while the share of investments capable of extending production capacity and creating new jobs has declined. These changes in the characteristics of the accumulation process are in a way effects of the "general disproportion crisis" which hit the entire industrial world in the '70s. The exogenous shocks produced by changes in the prices of some primary commodities and factors of production have brought about radical changes in relative prices which have affected different sectors to varying degrees, depending on the difference in input and labor coefficients. Consequently, the sectors hardest hit by the variations in relative prices are those which depend heavily on oil and those exposed to competition from the NICs. A basic tenet of economic theory is that of minimization of costs. Changes in relative prices thus oblige firms to modify their production processes, since at the new relative prices certain productions are no longer economic. Wide and deep restructuring has therefore to take place, but this happens only in part and only in a few countries. The fall in accumulation rates has in many cases hindered the required productive adaptations. Thus, in many industrial countries government industrial policy has been prevalently defensive, aimed mainly at shoring up industries and firms in crisis and postponing positive adjustments . . . This happened through a strong increase in state intervention in the production and accumulation processes. Public transfers in various forms have become one of the most important channels for sustaining firms, giving life to open or masked mechanisms of neo-protectionism which only exacerbate the tensions among the industrial countries. The common characteristics of the phenomena mentioned so far must not obscure the significant differences which have marked the productive restructuring processes in the major industrial countries. Some countries, notably Japan and Germany, have been able to go further in adapting their industrial sectors to the new terms of trade, at the same time accentuating a strategy of accelerated internationalization of certain sectors. It is thus foreseeable that in the '80s the hierarchy of the major industrial economies will tend to be reinforced in relation to the differences in the relative weight in the various national industrial structures of the advanced technological sectors on the one hand and of the services necessary to control the processes of territorial and sectoral decentralization of important production in the NICs on the other.

To conclude it can be pointed out that over the last few years the international economic system has undergone deep qualitative changes, whose results are still difficult to predict. But what arouses even more concern is that many structural problems produced by the economic events of the '70s have not yet been resolved. The industrialized countries' vulnerability to external shocks is still very high, just as the state of international monetary relations continues to generate dangerous jolts. Contrary to what happened in the postwar period, when growing integration had been a powerful vehicle for growth, the growing interdependence of the international system has increased its fragility and potential instability at the outset of the 1980s. In such circumstances it is very difficult to say if, when and how a new stable equilibrium might be reached in the international system. Current behaviors in international areas show signs of working in the direction of a strengthening of economic nationalism. But it would be a very serious mistake to think that national solutions might offer adequate responses. No country is or can be independent, and all must in some way manage their interdependence. This is the real challenge of the '80s which all major countries must face in formulating their medium-term economic policies.

chapter 3

POWER AND THE BALANCING PROCESS

> . . . *the balance of power is not a system in the sense that the states involved necessarily have the common end in mind of preserving the independence of rival participants, but only in the sense that, as the creation of one power grouping tends to beget another, it is relatively rare to find the one long existing without the other. . . . Further, the balance of power, insofar as balance is created between the opposing blocs [or powers] is almost entirely an accidental by-product of the existence of two alliance groupings, each formed to counter the power and ambitions of the other.*
>
> Frederick Hartmann,
> *The Relations of Nations,* 5th ed. (New York: Macmillan, 1977), p. 330.

Critics argue that the balance of power is nothing but a succession of imbalances which finally lead to war. First and foremost comes the observation that states and their governments want not equilibrium but superiority (in the sense of having a "balance in the bank"). This, of course, arouses competition and distrust. Second, it is argued that the balance of power produces two rival blocs, which makes war more likely, if not inevitable, because each side is bound to see any loss or defeat to one of its members as a threat to the entire alliance. At a certain point, it is said, the two blocs or alliances explode into war, as happened in 1914 and threatened to happen on several occasions in connection with the Cold War (such as the Berlin Crisis or the Cuban Missile Crisis of 1961). It is certainly true that the operation of the balance of power breeds tension and may make compromise difficult, especially if both sides feel that a concession would be diplomatic defeat or an unacceptable admission of weakness. It is also true that the balance of power may generate an arms spiral as each side feels the other is seeking an unacceptable advantage or superiority. We have seen the Strategic Arms Limitation Treaty (SALT II) treaty rejected because of the argument that it worked unequally to the advantage of the Soviet Union, a charge earnestly denied by the supporters of arms limitation agreements.

The balance of power, it is argued, favors the great powers at the expense of the small (often to the point of partitioning or even devouring the lesser states) as occurred in Poland in the eighteenth century and to much of Eastern Europe after World War II, when the Soviet Union annexed it as a buffer against Western aggression. Former U.S. Secretary of State Henry Kissinger defended the American efforts to overthrow the democratically elected government of distant Chile as necessary to prevent an unacceptable Marxist challenge in the Western Hemisphere, and Russia actually sent troops into neighboring Afghanistan to prevent an unfavorable reversal of its influence in that country. One of the greatest challenges to the balance of power occurs when a particular great power appears determined to upset the existing balance, come what may. One of the most trenchant and compelling statements of the logic of the balance of power in this regard is the memorandum Sir Eyre Crowe wrote for the British Foreign Office in 1907. Having become the dominant power on the continent, Germany, after 1900, appeared intent upon building a navy second to none and challenging Britain as a global power. One will find in Crowe's analysis the basic uncertainty that faced Britain concerning the intentions of imperial Germany, followed by the conclusion that it didn't matter what Germany's intentions were; what really counted was Germany's growing capabilities in the face of which Britain must abandon its splendid isolation and work for the preservation of the balance of power on the continent.[1] War followed in 1914. In 1938, Britain was alone too weak to maintain the global balance, and war followed in 1939. Traditionally, war has been viewed as the ultimate means by which the balance is maintained. Peace is *not* the basic object, however desirable an object.

In a brilliant essay reproduced in this chapter, the late Martin Wight identifies no less than nine manifestations or forms of the sometimes mystifying theory and practice of "the balance of power," an often used and often misused term in "I.R." In the aftermath of World War II, the balance of power took a bipolar form. Only two states—Russia and the United States—possessed the means and will to threaten each other. Moreover, each espoused an ideology hostile to the other's existence. Without similar means or will, other states decided that their only hope of maintaining their own security and independence was through allying themselves with one of the two superpowers. Thus the states of Western Europe and Japan entered into alliance with the United States, while Communist China allied itself with the Soviet Union. In the 1960s, however, global tensions eased and divisions surfaced within the two alliances. With the defection of China from the Communist bloc and of France partially from the NATO bloc, and with the evident inability of the two superpowers to dictate to their partners on all matters, we entered what was called, perhaps inaccurately and prematurely, a multipolar system. For a while, at the height of détente, the Nixon Administration tried to sustain the idea of a five–power balance: The

---

[1]Reproduced in part as selection 16 in William C. Olson and David S. McClellan, eds. *The Theory and Practice of International Relations,* 6th ed., Englewood Cliffs, N.J.: Prentice-Hall, Inc., 1983. pp. 180–183.

Soviet Union, the United States, China, Western Europe, and Japan. To some extent, the normalization of American relations with Peking gained for the United States a margin of diplomatic maneuvering, vis-à-vis Russia, characteristic of a three–power balance. By contrast, Western Europe and Japan have contributed little to any multipolar balance-of-power model. European power is essentially economic and limited to the defense of Western Europe. This was never more evident than in the reluctance of Western Europe or Japan to join the United States in sanctions against Soviet aggression in Afghanistan. Conversely, Western Europe's dependence on the United States was never more apparent than in its rallying against a threatened Soviet invasion of Poland, and Japan's defense capabilities are ever-increasing.

One of the most distinctive features of the post-World War II era is the fact that changes in the balance of power have been caused less by aggression and the annexation of territory than by changes in regime. Leaving aside the Soviet occupation of Eastern Europe, which posed a threat to the balance of power in the traditional mode, the greatest shocks to the balance have come from the Communist takeover of power in China in 1949 and in Cuba between 1960 and 1961. Similarly, the Sino-Soviet split and the realignment of mainland China with the West was the single most dramatic shift in the balance of power against the Soviet Union. Neither of these shifts involved aggression from the outside, although the United States threat to Cuba consolidated Fidel Castro's ties with Moscow, and China aspires to leadership of the non-aligned.

Other shifts—Yugoslavian President Marshal Tito's defection from the Soviet bloc, the demise of President Sukarno's regime in Indonesia, former Egyptian President Anwar Sadat's rejection of the Soviet Union as an ally, the establishment of a Marxist regime in Angola and the Sandanista government in Nicaragua—were caused by internal developments. Even the outcome in Vietnam was preordained because it was primarily a civil war, not a case of external aggression. Of course, this perplexes and baffles both superpowers. The United States gears itself to repulse changes in the balance of power caused by external aggression, but finds itself impotent to arrest the most significant power shifts because they have occurred through internal regime changes or, in some instances, by indirect aggression. The same development confronts the Soviet Union which, with its dogmatic emphasis upon the irreversibility of socialist advances, finds itself constantly harassed and affected by challenges to its authority—first in Yugoslavia, then in Hungary, China, and later in Poland. The development of Eurocommunism and the humiliation of seeing local Communist parties outlawed in many countries receiving Soviet economic and military equipment both represent setbacks to the Soviet global balance of power. These unpredictable and largely unavoidable shifts in the balance of power derive from the instability and desperation of many Third World regimes. Most Third World powers are hostile to both superpowers, and they cannot afford the luxury of casting their foreign policy in terms of some presumed stake in the Soviet-American balance of power. They are too intent upon economic survival and their own conflicts to make the global balance the touchstone of their foreign policy. The nonalignment movement was, and to some degree still is, an attempt to avoid becoming involved in the toils of-balance-of-power politics. The United

States finds its allies more and more reluctant to follow its leadership outside Europe.

The commitment of Third World states varies and is lukewarm at best. Iraq, Syria, and the Palestine Liberation Organization (PLO) are only interested in the Soviet Union for what it can do for them; not for what they can do for Russia. The most ardently anti-Communist regimes in Latin America contribute little, if anything, to the American side of the balance. They cynically exploit American security concerns to maintain their own grip on power. What stake does an impoverished regime have in the fate of either of the two superpowers? Local and regional circumstances rarely favor the kind of intimacy on which solid alliances must depend for their value. (For example, Jordan and Saudi Arabia, two conservative Arab regimes that presumably have a stake in the security of the Persian Gulf, bluntly rejected then U.S. Secretary of State Alexander Haig's argument that the Soviet threat take precedence over their conflict with Israel).

In much of the Third World, the prevalence of desperate conditions and the lack of any hopeful future generate instability and revolution, and lead one regime to invite in the Cubans or Soviets, and another regime to invite in the Americans, or to play one superpower off against the other. These regimes often have, at best, a half-life of a few years before exploding, such as that of the Shah of Iran (supposedly the guarantor of the balance of power in the Persian Gulf) or that of Ferdinand Marcos of the Philippines.

Both the Soviet Union and the United States have attempted, for thirty years, by every known technique of favor and influence—foreign aid, military equipment, support for clients against regional and domestic enemies—to secure a favorable alignment of Third World regimes, all to little avail. The competition has cost each superpower enormous sums in money and effort, but to minimal if any permanent advantage. Those states most obviously threatened by outside military aggression—South Korea, Vietnam, Angola, Cuba, Turkey—have lined up on one side or the other; but the farthest concern of most Third World countries is the effect of their behavior on the global balance. As Hedley Bull maintains, to the extent that the global balance depends upon the stability of regional balances, the United States is at a perplexing disadvantage. Regional states are far more intent upon using American (or Soviet) influence to perpetuate their own existence or to advantage themselves at the expense of a rival (with whom the United States would also like to maintain favorable relations) than they are in serving American interests vis-à-vis the Soviet Union. The examples of this are legion: Morocco vis-à-vis Algeria, Israel vis-à-vis the Arab states and vice versa, Pakistan vis-à-vis India, South Africa vis-à-vis its black African neighbors, the regimes in Latin America vis-à-vis their own populations. This is simply another reason why the East–West balance is so inherently unstable.

It is the skill and finesse with which military capacity is employed, together with the tactical advantages that inhere in a particular situation, more than crude military power, that determines the outcome in the obscure struggles in faraway places. Many of the shifts in the postwar balance of power (or political balance) have come about through regime changes or changes in ideological and social alignments within a country which admits very limited influence. United States military power could have done little to prevent the outcome of the civil war that brought Mao Tse-tung to power; and Soviet policy, which is offensive to China's national interests, had more to do with making China an "ally" of the West than did American military power. In fact, China shifted its alignment despite the United States' war in Vietnam. Sadat reoriented Egypt's foreign policy independently of the United States. Conversely, Castro's enmity toward the United States was a consequence of a century of American intervention in Cuban affairs, sealed, of course, by the Bay of Pigs. All this suggests that the operationalization of the balance of power in the Third World presents unique obstacles and limitations which neither superpower has ever entirely appreciated. Certainly the Kremlin has made many changes in its ideological and strategic line, as has Washington, for dealing with the Third World. But limitations and costs of managing relations with the Third World in traditional balance-of-power terms has not been fully grasped. The United States has suffered self-inflicted wounds in a number of situations (for example, when it sponsored the Baghdad Pact) by seeking to establish pro-American balances of power with local regimes whose people and interests were opposed to any such American connection. An obsessive effort to integrate every part of the Third World into the global balance of power is both costly and counterproductive, especially when so much of the effort neglects the underlying needs of the Third World for economic development. The need for balance in the Third World may be considerably overrated, the Middle East excepted. As will be seen in chapter 7, knowledge of other countries' political and social dynamics and the integrity of diplomats in reporting these dynamics and of leadership in evaluating their reports, may be more vital to success than an obsession with a mechanistic balance of power. Since America cannot halt these shifts caused by internal regime or policy changes, we should at least anticipate them. Just as many regimes might want to do business with the United States as with the Soviet Union if Americans were prepared to accept them.

With this complication in mind—the inherent instability of the Third World—one should be guarded against letting Professor Hedley Bull's reassuring analysis of the balance of power lead toward complacency.

A second dilemma that balance-of-power politics confronts is that of nuclear weapons. In this chapter, Bull seems to derive considerable confidence from the existence of a nuclear balance of terror for maintaining the peace which (he claims) has helped preserve the nuclear peace by rendering deliberate resort to nuclear war, by either superpower, irrational as an instrument of policy has contributed to the maintenance of a general balance by helping to stabilize the balance between the two protagonists. Bull also takes confidence in the stability of the superpower balance from the fact that a mutual nuclear balance does not require complete equality or parity in strength, because so long as either side possesses an invulnerable margin of nuclear weapons sufficient to wreak havoc on the other, equality is not necessary (all that is needed is an invulnerable nuclear retaliatory capability sufficient to survive the enemy's first strike).

Unfortunately, as nuclear weapons systems have become more sophisticated, the idea that complete equality or parity is unnecessary has become, especially among military planners, less acceptable. We are presently at the mercy of a runaway nuclear arms race, with nuclear war a real possibility. For a time, in the aftermath of the Cuban Missile Crisis, it appeared that the two superpowers might be engaged in a process of stabilizing the nuclear balance of power. The Test Ban Treaty of 1963 and the SALT I (1972) and SALT II (1980) agreements, raised high hopes that both sides might negotiate an equilibrium by outlawing certain types of weapons systems and by numerically limiting the numbers of strategic offensive missiles. Unfortunately, the essential preconditions for negotiating such an equilibrium have eluded the two superpowers. First and foremost, the rate of technological advance is now faster than the rate at which new weapons can be brought into service. Essentially, this means that it is difficult to build a stable relationship between the two superpowers because the penalty for failing to move at the frontiers of technology is seen as potentially dangerous. Second, there exists an asymmetry in the Soviet and American situations such that either's actions can plausibly be seen by the other as harboring the worst possible intentions. For example, during SALT I negotiations, the United States refused to agree to a limit of one warhead on each missile, and proceeded to multiply its strategic arsenal and immediately acquired a capability that the Soviet Union could only see as potentially threatening to its land-based InterContinental Ballistic Missiles (ICBMs). Conversely, when the Soviet Union deployed intermediate range missiles capable of targeting on western Europe, American strategists presumed that an advantage had been achieved by their prime adversary. This led to U.S. deployment of similar weapons (after initial opposition by peace groups in Europe) on the continent of Europe.

All of this simply demonstrates the complexity of one of the basic processes which operate in international politics, one which the student of IR should at least try to master.

DISCUSSION QUESTIONS

1. Why is the balance of power such an ambiguous concept? By what logic can Bull say that it exists at all?

2. What are the several functions of the balance of power that Bull describes? How do these compare with Wight's nine ways of understanding the meaning of the concept?

3. If you had represented the United States in negotiations with its European allies, what arguments would you have used to prove that it is to their advantage for American intermediate range missiles to be deployed on their soil?

4. How does Wight distinguish between *patterns* of power and *balance* of power?

5. What is the "sandwich system of international politics"?

8. Nine Variations of The Balance of Power

Martin Wight

The late Martin Wight taught at the London School of Economics and later as a Professor of History at Sussex University.

The theoretical analysis of international politics seems to move from a shallower to a deeper level, discovering at either level a 'law' or rule of political life. At the shallower level, it is the rule that neighbouring states are usually enemies that common frontiers are usually disputed and that your natural ally is the Power in the rear of your neighbour. Let us call this, for want of a better term, the conception of the pattern of power. It is developed with great elaboration in the *Arthashastra* of Kautilya, who did not however rise to the theory of the balance of power. The famous chapter in Commynes' *Memoirs*, which is usually credited with being the earliest account in modern European literature of the balance of power, is more truly a vivid description of the pattern of power, arguing that the universal hostility between neighbouring Powers must have been ordained by God to restrain 'la bestialité de plusieurs princes et . . . le mauvastié d'autres'.[1] Namier cogently restated 'the system of odd and even numbers' in international alignments, for the benefit of a generation that had chosen to forget it, and called it the 'sandwich system of international politics'.[2]

The idea of the *pattern* of power enables us to generalize about international politics in relation to their geographical framework. The idea of the *balance* of power involves a

Excerpted by permission from Martin Wight's "The Balance of Power," in *Diplomatic Investigations: Essays in the Theory of International Politics*. (Cambridge: Harvard University Press, 1968), pp. 149–75. (Most footnotes have been removed; those remaining have been renumbered.)

higher degree of abstraction. It means thinking of the Powers less as pieces on a chessboard than as weights in a pair of scales; we mentally pluck them out of their geographical setting and arrange them according to their alliances and affinities, with the underlying notion of matching their moral weight and material strength. The pattern of power leads to considerations of strategy; the balance of power leads to considerations of military potential, diplomatic initiative and economic strength.

Compared with the pattern of power, the notion of the balance of power is notoriously full of confusions, so that it is impossible to make any statement about the 'law' or principle of the balance of power that will command general acceptance. The sources of these confusions are at least three.

The first is the equivocalness and plasticity of the metaphor of 'balance' itself. In the notion of the balance of international power it may seem that the idea of equipoise is logically prior to the idea of preponderance. This is not borne out by the early history of the figurative meanings of 'balance' in the *N.E.D.* The meaning passed from the standard of justice or reason, through the wavering of fortune or chance, subjective uncertainty (hesitation), objective uncertainty (risk), to 'power to decide or determine: authoritative control', in a quotation from Gower as early as 1393. This was probably a hundred years earlier than the use of the metaphor in any European language to describe international politics, two hundred years earlier than the first recorded usage applied to international politics in English—and *that* happens to illustrate the sense of 'authoritative control'. If it has always been the supreme task of international statesmanship to preserve the balance of power, the difficulty of the task is prefigured in the mutability and inconstancy of the metaphor itself. If we put it in an over-simplified way, we may say that the essential meaning of the verb 'to balance' is 'to compare weights'. But weights may be compared, either in order to find them equivalent; or in order to find and measure the difference; or (when they are human and social weights) in order to minister to the sense of authority of the balancer. All these meanings coexist in the phrase 'the balance of power'.

The second source of confusion is the overlap between the normative and the descriptive. Most sentences containing the phrase 'the balance of power' combine a normative with a descriptive sense. They are statements not only about what foreign policy ought to be pursued, but also about the tendency, law or principle that governs international alignments. For the balance of power means two things. It is, first, a system of foreign policy: a system which the agents in international politics uphold, neglect or repudiate in favour of some other supposed system. It is, secondly, a historical law or theoretical principle of analysis which spectators of international politics (publicists, journalists, students) derive from or apply to their reflection on international politics. But agents and spectators are not distinct classes. All agents are partly spectators (of the other agents) and all policy presupposes some theory. And all spectators (above all in politically free societies) are frustrated agents.

The third source of confusion is that weighing in the balance implies an estimate, which requires judicial detachment. And the international agent who estimates the balance of power is involved in what he estimates, and cannot be detached. His judgment of the balance is expressed as objective but is necessarily subjective. This obliquity of vision is inherent in social life, but it is

most pronounced where the issue may be national survival or destruction.

This paper will try to show that 'the balance of power' has had the following distinct meanings in international politics.

1. An even distribution of power.

2. The principle that power ought to be evenly distributed.

3. The existing distribution of power. Hence, any possible distribution of power.

4. The principle of equal aggrandizement of the Great Powers at the expense of the weak.

5. The principle that our side ought to have a margin of strength in order to avert the danger of power becoming unevenly distributed.

6. (When governed by the verb 'to hold':) A special role in maintaining an even distribution of power.

7. (Ditto:) A special advantage in the existing distribution of power.

8. Predominance.

9. An inherent tendency of international politics to produce an even distribution of power.

It is the fascination of the subject that these senses are difficult to disentangle, and almost any sentence about the balance of power, as this paper will perhaps illustrate involuntarily more than deliberately, is likely to imply two or more meanings at the same time.

The original application of the metaphor of the balance to international politics is the sense of *an even distribution of power,* a state of affairs in which no Power is so preponderant that it can endanger the others. Let us call this sense 1. This is the primary meaning of 'the balance of power', to which there is always a tendency to return. If there are three or more weights that are thus considered as balanced (as with the five major Powers of Italy between 1454 and 1494, or the five Great Powers that formed the Concert of Europe in the nineteenth century) it may be called a multiple balance. If there are only two weights in consideration (as with the Habsburgs and France in the sixteenth and seventeenth centuries, Britain and France in the eighteenth, the Triple Alliance and the Triple Entente before 1914, or America and Russia since 1945) it may be called a simple balance. The conception of the simple balance involves a higher degree of abstraction than that of the multiple balance. It means a selective concentration upon the greatest Powers. There has never yet, in the history of Western international society, actually been a simple balance. When there have been rival predominant Powers, they have always had lesser Powers around or between them, capable of being considered as contributing to a multiple balance. Even the conformation of two world empires, as in the case of Rome and Persia, has been varied and enlivened by unreliable vassals and intractable buffers, an Armenia or an Osroene or a Palmyra; and the great contest between Heraclius and Chosroes was influenced, perhaps decisively, by the independent action of the Avars, Bulgars, Slavs, Gepids, and Chazars.

But the distinction between multiple and simple balance is immaterial to the conception of the balance of power as an even distribution. In both the multiple and the simple balance there is the idea of equipoise. When Machiavelli wrote that, before the French invasion of 1494, 'Italia era in un certo modo bilanciata', when Guicciardini wrote that Lorenzo de'Medici 'procurava con ogni studio che le cose d'Italia in modo bilanciate si mantenessino che piu in una che in un' altra parte non pendessino', they were trying to describe such an even distribution of power.[3] Thus Sir Thomas Overbury's description of the states-system a hundred years later, in 1609, when the Spanish attempt at predominance had been defeated:

'It is first to be considered that this part of Christendom is balanced betwixt the three Kings of Spain, France, and England; as the other part is betwixt the Russian, the Kings of Poland, Sweden and Denmark. For as for Ger-

many, which if it were entirely subject to one Monarchy, would be terrible to all the rest; so being divided betwixt so many Princes and those of so equal power, it serves only to balance itself, and entertain easy war with the Turk; while the Persian withholds him in a greater.'[4]

By a similar use of the metaphor, Churchill described the European situation brought about by the Locarno Treaties: 'Thus there was a balance created in which Britain, whose major interest was the cessation of the quarrel between Germany and France, was to a large extent arbiter and umpire'; and Eden wrote, 'The fighting in Korea achieved a balance of power, recognized and respected as such'. The same notion of even distribution appears in Lester Pearson's dictum that 'The balance of terror has replaced the balance of power'. In this usage the word 'balance' retains its meaning of 'equilibrium', and it is perhaps most likely to appear as the object of such verbs as maintain and preserve, upset and overturn, or redress and restore.

Almost insensibly, the phrase passes from a descriptive to a normative use. It comes to mean (2) *the principle that power ought to be evenly distributed*. When during the American Revolutionary War George III was seeking the assistance of Catherine the Great, she replied: 'Her ideas perfectly correspond with his, as to the balance of power; and she never can see with indifference any essential aggrandizement or essential diminution, of any European state take place'. The *Manchester Guardian* wrote in 1954: 'If there is to be coexistence there must be a balance of power, for if power is unbalanced the temptation to communism to resume its crusade will be irresistible'. In each of these quotations sense 2 can be seen emerging out of sense 1. In 1713 the phrase was written into the Treaty of Utrecht to justify the perpetual separation of the crowns of France and Spain: 'for the end that all care and suspicions may be removed from the minds of men and that the Peace and Tranquillity of the Christian World may be ordered and stabilized in a just Balance of Power (which is the best and most solid foundation of mutual friendship and a lasting general concord)'. Thenceforward, for two hundred years, the balance of power was generally spoken of as if it were the constituent principle of international society, and legal writers described it as the indispensable condition of international law. It was even ironically apostrophized as the condition of private prosperity.

> 'The *balance of pow'r*? ah! till that is restor'd,
> What solid delight can retirement afford?'

sang Isaac Hawkins Browne during the War of the Polish Succession. 'The balance of power had ever been assumed as the known common law of Europe,' wrote Burke in the *Regicide Peace*, 'the question had only been (as it must happen) the more or less inclination of that balance,' 'The balance of power in Europe,' said Lord John Russell sixty-five years later, 'means in effect the independence of its several states. The preponderance of any one Power threatens and destroys this independence.' The Concert of Europe was in origin and essence a common agreement on the principle of the balance of power.

But it is the trouble about international politics that the distribution of power does not long remain constant and the Powers are usually in disagreement on its being an even distribution. Most arrangements of power favour some countries, which therefore seek to preserve the *status quo,* and justify it as being a true balance in the sense of an equilibrium; and are irksome to other countries whose policy is accordingly revisionist. Just as such phrases as 'the hereditary system' or 'property' ceased to have a sacrosanct ring in domestic politics when they were uttered by men of the self-made or unpropertied classes, so 'the balance of power' loses its connotation of being grounded on morality and law when it is uttered by representatives of Powers that believe themselves at a disadvantage. This linguistic process can be seen at work in a discussion between Cripps and

Stalin in Moscow in July 1940. Cripps had been sent to Moscow as British ambassador with the task of persuading Stalin that Germany's conquest of Western Europe endangered Russia as well as Britain. 'Therefore both countries,' he argued, 'ought to agree on a common policy of self-protection against Germany and on the re-establishment of the European balance of power'. Stalin replied that he did not see any danger of Europe being engulfed by Germany. 'The so-called European balance of power,' he said, 'had hitherto oppressed not only Germany but also the Soviet Union. Therefore the Soviet Union would take all measures to prevent the re-establishment of the old balance of power in Europe.' Similarly Hitler to Ciano in 1936: 'Any future modifications of the Mediterranean balance of power must be in Italy's favour.' Here the phrase has lost any sense of an even distribution of power, and has come to mean simply (3) *the existing distribution of power.* The usage is not confined to revisionist Powers. When the Parliamentary Secretary to the Admiralty told the House of Commons in 1951 that 'the balance of sea power has tilted away from us very dramatically during the last ten years', he was using the phrase neutrally and unemotionally. And by a natural extension it comes to mean *any possible distribution of power,* future as well as present or past. Thus Churchill wrote to Eden in 1942: 'No man can see how the balance of power will lie or where the winning armies will stand at the end of the war.' This is possibly the most frequent usage—to describe the relationship of power prevailing at a given time. The word 'balance' has entirely lost its meaning of 'equilibrium'. There is less notion of stability, more of perpetual change about it than in sense 1; and it will frequently be found as the subject of a sentence (it will be said 'to have changed' or a new one will be said 'to be appearing') as though it lies largely beyond human control.

So far we have been considering 'the balance of power' roughly as a description of a state of affairs; it is now necessary to consider it as a policy; though it will be clear that the two conceptions are inseparable. The principle that power ought to be evenly distributed, raises the question, By whom? There seem to be three possible answers. a) It may be said that the even distribution of power will take place through the combined skill and effort of all the Powers concerned, or, in the case of a simple balance, of *both* the Powers or coalitions concerned. b) It may be said that the even distribution of power will be the responsibility of a particular Power, which is said 'to hold the balance'. This answer presupposes a multiple balance. Where there is a truly simple balance, a holder of the balance is excluded. The holder of the balance is, ex-hypothesi, a third force; he may be *tertius gaudens*. c) It may be said, again, that the even distribution of power will come about, over the widest field and in the long run, through a fundamental law or tendency of political forces to fall into equilibrium. Let us consider these answers in turn.

First, the argument that the maintenance of an even distribution of power can take place through the combined skill of all the Powers. If the broad test of an even distribution of power is the absence of a grand alliance against a Power aiming at universal monarchy, then there was such an even distribution from the defeat of Louis XIV to the French Revolution and from the defeat of Napoleon to the First World War. (Suitable qualifications must be made for the anti–British coalition in the American Revolutionary War, and the partial alliance against Russia in the Crimean. And by such a broad test, conflicts on the scale of the Polish Succession, Austrian Succession, and Seven Years Wars have to be rated as incidents in preserving an even distribution of power—a generous proviso.) The maintenance of a multiple balance of power during these periods must in some degree be attributed to the skill of the Powers concerned; but allowance must be made for external circumstances, especially the opportunity for expansion outside Europe. And it cannot be overlooked that these periods of multiple balance came to centre upon questions of

partition—of Poland and Turkey at the end of the eighteenth century, of Turkey, Africa and China at the end of the nineteenth. The balance of power, in effect, came to mean (4) *the principle of equal aggrandizement of the Great Powers at the expense of the weak.*

. . . Nothing in European history has done more to discredit the idea of the balance of power than the belief that it led naturally to such a crime as the Partition of Poland.

'The inventors of this evil project, in the whole course of their enterprise invoked the principles of the balancing system as their guide and polar star, and actually followed them, so far as circumstances would permit, in their division of the spoil, and whilst they inflicted the most fatal wounds upon the spirit and very existence of this system, borrowed its external forms, and even its technical language. *Corruptio optimi pessima*: To behold this noble system, which the wisdom of the European community had devised for its security and welfare, thus perverted, was an odious spectacle.'[5]

The battle of the concessions in China in 1897–8 was similarly an exercise in adjusting the balance. For the British, the sole object of their acquisition of Wei-hai-wei was 'to maintain balance of power in Gulf of Pechili, menaced by Russian occupation of Port Arthur'.[6]

The multiple balance lasts as long as no conflict of interests has arisen to make a decisive schism between the Great Powers. Sooner or later this occurs, and the Powers divide into opposite camps. The multiple balance now resolves itself into a simple balance: it is no longer a merry-go-round but a seesaw. The multiple balance of the eighteenth century dissolved directly into a state of war, near-general war in 1778–9, general war in 1792–3. The nineteenth century Concert of Europe was more skilful in prolonging the peace; the transformation of the multiple into a simple balance began with the Franco-Russian alliance in 1892, or rather, with the lapse of the Reinsurance Treaty in 1890, and peace was maintained by a simple balance for another twenty years. The corresponding transformation from multiple to simple balance between the two World Wars occurred in 1936 with the formation of the Rome-Berlin Axis against the League Powers.

In the circumstances of a simple balance, when each of two Powers or coalitions is trying to maintain an even distribution of power between them by a competition in armaments or a diplomatic struggle for alliances, the idea of the balance of power as equality of aggrandizement tends to be eclipsed (though it may still have a place) by another idea of the balance of power (which may also appear in the circumstances of a multiple balance). This is (5) *the principle that my side ought to have a margin of strength, in order to avert the danger of power becoming unevenly distributed.* Here the word balance acquires the sense it has in the phrases 'balance of trade' or 'bank balance', i.e., not an equality of assets and debits but a surplus of one over the other. And here the contradiction between the subjective and objective estimates of the balance of power, between a political position as seen from the inside and as seen from the outside, becomes acute. When Dean Acheson first formulated the policy of 'negotiating from a position of strength', he apparently meant a levelling up of America's strength to an equality with Russia's, the restoration of an equipoise; but the phrase was equivocal from the start, and quickly acquired the sense of possessing a margin of strength.[7] It was sharply illustrated by headlines in *The Times* newspaper in 1963: 'Mr. McNamara says West now has Superiority: US Forces nearing proper Balance for Peace.'

The logic of this development of the idea of 'balance' is illustrated by a story which Norman Angell somewhere tells. Angell as a young man heard Churchill as a young Cabinet minister making a speech in Oxford in 1913. 'There is just one way in which you can make your country secure and have peace,' Churchill said, 'and that is to be so much stronger than any prospective enemy that he dare not attack you—and this is, I submit to you, gentlemen, a self-evident

proposition.' Angell got up and asked him if the advice he had just given was the advice he would give to Germany. But it is not simple patriotism or nationalism which has given this interpretation of the balance its greatest potency, but a system where 'my side' is a coalition identified with international virtue and legality. Collective security under the League of Nations, as we shall note below, was built upon the assumption that the law-abiding Powers would have a constant preponderance over any possible aggressor.

The fullest transformation of the idea of the balance of power seems to arise out of the notion of 'holding the balance'. The Power that 'holds the balance' is the Power that is in a position to contribute decisive strength to one side or the other.

The figure is seen at its simplest in Camden's famous description of Queen Elizabeth:

'There sat she as an heroical princess and umpire betwixt the Spaniards, the French, and the Estates; so as she might well have used that saying of her father, *Cui adhaereo, praeest,* that is, 'the party to which I adhere getteth the upper hand'. And true it was which one hath written, that France and Spain are as it were the scales in the balance of Europe, and England the tongue or the holder of the balance.'[8]

There is a little confusion in the metaphor, since the tongue of a balance is an index to show which way the scales incline, not a stabilizer. The idea appears in an equally pure form in a letter from Palmerston to William IV in 1832. He is explaining the quarrels between France on the one side and Austria, Prussia and Russia on the other, about the treaty establishing Belgian independence.

'Upon the occasion of all these pretensions the British Government brought the three Powers to bear upon France, and France was upon all compelled to yield; latterly the three Powers have in their turn been unreasonable and deficient in good faith, and have endeavoured, under false pretences, to defeat the treaty they had ratified and to mar the arrangement they had guaranteed. The British Government then brought France to bear upon the three Powers, and it is to be hoped with ultimate success. Rivals in military strength, as France and the three Powers are, Your Majesty may be said practically to hold the scales of the balance of Europe. France will not venture to attack the three Powers, if she is also to be opposed by England; and the three Powers will pause long before they attack France, if they think that France could in that case reckon upon the support of England. Thus, then, it appears . . . that Your Majesty has peculiarly the power of preserving the general peace and that by throwing the moral influence of Great Britain into one scale or the other, according as the opposite side may manifest a spirit of encroachment of injustice, Your Majesty may . . . become on many occasions the arbiter of events in Europe.'[9]

This is the traditional conception, expressed in the simple terms suited to its recipient. Here, to hold the balance of power means, (6) *possessing a special role in maintaining an even distribution of power.*

It became part of the traditional British doctrine on the matter that a holder of the balance was essential to the very idea of the balance of power. Swift explicated the metaphor with characteristic clarity:

'It will be an eternal Rule in Politicks, among every free People, that there is a Ballance of Power to be carefully held by every State within it self, as well as among several States with each other.

'The true Meaning of a Ballance of Power, either without, or within a State, is best conceived by considering what the Nature of a Ballance is. It supposes three things. First, the part which is held, together with the Hand that holds it; and then the two Scales, with whatever is weighed therein. Now consider several States in a Neighbourhood: In order to preserve Peace between these States, it is necessary they should be formed into a Ballance, whereof one, or more are to be Directors, who are to divide the rest into equal Scales, and upon Occasions remove from one

into the other, or else fall with their own Weight into the lightest: So in a State within itself, the Ballance must be held by a third Hand, who is to deal the remaining Power with the utmost Exactness into each Scale. Now it is not necessary, that the Power should be equally divided between these three; for the Ballance may be held by the Weakest, who by his Address and Conduct, removing from either Scale, and adding of his own, may keep the Scales duly poised.'[10]

One of Swift's editors dogmatically contradicted his author on this point: 'Swift forgot that a balance ceases to be true, as soon as its adjustment is entrusted to anyone. It must either be maintained by its own equilibrium or it becomes a pretence sustained only by the application of arbitrary force.'[11] This comment illustrates the growing repudiation of the policy of the balance of power by a strand of British opinion in the nineteenth century, but it also indicates the ambiguities in the idea of holding the balance. They become apparent if we ask two questions: *Who* holds the balance in any given situation? and if the function of holding the balance be defined as an ability to contribute decisive strength to one side or the other, what is implied in the notion of *decisive strength*?

Who holds the balance? There are good grounds for the traditional British belief that it has been peculiarly Britain's role to hold the balance of Europe. From 1727 down to 1868 (with one or two lapses) the annual Mutiny Act described the function of the British army as 'the preservation of the balance of power in Europe'. To hold the balance has been a policy suited to an insular Power enjoying a certain detachment from Continental rivalries. But there have been other Powers with a degree of geographical detachment, particularly Russia. At the end of the War of the Austrian Succession the Tsaritsa Elizabeth controlled the balance of Europe. In the American Revolutionary War Catherine the Great held the balance between Britain and the anti-British coalition of France, Spain and Holland. In the War of the Bavarian Succession she was in a similar position, courted by both Austria and Prussia, and assuming the role of the protectress of the German constitution, hitherto played by France. Likewise, between March and September 1939 Stalin held the balance between the Western Powers and the Axis. In other words, a Power holds the balance only so long as it does not commit itself; and when it has committed itself, there is a new situation in which the balance will probably be held by another Power.

Indeed, holding the balance of power has its *n*th Power problem. It is not only the Great Powers that can aspire to the role. Sometimes a small Power, through the accident of strategic position or the energy of its ruler, can contribute useful if not decisive strength to one side or the other, as Savoy in the seventeenth and eighteenth centuries used to hold the balance on the Alps, or as Yugoslavia today holds a balance in South-eastern Europe between the Communist and Western blocs. The belief that they can hold the balance of power may soothe the pride of Great Powers in decline. Immediately after the War, de Gaulle stated his aim of grouping together the states which touch the Rhine, Alps and Pyrenees, and making of this organization the arbiter between the Anglo-Saxon and Soviet camps. 'France, in equipping herself with a nuclear weapon,' he said in 1959, 'will render a service to world equilibrium'. (The equilibrium between the Western and Communist blocs, or the equilibrium within NATO?) Many Japanese and some Germans have had the same idea for their own country. Acton argued that it was the Papacy itself which invented the system of the balance of power at the time of the Reformation to replace the Papal ascendancy of the Middle Ages. 'The Popes undertook to maintain their spiritual freedom through their territorial independence by the opposite plan to that of the *republicana Christiana* under pope and emperor, by *preventing* predominance of any one power, not by courting it. So they created the system of

balance of power as the security of their temporal power, as of old the imperial supremacy had been the implement and safeguard of their spiritual predominance.'[12] Others have attributed the beginnings of this policy to Venice. The Italian states aimed to hold the balance between the Kings of Spain and France as early as did Henry VIII. In 1553 Mary, Regent of the Netherlands, wrote to the imperial ambassador in England about the dangers which the Franco-Turkish alliance was bringing upon Italy, and added that if the Italian states knew their own interests they would confederate against the French King. . . .

Sometimes a balance has been held by barbarians outside the pale of international society: the Iroquois held the balance in the first half of the eighteenth century between the English and French in North America. Whenever a Power is courted by both sides, it holds in some degree the balance of power. Turkish policy in the Second World War held a delicate balance both between the two belligerent blocs and between the Western Powers and Russia. Many a Small Power likes to think that it holds a balance, if only between its allies. The balance of power (in sense 2) is incompatible with the doctrines professed by the Afro-Asian states, and Nehru argued that the neutralist states cannot be a third force to maintain the balance of power, because they lack military strength to throw into the scales—they can only be a third area, united on moral not military grounds, through which efforts at conciliation could be channelled. But this implies a devaluation of the moral element in politics which seems inconsistent with much of Afro-Asian doctrine. Indian mediation over the repatriating of prisoners taken in the Korean War, the role of Krishna Menon at the Geneva Conference in 1954, Indian chairmanship of the three international commissions for supervizing the Indo-Chinese armistice, seemed to show to many Afro-Asians and others that India could act as an arbiter. The *Manchester Guardian* early in 1953 described the Indian attitude in these words: 'Their view about their duties in Asia is like that of European statesmen of the eighteenth century, who, in a situation which was constantly changing, planned the combinations of the Powers by which a certain stability might be achieved.' There comes a point at which it is difficult to draw any clear distinction between 'maintaining' the balance of power (a function connected with sense 2) and 'holding' it. For any Power may find, in some circumstances, that it possesses a special role in preserving an even distribution of power. And we encounter here the confusion between the objective and the subjective estimates. There are many international situations in which an involved Power, and a Power relatively detached, will each interpret its policy by a responsibility for holding the balance. The notion of holding the balance shades easily into the hope of contributing some strength, whether decisive or not, which is almost equivalent to possessing some degree of freedom of action.

This brings us to the second question. What are the implications and consequences of holding the balance? If he who holds the scales is weaker than either of the Powers or coalitions which make the scales, his function will only be that of conciliator; but if he is as strong as either of them, or stronger, he will tend to become an arbiter. The answer lurks in Churchill's description of Locarno, and in the last sentence of the passage from Palmerston, both quoted above: 'Your Majesty may become the arbiter of events in Europe.' And a Power in this role may not always play it in a way that other Powers regard as just. It may be concerned less to maintain an even distribution of power than to improve its own position, 'The great danger of inviting, and accustoming Russia, on every emergency, to be the Mediatrix of Europe,' wrote the *Observer* in 1803, 'is that she will at length consider herself the Mistress of it also'. The activity of holding the balance easily slides from possessing a special role (which implies a sense of duty) to possessing a special advantage; as easily as the notion of the balance of power slides from *an even* distribution to *any* distribution. There is an equivocality about most of the English claims to hold the balance of power from the sixteenth to the nineteenth centuries. It is illustrated by the earliest recorded use of the phrase in English, in Fenton's dedication to Queen Elizabeth of his translation of Guicciardini: 'And lastly [God] hath erected your seate upon a high hill or sanctuarie, and put into your hands the ballance of power and justice, to peaze and counterpeaze [appease and counterpoise] at your will the actions and counsels of all the Christian Kingdomes of your time.' 'Balance' here means 'control'. Compare Waller's *Panegyric to My Lord Protector* in 1655:

'Heaven, (that has placed this island to give
    law,
To balance Europe, and her states to awe)
In this conjunction does on Britain smile:
The greatest leader, and the greatest isle!'

When an English politician in 1704 rejoiced that the battle of Blenheim 'has given the balance of Europe into the Queen's hands', he meant that it had made England the strongest Power on the continent, with a freedom of action greater than that of other Powers. Canning's doctrine that Britain should hold the balance between the conflicting ideologies on the Continent was similar. As he wrote to his friend Bagot, the British ambassador at St. Petersburg, soon after the enunciation of the Monroe Doctrine, 'The effect of the ultra-liberalism of our Yankee co-operators, on the ultra-despotism of our Aix la Chapelle allies, gives me just the balance that I wanted.' But this was Canning's private comment on what he afterwards publicly described as calling 'the New World into existence to redress the balance of the Old', and it contains perhaps a flavour of sense 5, that my side ought to have a margin of strength. Continental Powers have always noted that while Britain traditionally claimed to hold the balance of Europe with her right hand, with her left hand she was establishing an oceanic hegemony which refused for two centuries to admit any principle of equilibrium. Thus, from possessing a special role in maintaining an even distribution of power, holding the balance imperceptibly slides into (7) *possessing a special advantage in the existing distribution of power.* When Coral Bell writes:

'A consistent and in some ways a justified criticism of the policies of the western Powers in the period of the Cold War has been that they have tended to deliver the balance of power into the hands of Germany and Japan, both potential revisionist states'.[13]

It is the second rather than the first of these meanings of the phrase that is conveyed.

It will be seen that the idea of the balance of power as a description of a state of affairs tends to slip away from the meaning of an even distribution to that of any possible distribution of power; and that the idea of the balance of power as a policy tends to slip away from the meaning of a duty or responsibility for preserving an even distribution, to that of enjoying a margin of strength or some special advantage. By these routes the balance of power comes to mean possessing a decisive advantage, or (8) *possessing predominance.* In this sense Chester Bowles wrote in 1956 that 'the two-thirds of the world who live in the undeveloped continents . . . will ultimately constitute the world balance of power'.[14] In this sense Bonaparte wrote to the Directory in 1797: 'Nous tenons la balance de l'Europe; nous la ferons pencher comme nous voudrons.' And more dramatically, the Kaiser, visiting England for Queen Victoria's funeral in 1901, told Lord Lansdowne that the traditional English policy of upholding the balance of power was exploded: 'Die balance of power in Europa sei ich.' Here at last the word balance has come to mean the opposite of its primary diplomatic sense: equilibrium has become preponderance,

balance has become overbalance. Or, if you prefer, the word has returned to its still earlier pre-diplomatic sense of authoritative control. And the verbs that govern the phrase pass from possession to identification: from holding, through inclining, to 'constituting' or 'being'.

There remains to be considered the third answer to the question, By whom is power to be evenly distributed? 'The balance of power' sometimes implies an assertion that the groupings of Powers fall into everchanging but ever reliable conditions of equilibrium. Thus it means (9) *an inherent tendency of international politics to produce an even distribution of power.* This assets a 'law' of international politics that underlies and reinforces the 'principle' of the balance of power in sense 2; so that even if Powers neglect or repudiate the principle, the law will be seen at work overruling them . . .

. . . Between 1848 and 1914, says A. J. P. Taylor, the balance of power 'seemed to be the political equivalent of the laws of economics, both self-operating. If every man followed his own interest, all would be prosperous; and if every state followed its own interest, all would be peaceful and secure.'[15] 'The Balance of Power', says Toynbee, 'is a system of political dynamics that comes into play whenever a society articulates itself into a number of mutually independent local states.' It 'operates in a general way to keep the average calibre of states low in terms of every criterion for the measurement of political power . . . a state which threatens to increase its calibre above the prevailing average becomes subject, almost automatically, to pressure from all the other states that are members of the same political constellation'.[16] It might even be said that in contemporary political writings, the balance of power as this kind of sociological law has tended to replace the balance of power as moral and legal principle.

But even in this usage there is a tendency

to slide away from the notion of even distribution of power—to express rather the endless shiftings and regroupings of power, the scales perpetually oscillating without coming to rest. When Rostovtzeff writes 'The complicated political situation which constituted the balance of power among the Hellenistic States gave rise to almost uninterrupted warfare', the long perspective almost loses sight of the recurring equilibria of power, and the phrase becomes almost synonymous with the states-system itself. . . .

. . . Is then the balance of power the guarantee of the independence of nations? or is it the occasion of war? The only answer is that it is both. So long as the absence of international government means that Powers are primarily preoccupied with their survival, so long will they seek to maintain some kind of balance between them. It is easy to point to instances in which the final move in the rectification of the balance has been war. It is less easy, either to remember, or to establish, how often the balance of power has averted war. For the balance of power is not the 'cause' of war; the cause of war, however one chooses to identify it, lies in the political conditions which the balance of power in some degree regulates and reduces to order. The alternative to the balance of power is not the community of power: unless this means federation, it is a chimera. International politics have never revealed, nor do they today, a habitual recognition among states of a community of interest overriding their separate interest, comparable to that which normally binds individuals within the state. And where conflicts of interest between organized groups are insurmountable, the only principle of order is to try to maintain, at the price of perpetual vigilance, an even distribution of power. The alternatives are either universal anarchy, or universal dominion. The balance of power is generally regarded as preferable to the first, and most people have not yet been persuaded that the second is so preferable to

the balance of power that they will easily submit to it.

NOTES

[1]Commynes, *Memoirs*, Book V, Chap. xviii, Calmette ed., (Pan's: Champion, 1925) II, 211.
[2]L. B. Namier, *Conflicts* ([1]Macmillan, 1942), p. 14; cf. *Vanished Supremacies* (Hamish Hamilton, 1958), p. 170.
[3]Machiavelli, *Il Principe*, ch. xx (ed. Burd, p. 329). . . .
[4]Sir Thomas Overbury, *Observations in his Travels*, in *Stuart Tracts 1603–1693*, ed. C. H. Firth (Constable, 1903), p. 227.
[5]F. von Gentz, *Fragments upon the Balance of Power in Europe*, p. 77, as translated in Wheaton, *History of the Law of Nations*, pp. 279–80.
[6]*British Documents on the Origins of the War*, ed. Gooch and Temperley, vol. i, no. 47.
[7]Coral Bell, *Negotiation from Strength* (Chatto and Windus, 1962), chap. i.
The Times, November 19, 1963. The Washington correspondent wrote: 'In a policy speech today [18 Nov.] Mr. Robert McNamara, the United States Secretary of Defence, said that the west enjoyed a military superiority over the Soviet block in conventional forces as well as strategic and tactical nuclear weapons. The significance of this position of strength was manifold. . . . He rejected the idea that the Soviet block could ever achieve superiority and thus initiate another arms race, although new technological developments might require important expenditures in future. He saw the American forces rapidly approaching the proper balance required to maintain peace.'
[8]William Camden, *History of Elizabeth* (translated 3rd edition, 1675), p. 223.
[9]C. K. Webster, *The Foreign Policy of Palmerston* (Bell, 1951), ii, 801–2.
[10]*A Discourse of the Contests and Dissentions in Athens and Rome* (1701), chap. i, *A Tale of a Tub and other Early Works*, ed. Herbert Davis (Blackwell, 1957) p. 197.
[11]Henry Craik, *Selections from Swift* (Clarendon Press, 1892), i, 367.
[12]F. N. Gasquet, *Lord Acton and his Circle*, (Allen, 1906), p. 250. Cf. Ranke, *History of the Popes*, book I, chap. iii (Bohn Library, Bell, 1913) i, 67.
[13]Coral Bell, *Survey of International Affairs 1954* (Oxford University Press, 1957), p. 10.
[14]'Why I will vote Democratic', *Christianity and Crisis*, October 15, 1956, p. 137.
[15]*The Struggle for Mastery in Europe 1848–1918* (Clarendon Press, 1954).
[16]A. J. Toynbee, *A Study of History* (Oxford University Press, 1934), iii, 301–2.

9. The Balance of Power and its Present Relevance

Hedley Bull

An Australian, the author occupied the Montague Burton Professorship of International Relations at Oxford University before his untimely death at the prime of his intellectual and political influence.

We mean here by "the balance of power" what Vattel meant: "a state of affairs such that no one power is in a position where it is preponderant and can lay down the law to others." It is normally military power that we have in mind when we use the term, but it can refer to other kinds of power in world politics as well. The state of affairs of which Vattel speaks can be realised in a number of different ways.

First we have to distinguish a simple balance of power from a complex one, that is to say a balance made up of two powers from one consisting of three or more. The simple balance of power is exemplified by the clash of France and Habsburg Spain/Austria in the sixteenth and seventeenth centuries, and by the clash of the United States and the Soviet Union in the Cold War. The complex balance of power is illustrated by the situation of Europe in the mid-eighteenth century, when France and Austria, now detached from Spain, were joined as great powers by England, Russia, and Prussia. It is also illustrated by world politics at the present juncture, when the United States and the Soviet Union have been joined by China as a great power, with Japan as a potential fourth great power and a combination of Western European powers as a potential fifth.

Excerpted from Hedley Bull, *The Anarchical Society* (New York: Columbia University Press, 1977), pp. 101–124 Copyright © 1977 by Hedley Bull, Reprinted by permission of Columbia University Press and Macmillan, London and Basingstoke.

However, no historical balance of power has ever been perfectly simple or perfectly complex. Situations of a simple balance of power have always been complicated by the existence of some other powers, whose ability to influence the course of events may be slight but is always greater than zero. Situations of a complex balance of power are capable of being simplified by diplomatic combinations, as for example, the six-power balance of the pre-First World War period was resolved into the simple division of the Triple Alliance and the Triple Entente.

Whereas a simple balance of power necessarily requires equality or parity in power, a complex balance of power does not. In a situation of three or more competing powers the development of gross inequalities in power among them does not necessarily put the strongest in a position of preponderance, because the others have the possibility of combining against it.

In a simple balance of power the only means available to the power that is falling behind is to augment its own intrinsic strength (say, in the eighteenth century its territory and population; in the nineteenth century its industry and military organization; in the twentieth century its military technology). Because in a complex balance of power there exists the additional resource of exploiting the existence of other powers, either by absorbing or partitioning them, or by allying with them, it has usually been held that complex balances of power are more stable than simple ones.

Second, we must distinguish the general balance of power, that is, the absence of a preponderant power in the international system as a whole, from a local or particular balance of power, in one area or segment of the system. In some areas of the world at present, such as the Middle East or the Indian subcontinent or Southeast Asia, there may be said to be a local balance of power; in others, such as Eastern Europe or the Caribbean, there is a local preponderance of power. Both sorts of situation are consistent with the fact that in the international system as a whole there is a general balance of power. . . .

Third, one should distinguish a balance of power which exists subjectively from one that exists objectively. It is one thing to say that it is generally believed that a state of affairs exists in which no one state is preponderant in military strength; it is another to say that no one state is in fact preponderant. It is sometimes generally believed that a rough balance of military strength exists between two parties when this does not reflect the "true" position as revealed by subsequent events; in Europe in the winter of 1939–40, for example, it was widely held that a military balance existed between the Allies and Germany, but a few weeks' fighting in the spring showed that this was not the case. A balance of power in Vattel's sense requires that there should be general belief in it; it is not sufficient for the balance to exist objectively but not subjectively. . . .

But if the subjective element of belief in it is necessary for the existence of a balance of power, it is not sufficient. If a power is in fact in a position to gain an easy victory over its neighbour, even though it is generally thought to be balanced by it, this means that the beliefs on which the balance of power rests can quickly be shown to be false, and a new subjective situation brought about. A balance of power that rests not on the actual will and capacity of one state to withstand the assaults of another, but merely on bluff and appearances, is likely to be fragile and impermanent.

Fourth, we must distinguish between a balance of power which is fortuitous and one which is contrived. A fortuitous balance of power is one that arises without any conscious effort on the part of either of the parties to bring it into being. A contrived balance is one that owes its existence at least partly to the conscious policies of one or both sides. . . .

The most elementary form of contrived balance of power is a two-power balance in which one of the parties pursues a policy of preventing the other from attaining military preponderance. A more advanced form is a three-power balance in which one power seeks to prevent any of the others from attaining preponderance, not merely by augmenting its own military strength, but also by siding with whatever is the weaker of the other two powers: the policy known as "holding the balance." This form of balance-of-power policy was familiar in the ancient world, as David Hume argues, relying mainly on Polybius's celebrated account of the policy of Hiero of Syracuse, who sided with Carthage against Rome.

It is a further step from this to the policy of preserving a balance of power throughout the international system as a whole. This is a policy which presupposes an ability to perceive the plurality of interacting powers as comprising a single system or field of forces. It presupposes also a continuous and universal system of diplomacy, providing the power concerned with intelligence about the moves of all the states in the system, and with means of acting upon them. The policy of preserving a balance throughout the international system as a whole appears to have originated only in fifteenth-century Italy, and to have developed along with the spread of resident embassies. It became firmly implanted in European thought only in the seventeenth century, along with the notion that European politics formed a single system.

It is a further step again to the conception of the balance of power as a state of affairs brought about not merely by conscious policies of particular states, but as a conscious goal of the system as a whole. Such a conception implies the possibility of collaboration among states in promoting the common objective of preserving the balance, as exemplified by the successive grand alliances of modern times against potentially dominant powers. It implies also that each state should not only act to frustrate the threatened preponderance of others, but should recognize the responsibility not to upset the balance itself: it implies self-restraint as well as the restraint of others. The idea that preservation of the balance of power throughout the international system as a whole should be the common goal of all states in the system was one that emerged in Europe in the seventeenth and early eighteenth centuries, especially as part of the coalitions against Louis XIV, and which came to fruition in the preamble to the Treaty of Utrecht in 1713.

Functions of the Balance of Power

Preservation of a balance of power may be said to have fulfilled three historic functions in the modern states system:

1. The existence of a general balance of power throughout the international system as a whole has served to prevent the system from being transformed by conquest into a universal empire;
2. The existence of local balances of power has served to protect the independence of states in particular areas from absorption or domination by a locally preponderant power;
3. Both general and local balances of power, where they have existed, have provided the conditions in which other institutions on which international order depends (diplomacy, war, international law, great power management) have been able to operate.

The idea that balances of power have fulfilled positive functions in relation to international order, and hence that contrivance of them is a valuable or legitimate object of statesmanship, has been subject to a great deal of criticism in this century. At the pre-

sent time criticism focuses upon the alleged obscurity or meaninglessness of the concept, the untested or untestable nature of the historical generalizations upon which it rests, and the reliance of the theory upon the notion that all international behavior consists of the pursuit of power. Earlier in the century, especially during and after the First World War critics of the doctrine of the balance of power asserted not that it was unintelligible or untestable, but that pursuit of the balance of power had effects upon international order which were not positive, but negative. In particular, they asserted that the attempt to preserve a balance of power was a source of war, that it was carried out in the interests of the great powers at the expense of the interests of the small, and that it led to disregard of international law. I shall deal with these latter criticisms first.

Attempts to contrive a balance of power have not always resulted in the preservation of peace. The chief function of the balance of power, however, is not to preserve peace, but to preserve the system of states itself. Preservation of the balance of power requires war, when this is the only means whereby the power of a potentially dominant state can be checked. It can be argued, however, that the preservation of peace is a subordinate objective of the contrivance of balances of power. Balances of power which are stable (that is, which have built-in features making for their persistence) may help remove the motive to resort to preventive war.

The principle of preservation of the balance of power has undoubtedly tended to operate in favor of the great powers and at the expense of the small. Frequently, the balance of power among the great powers has been preserved through partition and absorption of the small: the extraordinary decline in the number of European states between 1648 and 1914 illustrates the attempt of large states to absorb small ones while at the same time following the principle of compensation so as to maintain a balance of power. This has led to frequent denunciation of the principle of the balance of power as nothing more than collective aggrandisement by the great powers, the classic case being the partition of Poland in 1772 by Austria, Russia and Prussia. Those who, like Gentz and Burke, argued that the partition of Poland was an aberration and a departure from the true principles of the balance of power, which enjoined respect for the independence of all states, large and small alike, took as their starting-point an idealised and legalistic conception of the balance-of-power doctrine which misconstrues its essential content. The partition of Poland was not a departure from the principle of balance of power but an application of it. . . .

From the point of view of a weak state sacrificed to it, the balance of power must appear as a brutal principle. But its function in the preservation of international order is not for this reason less central. It is part of the logic of the principle of balance of power that the needs of the dominant balance must take precedence over those of subordinate balances, and that the general balance must be prior in importance to any local or particular balance. If aggrandisement by the strong against the weak must take place, it is better from the standpoint of international order that it should take place without a conflagration among the strong than with one. . . .

It is noticeable that while, at the present time, the term "balance of power" is as widely used as at any time in the past in the everyday discussion of international relations, in scholarly analyses of the subject it has been slipping into the background. This reflects impatience with the vagueness and shifting meaning of what is undoubtedly a current cant word: doubts about the historical generalizations that underlie the preposition that preservation of a balance of power is essential to international order; and doubts about its reliance on the discredited notion that the pursuit of power is the common denominator to which all foreign policy can be reduced.

The term "balance of power" is notorious for the numerous meanings that may be attached to it, the tendency of those who use it to shift from one to another and the uncritical reverence which statements about it are liable to command. It is a mistake, however, to dismiss the notion as a meaningless one, as von Justi did in the eighteenth century and Cobden in the nineteenth, and some political scientists are inclined to do now. The term is not unique in suffering abuses of this kind, and as with such other overworked terms as "democracy," "imperialism" and "peace," its very currency is an indication of the importance of the ideas it is intended to convey. We cannot do without the term "balance of power" and the need is to define it carefully and use it consistently.

But if we can make clear what we mean by the proposition that preservation of the balance of power functions to preserve international order, is it true? Is it the case that a state which finds itself in a position of preponderant power will always use it to "lay down the law to others"? Will a locally preponderant state always be a menace to the independence of its neighbors, and a generally preponderant state to the survival of the system of states?

The proposition is implicitly denied by the leaders of powerful states, who see sufficient safeguard of the rights of others in their own virtue and good intentions. Franklin Roosevelt saw the safeguard of Latin America's rights in U.S. adherence to the "good-neighbour policy." The United States and the Soviet Union now each recognize a need to limit the power of the other, and assert that this is a need not simply of theirs but of international society at large. But they do not admit the need for any comparable check on their own power. . . .

Criticism of the doctrine that the balance of power functions to maintain international order sometimes derives from the idea that this is part of a theory of "power politics," which presents the pursuit of power as the common and overriding concern of all states in pursuing foreign policy. On this view the doctrine we have been discussing involves the same fallacies as the "power-political" theory of which it is part.

Doctrines which contend that there is, in any international system, an automatic tendency for a balance of power to arise do derive from a "power-political" theory of this kind. The idea that if one state challenges the balance of power, other states are bound to seek to prevent it, assumes that all states seek to maximize their relative power position. This is not the case. States are constantly in the position of having to choose between devoting their resources and energies to maintaining or extending their international power position, and devoting these resources and energies to other ends. The size of defence expenditure, the foreign-aid vote, the diplomatic establishment, whether or not to play a role in particular international issues by taking part in a war, joining an alliance or an international organization, or pronouncing about an international dispute—these are the matters of which the discussion of any country's foreign policy consists, and proposals that have the effect of augmenting the country's power position can be, and frequently are, rejected. Some states which have the potential for playing a major role—one thinks of the United States in the interwar period and Japan since her economic recovery after the Second World War—prefer to play a relatively minor one. But the doctrine I have been expounding does not assert any inevitable tendency for a balance of power to arise in the international system, only a need to maintain one if international order is to be preserved. States may and often do behave in such a way as to disregard the requirements of a balance of power.

The Present Relevance of the Balance of Power

It is clear that in contemporary international politics there does exist a balance of power which fulfills the same functions in relation to international order which it has per-

formed in other periods. If any important qualification needs to be made to this statement it is that since the late 1950s there has existed another phenomenon which in some respects is a special case of the balance of power but in other respects is different: mutual nuclear deterrence.

There clearly does now exist a general balance of power in the sense that no one state is preponderant in power in the international system as a whole. The chief characteristic of this general balance is that whereas in the 1950s it took the form of a simple balance (though not a perfectly simple one), and in the 1960s was in a state of transition, in the 1970s it takes the form of a complex balance. At least in the Asian and Pacific region China has to be counted as a great power alongside the United States and the Soviet Union; while Japan figures as a potential fourth great power and a united Western Europe may in time become a fifth. However, the statement that there is now a complex or unilateral balance of power has given rise to a number of misunderstandings, and it is necessary to clear these away.

To speak of a complex or multiple balance among these three or four powers is not to imply that they are equal in strength. Whereas in a system dominated by two powers a situation of balance or absence of preponderance can be achieved only if there is some tough parity of strength between the powers concerned, in a system of three or more powers balance can be achieved without a relationship of equality among the powers concerned because of the possibility of combination of the lesser against the greater.

Moreover, to speak of such a complex balance of power is not to imply that all four great states command the same kind of power or influence. Clearly, in international politics moves are made on "many chess-boards." On the chess-board of strategic nuclear deterrence the United States and the Soviet Union are supreme players, China is a novice and Japan does not figure at all. On the chess-board of conventional military strength the United States and the Soviet Union, again, are leading players because of their ability to deploy non-nuclear armed force in many parts of the world. China is a less important player because the armed force it has can be deployed only in its own immediate vicinity, and Japan is only a minor player. On the chess-boards of international monetary affairs and international trade and investments the United States and Japan are leading players, the Soviet Union much less important and China relatively unimportant. On the chess-board of influence derived from ideological appeal it is arguable that China is the pre-eminent player.

However, the play on each of these chess-boards is related to the play on each of the others. An advantageous position in the international politics of trade or investment may be used to procure advantages in the international politics of military security; a weak position on the politics of strategic nuclear deterrence may limit and circumscribe the options available in other fields. It is from this interrelatedness of the various chess-boards that we derive the conception of overall power and influence in international politics, the common denominator in respect of which we say that there is balance rather than preponderance. Overall power in this sense cannot be precisely quantified: the relative importance of strategic, economic and politico–psychological ingredients in national power (and of different kinds of each of these) is both uncertain and changing. But the relative position of states in terms of overall power nevertheless makes itself apparent in bargaining among states, and the conception of overall power is one we cannot do without.

Furthermore, to speak of the present relations of the great powers as a complex balance is not to imply that they are politically equidistant from one another, or that there is complete diplomatic mobility among them. At the time of writing a *detente* exists between the United States and the Soviet Union, and between the United States and China, but not between the Soviet Union and China.

Japan, while it has asserted a measure of independence of the United States and improved its relations with both the Soviet Union and China, is still more closely linked both strategically and economically to the United States than to any of the others. While, therefore, the four major powers have more diplomatic mobility than they had in the period of the simple balance of power, their mobility is still limited, especially by the persistence of tension between the two communist great powers so considerable as to preclude effective collaboration between them.

We have also to note that the complex balance of power that now exists does not rest on any system of general collaboration or concert among the great powers concerned. There is not any general agreement among the United States, the Soviet Union, China, and Japan on the proposition that the maintenance of a general balance of power is a common objective, the proposition proclaimed by the European great powers in the Treaty of Ultrecht. Nor is there any general agreement about a system of rules for avoiding or controlling crises, or for limiting wars. . . .

The present balance of power is not wholly fortuitous in the sense defined above, for there is an element of contrivance present in the "rational" pursuit by the United States, the Soviet Union and China of policies aimed at preventing the preponderance of any of the others. It may be argued also that there is a further element of contrivance in the agreement between the United States and the Soviet Union on the common objective of maintaining a balance between themselves, at least in the limited sphere of strategic nuclear weapons. There is not, however, a contrived balance of power in the sense that all three or four great powers accept it as common objective—indeed, it is only the United States that explicitly avows the balance of power as a goal. Nor is there any evidence that such a balance of power is generally thought to imply self-restraint on the part of the great powers themselves, as distinct from the attempt to restrain or constrain one another.

The United States and the Soviet Union have developed some agreed rules in relation to the avoidance and control of crises and the limitation of war. There is not, however, any general system of rules among the great powers as a whole in these areas. Neither in the field of Sino-Soviet relations nor in that of Sino-American relations does there exist any equivalent of the nascent system of rules evolving between the two global great powers. In the absence of any such general system of rules, we cannot speak of there being, in addition to a balance among the great powers, a concert of great powers concerned with the management of this balance.

Finally, the present complex balance of power does not rest on a common culture shared by the major states participating in it, comparable with that shared by the European great powers that made up the complex balances of the eighteenth and nineteenth centuries. . . . In the European international system of those centuries one factor that facilitated the maintenance of the balance itself and cooperation among the powers that contributed to it was their sharing of a common culture, both in the sense of a common intellectual tradition and stock of ideas that facilitated communication, and in the sense of common values, in relation to which conflicts of interest could be moderated. Among the United States, the Soviet Union, China and Japan there does exist, as will be argued later, some common stock of ideas, but there is no equivalent of the bonds of common culture among European powers in earlier centuries. . . .

This presently existing balance of power appears to fulfill the same three functions in relation to international order that it has performed in earlier periods, and that were mentioned in the last section. First, the general balance of power serves to prevent the system of states from being transformed by conquest into a universal empire. While the balance continues to be maintained, no one

of the great powers has the option of establishing a world government by force. . . .

Second, local balances of power—where they exist—serve to protect the independence of states in particular areas from absorption or domination by a locally preponderant power. At the present time the independence of states in the Middle East, in the Indian subcontinent, in the Korean peninsula and in Southeast Asia is assisted by the existence in these areas of local balances of power. By contrast, in Eastern Europe where there is a Soviet Preponderance and in Central America and the Caribbean, where there is a U.S. preponderance, local state cannot be said to be independent in the normal sense. It would be going too far to assert that the existence of a local balance of power is a necessary condition of the independence of states in any area. To assert this would be to ignore the existence of the factor of a sense of political community in the relations between two states, the consequence of which may be that a locally preponderant state is able, up to a point, to respect the independence of a weaker neighbour, as the United States respects the independence of Canada, or Britain respects the independence of Eire. We have also to recognize that the independence of states in a particular area may owe less to the existence or non-existence of a balance among the local powers than to the part played in the local equilibrium by powers external to the region: if a balance exists at present between Israel and her Arab neighbors, for example, this balance owes its existence to the role played in the area by great powers external to it.

Third, both the general balance of power, and such local balances as exist at present, help to provide the conditions in which other institutions on which international order depends are able to operate. International law, the diplomatic system, war and the management of the international system by the great powers assume a situation in which no one power is preponderant in strength. All are institutions which depend heavily on the possibility that if one state violates the rules, others can take reciprocal action. But a state which is in a position of preponderant power, either in the system as a whole or in a particular area, may be in a position to ignore international law, to disregard the rules and procedures of diplomatic intercourse, to deprive its adversaries of the possibility of resort to war in defense of their interests and rights, or to ignore the conventions of the comity of great powers, all with impunity.

chapter 4

RULES AND ORDER IN THE RELATIONS OF STATES

Therefore doth heaven divide
The state of man in divers functions,
Setting endeavor in continual motion;
To which is fixed, as an aim or butt,
Obedience: for so work the honeybees,
Creatures That by a rule in nature teach
The act of order to a peopled kingdom.

William Shakespeare
Henry V Act I
Scene 2.

Given the regrettable fact that international law does not appear noticeably to control nor even noticeably affect many states in the actual pursuit of their "vital national interests," which are often narrowly self–seeking, doubts have often been expressed as to whether international law is really law at all. But this is not the point. In the absence of a value consensus and a common power base for the entire world, international law is qualitatively different from domestic law, and in many ways is hardly comparable to it. What is important for the student to understand at the outset, however, is that legal processes *are* at work in the international system and have been for three centuries or more.

If interests are defined and asserted in terms of power, then it would appear that international law enjoys only a vestigial reality in the absence of authority. Even the terms *international community* and *international society* are all too often invoked without much conviction of their order-generating possibilities, but we share Professor Nicholas Onuf's view that the notion of international society and international law deserve better. Concepts like international society *can* be endowed with order–explaining content provided scholars and statesmen are willing to look for and cultivate that content. The same holds true for international law. It cannot just be assumed that, in the absence of an authority to enforce international law, it only gets its authority from the existence of an international society of which the law is a guiding expression. What international law is presumed to do "is communicate assumptions and predispositions about the system among its members."[1] This view takes for granted an influence that needs to be explained. We should understand the functioning of international law as it really operates—as a system of rules and norms, displaying a lawlike character, "yet substantially bereft of the authority needed to produce order through the agency of law . . ."[2]

This is not to say that extensive and effective legal processes are not constantly at work in the adjustment of differences and in the daily conduct of affairs among states which could never accept each others' basic values and legal norms. Diplomats are exchanged and granted diplomatic immunity; transportation and communications are regulated by universally accepted legal rules; detailed agreements with the virtual force of law have been reached on everything from monetary policy to nonproliferation of nuclear weapons. Nevertheless, it is difficult to contest the view expressed by A. V. Lowe that merely to recognize that international law exists is not tantamount to saying that, as a legal system, it is as effective as the legal system that operates within each state.

The following delineation of basic principles, set forth by the late Wolfgang Friedman of Columbia University some years ago, is still one of the most useful for the student of this oftentimes elusive subject:

1) International law is based upon a society of sovereign states, regardless of structure and ideology.

2) Any attempt by a foreign power to interfere with internal change by assisting either rebels or the government is probably contrary to international law.

3) It is within the right of any sovereign state to surrender its national sovereignty by federation of amalgamation with another state (or states).

4) Any state is, under international law, at liberty to tolerate or suppress a subversive political movement by whatever means it chooses, except insofar as its action threatens the security of a third state by demonstrable preparations for aggressive action.

5) The evolution of lesser and indirect forms of aggression, falling short of armed attack, justifies countermeasures that are intermediate between peace and war. . . .[3]

In his treatment of international law in this chapter, Professor Lowe of the United Kingdom further develops some of these points.

In an effort to make international law more effective, states have resorted to the creation of international organizations. Prior to World War I, a number

---

[1]Nicholas Greenwood Onuf, "International Legal Order as an Idea," *The American Journal of International Law,* 73, no. 2 (April, 1979).

[2]*Ibid.,* p. 251.

[3]Wolfgang Friedman, in *The Changing Structure of International Law* (New York: Columbia University Press, 1964), p. 378.

of international organizations and commissions had been established to manage specific areas of international relations—the Universal Postal Union, international fisheries commissions, and the like. But the first international organization with a political mandate was the League of Nations, which was designed to provide an institution through which states, acting collectively, might identify threats to the peace and take measures such as sanctions and even military action to stop an aggressor. Unfortunately, the strength of the League was sapped from the beginning by the failure of the United States and Russia to join, and by the difficulty of the remaining so-called "great powers" in deciding to act when first one (Japan) and then another (Italy) and yet another (Nazi Germany) country committed aggression. Britain and France meanwhile pursued their "national interests" at the expense of "world order."

During World War II, Washington determined to take the lead in creating the United Nations organization. The keystone of the United Nations was to be the Security Council, on which were permanently represented the five great powers—the United States, the Soviet Union, Britain, France, and China—plus several other states periodically elected by the General Assembly. Recognizing that it would be impossible for the United Nations (UN) to act against one of the major powers if it was unwilling to be restrained, the UN charter provided each permanent member of the Security Council with the power to veto any resolution with which it did not concur. Almost immediately after the cessation of hostilities, the cold war erupted between the Soviet Union and the West, and the actions of the Security Council were largely stymied by the Soviet veto. It was only by chance that the Soviet Union was boycotting the United Nations, for failing to admit the government of Communist China, when the Korean War broke out (June 25, 1950), thereby permitting the United States to secure the endorsement of the Security Council for the United Nations' armies to intervene. On this occasion, the system worked as designed.

When the UN was founded in 1945, it had 51 members, each of whom was represented in the General Assembly. So long as the UN remained small, the United States enjoyed an automatic majority among the membership (principally the Latin American states and NATO allies), and the UN consistently endorsed what the United States wanted done. After 1956, however, the majority of the new members were either opposed to Western capitalism or determined not to become involved in the cold war struggle. For years, a majority of the Assembly, usually assisted by the Communist bloc, concentrated on pushing for the independence of the remaining colonial possessions. They refused to view the Soviet suppression of Hungarian freedom as being of the same illegality as the Franco-British attack upon Egypt in 1956. In fact, the majority refused to support the Western position on Berlin in 1961 and even less willing to give its sanction to the American effort in Vietnam. Professor Henkin's contribution to this chapter very clearly explains the changing UN system.

The Third World voting majority has promoted the advancement of economic development as the UN's first concern. Their emphasis is the need for more investment funds and a more equitable redistribution of wealth. On these issues, the United States has found itself at loggerheads with a UN majority comprised of Third (or Fourth) World and Communist states.[4]

As a result of these changes, Americans have felt frustrated, if not downright disillusioned, with the United Nations. Having invested so much ideological faith in the UN as a panacea and then finding it to be at the mercy of hostile majorities, some have called for withdrawal. Inis Claude has suggested that Americans would do better to view the United Nations as "a symbol of the inhibitions that their country should respect, of the limitations that it should observe in the conduct of foreign policy."[5] The United Nations should be a forum in which the collective destiny of states must be worked out in place of unilateral American efforts to remake the world. The UN cannot act in the absence of the United States, which should continue its membership in its own "national interest."

At a time when the international system, tends toward chaos and anarchy, the UN and its associated organs provide a medium through which urgent Third World demands may be heard. By belonging to and participating in the one organization that most fully exemplifies the principles and norms of law and justice in the international system, members gradually are conditioned to conform with those principles and norms.

As the preceding chapters have tried to make clear, states and their governments remain the most important actors on the international scene; but they have more recently been joined by other, nonstate actors as well. International organizations have attempted, with varying degrees of success, to link states and governments in networks of contact and communication; and also to draw into that network the nonstate actors in international relations—multinational corporations, ethnic groups, and the like. Usually this has taken the form of placing N.G.O.'s (nongovernmental organizations) in a consultative capacity, primarily in the work of the Economic and Social Council and various specialized agencies of the United Nations system.

In addition, the United Nations managed some years ago to perform a crucial peace–keeping function in such places as the Congo, Lebanon, and Cyprus. On more than one occasion, the UN capacity to dispatch a military force drawn from the armies of its members to enforce cease–fires and truces, and even to establish peace between the parties, has kept the Soviet Union and the United States from becoming embroiled. The peacekeeping function of the United Nations should be regarded not as a device for defying aggression and certainly

---

[4]These terms may require some amplification. The *first world* consists of highly developed capitalist/democratic countries; the *second world* consists of highly developed Communist states. The rest of the world was previously classified as *Third World*, but it now appears that there are large distinctions among these countries. *Third World* is defined today as those societies, still underdeveloped, who possess the *capacity* to develop and modernize rapidly. But some countries are so poor that it remains doubtful whether they can develop, even with massive foreign assistance—the *fourth world*. There is, to some, even a *fifth world* absolutely hopeless of meaningful modernization.

[5]From "The Symbolic Significance of the United Nations," used as a selection in the fifth edition of this book, p. 232, and written in 1971.

not for coercing the great powers, but as a means of helping those powers to contain their conflicts. In the words of a leading authority in the field:

> The greatest political contribution of the United Nations in our time to the management of international power relationships lies not in the implementing collective security or instituting world government, but in helping to improve and stabilize the workings of the balance-of-power system, which is, for better or worse, the operative mechanism of contemporary international politics.[6]

It is probably clear by now that this is a distinctive age—the culmination of processes that had their origins in the political, scientific, and industrial revolutions of the eighteenth and nineteenth centuries. Although we are still compartmentalized into national states and expect our governments to guarantee us security, economic well–being, and an orderly life, the conditions of that life are increasingly dependent upon economic developments beyond our control.

There are generally two alternatives now presented for achieving a manageable world order. One is the balance–of–power model, taken up and popularized by Washington as a replacement for the old cold-war, global–leadership model that broke down so badly in Vietnam when the United States was unable to mobilize world support for its efforts there. The balance–of–power model postulates that each state, by acting to preserve and enhance its security and national capability, needs to maintain a stable system. This does not rule out the threat of international violence or the danger of war. But it means that, despite increasing scarcity, technological uncertainties (new nuclear powers, new weapons) and interdependence, there is sufficient adaptiveness and innovativeness in the sovereign–state system that order can be preserved. Under the balance–of–power model, no change will be required in the values by which we presently manage our affairs; each state will be the judge of its own best interest. No motivation for questioning the present distribution of wealth and values within and between societies will be needed, because any disruptive tendencies will be handled by the efficacious workings of the balance of power.

An alternate model for behavior is one which, while not doing away with the nation-state—with which people identify too strongly for it to be abolished—calls for a modification of the values which until now have governed the conduct of states. This might be termed the *mutual interest* or world–order model. The traditional state system assumes that domestic politics "stop at the water's edge"[7] and that national goals and policy are framed exclusively with an eye to security and other so–called national interests of the state, as distinct from the individuals who live within it. But the view of the state as an autonomous actor is anachronistic. International relations now involve as many economic, ethical, ideological, and moral determinations affecting both individuals and domestic interests

---

[6]Inis Claude, in *Power and International Relations* (New York: Random House, 1964), p. 285.

[7]A term popularized by the late Senator Arthur Vanderberg (R., Michigan) when he chaired the Foreign Relations Committee and a Democrat, Harry S. Truman, was President in 1949.

as do domestic politics; and, vice versa, the content and style of domestic policymaking is having an increasing impact upon international politics. Political and economic values can no longer be separated. Just as order at home has required that the weak and poor be included in the national community, so too they cannot be ignored if order is to prevail in the world community; domestic tensions of all industrial and industrializing societies are increasingly spilling over onto the international scene. Professor Khadduri's learned discourse in this chapter on the relationship between international—mainly Western—Law and the Law of Islam is particularly useful and relevant.

Under these circumstances, acting out of exclusive self–interest is only likely to worsen the crisis for the weaker countries. Going abroad with "no acceptance of the mutuality of obligations, no felt need to compromise, and no desire to establish a community of interests involving the happiness of living and sharing together [conversely, acting multilaterally] . . . is much the same as one seeks to create a national community within one's own borders."[8] Such an approach cannot exclusively rely upon *technique* to achieve international order. Nor is value-free pragmatism and neutrality possible when the nature of the world system is itself in contention.

But what about the individual?

Professor Rosalyn Higgins questions why individuals who often suffer from violations of the law at the hands of their own governments, or who may be victimized by the operations of other governments, should not have a recognized legal status under international law with the right of appeal to higher authority outside the confines of their own state. In many areas, particularly in the sphere of human rights and the protection of property rights against arbitrary treatment by national governments, the rights of individuals to have recourse under international law (through treaties, conventions, precedents, etc.) is gaining ground, especially in the European community. How can the right of the international community to be protected against terrorism, however, be reconciled with the traditional right of an individual to political asylum?[9] The issue has been well stated by the former U.S. Secretary of State, William P. Rogers:[10] "We all recognize that issues such as self–determination [meaning the right to freedom and justice under a government] must continue to be addressed seriously by the international community. But political passion, however deeply held, cannot be a justification for criminal violence against innocent persons." To representatives of the Third World, terrorism is not a new phenomenon. It has only been brought closer to home because world opinion—which accepted violence and

---

[8]Kalman Silvert, *Essays in Understanding Latin America* (Philadelphia: Institute for the Study of Human Issues, 1977), p. 149.

[9]See Chapter 11, William C. Olson and David McLellan, eds., *The Theory and Practice of International Relations*, 6th ed. (Englewood Cliffs, N.J.: Prentice-Hall, Inc., 1983), pp. 241–49.

[10]More recently, head of the Presidential Commission which investigated NASA (National Aeronautics and Space Agency) in light of the Challenger disaster and issued its report in June 1986 (Washington: A.P.O., 1986). NASA is a striking example of a *national* agency subject to little, if any, international control of its operations.

terror as the natural lot of the poor, the weak and the oppressed—is shocked to see terrorism applied to the rich and successful as well.

Proving unable to contribute much to the resolution of the Soviet–American conflict or other issues involving peace and security, the majority of UN members, coming now from the Third World, are using the United Nations as a forum for solving their own problems of development. Meanwhile, rules and order in the international system seem as elusive as ever, if indeed not more so, as unilateral approaches to problem–solving are relied upon by the powers, great and small.

DISCUSSION QUESTIONS

1. In what way is international law qualitatively different from domestic law? What are "truly general laws"?

2. Why does Professor Lowe urge us to understand that, despite the absence of an authority to enforce international law, a system of legal rules and norms does exist because states find it convenient to have and observe such a code?

3. What according to Friedman, are the basic principles of international law? In what significant ways do these differ from Islamic Law? How does Professor Khadduri relate both to moral principle as the basis of law and of world order?

4. What does Professor Henkin mean when he argues that the greatest influence of the UN for peace "can neither be measured nor proven"?

5. How does it happen that a terrorist who flees to another country to avoid punishment may be better protected under the laws of political asylum and against forced extradition than other categories of individuals under existing international law? Why is this also a domestic problem for the United States?

6. The United Nations was founded to provide the international community with a means of responding to aggression and threats to the peace. Yet many of its present activities are directed toward meeting economic demands and problems. How is this an example of the difference between theory and practice in international relations?

10. International Law: Myth or Reality?

A. V. Lowe

Having been a Visiting Scholar at Cambridge University, A. V. Lowe is currently Lecturer in Law at Manchester University, England.

The aim of this short paper is to explore the concept of 'general' rules of customary international law (i.e., rules in principle binding upon all states, as contrasted with 'special' rules binding only on a few states, usually on a regional or local basis), and the tension which exists between that concept and the consensual basis of customary international law. It will be suggested that it is possible to hold a view of international law which denies the general applicability of most rules of customary law and preserves its consensual character, while admitting that a few rules of truly general application do exist which, however, must derive their binding force from outside the framework of consensual law creation.

Consent

General rules of customary law are undoubtedly thought to exist. Thus, article 38 of the Statute of the International Court of Justice refers to 'international custom, as evidence of a general practice accepted as law': while it is more properly the 'general practice' which evidences the rule of 'custom', the concept of a rule of general application inferred from widespread state practice is clear enough. Such rules are considered to be binding upon all states. As O'Connell put it,

> . . . (customary international) law is dependent, not upon unanimity, but only upon gen-

Review of International Studies, Vol. 9, no. 3 (July 1983). Copyright © 1983. Reprinted by permission of the publisher from A. V. Lowe's, "Do General Rules of International Law Exist?"

erality of will. The dissentient minority of States are as much bound by the formulated rule as those who actively participated in its creation, the source of their obligation residing in the moral necessity which underlies observance of all law.[1]

Customary international law is also said to be consensual, and to derive its binding force from the will of states. Thus, it was said in the judgment of the Permanent Court of International Justice in the *Lotus* case that

> International law governs relations between independent States. The rules of law binding upon States therefore emanate from their own free will as expressed in conventions or by usages generally accepted as expressing principles of law and established in order to regulate the relations between those co-existing independent communities or with a view to the achievement of common aims. Restrictions upon the freedom of States cannot therefore be presumed.[2]

This consensual basis is clearly evidenced in the right accorded to states to exempt themselves from emerging rules of customary law by means of persistent objection to such rules. Perhaps the clearest example of this is the well-known response of the International Court of Justice to the British attempt to prove that Norway was bound by a rule of customary international law not to employ closing lines (which render the enclosed waters part of the national territory) longer than ten miles across bays: '. . . the ten–mile rule would appear to be inapplicable as against Norway inasmuch as she has always opposed any attempt to apply it to the Norwegian coast'.[3] If this extract from the *Anglo–Norwegian Fisheries* case illustrates the proposition that the consent of a state is necessary if it is to be bound by a rule of customary law, the complementary proposition that such consent is also sufficient to render the state bound can be illustrated by reference to the *Right of Passage* case. In that case the International Court found that because the parties to the case, Portugal and India, had consented to a practice constituting a right of passage over Indian territory between Portuguese enclaves, that practice had acquired the status of a 'local custom'. Noting that the existence of the local custom rendered it 'unnecessary . . . to determine whether or not, in the absence of the practice that actually prevailed, general international custom . . . could have been relied upon', the Court stated that

> . . . where the Court finds a practice clearly established between the two States which was accepted by the Parties as governing the relations between them, the Court must attribute decisive effect to that practice for the purpose of determining their specific rights and obligations. Such a particular practice must prevail over any general rules.[4]

The questions then arise, if the consent of a state to a rule is necessary and sufficient to establish that the state is bound by the rule, why is the 'general practice' of *other* states relevant to that task, and what legal status may be attributed to a rule which has the support of such general practice?

Two Interpretations

There are at least two interpretations of the nature of customary international law in which the concept of a rule of customary law generated by a general practice of states may be reconciled with the principle that it is the consent of each state to be bound which gives the rule its binding force in relation to that state. First, we could say that all states consent to a secondary rule of law–creation which deems all states which have not persistently objected to an emerging primary (i.e., substantive) rule of law to be bound by it, without being at all concerned with the question whether or not such states consent to the primary rule, whenever that primary rule is 'generally accepted' by states. Here the consensual nature of internal law is preserved in the requirement of consent to the secondary rule, although it is excluded in the case of the primary rule. Primary rules established in this way have a truly general applicability, applying to all cases which fall within their purview, and may properly be called laws. The problem of persistent objection, putting states outside the binding force of the rule, can be explained by distinguishing between the abstract question of the nature of the rule, which is general, and its opposability to particular states by a court,[5] which is excluded in the case of persistent objectors. Local customs may be accommodated by describing them as a sub–species of custom,[6] prevailing over general rules by virtue of the traditional principle of interpretation that special rules prevail over general ones.

A second way of interpreting customary international law is to say that all states consent to a secondary rule of law–creation according to which a general practice among states creates a presumption that all states have consented to the primary rule embodied in the practice, subject to the possibility of that presumption being rebutted in the case of any state which can show that it has persistently objected to the emergent rule. Unlike the previous interpretation, this one attaches a central importance to each state's consent to the primary rule; the presumption goes only to the question of the manner in which that consent is proved. This is the approach adopted, for example, in the statement that 'whatever has received the common consent of civilised nations must have received the assent of our country'.[7] It is necessary that some secondary rule such as this presumption exist, in order to deter-mine precisely what will qualify as consent to the primary rule; but this no more de-tracts from the consensual nature of the pri-mary rule than the existence of rules con-cerning the formation of contracts detracts from the consensual nature of contracts.

The essence of this second interpretation is that any primary rule binding on a state is so binding because the state has consented to the rule in question, and not because the majority of other states in the world have accepted it in their practice. Accordingly, the binding force of the rule is co–extensive with voluntary subscription to it: the rule has no binding force independent of consent, and arguably should be called an obligation rather than a law. Local custom and persistent ob-jection need no special explanation under this view: they simply represent cases where states have consented to a rule which hap-pens to differ from that widely adopted by other states, or have not consented to an otherwise widely adopted rule.

The first point which this note seeks to make is that there is no obvious reason for preferring the first to the second interpre-tation. The secondary rule of law–creation in question will itself be a rule of customary international law derived (whichever inter-pretation is adopted) from state practice, and state practice on this point does not appear to support unequivocally one solution or the other, although much more work is needed on this question. Without wishing to pre-judge the outcome of future investigations into the question of which is the correct interpretation, it is perhaps worthwhile to point out some of the consequences of the second interpretation.

Network of Obligations

Unlike the more traditional first interpre-tation, the second excludes the possibility of a general practice among states generating rules of customary law which have an in-dependent existence in the sense that they are binding upon other states not consenting (within the terms of the secondary rule con-cerning presumed consent) to the rule. Thus, international law becomes not a set of gen-erally applicable laws, but rather a network of obligations. A rule may only be said to be general in the *descriptive* sense that it is a rule to which states in general subscribe, but this does not imply that it is general in any *pre-scriptive* sense, applying in principle to all states.

The resolution of international disputes by adjudication would proceed, according to the second approach, by determining the ob-ligations accepted by the parties to the dis-pute, and it would not in principle be nec-essary to have regard to the practice of any other states, although it may in practice be necessary to do so in order to operate the secondary rule of presumption and decide what the parties have accepted. If they have accepted the same obligation, it would be applied, as it was in the *Right of Passage* case. If state A has made a claim to some new right to which state B has persistently ob-jected, state B would not be obliged to accept it and could continue to rely upon its rights under the 'old' law. Such a view explains, for example, the United States' belief that it has by persistent objection retained its right to treat seas more than three miles from the coast as high seas, and that the resources of the deep seabed remain free for exploitation by its corporations, despite the view of the overwhelming majority of states that both positions are contrary to recently–emerged rules of customary law.

The latter point also suggests how changes in international law can be explained. A new rule may be put forward by one state and accepted by some others, whereupon they become bound by it among themselves, leav-ing all other states bound among themselves by the old rule and entitled to insist on ad-herence to the old rule in their dealings with states adopting the new practice. As states change from one group to the other, the balance of states accepting old and new obligations changes. Traditionally, this is described as the replacement of the old rule by the new, giving rise to problems concerning the legality of the actions of the first adherents to the new rule, and the time and manner in which the replacement can be said to occur. Under the view here advanced no such problems arise, there being simply a change in the pattern of obligations of individual states, from the position corresponding in traditional terms to the existence of a 'local custom' between two states to the point where, as more and more states shift to the new position, only a few 'persistent objectors' remain. Local customs and persistent objectors are not then special categories of customary law, they are merely stages on the continuous road towards universal recognition of a new customary rule. Similarly, the distribution of adherents to the respective rules at other points along the path may be such that it is possible to speak of rules of Latin American or socialist or bourgeois international law, for example, co–existing. It would, indeed, be misleading to speak of *the* rule of customary international law on any particular subject unless, coincidentally, all states had accepted the same obligation. It would only be correct to speak of the rule applicable in a particular context, which rule may well not be the same for every state, nor even for any one state in its dealings with all others.

Clearly, these consequences of the second interpretation of international law render customary law much more complex than the statements of the set of customary rules in textbooks, apparently based upon the belief that those rules are general laws, would suggest. In truth, the result is no more complex than is the network of treaty obligations which bind states and to which, indeed, customary law as here interpreted is precisely analogous. There are, none the less, good reasons for continuing to attend to the rules which can be discerned in the general practice of states, and not concentrating solely upon individual states' obligations. First, this may be necessary in order to operate the secondary

rule of presumption, as described above, so as to determine what obligations a state has accepted. Secondly, in considering the operation of legal rules outside the context of judicial settlement of disputes, it is undoubtedly true that general practices have a significant normative effect, creating an expectation that all states will subscribe to them, and such practices will often be cited in diplomatic exchanges and so on as a reason for some state to follow the 'general rule'. Thirdly, statements of general practice are an invaluable tool for the teaching and analysis of international law, allowing a broad view of the patterns and trends in the network of international obligations, where close attention to the actual rules applicable in the dealings of a specific state may be inappropriate. However, it should always be kept clear that, if the second interpretation is correct, implications and statements that a particular rule is a general rule of customary law are descriptive and not prescriptive.

Truly General Laws

If the view that customary international law consists in obligations rather than laws is correct, it would still have to be admitted that some truly general laws do exist, although it would be necessary to find a basis for their binding force outside the framework of consensual law formation. There are two bases which are suggested by current practice in international law. The first is the logical necessity which demands that, if a legal system exists at all, some basic rules must be admitted. For example, international law as a coherent system must contain some such rule as *pacta sunt servanda*,[8] whether or not such a rule has attracted the consent of states, because without the rule it would not be possible to speak of an international legal system. Other rules in this category may be of more specific significance. For example, it is arguable that the concepts of sovereignty and independence of states are similarly elemental,[9] and from these it may be possible to infer more specific rules concerning, for instance, sovereign immunity, extraterritorial jurisdiction, and the act of state doctrine.

Apart from rules logically inhering in the concept of a legal system, there may be a second category of truly general rules deriving their validity from outside the legal system. The conviction that international law ought not to be morally neutral in the way in which it could be said to be were it not to prohibit, say, genocide in the absence of any consensually-created obligation not to commit genocide, seems to have led to the rapid and universal acceptance of rules prohibiting genocide, the waging of aggressive wars, and so on. But these rules are also said to have a validity which transcends this acceptance and renders them binding on all states, regardless of their consent, and which automatically invalidates any treaty agreement purporting to exclude the rules in relations between the parties. It seems that the binding force of such rules as these derives from what in earlier times would have been called natural law. Both this and the previous category of rules are commonly described as peremptory rules of international law or rules of *jus cogens*. But while there is widespread agreement about the existence of a body of peremptory rules, there is very little agreement upon its content.

Even if the view that customary international law is no more than a set of obligations is rejected in favour of the first interpretation offered above, that rules of customary law are properly regarded as being of general application, the categories of peremptory rules remain significant. While the technical objections to claiming general effects for rules do not arise, practical objections do, in that the existence of persistent objections and local customs will distort the picture presented by the general rules. Here too, only the peremptory rules may claim a truly universal applicability. The potential significance of these rules in future can best be approached by way of a backward glance at the development of international law.

Natural Law Origins

While international law was tied to natural law it was proper to regard rules as being generally binding upon states. When in the seventeenth and eighteenth centuries, international law began to separate from natural law, the content of its rules remained largely undisturbed by the change in its theoretical basis—a fact greatly facilitated by the supposition that the creation and enforcement of international law was the prerogative of the 'civilized' European powers whose interests in the law were broadly similar. The notion of general rules was thus carried over from its natural law origins (possibly wrongly, as was suggested above) when international law was put on a 'consensual' basis. Those rules were often enforced by the European powers upon other countries and newly emerged states. But with the emergence of so many newly independent states in the wake of the post-war decolonization movement, the community of interest which this presupposed has largely disappeared in many spheres.

Newly independent states have sometimes sought to avoid obligations under the 'old' law by arguing that they cannot be bound by rules to which they have not assented. But of greater long–term significance, given the rapid development of the substantive rules of international law in the post-war years, are the attempts to create rules binding on all states. This cannot be effected through ordinary customary law formation, because of the rights of the persistent objector, and so developing states have claimed that some rules have the status of peremptory rules. This has been alleged, for example, in the case of the rule prohibiting mining of seabed resources outside the international regime currently being established, and in the case of some rules concerning sovereignty over natural resources. In this way they hope to be able to convert the ability which their numerical strength gives them to create a 'general practice', into a power to create generally applicable rules admitting of no derogations in favour of dissentient states.

It seems likely that much activity will centre in future upon attempts to escape the implications of the consensual basis of international law by invoking the notion of peremptory norms, of both kinds, as the law follows governments into more and more areas of activity in which the interests of states do not all coincide.

Conclusion

It may be helpful to draw the threads of this note together. The argument is, in short, that there is no obvious reason for regarding any but a small number of peremptory norms of law as being of general applicability, or for denying that customary law is essentially a set of obligations rather than laws. This argument may be proved wrong when tested against state practice, in the unlikely event of state practice providing a conclusive answer to the question. But whatever the outcome of that inquiry, the category of peremptory norms remains the sole body of laws of truly general applicability and is likely to increase in its significance as the community of interest which allows a system of consensual law–creation to operate effectively diminishes with the expansion of the inter-national community and of international law. Within this category, natural law may find a new lease of life.

NOTES

[1] D. P. O'Connell, *International Law*, 2nd ed. (London, 1970), pp. 15–16.

[2] Permanent Court of International Justice Reports, Ser. A, No. 10, (1927), p. 18.

[3] (1951) International Court of Justice Reports 116, p. 131.

[4] (1960) International Court of Justice Reports 6, pp. 43–4.

[5] See, e.g., I. Brownlie, *Principles of Public International Law*, 3rd ed., (Oxford, 1979), p. 10.

[6] See, e.g., A. A. D'Amato, 'The Concept of Special Custom in International Law', 63 *American Journal of International Law* (1969), p. 211.

[7] Per Lord Alverstone C. J., in *West Rand Central Gold Mining Co., Ltd. r. The King* (1905) 2 K. B. 391, at p. 406.

[8] See, e.g., Sir G. Fitzmaurice, 'The Formal Sources of International Law'. *Symbolae Verzijl*, (The Hague, 1958), p. 153 at p. 164.

[9] See, e.g., G. Tunkin, *Theory of International Law*, Trans. W. E. Butler (London, 1974), p. 223.

11. The Utility of the United Nations

Louis Henkin

As Harlan Fiske Stone Professor of Constitutional Law at Columbia University in the City of New York, Professor Henkin has written a number of significant works relating to politics and law, among the most useful for students of international relations being *Foreign Affairs and the Constitution* (1972)

Although students of international relations would probably agree that technology, cold war, and the proliferation of nations shaped international politics in the decades following the Second World War, few would argue that the United Nations ranks with these in significance. For the influence of law on foreign affairs, however, the relevance of the United Nations cannot be denied. The major development in contemporary international law is contained in the United Nations Charter. The organization is charged with enforcing this law and has involved itself in the creation and enforcement of other international law. The effect on law of modern technology, of cold war, and especially of the proliferation of new nations is enhanced and modified through the United Nations.

The United Nations is a political body, but its principal *raison d'être* was to have been the enforcement of law, the law of the Charter against war and the use of force between nations. Its other purposes—political, social, and economic—have also engaged various U.N. organs in the development and enforcement of international law, usually of international agreements. In some areas, the principal organs have exercised legislative influence, the General Assembly promoting law in many fields—outer space, disarmament, defining aggression, the sea–bed, human rights. Sometimes it has purported even to declare law by "parliamentary" majority.

The United Nations and the Law Against Force

The extent to which the existence of the United Nations and its processes have influenced nations to observe the norm against unilateral force need not be exaggerated; neither should it be discounted, although that influence was far greater in earlier years. Because the United Nations has existed, issues of war and peace have become the active business of all its

"The United Nations" is excerpted from *How Nations Behave*, a Council on Foreign Relations Book, 2nd Ed. (New York: Columbia University Press, 1970) pp. 165–174, 185–188. Copyright © Council on Foreign Relations, Inc. (Footnotes have been deleted.)

members, and they have not been able to avoid taking a stand and doing so in support of peace. All of the nations there assembled are eager to avoid a nuclear holocaust. All have had some sense that the norm against force is important and that the organization, which they value, is diminished when it fails in its principal purpose of maintaining international peace. All have had some recognition that any war concerns them, that peace is indivisible, that war anywhere might spread and escalate. All have had some desire to assert authority and influence events in world affairs. In the absence of special factors, principally colonialism or racial oppression, only private quarrels have threatened war (Arab-Israel hostility, Sudan-Ethiopia, Somalia-Ethiopia, Cyprus, Indonesia-Malaysia, India-Pakistan, Latin American quarrels), while almost all the other nations pressed for peace. Where international fighting broke out, U.N. organs have generally called for an end to hostilities, and the call was generally heeded, although sometimes only after some delay to achieve some political end.

At the center of efforts to maintain international peace, the United Nations was for many years the focus not only of world opinion but of the many diplomacies concentrated there. We sensed its influence, even if we are unable to weigh it, in the early confrontation between the Soviet Union and Iran in 1946; in the Indonesian case, when the forces for peace may have been more significant in resolving the controversy than the new forces for ending colonialism; in continuing tension and occasional fighting between the Arab states and Israel, in Korea, where virtually all the nations outside the Communist bloc followed the lead of the United States and placed the resistance to aggression under the aegis of the United Nations; in the Congo and in Cyprus, where internal hostilities threatened to ignite external wars; in ending actual fighting over Kashmir. In different cases, in different ways, the United Nations intervened to discourage, prevent, or terminate hostilities, and provide "peace-keeping."

Perhaps the United Nations' greatest influence for peace can neither be measured nor proven. But it is not wholly an assertion of faith to insist that the existence of the organization reaffirmed the norm of the Charter and enhanced its deterrent influence. (Corridor diplomacy in the United Nations also serves to discourage threatened violations and helps terminate any that materialize.) A nation could initiate the use of force only with full awareness that it would have to answer in this world forum, a prospect which few nations faced with equanimity. Even if a proceeding produced nothing more than condemnatory addresses and resolutions and hostile headlines in the world press, the prospect of being accused was a significant cost of violation that all governments take into account. (The universal and intense concern of members with the outcome of votes on U.N. resolutions is evidence that resolutions matter.) The effect of a violation on the aggressor's relations with the victim was also magnified by public accusation; because others had to take sides, its relations with other nations would also be affected. Though rare, there was also the threat of sanctions—as against North Korea and Communist China. Even the response of an individual nation to a use of force by another had increased justification and effectiveness because the United Nations and the Charter exist: in 1956, the Russian threat to intervene if invading forces were not withdrawn from Suez-Sinai was more credible and effective because the United Nations was seized of the issue and was prepared to find that there had been a violation of the Charter.

Even in earlier years the deterrent influence of the United Nations, however, was not simple and certain. For the United Nations is legislator as well as judge and executive, and its judgments are political, not juridical. Its members have adverse national interests as well as the common ones reflected in their U.N. membership. No matter what a court might do, the members of the U.N. political organs will reach political judgments. They may condemn where a court would not; they will not condemn if they do not wish to. And the response of the United Nations will continue to reflect both ideological conflict and the emergence of the Third World which effectively dominates the organization.

In regard to the law against force in particular, I have written:

The law of the Charter forbidding unilateral force is, of course, intertwined with the institutional pattern created by the Charter. One may say, indeed, that the primary purpose of the institution was to implement and enforce the law of the Charter against war.... The relation of the law to the institution, however, is more complicated than merely that of law to law enforcement. Authority to enforce includes the power not to enforce.... In order to decide whether and how to enforce, moreover, the Security Council and the General Assembly must first sit in judgment on the action of member nations. And in the process of judgment and enforcement, inevitably the Council, and particularly the Assembly, exercise also legislative influence modifying the law of the Charter. In the first instance, of course, the actions of members, and the reactions of other members, have the effect of interpreting what the Charter obligations mean. Then, deliberations, recommendations, resolutions, and actions in the Council or Assembly inevitably determine what the law of the Charter means or may be held to mean in the future.

Policy-makers considering whether to use force had to take into account what might or might not happen in the United Nations. The expectation that members would condemn and the organization would take a strong stand was likely to serve as substantial deterrent. On the other hand, would-be violators might expect—and find—protection against effective U.N. judgment. In 1964, Indonesia was saved by Soviet veto from condemnation by the Security Council for its attacks on Malaysia. The veto did not of course save Indonesia from criticism by a majority of the Council. Surely, the promise or hope of U.N. blessing, acquiescence, or even inaction or mild reaction would not discourage violation. India, for example, may well have been encouraged in its action in Goa by an estimate—proven correct—that the United Nations would do nothing, that some members in the Communist bloc and among the new nations would condone or approve, some even condemning the "victim" in the case. In such a case the organization not only fails to deter, or prevent, or restore, or punish; it may also prove a haven for the violator, serving as a lightning rod to help protect him even against sanctions outside the United Nations. In fact, when the U.N. majorities fail to condemn, its failure tends to remove the stigma of a violation by suggesting that the Charter provision, properly interpreted, was not violated.

Goa might have proved to have been a "sport" or a case of the special "law" of anticolonialism, but it reflected, quite early in the U.N.'s history, the temptation of political bodies to judge by a double or multiple standard, or by no standard at all but only on the basis of political sympathies in the particular case. It showed that this might become a common occurrence, and war and peace might revert from the domain of law to that of politics and power. Concerned observers began to warn that the influence of the U.N. organization too might not survive, for even small nations will not respect unprincipled votes of powerless majorities.

Different weaknesses in the United Nations were revealed in the Kashmir war of 1965. As a matter of international law for our hypothetical court, the hostilities that erupted in September 1965 did not perhaps represent a clear violation by one party or the other. Politically, too, Kashmir was a unique situation: a territory long in dispute and in joint occupation without political solution in sight; military forces in close confrontation; political maneuvers that became a military skirmish and, both sides probably unwitting, exploded into war. Still, the fact that war happened seemed to bode badly for the United Nations. In South Asia, in particular, political forces conspired to weaken the forces for peace. The United States and the Soviet Union were effectively neutralized, politically and militarily, leaving nearby China dominant, and emboldening China's friend (Pakistan) which had a grievance against China's enemy (India). The influence of the United Nations was at its weakest: Chinese exclusion from the organization and Indonesian withdrawal had created a focus independent of, even hostile to, the United Nations, and attracted countries, like Pakistan, which might see their future in China's friendship. The United Nations' authority was further weakened by its long failure to achieve a political solution in Kashmir. For its part, India had lost its position of political and moral leadership in the United Nations and was less concerned with the institution; on Kashmir, it had long been in embarrassed opposition, refusing the plebiscite that had been U.N. policy for many years.

But whatever the particular explanation of Kashmir, it represented the first war between established nations since the Charter had been signed, the kind of war that the organization was designed to prevent. It led to wonder and to worry whether there was worse to be expected, especially in Asia; whether the weakening influence of the institution might impair the authority of the Charter and its law against force; whether assumptions of the Charter that nations will forgo the use of force to change the existing order were in fact accepted in Asia; whether nations elsewhere might also begin to think of force to effect political change; whether the big powers and the U.N. members were prepared to enforce the status quo against threats of forcible change; whether, in short, the skeptics were right who had insisted that the law of the Charter was an idle hope, that war cannot be governed by law. But the war was quickly terminated, under pressure of a strong and unanimous stand in the Security Council; the influence of China did not prevail, but rather impelled the United States and the Soviet Union to assume a common position for peace; in the end, perhaps, the law of the Charter and the influence of the United Nations were enhanced rather than weakened. (Subsequently, agreement at Tashkent bolstered the peace in Kashmir, the disruptive influence of China was further weakened, and Indonesia changed direction and returned to the United Nations.)

The United Nations was tested again by the Arab-Israel wars of June 1967, and October 1973, chapters in a long unhappy story that began soon after the United Nations approved the creation of a Jewish state in Palestine. In 1948, claiming that the establishment of Israel in Palestine was a continuing "aggression" against the former inhabitants of that territory, the Arab states went to war against Israel. Despite the armistice agreement that followed Israel's victory, the Arab nations later insisted that a state of war continued, denied to Israel's shipping passage through the Suez Canal and blockaded its port on the Gulf of Aqaba, launched or encouraged border raids, and threatened eventual revenge. From time to time, Israel retaliated by single military actions. On two occasions there were major hostilities. In 1956, Israel (in "collusion" with France and Great Britain) launched a major attack at Suez and Sinai; the invading forces were withdrawn at the request of the United Nations, but a U.N. peacekeeping force was stationed on Egypt's side of the border, and the blockade of Aqaba was lifted. The fighting in June 1967 began after Egypt requested the withdrawal of U.N. forces and reimposed the blockade of Aqaba; Israel, claiming self-defense against armed attack, again fought and defeated the Arab states. In 1973, the Arab states launched a surprise attack on Israel; again, under pressure from the United States and the

U.S.S.R., there was a cease-fire pursuant to a U.N. resolution.

During the first two decades of Arab-Israeli hostilities the law of the Charter and the U.N. organization made important contributions to peace in the area. After their defeat in 1948, the Arab states continued to threaten revenge but refrained from resuming major hostilities. While no doubt they were deterred by their military weakness in comparison with Israel, they also knew that nations outside their own bloc would consider any attack on Israel a violation of the Charter. Israel, too, was deterred by law and U.N. authority. Despite its confidence in its military superiority, despite substantial provocation and the temptation to take the old city of Jerusalem and other border territories which would strongly improve its defensive position, Israel refrained from major action from 1948 to 1956 and again from 1956 to 1967. Israel knew that, although there was considerable sympathy for its position, even its friends in the United Nations would not tolerate offensive action in violation of the Charter. Major actions—in 1956 and 1967—came in response to intensified Arab threats and pressures, in circumstances which gave Israel a respectable claim that it was acting in self-defense consistent with the law of the Charter. In 1956 the United Nations was the stage for great drama: it compelled the United Kingdom, France, and Israel to justify their action, helped concentrate the other pressures that brought about the withdrawal of their forces from Egypt, established a U.N. force to prevent and deter further hostilities. For eleven years U.N. forces helped maintain the peace in the area; fighting erupted only after these were withdrawn. In 1967, too, the United Nations helped limit the war and terminate it in a few days. The resolution which was adopted, acceptable to both sides and to the powers, served as a kind of armistice agreement and offered the outline of a peace settlement.

Alas, the peace settlement did not come,

and has not come yet, though another war and another cease-fire, an Egypt-Israel interim disengagement agreement and dramatic meetings and negotiations have intervened. The law of the Charter was hardly mentioned when the Arabs attacked Israel in 1973; perhaps the Arab-Israel hostility has been accepted as one continuing violation or deviation. The cease-fire was adopted after extended U.N. debate and pursuant to U.N. resolutions, but, skeptics might say, the United Nations added nothing to the influence of the United States and the U.S.S.R., both of which desired the cease-fire. Since then, surely, the United Nations' influence in the Middle East has sharply declined as substantial Third World solidarity and the particular influence within the Third World of the Arab states—"its own rich," on whom others depend for oil and aid—impelled majorities to support pro-Arab, anti-Israel resolutions in various contexts, including the infamous resolution identifying Zionism with racism. For Israel the United Nations—for the present, at least—became the enemy. For the United States and some others, U.N. majorities have, especially where Israel is concerned, abused their voting power, and violated constitutional limitations, fair process, and equal treatment.

The dominance of the Third World has politicized U.N. implementation of the law of the Charter in other ways. Although the five permanent members retain their veto, Third World members have important weight even in the Security Council. Peace-keeping, however, is not as high on the Third World agenda for the United Nations as other purposes—ending white rule in southern Africa and a new economic order. Big-power wars would indeed concern them but these are highly unlikely, and the Third World has little disposition to invoke and assert U.N. machinery in hostilities between Third World countries (where hostilities are increasingly likely to occur, as they have, *e.g.*, between Somalia and Ethiopia). It remains to be seen, of course, whether Third World solidarity will continue to politicize also issues of war and peace. Some hope that increased responsibility, increased recognition of the crucial importance of international peace and stability, and concern for the organization which they value might yet restore both the law and the institutions of the United Nations to their intended major significance in international relations. A settlement in the Middle East would make a major contribution to that end.

The United Nations and General Law Observance

The existence of the United Nations, I have suggested, creates a threat that certain violations of law will be aired there. As in regard to the use of force, the United Nations has had influence to undo and to deter other violations that might come into its ken. While a member can bring virtually any dispute to the organization, if only because it spoils friendly relations and may threaten the peace, to do so would generally further aggravate the dispute and impair relations; the membership at large may also resent being drawn into the controversy. The political fare of the United Nations, therefore, still consists almost entirely of the especially "political" issues that were expressly made its business. The questions of law they involve are those relating to use of force, threats to the peace, colonialism and race, and kindred subjects. (U.N. bodies have assumed some small responsibility for monitoring gross violations of human rights.) As to these political issues, the influence of the United Nations—like that of law—is complex and not readily demonstrable. Although there is no way of proving it, one may assert confidently that the existence of the United Nations tends to discourage some of the grosser and more devastating programs of racial discrimination. In regard to colonialism, too, the United Nations has largely achieved its goals;

in Rhodesia and in Namibia, the United Nations is, again, the "legislator" of sanctions imposed against states that are charged with "violations."

Whether the political influence of the United Nations will be extended to seek observance of other law or agreement is uncertain. There have been isolated cases where the United Nations was invoked to vindicate other law. The future may bring additional cases, but until they begin to multiply, the fear of accusation in the United Nations will not be sufficient to figure in a violator's accounting.

The International Court of Justice

One organ of the United Nations deserves special mention in any discussion of contemporary influences on compliance with law. The likelihood of being brought before the International Court of Justice would be a deterrent to a violation, even if a nation did not fear enforcement of its judgments by the Security Council (Article 94). The judgments of the Courts are complied with, the onus of noncompliance with a judicial judgment weighing substantially in world opinion.

Still, the existence of the Court has not proved a major deterrent, because nations have not been prepared to submit to its jurisdiction or even to invoke it when the other side had accepted jurisdiction. The reasons for this negative attitude of nations—old and new, capitalist and socialist—have been much discussed. Briefly, it is based on a reluctance by political officials to let their interests in a dispute get out of the control of their own diplomacy for final determination by others; a sense of ignorance and unfamiliarity about the world of law and adjudication; a preference for flexibility and possible compromise rather than the all-or-nothing of a law suit; the law's delay and uncertainty; the weakness—in many cultures or countries—

of the habit of adjudication; a lack of confidence in "foreign judges" and fear that a court might extend its authority and the scope of law to "strictly internal" matters; the feeling that a law suit is an unfriendly act that might exacerbate relations, and that loss of a case would be a blow to national prestige. Resentment over a particular action of the Court—as in the South West Africa case in 1966—may also enhance mistrust of the institution or of the process. The issues of particular cases, moreover, will often discourage its adjudication. A nation will not normally come to court where its case is weak and its chance of winning slim. Political law or agreement, where the stakes are high, are especially unlikely candidates for adjudication: nations will not adjudicate matters which, they feel, they could not afford to lose or where, if they lost, they could not afford to obey the judgment. Those confident of political support for their cause, as in the General Assembly, will not risk a loss in court. That the Court is an organ of the United Nations and is invoked by majorities for advisory opinions to support political actions has "politicized" the Court to some extent and made it less acceptable to all as an impartial supreme court on international law.

Many of these reasons are "irrational." None of them explains reluctance to turn to the Court in some cases, say, for interpretation of multilateral treaties, or for advisory opinions. The Western observer is committed to hopes that adjudication may yet play a great role. At present, few would claim that it figures significantly as an inducement to law observance. It is relevant to add that reluctance to submit to adjudication is not necessarily evidence of an intention to violate international law. Even the nations with the best records of compliance and with every intention to comply in the future, have not been willing to submit to the Court. Nations seem eager to maintain that extra measure of "freedom" to decide whether they will observe the law, even when they know that they will probably do so.

12. Islamic Law and International Law

Majid Khadduri

Majid Khadduri is Professor Emeritus at The School for Advanced International Studies, Washington, D.C. In this article, he has drawn freely from a number of his published works on the subject, particularly his recent book, *The Islamic Conception of Justice* (Baltimore: The Johns Hopkins Press, 1984).

The purpose of this paper is not to discuss the rules of law that might be drawn from Islamic law for the future development of modern international law, for obviously a system of law that had evolved in a society far different from the Western can scarcely be expected to provide us with specific legal raw material. Several non-Western scholars have pointed out that modern international law is essentially the product of Western European experience and outlook and that a universal system of law should draw not only on Western but on other non-Western systems. The protest of non-Western jurists has been responded to by the growing interest among Western jurists to pay attention to non-Western laws and an emphasis on the comparative law method. The interest in comparative studies should be useful for the interpretation of Article 38 of the Statute of the International Court of Justice, under which the Court seeks to apply "the general principles of law recognized by civilized nations". What we should look for in non-Western societies, however, is not specific precedents or parallels, but fundamental concepts of law and general principle which might provide guidance for the future development of international law in a multinational world.

Like other great systems of law, Islamic law reveals the stored experiences of its followers with the problems of establishing an ordered society among men and its relationship with other contemporary communities in accordance with a set of general principles and rules under which a certain standard of justice is acknowledged. The part of the law dealing with Islam's relationship with other communities is called the Siyar (conduct of State), but this law is not necessarily a separate system of law. Like the *jus gentium*, an extension of the *jus civile*, the Siyar is an extension of Islamic law which governs the relationship of Muslims with non-Muslims, whether inside or outside the dominium of Islam. The binding force of the Siyar was based partly on reciprocity and mutual interest (derived from agreement and custom), but in the main it is a self-imposed system, the sanction of which was moral, binding on its followers even though its rules might not always be consistent with their interests. Before we discuss the concepts and principles of the Islamic law of nations (the Siyar), perhaps a brief account of the nature and character of that law might be illuminating.

To begin with, the Siyar, though consisting of some elements of positive law, was as a whole taken to be ultimately derived from divine sources (the Qur'an and Traditions). Since both law and State were considered ecumenical (universal) in nature, the Siyar was potentially capable of application to all people regardless of race or colour, individually and collectively. It follows that "persons" under the Siyar were not only "States", but both individuals, groups and political communities (the latter were not necessarily States, in the strict legal sense).

In reality, however, Islam—not unlike other ecumenical systems—could not claim monopoly of the universality of its law. In the application of its law to other nations, Islam played three distinct though not unrelated roles. First, Islam tried to play the role of an imperial State and sought to maintain peace and justice in the form of *Pax Islamica*. This role was challenged by Western Christendom which insisted on the maintenance of peace and justice in accordance with its standards of peace and justice. The rivalry between these two ecumenical States lasted from the 8th to the 13th century. Secondly, Islam played the role of a regional hegemonic State and sought in cooperation with other States (not without resort to violence) to maintain peace and justice. This period lasted from the 13th to the 19th century. Thirdly, Islam (now split into several political communities) became part of the world community and participated as a member of international organizations to maintain peace and security in accordance with the modern law of nations. In the period of confrontation, both Christendom and Islam claimed that their systems of law were truly universal and capable of application to all mankind. Continuous resort to violence taught both the lesson that neither one could claim monopoly of peace and justice without regard to the interests of other nations. In the modern age the division of Christendom and Islam into several States created new conditions which compelled them to accept the principles of competition and coexistence within the system of a world community of nations.

Owing to the ecumenical character of the State, Islamic law was personal and not territorial, as territorial limitation was irrelevant to the concept of the State claiming ultimately to embody the whole of mankind. The division of Islam into several territorial subdivisions introduced the concept of territorial sovereignty and its legal system necessarily recognized territorial concepts. Islam, however, some six centuries younger than the Western state-system, remained ecumenical in principle and its law is essentially personal, qualified by territorial limitations.

Finally, despite its apparent rigidity, Islamic law has revealed remarkable qualities of flexibility and accommodation to changing conditions. In the formative period, when the Islamic State played the imperial role, its law of nations scarcely made a distinction between defensive and offensive war (jihad). When conditions began to change and Islam assumed a defensive attitude, Muslim rulers were bound to make peace, although the classical doctrine of the jihad (equivalent to a "state of war") continued to exist in principle until early modern times.

In the light of Islam's experiences of rivalry and conflicts with Western Christendom, the first lesson that might be drawn is that no nation can claim the right of imposing its standard of order on other nations and that diverse legal systems would be more useful for the future development of the law of nations than a heavy dependence on one or on a limited number of nations. A step in the right direction is the adoption of the Universal Declaration of Human Rights by the United Nations (1948), drawn from diverse public orders, which demonstrates the possibility that nations can agree on a general standard of public order acceptable to all nations.

Second, in the Islamic experience the individual was considered a subject of the law of nations, and the central authorities dealt with him directly, apart from the State. The Islamic State recognized the individual as a subject because its law was personal, but in a shrinking world it would seem that the individual's claim to protection under the modern law of nations has become a pressing necessity. It can be taken for granted that Muslim States would welcome the adoption of such a principle, since traditionally Islamic law recognized the individual as a subject on the international plane.

Third, the confrontation between Islam and Western countries demonstrated that religious doctrines as a basis for the relationship among States tended to intensify conflicts among nations; only when religious doctrine was relegated to the domestic level did Islam, and later other nations, agree on a common standard on law devoid of religious dogma. The historical experiences of Islam and Christendom demonstrated that the fusion of religion or any other form of ideology with the foreign conduct of the State tends to increase tensions rather than promote peace among nations. It is unfortunate that when Islam and Christendom, following a long period of rivalry and conflicts, finally learned to divorce ideology from the law governing relations among nations, both have found themselves confronted today by nations advocating new standards derived either from religious or other ideological doctrines which their followers appear to insist on re-introducing into the relationship among nations.

Finally, should morality, like religion, be divorced from the law governing the rela-tionship among nations? Some scholars have advocated a completely positive viewpoint and argued that law is a set of norms which regulate the conduct of States irrespective of values. Western States claim to conduct their relations with other States to protect their national interests, whereas Muslim States still assert values and subjective criteria. Indeed, neither Western nor Muslim States are prepared to compromise their national interests, but their leaders claim to pursue their moral values and State ends.

What should the relationship between means and ends be, it may be asked, in the relations among nations? Perhaps neither one should, we may argue, be completely divorced from the other and the subordination of one to the other necessarily raises a moral question. The historical experiences of Islam demonstrated a paradox: that religion as a basis for the conduct of State-promoted conflict and continuous hostilities with other nations, but religion as a source of moral values prompted Muslims to observe moral principles still considered important in the relationship among nations. The historical experiences of Islam—indeed the historical experiences of all mankind—demonstrate that any system of law on the national as well as the international plane would lose its meaning were it divorced completely from moral principles.

chapter 5

CHANGE IN THE INTERNATIONAL SYSTEM

The growth of complex interdependence and the changes associated with it are causing important modifications of traditional "realist" premises regarding the essential characteristics of international systems and politics. Thus, the long-standing assumption that states are the dominant actors in world politics has been challenged by the growth in numbers and strength of nongovernmental actors such as multinational firms engaging in international transactions more or less independently of governments. The related "realist" assumption that states act as coherent units in international relations is also being substantially modified in view of the fact that subunits of different national governments tend increasingly to interact directly with each other on specific matters engaging their specialized responsibilities, sometimes with little direction or control by their own governmental leaders.

Gordon Craig and Alexander George,
Force and Statecraft: Diplomatic Problems of Our Time (New York and Oxford, Oxford University Press, 1983) p. 151. Reprinted by permission Oxford University Press, Inc.

It is not enough to define the characteristics of the state independent of the economic context in which it functions. Much of the behavior we observe to be characteristic of those responsible for the conduct of a state's foreign policy derives from the fact that the states must coexist with one another. Because of the condition of potential anarchy to which the principles of sovereignty and nationalism give rise, one simply cannot ignore the way in which that condition affects the way states behave.

The fact that states are all exposed to the same set of circumstances and are compelled to coexist and interact with each other according to terms imposed by their common condition has given rise to the notion that they are all part of a system, and that if we would understand how they behave we must understand and think in terms of a collective interdependency which imparts a uniformity and regularity to their behavior—or at least up to a point. As Professor McLellan so cogently brings out in his essay, they are certainly not equal and therefore, cannot possibly respond to the same set of circumstances in the same way. Other contemporary theorists have carried the notion of the international system beyond the merely descriptive or metaphoric to argue that, like an ecological system or a clock, the parts (the states) are so related each to the other and to the whole that the behavior of the parts cannot be understood apart from the functioning of the whole system. How is the "system" of international relations supposed to work? Or, *does* it work, as Sir Harry Hinsley wonders in his Martin Wight lecture of 1981, reprinted in this chapter?

According to Joseph Frankel, "a political system denotes a collection of independent political entities [states] which interact with considerable frequency and according to regularized processes."[1] Conceiving of international society as a system, and its major components—the states, as well as non-state actors—as subsystems, "conceptualizes reality in a sensible manner."[2]

It recognizes that the whole is greater than the sum of its parts and that the structure or distribution of power within the whole determines how each part—namely each government—will act in response to the whole. When power is concentrated in two states—we call this a bipolar system—it is the interaction between them that will have the greatest effect with how the system functions and how the other states behave.

This "system" concept of international relations assumes that each state, by pursuing its own self-interest, contributes to the maintenance and stability of the whole. Each state will so act as to maintain the condition which guarantees its continued existence as a sovereign entity. Unfortunately, there is no outside force or authority capable of stepping in and preserving stability if the relationship or balance among the parts begins to tip or break down. In the course of events tensions may reach such a point that the stability of the system *does* break down and wars occur—"because the world community of nations is not yet a maturely functioning homeostatic unit in equilibrium."[3]

Actually, big wars take place because leaders and governments fail to account for or become dissatisfied with the existing equilibrium and attempt to improve or protect their positions—in terms of security, power, or prestige—at whatever cost. In any case, it is the nature of the international system—the condition of uncertainty and insecurity, and the absence of a higher authority—that determines the behavior of most, if not all, states and hence obliges us to analyze international relations not simply with regard to each state individually, but with regard to the character and interactions of the entire system as they influence the behavior of all states.

The most suggestive part of the system-level of analysis is the emphasis placed upon the importance of the distribution of power among the states members

---

[1] Joseph Frankel, *International Relations in a Changing World* (New York: Oxford University Press, 1979), p. 147.

[2] *Ibid.*, p. 148.

[3] Keith Nelson and Spencer Ohlin, Jr., *Why War: Ideology, Theory, and History* (Berkeley and Los Angeles, University of California Press, 1980), p. 56.

and upon the effects that advances in technology and weapons (especially nuclear weapons) have for the danger of war.

Not only have nuclear weapons made war potentially suicidal, but they have made the game of power competition a "strange blend of arms race and restraints."[4] An equally profound change in the nature of interstate relations has been brought about by technology and economics. Modern states are highly dependent on foreign trade and investment and upon access to vital resources like oil. They cannot secure their ends simply by imposing their will on others. This has given rise to a condition of "interdependence" that limits even the strongest states from acting at the expense of others.

Those who stress the importance of system-level analysis point to the difference in the distribution of national power that existed in the eighteenth and nineteenth centuries with what exists today. Eighteenth- and nineteenth-century Europe was comprised of half a dozen more or less evenly matched states— Britain, France, Prussia, Austria, Russia—whereas today, there exists a marked hierarchy (bipolarity) in which the U.S. and the Soviet Union are superpowers and all the rest lack the essential requisites of a superpower, at least so far, as some see China, India or Brazil as future superpowers. The European system was more stable because the defeat of any one state would not give the victor automatic domination over all the rest, whereas today, if either the U.S. or the Soviet Union were threatened or defeated, no other state could come to its aid or offset the consequences. It does make a difference whether the distribution of power is spread evenly or concentrated in two states. When examining the effect the distribution of power has upon each state's foreign policy we must also consider the importance of ideology (lack of a common culture or commitment to the existing order) and the difference in weapons between nineteenth-century firearms and modern ICBMs and nuclear warheads. During the darkest days of the Cold War, it became a commonplace to predict that World War *IV* would be fought with bows and arrows!

Certainly any understanding of international relations will benefit both in practical as well as in theoretical aspects from the analysis of how bipolarity affects the foreign-policy behavior of the member states. A system-level approach also enables us to take account of the situation with which the Third World confronts the international system upon which the emergence in the period since 1948 of about 100 new states has had a drastic impact. Quite apart from the sheer number and variety of societies involved, most of which are non-Western in religion and culture, their struggle to make good their sovereignty and to meet the needs of their people has introduced an element of volatility and instability into the international system. One might well ask if conditions of international order any longer exist. Such states are frequently the scene of coups and revolutions. Many exist economically on the margin of subsistence; others are riven by tribal, religious, and social conflict. They are often the victims of proxy wars fought by the superpowers. Many challenge and some even deny the proposition that they have a common stake in preserving the existing inter-

---

[4]Stanley Hoffmann, "The Diplomatic-Strategic Chessboard," *Primacy or World Order* (New York: McGraw-Hill Book Company, 1978), p. 119–32.

national order; a major objective of the Third World countries is to bring about a massive redistribution of the global economic wealth and they have raised a challenge to the legitimacy of many of the present norms of international law. Hence no understanding of contemporary international problems would be possible without a recognition of the extent to which the behavior of the Third World challenges the existing international system, the unequal and revolutionary nature of which is the subject of Professor McLellan's updated essay.

Finally, there is the extent to which transnational forces have undercut and usurped the authority of the nation-state. With the growth of communication and technology, movements linking people and activities that go beyond the nation-state have been on the increase. We call these "transnational" movements, and to the extent they take an institutional form that has an impact upon the international system or upon the states themselves, we refer to them as "transnational actors." The recent efforts both within and outside the United Nations to negotiate an agreement to condemn and punish acts of terrorism against airlines is a good example of the problem of emergent transnationalism.

With the increase in communications and technology, new relations of dependence and interdependence are being created which political leaders can ignore only at their peril; new forms of power have arisen—such as the multinational corporation—which have the potential to challenge the nation-state. One need not go as far as to argue that the nation-state is defunct as an economic unit, or to accept the theory that the nation-state is becoming "functionless" and that the base for an alternative world order is already being formed by technicians, managers, and political elites who think in extranational terms. Nevertheless, one could agree that new transnational forces are impinging upon the sovereignty of the state and forcing governments to adjust to a new level of activity in order to control and manage these forces.

The focus on transnational movements is also an aspect of the ongoing debate between the federalists who favor a supranational organization at the regional or world level, and the functionalists who have advocated a more practical path to unification through the organizing of transnational activity on a function-by-function basis. The stunning rise of a number of new transnational movements and actors, whose activities escape the control of states and force governments to negotiate functional agreements in order to regulate them, has given new life to the argument that it is through such transnational activities that states will be forced to knit an ever widening web of supranational authority.

As noted in Chapter One, transnational actors may include such groups as the Roman Catholic Church, the world Zionist movement, the guerilla and terrorist movement associated with the Palestinian Liberation Front, as well as multinational corporations and worldwide labor associations that transcend national jurisdiction and have an economic or political impact upon the international system or upon the individual states, either directly or indirectly, by exerting pressure upon national governments through domestic affiliates or adherents. It is not hard to understand why some observers can see the emergence of a true world society, one in which international relations—if by that term one means relations between completely separate units—is fast becoming an anachronism. Harlan Cleveland, a man of extraordinary practical experience internationally, combined with deep philosophical insight expressed with a sense of humor, deals with this in his article, "The Passing of Remoteness", part of which is reprinted in this section.

DISCUSSION QUESTIONS

1. Why can we speak of interstate relations as forming a "system"? How does Hinsley explain its "rise and fall"? What does Cleveland mean by "power leaking out of sovereignty"?

2. Do you conclude from McLellan's essay that inequality in power inevitably leads to revolutionary activity? Why or why not?

3. Why do the weaknesses of many newer states make them less able to perform effectively the two vital functions of sovereignty: providing for the security and well-being of society?

4. How has the weakness and inequality of the Third World countries that sets them apart from the longer-established states complicated the conduct of international relations?

5. How has their condition complicated American foreign policy, according to Cleveland? What does he say about the old distinction between "domestic" and "foreign" policy?

6. In the final analysis, is it not still true that world politics continues to be dominated by the few most powerful countries?

7. Which of the two contradictory forces in world society—integration or fragmentation—do you think is the more influential today? Do Hinsley and Cleveland appear to agree or disagree on this issue?

13. The Rise and Fall of the Modern System

F.H. Hinsley

Knighted after having served as Vice-Chancellor at Cambridge University, England, Sir Harry has now returned to St. Johns College to teach and write. He is a leading Naval authority on British Intelligence in World War II.

In the history of relations between the world's leading states since the end of the eighteenth century certain features stand out prominently. One is that infrequent wars have alternated with long periods of peace. From the 1760s to 1790s these states were at peace: from the 1790s to 1815 they were at war; from 1815 to 1854, peace; 1871 to 1914, peace; 1914 to 1918, war; 1918 to 1939, peace; 1939 to 1945, war; and since 1945 another 36 years to peace already. Another feature, no less pronounced, is that each of these infrequent wars has been more demanding and devastating for all participants, more nearly total, than that which preceded it. In these respects, as also in a third on which I shall enlarge later on, international conduct in the past 200 years has differed from international conduct in all earlier times, when states were more or less continuously engaged in wars that remained limited in scale—and so much so that the rise of the modern system may safely be traced back to the end of the eighteenth century.

It is possible to exaggerate the distinctiveness of the modern system; and it is certainly true that its defining characteristics have become more prominent as it has aged. Thus, the years from 1854 to 1871 did not witness unremitting war between the leading states, but several separate wars, and from each of these wars to the next there was no escalation

"The Rise and Fall of the Modern International System," *Review of International Studies*, Vol. 5, No. 1, © 1982, British International Studies Association, pp. 1–8. Reprinted by permission.

in the scale of fighting. But this qualification, like others that might be made, pales into significance when we contrast the modern pattern of conflict with conflict in earlier conditions. Before the end of the eighteenth century it had commonly been the case that war and peace had not been sharply differentiated—that public war and private war, inter-state war and civil war, civil war and rebellion, rebellion and crime had been barely distinguishable. At some times, in some places, on the other hand, war had become a specialized activity, oragnized by the state, undertaken after due preparation, engaging professional forces. Yet even when it was so organized, war had remained a natural activity, indulged in with great regularity, not to say seasonally. It had also remained limited in scale. That escalation in the destructiveness of war which has accompanied its almost every renewal since the end of the eighteenth century had not set in.

We generally recognize that warfare even now retains these characteristics in the extreme condition of relations between primitive societies which we call tribes—that for such societies as the Papuan, for example, it was till recently both central to the economy and akin to play, and took the form of a universal seasonal competition. What we do not always remember is that in conditions less extreme than those far less removed from our own, conflict conformed to the norms of primitive societies rather than to those of modern times until so comparatively recently as 200 years ago. During the whole of the seventeenth century there were only seven years in which none of the European states was at war. In the first two-thirds of the eighteenth century some or other of the European states were still at war during two out of every three years, and of the individual states the United Kingdom, which was not abnormally belligerent, was at war during two and a half years out of every five. As for the scale of warfare, its very frequency reveals how restricted it was, what lack of intensity marked its conduct, and there is no lack of detailed evidence to that effect.

Modernization

When we ask why this situation gave way to the modern one and why it did so when it did, we should bear in mind a consideration to which I have already drawn attention: for a long time after the end of the eighteenth century the transition was confined to the relations between the more developed states and societies. A condition of affairs evocative of the primitive one was not abnormal throughout the nineteenth century for such parts of the world as escaped Europe's control or were failing to share in Europe's advance, and in some areas it is not abnormal to this day. For the different experience of the developed states, on the other hand, the phenomenon of Europe's advance from the end of the eighteenth century provides the sufficient, if also the obvious answer to our question. In the last resort it was as a result of the subjection of societies and states of the process of modernization or industrialization—a process based to an ever-increasing extent on science and technology—that international conduct acquired the characteristics that have distinguished it in modern times. In particular, it was because that process had so great an impact on the destructiveness of weapons, on the structure of societies and on the capacities and concerns of governments that—between the industrializing societies, if only between them—the modern pattern of war came into being.

The continuing and accelerating increase

in the deadliness of weapons began only in the eighteenth century. By the middle of the nineteenth century it had already advanced so far as to ensure of itself that war would be fought at a higher level of violence each time it recurred. In the 1860s the fear that this would be so produced the first attempts by states to place international restrictions on the development and use of new weapons; and we need not doubt that although all such attempts have been ineffective, the first of them marks the point at which anxiety about the weapons revolution began to contribute to that other feature of the modern system—the alternation of bouts of war with long periods of peace—by making states more hesitant to fight each other.

By the same date the huge power of technology to transform the nature of society had begun to create out of rural, provincialized communities societies that were so much more integrated, more centralized, more nationalized than ever before that as a natural consequence the leading states were abandoning long-service professional armies and replacing them with national conscription. By 1900 this change was reinforcing the weapons revolution by making it still more certain that any future war would be more nearly total than any previous conflict; and in 1914 it was to be confirmed that the greatly increased integration, articulation and regulation of the European societies had made the exhaustion of the enemy's national resources, and of his national will to fight on, the inescapable objective in war, the only war aim, even as the weapons revolution had erected mechanical and mass attrition, on a dreadful scale, into the centrepiece of battle. But the greater integration of societies had been accompanied, in the wake of the same industrializing process, by their greater material sophistication. Ever since the beginning of the industrial revolution, and at an ever increasing rate, the range of a society's forms of enterprise, and of its means of maintaining and multiplying power and wealth, had been widening and becoming more complex, and by the 1860s the days were fast receding when land had been the main source of wealth and when, next only to marrying it, conquest had been the most cost-effective way of acquiring it. Industrialization was presenting fast-developing societies with opportunities for advancement and satisfaction other than war at the same time as it was increasing the inescapable destructiveness and risk of war. In this way, also, by producing a changing balance of calculation, it explains why wars between these societies were now separated by long periods of peace.

This was all the more the case because industrialization. by exerting a profound impact on the character and capacity of government, was creating state structures which could calculate with some consistency and channels through which their conclusions could be imposed. Until the eighteenth century war was an undertaking for which, like agriculture then or manufacturing now, large sections of society were naturally organized. It was also an activity on which, appearances notwithstanding, societies embarked with scant regard for the wishes or the warnings of their states. Indeed, communications remained so negligible, and state apparatuses so weak, that it may be questioned whether rulers did more than merely reflect and express the social consensus that pressed for war until men were tired or satisfied enough to press for peace. But if the impact of science and technology was producing societies that were more integrated and more capable of sustained and systematic warfare, it was also facilitating from the end of the eighteenth century the rise of regulatory government—indeed, it was necessitating it— and this at a time when the growing burden of being prepared for war and the risks involved in increasingly destructive war were forcing governments to apply their growing competence to the task of avoiding war.

Rights and Reforms

The states of the modern international system failed in this task. If only at long inter-

vals, peace between them continued to break down; and in the fact that each next war was more catastrophic than the last lay one reason why in the twentieth century the system itself became bankrupt and declined. Why did they fail?

Some historians of the detailed diplomacy of the system, and especially of those of its international crises from which, as in 1914 and 1939, war ensued, have concluded that this is the wrong question. In their judgement, governments did not fail in the task, but failed to address themselves to it seriously. And it is, of course, no answer to their argument to point out that at just those junctures when peace was breaking down most of the states, and important elements in all of them, displayed the greatest anxiety to preserve it. But a proper study of the crises will show that, if war still broke out, it was not so much because anxiety was less prevalent than belligerency and bravado as for other reasons.

No one who has reflected on the disarray of government machines and the anguish accompanying government decisions in the years before 1914 and before 1939 will doubt what those reasons were. For all the increase in their competence over 100 years, governmental structures were still unable, in the long run, to exercise adequate control over domestic pressures and international tensions which had themselves intensified in the wake of the industrializing process. For all their increasing reluctance to fight each other, governments could not in the last resort relinquish a basic right which had itself been consolidated—freed from external moral and theological sources of restraint—under the impact of the same process. Throughout the history of the modern international system states retained the *ius ad bellum*—the legal right to go to war for any reason whatever— indeed, for no reason at all—to preserve the security or advance the interests of their societies. All states conceded that any state invoking this right acquired the privileges of belligerency, and these privileges included the legal right to the spoils of war. The right to challenge the status quo was matched by the right to change it by holding on to conquests.

In view of their tenacious retention of this right, if not of their continuing inadequacy in crises, it may be thought that governments cannot be said to have been increasingly absorbed by the wish to avoid war. The two preoccupations certainly conflicted; but they are not mutually exclusive or logically incompatible. Moreover, a third outstanding feature of the modern international system may now be brought into account. At the end of every war since the end of the eighteenth century, as had never been the case before, the leading states made a concerted effort, each one more radical than the last, to reconstruct the system on lines that would enable them, or so they believed, to avoid a further war. These successive efforts at reform produced the Concert system set up after 1815; the arbitration measures that were adopted in the 1890s in the aftermath of the wars of 1854–71; the League of Nations that was established at the end of the first world war; the Kellogg Pact by which in 1928, when the League was visibly failing, the states renounced the right to use force for the settlement of their disputes. These initiatives are as characteristic and distinctive of the operation of the system as are the dynamics of its wars. So is the fact that they all came to nothing. But their failure adds significance, and also gives poignancy, to their persistent renewal. When the states embarked on the first of them they had come to recognize that the next war would be more destructive than the war they were bringing to a close. They renewed their efforts in the knowledge that the latest war had amply confirmed their earlier forebodings. And yet in spite of the last reform they had adopted, the system again broke down; and if one reason for the decline of the system was that each war was more catastrophic than the last, another was that each increasingly radical attempt to guard against the danger of another war failed in its objective.

The League and the United Nations

The most recent of these initiatives is the United Nations, the peace-keeping organization set up at the end of the second world war. What if it were to be as ineffective as its predecessors? What if the period of peace between the leading states which has lasted since 1945 were not to last much longer? In that event the modern system, continuing to be in force, would have sustained another of the periodical collapses that have characterized its operation throughout its existence—though it might be the final collapse. But what if this catastrophe were not to materialize? We and our successors would then be justified in concluding that after the collapse of the second world war, the modern international system had entered upon a process of decline and that a new system had arisen to take its place. The argument that the system is declining will meanwhile be unconvincing without evidence that another is replacing it, and it remains to consider whether any such evidence yet exists.

We may begin by glancing at the ways in which the United Nations Organization differs from the League of Nations. The Covenant of the League placed great emphasis on the difference between the legal and the illegal resort to war—between just war and unjust war—and it imposed on member states both the obligation to refrain from unjust war and the obligation to uphold legality against such states as embarked on war illegally. The states which drew up the Charter of the United nations placed all the emphasis on avoiding war at almost all costs; and they thus refrained from imposing legal rules and obligations upon the member states. Instead, they required the member states to impose a new standard of conduct on themselves by resolving that the renunication of the right to go to war, the principle embodied in the Kellogg Pact, should be a condition of membership of the United Nations.

It is not difficult to account for these differences between the League and the United

Nations. The UN, set up after the modern international system had collapsed for a second time, was also set up at a time when a second total war had revealed the extent to which the process of industrialism had accelerated in momentum, in the wake of the continual advance of science and technology, since the foundation of the League. It was set up by states which could not fail to know that since 1919—indeed, in the few years since 1939—the impact of that process on the scale of weapons, the structure of society and the capacity of government had had more effect than in the whole of the previous history in raising the potential destructiveness of war and reducing its potential utility for the more advanced societies. Nor need we doubt that it is on this account that, although the renunciation of the right to war constitutes a greater limitation on the freedom of states than any that was created by the Covenant, states have not subsequently disowned the United Nations in the way they disowned the League of Nations—by deserting it.

You may feel that this last fact is no great testimony to the importance of the differences—so dismal has been the performance of the UN since it was established. And you may feel distinctly sceptical of their significance when I remind you that the renunciation of the right to go to war is qualified—it is subject to the right of self-defense and is waived when states are carrying out the instructions of the Security Council—and point out how easily states have exploited these loopholes. No state now has a War Office, but all retain the department and call it the Ministry of Defence. No state now declares war when it uses force in contravention of its pledge; if a state cannot plead self-defence or UN instructions for declaring war, it either resorts to force without admitting that it is doing so or finds some other justification by claiming that it is helping a legitimate government against rebellion or helping rebels to advance an indubitably moral cause. But these subterfuges confirm

rather than weaken the argument that in 1946 the states achieved a great advance. They are subterfuges to which states descend in order to remain within the letter of a new rule of conduct, and you do not make efforts to appear to obey a rule which you do not accept. We must not forget, moreover, the difference between rules and the laws of thermodynamics. You do not make a rule to the effect that water must not flow uphill; but man-made law would not be law—indeed, it would not be made—unless it could be broken or bent. It lays down rules but does not ensure that they will be observed. What came about with the abolition of the right of the state to go to war was a shift of norms, and involving, as it did, the recognition that war had ceased to be a legalized or sanctified form of force, it constituted a greater displacement of assumptions about relations between states than any that has taken place in history.

When a shift is so fundamental we may be sure of two things. It will have been a long time in preparation. And once it has been made, and if it is consolidated, it will have multiple and far reaching repercussions. In the case of this shift, it was being prepared for throughout the history of the modern international system: indeed, its completion was nothing less than the logical outcome of those developments, and of those responses to developments, which explain the history of that system and account for its distinctive features. But is it possible to claim that the shift has as yet produced any noticeable repercussions? I believe it is. There has been much evidence to suggest that other displacements of belief or ideology, subsidiary to and consequential upon the first, have been taking place in recent years.

Most prominently—and this should cause no surprise since Marxism-Leninism is the most rigourous and self-conscious of all modern ideologies—the evidence is to be found in the steps that have been taken to adjust the doctrines of Marxism-Leninism. The central doctrine of Marxism-Leninism relating to the issue of peace and war used to be the doctrine that war is inevitable between socialist and capitalist societies. Whether this doctrine issued from the conviction that capitalism would not be satisfied until socialism had been destroyed, or from the conviction that socialism must not be content until capitalism had been abolished, is a question of no consequence; the doctrine was beyond dispute. But in 1956, at the XXth Congress of the Communist Party of the Soviet Union, it was formally cancelled. No less important, another doctrine was made central in its place—the doctrine of peaceful coexistence which insists that the rivalry which is inevitable between societies with different structures and ideologies, but is supposedly inevitable only between such societies, must for ever be kept short of war by the states.

It was perhaps inevitable that at the time, and for years after, the capitalist societies should have regarded this change as constituting no more than a dangerous tactical twist in the Bolshevik offensive, one that was designed to lull them into a false sense of security while Stalin's successors rescued Russia from Stalin's excesses and prepared to return to the true Bolshevik path. Even now, this suspicion is not wholly stilled. But this residue of distrust is of little significance compared with the fact that since the 1960s capitalist states have embraced the Marxist-Leninist new-model doctrine of peaceful coexistence and made it their own over-riding doctrine in the field of relations between states. At least in this field, East and West, Communism and capitalism, now subscribe to a common view for the first time since the Bolshevik revolution of 1917. Nor does China any longer remain outside the consensus. It is sometimes claimed that the Chinese Marxist-Leninists, the fundamentalists of the movement, still proclaim that war is inevitable between socialism and capitalism. On closer inspection it will be found that they now insist only that war will be inevitable unless an expansionist Russia is contained by the combined efforts of other states.

That this adjustment has not been made easily in Russia and China we may be sure from what we know about the rigidity, almost theological, of the Marxist-Leninist laboratory of thought. And we know that the West was hardly less reluctant to make it, for here we may examine in some detail how and why it was brought about when impasse had been reached after a decade or labour in the field of strategic studies. Strategic studies became a major academic industry in the West in the early 1950s. Nor is this surprising; it was then that the nuclear weapons were superseding the atomic bomb, that the missile was superseding the bomber, that the submarine was emerging as the perfect moving missile platform—and that the West's monopoly of these advantages was shattered by developments in Soviet Russia. It is in no way surprising, either, that until the middle of the 1960s the object of the studies was, as all the literature proclaimed, to reintegrate strategy with policy—to restore to policy the flexibility and the range of options that the latest weapons were taking away from it. But the real, as opposed to the proclaimed objective of the literature was to discover whether nuclear states could evolve strategies and weapons by which they could preserve the options of threatening war with each other and of going to war with each other despite the fact that they had become nuclear states. Techniques of crisis management; theories for the control of escalation; strategies of flexible retaliation; the development of tactical or little nuclear weapons—these suggestions were all advanced in the hope that by enabling nuclear states to evade the logical outcome of nuclear deadlock, the strategy of 'the great deterrent', they would preserve for them the possibility of more limited war.

If we read these elaborations today we bring away from them one unmistakable impression. They possess all the cogency, all the intellectual rigour and all the irrelevance of the scholastic writings of the middle ages. And whence their irrelevance? The answer lies partly in the fact that they did not pause to ask whether disciplines accepted by one nuclear state would be accepted by another, or whether disciplines accepted by all nuclear states before the outbreak of hostilities would be observed by all after hostilities had broken out. But it lies mainly in the fact that since the mid-1960s, no doubt as a result of deeper reflection, the response of strategic thinkers had undergone a fundamental change.

Their message since then has been that should provocation lead to war between the world's most developed states—or should accident or miscalculation do so—there is no reasonable hope of avoiding massive nuclear exchanges and no possibility of providing civil defence against them; that if it is thus imperative to avoid war, then, far from trying to avoid dependence on the great deterrent of massive retaliation, it is imperative to ensure against provocation and miscalculation by seeing to it that all nuclear states shall be able to rely on deterring each other; and that they will be deterred by the risk of massive retaliation if all possess a retaliatory nuclear armoury that is invulnerable to a nuclear first attack. They have concluded—to put this message in other words—that whereas the chief purpose of military establishments has hitherto been to fight wars, from now on their chief purpose is to avert war, and that the advance of technology has at last made it possible for them to fulfil it.

Abstention from War

You may grant the interest and the significance of these developments and yet remain apprehensive lest they prove to be reversible. The initiative which produced the establishment of the League of Nations was significant; but the League was ineffective and short-lived. It was already a feature of the modern international system before 1945 that its leading states contrived to enjoy long periods of peace; and the fear that the present period of peace between the leading states will break down in its turn in understandable at a time when the world economy is again in serious disarray, *détente* is again under strain and some voices, however few, are again suggesting that nuclear war would not in the event be total and devastating. There is much force in these points; it would indeed be unwise to assume that the advances to which I have drawn attention cannot be reversed. But I derive some comfort from the belief that the conjunction of circumstances which proved fatal to the international system in 1914 and again in 1939 is unlikely to be repeated.

The modern international system collapsed on those occasions because states continued to hold the view that they had the legal right to go to war. It also collapsed because states holding this view were confronted with massive shifts in their relative power which persuaded them in the last resort that war was a reasonable means of defending or advancing their interests. States hold this view no longer, and in the wake of the great acceleration of scientific and technological development that has taken place in the last forty years and that has ensured that even conventional war between developed states would produce insupportable damage, they are unlikely ever again to make this judgment. Indeed, they are unlikely, such of them as have been caught up in this acceleration, to be confronted ever again with shifts in their relative power that will disturb the equilibrium between them. That shifts of power will continue to take place—this goes without saying, as does the fact that interests will continue to conflict. But these states have passed so far beyond a threshold of absolute power that changes in relative power can no longer erode their ability to uphold the equilibrium which resides in the ability of each to destroy all.

Such are the grounds for suggesting that we are now witnessing the formation of an international system which will be even more different from the modern system than that system was from all its precursors, and which will be so because its leading states will abstain from war with each other. But since it will also be a system in which conflict and confrontation continue, between those states as between the others, let me conclude by reminding you that Immanuel Kant, he who first foresaw that precisely such a system would one day materialize, allowed that it would remain subject to constant danger from 'the law evading bellicose propensities in man' but judged that, once constructed, it would survive for that very reason. . . .

---

14. The International System: Unequal and Revolutionary

David S. McLellan

Dr. McLellan is a Professor of Political Science at Miami University in Oxford, Ohio.

A most distinctive feature of the contemporary international system is the combination of vulnerability and external assertiveness that characterizes the situation and the behavior of many of the newer states that were established after 1950. Traditionally the smaller European states did not count for much, although the world was given a preview of what the future might hold when little Serbia refused to yield to the Austrian ultimatum that brought on the First World War. By contrast, the role and actions of smaller states, particularly those in the Third World, has been a major contributing factor to the crisis in international politics that has marked the decades of the 1960s and 1970s. Almost all of the wars that have occurred since 1950 have been fought in the Third World; the Soviet and American conflict since the early 1960s has been at its most intense in the Third World; each side has made its

Coeditor of previous editions of this book, David McLellan drafted this essay while a Visiting Fellow at Clare Hall, University of Cambridge, England, in 1981. He later updated it.

greatest gains and suffered its severest setbacks here; the difficulties of managing the European alliance have been minor until now compared with those Washington has encountered in its relations with the Third World, and in particular with the states in the Middle East and southern Africa. The threat of a local conflict drawing the Soviet Union and the United States into a nuclear confrontation such as occurred over Cuba and in the Middle East has been more frequent in the Third World than in Europe, where the NATO and Warsaw Pacts confronted each other directly. Finally, the most significant and ominous shifts in the balance of power since 1945 have come not in the traditional form of aggression and territorial conquest but from regime changes within Third World countries. For example, the greatest shifts in the global balance occurred when the Communists attained power in China in 1949, and when Peking broke with Moscow and aligned itself with the United States in the early 1970s.

Why has the Third World been such a

cockpit of conflict and crisis and why is it likely to remain so for an indefinite future? The principal explanation is that much of the Third World is comprised of states that either do not yet constitute nations (which lack important qualities of effective nation-statehood) or are too weak politically and economically to provide for the welfare and security of their people. There is no single explanation for this, and the situation varies somewhat between long-established Third World states, such as Brazil or Chile, and newly formed states.[1]

Many of the newer states of Africa and Asia were established on the basis of territorial boundaries carved out by the European colonial powers without regard for the ethnic, tribal, or religious distinctions of the people involved. Even before the Europeans arrived, the native peoples were comprised of congeries of disparate tribal, religious, ethnic, and caste groupings, often at different levels of economic and social development. Upon this basic mélange the European imperialists imposed artificial territorial boundaries, so that in many instances the successor states consist of a heterogeneity of groups not yet coalesced into nationhood. Or, as in the case of Latin America, the Spanish left behind a ruling class separated economically and socially (and sometimes ethnically) from the mass of the population. Governments of such states are often in the hands of a dominant tribe or religious group or a ruling class, and are therefore less than fully legitimate in the eyes of the population that is excluded from power. Elsewhere, governments reflect an uneasy balance between rival groups that is all too susceptible to collapse (as happened in the case of Pakistan when Bangladesh seceded and in Lebanon where Christians and Muslims war on each other).

Second, many Third World states are economically underdeveloped and cannot adequately provide for the welfare of their population. Many are resource poor or subsistence economies confronted by the pressure of too many people on too little land.

Where development has taken place, it is often in a small, modernized sector serving the needs of the international market rather than the needs of the local population. Precisely because they find themselves dependent on outside investment capital and outside markets for their products, such regimes are dependent upon and vulnerable to unpredictable economic forces (such as recessions) over which they have no control. The result has been that the privileged elites in many of these countries—the large landowners, merchant and banking interests, the political class—fearing that any change might destabilize or deprive them of their power, hesitate to institute reforms and so tend to rely upon authoritarian and repressive rule.[2]

National unity and economic welfare—the two indispensable conditions of the modern state's existence—are often lacking. Is it any wonder that the absence of the requisites of statehood should figure so heavily in determining the international role and foreign-policy behavior of most of the countries of the Third World?

To the legacy of colonialism which still lingers on in many forms must be added the insecurity and frustrations of ineffectuality both at home and in external relations. This perhaps explains the instability and prevalence of wars and coups that are such a prominent feature of international relations in the Third World. Weakness generates insecurity and a preoccupation with one's ability to control one's existence. It may also inspire foreign adventures against one's neighbors as a means of directing attention away from domestic failures. As Klaus Knorr points out in a later chapter, most wars since 1945 have occurred in the Third World, partly because of the unsettled nature of many Third World frontiers, partly because Third World regimes are tempted to use war to divert attention from their own inadequacies, and partly because the Third World offers the superpowers the option of *fighting wars by proxy.*

Shortly after gaining independence, a number of these regimes espoused a largely symbolic policy of "nonalignment," vowing to eschew great power entanglements in favor of a virtuous independence (the same freedom from entangling alliances, incidentally, that George Washington recommended to the new American nation in his Farewell Address). But many Third World governments soon found the temptation of economic and military benefits from identification with one or the other superpower too great to resist. This did not mean they had given up their aspiration for independence or their sensitivity to any indications of outside control. On the contrary, except for those directly threatened by one superpower and therefore dependent on the other for its security and survival (examples: Castro's Cuba, South Korea, Vietnam), the nonaligned sought to secure benefits from both sides without abandoning or compromising their independence. Nasser's comment about Tito illustrates this point of view: "Tito is a great man. He showed me how to get help from both sides—without joining either." As a result, the United States and Russia have competed for over a generation for influence in the Third World; in contrast, most of these countries were largely unconcerned with how their behavior affected the global balance of power. (Nowhere is this more evident than in the Middle East, where both Jordan and Saudi Arabia, two conservative Arab regimes, presumably with a stake in the security of the Persian Gulf, spurned [former] Secretary of State [Alexander] Haig's argument that the Soviet threat take precedence over their conflict with Israel.)

As a result, the situation in the Third World poses a constant challenge to the international system and to international stability and order (at least as Washington would like to see it). The vulnerability of many Third World regimes to revolution and perforce to Soviet or Communist influence has been a constant nightmare for Washington policymakers. In the ensuing competition, the United States has spent more than $100 billion in economic and military aid, has intervened numerous times (both directly—in the

Dominican Republic and Grenada—and indirectly—in helping to overthrow the Allende regime in Chile), has fought at least one major war (Vietnam), and is now intervening in Nicaragua. It has endeavored to limit the spread of nuclear weapons to Third World countries while taking the lead in the sale and distribution of conventional weapons. In each case it has the same objective in mind, namely, to insulate the United States against unpredictability and disorder.

Furthermore, in the last decade both the United States and the international system have faced constant pressure to modify certain traditional principles of the Western, capitalist order so as to give favorable treatment to help the development of the Third World economies. The United States and its capitalist partners have largely resisted their demands, but only at the price of disfavor and hostility from the Third World. More recently, American and Western diplomats as well as private citizens have been the victims of official and unofficial acts of terrorism. The most marked feature of the international system for the rest of this century and well into the next will be instability, revolution, and hostility toward the advanced capitalist states.

In some instances, anti-Western activities are the work of Marxist and radical movements. In other instances, the hostility is inspired by religious or cultural fundamentalism (as in the case of Iran and Lebanon), where the fruits of modernization (and American influence) ran counter to traditional Islamic values or where it has not produced a meaningful social and economic life for the millions uprooted by change. In Latin America, elements of the Catholic Church have for some time supported the forces of social and political change opposed to the status quo which the United States traditionally supports. While annoyed and upset by the support for revolution by some Catholic bishops, the United States has failed to recognize or accept the changes being wrought by the Catholic clergy. Instead, there is a dangerous tendency for American foreign policy to assume that such "radicalism" (which amounts to no more than a demand for economic survival and justice) is caused by Marxist agitators or supported by Soviet arms shipments and to ignore that such revolutions are being stirred by more powerful forces: hunger and a desire for a better life. Fundamentally, the crisis to the international order is produced by the conflict between a Western capitalist system that possesses the economic wealth and organization to provide its people with reasonable abundance, and a Third World in which order is breaking down and justice seems as far off as ever. Moscow does not create this conflict, although it is clearly in a position to exploit and benefit from it.

Poverty is so endemic and the sense of powerlessness or fear on the part of Third World governments so pervasive that a tragic pattern of revolution and repression seems inescapable. Since it is against the abuses and moral insensitivity of capitalism that many revolutions are directed, the United States finds itself the target and scapegoat for much that is wrong in the Third World. Anti-Americanism is not limited to radical regimes but also manifests itself under right-wing authoritarian regimes and under regimes that reflect a religious and social reaction against the capitalist and Western threat to traditional values. Time after time Argentina, Chile, Zaire, the Philippines, Guatemala, and Indonesia—all conservative regimes and clients of the United States—have voted against America in the United Nations, not because we espouse human rights, but because it is a relatively painless way to vent their frustrations and demonstrate to their people their independence from American domination.

We can expect few of these regimes to be swayed by a traditional concern for the stability of the balance of power. In many instances, local conflicts weigh far more heavily in Arab and Israeli calculations than does the threat of Soviet penetration into the Persian Gulf. The Shah of Iran sought security ties with the United States to reinforce his personal power, not because he feared an external threat from the Soviet Union.

The United States, being the status quo power, is at the greatest disadvantage in its efforts to establish and maintain local and regional balances in the Third World. In 1956 the United States took the lead in establishing the Middle East defense treaty known as the Baghdad Pact; two years later, forces opposed to the Western alliance overthrew the Baghdad government. Another American alliance, the Southeast Asia Treaty Organization (SEATO), had a divisive and highly disastrous impact on our relations with India and contributed practically nothing to the defense of Southeast Asia.

In other situations, religious and nationalist hostility to foreign influences which seem evil and inimical to the local culture undercuts and vitiates whatever security interest a state may have vis-à-vis the Soviet Union. The last thing an Islamic or African or any other Third World government wants is to have American (or Soviet) bases or troops stationed on its territory; when it does accept them it attaches conditions and assumes a posture toward the superpower that is politically and psychologically quite different from that which obtains, say, between the United States and its NATO allies. The NATO alliance is based upon an identity of agreement about the common enemy—Russia—and upon an affinity of culture and interest; in the Third World, United States support is often a purely expedient means by which an unpopular regime secures American backing against its own people, as with the Shah in Iran. The Egyptian and Saudi governments' reluctance to have elements of an American rapid-deployment force based on their territory is a good example of the extent to which many governments fear too close an identification with the United States. The Soviet Union suffers from a similar situation. In 1972 Soviet influence and Soviet advisers were summarily ejected from Egypt as an affront to Egyptian dignity and national interest. Having backed an incompetent and unpopular regime in

Afghanistan, the Kremlin found itself forced to choose between abandoning its puppet or sending in its own forces. Nor is the Soviet Union able to control its clients or keep them subservient. . . . While the Kremlin arms and supplies its Arab allies, Syria and Iraq, it is forced to acquiesce in their imprisonment or execution of Communist Party members, and it has little if any influence over their decisions to go to war—wars which often involve a risk for the Soviet Union of nuclear confrontation with the United States.

For these reasons, the traditional techniques of foreign aid and arms transfers to win an ally or control local or regional conflicts have not had great success. Third World regimes cannot afford to show gratitude or align themselves too closely with either superpower. The Cold War is not their concern, except as it can serve a purely local interest or cause. The support of and transfer of arms to Third World countries only prompts governments to engage in greater repression at home and vendettas against their neighbors; it also identifies the supplier with the evils of the incumbent regime in the eyes of its people. Because most Third World regimes face such desperate economic and political circumstances, our security concerns cannot be shared by them in the same manner and to the same degree as they are shared by our NATO and Japanese allies. The combination of poverty and relative powerlessness to achieve effectuality either at home or in the global economic and political arena (often attended by corruption and by ruthless repression) does not really permit Third World countries to enjoy the legitimacy and stability that comes to a government strongly supported by its people. For this reason, the Third World imparts to the contemporary international system a potential for disorder and crisis with which the traditional theory and practice of international relations is unfamiliar. The Third World situation is yet another in a series of challenges, beginning with the Great War and the rise of totalitarian dictatorships, with

which the twentieth century has confronted the international system. It is a situation that has been rendered all the more dangerous by the often counterproductive efforts of the two superpowers to pursue their own objectives—the West by ignoring the Third World's poverty and despair and the Soviet Union by exploiting it.

To compound the problem, Americans still lack rapport with alien customs and mentalities. As one author writes, "U.S. foreign policy specialists often show a distressing lack of interest or understanding in the rest of the world. For example they viewed Iran as a characterless cipher: a less developed country, an oil exporter, an arms market, a strategic ally—not as a nation whose history, religion, and social mores made it unique."[3] The same national security specialists who treated Iran as a cipher now fuel the debate over "who lost Iran" with tendentious accounts of what happened. The real need, as Daniel Pipes observes, is to recognize "the American inability to shed our own cultural context and pay attention to the ways of other people." Instead, our national security specialists approach other nations as pawns in the Cold War and not as unique and sovereign actors in their own right. Pipes concludes that "something can be salvaged from the American failure in Iran if it spurs the foreign policy establishment to take other cultures more seriously."[4] The failure of the Reagan administration's policies in Lebanon suggests that this has not occurred.

When Nixon and Kissinger came to power they found the United States involved in a painful Third World situation, namely a hopeless war in Vietnam. They recognized, in theory and rhetoric at least, the costly price that America was paying for its "undifferentiated globalism"—that is to say, its attempt to preserve an anti-Communist status quo throughout the Third World, regardless of the relevant political circumstances. In effect, the United States had made alliances with and commitments to over forty countries, many of which did not possess the requisites of popular support or authority or effectiveness essential to their own self-preservation. As a consequence, the United States had become trapped into defending regimes such as the one in Saigon or the Maronite Aristian action in Lebanon, which were totally dependent for their survival upon American military forces.

In an effort to understand this crisis in American foreign policy, Nixon and Kissinger sought to distinguish between "interests" and "commitments." The United States, they said, had gotten itself into trouble in Indochina and elsewhere in the Third World by failing to limit American commitments to those countries which were clearly within America's interest and ability to defend. Henceforth, Nixon announced, "our interests must shape our commitments rather than the other way around." Henceforth the United States, Nixon declared, shall look to the nation directly threatened to assume the primary responsibility of providing the manpower for its defense. As a statement of principle, Nixon's distinction between "interests" and "commitments" was quite commonplace.

But as a statement of intelligent American strategy for dealing with the Third World, it was seriously deficient. As the Australian writer J.L.S. Girling points out, all Nixon proposed to do was to reduce the amount of the military burden the United States would bear by trying to shift it onto our local allies and clients. The Nixon Doctrine never really came to grips with Third World political realities as they affect the United States.

The next Nixon-Kissinger strategy for combining détente at the superpower level with reduced costs for maintaining American influence and control at the Third World level did not come to grips with the fact that poverty and instability would continue to undermine the status quo and work against the United States' attempts to impose order.

Despite their attempt to distinguish between necessary interests and unnecessary commitments, the Nixon-Kissinger strategy did not propose to abandon any existing American commitments or assets, however dubious they might be, ostensibly because this might undermine American credibility and the confidence of allies in whose security we have a "real" interest. As a result, Nixon and Kissinger felt obliged to continue their commitment to Saigon and added additional commitments, such as that of all-out support to the Shah of Iran. As Girling observes, in dealing with the Third World the inescapable problem of what situations involve real interests that must be defended cannot be resolved according to facile statements of global principle of geopolitics, but only by a process of discrimination that establishes concrete priorities and terminates unsound and unnecessary commitments, even if it means giving up a self-proclaimed "old friend" or ally who in fact is primarily a burden and a troublemaker. As a statement of American strategy for dealing with the Third World, it was wholly inadequate. As we have observed, it only reduced the military burden the United States would bear by shifting it onto the shoulders of local allies. It did not represent any diminishment of the actual number of American commitments, nor did it usefully discriminate between existing commitments.

In place of anticommunism as the *raison d'être* of American foreign policy, Kissinger and Nixon put the maintenance of order. But, as we have shown, the Third World is not an orderly place. Trying to maintain order everywhere in the Third World is the work of Sisyphus. Nixon and Kissinger hoped to make their task easier by burying America's ideological feud with the Soviet Union so that the Kremlin would stop challenging American desire for order in the Third World. Unfortunately, the Soviet Union chose not to be as accommodating as that. But even if it had, would that have made the dilemma of the Third World any less complex and challenging? It is not the Soviet Union that creates guerrilla movements in Africa and

Central America, and it is not the Soviet Union that inspired the Arab-Israeli wars or overthrew the Shah of Iran. The situation in the Third World presents a challenge to the United States precisely because its conditions and goals are a challenge to the existing order. As long as we approach the Third World exclusively in terms of how to maintain that order, both locally and globally we are bound to fail. (This does not rule out the strategic importance of certain parts of the Third World, such as the Middle East.)

Confronted by the failure of his strategy of maintaining order in the Middle East and southern Africa, through support for Israel and the white regimes, Kissinger adopted a more productive approach—the attempt via diplomacy to regulate the Arab-Israeli conflict and the recognition of the principle of black majority rule in Zimbabwe—to put our pursuit of order on a more enduring and legitimate footing. President Jimmy Carter endeavored to carry this approach a step further by abandoning the last vestige of American colonialism in Latin America (the Panama Canal), by negotiating the Camp David Accord establishing peace between Egypt and Israel, and by mediating the conflict between the blacks and whites in Zimbabwe and bringing about a peaceful transfer of power. Unfortunately these efforts, constructive though they were, could not solve the underlying crisis of which we have spoken earlier in this essay: the poverty and illegitimacy of many of the regimes. It is in the context of this pervasive condition that Carter's human-rights policy met its greatest defeat. It is in part, at least, because of their country's weakness and the illegitimacy of their rule that many Third World regimes have resorted to repression and terror as a technique of control. An emphasis on human rights is incompatible with the means by which many Third World governments exert their authority. Thus the application of a deeply moral ideal—respect for human rights—is at odds with the presently prevailing agony under which the Third World

exists. (This does not excuse many of the more barbaric acts of torture and killing, of course.)

To return to our initial hypothesis, the poverty, weakness, and disunity that afflict most countries in the Third World (even the oil-rich Arab states recognize the precariousness of their political situation) make their existence a unique feature of the contemporary international system. Because they cannot achieve a condition of legitimate order vis-à-vis their own people, they cannot accept the existing international order as legitimate, nor can they contribute effectively to such an order. Religious and other passions run deep because they are under such stress, as much from the forces of modernization and exploitation fueled by the United States and the West as by Soviet-backed radical movements. Any adequate theory of international relations and any adequate strategy for American foreign policy must recognize the magnitude and intractability of the forces of disorder presented by the Third World and not expect to impose an American-inspired order—least of all an order inspired almost exclusively by American self-interest.

NOTES

1   Third World states vary enormously in their backgrounds but they have two things in common: economic poverty or underdevelopment and an unstable political situation marked by repression and civil strife.

2   It is sometimes argued in defense of America's support for these regimes that unlike a Communist state where no change is possible, it is always possible for a non-Communist authoritarian regime to give way to democracy. The only trouble with that argument is that most Latin American regimes have been based on repression and exploitation of their people for the past 300 years!

3   Daniel Pipes, *The New Republic,* April 25, 1981, p. 38.

4   Ibid.

15. The Passing of Remoteness

Harlan Cleveland

Dean of the Hubert H. Humphrey Institute at the University of Minnesota, Dr. Cleveland has served in a number of high-level government and academic posts.

For almost a century, from Andrew Jackson to Woodrow Wilson, the strength of the United States lay in its isolation. We could get on with our development without outside interference—except, of course, for large railroad loans and massive immigration which Americans didn't think of as "world affairs." We tried, for nearly two decades after World War I, to reenter the cocoon of remoteness, but we got involved again—this time, it seems, forever.

The idea that location is a form of power, that the political importance of communities is due to their geography, dies hard. The political relevance of geography was one of the cardinal principles of the founding fathers and mothers of the postwar world in the 1940s and early 1950s. For issues that could not be handled by global institutions (the U.N. and its specialized agencies, the World Bank and International Monetary Fund), their assumption was that regional organizations, continent by continent, would take charge.

It soon developed that for the most part (a partial exception has to be made for the European Community and ASEAN, the Association of Southeast Asian Nations), regional organizations did not amount to very much; they tended to be overstaffed and underemployed. On the other hand, functional

Reprinted by permission, *HHH Newsletter*, May 1985, Vol. 8, No. 1, Hubert H. Humphrey Institute of Public Affairs, University of Minnesota. Copyright © by Harlan Cleveland.

international organizations such as OPEC (the Organization of Petroleum Exporting Countries, which set the price of oil as long as it was in short supply) and OECD (the Organization for Economic Cooperation and Development, the club of rich countries banded together for mutual cooperation and for dealing with the poor) turned out to be fully employed.

Communications satellites and fast computers are gradually erasing distance, eroding the idea that some places are world centers because they are near other places, while other areas are bound to be peripheral because they are remote from the "center of things."

Octavio Paz, a poet, caught on to what was happening well before most of the systems analysts and political pundits. "We Mexicans," he wrote in the early 1970s, "have always lived on the periphery of history. Now the center or nucleus of world society has disintegrated and everyone—including the European and the North American—is a peripheral being. We are living on the margin . . . because there is no longer any center. . . . World history has become everyone's task and our own labyrinth is the labyrinth of all mankind."

The passing of remoteness is one of the great unheralded macrotrends of our extraordinary time. You can now plug in through television to U.N. votes or a bombing in Beirut or a Wimbledon final. You can sit in Sydney or Singapore or Bahrein and intervene directly in the markets that determine the prices of goods or of money. Distant farmsteads can, if they will, be connected to the central cortex of their commodity exchanges, their political authorities, their global markets. Once you can participate in rule, power and authority according to the relevance of your opinion rather than the mileage to the decision-making venue—then the power centers are wherever the brightest people are using the latest information in the most creative ways.

There are, of course, alternatives to geography as principles of organization. A revised proposition is suggested by futurist Magda McHale: in the changing information environment, civilization will be built more around communities of people, whether or not they happen also to form communities of place.

That this trend is well advanced can be seen in a quick review of the changing context of three familiar kinds of organization: State, Nation and Organized Religion.

The State is not withering away, as with their different motives Karl Marx and the advocates of world government would have desired. But power is leaking out of "national sovereignty" in three directions at once.

The State is leaking at the top, as more international functions require the pooling of sovereignty in alliances, in a World Weather Watch, in geophysical research, in eradicating contagious diseases, in satellite communication, in facing up to global environmental risks.

The State is leaking sideways as multinational corporations conduct more and more of the world's commerce, and operate across political frontiers so much better than committees of sovereign states seem able to do.

The State is also leaking from the bottom, as ethnic minorities, single-issue constituencies, functional communities and special-purpose neighborhoods take control of their own destinies, legislating their own growth policies, their own population policies, their own environmental policies.

And what does Nation mean nowadays? Increasingly it means not location but ethnicity—the Frenchness of Quebec, the tribal loyalties of the Ibo in Biafra, the separatism of the Scots, the rhetorical nationhood of the Arabs, the world's many diasporas ranging from the Overseas Chinese to the Zionist and non-Zionist Jews outside Israel.

In the information game of global ethnicity, for example, Israel is certainly one of the "advanced" countries: the Jewish people have been at it for so long. The potential of real-time networking is now a powerful new means of communication with the electronic diaspora—whenever Israel has ideas to sell to, or wants to solicit ideas from, the information-rich global community which is world Jewry.

And Organized Religion? In a world of people-communities, the "parish" cannot be mostly geography-based. All of the great religious traditions have had to settle, so far in world history, for predominance in one or another part of the world. But now, even "established" religions are trying to break free from their national and regional parishes.

The prospect of people rather than place as a basis for community has interesting implications for universities and school systems trying to serve a "local" clientele; for corporations that have bet heavily on regional organization; and for political systems that have bet heavily on geography-based constituencies. It implies that those institutions which exploit the electronic answers to remoteness will be "catching a wave" in the new knowledge environment.

The fusion of rapid microprocessing and global telecommunications thus presents all peoples with a choice between relevance and remoteness. There will be costs and benefits to either choice—but the necessity to choose is new, and inescapable.

The world's least remote people are Americans.

As of 1985 the United States of America is more pervasively engaged with other societies—more intimately involved in the destinies of more peoples around the world—than any other country. Indeed, in most senses of the phrase the United States is the only global power—not because of its geography (rather, in spite of it), but because Americans are able to compute and communicate on more subjects in more places, around the clock and around the globe, than any other people. This is partly because of what the U.S. Government can do. But it is mostly because the American people are directly engaged—whether they know it, and like it, or not—in the making and carrying out of U.S. foreign policy.

What about the Soviet Union, you say? The Soviet Union is a superpower in space exploration and military might (which may turn out to be the same thing), but very little else. That is why, whatever the problem, the Kremlin looks for a military solution. Quite a lot of people in the world are using Soviet weapons. But hardly anyone outside the U.S.S.R. is singing Soviet songs, listening to Soviet rock, drinking Soviet colas, flying in Soviet airliners, hoarding Soviet rubles, buying Soviet computers and electronics, aping Soviet agriculture, or copying the Soviet political system. The U.S., by contrast, has a global reach in all such fields, and many more.

To the surprise of many Americans disheartened by the doleful diet on TV's evening "bad news," the United States is also the world's most attractive society. The evidence? There are now some 16 million refugees world-wide—a million more than all the displaced persons just after World War II. Given a free choice, more of these refugees would like to come to the U.S.A. more than anywhere else—by hook if possible, by crook if necessary.

Those of us who seek or are sought for generalist roles need, therefore, to think hard about the kind of world in which Americans are going to have to live and work as an interdependent part of the whole. We also need to think hard about the kind of world we want; no one runs the world, but the United States always seems to get on the executive committee.

"A civilization," Raymond Aron wrote, "is usually composed of combative states or of a universal empire." But what we have achieved is much more complicated: ". . . quarreling states, more subjected to asymmetric interdependence than they would like, . . . too different to agree, too interconnected to separate."

The world we are not remote from is leaderless, dangerous, uneconomic, unjust and ungovernable. The problem for the "executive committee" is to exercise leadership in moderating its dangers, enhancing its efficiencies, rectifying its injustices, and arranging the governance of its necessarily international functions.

It's obvious enough that the world's nonwhite majority thinks the cards are stacked. The nations that first became "powers" are indeed reluctant to share their power with the developing countries that achieved their nationhood later on. Let's look at the rest of the picture.

- It is a world with nobody in general charge. That is, of course, the way we Americans wanted it. We didn't want the Kaiser or Adolph Hitler or Josef Stalin to be *über alles*—but we also didn't want to be global policemen or overseers ourselves. Through alliances and aid programs, we have done what no leading power in history has done—shared some of our power with others, tried to build up other nations (including recent ex-enemies) and international agencies. Let's not be carried away with our own generosity, because it was really enlightened interest: we didn't want all those foreigners on our back. We wanted our brothers to keep themselves.

- It is a world where what peace we have is an international balance of terror, based on the built-in uncertainty of nuclear weapons. "Mutual deterrence" works this way: The Soviets don't know what we would do if . . . and their uncertainty is soundly rooted on our own: we don't have the slightest idea what we would do if. . . either. Our uncertainty is therefore credible, and that's the deterrent.

We may indeed have invented, not just the ultimate weapon but the ultimately unusable weapon, the explosion which is too powerful to be a military instrument and cannot even be profitably brandished. (The last good brandish was Nikita Khrushchev's promise to "incinerate the orange groves of Italy and reduce the Acropolis in Athens to radioactive ash." That empty threat only served to galvanize Italy and Greece as loyal members of the NATO alliance—which, considering politics, wasn't easy.) Strategic nuclear weapons have been usable, since 1945, only to deter their use by another.

- The intriguing unusability of very large explosions is only one aspect of a transition from concepts of national security as military defense based on complex weapons systems, to concepts of security as including oil, environmental risk, nuclear proliferation, population growth, unsafe streets, Islamic revolutions, and a global epidemic called inflation. The most frightening security nightmare of the 80s and 90s may not be the familiar mushroom cloud but the unfamiliar and unsettling collison of the modernization process, in the developing world, with resentments about fairness and resentments about the rape of cultural identity. The triple collision at this dangerous crossroads is what's producing the Irans, the Lebanons, the Cambodias, the Northern Irelands, the El Salvadors and who knows how many future examples of the incapacity of governments to cope.

- It is a world full of dangerous weapons. Two-thirds of a trillion dollars of annual defense spending worldwide. . . . One nation per year gone nuclear for energy production, all of them together producing as a by-product the starting kit for several thousand Hiroshimas a year— if they wish. A massive trade in conventional arms, amounting to more than $13 billion per year in 1982—with American ingenuity and marketing skills accounting for 37.7 percent of the worldwide. The prospect of terrorists brandishing much bigger bangs than any terrorist has yet found it useful to set off. And an escalating capacity by smaller nations—or guerilla groups, criminal conspiracies or individual desperadoes—to make a less-than-global mess of the complexity we call civilization.

- It is a world full of wars. In 1980–82, six new wars were started and only two were turned off. In 1983 there were 40 major and minor conflicts in the world, involving 45 of the world's 164 nations—ten conflicts in the Middle East and the Persian Gulf, ten in Asia, ten in Africa,

seven in Latin America and three in Europe. As many as four and a half million soldiers (of the 25 million in standing armies worldwide) were engaged in combat that year. The total casualties in these wars are uncounted, but estimates of deaths run from more than one million up to five million. The number of wounded may well have been three times the number of dead. The financial cost of these wars runs into many hundreds of billions of dollars. (The 45 nations involved in the 40 wars spend more than $500 billion a year on their armed forces.)

- Some of the industrial democracies face a chronic crisis of governance—their leaders baffled by the dirt, danger and disaffection that urban systems seem to generate, their young people educated for nonexistent jobs, their middle classes periodically squeezed by inflation, disemployed by recession and harrassed by regulation, their industries and farms hosting an enormous migratory proletariat, their governments revolving in endless and ineffective coalitions. The leading "centrally-planned economy" is, by contrast, so stable as to be static—its leaders unable to generate the morale or productivity to compete in the trading world, incapable 68 years after the Bolshevik Revolution of feeding their own people, incompetent to enforce their system dependably on their key neighbors, let alone create a durable market for it around the world.

- A world population of four thousand six hundred seventy seven million is already programmed to double in four decades. Annual population growth decreased from 2 to 1.7 percent in the decade just past, but the same period still saw global population rise by 800,000,000. The world food situation—not yet organized enough to call it a "system"—is too dependent on the North American granary, where public policy is still afflicted with a hundred-year bias in favor of scarcity. At its tenth anniversary session the World Food Council affirmed "that hunger can no longer be blamed solely on humankind's inability to produce enough food for all. Hunger today is largely a natural and man-made phenomenon: human error or neglect creates it and human resolve can eradicate it."

- It is a world where national energy policies still discourage plentiful solar sources, and draw down too fast on the complex petroleum molecules that are really too valuable and versatile to be burned. The way things are going, we might have to settle in desperation for coal (which risks overheating the earth through the "greenhouse effect" of spewing carbon dioxide and other gases into the global atmosphere) or nuclear power (which facilitates the proliferation of nuclear weapons and produces radioactive wastes for which no reliable garbage dump has yet been found).

● It is a world under chronic threat of a nervous breakdown in the fatefully interconnected world economy. Whatever it is triggered by (at this writing a cascade of defaulting debtors seems a likely trigger), the scenario is all too readily imaginable: bank failures, wild speculation and financial panic . . . the ungluing of alliances induced by epidemic inflation and depression at the same time . . . a hardening North–South confrontation leading to government-sponsored terrorism and the interruption of ocean choke-points . . . violent revolutions in a dozen Irans or Lebanons at once . . . and paralysis of will in the world's islands of affluence as the "power of poverty" pits guilt and resentment against each other in the politics of the industrial countries.

● It is a world where science, which has always been transnational, keeps inventing inherently global technologies—for weather observation, military reconnaissance, telecommunications, data processing, resource sensing, and orbital industry. As a result, for the non-land environments at least, we find ourselves moving beyond concepts of national ownership, sovereignty and citizenship to ideas such as the global commons, the international monitoring of global risks, and "the common heritage of mankind."

● It is a world in which a growing number of functions that simply must be performed cannot be contained in national decision systems at all—the management of transborder data flows, the allocation of radio frequencies, the regulation of satellite communications, global pollution, ocean fishing and mining, weather forecasting and modification, the nuclear fuel cycle, the potentials of earth-sensing space vehicles, and a complexity of transnational corporations which provide much of the enterprise in world trade and investment yet remain the most popular villains in world politics.

● It is, in sum, a world whose international institutions and practices are not yet able to cope with the international functions modern science and technology have made possible, or resolve the conflicts generated by the modernization process itself.

In the most creative celebration of the Bicentennial of our Declaration of Independence, a group of citizens in Philadelphia commissioned historian Henry Steele Commager to draft a "Declaration of Interdependence;" 128 Members of Congress signed it, and the new Declaration became the basis for a year of Philadelphia-based discussions of world affairs.

The Philadelphians were on the right track. Durable though the nation-state has proved to be, interdependence has caught up with most of the issues, practices and policies that used to be regarded in the United States as essentially "domestic"—energy, pollution, civil rights, race relations, feminism, poverty, education, research, science, technology, business, labor, food, transportation, population, culture, communication, terrorism, revolution, law enforcement, arms, narcotics, religion, ideology.

No nation controls even that central symbol of national independence, the value of its money: inflation and recession are both transnational.

The communications media operate all over the world. One-fifth of the world's gross product is created by multinational enterprises, more of them based in the United States than anywhere else; something like one-quarter of what I learned in school to call "international trade" is the internal transactions of international companies.

The content of international affairs is now mostly the internal affairs of still sovereign nations. At the White House level, every major issue for policy decision is partly "domestic" and partly "international."

What we mostly want from other countries—and what they mostly want from us—is changes in "domestic" preconceptions, priorities, policies and practices. By the same token, most major "domestic policy" actions we take—decisions about the levels of farm subsidies, the direction of research and development, the degree of emphasis on energy conservation, the supply of American dollars, the amount of unemployment we will stand for, the size and shape of our budget deficit, and many, many others—are enormously important to nearly every other nation on earth.

Despite these well-known facts, the U.S. Government is still unambiguously divided between people who are supposed to work on "domestic" matters and people who work on "foreign affairs." To paraphrase Gilbert and Sullivan, each matter of public policy is born a little "domestic policy" or a little "foreign policy"—and is so treated as it grows up through the processes of decision, both in the Executive Branch and on Capitol Hill.

One of the most elementary doctrines about the management of large-scale systems is that a supervisory office should not be organized in the same way as its subordinate offices are—that, indeed, it should be deliberately organized to cut across the vertical divisions below, in order to throw new light on their interrelationships and inconsistencies before issues come to the top executive for decision (which can mean resolution of differences or, more commonly, confirmation of a consensus already reached among subordinates). Each of the Cabinet departments was established essentially to deal either with national security/foreign policy matters, or with "domestic policy." Yet the White House has for three decades been organized the same way, coordinating State and Defense and the Intelligence community through a National Security Council and channelling the rest of the government through a "domestic policy" staff, the lineal successor of a function performed by White House assistants under a variety of names ever since the Truman Administration.

Despite the melding of "domestic" and "international" issues out there in the real world, it is still almost literally true that only one person in the Executive Branch is overtly hired to work on both domestic and foreign policy. We call him President of the United States. The policy officials with "domestic" or "foreign affairs" job descriptions have to cheat, of course; nearly everybody with public policy responsibilities works on both.

The only option, in the mid-80s, is to view foreign policy, as Adam Yarmolinsky has suggested, as "not a subject matter for government decision-making; it is rather an aspect of every important government decision." The implications are far-reaching, and not for the federal government. Taking our interdependence seriously will require changes of purposes and priorities in education, in research and development, in business practices, in the orientation of labor unions, in the communications media with their global impact, and in the voluntary sector with its grass roots base.

The chronic crisis of interdependence, of which the troubles called energy and food and arms and inflation and jobs and money are only the most obvious examples, requires actions by dozens of government agencies, hundreds of state and local governments, thousands of business executives, hundreds of thousands of teachers, and millions of householders, automobile owners, investors, and organized and unorganized workers.

The style of national governance appropriate to these circumstances is akin to wartime leadership, engaging the cooperation of whole populations to take "domestic" actions without which the requisite international cooperation cannot be arranged by even the most skillful diplomats. Such leadership goes far beyond the capacity to guide legislation through the labyrinth of enactment, to the capacity to educate whole populations. For modern interdependence and national security require changes in attitudes and assumptions, lifestyles and workways—the capacity to elicit millions of willing actions, more or less voluntary, backed up by self-interest, market economics, social pressure and only at the margin by government intervention.

In a polity where ultimately the people make the policy, even individual citizens have to try to get their minds around the whole of this complexity. *A fortiori,* the leaders who interact with citizens in the formulation of policy have to wrap their minds around the world, develop for their own personal use a strategic global agenda—which can serve both to help educate the American constituency and to guide the day-to-day tactical actions and reactions that constitute "American foreign policy."

chapter 6

NATIONAL BEHAVIOR IN CRISIS

History teaches that history does not teach.

—Anon.

I begin with the premise that beyond our individual, professional and national self-interests we do need to give higher priority to the welfare of the entire human race, including those global citizens yet to be born. This requires that we demand higher standards of competence and compassion from our governments, parties and associations before lending our support. This also requires us to attend more carefully to the legitimate interests of other groupings, and perhaps most important, to recognize that 'the national interest' may often be contrary to the very real and human interests of those diverse groups that make up our own society.

J. David Singer, "The Responsibilities of Competence in the Global Village" *International Studies Quarterly* (U.K.), Sept. 1985, p. 246.[1]

Even though they are obliged to operate within the international system, states nonetheless invariably serve their own particular *national interests*—or at least try to.

The term *national interest* has traditionally been used as the key to understanding why governments frame their goals and objectives the way they do, or in another sense, as the ultimate justification by leaders in explaining to their people (in America often to Congress) why they have done whatever it is that they did. Inevitably this can often be little more than a *post-hoc* rationalization. Because most nation-states exist in a relationship of potential insecurity and competition with each other, it has seemed reasonable to declare that each government acts so as to preserve and enhance its national (or collective) interest vis-à-vis every other state. By the same logic, it has been taken for granted by practitioners and theorists alike that each state counts among its vital interests

---

[1]The first section of Singer's Presidential address to the 1985 International Studies Association Convention from which this paragraph is taken, is reprinted as the final selection in this edition of *The Theory and Practice of International Relations.*

such things as security and survival, independence, economic well-being, power, and prestige. For example, one reason American leaders hesitated to abandon South Vietnam for so long was the fear that its fall would be a blow to American prestige; in this aspect of their pursuit of the national interest, hindsight reveals that they were right, though the loss of prestige was probably greater by virtue of staying too long. Pressure from congressional representatives mounted as their constituents at home turned against the war, which voters no longer felt was in the national interest (and draft-age young men, in their personal interest).

Framing foreign policy, it has often been assumed, follows automatically by deducing what territorial acquisitions, bases, allies, and distribution of power and influence would be most favorable to one's own nation's security, independence, power, and prestige. Unfortunately, as the late Professor Sondermann observed in his article, the ambiguities associated with the concept of the national interest have led more than one observer to turn away from the concept altogether, or conversely, to try to bring the theory of how governments form and implement their foreign-policy goals into line with a reality that is much more complex than its simple description assumes. In this case, theory follows practice.

The survival or self-preservation of the nation-state is often cited as the *sine qua non* of its foreign policy. But what is this "self" that is to be preserved, and what do such terms as *preservation* and *survival* really mean? If 50 million Americans were to die in a nuclear war with Russia, could one say that the nation has been preserved? Another such term used to describe state objectives is *independence*. Yet no country, not even the most powerful one, is ever fully independent of decisions made in other countries, decisions over which only a very imperfect control can be exercised. Just how "independent" was the United States on the day following Pearl Harbor? The decision to declare war on Japan was made by the Congress at the request of the President; but the real choice for war had been made weeks before in Tokyo (which in turn had made its "independent" decision in response to prior moves that had been made elsewhere, including in Washington). Andrew Burns, in his selection following, illuminates the failures of British diplomacy, including the complicating role of Parliament, in the crisis with Argentina over the Falklands (or the Malvinas) Islands.

Another ambiguous expression, "the maintenance of territorial integrity," is often used to define the interest of states; however, it fails to specify precisely which territory is to be defended and against whom. Does the term *territorial integrity* imply that the United States would defend only its own territorial boundaries, or does it include the territory of its European allies and the bases established overseas in order to better protect the national realm? Was former Prime Minister Menachem Begin correct in asserting that Israel's air strike against nuclear facilities in Iraq was *defensive* in nature? Or President Ronald Reagan in *his* against terrorist bases in Libya?

Some students of international politics maintain that all human behavior, including the behavior of actors on the international stage, is characterized by a *power drive*. Bertrand Russell, for example, wrote that of the desires of humankind, the chief are for power and glory; and he added that some human desires, unlike those of animals, are incapable of complete satisfaction. Other competent observers agree, and although some of them might not classify the power drive as either unlimited or omnipresent, they feel that the concept of power provides the best organizing focus for analyzing relations among individuals and groups, including the sometimes gigantic and always complex groups whose interaction is the subject matter of the study of international relations.

Before accepting this or any single-motive explanation of behavior and applying it to the infinite variety of patterns found in international relations, one should recognize (as did Machiavelli, whose *Prince* symbolizes this approach) that there are other values in the minds of decision-makers. Considerations of power are hardly a first priority in each and every type of situation. Much will depend upon how power is defined. If it is equated with physical force alone, one finds many contemporary international relationships which simply cannot be explained by sole reference to relative possession of military strength. But if "power" implies not only military but also psychological, economic, and even moral influence or control, then one may wonder whether the concept has not become too broad to be useful for analytical purposes. On the other hand, it cannot be denied that in today's world, power, however defined, is not only an immediate means, but a long-range foreign-policy objective in itself in many states' "shopping bag" of things to be acquired.

The difficulty lies in how we specifically define the national interest, and what actions must be implemented to make the pursuit of it successful. Thus, after defining the motivations underlying states' behavior in terms of national interest, one is still left with the same problem: defining the national interest. As a high Soviet official put it at the 27th Party Congress in Moscow recently, "How many times can we permit the same mistakes to be made, without taking into account the lessons of history?"[2]

A second complicating factor in formulating and implementing policy in light of the concept of the national interest is the assumption that states or governments are single-purpose organizations, when in fact they are multi-purpose organizations pursuing many varied, and often competing, objectives. It is no longer possible to define national interest in terms of objectives proclaimed by a group of experts in the State Department or foreign ministry, because the influence of domestic objectives has become a more prominent feature of foreign-policy decisions. Citizens (of democracies, at least) demand that their particular group interests and economic well-being be incorporated into the national interest.

The framing of a nation's objectives may be skewed by the personal or collective power drive of the national leadership or by the stake that foreign policy and military bureaucrats have in maintaining the image of another country as an enemy in order to perpetuate their own power needs. Then, too, powerful economic interests may impose their will upon a government in the *name* of the national interest, when in fact, they are really seeking their own profits. Immigrant groups are becoming more effective in identifying the national interest of their adopted country with the interests of the places from whence their

[2]February 9, 1986 by Boris Yeltsin; candidate member of the Politburo, quoted by Peter Frank, "Gorbachev's dilemma; Social justice or political instability?" *The World Today*, 42, no. 6, (June 1986), 94, published by the Royal Institute of International Affairs.

forebears came. If a president or prime minister fails to respond to these interests (even though their claims do not represent any values but their own), the political office is sure to suffer in the next election. So, in any theory of the national interest (of how foreign policy is made) we have to consider that states are multipurpose organizations, not simple guardians of abstractions called the national interest. Any theory of foreign policy-making must take into account the influence that domestic (or subnational) groups exert upon the process—often in ways that may defeat other, more important values and goals of foreign policy.

This brings up another practical matter that qualifies the determination of a country's goals and policies designed to implement those goals. Bayless Manning, former head of the prestigious Council on Foreign Relations, once observed that, "in real life situations, the problem of the policy-maker is usually how to choose between two or more results that are all desirable but conflict with one another; or how to choose between two or more results, all of which are undesirable; or how to move toward a desired result where one has little or no leverage on the situation. . . ."[3] National and subnational interests of a country are often in conflict with each other, which greatly complicates the practical matter of deciding which value or goal is to be pursued and which one sacrificed, particularly in managing crisis situations.

The choice of goals and policies will also be conditioned by those capabilities and leverage a country has at its disposal. Clearly, in a situation as complex as international politics, no one state will be able to achieve all of its objectives. Sooner or later, it has to make some choices, choices which the concept of the national interest can illuminate, but which it cannot determine. One reason for this is the simple physical environment within which policy-makers operate and which they may often overlook or misconstrue. As Richard Neustadt and Ernest May so clearly demonstrate in their new book, *Thinking in Time: The Uses of History for Decision Makers*,[4] resort to history has demonstrably contributed to more intelligent decisions, which they call "success stories." Unfortunately, both history and geography are all too often overlooked.

On the basis of many years' experience in policy formulation and crisis management analysis, Ray Platig describes in his article in this chapter some of the complexities of the process. While certain leaders and nations have determined that war is the only means of attaining their ends, there is a great deal of evidence showing that crises assume a life of their own and that, in the process, governments are heavily influenced by nonrational factors. For one thing, crises are often the outcome of a stimulus-response pattern in which the words and actions of one side are perceived and interpreted as hostile and threatening by the other. This, in turn, stimulates counterexpressions of hostility, touching off a vicious cycle of constantly escalating actions and emotions. A constant, unrelenting crisis situation such as that which characterizes the Arab-Israeli

---

[3]Bayless Manning, "Goals, Ideology and Foreign Policy," *Foreign Affairs* 54, no. 2 (January 1976), p. 221.

[4]In this highly original article reproduced in part in the 6th edition of this book, Manning created a new term which, perhaps unfortunately, has not taken hold in the decade which followed: "intermestic."

conflict fosters attitudes of fear and hostility that are almost impossible to overcome.

As stress increases in a crisis situation, the decision-maker's perceptions of the factors that are involved also change. In his study of the coming of World War I, Ole Holsti observes that "in a crisis situation, decision-makers will tend to perceive their own range of alternatives [and that of their allies] to be more restricted than those of their adversaries; that is, they will perceive their own decision-making to be characterized by necessity and close options, whereas those of the adversary are characterized by open choices."[5]

As the crisis mounts, there seems to be less time available to examine options and arrest the race to war. As a result, decision-makers limit the range of information available to them and foreclose alternatives more quickly than necessary. Members of the decision-making groups tend to abandon their individual judgments and to coalesce around the group judgment. "Group-think" takes over and no one is willing to challenge it. Hostility and threat are perceived to be greater than they really are. The sense of "injury" done to one by the adversary grows apace, as does the degree to which one feels one's honor and prestige to be at stake and "stress may cause an actor to misperceive the actions of another, thus giving him an inaccurate definition of the situation."[6] Thus even when the adversary tries to make reassuring signals, they are perceived as threats or dissimulation. The U.S.-U.S.S.R. relationship, affected as it is by ideology on both sides, has been disturbingly prone to this reaction pattern.

The nation may, through its leaders, be willing to take greater risks than would be true of individuals. A collectivity cannot calculate the consequences of its action in quite the same direct and personal way that we, as individuals, calculate the likely consequences of our actions. Amidst all this, the decision-maker may feel under pressure from the public and press, or from rivals. As a result, there really is no limit to the failure or breakdown that is capable of afflicting the processes of rationality in facing a national crisis. This presents decision-makers on both sides with a complex trade-off relationship. On the one hand, decision-makers want to avoid a costly war, especially a nuclear war; on the other hand, they do not want to give in, especially if giving in is perceived to involve a sacrifice of prestige or interest that would have strongly adverse effects. Once engaged in a crisis situation, the conflict between the two values may be so severe that as President John Kennedy set forth as his own cardinal rule: "above all, while defending our own vital interests, nuclear powers must avert those confrontations which bring an adversary to the choice of either humiliating retreat or a nuclear war."[7] Stated that way, a crisis clearly involves a complex cognitive or analytical problem. How do we define our terms for managing or ending a crisis while avoiding the risk of a nuclear war?

Because of their suicidal potential, nuclear weapons have fostered a greater

---

[5]Ole R. Holsti, "Perceptions of time, perceptions of alternatives, and patterns of communications as factors in crisis decision-making," *Peace Research Society Papers, 3,* 79–120.

[6]Patrick J. McGown and Howard R. Shapiro, *The Comparative Study of Foreign Policy: A Survey of Scientific Findings* (Beverley Hills: Sage Publications, Inc., 1973), pp. 4, 59.

[7]Commencement address at The American University, Washington, D.C., June 10, 1963.

concern to avoid war in the thinking and policy decisions of Soviet and American statesmen. This is really what is meant by the term *crisis management.* Beginning with the Korean War (1950 to 1953), both the Americans and the Chinese acted to limit the war to the Korean peninsula. Subsequently, both the Soviet and the American sides have sought to exploit the coercive possibilities of their position while consciously avoiding actions that might escalate into a nuclear war.

The differential consequences that would ensue from a nucelar war as opposed to a conventional war have served as a "fire break," preventing both superpowers from reaching the point in a crisis at which either one might feel compelled to resort to nuclear weapons. Under conditions of crisis, the most powerful signal that one superpower can send to the other is the warning that a resort to nuclear weapons is being contemplated. The holocaust that would ensue upon any use of nuclear weapons constitutes a threshold in the calculations of the two superpowers between a crisis outcome that would be tolerable and one that would *be* intolerable. In this context, Dr. Platig's "four guidelines" are particularly illuminating. They beautifully demonstrate the link between theory and practice.

DISCUSSION QUESTIONS

1. Is "pursuit of the national interest" a vain quest, since it is really only a justification of what a nation's leaders are trying to do in foreign as well as domestic policy? Or is it really *the* ultimate and honorable value in foreign affairs after all?

2. How can two nations both achieve their vital interests if each wants the same thing?

3. Do you think the *public interest* is the same as the *national interest?* Is it a collection or combination of "special interests"? What does Sondermann say about this?

4. Why do crisis situations confront decision-makers with such emotional stress? How does Burns describe British behavior in this context, particularly in relating theory and practice?

5. Do you think the superpowers have learned anything about crisis management from their past nuclear confrontations? Are lessons in world politics "learned" or is history merely bound to repeat itself, in your view?

6. Does Raymond Platig's "modest proposal" have any utility for *smaller* states in world politics? Or only for superpowers? What are his "four lessons of history"?

16. The Concept of the National Interest

Fred A. Sondermann

Professor of Political Science at Colorado College and coeditor of the first five editions of this book, Dr. Sondermann was active in public affairs at the municipal and state level as well as serving as one of the first presidents of the International Studies Association.

. . . . The term "national interest" is of relatively recent vintage. It was and remains an effort to describe the underlying rationale for the behavior of states and statesmen in a threatening international environment. But the idea of preserving and protecting one's values against others, goes back into antiquity. The word "interest" derives from the Latin, meaning "it concerns, it makes a difference to, it is important with reference to some person or thing."

We have the example of the early Israelites' continuing efforts to assert and maintain their characteristics and their values. We know of the Greeks' devotion to their city-states—Pericles' Funeral Oration is a statement to which we still respond. We know of the Romans' pride in their empire and the status of their citizenship within it. These feelings, and the behaviors that followed from them, may have been confined to relatively small groups at the top; the popularization and democratization of foreign policy would come much later. But for those who formulated and executed their tribe's, their city's, their kingdom's, their empire's policy vis-à-vis the outside world, the idea, if not the term, was always there.

Charles Beard, whose book on national interest was written in the early 1930s, traced the evolution of the concept in the more modern period through several stages. In

Excerpted by permission of the publisher from Fred A. Sondermann, "National Interest," in *Orbis: A Journal of World Affairs* 21, no. 1 (Spring 1977). Copyright 1977 by the Foreign Policy Research Institute, Philadelphia. (Most footnotes have been removed; those remaining have been renumbered.)

the first of these the relevant concept was the "dynastic" interest—the desire of each monarch to maintain and, if possible, extend his domain and his control over land and people. As more and more groups within the domain came to attach their specific interests to those of the monarch, the dynastic phase gave way to the concept of *raison d'état*, which became, in turn, intermingled with the idea of national honor. Beard argued that the idea of national honor was weakened as economic issues gained an ever greater share of attention. Honor and profit do not always go hand in hand, it seems. He suggested that "with the emergence of the national state system, the increase in influence of popular political control, and the great expansion of economic relations, the lines of [the] new formula—national interest—were being laid down." Links with the past remained strong, however. The characteristic of unity associated with the dynastic phase remained; so did the element of "compelling absolutism," making national interest "no less sovereign and inexorable than the 'will of the prince' had been."

To understand the impact of the concept of the national interest on a generation of scholars of foreign policy, a brief detour into intellectual history is appropriate. The interwar period was characterized by a high level of academic attention to, reliance upon, and value placed in the processes of international law, international organization and international trade. The hope was that reliance on these could reduce the harshness of "realpolitik" which had culminated in a disastrous world war. These hopes were disappointed, and in the post–World War II period a new school of thinkers and writers promoted a "realist" stance on issues of foreign policy and international politics. Charles Beard, having written on national interest in the early 1930s, had in a sense been outside the mainstream of scholarly thought at that time, a situation to which he was accustomed and which he seemed to relish. E. H. Carr weighed in at the end of the decade with his important book *The Twenty Years Crises, 1919–1939*. By then, World War II was upon us, and it remained for writers like George Kennan, Walter Lippmann, and above all Hans Morgenthau to make the postwar case for the relevance—indeed, the centrality—of the national interest as a focus around which the complex and diverse issues of foreign policy could be organized, as a concept by which the behaviors of states and their governments could be understood.

The crux of the concept, as advanced in the postwar years, was that in a world in which states are "the major units of political life, which command the supreme loyalty and affection of the great mass of individuals," statesmen who are responsible for and to their separate publics, and who operate in an uncertain and threatening milieu, have little choice but to put the interests of their own entity above those of others or those of the international system. National interest, thus, became a synonym for national egoism. One could not rely on others, nor could one rely on international institutions and processes to protect one's key values. These values were thought to be national in scope. Their protection was the concern and responsibility of those who governed each separate entity. Osgood put it as follows: "National interest is understood to mean a state of affairs valued solely for its benefit to the nation. The motive of national egoism, which leads men to seek this end, is marked by the disposition to concern oneself with the welfare of one's own nation; it is self-love transferred to the national group."[1]

It must by now be clear that when we speak of national interest, we speak of values; values held by some, many, perhaps even all of the members of a given society. Whether it be some, many or all is a separate question that will be addressed in the next part of this paper. But the more immediate question is, How can these values be defined? Surely, not everything anyone desires is automatically transformed into an interest, let alone a national one. Hopes, wishes, aspirations and dreams are not the same as practical and concrete interests. They are not always, or even often, reflected in the policies of states and their governments.

The problem of definition, or more accurately of description, has been approached in two ways. Some observers have tried to define the national interest of a given state by looking at the state's actual policy output and, finding repetitive behavior patterns, have deduced from these what the national interest must have been. For instance, John Chase suggested four "aspects of the American national interest which . . . actually guided and motivated the development of our foreign policy": (1) to deprive potential aggressors of bases from which they might launch attacks against the United States; (2) to support self-government and democracy abroad; (3) to protect and advance commerce; and (4) to help establish and maintain a favorable world balance of power.[2] Beard stressed the economic/commercial element in American statecraft throughout the Federalist-Whig-Republican succession. He attached the development and maintenance of a superior navy to this basic goal, and leaned heavily on the writings of Admiral Mahan, who expanded the reasons for needing a superior navy from mere defense of territory to "defense of our just national interests, whatever they be and wherever they are."[3] Mahan included among those interests the defense of national territory, the extension of maritime commerce, acquisition of territorial positions that would contribute to command of the seas ("when it can be done righteously"), maintenance of the Monroe Doctrine, hegemony in the Caribbean, and active promotion of the China trade. Modern revisionist writers on American foreign policy could hardly express their case more clearly and succinctly.

Other scholars went at the task of defining the national interest in a different manner, basing their analysis on logical reasoning and induction; framing their conclusions in less tangible, more conceptual terms. Thus, Robert Osgood along with many others put national survival or self-preservation at the head of the list, because everything else would clearly depend on the achievement of this goal. He defined survival or self-preservation in terms of territorial integrity, political independence, and maintenance of fundamental governmental institutions.

Osgood proceeded to other categories of national interest: self-sufficiency, prestige, aggrandizement. Beard, on his part, talked about territory and commerce as two of its fundamental aspects. George and Keohane, in a major recent effort to imbue the term with specific meaning, wrote about three "irreducible" national interests: physical survival—by which they meant the survival of people, not necessarily the preservation of territory or sovereignty; liberty—by which they meant the ability of inhabitants of a country to choose their form of government and to exercise a set of individual rights defined by law and protected by the state; and economic subsistence—the maximization of economic welfare.

Finally, since he is clearly the contemporary scholar most closely connected with the concept of national interest, let us consider Hans Morgenthau's work. He defined the "survival of a political unit . . . in its identity" as the irreducible minimum of a state's interest vis-à-vis other units, encompassing in this the integrity of a state's territory, its political institutions, and its culture. He asserted that it had been the perennial national interest of the United States to remain the predominant power in the Western Hemisphere—leading it to support the European balance-of-power system whose breakdown alone could threaten our hegemony in the Americas. With respect to Asia, he stipulated

that maintenance of the balance of power there had been the consistent ingredient of American statecraft, hence part of our perennial national interest.

Although there are some variances in all of this, one detects a high degree of convergence of definitions and descriptions. Certain terms and ideas recur frequently. Most of them relate to tangible things—to concrete conditions or advantages, concretely experienced. But a few (culture, liberty, prestige) refer to intangibles—to how a society feels about itself, how it maintains and strengthens its morale, its élan.

Yet the picture is clouded. Difficulties and complexities have caused many analysts of the foreign policy process to turn away from the concept altogether, in spite of the fact that the term clearly remains a part of the rhetoric of foreign policy. Its use for analytic purposes has declined from the high point reached in the late 1940s and early 1950s. Some students of the subject suggest that it will not be used much in the future.

One way of explaining this state of affairs is to speculate that in the late 1940s and early 1950s the concept's function differed from the one for which scholars in the field now strive. The idea of the national interest was useful to Morgenthau and others in the then-current debate between "realists" and "idealists." In my judgment, this debate was won by the realists. But the victory was transient. The study of international relations, having conquered that particular piece of intellectual territory, proceeded in directions different from, and in fact somewhat irrelevant to, those staked out by the realists.

Of the many areas of doubt about, and criticisms of, the concept of the national interest, we present five as concisely as the subject matter permits.[4]

The first criticism is, simply, that the concept is too broad, too general, too vague, too all-inclusive to perform useful analytic functions, to serve as a guideline for policymakers, as an organizing concept for scholars, or as a criterion of judgment and evaluation for the citizen. . . .

Morgenthau, of course, tried to give the concept a specific meaning—namely, that national interest could be ascertained as well as advanced by the possession of power. The difficulty with this formulation is that it merely pushes the analytic task back a step: now one has to determine what "power" means, what it consists of, and how it can be measured. This task, far from becoming easier, has become ever more complex.

But what is true regarding power is also true of other formulations of the content and meaning of the national interest. Such terms as survival, self–preservation, independence, sovereignty—usually said to constitute the rock-bottom purposes of the foreign policies of states—will be found, upon closer inspection, to hide a host of ambiguities.

In short, there is concern that the "great generality" of the phrase "national interest" obscures from the view of policymakers, analysts and the public the fact that foreign policies are designed to achieve specific goals, often short-term in nature; and that the study of these specific goals is likely to provide a better basis for the understanding of a country's political behavior in the external realm than reference to a general, vague, ambiguous term such as the national interest.

A second major problem is that of distinguishing between ends and means in foreign policy. The question the national interest concept is meant to answer relates to the ends, the goals, the purposes of foreign policy. This is an area of inquiry that, in my judgment, has not been satisfactorily addressed in the literature of international relations. It appears that, having tried to find the explanation for foreign policies in the external realm—in the behaviors and actions of other states—and having failed at this task, observers have more recently turned inward, and now seek to find that explanation mainly within the motivations and operations of domestic bureaucracies. One may be forgiven for doubting whether this approach, by itself, will provide the desired key to understanding.

In any case, on closer inspection ends tend to become means toward some other ends; and conversely means—because they are desired, because they are thought to be useful—tend to become, at least in the short run, ends. Van Dyke put it this way: "When we use the language of means and ends, we say that means can themselves be ends and that ends can be means."[5] (Unfortunately, however, neither the distinction between, nor the merging of, the concepts is always as clear as it might be.)

This problem was obscured by Morgenthau's formulation that stipulated power as the yardstick by which achievement of the national interest could be measured, thereby making power a goal of foreign policy behavior. But is it? Many would, no doubt, agree with George and Keohane, who suggested that "power is . . . only one subgoal of national interest, and an instrumental goal at that, rather than a fundamental value in and of itself."[6] Furthermore, even if one could use power in the way Morgenthau intended to have it used, the issue would by no means be resolved, because in many ways power is as "elusive and ambiguous" a concept as is national interest itself. How many efforts to specify the components of power, to weight them accurately, to aggregate them suitably, and to utilize them appropriately have come even close to success? . . .

Thirdly, any student or user of the concept of the national interest must face perplexing questions: Whose interests? How determined? By whom?

One can argue that the national interest is the culmination, the aggregation, of all the specific interests contained in the society. But this is a difficult argument to sustain or to act upon. A modern society, by definition, contains a multitude of interests—personal, ethnic, religious, racial, economic, regional, occupational/professional, ideological, to name some. It is one of the tasks of government to satisfy the largest possible number of these interests, or at least to keep dissatisfaction to a level low enough to avoid instability and upheaval. But it is also in the nature of politics that not every interest can be equally satisfied; some cannot be satisfied at all; and painful choices and tradeoffs are the order of the day. Some interests will gain while others lose—sometimes absolutely, always relatively—from any political act.

This is harsh doctrine, difficult to accept. It has become more difficult as the "revolution of rising expectations" we used to attribute to the developing countries has spread to the developed ones as well and has, in the words of Daniel Bell, led to a "revolution of rising entitlements." Each subgroup in a modern society, including governmental bureaucracy, seems to feel entitled to make claims for the satisfaction of its wants and desires, if need be at the expense of other subgroups.[7] Nor is this new. More than forty years ago, Beard put the case as clearly as anyone could:

> The conception of national interest revealed in the state papers is an aggregation of particularities assembled like eggs in a basket. Markets for agricultural produce in the national interest; markets for industrial commodities were in the national interest; naval bases, territorial acquisitions for commercial support, an enlarged consular and diplomatic service, an increased navy and merchant marine, and occasional wars were all in the national interest. These contentions were not proved; they were asserted as axioms, apparently regarded as so obvious as to call for no demonstration.[8]

Various subinterests are likely to be at cross–purposes with one another. Given a limited pie to be distributed, the claims of one group are apt to run counter to those of another; the aspirations of the military for additional appropriations, claimed to be in the national interest, run counter to the pleas of cities for additional resources for urban services, equally claimed to be in the national interest. How does one determine priorities? The only possible answer is that it is done through acts of political choice,

which are likely to be outside the realm of the national interest concept.

Within any society, including ours, some subinterests are less successfully represented in the policy process than are others. But let us assume, unrealistically, the best of all possible societies; one in which all interests have an equal opportunity to make themselves effectively heard; one in which there is a minimum (there can never be an absence) of conflict among various claims and expectations. We would still have to decide whether these various claims and expectations, these values and interests, could be aggregated, and if so, whether the aggregate could be said to represent the national interest. Both parts of this problem are extremely complex. Aggregation is particularly difficult because the depth and intensity of separate goals can never be known. But the second question—whether such an aggregation, if it could be performed, would constitute something to be known as national interest—is more difficult still.

Is the national interest merely the aggregation of specific interests? Or, assuming that there is such a thing as a national interest, could it be larger than, perhaps even different from, such an aggregation? Is a "general will" à la Rousseau, or a "public philosophy" à la Lippmann something real, reflecting values that transcend the accumulation of specific interests? This is not an easy question to answer with confidence, especially within the framework of a society in which government is said to serve the citizens, rather than the other way around. But however one responds, the question is of surpassing importance.

The third subquestion is, Who specifies what the national interest is? Since that can be debated endlessly, let us be brief. After much agonizing, analyzing and debating; after bravely marching up the sides of hills only to march down the other side, the end result is that most of us, most of the time, accept the definition of the national interest provided by a nation's high officials and policymakers.

There is hardly an alternative to this practice. The term national interest is political in nature. Public disputes arise over its meaning in concrete situations. Policymakers have the penultimate word in such disputes; the ultimate word is spoken by the process by which those policymakers can be replaced if their judgments have been faulty. What seems less clear is whether those of us who try to understand or predict a nation's policy are entitled to build our structure of understanding and prediction on the words and acts of the policymakers, imbuing these with a sense of purpose and rationality that may not be justified. This brings us to the fourth major area of criticism of the national interest concept.

We all know how self-serving statements of policymakers are apt to be. We know that a given policy may lend itself to quite different interpretations of its basic purposes, and that much of foreign-policymaking is accidental, *ad hoc*, fortuitous. The incremental nature of decision-making is known to us. The input of bureaucracies, both in the early stages of decision–making and in the implementation of decisions made at higher levels, has been the subject of a large recent literature. Thus, while we may have no options but to accept the official definition of the national interest, or to infer interest from behavior, utmost caution is indicated in doing so. The case may well be that by holding on to the only thing we have we may go seriously astray.

For all its shortcomings, the best and perhaps the only available procedure may be to take the official definition and the policy output as the basis for our understanding. If one focuses on such official definitions, on the rhetoric that surrounds the policy output, he must make allowance for the fact that in such rhetoric the term national interest can easily serve to justify actions, hide mistakes, rationalize policies, disarm the opposition. Sometimes one suspects that it may be little more than a debater's point: if your side gets to use the term before the other side comes to it, you win the argument.

Compared to previous eras of statecraft, there is now a much greater need for policymakers to justify their choices to broader publics. In fact, a great deal of discussion in recent years has revolved around the idea of government officials' accountability for their conduct in office. But as everyone knows, public justification is an invitation to the use of the rhetorical arts. And within the rhetorical arsenal, few concepts are more effective than that of the national interest. Some students of foreign policy have suggested that the same ingredients that make the term so difficult to use for analytic purposes make it easy, inviting, tempting to use in political discourse.

Of the concerns surrounding the concept of the national interest, we have spoken thus far of its ambiguity; of the complexity of defining ends and means in foreign policy; of the problem of aggregating special interests into a national interest; of the risk that national interest is retroactively read into public policies in the formulation of which it may have played no, or at best only a marginal, role; and of the problem of attempting to use a phrase so serviceable in public rhetoric as a concept in scholarly inquiry which is supposed to rise above debaters' ploys. There is one other issue.

Professor Rochester framed this final issue as follows: "The two-fold assumption which appears to be embedded in the concept of national interest is that (1) there exists an objectively determinable collective interest which all individual members within a given society share equally; and (2) *this collective interest transcends any interests that a particular subset of those individuals may share with individuals in other societies.*" The traditional critiques of the concept have focused on the first of these assumptions. But what about the second? Rochester argued that it "runs squarely up against what a number of observers believe to be major new forces in world politics."[9]

Much has been written on the old versus the new, the "classical" vs. the "modernist" paradigms of international relations. One has no wish to add to the volume of literature on this subject. Clearly, not everything has changed, not everything is different than it was before. But equally clearly, there have been changes, because there will always be changes in an environment of great variety and complexity. There are new actors, such as multinational corporations, functional organizations, terrorist groups. There are new goals of foreign policy that de-emphasize physical conquest and occupation, and stress instead economic and ideological influence. There are certain disintegrative trends within at least some societies, and some integrative trends within the international system. There are new developments in the means used to affect events in other countries. Power has become more diffused; new interdependencies have arisen, though not evenly across the board. There are new problems, new issue–areas to which some of the devices and categories of traditional statecraft are only marginally relevant: the protection of the environment, the allocation of dwindling resources; problems of food supply and of population increases.

Let us leave the relevance of the concept of national interest to such developments as a question, not presuming to be able to answer it fully. No one would suggest that the classical paradigm of international politics is no longer useful. All that is suggested is that the world is changing: that those of us who find ourselves in the midst of these changes are probably not clearly aware of them and cannot know their eventual outcome; and that in such a situation, a healthy skepticism is most suitable for the policymaker, the observer and the public alike: skepticism about the continuing validity of one's accustomed conceptual and operational equipment. . . .

Whatever our search for a more specific and adequate conceptualization of the national interest may reveal; and wherever that search may take us, it seems appropriate to suggest, in conclusion, that in the long run a system based solely on the self–centered pursuit of goals by its individual members can give no assurance of stability or safety, to say nothing of justice and equity, or of peace.

To make this point clearer, let us counterpose the two great events of the year 1776: the publication in Great Britain of Adam Smith's *Wealth of Nations* and the signing in Philadelphia of the American Declaration of Independence.

Smith held, among many other things not so well remembered, that if each individual were left free to pursue his own self-interests, in the long run—by the operation of an "invisible hand"—he would thereby contribute to the well-being of the entire community. The Declaration also stressed individual rights, including the right to pursue personal happiness. But it clearly sought the ultimate expression of those rights in an act of union, of contract, of "decent respect" for the opinions, judgments and (one can reasonably infer) interests of others.

Both sets of ideas have been influential in the history of the last two hundred years. Both have endured. But the second has worn rather better than the first. Men and women around the globe still believe in the principles of the Declaration, even when they are not being practiced. But how many really still believe in the "invisible hand" that encourages the untrammeled pursuit of self-interest? How many still believe that others, and the community at large, cannot be grievously injured by such pursuit? Some do, no doubt; but most of us feel that there must be limits, there must be restraints on the exercise of the pursuit. Most of us understand that some of us, pursuing purely our own interests, can do great damage to all of us; and that this damage must somehow be restrained and limited.

If this is true within a city, a state, a nation, then it must also be true within an international environment—especially one that has changed and continues to change. The requirements of the situation therefore argue for a possible redefinition of the national interest, one that explicitly takes account of the interests of others. Addressing themselves to the "intensity problem," Kendall and

Carey in an important essay some years ago noted that stability is important to an entire community, especially to those of its members who—temporarily or otherwise—are in a majority. They concluded that it was inadvisable to force one's interests on others unless the issue at stake was absolutely vital. What this conclusion amounts to is a counsel to practice restraint, not only out of generosity or other appealing human traits, but as a matter of enduring self-interest, albeit more broadly defined than is usually the case. It seems that a similar case can be made for those who operate within the international system.

Given the international context, given the continuing need to conduct foreign policy, to frame goals and to seek to achieve them, three qualities—modesty, restraint, and openness to change—should be cultivated by decision–makers, observers, and citizens alike:

- *modesty* in assuming that one can know what is best for others—indeed, sometimes what is best for oneself;

- *restraint* in the assertion of one's own interests (personal, organizational, group or national) as against those of others. In fact, one might make a conscious effort to frame his interests and goals so as to include those of others as much as possible. Morgenthau, much more sophisticated than some of his followers were or than some of his critics gave him credit for being, said it well, ". . . the national interest of a nation . . . must be defined in terms compatible with [the interests of other nations]." More recently, George and Keohane questioned the tendency to use the concept of national interest in only one context—which they call "self-regarding," excluding "other-regarding" and "collective" interests. They point out that this limited usage may be appropriate in periods of great danger, but that such periods occur only rarely, and that "to argue *a priori* that self-regarding interests must always be given priority over other interests is not morally tenable."

- *openness* can mean two things: (1) a willingness to accept national self-interest as a fact without accepting it as a norm, which was Reinhold

Niebuhr's position, and (2) a willingness to entertain alternative forms of the national interest and national policy.

One should try not to close off alternatives, but to leave the future open. Given the world in which we find ourselves—and, let us face it, which we helped make—that may be the best we can do, until such time as others can do better.

NOTES

[1] Robert E. Osgood, *Ideals and Self–Interest in America's Foreign Relations* (Chicago: University of Chicago Press. 1953), p. 10.

[2] John L. Chase, "Defining the National Interest of the United States," *Journal of Politics* (November 1956), pp. 720–724.

[3] Quoted in Charles A. Beard, *The Idea of National Interest* (New York: Macmillan, 1934), p. 339.

[4] One area of criticism omitted is the moral/ethical one—not because it is unimportant, but because the debate is based on assumptions that would require a separate paper to do them full justice. In the final section of this article, we will briefly refer to some considerations pertaining to the moral/ethical dimension of the subject.

[5] Vernon Van Dyke, "Values and Interests," *The American Political Science Review* (September 1962), p. 568.

[6] Alexander L. George and Robert Keohane, "The Concept of National Interest: Uses and Limitations," in Commission on the Organization of the Government for the Conduct of Foreign Policy. *Appendices*, vol. 2. pp. 67–8.

[7] The author can testify to the strength of these claims from his experience as a member of a city council. Each group, each section, each neighborhood looked after itself. It was relatively easy to achieve general agreement on such issues as the need for better thoroughfares or for social service agencies, as long as these were located in another part of the community. It was often difficult to perceive what the general interest was, or how many people

cared enough about it to be willing to make some sacrifices for it. To serve the general interest, however defined, without injuring some individual or group was impossible.

[8] Beard, *op cit.*, p. 167.

[9] J. Martin Rochester, "The 'National Interest' in the Context of Contemporary World Politics: Shifting Conceptions and Perceptions," paper prepared for the National Security Education Seminar, Colorado College, July 1975, p. 1.

17.   Crisis and Superpower Behavior

E. Raymond Platig

Dr. Platig is director of the Office of Long-Range Assessments and Research, U.S. Department of State, and recently served as vice-president of the International Studies Association.

International crises are characterized by the threat or presence of military conflict between or among states. At times these crises arise in areas in which neither the United States nor the USSR appears to have vital interests. Such crises would seem to offer opportunities for the superpowers to behave in ways that would contain or even ease tensions in their own relations. This article focuses upon the feasibility of guidelines for superpower crisis behavior in such areas of secondary interest to them.

An Apologia and a Basic Principle

Certain objections can be made to this focus, and they should be acknowledged at the outset.

It can be argued that to focus on the superpowers is wrong for one or both of the following reasons: (1) such a perspective as-

Excerpted from E. Raymond Platig, "Crisis, Pretentious Ideologies, and Superpower Behavior." *Orbis: A Journal of World Affairs*, 25, no. 3, Fall 1981, 511–22. (Copyright © by The Foreign Policy Research Institute, 1981. Reprinted by permission. (Footnotes have been deleted.)

sumes that the international political system is essentially bipolar in structure; and (2) the perspective assumes that the superpowers are equally capable of abiding by a minimal set of common behavioral norms. I plead guilty to the assumption of bipolarity, while recognizing that the rapid diffusion of power is also characteristic of the current state of bipolarity. That is a premise of this paper, not to be further argued here but to be challenged by those who do not accept it.

The search for a set of common behavioral norms is, of course, what this paper is all about. To date, the superpowers have found such guidelines elusive. What justifies a continuing effort is the overriding importance of the subject and the belief that, despite their many different attributes, the superpowers do share some important needs that stem from their continental, population, and industrial bases, their nuclear arsenals, and the perception each has of the other as well as of itself as a superpower. The two superpowers have, of course, important ideological and other differences that inhibit the search, and these are considered in the following discussion.

A second objection to this focus could be that by concentrating on crises in areas of secondary interest to the superpowers we ignore the tougher cases. It is true that we de-emphasize those crises in which the super-powers confront one another directly (as in the Cuban missile crisis of 1962), and those in areas in which one or both have vital interests (as in the Czech crisis of 1968 or in the intersecting Iranian and Afghanistan crises of 1979–1980).

It is not necessarily true, however, that the cases thus eliminated are the tougher ones. It could be argued that nothing concentrates the attention and heightens the superpowers' sense of their own limitations and vulnerabilities as does a crisis affecting their vital interests. In any event, since locating the line separating vital from secondary interests is an uncertain art, I have felt free to wander across that line in order to gain perspective on the subject of crises in areas of secondary interest to the superpowers.

A final objection could be that there is a moral deficiency in judging the desirability of superpower crisis behavior first and foremost from the perspective of easing tensions in superpower relations, rather than from one that seeks to minimize violence on the scene, ensure that justice is done, or further some other humane-sounding goal.

Neither separately nor together do the superpowers have an exclusive legal or moral duty to eliminate all violence from the world or to guarantee justice to all. They both have a moral and practical interest in the survival of humankind so that the search for justice and peace within and between subgroups of the species can continue. It is a search that started before the dawn of history and has been ever changing, always contentious, and frequently violent. There is little reason to believe the search will be different in the future unless strategic nuclear war catapults it into an environment of devastation and hazard unparalleled in recorded history. Thus, the greatest moral imperative of the age is the avoidance of strategic nuclear war between the superpowers.

In the long run, continued avoidance requires that the superpowers manage their relations so that neither feels that capitulation to or by the other is the only alternative, for that alternative will ensure the nuclear disaster it is imperative to avoid. Growing confidence in each superpower's commitment to the survival of both is what is required.

Mutual confidence can grow only through the common experience and common perception that both superpowers understand and abide by the most fundamental principle of international politics in the nuclear age. That is *to be extremely sensitive to and restrained regarding the adversary's security interests—to eschew the search for a "decisive" advantage*. It is a principle clearly understood and applied in the context of strategic arms limitation negotiations. It is the principle that made possible the Helsinki agreements and on which the further development of peaceful relations in Europe depends. It is the principle against which superpower behavior in the Middle East has to be measured over the past several years and the immediate future. Given the importance of public as well as of official perceptions, and given the ways in which events reverberate through the tightly knit, contemporary international system, it is a principle not to be ignored by either superpower, even during crises in areas where their interests are presumed to be secondary.

The Precrisis Phase

International crises do not spring full-blown from the barrel of a gun. They have their roots in the dynamics of relations between nations, dynamics that can often be profoundly affected by political violence within a single nation. Many observers hold that in the decades ahead domestic political instability and violence will be an even more common phenomenon than it has been. For that reason, and also to help focus the discussion of superpower behavior, it is useful in considering the precrisis phase to narrow attention to crises that are preceded by domestic political violence. This serves also to highlight the role of ideology in superpower interactions.

The Need for Astute Analysis

Like an international crisis, domestic political violence has its causes, most of them found in the conditions of the society experiencing it, some of them found in external factors impinging on the society. The relationships between preconditions and political violence is not well understood. The relationship appears to differ widely from one political culture to another and from time to time within a particular society. Nonetheless, astute observers of particular societies do watch what they consider to be social, economic, and other indications of political trouble that could turn into violence. Such observers are familiar with the history and culture of the society and with its foreign relations, benign and hostile. They may overlook factors, misestimate forces, misread trends, and be caught by surprise. Such observers, though, ought to be right on occasion and in a timely enough fashion to be able to consider whether any feasible course of action would help dampen the pending violence and its international repercussions.

Foreign embassies are supposed to be staffed with astute observers of a host country's affairs. Assume that the embassies of the superpowers are. And assume that each embassy makes a separate analysis concluding that the eruption of serious and potentially dangerous internal violence is a highly likely possibility. And further assume that, after consultation between the embassy and its capital, each superpower concludes that the threatened political violence might enmesh the superpowers in ways that would increase tension between them. Each concludes therefore that it has an interest in avoiding or at least containing the eruption of political violence.

Under these conditions, it is possible to envision the superpowers pursuing parallel or even joint policies. Logic would suggest that they could increase their chances of success by sharing the analyses made in their embassies and governments. But such sharing encounters major difficulties.

Ideology and Analysis

One difficulty arises out of the fact that embassies are not staffed solely by dispassionate an disinterested analysts. Each is staffed also by representatives of the government of one of the superpowers. They are there to represent, protect, and advance their nation's interests. However secondary these interests may be, they are nonetheless real. Each superpower embassy, then, has certain preferences—not necessarily shared—concerning the political, social, and economic performance of the host country, as well as certain assets (seldom equal in type and scope) with which to influence that performance.

It is the superpowers' preferences concerning the political performance—and even the system—of the host country that are most likely to diverge. Each superpower exemplifies a political system that, however it differs from the other, shares a common feature with it: each political system is typically presented to the world as exclusively and universally valid for all countries. Each proclaims itself to be the progenitor of the wave of humankind's political future and the protector/liberator of all peoples from the predatory imperialism of the other.

When the superpowers give a central policy role to these contending ideologies, then it is difficult to envision any but fragmentary exchanges of embassy (or foreign-office) analyses as part of mutual soundings to decipher the role of the other. The end result of this ideologically enforced isolation is that the superpowers are more likely to become part of the problem (each perceiving only the other as such), rather than problem solvers in concert during the precrisis phase. The ideologically based aspirations and suspicions of each make it more difficult—perhaps impossible—to manage what otherwise might be manageable differences between their tangible secondary interests.

Ideology and Culture

If competing, universalized ideologies are indeed among the core obstacles to envisioning practical guidelines for desirable superpower foreign policy behavior, then it is tempting to draw the logical conclusion. Both superpowers need to give up the universal pretensions of their ideologies, to cease trying to export their political forms and values, to desist from the effort to transform other nations according to the superpower's political image. But how likely is that?

History offers few grounds for optimism. One lesson of history is that universalistic political movements eventually exhaust themselves through their own failures. Another is that the intensity of American universalism has risen and fallen over the past 200 years. In addition, over a shorter period of sixty-some years, the intensity of Soviet universalism has been less, but still notably, marked by ebbs and flows. And a fourth lesson from history is that neither the Americans nor the Soviets have met with marked success in the peaceful exportation and foreign institutionalization of their political values. That point is starkly evident in the multitude of political forms that have become manifest in the wake of post-World War II decolonization. Though at times the words used to describe these forms may sound familiar in Moscow or Washington, actual political practice frequently appears strange if not repugnant.

Soviet experience in Afghanistan and American experience in Iran, along with stirrings elsewhere in the Islamic world, are powerful and current reminders that outside the Western and Soviet worlds there are deep-rooted political traditions profoundly foreign to both. That larger world harbors forces capable of generating political systems quite alien to what can be dreamed of in Washington or Moscow. To be sure, these forces have to contend with the realities of modern science, technology, and productive enterprise, all integral parts of modern Soviet and American life and presence. Nevertheless, only those suffering an advanced case of colossal hubris can seriously believe that out of the numerous struggles between traditional cultures and modern forces and aspirations will there emerge political and social practices that fall into the Soviet or American mold.

It has been argued that the foreign policy of neither superpower is as ideologically pure as its rhetoric suggests, that the ideology serves as both an instrument and cover for the pursuit of more self-interested, pragmatically calculated goals. To the extent that argument is true, it provides a basis for some hope that the superpowers can find practical ways of managing their relations. But it does not offer all that much hope. For even rhetorical ideologies poison the atmosphere when their claims to exclusive universality encounter each other, as inevitably they must. The temptation is then irresistible for the superpower proponent of one ideology to denounce the proponent of the other, and to evoke a response in kind. Reverberating in different but magnifying ways through the American, Soviet, and other media, this language of mutual denunciation is hardly conducive to the development of mutual confidence and the workings of quiet diplomacy.

A Modest Proposal

This excursion into universalistic claims, cultural multiplicity, and political diversity leads not to a guideline for superpower foreign policy behavior but to a more modest proposal that might help both arrive at a better understanding of the kinds of societies they are dealing with in areas of their secondary interests, and perhaps even help them achieve a degree of ideological modesty. The proposal in its most general form is for the superpowers to engage in joint analyses of the political systems and dynamics of selected third countries in areas of their secondary interest.

If accepted in principle as the basis for experimentation, the details could be worked out. They could vary over a broad spectrum of possibilities involving foreign offices, embassies, and scholars. One pattern would be for each superpower to attach to its embassy in a particular country one of its most astute observers of that country (who could be either an official or unofficial scholar) to engage in collaborative work with the other and with one or more indigenous astute observers of the same scene, with the work conducted in the local language.

The proposal is less radical than it may at first appear. Over the past several years, there have been exchange visits and joint conferences of scholars from various Soviet foreign area or international studies institutes and American research centers. The focus has usually been broad, the prepared papers predictable, the discussion sometimes less predictable, the changes of positions minimal. No ideological tigers have been defanged, but removable ideological teeth have sometimes been pocketed at least temporarily. To some, these events suggest a possibility for the eventual emergence of a common framework for international political analysis. To others, these events demonstrate that two charades can be performed simultaneously; or the events are seen as an opportunity to "know thy enemy," or to confirm the animosity, or to delude the innocent. My own view is that exchanges and conferences have done all of these things, and that the search for a common framework for political discourse is worth pursuing, but on a differentiated rather than universal basis.

The proposal set forth here would direct the search to different settings, focus it on the domestic affairs of a particular third state, pursue it in the culture and practices of that state, and embed it in the local idiom. If the search for a common framework failed, the results might still include improved understanding by both superpowers of the third state and of each other. If the search succeeded, it could open up the possibility of more extensive and timely exchanges of superpower embassy analyses in precrisis situations, with the further possibility that this could lead to the types of crisis-averting superpower behavior discussed earlier.

Nonideological Obstacles

If over time successful searches were conducted in a number of third states, it is even conceivable that some superpower ideological pretensions of universality would be humbled by shared perceptions of persistent particularities worthy of respect. That would hardly usher in an era of permanent superpower amity. It would dimish, however, the danger of stereotyped, zero-sum reactions to all political change in the vast, tenaciously different, and highly diverse Third World.

What would continue to bedevil superpower amity would be their remaining and likely divergent interests—interests in resources, trade, military ties, relative status and influence, prestige, and reputation—all of the tangible and symbolic advantages for which great powers have competed throughout history and which seldom are available sufficiently to satisfy all competitors. Superpower rivalry in these realms would not disappear even if the "age of ideology" were actually terminated. And such rivalry needs to be considered when discussing superpower behavior in international crises.

The Crisis Phase

The type of international crisis of interest here is one that arises because one or more states intervene or threaten to intervene forcefully in another state experiencing domestic political violence. The superpowers' behavior during such a crisis will be shaped, but need not be determined solely, by their behavior in the precrisis phase. Consider the two extremes of superpower ideological intensity.

At the one extreme, each ideologically intense superpower in the precrisis phase has been backing a different domestic political force, denouncing and seeking to discredit the other superpower, and consequently escalating the tension between them. Angola on the eve of independence is an apt example of this syndrome.

When other states intervene and the international crisis is at hand, it is difficult to imagine that the superpowers could quickly shift to behavior calculated to moderate tension between them. Nevertheless, the fact that other states are now forcefully involved introduces new factors into the relationship. Whether these can be used to moderate or intensify the tension in superpower relations is a question best addressed by looking at the other end of the spectrum.

At this other extreme, the ideologically less pretentious superpowers have kept tension between them at a minimum during the precrisis stage through a series of steps. Each has made, and perhaps even shared, astute political analyses of the potential for domestic political violence. They have concluded that parallel or in-concert action to avert political violence would be either undesirable or unavailing, or else they have tried such action and failed. In either case, the threatened or actual forceful intervention of other states means that the international crisis phase has opened. In these circumstances, the search for feasible behavioral guidelines for the superpowers is more readily pursued.

Guideline 1

An obvious guideline for the superpowers emerges readily from the logic of the situation. It reads: *Assess and discuss candidly the importance of those superpower interests likely to be affected by the crisis.*

This guideline is not feasible for ideologically intense superpowers. It is a prudent first step under the assumption of ideological relaxation. What the superpowers need to determine is which of their interests provide them with leverage with (and vulnerability to) the various states active in the crisis. If each has roughly equal leverage and roughly equal vulnerability, then they can at least consider the possibility that the concerted use and nonuse of leverage can dampen the crisis under conditions of roughly sharing risk and cost. A few superpower successes of this type would substantially lessen and stabilize at that lower level the tensions between them.

Opportunities for such successes, however, are likely to be rare. One reason is that in many theaters of crisis, superpower interests and leverage are likely to be divergent or out of balance. The more disparate they are, the more it takes an extraordinary degree of magnanimity for the superpower with greater leverage to use it to shield not only its own interests but those of the more vulnerable other. When the disparity and divergency are great enough, one superpower will wind up on the sidelines while the other advances its interests as best it can. The active superpower will be tempted to ignore the interests of the other, which in turn will suspect the first of yielding to that temptation and, at a minimum, start denouncing its rival from the sidelines.

Moreover, if the weaker of the two is capable of more than denunciation, it will be sorely tempted to find in the crisis an opportunity to redress the imbalance, an opportunity to provide decisive support to the forces inimical to the stronger superpower's interests and thus win for itself an equal or superior presence and status. In the conflictual context of almost any crisis, "decisive support" is likely to take the form of military supplies and advice, either direct or through surrogates, and either overt or covert.

This type of superpower behavior, discernible in the October War in the Middle East, can hardly be undertaken with the expectation that it will not increase tension in superpower relations. The Angolan crisis also followed this pattern. Like the October War, it came after Nixon and Brezhnev denounced "efforts to attain unilateral advantage at the expense of the other, directly or indirectly." Such efforts, they said, were "inconsistent" with various worthy objectives, including that of "preventing the development of situations capable of causing a dangerous exacerbation of their relations." How much exacerbation is dangerous is open to speculation, but these and other recent events as well as the long history of international politics, demonstrate how unrealistic it is to try to put beyond the pale of acceptable behavior efforts by great powers "to attain unilateral advantage at the expense of the other," especially when one power is dissatisfied with its relative inequality in a particular arena. Far into the future the superpowers will have to live with situations in which one or the other seeks and at times achieves a unilateral but not strategically "decisive" advantage.

Guideline 2

Can the superpowers comport themselves to contain the inevitable rise in tension between them in crises in which one is in fact positioned to achieve a less than decisive advantage over the other? One suspects that they could do this only by invoking an ordinance of rhetorical self-restraint. It might read: *Upon achieving a unilateral advantage in a crisis, don't trumpet victory; when sidelined or disadvantaged, don't embrace a setback as a defeat.*

This requires a degree of self-restraint not likely to be found under conditions of ideological intensity. From its sidelined or disadvantaged position, an intensely ideological superpower will not only envy the other's advantage but also see it as reconfirmation of its rival's unlimited ambition. And the equally intense rival will proclaim itself the ideological "winner," heightening the other's sense of loss and strengthening its de-

termination to suffer no more "humiliations." Thus what in fact may be nothing more than a marginal shift in the power relations of the superpowers in an arena of secondary importance to each is seen instead as an event of cosmic significance.

Under conditions of ideological relaxation, the requisite self-restraint may be possible. The superpowers then might be able to perceive the event in the context to two longer-run realities. First, given the strength of indigenous forces in the theater of crisis, the immediate fortunes of the superpowers are quite likely to prove short-lived, with the distribution of advantages and disadvantages appearing quite different in the years ahead from how they appear at the moment. Egyptian, Ethiopian, and Somalian realignments in recent years all illustrate the point. Second, in some future crisis, superpower fortunes are likely to be reversed, conferring upon them a quite different distribution of immediate advantages and disadvantages, however fleeting. Admittedly, advice to take the longer view is more easily rendered than accepted, but its acceptance is not unknown in the long history of statesmanship and diplomacy.

Admittedly, too, not everything is automatically benign or balanced in the long run. Hypothetically, it is possible for a series of less than decisive advantages to bring one superpower to the brink of a decisive advantage. In practice, however, each superpower can be expected to be alert to such a trend and to react with steps designed to disrupt it before it takes on such ominous dimensions. Indeed, such steps can add to the basic stability of the relationship, provided they are measured and not accompanied by rhetorical overkill.

A second reason why it will be the rare crisis that is successfully dampened simply through the concerted use of superpower leverage is that, in their areas of secondary interest, the combined leverage of the superpowers is seldom that great. In many cases other states or groupings of states will be better situated to take the initiatives toward conflict resolution. If none is willing or able to, then the superpowers have little choice but to try to minimize damage to their own interests. But neither the unwillingness nor the impotence of others ought to be assumed. States more proximate than the superpowers to the theater of crisis may have more substantial interests in its outcome, as may more distant economic partners and those with cultural or status affinities with the states in conflict.

An important feature of the present era of international politics is the fluidity with which states group and regroup themselves for a great variety of overlapping purposes. Familiar alliances, blocs, and regional groups are increasingly penetrated and overlaid with subregional, commodity, producer, trading, users, religious, cultural, and even nonaligned alignments of states.

This phenomenon is no doubt related to growth in the sheer number of sovereign states, to the tremendous disparities of power and interest among them, to the burgeoning insistence with which the weak press their demands for more, and to the conveniences of instant communication and jet travel. Whatever the underlying causes, it is a phenomenon with which the superpowers must deal. For them, and for other established powers accustomed to the simpler patterns of an earlier era, it can be an unsettling phenomenon. Even so, it offers alternative ways of handling some of the world's international concerns, even international crises. It is a phenomenon that bespeaks a certain vigor and inventiveness in the international system. While it does not mean that an international crisis anywhere is a crisis for all, it does mean that a larger number of states will have interests affected by the outcome of any particular crisis. The nature of those interests and the means and modalities through which they are pursued will determine whether the presence of a larger number of concerned parties exacerbates or moderates the crisis. But there is no *a priori* reason to expect the worst. On the contrary, the better assumption is that the parties at

interest are those most likely to work out a more lasting resolution of the crisis. It is an assumption borne out by the drawn-out Zimbabwe-Rhodesian crisis, in which the United Kingdom effectively orchestrated the eventual resolution.

Guideline 3

All of the above suggest another guideline for superpower foreign policy behavior in a range of international crises. Simply put, it reads: *Stand back; do not assume that every crisis calls for a public display of your leadership; expect the parties or other states or agencies to take initiatives; allow a reasonable interval for these to unfold; keep open the channels of communication between you and with the others.*

At first blush, this guideline would seem to be particulary apt for crises in areas where the superpowers have only secondary interests. The Polish and Iraq–Iran crises, however, on which the returns are not yet in, raise the possibility that this guideline may have broader applicability. In these areas, where the interests of the superpowers are substantial, they at this writing have avoided massive intervention while domestic political forces in Poland have shown great vigor and Islamic diplomatic initiatives in the Persian Gulf have been numerous. This suggests anew that what we have called the fundamental principle of international politics in the nuclear age is well understood. But it may also suggest that the superpowers attach some value to allowing room for initiatives by the parties and others.

There is another feature of the present era of international politics that both deserves comment and suggests one more guideline. That feature is a legacy of the ideological intensity of the superpowers. Because of that intensity, many national leaders and aspirants have learned to manipulate the languages of communism and liberal democracy to advance their own causes. If the cause is stated in one or the other of these self-proclaimed universal languages, it is sometimes possible to achieve a level of superpower commitment quite in excess of the superpower's real interest. Expanding Soviet commitments to Afghanistan beginning around 1977 and American commitments to the Republic of China on Formosa beginning around 1950 provide stark if only partial and not fully comparable examples of this syndrome at work. The costs to the overcommitted superpower have sometimes been high. The rewards have often been disappointing, illusory, or ephemeral. And the escalation of tension between the superpowers sometimes has been irresistible and costly to both.

It should not be surprising that political leaders and aspirants seek to put more power behind their purposes by inducing others to support them. What is surprising is that a presumably sophisticated superpower could be induced to take costly action by words behind which there is so little substance. The only explanation can be that ideological intensity creates translucent blinders that filter out the reality of cultural and political diversity and local ambitions while admitting the bright flashes of comforting rhetoric.

Guideline 4

Thus, one can formulate yet another guideline for the superpowers, but one they will not be inclined to follow when they are ideologically intense. It reads: *Don't underestimate the mischievous power of the weak; beware especially foreign supplicants fluent in your political idiom. . . .*

---

18.   Lessons from the Falklands

Andrew Burns

Andrew Burns is counselor at the British Ambassy in Washington; he received the "Benjamin H. Brown Award" at the Center for International Affairs at Harvard for this paper, written as a Fellow at the Center in 1982–3.

The confrontation in 1982 between Argentina and the United Kingdom over the Falkland Islands meets in all respects the classic definition of a crisis: a situation characterized by surprise, a high threat to important values, and short decision time. For the first time in a generation, the British public and its leaders had to grapple with the broad

Excerpted from Andrew Burns, *Diplomacy, War and Parliamentary Democracy: Further Lessons from The Falklands on Advice from Academe* (New York: Lanham 1985) pp. 3–19. Reprinted by permission of the publisher. Copyright © 1985 by the President and Fellows of Harvard College. (Footnotes have been deleted.)

issues of war and peace and the practical implications of a large-scale naval and military deployment to the other side of the world. They did so with surprising seriousness and unity of purpose, given the unexpectedness of the crisis and the apparently trivial nature of the problem itself. Few, however, of those who were called upon to manage or describe the crisis had had much previous knowledge of the substance or the geography of the problem.

On one point there was wide agreement: British diplomacy had been found wanting. The government had failed to anticipate or deter the Argentine invasion of the Falkland Islands. Thereafter, diplomatic efforts to persuade Argentina to the virtues of a peaceful withdrawal proved unsuccessful. Some said that the British government tried too hard, some said not hard enough. Either way, the task of restoring the Islands to British administration had to be left to a Task Force. It took 28,000 men and over 125 ships to rescue the Islands and their 1,800 inhabitants, at a cost of 1,000 men killed and many more wounded on both sides. The price of diplomatic failure was high. Was it avoidable? . . .

. . . the crisis posed real and thoroughly contemporary challenges, both in terms of diplomatic maneuvering among friends, allies, and critics, and in terms of securing legitimacy for British actions against skeptical world opinion. There may have been an air about it of 19th century gunboat diplomacy, but the affair took place long after the diplomatic revolution which has brought so many new actors and institutions onto the international stage since the Second World War.

Moreover, the Falklands affair had a lifecycle which, though compressed, involved some of the basic concerns of crisis management and conflict resolution in any age: negotiation, deterrence, defense, prevention of surprise attack, mediation, coercion, escalation, war termination. It was a vivid demonstration of the use, and the threat of use, of conventional force to back up national diplomacy.

In the Falklands affair, we see the lamentable consequences of allowing diplomacy to become divorced from political and military support. We have a telling demonstration of the failure of deterrence. We have yet one more example of a technologically sophisticated power becoming the victim of a surprise attack by an enemy which it has long suspected of harboring hostile intentions. We have an instructive illustration of how a government copes in conditions of sudden stress and conflict. We see the possibilities and contradictions in the processes of mediation and coercive diplomacy. We

can see some of the challenges to government for the political management of war in a liberal Parliamentary democracy . . .

It is difficult for policy-makers laboring under the stresses and time pressures of a crisis to stand back from what is happening in order to draw upon and apply either the lessons of the past or any but the most commonplace theories of the present. Recently, however, much good work has been done to help current practitioners apply the lessons of past history and the theories and models of conflict resolution and crisis management which diplomatic historians and political scientists have begun to evolve.

Three broad questions deserve attention: What useful guidance could the theories have offered on each phase of the Falklands crisis? How does this crisis correct or illuminate the theories? What are the particular challenges which a Parliamentary democracy presents for crisis management? . . .

The phases of the Falklands conflict divide conveniently into those that predate and those that follow the Argentine invasion of April 1982. What follows is a summary of eight detailed studies—not for publication—comparing theory and practice in each of the phases of diplomacy and war.

The phases of the conflict before the invasion were (1) the inability of British diplomacy to produce or to mobilize domestic political support for a negotiated settlement with Argentina; (2) the failure of British diplomatic and military strategy to deter the Argentine attack; and (3) the failure of the British to anticipate a surprise attack. After the invasion, the phases were (1) the problems of maintaining political control over both the development of the crisis and the momentum of military events through the choice and presentation of issues and the search for constitutional legitimacy; (2) the conduct of a strategy of coercive diplomacy; (3) the theory of escalation; (4) the theory and practice of mediation; and (5) the problems of maintaining political control over the development of a crisis and the momentum of military events through effective crisis management and close diplomatic-military coordination. . . .

Failure of Negotiations

Insights emerge from an examination of these events through two different theoretical perspectives which have received much attention in recent years: an analysis of the decision-making process and a review of the negotiating practice.

In terms of the formal decision-making process, the system worked fairly well. Rational decisions were the result of "consistent value-maximizing choice within specified constraints." The trouble was that the key decision was a tough one, not because the choice was difficult to identify (to negotiate a cession of sovereignty because the cost of continuing defense would be too high), but because it was controversial. Much political capital would have to be spent on what was considered a minor issue. In consequence, when faced with Argentine or Islander recalcitrance, successive governments played for time without adequately recognizing that the choice was not a pure one between two equal alternatives. If Britain could not obtain a negotiated settlement, it was automatically saddled with maintaining an expensive defense.

An examination of the decision-making process suggests four explanations for this inability to act effectively. First, the choice, however rational, is meaningless if the "specified constraints" are not constantly analyzed and revised. Officials seemed to have become prisoners of past decisions, pursuing an ever-narrowing set of options in a persistent effort to keep negotiations going. Plainly, negotiation was better than confrontation. Yet it was not until 1981 that serious thought was given to a "sales campaign" designed to persuade both the Islanders and domestic political opinion of the wisdom of a negotiated deal over sovereignty. It is part of the tradition in Great Britain that the elected members of Parliament be left to as-

sess, influence, and determine Parliamentary opinion. Yet Parliament's objection to considering a cession of sovereignty was such a constraint that the task of changing Parliamentary attitudes should have been recognized earlier as a key requirement for success.

Second, in organizational terms, the Foreign and Commonwealth Office was on its own; it had no allies on the issue and therefore could not mobilize adequate support for its recommendations either from Parliament or from other government departments. The problems caused by the F.C.O.'s isolation were compounded by intragovernmental politics. The key bureaucratic battles after 1979 took place over reductions in public expenditure plans and the establishment of a new system of cash limits on the overall annual budgets of individual government departments. It had become almost impossible for a department to propose additional expenditures on old commitments (such as Falklands defense) without leaving itself vulnerable to demands for corresponding financial cuts in other areas of its responsibilities. Thus, the Foreign Office felt impelled to pursue negotiations with Argentina despite the seriousness of the Parliamentary obstacles and even though it was unable to identify a manageable fallback position should a deal fail to materialize.

Third, the Foreign Office failed to realize that a decision to postpone a decision is, in fact, a decision. Playing for time may be a suitable tactic when circumstances are favorable. In the case of the Falklands crisis, however, playing for time had the effect of passing the initiative to Argentina, leaving the British government with no strategy and vulnerable to surprise developments.

Fourth, the British government proceeded as though it were playing from strength when, in fact, it was playing from a weakened deterrence posture and an inadequate negotiating hand. These were compounded by a failure to keep the basic balance of interest under constant review. For reasons of organization and internal pol-

itics, there was an inadequate assessment of the constraints on rational political action and only a belated effort to try to change those constraints.

In terms of negotiating procedure, a number of lessons emerge, of which perhaps the key is this: When a negotiation becomes very drawn-out and different actors take part over the years, it is important to see the evolution of the negotiation as a whole and to understand its internal dynamics, rather than treat each phase as a separate negotiation. British governments failed to understand that their negotiating credibility in Argentine eyes was progressively eroded because the British were unable or unwilling to carry the Islanders with their policy. To negotiate is to be willing to compromise and to concede something of value to the other side. Otherwise there is nothing to negotiate about in good faith. On the other hand, it is far from easy over an extended period to ensure that both parties remain equally committed to the negotiation, i.e., that both remain serious about reaching an agreement, that both continue to see the same fundamental negotiating issues, and that both see the essential shape of an acceptable bargain.

The Foreign Office also failed to develop satisfactory alternatives. Since it was unable to persuade the government to spend more money on defending the Islands, it would have been better had the Foreign Office faced up to the fact that nothing more than an uneasy truce was possible pending later developments, rather than suggest that it was still possible to pursue an agreement on sovereignty which was not politically viable. In this respect, the negotiations demonstrate that the way to lead public opinion in such circumstances is to reexamine and reformulate one's objectives often enough to encourage free discussion and to avoid becoming bound by rigid or unrealistic positions. The commitment to respect the wishes of the Islanders acquired, without much considered public debate, a status which does not seem to have reflected the real relationship between the colony and the Parliament at Westminster or any objective calculation of the British national interest. Of course, no one wanted to hand the Islanders over to non-democratic rule. The lease-back idea was one way of avoiding that. Its merits were unfortunately never given an adequate hearing in London or on the Islands.

The conclusion from analysis must be that British governments did not understand their own negotiating position well enough. They did not recognize, nor act to remedy, the weaknesses and vulnerabilities that developed in their position over the years. They should have been more sensitive to the changes in the relative importance of the issue for either side and to the influence of changing attitudes in third countries. A knowledge of some of the theoretical literature could have been helpful. . . .

chapter 7

DIPLOMACY, OLD AND NEW

. . . before embarking upon so wide a field of examination, it is, as has been said, necessary to define in what sense, or senses, the word "diplomacy" will be used in this study. I propose to employ the definition given by the Oxford English Dictionary. It is as follows: "Diplomacy is the management of international relations by negotiation; the method by which these relations are adjusted and managed by ambassadors and envoys; the business or art of the diplomatist.". . . [But what are his or her qualities?]

These, then are the qualities of my ideal diplomatist. Truth, accuracy, calm, patience, good temper, modesty and loyalty. They are also the qualities of an ideal diplomacy.

"But," the reader may object, "you have forgotten intelligence, knowledge, discernment, prudence, hospitality, charm, industry, courage and even tact." I have not forgotten them. I have taken them for granted.

Sir Harold Nicolson
(New York: in *Diplomacy*, 3rd ed.
Oxford University Press, 1963), pp. 4–5; 67.

An Ambassador is an honest man sent abroad to lie for the good of his country.

Attributed to Sir Henry Wotton (early seventeenth century)

Diplomacy, in a very real sense, is older than international relations themselves. Wherever people have existed in separate tribes or other groupings they have needed some means of communicating and regulating their relationships. Long before the appearance of the modern state system, the practice developed (in the absence of common councils among states) of establishing permanent legations or embassies at each other's court or capital as a channel of information and negotiation. Inasmuch as the ambassador was the personal representative of the ruler or monarch, he enjoyed all the privileges and immunities that would normally be extended to the monarch, say Elizabeth I, were she herself to appear in person. Diplomacy gained its unique status from the special need which sovereigns had from the beginning for keeping in regular touch with one another and resolving their differences, if their relations were not to break down to their mutual disadvantage. Elizabeth happened to be a great statesman, and England became a great power.

Even though the term *diplomacy* is sometimes used interchangeably with *foreign policy* (that is, "Israeli Diplomacy Seeks Security in Middle East"), the two are not the same. Diplomacy is the *process* or *method* by which governments pursue foreign policy; it is not policy itself. It is helpful in clarifying how the process works if we draw a distinction between the making of foreign policy and the conduct of diplomacy. As we have seen, foreign policy is what heads of state and their government advisers decide should be done in order to implement the nation's goals; diplomacy and negotiation are among the methods or techniques whereby ministers and envoys pursue that policy. Thus, diplomacy is neither the substance of policy nor the process whereby the government *formulates* policy, although it may influence that process. The diplomat's primary task is to negotiate with representatives of other countries (often called "plenipotentiaries") to try to arrive at solutions to problems acceptable to all sides of the negotiating process. In today's world, it is the closest direct, official, and regular contact in international relations. Policy is formulation; diplomacy is, as Professor James puts it in a delightful contribution to this chapter, communication.

Diplomacy is conducted by governments through the agency of the foreign ministry (in the American case, the Department of State). The foreign minister or secretary of state is responsible for the overall coordination between the home government and the diplomats serving abroad and, in democratic countries, for interpreting, defending, and often "selling" policy to parliaments and publics. Authoritarian governments are not concerned with domestic approval.[1]

The Department of State is expected to provide the President with the information and advice necessary for making policy. The department relays decisions and instructions for their execution to ambassadors serving in foreign capitals. They are expected to discuss these decisions with the governments to which they are assigned or within the international organizations where they see representatives of many governments at the same time in the same place. The United States ambassador is the President's personal representative. Foreign ambassadors in Washington are performing similar functions for their governments. They are expected to carry out the instructions they have been given but seldom, if ever, to act upon their own initiative. They may refer questions back to the foreign ministry or make suggestions of their own, but their primary task is to induce the government to which they are assigned to respond favorably to

---

[1]Professor Jeanne Kirkpatrick is said to have become Ambassador Kirkpatrick partly because of the distinction she drew between *totalitarian* and merely *authoritarian* states. Thus justifying support of certain anti-communist, but non-democratic, regimes. At the United Nations she, in a very statesmanlike way, dealt with both.

their home government's request. Conversely, effective ambassadors (about fifty of whom have been American women) can make a personal contribution to international understanding depending on how well they interpret to their home capital the views of the government to which they are assigned.

Occasionally, diplomacy may take the form of an actual visit by a head of state to another country to negotiate personally with that country's leadership, or even with several other leaders. In recent years, this phenomenon has been called "summit diplomacy." On other occasions, foreign ministers may become involved in complicated negotiations concerning several foreign countries. Such was the case with Former U.S. Secretary of State Henry Kissinger, and later with President Carter and Secretary Cyrus Vance in the Middle East. This more recent practice has been dubbed "shuttle diplomacy." The diplomats are usually advised in these matters by a corps of Foreign Service officers and State Department specialists versed in the complicated economic, political, social, and religious issues of the area. In these instances, the President or the secretary of state are themselves acting as diplomats. They must be exceedingly careful when undertaking this role. When negotiating, a diplomat is acting as a professional agent, versed in the art of negotiation; when a president or leader enters into negotiations, he (or she) may be pressured to refuse any significant concessions, so that public opinion will not decide that too much is being sacrificed for the sake of agreement. Few professionals regard either summit or "shuttle" diplomacy very highly: former Undersecretary of State George Ball, for example, concluded that Kissinger's spectacular efforts "established a clumsy pattern,"[2] which Secretary of State Alexander Haig later discovered in trying to resolve the Falklands/Malvinas crisis in the South Atlantic.

Traditionally, the function of diplomacy has taken its form from the nature of the state system itself. In the absence of a common forum such as a parliament, states had to regulate their relations indirectly and diplomats were sent abroad to negotiate with other diplomats or directly with foreign sovereigns to accomplish their ends. For hundreds of years, foreign policy was seen as the exclusive province of the monarch's inner circle. The preoccupation of traditional diplomacy was war, sovereignty, territory, and the personal ambitions of rulers. Diplomats were sent abroad to win over other monarchs to their leader's point of view. Hence, a premium was placed upon the arts of charm, guile, flattery, threat, and persuasion. As relations became more complex, diplomats had to be knowledgeable about the state to which they were sent, skilled in representing their country's interests to a foreign government (and vice versa), and adept at bargaining. The well–known scholar of the theory and practice of diplomacy, Kenneth Thompson, describes the background to nineteenth–century European diplomacy as follows:

> In theory at least, it sought to mitigate and reduce conflicts by means of persuasion, compromise, and adjustment. It was a diplomacy rooted in the community of interests of a small group of leaders who spoke the same language, catered as often to one

---

[2]George Ball, "Shuttle Diplomacy—The Preference for Tactics Over Strategy," in *Diplomacy for a Crowded World* (Boston: Little, Brown, 1977), p. 136.

another as their own people, and played to one another's strengths and weaknesses. When warfare broke out, they drew a ring around the combatants and sought to localize and neutralize the struggle. The old diplomacy . . . carried on its tasks in a world made up of states that were small, separate, limited in power, and blessed, ironically enough, by half–hearted political loyalties. Patience was a watchword; negotiations and talks would be initiated, broken off, resumed, discontinued temporarily, and reopened again by professionals in whose lexicon there was no substitute for "diplomacy."[3]

In the twentieth century, especially the second half of this century, diplomacy has become a highly organized and even specialized enterprise. There are, in addition to the more traditional military "attachés," cultural, commercial, labor, and even scientific attachés. Frank Ninkovich describes one of these in detail in his contribution to this chapter—cultural diplomacy.[4]

Much of modern diplomacy still involves secrecy and bargaining over conflicts of interest. The United States and the Soviet Union could only reach their first agreement on strategic arms control after extensive secret bargaining. In Vienna, the Soviet and American delegations engaged in the formal SALT negotiations. But behind the scenes in Washington, and unbeknownst to the American negotiators in Vienna, then National Security Adviser Henry Kissinger and Soviet Ambassador Anatoly Dobrynin were secretly negotiating to remove the roadblocks encountered in the deliberations going on in Vienna. The formal negotiating positions on the Soviet and American sides were severely circumscribed by the interests of the military in maximizing their weapons' advantages; Nixon's overwhelming desire to reach an agreement prompted the President to bypass these limitations by having Kissinger directly explore other alternatives with Brezhnev in the Kremlin. Had they not been able to bargain in secret, they would have been under such pressure from opponents of the SALT treaty that neither could have made the necessary concessions to the other's point of view. The same was true of the negotiations to end the war in Vietnam, to establish terms for ending United States control of the Panama Canal, and to bring the Iranian hostage crisis to a successful conclusion. It is in the nature of many issues that only after the bargaining has been consummated and the terms to an agreement reached can results be revealed. It is then to be hoped that, with the knowledge of the whole package, including what each side has conceded, Congress and the public can be persuaded to accept the agreement. All too often, however, as Charles Maechling puts it in his selection in this chapter, modern diplomats must expect to "operate in a goldfish bowl."

Diplomacy today is less an art than "a management process.,"[5] This is because states and societies are more interdependent and the issues are increasingly complex. In the old days, the outcome of negotiations was likely to have little

---

[3]*Christian Ethics and the Dilemmas of Foreign Policy* (Durham, N.C.: Duke University Press, 1959), pp. 81–82.

[4]See in this context, a plea for upgrading this dimension by John Russell, "Cultural Exchange Must Not Be Second Best," *New York Times*, Sect. 2, March 9, 1986, pp. 1, 33.

[5]Gilbert R. Winham, "Negotiation as a Management Process," *World Politics*, 30, no. 1 (October 1977), pp. 87–114, reproduced in the fifth edition of this book.

effect upon the people at home unless it led to war. But today here are endless problems that can only be solved in conjunction with other nations, and they are not problems that can be neglected or easily postponed. Nuclear–arms control; tariff and monetary matters; agreements to regulate air travel and communications; the avoidance of danger from pollution or terrorism or economic collapse—all are less a matter of conflict over issues than a matter of finding solutions to common problems. The difficulty encountered in obtaining landing rights for the Concorde at New York's Kennedy Airport is a perfect example of the way in which technology has created problems at the domestic level, the solution to which must be found at the international level if serious misunderstanding is to be avoided.

Internal pressures indirectly affect the negotiation process. Even more private as well as public interests in each country must now be taken into account. The complexity of the issues frequently requires large teams of experts on each side. In effect, many problems can no longer be exclusively solved at the national level or left to the uninhibited play of nations' self–interest. As the Canadian scholar Gilbert Winham observes:

> Modern international negotiation represents a machine of great systems. It is commonplace today to observe that the world is becoming more interdependent. . . . Today, negotiators function as an extension of national policymaking processes rather than as a formal diplomatic representation between two sovereigns. . . . It is now more akin to the art of management as practiced in large bureaucracies than to the art of guile and concealment as practiced by Cardinal Mazarin.[6]

Governments need more control over forces in the international system than they can achieve independently. In the absence of the policy debate and consensus that occurs at the national level, they must resort to often delicate negotiations.

Diplomacy today requires quite a different psychology and perspective from that of the past. Negotiators must approach their task with problem–solving orientation rather than with a view of winning points at someone else's expense, although the latter may still be an element in the bargaining process. They must also be able to effect change in their own government's negotiating position. One diplomat remarked to Winham that as much as 90 percent of his delegation's time was spent in securing modifications of position from the government back home. In this sense, much of modern negotiation is indeed the extension of the national bureaucratic bargaining and policy process to the level of the international system.

Nevertheless, nations often come to the negotiating process with important differences in style and motive. The most persistent question about style and motive has been raised concerning Soviet diplomacy. The Bolshevik government came to power in 1917 forsworn to the overthrow of the capitalist system. Lenin made no secret of his belief that all relations with capitalist countries were to be conducted on the presumption that friendly or even normal relations were not

---

[6]Ibid., p. 89.

possible between two ideological systems, one of which was historically destined to triumph over the other. According to the Marxist–Leninist interpretation of history, capitalism is an outmoded system against which socialism must carry on a life–and–death struggle. That does not mean capitalism will not fight back. Under the socially determined laws of history, peaceful or harmonious relations between socialist and capitalist states are not possible; the only relevant question is "Who will kill whom?" The Soviet view that a good Bolshevik must advance the victory of communism wherever possible, and be ever on guard against the efforts of the capitalists to reverse the gains of socialism, does not make the task of diplomacy an easy one. Short of war, diplomacy presupposes some degree of mutual interest among capitalist states on the one hand and Communist states on the other that relations between them must be governed by historically de-termined laws of conflict; it is not possible for Soviet diplomacy, however, to possess that degree of common interest and trust that hitherto marked diplomatic relations between states not on the verge of war.

This outlook has led the eminent diplomatic historian Gordon Craig to write:

> Despite the excellence of their training in the external forms of diplomacy, and their skill in using it, Soviet negotiators have always had a fundamentally different ap-proach toward diplomacy from that of their Western Colleagues. To them, diplomacy is more than an instrument for protecting and advancing national interest; it is a weapon in the unremitting war against capitalist society. Diplomatic negotiations, therefore, cannot aim at real understanding and agreement; and this has had pro-found effects upon their nature and techniques.[7]

It should be noted that a considerable evolution has occurred in the Soviet approach to diplomacy. At first, states under Communist rule tended to regard diplomacy as an outworn bourgeois institution. The Soviet government still pursues a two–track course in its relations with other states—one track that of conventional diplomacy and government–to–government relations, the other that of support for revolutionary movements aimed at the overthrow of estab-lished governments. Still, Soviet diplomacy has shifted in the direction of ex-ploiting the possibilities of diplomacy as much as possible to achieve the objectives of the Soviet state—objectives which are less those of world revolution and more those characteristic of every great power with global pretensions. At the same time, strong suspicion remains that the Kremlin views negotiations less as a means of achieving a mutual accommodation of national interests than as another terrain on which to continue the struggle against capitalism. By contrast, Western governments are often under public pressure for quick results and are, therefore, prone to accept illusory concessions or dangerous agreements in principle. Soviet negotiators are free to proceed with infinite patience, knowing that sooner or later they may be in a position to exploit the Western need for agreement. This does not necessarily mean that the Soviets are duplicitious, but rather than their operational principles and conditions give them negotiating advantages that are

---

[7]Gordon Craig, "Totalitarian Approaches to Diplomatic Negotiations," in A. O. Sarkissian, ed., *Studies in Diplomatic History and Historiography* (London: Longmans, Green and Co., 1961), p. 120.

denied to Western diplomats. On the other hand, it is often argued that the rigidity and secrecy with which the Kremlin surrounds its diplomacy limits its negotiators from securing terms that would be more in the Soviet interest than would prolonging negotiations and relationships.

The greatest criticism advanced by those who feared that the United States would be giving away too much in the SALT talks was that the United States did not approach the talks as a bargaining process or a competitive one, but as a cooperative process; whereas the Soviets have regarded SALT as another competitive endeavor designed to catch up or get ahead of the United States and to make gains in other political areas. Critics of SALT II and of détente argued that American negotiators entered into the talks with excessive preoccupation with technical details at the expense of a thorough consideration of the basic political and strategic questions involved. By contrast, they contended that the Soviets approach these negotiations with a comprehensive strategico–political view as to what kind of agreement will most enhance Soviet strategic and political superiority. What is common to both sides is a determination to serve the national interest as each sees it, and the great question is how mutual self–interest can be achieved.

DISCUSSION QUESTIONS

1. Discuss the contemporary relevance, if any, of the two quotations at the beginning of this chapter. Is Nicolson now out-of-date?

2. In light of its abuse for purposes of political rhetoric by which presidents and their advisors justify their decisions, does the *national interest* concept have any value for the diplomats who have to implement these decisions in their posts abroad? Do you agree with Ambassador McGhee on this?

3. Can diplomats overcome the propensity of presidents and their advisors either to avoid or to over-react to critical situations or choices, according to Maechling? What does he think of theoreticians?

4. In what sense does McGhee use the term *twilight of diplomacy?* Is this not incompatible with James's view of it as an essential means of communication between countries?

5. Why is it essential that diplomats recognize the complexity, ambiguity, and situational referents involved in the use of terms like *security, independence, prestige,* and even *peace* to explain what their countries are striving for?

6. Even if we think we know what some particular national interest is, why is it so difficult for diplomats to decide how to implement the goal or objective their superiors have in mind? In what ways does Frank Ninkovich think cultural relations can be useful in this regard?

19. Diplomacy as Communication

Alan M. James

Alan M. James is a professor in the Department of International Relations at the University of Straffordshire, England and has served as President of the British International Studies Association (BISA).

. . . . I intend to draw attention to certain phenomena which seem to me to be essential for the maintenance of international relations. That is not to say that I think they are sufficient for states to have frequent and often far–reaching relations. I do not. But I am of the view that they are necessary conditions of international relations as we know them. It also happens that I think these phenomena clearly point to the existence of an international society and that the choice of the word society in preference to another is not a matter of indifference. "Mankind," said Gibbon, "is governed by names"[1] and in many cases the words we use do influence our perception of the objects to which they refer. I, therefore, hope that the concept of society which will emerge from what I have yet to say will not be regarded, either within or beyond the academic world, as too idiosyncratic. But, as I have said, this is not an area in which one can be dogmatic. It is not my purpose to try to sell you a particular concept of society. What I am going to do is to claim importance for certain phenomena and to suggest that together they indicate the presence at the international level of what might reasonably be called a society. . . .

I want first to mention diplomacy, by which I mean the system whereby officially accredited representatives are sent by states to reside in each other's capitals, together with an accompanying staff which is often of considerable size. It is a colourful subject and

not just because its practitioners occasionally wear elaborate dress and behave in a manner which caused the young Bismarck to say in 1851: "No one, not even the most ill-disposed cynic of a democrat, could believe how much charlatanry and pompousness there is in this diplomatic business."[2] It is also colourful in the sense that diplomats sometimes find themselves in situations which, when recounted at leisure or reported by an observer, make good stories. . . .

One can tell of diplomats resorting to fisticuffs in the seventeenth century over questions of precedence and taking elaborate precautions in the twentieth to counter the 'bugging' of their premises and communications: in this connection the Celtic languages have sometimes been very useful. Embassies have been known to abuse their privileges, for example using what is called the diplomatic bag for a variety of illicit purposes. One of the most ambitious such enterprises in recent years was the attempt by some members of the Egyptian Embassy in Rome to ship a drugged Moroccan out of the country by air freight. There have been many modern variants of the 'go-out-and-govern-New-South-Wales' gambit. A difficult general in the Dominican Republic, for example, was ordered to Miami in 1965 as Consul–General. He was escorted to the airport by what the occupying American force called an 'honour guard,' but which the General himself insisted was the point of a bayonet. Embassies have been besieged and even sacked when their countries' foreign policy has given offence to nationals of the host state. British missions have often been in this particular firing line. As an abusive crowd

Excerpted from Alan M. James, "International Society," in *Review of International Studies* 4, no. 2 (July 1978), 97–100. Copyright © 1978. Reprinted by permission. (Some footnotes have been removed; those remaining have been renumbered.)

gathered outside the embassy in Djakarta in 1963, Ambassador Gilchrist (a Scot) defied them both vocally and by sending his military attaché to march up and down inside the railings playing the bagpipes. In the event his efforts were unsuccessful and possibly even counter–productive, for the rioters broke inside and set the new Embassy building on fire. But evidently the Ambassador was thought to have shown appropriate spirit for it was only a matter of months before he got his knighthood. Some years before, at the time of the Suez crisis, the Ambassador in Moscow, Sir William Hayter, listened to the chants of the inevitable demonstrators. Then, however, they invaded the Embassy's garden and pinned slogans to its walls. This was too much. He had a General of the Russian civil police who was amongst the rioters brought inside the building. "How much longer is this disgraceful scene going on?" the Ambassador demanded crossly. The policeman seemed taken aback by his reception. But clearly he knew a man having authority when he saw one. He looked at his watch and said: "About another quarter of an hour."[3]

The importance of the diplomatic system is generally thought to have considerably diminished. This is sometimes attributed, especially by diplomats of the 'old school,' to the deterioration in the relations of states which has occured in the twentieth century as compared with the nineteenth. In the past 60 years or so states have exhibited a much greater degree of hostility toward each other than during the previous 100. This, combined with the democratization of all political affairs, has produced open stridency and insults, which have inevitably been reflected in the world of diplomacy. Many of the old assumptions and conventions regarding diplomatic behaviour have been swept aside. But in speaking of the decline of diplomacy, many observers give much more significance to technological developments. No longer can an American secretary of state, or any other foreign minister, observe, as Jefferson did at the end of the eighteenth century, that he had not heard from his Ambassador in Ma-

drid for over two years and that if another year went by without news he proposed to send him a letter. Nowadays our man in Madrid, Mogadishu, or wherever, can be in instant touch with his policymaking superiors at home and they with him. He knows, too, that his foreign minister or even his prime minister or president can descend on him at any moment and may well do so if anything important is afoot. Additionally, summit meetings and other international gatherings of a more regular kind deprive him of much of his former potential thunder. In this sense it can truly be said that diplomats have gone down in the world.

As against this, attention can be and often is drawn to the usefulness of diplomats on account of their reports on the countries to which they are accredited, which can play an important part in the making of foreign policy. The information they contain cannot, it is argued, be picked up by foreign offices from the published work of journalists and other agents of the media. States need to have their own team on the spot, whose impartiality, loyalty and appreciation of the wider perspectives of policy can be relied upon. Another increasingly important aspect of a modern embassy's work concerns the promotion of its country's trade, both by trying to obtain profitable governmental deals and by providing advice and assistance for private exporters. This, too, underlines the usefulness of a diplomatic service and is often referred to.

But what receives quite remarkably little comment is the indispensability of diplomacy for the simple but essential task of maintaining day–to–day contact with other states on a whole range of issues. States, being notional persons, cannot speak to each other in the manner of individuals. They have to do so through their official representatives and there has to be no doubt regarding the authenticity of those who claim to speak for them. Further, most of what is said needs to be said in conditions which are assuredly private. It is hard to see how these requirements could be adequately met other than through the exchange of officially accredited representatives. No doubt a series of electronic devices would be set up, similar to the 'hot line' which presently runs between Washington and Moscow for use in situations of great emergency. But problems of eavesdropping and authenticity would presumably arise in connection with the regular use of such arrangements and they would in any event lack that personal touch which is said—and I imagine rightly—to be an important element in diplomacy.

Be that as it may, the fact is that the diplomatic system is at present, as it has been for centuries past, the means by which states communicate with each other. A country wishing to pass a message to another will normally transfer it through its embassy in the foreign country, or alternatively through the foreign country's embassy in the 'home' capital. Thus, if states have interests in common they almost invariably (the only clear exception I am aware of being Syria and Lebanon) find it highly inconvenient not to have diplomatic relations with each other. Such inconvenience occurs not infrequently, for the breaking off of diplomatic relations as a gesture of displeasure is resorted to much more often than used to be the case. In these situations contact has to be maintained through a willing and reliable third party—Switzerland being a popular choice for this role—but it is not the happiest arrangement.

In sum, the communications aspect of diplomacy seems to me to be its core. Moreover it is an essential core if states are to have regular and complicated relations with each other, relations being impossible in the absence of communication. This, too, is one of the reasons why, in my book, there is an international society. As I conceive it, a necessary condition of society is communication. Internationally, this crucial element is provided by the diplomatic system.

NOTES

[1] Quoted in G. F. Kennan, *Memoirs, 1950–1963* (Boston: Little, Brown, 1972), p. 289.

[2] Quoted in G. A. Craig, *From Bismarck to Adenauer* (Baltimore: Johns Hopkins University Press, 1958), p.16.

[3] W. Hayter, *The Kremlin and the Embassy* (London, 1966), p. 149.

---

20. The Future of Diplomats

Charles Maechling, Jr.

Charles Maechling, Jr., an international lawyer, was a decision-maker in the Department of State from 1961 to 1967, taught the law of the sea at the School of International Service, Washington, D.C., and is a visiting Fellow at Wolfson College, Cambridge University.

Diplomacy stands at a crossroads in the turbulent '80s and with it the future of the career service. No one questions the need for

Excerpted from "The Future of Diplomacy and Diplomats," *Foreign Service Journal* (January 1981), pp. 17–22. Reprinted by permission © 1981 American Foreign Service Association.

a corps of trained foreign service professionals to represent the nation overseas, or the role of the State Department as the formal vehicle for conducting foreign relations, but in practice the department's leadership role in foreign affairs within the government is increasingly subject to challenge. Not only has there been a shift in bureaucratic power from the State Department to the National Security Council, but in many eyes the department is viewed as merely a bureaucratic mechanism to formalize policies and implement decisions arrived at through other channels.

Fifty years ago, in the aftermath of the world war that shattered the old order in Europe, Sir Harold Nicolson sought to identify the reasons for the inability of diplomacy to solve the pressing problems of the postwar era. He set down his answer in a small book entitled *Diplomacy,* subsequently updated in his Chichele Lectures at Oxford in 1953, which called for a return to the traditional methods of the old diplomacy, which he defined as the "conduct of relations between civilized states." With impeccable literary grace—and remarkable selectivity of historical example—he traced the evolution of the diplomatic method from its origins in the Greek city states, through Byzantium, Venice and 18th century France, to its apotheosis in Edwardian Europe. He concluded his analysis by scathingly enumerating the anarchical and barbaric forces that were threatening to destroy it.

In Nicolson's idealized picture the old diplomacy, grounded in the European system of nation-states, was the outgrowth of a natural hierarchy of power, in which larger states assumed responsibility for the conduct of smaller states, and diplomatic intercourse was entrusted to a corps of professionals who insured that relations were conducted according to principles of "courtesy, confidence and discretion." Nicolson seems to equate the diplomatic method almost exclusively with negotiation, though not in the operational sense we think of today; he saw it as a continuous, confidential and discreet process of adjusting relationships and differences between sovereigns. He says nothing about other aspects of diplomatic representation—military, commercial, public information. The reporting function is taken for granted.

Nicolson saw the primary threat to traditional diplomacy as originating not so much from the break-up of colonial empires or dramatic advances in transportation and communication, disruptive as these were to the civilized tenor and measured pace of diplomatic intercourse, as from the rise of popular democracy and the application to the conduct of external affairs of the "ideas and practices which in the conduct of internal affairs, had for generations been regarded as the essentials of liberal democracy." In brief, like his later American counterpart, George Kennan, Nicolson bewailed the intrusion of domestic factors into the conduct of foreign relations.

Today, Nicolson's historical perspective seems almost ludicrously culture-bound and his standards of international behavior unbelievably artificial. (Can the term "responsibility" be seriously applied to the three partitions of Poland? to the rape of the Danish duchies by Prussia? to the repeated invasions of Italy by France? to the suppression of the Hungarian rising by Russia?) Profoundly disturbed by the impact of messianic Wilsonian idealism on the peace negotiations of 1919, and the rejection of the Versailles treaty by the Senate, Nicolson viewed the diplomatic method as one of the last entrenchments of civilization—an extension of the upper-class norms of Edwardian Europe, whose stratified class distinctions and traditions of civility he unconsciously extrapolated to the international arena. In order to nail down the indispensability of his class and educational tradition to diplomacy, he rather artfully narrowed the definition of the diplomatic function to exclude such difficult and inconvenient areas as the economics and technology that had already transformed European society and were rapidly revolutionizing warfare.

Dismayed by the League of Nations—and even more by the United Nations—Nicolson regarded their proceedings not as part of the "negotiating" (i.e., diplomatic) process but as "exercises in forensic propaganda." Appalled by the "diplomacy by insult or diplomacy by loudspeaker" which first made an appearance in the era of the fascist dictators, he equally rejected the intrusions of popularly-elected politicians, especially American ones.

Nicolson's analysis (if it can be flattered by such an appellation) is useful today for its advocacy of certain timeless virtues in the conduct of relations between states—reliability, truthfulness, discretion, firmness, and consistency. Where his analysis failed fifty years ago—and where similar attempts fail today—is in its incomplete comprehension of the underlying idiom of history and human development, of which relations between governments and modalities of international intercourse can only be a reflection. Today the forces destructive of the old diplomacy that were operative in the '20s and '30s have been intensified and multiplied many times over. A return to the past is impossible.

The crisis confronting diplomacy in the 1980s can only be understood as part of the much larger crisis confronting the nation-state. Despite all the frenzied manifestations of nationalism and the proliferation of new nations, the basic reality to the latter part of the 20th century is that "One World" is rapidly becoming a fact. The steady and inexorable shrinkage of the planet to the dimensions of a global village, combined with quantum leaps in the advance of technology and the social and economic development of hitherto backward regions is daily making the nation-state more obsolete at every level of international intercourse. As this process accelerates, the traditional modalities and instrumentalities have become too narrow and stereotyped to accommodate the traffic.

At the risk of belaboring the obvious, here are some of the factors that are rapidly changing the shape of diplomacy:

(1) The Revolution in Communications and Transportation This is not merely a question of the extension overseas of the long arm of the executive branch, thereby reducing the importance of ambassadors and diplomatic missions. Of far greater impact are the multi-level channels of communications and transportation that now bind societies together, and saturate them with information on every facet of political, economic and social life. The proliferation of news and information media—ranging from scholarly and technical journals at one end of the spectrum to radio and television at the other—has created so many information outlets that no significant development can be kept in isolation and analyzed for long.

In addition, the breadth of media coverage now dwarfs official coverage to the point of making the latter hopelessly narrow, no matter how much deeper its penetration. Mass communication also unleashes governmental propaganda, directed at a nation's own citizens, neighboring countries, and the rest of the world, on an unparalleled scale. Air transportation has compressed the time frame of international intercourse and made isolation of criminal activities inside national boundaries impossible.

(2) Extension of the Role of Government In every nation today, whether socialist or nominally free, the role of government in regulating the social and economic welfare of its citizens has projected the state into every level of commercial and financial life. In the United States, a governmental interest is present in a whole range of transactions untouched by government thirty years ago. This has generated corresponding pressures on government from the business, labor and societal sectors affected. Government has everywhere extended its control over society and the person to the point where even in free societies the citizen has little redress except at election time. The effect on foreign relations is to expand government's constitutional mandate to intervene in transactions and activities extending overseas.

(3) Advanced Technology The transformation of warfare by science and technology has not only created a "balance of terror" in nuclear armaments, but made the technology factor a crucial element in military readiness and comparative military strength. It is also transforming industry all over the world, on the one hand increasing productivity, on the other increasing energy consumption and vulnerability to economic and military disruption. The march of technology introduces an element of perpetual change into society, strongly accentuating the interdependence factor, discussed below.

(4) Global Interdependence The voracity of advanced industrial societies for fuel and raw materials has made national self-sufficiency a thing of the past. The economies of advanced industrial societies like the United States, Japan and Western Europe have become vulnerable. But dependence on foreign energy sources is only one aspect of the *interdependence* of advanced industrial societies on each other and the Third World. For nearly all countries, exports provide the foreign exchange to pay for food, fuel and other imports on which the standard of living, and in a few cases like Britain and Japan, the physical survival of the population, depends. Economic self-sufficiency is almost everywhere an idle dream, except at the price of return to a subsistence economy and a medieval way of life. Environmental effects are also global in character, inextricably linked in such matters as toxic discharges and oil spills to the economic life of industrial societies. Moreover, multi-level relationships between nations now continue through periods of extreme political hostility and even war.

(5) Egalitarianism—Mass Education A rising level of general education and social equality has become both a precondition and inevitable consequence of technological progress and economic development. As mass education takes hold there is no way of containing popular participation in the governing process, however crude or indirect. There is no longer any way of containing ideas—and ideologies. Even the most repressive governments pay involuntary tribute to pop-ular sentiment by feeling the need to justify their policies. Egalitarianism is replacing stratification by class whether or not accompanied by political freedoms.

(6) Acceleration of Change Every nation, whether advanced or less developed, now stands on a moving walkway from which it falls off at its peril. Economic development is the name of the game in the Third World, and technological progress in the advanced industrial countries. Together with mass education they stimulate societal change and fuel rising expectations. Constant political and economic adjustment becomes necessary to make society work, introducing a component of instability into foreign relations, as well.

The convergence of these factors produces effects that make obsolete the conduct of foreign relations as a distinct and separate field of political activity. Internal and external affairs are now inextricably mixed up. Overseas developments frequently dictate popular responses at variance with foreign policy goals or commitments; these translate into internal political imperatives that cannot help but interfere with the steady pursuit of foreign policy goals. The points of impact where overseas developments strike the domestic economy and social structure have now multiplied to the point where it has become virtually impossible for an administration to consistently pursue foreign policy goals without being subject to pressure from special interest groups, usually applied through Congress.

There is, of course, nothing new in the role that special interest pressures play in the formation of foreign policy—witness the effects of tariff policy and racial discrimination on US relations with Japan during the '20s; of the China lobby on US relations in East Asia during the '50s. What is different today is the degree to which the breakdown of a native American ethos has lowered resistance to ethnic, racial and special interest particularity. This trend has been so encouraged by governmental demagoguery that decision-making, both in the domestic and foreign fields, is in danger of being paralyzed by pressures at best irrelevant and at worst actually inimical to the national interest. In the last four years alone, the influence of the Greek lobby on arms sales to Turkey; of the Jewish lobby on West Bank settlement; of the farm lobby on the grain embargo against the Soviet Union; of the black lobby on relations with South Africa; and of the steel and automobile industries on competing Japanese imports, has each been allowed total latitude of influence, without regard to countervailing strategic or political considerations. This intrusion of special interest pleading into the policymaking process is of course given full exposure by the press and mass media, thereby reinforcing pressure on members of Congress who might otherwise feel free to exercise independent judgment.

A second consequence has been the proliferation of non-governmental links between countries. Every region and especially the advanced industrial areas, is now interconnected with a complex network of economic, communications and societal ties no longer susceptible of containment with established channels of government. The transactions of the international banking community in any given week now totally swamp the capacity of the leading industrial nations to trace them, let alone control them. Technology flow proceeds at so many levels, and by so many different routes, that the export control system can only hope to cover major categories of military equipment and then imperfectly.

To the extent that states extend their regulatory coverage to a given field of activity, that coverage now automatically spills over into foreign territory, creating conflicts of jurisdiction and ripple effects on foreign relations. The US government now asserts the right to regulate *any* overseas economic activity, including stock and commodity trading that has a substantial effect within the United States. The statutory mandate of US regulatory agencies to enforce the anti-trust laws and curtail unfair trade practices has led them to police transactions in the stream of US foreign commerce that not only fall within the jurisdictions of foreign governments but are regarded as perfectly legal by those governments.

Some agencies of government, hitherto regarded as exclusively domestic in character, now conduct their own specialized forms of foreign relations, using State Department channels for communications purposes only. The Departments of Justice and Treasury regularly conduct business with counterpart ministries overseas without going through diplomatic channels, and frequently make assertions of US jurisdiction that are regarded by foreign governments as trespasses on sovereignty. Base rights and status-of-forces agreements are negotiated by the Defense Department, and scientific agreements by the National Science Foundation and White House science office, under only the loosest of supervision by the State Department, which has neither the personnel nor the expertise to assert effective control.

One little-noticed example of agency independence took place in 1975 when Secretary Kissinger was engaged in a delicate bit of carrot-and-stick trading with the Soviets. Without informing State, the chairman of the US Maritime Commission negotiated an agreement with the Soviet government establishing reciprocal access to a limited number of ports in each country for US and Soviet-flag vessels. Kissinger was infuriated but had to back down—the Maritime Commission is covered by a statutory mandate unlimited in scope, its chairman is not part of the executive branch.

A side effect of the multiplication of financial and economic relationships and the corresponding spread of governmental regulation has been the introduction of law and legal approaches into areas of foreign relations hitherto the province of traditional diplomacy. Contributing has been the breakdown of European hegemony and the challenge to the consensual methods of the old diplomacy posed in international forums by the socialist *bloc* and the more radical regimes of the Third World. As a result, the American style of international agreement, based on a contractual model that aims at covering every conceivable contingency, is gradually replacing the traditional European-style treaty or agreement, which tends to be tersely worded and aimed primarily at defining the intent of the parties. Moreover, the multilevel nature of international relationships has entangled virtually every act of state in a thicket of legal complexity—witness the recent inability of the US government to take prompt action in freeing Iranian government assets and pursuing the ill-gotten wealth of the shah.

. . . Within the United States the complexity of the subject matter of diplomacy has opened the way to formation of a new foreign policy elite of full-time specialists in defense and foreign affairs matters, centered in foundations, universities and think tanks. Special interest pressures exerted through Congress and other public channels by business, labor or farm groups at least reflect legitimate economic and societal interests that in any event would have to find expression through the political process. Their objectives are tangible and their methods plainly visible. Much more elusive are the goals and methods of the new elite, which has replaced the traditional establishment of bankers, politicians and lawyers. Its members employ words and ideas as weapons, gauge success and failure by the influence they exert over the political leadership, and camouflage a remorseless quest for power and riches under a protective mantle of selfless scholarship.

The creation of an outside community of academic specialists capable of infiltrating the bureaucracy and imposing its ideas on experienced military and civilian leaders is unique to the United States. Originally confined to areas of science, technology and advanced engineering, where expert advice could only be obtained from outside the government, the thirst for ostensibly objective scientific opinion has now spread to areas of foreign relations formerly reserved to the diplomatic practitioners. No other country would permit the career ranks of its government to be infiltrated by theoreticians with free license to impose their ideas on foreign policy and no accountability for the success or failure of their advice except to the politician who for a brief period gives them employment.

Unlike the old establishment, with deep roots in society and no personal advantage to be gained from public service other than enhanced standing in the community, the new elite is dominated by ambitious intellectuals whose entire life is wrapped up in their professional achievements, and whose ambitions—social and financial, as well as academic—depend on the influence they can exert on the decision-making process. Secure in tenured positions, with no obligation to actually educate, its more influential members are given facilities, research assistance, and travel opportunities on a scale impossible for business and professional men in other fields to match. Battening on government or industry grants, they have the mobility to shuttle from outside consultancies to inside policy jobs in a way denied to professionals locked into corporations and law firms by business commitments, retirement plans and shareholdings. Their continued access to colleagues in power is assured by the community's operation as both personnel recruiting ground and source of future employment.

The ascent to power of this new elite has a conspiratorial side inimical to good government. The financing of some of its leaders has been concealed from public view and is on a scale that leaves them in some degree captive to the policy biases of their patrons. The links between Kissinger, the Rockefeller interests and the late shah certainly distorted US policy toward Iran. The Trilateral Commission, while certainly not a conspiracy in the crude sense portrayed by the right-wing fringe, was nevertheless converted into an *instrumentality* advancing the political fortunes of Governor Jimmy Carter at an early stage of his presidential candidacy—with the predictable result that after Carter was elected to office key national security jobs were given to the commission's directorate, headed by Zbigniew Brzezinski, who in effect dictated his options in accordance with their own predilections and those of their sponsors.

The creative talents of the more gifted members of the new elite should not blind the public to the fact that they have imported values into government that are alien to the American tradition in both the figurative and literal sense. Their addiction to grand designs and resounding formulations, coupled with Old World affinities and hatreds brought over in their baggage, has severely damaged the American reputation for pragmatism, candor and moral principle. Their public pronouncements sometimes betray a shocking ignorance of the Constitution and separation of powers. Their personal traits, ranging from paranoia and deviousness to loose-lipped braggadocio, have repeatedly poisoned the climate of confidence so essential to a healthy relationship between colleagues and allies. As a result, honest reporting and the frank interchange of conflicting viewpoints have been made extremely hazardous for senior officials with careers at stake.

These strands come together in the phenomenal growth of the National Security Council NSC, headed by the president's national security adviser, at the expense of the secretary and Department of State. The interrelationship between foreign and domestic affairs, often invoked by apologists to justify this trend, is not the determinative factor—that connection is divisible by the very nature of government and, until recently, was never permitted to diminish the supremacy of the secretary in his own sphere. The intractable new development is the encroachment of powerful departments and agencies with legitimate interests and independent statutory missions in the foreign affairs field that give them a degree of operational autonomy impossible for the department to control. The need for a coordinating mechanism to weigh the diverse interests and present balanced policy options to the president is obvious. Repeated

efforts to endow the secretary of state with enough authority to exercise a coordinating role have run into a wall of departmental and congressional resistance. The rise of the NSC has been the inevitable result.

What do these lessons portend for the future? Can diplomacy survive the welter of conflicting forces that threaten to swamp it? Will the career services disintegrate into an aggregation of specialists bound together at the top by the small minority of managerial generalists who have managed to rise above the specialities that gave them a head start in the fist place?

. . . an analogy to the British legal system may be in order. Just as the career diplomatic service of every nation seeks to maintain a monopoly on the conduct of foreign relations with other governments, so has the elite corps of barristers sought to remain the exclusive channel for litigating disputes between private parties in the British courts. That system is now in a continual state of crisis. As the subject matter of commerical and financial disputes has grown in size and complexity, the necessity of prosecuting a claim in the courts through an intermediary totally unversed in the technical intricacies of the subject matter has confronted the system with a dilemma. Either the issues must be broadened to allow a wide range of economic and sociological data to be introduced as evidence, or the issues must be narrowed and refined until they turn on a few critical questions of law and fact capable of being addressed by a classically-trained barrister and adjudicated by a classically-trained judge (there are no juries in British civil cases). The United States has taken the former route—the only feasible way of rendering justice in anti-trust cases and regulatory proceedings. The British have taken the other route, squeezing out substance until they reach an authentic legal question at the core. The price, however, has been judicial restraint that amounts to retreat from the burning social and economic issues of British life.

Diplomacy faces a similar predicament. Unless its institutions and practioners can master the complex transactions making up the network of transnational relationships, they cannot hope to deal with the disputes that these transactions generate. Once again, the options are contraction to preserve institutional integrity versus diversification to achieve broader horizons. In the United States these choices have been sharpened by the emergence of the new foreign policy elite, ready and eager to fill any vacuums created by the incapacity of the career services. . . .

Operating in a Goldfish Bowl: Sooner or later the department is going to have to tighten its rules on public disclosure or risk having its hand forced at every turn of the diplomatic wheel. Foreign governments have not become quite expert at manipulating the media; and the media are now locked into a competitive cycle that makes them willing collaborators. Absent official authorization, the standard reply of the working level to all requests for information for the press should be "no comment," and referral of the questioner to the department's spokesman. The "anonymous official source" label should be especially avoided: it has been thoroughly abused by the press in the form of unverifiable inventions.

Even the most inflexible traditionalist now understands that policies and negotiating positions must be formulated with unexpected exposure in mind. Sooner or later, the proliferation of leakage points and the compulsion of even the most authoritarian government to show achievement, or at least purposeful activity, makes disclosure inevitable. Less understood is that the currency of private undertakings and corridor assurances on which diplomats set such store is now of such transient and uncertain value as to be almost worthless. Statements on the public record, no matter how opaque or misleading, provide the only firm basis from which to derive the intentions of other governments and frame the policies of one's own. For a brief period at least, these represent a commitment by the leadership to its own people and the rest of the world.

If any conclusion is possible, a prediction can be made that the diplomat of the future is doomed to perform his functions in precisely that atmosphere that Harold Nicolson so justly abhorred. The profession has become both impossibly demanding and physically dangerous; the amenities and privileges to diplomatic life greatly attenuated. The consolation is that no other profession provides such a ringside seat to history in the making—and a chance to make history oneself.

---

21.   The Twilight of Diplomacy

George C. McGhee

George C. McGhee, who was with the State Department for 20 years, served as ambassador to Turkey and the Federal Republic of Germany and as undersecretary for political affairs.

Today the nations of the world seem incapable of conducting successful diplomacy. Incidents that in the past would have been re-

Excerpted from the *Foreign Service Journal* April, 1985, pp. 34–37. Reprinted by permission Copyright © 1985 The American Foreign Service Association.

solved through negotiation, now all too frequently become nagging problems or even wars. The cost has been high in both lives and resources.

There are many reasons behind this setting of the diplomatic sun, and some of them are due to irreversible changes in the structure of governments and societies around the world. Others, however, can be reversed, or at least coped with. In particular, a greater willingness by our leaders to make decisions instead of simply letting policy evolve haphazardly, and to instruct the public as to what can realistically be accomplished, would do much to make a new dawn possible.

Diplomacy is used here in the broadest sense, and includes all negotiations and exchanges of views across national borders that are intended to lessen tensions or bring about agreements between countries. Diplomacy is at its best when, unseen and unheard, it works successfully through secret channels to avoid open breaks between governments. Such efforts usually go unrecognized and unrewarded but are nevertheless essential to effective management of foreign relations. Diplomacy is often conducted openly in bilateral or multilateral forums. It is also—perhaps increasingly so—carried out in public, through both official speeches and the media.

It has not been long since our last diplomatic heyday. During World War II and in the immediate postwar era, there were many examples of successful diplomacy. Drawn together by the threat of Nazi domination, the Allied governments resolved their difficulties sufficiently to fight a successful war and reach general agreement on organizing the peace. When Soviet communism threatened Western Europe, those countries took up our suggestion and organized the Marshall Plan to rescue their economy. Soon afterward, NATO was established to defend Western Europe against Soviet aggression. And there were many other examples of successful negotiations and cooperative efforts during this period: The financial agreements of Bretton Woods of 1944, the preservation of Greece and Turkey through the Truman Doctrine and Greek-Turkish aid in 1947, Ralph Bunche's mediation in behalf of the United Nations during the 1948 Arab-Israeli war, the defense of Berlin in the face of the 1948 Soviet blockade, the Tripartite Declaration of 1950, the Japanese Peace Treaty and the Austrian State Treaty of 1955, and others. There have in recent years been other successful negotiations: President Nixon's and Henry Kissinger's agreements creating SALT I, establishing relations with China, and the separation of Arab-Israeli forces in the Sinai. After a lull under President Ford, President Carter negotiated SALT II (not ratified), and the Camp David agreement and Panama Canal Treaties.

There have been no such successes during the Reagan administration. The recent Geneva negotiation between Secretary of State George Shultz and Soviet Foreign Minister Andrei Gromyko was promising, but it resulted only in an agreement on the format for further arms talks. Even though the negotiations themselves have finally begun, it will be at least two to three years before all three sets of related negotiations can be completed—if they ever are completed. The positions of the two sides remain unchanged.

Since the postwar successes of diplomacy, the world has seen major changes in the relations among countries. The colonial system has ended, and peace has lasted long enough for us to hope that the cycle of world wars has broken. Unparalleled prosperity, although interrupted by a world recession, has come to the industrialized states. Western Europe has enjoyed great benefits from this economic resurgence, but it has not been able to generate enough political power to regain its pre-war role in the world. The United States, too, is no longer the pre-eminent power. The Soviet Union, although weak economically, has gained on us in military strength, solidified its position in Eastern Europe, conquered Afghanistan, and established strong influence in Cuba, Angola, Ethiopia, and South Yemen. Along with these shifts, there has also been a marked diffusion of power. Germany and Japan have emerged as economic giants, while the OPEC countries, Brazil, Mexico, South Africa, and South Korea have also increased their importance in the world economy. The United Kingdom, on the other hand, has declined both economically and as a world power.

During this same period, there has been

a startling decline in the ability of governments to settle their conflicts through negotiation and agreement. This applies not only to conflicts between communist and anticommunist countries, but even to those between members of the "free-world." Instead of negotiations and despite the foundation of the United Nations, local wars have proliferated. Severe tensions have arisen, which may well lead to even more wars. Relations between the United States and U.S.S.R. have worsened. Until recently, there was a complete lapse of arms control negotiations. The SALT talks, which had shown fruitful results since their inception in 1969 have, following U.S. failure to ratify SALT II in 1980, ceased to exist—drying up one of the most fruitful U.S.-Soviet points of contact. Open denunciation and threats, confrontation, unilateral action, invasion without negotiation, have all become the order of the day.

In 1980, Iraq invaded Iran without warning over the control of the Shatt-al-Arab waterway and Iranian provocations with the Kurds and Shiites. Both countries are being destroyed by the conflict, but neither is making a serious effort at negotiation despite U.N. efforts. Likewise, neither the United Kingdom nor Argentina made a serious effort to resolve their long-festering dispute over the Falkland Islands before the Argentine invasion, and former Secretary of State Alexander Haig's efforts to mediate fell on deaf ears. In addition, Haig, his successor, and others in the U.S. government have made little effort to negotiate our basic differences with Nicaragua, against whom we are fighting an undeclared war. Even after Nicaragua's acceptance of the Contadora Group proposals, we raised some new exceptions, and the President and others have stated that their goal is to make the Sandinistas cry "uncle."

When the Soviets had difficulties with neighboring Afghanistan, they did not stop to negotiate, but invaded the country on the pretext of aiding the existing communist regime, whose leader they immediately killed. But despite U.N. efforts, there is no prospect of negotiations leading to Soviet withdrawal. And, whether or not the recent U.S. action in Grenada was justified, the fact is that we made no effort to obtain a peaceful solution before we invaded.

In the Middle East, there have been a number of attempts to negotiate differences, but the unwillingness of many parties to resolve these peacefully has made for a catalogue of failures. The Camp David accords were flawed by a failure to understand Israel's firm intentions to continue West Bank settlements. President Reagan's peace proposals of September 1982, which were both sound and consistent with previous U.S. efforts, were spurned by all the parties concerned. The Israeli invasion of Lebanon, a unilateral action the United States at least officially opposed, disrupted the fragile fabric of that country beyond repair.

We later managed to negotiate the withdrawal of Palestine Liberation Organization forces from Lebanon, but these efforts were negated by the ensuing Christian-Shiite war. Secretary Shultz's efforts to obtain the withdrawal of Israeli and Syrian forces foundered over the latter's refusal. The Saudi peace proposals met a similar end and the Middle East is still in general disarray. The United States has stepped back from its leading role and for the first time since 1948 has no active peace proposal on the table. The recent Arafat-Hussein accord, although rejected by Israel, and the Mubarak initiative, raise hopes, but many road-blocks lie ahead.

As a result of these many conflicts, the world has drifted more and more into a state of international anarchy. Agreements such as the Panama Canal treaties are now lonely and isolated events. They would not be possible today because of Republican opposition. British diplomacy at its best created the new state of Zimbabwe out of Rhodesia, but the U.K. government has had no such success in the Falklands or Northern Ireland.

One of the major reasons for this inability to resolve disagreements without resorting to war has been an apparent breakdown in traditional bilateral diplomacy. The secret day-to-day flow of information and quiet discussions between governments that allow accommodation to develop, instead of conflict, seem to have just about dried up. Ambassadors no longer seem to play the central role they once did in keeping bilateral channels open. Our ambassador in London, for instance, though apparently a well-meaning man, was unceremoniously removed because, having no previous diplomatic experience, he was not considered effective. Our ambassador in Paris was reprimanded by the French government for publicly attacking a communist cabinet member. A recent *Wall Street Journal* article highlighted the increasing irrelevance of ambassadors, in some cases, according to the *Journal,* because they are incompetent political appointees, or because they are career officers who are not trusted by the President, or because the President and secretary of state prefer to bypass the ambassador.

Why are we in this situation? What has changed in the world that has caused it? What are the prospects for the future? In the first place, there is a change of atmosphere in the West. As brought out by a recent Atlantic Institute poll, the citizens of the United States and Europe perceive no present threat of general war, or any other imminent critical danger, that would force the Western nations to subordinate their national interests to common goals, even among allies.

There have also been other structural changes affecting diplomacy. Until World War I, Europe was largely run by monarchs, who had almost complete freedom to wage war and make peace. Their plenipotentiaries, usually members of the royal family, were given full powers to negotiate the terms of surrender or conquest, as at the Congress of Vienna at the end of the Napoleonic wars. Rulers then were willing (and unconstrained by public opinion, were able) to accept the most onerous terms of defeat, so they could start re-arming to win the next round.

In the case of democratic governments, however, the chief executive holds much less power and in fact is often a hostage to the political system. The president or prime minister basically represents only his or her own political party and in many cases cannot control its extremist elements. The right wing of the Republican party, for example, can block almost any treaty or policy intended to establish an accommodating relationship with the Soviets. Similarly, the left wing of the Democratic party pushed for protection of human rights over security interests. A head of government today must overcome constant public harassment by opposition parties, who often ignore the merits of the case.

Today, the makers of foreign policy must always consider the political implications of their decisions. This is hardly the basis on which foreign policy should be constructed and often leads to unwise international commitments. In the recent U.S. election, for example, both candidates made promises to the supporters of Israel, Walter Mondale going as far as to advocate moving the U.S. embassy to Jerusalem and accepting the legality of Israel's West Bank settlements.

Another complicating factor in recent years has been the massive invasion of the foreign policy-making process by almost all elements of the government. Secretary of State Dean Acheson, aided by the full confidence of President Truman, had much more freedom of action than Secretary Haig, who in his recent book *Caveat* complained about his inability to obtain access to the president, his irreconcilable differences with the secretary of defense, and his harassment by White House assistants. It is a hopeful sign that Secretary Shultz appears to have succeeded in gaining control of the State Department, and supremacy as the president's foreign affairs adviser. Today, however, the secretary of state must contend with a bloated National Security Council staff, other federal agencies, and an active and involved Congress. The media increasingly pry into the conduct of foreign policy, often in an overly critical way. As a result, diplomacy is now plagued by premature leaks and conflicting press interpretations, which dry up foreign sources of information and lead to damaging prejudgments and interference.

The growing interdependence of the world—and awareness of that interdependence—has added another burden to diplomacy. The behavior of foreign countries and other international factors have become inextricably intertwined with domestic political interests. Issues that previously were left to the purview of the diplomats now have powerful constituencies. Various ethnic groups in the United States, for example, affect a large portion of our foreign relations: the Israeli lobby's influence over the Middle East policy and relations with the Arab and Islamic states; the Greek and Armenian lobbies' effect on relations with Turkey; the South Asian Indian lobby's growing voice concerning relations with Pakistan; the Polish and other Eastern European lobbies' influence over relations with the U.S.S.R. (although more balanced by overall U.S. interests); the Hispanic community's control over immigration policy and influence on relations with South and Central America; the black concern over relations with South Africa; even the influence of the various descendants of Western European immigrants. In such a situation, few are left to speak for the interests of the country as a whole.

Policymakers must also contend with the special pleading of liberals and conservatives, labor and management, and countless industries, including banking, automobiles, petroleum, steel, and agriculture. More recently, religious groups have begun to exert their influence on international politics. The most extreme example is the Khomeini regime in Iran. In the United States, we see the disruptive effect of various religious groups—Islamic organizations, South Asian sects, Moonies, and the Moral Majority and other rightist Christian organizations—on our relations with other countries.

Extremism is also evident in the growth of international terrorism. Assassinations, kidnappings, airline hijackings, boycotts, and destruction of property will undoubtedly continue, and even increase, further disrupting the delicate fabric of international relations, which relies on the safe passage of government officials, businessmen, and tourists throughout the world. Meaningful negotiations over outstanding issues are much more difficult against such a background. But terrorists are not the only ones exerting extremist pressures on government decision-makers. In many countries, the legitimate political opposition, such as the British Labour party and the West German Social Democrats, have become more polarized against the party in power. Despite having recently been in government themselves, these parties are becoming anti-nuclear, anti-NATO, even anti-United States. Support for the alliance is no longer assured should the governments change; this has enormously complicated our relations.

Governments also contribute to the overwhelming of diplomacy by extremism. In recent years the world has seen the re-emergence of the equivalent of the holy wars of past eras, in the form of ideological conflict. In those earlier times it was not possible to negotiate except after capitulating. One side or the other had to be annihilated. This was as true of the Crusaders as of those who conquered Christians in the name of Allah. Today, the most obvious examples of governmental extremism are the many statements issuing from Moscow, Libya, and Teheran toward the West, particularly the United States. But even President Reagan, by calling the Soviets an evil empire, liars, and cheats, made successful negotiation with them much more difficult. Many right-wing Americans consider the establishment of a government they believe to be "Marxist-Leninist"—in countries such as Nicaragua, where the meaning of the term is barely understood—as *ipso facto* justification for a preventive war. Negotiations are too often undertaken to "win a victory" rather than to solve a problem. If this is the wave of the future, the opportunity for successful diplomacy will be greatly diminished. . . .

22.   Cultural Relations

Frank A. Ninkovich

A frequent contributor to *Diplomatic History,* Frank Anthony Ninkovich received his Doctorate with Distinction from the University of Chicago before entering the foreign service.

Cultural relations can be thought of as two different yet related processes. For students of diplomacy, they are first and foremost a specialized form of statecraft concerned with the management of intellectual influences in international politics. This intellectual diplomacy has deep historical roots. The pharaohs of Egypt, to take only one example from antiquity, demanded young aristocratic hostages of their vanquished foes, not so much as guarantees of good behavior as to inculcate these future leaders with an Egyptian outlook and style of life. Despite an impressive historical pedigree, however, the cultural zone of foreign policy has always remained a fringe area of diplomatic activity and historians have been satisfied by and large to concentrate on the political, economic, and military aspects of foreign policy. In the United States, with which this study is concerned, cultural relations have repeated this pattern of diplomatic marginality and scholarly indifference.

This neglect, if not justifiable, is at least understandable. The U.S. Department of State's programs in cultural relations have been a minor cog in the gearbox of foreign policy. Major questions of "high policy" or even more mundane foreign policy concerns—in other words, the usual stuff of diplomatic history—were not debated, much less decided, by cultural officers. True, over the

Reprinted by permission of the publisher, © Cambridge University Press 1981 *The Diplomacy of Ideas: U.S. Foreign Policy and Cultural Relations* (New York: Cambridge University Press, 1981), (Footnotes have been deleted.)

years the cultural programs have increased greatly in size and, if for no other reason, in importance. Nevertheless, they have continued to occupy a lowly position in the diplomatic pecking order. Given this relatively inconsequential status, it might seem only sensible to view the study of cultural relations as a scholarly analog of the "tertiary recovery" procedures employed by oil producers—that is, as a marginal supplement to played-out political and economic modes of analysis. Be that as it may, this study's aim goes beyond an incremental extension of our knowledge of the policymaking process or the addition of an extra "dimension" to our understanding of U.S. foreign policy.

Although cultural relations are a minor form of diplomacy, at the same time the entire foreign policy process is itself subordinated to larger cultural dynamics. Going beyond the fixation with transnational intellectual contacts, from a macroanthropological perspective cultural relations can be viewed as no less than the totality of relations between cultures. Here one confronts the truly grand processes of diffusion and acculturation that, when viewed as a whole, form a global pattern of intercultural interaction and adaptation. The study of such contacts and their effects provides a lofty conceptual perch from which to survey the dynamics of world history. From such a theoretical height, diplomatic relations of every stripe, the cultural included, constitute but a fraction of all intercultural transactions and exercise a relatively modest influence in the overall scheme of things. By this standard, a nation's foreign policy is only an expression of powerful cultural forces beyond its grasp.

To study one form of cultural relations is inevitably to confront the other, for the diplomatic pursuit of cultural influence is obviously conditioned by its cultural environment. Unfortunately for the study of international relations, the anthropological conception is at present little more than a blunt instrument, well suited only to world-historical speculations. For the elucidation of specific foreign policies, it must give way to more restrained concepts and to more sharply defined choices of subject matter. It is here that the study of cultural diplomacy, traditionally perceived as too narrow to be of much value to students of foreign policy, can serve as a peephole affording at least a partial glimpse of broader vistas. Acknowledging beforehand its inability to penetrate to the source of cultural processes, such a study can at least explore particular visions of those dynamics. It might also shed some indirect light on the nature of cultural influences, internal and external, upon foreign policy.

There are a number of reasons why this should be so. First, the founders of the American cultural programs and their successors possessed a weighty anthropological sense of their task, though it was less than sophisticated in terms of theory. Their conceptions possessed an amazing degree of elasticity, beginning with an elitist fixation on the virtues of intellectual exchanges and expanding in later years to embrace the manipulation of mass education and technological diffusion, but they were always informed by a belief that diplomacy was only a small part of a larger, more fundamental, and ultimately benevolent dynamic of historical change. It was their objective not only to work in harmony with this process by becoming its allies, but also to expedite its self-realization. By the very nature of their concerns, the cultural personnel were forced to confront, if not traditional foreign policy issues, the assumptions underlying those issues. Their consignment to the diplomatic basement, so to speak, gave them access to the foundations of U.S. foreign policy.

There is another point at which this study embraces larger concerns. Culture involves more than patterns of ideas, for ideas are always intimately connected to technological forms and to social structures; that is, they are part of a social geography. The State Department's policies in cultural relations were an organic development, not simply an intellectual response, rooted in an institutional and social environment that mirrored the fundamental values of the larger society. The same was true of other nations to undertake cultural diplomacy in the twentieth century. With a circularity that inheres in the topic, each nation attempted to shape the factors that were in turn shaping it, each in accordance with its traditions. The point is that these peculiarities of "national character" make the cultural programs good material for studying in some detail the influence of domestic factors in the foreign policy process. In particular, the U.S. programs, where tradition played a prominent part, provide an opportunity to study an evolving relationship between ideas and institutions in the context of a rapidly changing international environment. In this way, the study of the cultural programs can illuminate suggestively some of the connections between foreign policy ideas and their social underpinnings.

Finally, the fact that the cultural programs were relatively unburdened by the day-to-day complexities of foreign policy makes them an excellent vehicle for tracing in outline changes in the basic patterns of U.S. foreign policy, patterns that are normally obscured in the study of more intricate diplomatic topics. If the traditional matter of foreign policy is here lacking, its form is enhanced. Even a narrow study of the cultural programs would have been impossible without some inquiry into the major shifts in the conduct and structure of American foreign policy caused by the nation's absorption into the mainstream of international politics. It would be too much to claim that the programs formed a microcosm of U.S. foreign policy. Their development might more usefully be viewed as a metaphor or trope than as a literal model for other policy developments. In addition to providing a general survey of the cultural programs, this history has kept such a larger interpretive purpose in mind.

The programs, then, have a dual significance: as part of the policy process and as symbols of the larger cultural forces at work upon policy. Consequently, the scope of this work is both narrow and broad, modest and ambitious. It is narrow in the sense that it confines itself to a relatively obscure subdivision of the diplomatic community, treating it for a brief time span. It is broad because the events treated herein have a significance that transcends their modest bureaucratic horizons. It is a study of cultural relations, and of culture at work. Considerations of manageability and professional competence dictated restricting the study to a form of cultural relations that is but a pale shadow of the grand anthropological process; but this acknowledgment of limits coexists with a recognition that the resemblance, even though a poor caricature, nonetheless illustrates important features of foreign policy too long neglected. This dualism comes with the topic. Indeed, it is the reason for my fascination with it as well as the source of any importance that it might possess.

Having said this much, I am obliged to make a few remarks on the meaning of that slippery term, "culture." Obviously, it would be presumptuous as well as foolhardy for a historian to tackle a concept that has puzzled generations of anthropologists. Nevertheless, because the word will be repeated until it might come to appear drained of meaning altogether, some comment is in order. The temptation is to make do with some minimally acceptable definition of culture, such as the truism that it is learned behavior or that it represents social heredity. It is, of course, both of these. But this study assumes

more than that. I am among those who hold that culture and culture change are more than simply intellectual or mental phenomena. From the standpoint of the study of diplomacy, material and institutional factors need to be taken into account, if only because power, which lies at the core of international relations, assumes at bottom a palpable form. Thus in the debate over the nature of culture that still rages in anthropological circles, I would ultimately, if only halfheartedly, take my stand with the so-called cultural materialists. By contrast, the cultural enthusiasts of whom I write were zealous proponents of a cultural idealism, an outlook dependent ultimately upon idealistic metaphysical premises concerning the nature of reality. Employing a reductionist logic more often found among materialist thinkers, they viewed the large process of cultural relations as being a function of intellectual relations.

Their views coincided nicely with the anthropological theory of the day. Admittedly, the cultural personnel within the State Department never discarded the crude nineteenth-century evolutionism that had been discredited by Franz Boas and his disciples, a view that saw cultures evolving from primitive, irrational forms into modern liberal-rational entities. Despite the widespread scholarly acceptance of a nonnormative cultural relativism, they preferred to retain their faith in the ultimate triumph of rationality and progress. For the most part, though, their thinking paralleled the mentalist, psychological outlook then enjoying great popularity in American anthropological circles. The American school of historical ethnology, according to one of its prominent practitioners, conceived of cultural diffusion as "a process psychological in essence." This emphasis on psychological factors elevated the role of individually transmitted ideas to supreme importance in explaining externally induced culture change or acculturation. Diffusion came to be perceived largely in terms of the transmission of abstract "culture traits." Consistent with this idealist orientation, the scholars of the Boas school displayed little interest in the material or economic aspects of culture. There is no evidence, however, to suggest that the State Department's cultural personnel were deeply affected by anthropologists' dogmas; more likely both reflected dominant American cultural values and assumptions.

There is no denying the obvious fact that culture is transmitted by individuals or that ideas play a significant role in the processes of diffusion and acculturation. But there is strong reason to question whether the overall workings of intercultural change are dominated by intellectual and individual processes to the exclusion of material and systemic factors. One way of looking at the matter is to conceive of cultures as possessing a permeability gradient that allows material goods and technologies to penetrate their barriers far more rapidly and readily than new ideas. That is why military power ranks first in the concern of nations (and cultural affairs last, usually); it is also the reason why intellectual penetration follows only in the wake of demonstrations of military-economic superiority, and even then to only a limited extent. Where the introduction of new intellectual outlooks appears to precede technologically powered diffusion—the so-called reverse cultural lag—it is usually because of a prior understanding of the concrete power of modern technological forms and a desire to more readily acquire them for domestic use.

This is not an argument for a straightforwardly materialist interpretation of culture and culture change. To say that material forms penetrate more readily is only to point to the strongest feature of culture—its systematic symbolic function. The wisest statesmen have long recognized that military power was of only limited use in dealing with flourishing cultural traditions. China's long history of sinicizing its conquerors provides perhaps the strongest example of the tendency toward cultural inertia. Although one can point to instances of cultural extirpation caused by outside contact, foreign ideas and technologies usually end up adjusting to the limitations imposed by local traditions. Cultures are especially resistant to new patterns of thought, so much so that the introduction of new ideas usually comes to resemble domestication rather than assimilation. The implantation of ideas might make sense from an individual perspective, but it is problematic at best if cultures are viewed as systems.

Thus the arguments for culture as a symbolic organizing medium are well taken, as far as they go. But I think that the symbolic nature of culture is best understood, from an international perspective at least, by jettisoning the idealist view of culture change. To my mind, the crude idealism of the cultural enthusiasts does not provide a tenable historical perspective. Philosophically, the gap between us yawns wide. However, as the foregoing remarks were intended to indicate, I have no wish to deny the significance of ideas or ideals in history; quite to the contrary, this study confirms their importance although it denies their exclusive sway. . . .

chapter 8

THE MANAGEMENT OF ALLIANCES

An alliance may merely involve an agreement to come to each other's assistance should one or another party to the alliance be attacked; or it may provide for joint military plans and strategy in advance of an attack. An alliance may be either offensive or defensive in purpose, or both. If offensive, it may be the means by which one state gains sufficient strength to launch an attack; if defensive, it may be the means by which its members mobilize sufficient strength to deter an attack or, if war occurs, to defend themselves successfully.

In principle, states enter alliances at will, according to their perception of how the balance of power bears upon their own security, interests or objectives. Statecraft acquired a certain reputation for treachery from the frequency with which allies betrayed each other and switched sides for the sake of expediency. In reality, however, modern alliances have been long enduring, reflecting an identity and permanency of interest that itself reflected a distribution of power and ambition among significant powers of considerable historic duration. For example, the pattern in European (and North Atlantic) history for the past 400 years has been for alliances to form as a defense against a single hegemonial power—first against Spain, then against the France of Louis XIV and Napoleon, then against Imperial and Hitlerian Germany, and now against the Soviet Union. For several centuries, England was very much the leader in encouraging these alliances; in the twentieth century that role has fallen to the United States, which has created pacts in different regions of the world, for somewhat different purposes, at the same time.

An alliance may take the form of a treaty or it may be simply an understanding; in either case, it must have the confidence of each party for it to be effective. The North Atlantic Treaty is a legal instrument by which the United States, Canada, and the countries of Western Europe agree to come to each others' support should they be attacked. After the treaty was signed in April 1949, the member nations agreed to form an integrated defense system known as the North Atlantic Treaty Organization (NATO). It was hoped that, by implementing the treaty in advance of hostilities, the Soviet Union would be discouraged from attacking. It was also a condition of European support that American forces be part of the integrated defense system in Europe. The Warsaw Pact was organized by the Soviet Union among the Communist states of Eastern Europe under its control ostensibly to counter the Atlantic alliance. A constant problem for the United States government has been to maintain the confidence of its European allies that it would come to their defense in the likelihood that America itself would come under nuclear attack in a war. John Holmes, a sympathetic Canadian diplomatist, expresses the view in his article in this chapter that one reason for this is that the very form of government in the United States makes *true* consultation difficult if not impossible.

It can thus be seen that alliances have long been characteristic of the international system. If state *B* fears that state *A* harbors aggressive designs, or if state *B* feels itself weaker than state *A* and that state *A* might be tempted to attack, then state *B* can look to an alliance with other states to augment its strength. Alliances are formed as a consequence of the insecurity and unpredictability that prevails among states. They exist primarily to enhance the security of its members. Alliances do not exist to eliminate war but to eliminate insecurity; if by deterring an attack or maintaining the status quo an alliance also achieves peace, then so much the better. But it ought to be kept clear that, while alliances arise out of conflict and insecurity, they may have the effect of increasing tension and hostility. In entering into an alliance, states seek to augment their strength and thereby improve their chances of deterring an attack or of defending against an attack. Alliances do not eliminate or necessarily reduce the likelihood of war. While prevention of war is obviously desirable, the ultimate test is victory should war break out.

Hence, an alliance may rest upon one or several foundations. These include:

(1) an identity of interest among its members in security against a common enemy;

(2) a common or similar ideology; or

(3) parallel but not common or identical interests.

The strongest motive among nations for forming an alliance is a sense of threat from some other power or powers to their security and independence. In the absence of any other assurance, states look for allies to augment their own strength. On the other hand, if no such threat exists, there is no need for allies.

A second basis for forming an alliance is ideology. As Holmes points out in this chapter, the North Atlantic Treaty alliance is reinforced by its members sharing a common ideology: democracy, free elections, individual rights, and a similar economic system. The Sino-Soviet conflict provides a contrasting illustration of the weakness of ideology alone as the basis of an alliance. Immediately after the communists came to power in China, Mao Tse-tung formed an alliance with Moscow. According to Marxist-Leninist ideology, history is fated to be the story of mortal enmity and conflict between the capitalist and socialist states. What could be more inevitable than two Communist states sharing a powerful ideological bond also forming a political and military alliance? Fortunately, the history of Sino-Soviet relations demonstrates the weakness of ideology as the basis for an alliance in the absence of other requisites. As soon as it became apparent to China that Moscow was intent upon advancing Russia's national interests at China's expense by withholding nuclear technology and support in China's struggle against the United States and India, the underlying fear and resentment each has of the other came to the fore and quickly revealed the superficiality of their common ideology as a bond of alliance. The rival claims of each to the leadership of the world communist movement only reflected and reinforced the underlying national and cultural hostilities rooted in insecurity and rivalry along a common frontier extending from central Asia to the Pacific Ocean. As Wolfowitz explains in his selection, keeping such a system in working order takes real diplomacy.

A common ideology may reinforce and facilitate the working of an alliance, but it is no guarantee that the interest of all members will remain identical, especially if changing circumstances reduce the degree of fear and insecurity that provided the initial impetus for the alliance. General Charles de Gaulle withdrew French forces from NATO in 1965 (though he did not abrogate France's membership in the treaty) because he believed that it was being used to maintain American control over Western Europe. It also suited the needs of his own leadership to claim that the interests of the European states were being sacrificed to the interests of the United States. The French people did not repudiate de Gaulle's action because by 1965 the magnitude and immediacy of the Soviet threat appeared to be receding. With the Soviet invasion of Czechoslovakia in 1968 and the subsequent growth of Soviet military power, France returned to a closer association with NATO. Although somewhat weakened, the identity of interest felt by its respective members remains remarkably strong.

Not every alliance rests upon an *identity* of interest between its members. Some alliances are based upon *parallel* interests. For example country *A* may be interested in securing an air or naval base in country *B* as part of its security: country *B* may consider the threat that *A* perceives as irrelevant to its own interests, but *B* wants economic and military assistance from *A* against a neighbor. In that case *A* and *B* may form an alliance based not upon identical interests but upon parallel interests. The weakness and danger inherent in this kind of alliance is that with neither having the same purpose or objective, each may employ the alliance more to its advantage that the other is willing to concede. Both the United States and the Soviet Union have entered into many such alliances which have seldom enjoyed the same record of success as NATO. For example, Pakistan joined the U.S.-sponsored Southeast Asia Treaty Organization (SEATO), not as a bulwark against communist expansion, but to secure American military equipment for its conflict with India. As a consequence, the United States antagonized India and gained little tangible benefit from its alliance with Pakistan. Although the Southeast Asia Treaty, signed by England and France and several Asian states, called for a common defense against communist aggression; in the absence of any genuine commitment, only Thailand voluntarily supported the United States in Vietnam. Similarly, other Third World regimes have formed alliances with the United States, not because of a shared identity of interest in stopping communism or maintaining regional stability, but to strengthen the regime against its own population, or to reinforce its ambitions at the expense of its neighbors. The case of Iran provides a classic example of this type of alliance. In principle, Washington and the Shah shared parallel interests, but the alliance led the United States to ignore the danger of the ends to which the Shah was using the relationship prior to his replacement by the intensely anti-American Ayatollah Khomeini. Conversely, when the Egyptian leader Anwar Sadat became distrustful of the ends to which the Soviet Union was using its alliance with Egypt, he broke the alliance and today Cairo works closely with Washington though they are not formal allies.

It must be noted that alliances, like foreign aid, are a vital tool of any great power's diplomacy, but they cannot be made to serve too many purposes without destroying their integrity and usefulness. The strongest type of alliance is one whose members share an identical security interest. The weakest and most dangerous type of alliance is one in which the parties are pursuing disparate ends which may prove to not even be parallel. An alliance can suffer if it is made to serve objectives, too many of which are tangential to or derogative of its principal purpose. For example, the Pentagon and American arms manufacturers may find the sale of military equipment so advantageous that they turn the alliance into an arms bazaar and fuel the resentment of the local population against the alliance. Iran is the most striking example to date.

An alliance may exist without a formal treaty. This is the situation that exists between the United States and Israel. Successive administrations backed by Congress have made commitments to the security of Israel in lieu of a formal alliance. The basis of the "alliance" is twofold: a moral commitment to the right of the Israelis to a homeland and a stake in the stability of the region. Washington fears that if it abandoned Israel, more, not less, chaos would ensue. This puts Israel at an advantage in exploiting the relationship to its benefit, which brings us to yet another controversial feature of alliances.

Alliances frequently involve an unequal sharing of costs and benefits. An alliance may well be, in Mancur Olson's terminology, a "collective good"—something in which all share equally in its benefits, although all may not be obliged to contribute equally to its costs. The North Atlantic Treaty Organization provides ample evidence of the controversies to which this unequal sharing may give rise. The North Atlantic Treaty was established at a time when Europe was still recovering from the war and too weak to defend itself. The entire burden of both the alliance and of Europe's economic recovery had to be borne by America. Nearly four decades later, Europe (like Japan) not only has recovered but constitutes a powerful trade partner as well. Yet the United States must continue to bear the burden of the costs. Try as it may to shift the burden, it has not been able to do so. Why? Because the American stake in NATO is so substantial that the other members know even if they do not carry an equal share of the military costs, Washington has little choice but to go along. This does not mean that the Europeans do not make a very substantial contribution both in the form of money and manpower (France and Germany still retain conscription). The United States has also tried, without much success, to make its contribution to NATO a condition of favorable economic treatment by its European allies, but as Clive Archer has pointed out, the "idea that the United States inveigled the Europeans into NATO by a mixture of Cold War rhetoric and Marshall Aid no longer stands up to the evidence."[1] As Washington encountered economic difficulties—balance-of-payment deficits, loss of jobs in certain industries, inflation—it sought to get the European governments to afford the United States relief through favorable treatment. The Europeans made some concessions, but refuse to weaken or sacrifice their own economies to save America the trouble of correcting its own mistakes and failings.

NATO was originally established to defend Europe, not the Middle East or Indochina. As the American role as a world power became more marked and the struggle with Russia has taken on a global aspect, Washington has found the Europeans unwilling to back the United States everywhere. This has led to some harsh disagreements, especially over Afghanistan, but also over the Arab-Israeli conflict particularly over the military strike against Muammar Qaddafi. Nevertheless, the logic behind the NATO alliance is so powerful that the disagreements so far have not led to either a breakup or significant weakening of the alliance. As long as Russia appears as a military threat, Europe will continue to rely upon the United States and NATO for its security. Unity and morale among its members depends upon coordinating economic relations, policy vis-a-vis the alliance's principal opponent, and military strategy. As Wolfowitz points out, there is no substitute for fear in making an alliance work.

An alliance exists to augment its members' security, not to avoid war. The research of Kegley and Raymond in this chapter shows that historically peace is best preserved when there is flexibility in alliance commitments. Nonalliance states like Switzerland and Sweden escape war; they benefit from their geographic position but also from the "collective good" in that their security, too, is protected by the alliance system which constrains the Soviet Union.

It stands to reason that if alliances exist because of insecurity and conflict that characterize international politics, they do not exist to eliminate war but to eliminate insecurity. An alliance exists either because one side wants to *change* the status quo, as was clearly the intent of the anti-Comintern (communist international) pact of the 1930s which joined Germany, Italy, and Japan in a course

---

1. Clive Archer, "NATO then and now," *The World Today*, 42, no. 3, (March 1986); 55, a useful review article of five recent analyses of the Alliance by European writers.

of aggression or to *defend* the status quo. It also stands to reason that if conflict and insecurity are the motives for joining an alliance, alliances themselves may increase rather than reduce the incidence of conflict and hence, insecurity. Alliances, by augmenting each side's strength, may deter the other side; but they may also increase tension and hostility, especially if neither side feels it can afford to let the other get away with anything. World War I appears to have been inevitable because of the combination of tension, hostility, emotionalism, and rigidity that was engendered by the opposing alliance systems. The "guns of August" 1914 did not go off entirely by themselves, but the chance to cool them off had been progressively eliminated by the unwillingness on either side—the German or Entente side—to avoid the showdown over the Sarajevo incident for fear of weakening its alliance system. The Soviet Union and the United States have probably not gone to war, in spite of their alliances, because of the threat of self-destruction that nuclear war poses. Hence, the supreme irony of the past generation is that peace has been served by the most terrible weapon of war yet devised by man.

DISCUSSION QUESTIONS

1. Upon what values or aims are the three types of alliance discussed in this introduction based?

2. What type of alliance is most conducive to peace, according to Kegley and Raymond?

3. Why does the North Atlantic Treaty alliance exemplify the problem of unequal sharing of costs? Are Warsaw Pact costs equally unequal? In what sense?

4. Can the United States expect its NATO, ANZUS, and Japanese allies to share its global responsibilities? Does this mean that the alliances are not worth anything to the United States? What might Wolfowitz say about NATO?

5. Why is it so necessary to the United States to convince its European allies that, despite or perhaps because of changes and gains by the Soviet Union in weapons systems, the United States commitment is still valid? What is the ultimate price that the commitment may entail?

6. Why is it that, according to Holmes, "the dumbbell won't do"? Is his symbolism or analogy a useful or sound one, in your opinion?

23. The Dumbbell Won't Do

John W. Holmes

Assistant Undersecretary of State for external affairs in the Canadian government from 1953 to 1960, John W. Holmes is counsellor at the Canadian Institute of International Affairs and professor of international relations at the University of Toronto.

If wars begin in the minds of men, then so may quarrels among allies. Although it would be rash to describe the differences among the members of the North Atlantic Treaty Organization (NATO) as mere phantoms, perceptions of the Atlantic Alliance tend to accentuate the conflicting interests, needs, and views of peoples straddling two continents and an ocean. The media and politicians aggravate the problem because they insist on describing the quarrels as a struggle between a mythical being called "Europe" and a fabulous creature called "America." Western Europe, they say, does not think the same as America does about Afghanistan, the Middle East, or interest rates. Each side becomes identified with personalities of the left or the right whose positions are, or are perceived to be, extreme.

The habit of viewing NATO not as a community of states but as a bilateral deal—the pattern known traditionally as the dumbbell or two pillars—undermines the spirit of fraternity. This perception denies the essence of the alliance created in 1949 and could well become a self–fulfilling prophecy. It is not based on political, economic, and strategic realities in the two continents. The distortion influences West European and American thinking equally.

A modest advantage of a Canadian perspective on the alliance is that Canada has remained outside the fictions and that its perceptions and policies resemble those of

Foreign Policy, 50, (Spring 1983) copyright © 1983 by The Carnegie Endowment of International Peace. Reprinted by permission of the publisher.

West Europeans as often as those of Americans. Canadians find natural company with other lesser allies who share an interest in resisting the cabal of more important NATO members. Canada and Italy live in constant danger of being excluded from Western summit meetings. Canada is more aware of the causes that divide West Europeans and also realizes that North America is not a political entity and that the United States occupies a unique position in the alliance— facts ignored by West Europeans and casually forgotten by Americans. Seen from the Canadian perspective, the divisive strains in the alliance are not the result of historical phobias between the Old World and the New but largely the inevitable differences between a superpower and its associates.

NATO has never been a symmetrical alliance of equal states. The superpower has always possessed special authority and shouldered greater obligations. How to accommodate itself fairly and pragmatically to that fact has posed a continuing challenge to NATO and remains the real issue. Now the allies must adjust to a decline of American power and responsibility. Doing so now, at a time when the Reagan administration appears determined to turn back the clock, is merely the latest challenge to an alliance constantly seeking equilibrium.

NATO came into existence primarily to deter Soviet aggression. Its founders considered alternative structures but chose to create a multilateral alliance based on the recognition that the members had and always would have divergent interests. They needed a framework that would help minimize that divergence. Conflict in NATO and perpetual crisis, therefore, are not unnatural.

Canada for its part never endorsed the dumbbell concept. The interests of the alliance as a whole take precedence over those of one middle–sized member, and it would be folly to revise a sound concept of NATO for Canadian convenience. But the dumbbell concept is not sound. It offers the East tempting grounds for mischief and undermines the ability of the West to meet the needs of the South.

Canada has objected to the dumbbell theory first because in such an alliance the Canadians—regarded as docile or expendable or just forgotten—might lose their voice. Although certainly not crucial, the Canadian contribution to NATO does have a certain significance. Canada maintains limited army and air forces in West Germany, perhaps more as a political gesture, and has a naval role under SACLANT (Supreme Allied Commander, Atlantic). NORAD (North American Air Defense), a U.S.-Canadian arrangement for joint air defense of North America, exists outside the NATO framework but is an essential element in alliance strategy. Canadians from former Prime Minister Lester Pearson to former Prime Minister Pierre Trudeau have insisted that NATO defends two continents and that Canadian forces could be deployed for use on the European or the home front.

True, the declining significance of the north-west sector of NATO has something to do with Canada's comparatively low levels of defense spending. But Canada's defense budget may reflect a more basic problem. It seems that only when Canada grows restless do others notice its participation at all. As one former Canadian defense minister said: "We are expected to put up the minimum fee and to do what we are told." When Canada withdrew one-half of its forces from Western Europe beginning in the late 1960s, the decision produced a great outcry. The West Europeans feared the Americans would consider the Canadian withdrawal a prece-

dent. But Washington, as usual, hardly noticed what Ottawa was doing. If the major powers pay no attention to an awkward lesser power, Canadians are inclined to let them assume a heavier share of the burden.

Canada's importance might attract attention if Canadians threatened to withdraw into splendid isolation. It would create quite a stir if the largest country in the alliance— equal in size to all Western Europe, obviously important to NATO's northern defenses, and possessor of potentially crucial gas and oil reserves—decided to withdraw from NATO's military plans. The lack of even a mention of Canada in U.S. or West European articles and pamphlets about the alliance and its problems increases the temptation to do something shocking. Yet an idle threat to withdraw would be unrealistic because most Canadians still believe in NATO's importance and support Canada's membership. But their sense of obligation, their zeal, and the will to spend more on defense despite budget pressures are at stake.

Consider, for example, the feelings of Canadians on reading a report published recently by the directors of eminent institutes in London, New York, Paris, and Bonn.[1] Although the authors grapple with contemporary issues and even note the advantages of diversity, they fail to break the grip of the orthodoxies of the 1950s—West European unity, two pillars of freedom—along with the Trilateral Commission's efforts to embrace Japan. The smaller West European countries do not count for much, but at least they receive mention. The report ignores Canada totally.

Paradoxically, to be forgotten is an improvement on the tendency to remember Canada at the last moment and include it in something called North America to match something called Western Europe. Although Canadians and Americans have some coincidental interests and perspectives, no single North American economic or political entity with a common foreign or defense policy exists. The West Europeans, conversely, aspire to a common voice and tend to impose that aspiration on North America, where the circumstances differ greatly.

Canadian strategists have begun to make efforts to work out a northern perspective, not so much to argue against the West European priority as to remind those focused on Europe and the Middle East of the importance of the Arctic rim. Canadians should push this angle of vision more effectively. The relative lack of original Canadian strategic thought since the 1950s is largely Canada's own fault. But a greater willingness on the part of others to pay attention to Canada and its views might encourage Canadian thinkers.

Prompted and to some extent goaded by the paper on Western security mentioned above, a Canadian review on the same subject has just been published. The views presented approximate the Canadian norm. The authors call for the formulation of a long–range NATO strategy, replacing flexible response with a doctrine appropriate to the 1980s, strengthening conventional forces in Western Europe and at sea, and vigorously pursuing arms control negotiations. They criticize Canada's contribution to the allied defense and to strategic theory and also demand greater attention to security policy and a re–examination of the traditional disposition of Canadian forces. The views reflect impatience with orthodoxy but are neither startling nor revolutionary. A central proposition is that Canadians should recall the alliance to its original nature and purpose to ease transatlantic tensions.

A Collective Defense

Contrary to views widely held, especially by American revisionists, the United States did not create NATO. If it was a plot, as they allege, it involved the British and Canadians along with some West Europeans and some members of the U.S. State Department who wanted the Senate to commit the United States to Western Europe. Former Canadian Prime Minister Louis St. Laurent first publicly proposed the idea of collective defense. British, Canadian, and U.S. representatives drew up the outlines at highly confidential meetings in Washington in spring 1948 before the other prospective members assembled that summer.

The essential difference of opinion in 1948 was over whether to create a transatlantic alliance or to settle for a U.S. guarantee of a West European union. Europeanists like Belgian statesman Paul–Henri Spaak feared that creating a transatlantic defense community might contradict the movement toward West European unity. Others worried whether the U.S. Senate would accept permanent obligations. The Canadian view of how best to meet the Soviet threat triumphed, although not solely because of the effectiveness of Canadian negotiators. Others—especially the British—shared similar views and had their own reasons for opposing bilateralism.

Canadians based their argument for an Atlantic Alliance community on national and international considerations. The commitment to joint defense of North America raised awkward problems because of the disparity of power between the United States and Canada. Canadians thought they would be more comfortable in a multilateral alliance—particularly one that included their two mother countries as well as the United States. More important, Canadians were convinced that an institution based on mutual pledges of support would survive longer than a guarantee of one continent by the other. How Western Europe could come to North America's aid was unclear. But unlike the United States, Canada has promptly and voluntarily intervened twice in European civil wars, and Canadians generally felt that the West Europeans owed something in return.

The so–called North Atlantic Triangle—Canada, the United States, and Great Britain—has served as the basis of Canada's security for a century. The North Atlantic community was a natural extension of the concept. Canadians worried that a breach seemed inevitable as wartime emotions subsided and the stark differences between the war–strengthened North American economics and the war–weakened West European economics produced tension. Thus Article 2 of the North Atlantic Treaty— sometimes called the Canadian article—emphasizes the commitment to free institutions and pledges the parties to "seek to eliminate conflict in their international economic policies and . . . encourage economic collaboration between any or all of them." Although a few Canadians had hoped for a community along federal lines, the essential argument for Article 2 was not institutional but attitudinal: Countries prepared to fight together must not conduct economic war against one another or the alliance will not last.

Some mistakenly believe that Article 2 aimed to give NATO economic functions. In fact, Canada and others recognized the Organization for European Economic Cooperation—later the Organization for Economic Cooperation and Development (OECD)—as the best way to handle economic collaboration. But Article 2 is not simply a dead letter. The record is more encouraging. The member countries have not subordinated all their national interests to the communal good. No one would have expected that. Nevertheless, they have up until now shown forbearance and recognized that the economic health of every member is a strategic interest of the alliance. The United States did not object to Article 2 in principle, but then Secretary of State Dean Acheson thought it would frighten a U.S. Senate wary of perpetual obligations to a bankrupt West Europe. The Marshall Plan, however, offered the strongest evidence of the U.S. commitment to the spirit of Article 2. And although he did not cite it, former Secretary of State Henry Kissinger's call for spirit of mutual obligation during a "Year of Europe" echoed the essence of the article. Regular summit sessions are a contemporary mechanism to carry out the pledge. It should be of greater concern than it is to NATO strategists that Western economists are also in heated disagreement with one another.

Canadians frequently quote columnist James Reston's 1948 comment that Canada's membership made NATO a mutual alliance rather than a scheme to provide U.S. aid to Western Europe. Nevertheless, the unhealthy view that NATO exists for bilateral aid purposes persists, encouraged by Western Europe's efforts to become a bloc and by America's interpretations of its leadership role.

The European Economic Community (EEC) and its attempts to forge a common foreign policy undoubtedly have positive aspects, but they often have damaging effects on NATO. Americans strongly believed in the 1950s and 1960s that Western strength required West European unity. Canadians could not oppose unity. But they did not consider continental protectionism more progressive than the nationalist kind or believe a united West European foreign policy would necessarily be strong and wise. The West Europeans have rarely questioned this sublime search for unity. They may have condemned themselves to a foreign policy based on the lowest common denominator and made their frequent inability to agree more debilitating by making it seem unnatural. West European caucusing probably has made the path to consensus within NATO more difficult. The attempt to reach a united stand encourage the West Europeans to set themselves apart from the Americans as an end in itself.

A close look at U.S. comments on Western Europe reveals that they usually focus on West Germany alone or West Germany with France. The British receive little notice and seem doomed to fall into the second division or to become an odd man out with the Canadians. Sometimes the dumbbell seems to consist of the West Europeans on the Continent versus the Anglo–Saxons. But West Germany, as British scholar Philip Windsor has pointed out, is not just a dependent variable.[2] Its strategic location, its unavoidable and inseverable ties to East Germany and Eastern Europe, and its vital need for détente, make it a unique power in the alliance. Thus, if a dumbbell exists, then perhaps the two elements are West Germany and the United States. But West Germany's lack of nuclear weapons sets it apart from France and Great Britain in strategic calculations. On reflection, there are many odd men out in NATO—including, of course, the United States.

Experience shows that no formula can guarantee a united voice. The dumbbell formula, while disarmingly simple, does not fit the complexity of the real world. A bilateral alliance might work if it consisted of two strong governments with the capacity to act swiftly and surely. Neither Western Europe nor America can do so. Western Europe will have to achieve far greater integration before it can speak with a single voice; that prospect remains years in the future. And as the EEC expands, the problem of forging a single foreign policy will surely worsen. Meanwhile, the strong voices of West Germany, France, and Great Britain are muffled, and the United States lacks the form of government required for a true consultative alliance. The division of powers sets the United States apart from its allies, many of which have a parliamentary system of government that enables representatives to negotiate commitments. Nothing has disrupted the alliance more than the recent West European and Canadian perceptions that Congress will not honor agreements between foreign and U.S. leaders—even those reached with the president.

The U.S. habit of acting unilaterally—over Afghanistan or Poland or the Middle East—and then measuring its allies' fidelity according to their willingness to follow seems unshakable. Nevertheless, the United States has, and its allies have endowed it with, a responsibility for action in the last resort. Americans can justly protest that friends and antagonists complain about U.S. unilateralism, but nevertheless expect the United States to intervene, as in Lebanon, and criticize it

if it does not. The U.S. media demand instant stances from their government. Although its members preach lessons to others, especially the Canadians, on the evils of nationalism, the U.S. Congress guards its own sovereign independence more jealously than any democratic legislature in the world. It will not even allow an American administration to make foreign policy.

The Argument for Diversity

Thus neither Western Europe nor America can sustain a bilateral alliance, and thinking they can will not make it so. The alliance can defuse conflict, however, by diffusing it if the allies cannot agree and then letting the confrontation be many-sided. Thomas Hughes argues persuasively that the alliance could facilitate the Reagan administration's transition from its campaign postures to more realistic policies. He suggests the Commonwealth community performed such a role in bringing British Prime Minister Margaret Thatcher to compromise over Zimbabwe. Rather than succumb to "its own disintegrative tendencies," the alliance can "become a vehicle for the opening up of ideologically closed circuits."[3]

Hughes extends the argument for diversity by emphasizing that the variously shaded governments speak not only for themselves but also for constituencies in other countries. A conservative British government and an important constituency of West European and Canadian conservatives staunchly support the Reagan administration. The left-center in the United States and elsewhere looked to former West German Chancellor Helmut Schmidt and look now to French President François Mitterrand to speak for them in NATO councils. Fortunately, the random emergence of regimes in the West makes them more broadly representative of Western interests and attitudes when taken together than any of them is when taken separately.

The Canadian need to participate in the

alliance as a consultative community is typical of members other than the big three or four. Canadians know that although they will not have decisive voice, the influence of any one member depends on the nature of the issue. Canada and Norway expect a larger voice on issues involving energy resources or northern strategy; no decision to impose a grain embargo should be made without Canadian participation, as happened under former President Carter. Canada has played a modest part in persuading the allies to seek together appropriate policies toward the Third World. Canadians, like other allies, feel they have a right to a say in U.S. policies that could involve all in war. The 1962 Cuban missile crisis showed that the allies could not hope to participate in crisis decisions—especially when the forces in question are largely American—and probably they would not want to. However, all the allies must feel they have some role in determining grand strategy. The cynic may not rate consultation in Brussels, or the perpetual NATO diplomatic network as important, but both have undeniable significance. When the ministers officially assemble in Brussels, the cross-currents become obvious and the dumbbell is hardly apparent. The table is round. The U.S.-West European stand-off is more a mischievous creation of the media, the foreign policy elite, politicians, and picketers than a description of North Atlantic councils in session.

In practice the Atlantic Alliance must accept some kind of U.S. priority, preferably not spelled out precisely. But the alliance must break the pattern in which the United States makes unilateral decisions and expects loyalty. The United States rationalizes its behavior on the grounds that none of the allies—or Japan—plays its military part. The U.S. grievance is understandable. American nationalists at home and anti-American nationalists abroad have always exaggerated the U.S. role. Protesters in Western Europe assume that the United States wants to force them to accept intermediate-range nuclear forces. They ignore that their own govern-

ments asked for the missiles to protect West Europeans. The protesters may have a case against the missiles. But that they see NATO decisions as U.S. commands is unhealthy for the alliance. That view is unfair, but the present administration has done little until recently to correct the impression that the United States cracks the whip.

The wide gap in responsibility inherent in any alliance composed of unequal blocs— a superpower, a few major powers, and some lesser powers—renders the issue of strategic arms especially acute. When President Reagan finally moved on arms negotiations, NATO applauded him. The allies understand the terrible dilemmas of strategic arms and the need for American strength. But they honestly feared that some of the president's advisers had abandoned hope of avoiding a nuclear contest. Reagan's November 1981 speech on negotiations did a great deal to restore Canadian and West European confidence in the good sense of Americans, who too often gave the impression of wanting only to escalate Western military clout. The allies cannot negotiate arms control agreements, and they dislike harassing the United States to do so. They are worried, as are a great many Americans, about complacency over simple deterrence. The Canadian government and others insist in low voices on a comprehensive approach to arms and arms control.

The contradictions came to a head over the response to martial law in Poland—a crisis in the alliance that illustrates both the shortcomings of the bilateral perspective and American unilateral action as well as the probable advantages of a more consensual approach. The United States, as usual, acted promptly and alone in imposing economic sanctions against Poland and the Soviet Union. Washington probably knew it would not get agreement and thought it better not to try. Prompt and firm response by the country that counts most is defensible provided the policy is not rash. But sanctions against the USSR over Afghanistan had provoked disunity and handed the Soviets a kind of victory when the sanctions lost their effectiveness. Many allied leaders feared the same results again. At least at first, some of them also found events in Poland sufficiently enigmatic to require caution. By imposing an embargo on the Poles and Soviets, Washington employed a blunt instrument without carefully considering what it could actually achieve for the Polish people.

Americans widely attributed the honest doubts of the allies about this tough diplomacy to cowardice, economic selfishness, disloyalty, and naiveté about the Soviets—the allies had let down their champions again. Whereas Americans tend to view détente as a superpower relationship in which the Soviets cheated, West Europeans and Canadians do not because they see gains from détente: Trade opened up, families were reunited, and arms negotiations progressed. For each ally sanctions present different dilemmas. For Canada economic sanctions mean cutting off food exports. And Canadians recall how they loyally agreed not to undermine the U.S. grain embargo over Afghanistan, even though the United States ignored the Canadian position as a major exporter when it made the decision. Then to help win an election, a presidential candidate—Ronald Reagan—renounced the embargo in the interests of the American farmer.

West Germans recall that although the United States denounced them for taking sorely needed gas through a Soviet pipeline, Washington would allow a U.S. company to sell the pipe. The United States eliminated that inconsistency later when it imposed sanctions over Poland. But in the process it triggered a more acute controversy when it tried to impose its ban extraterritorially on the foreign subsidiaries of U.S. companies and on foreign companies manufacturing equipment under U.S. license for the Soviet-West European pipeline. This time even the British took umbrage. Canada strongly supported the West Europeans, as did Japan.

It is important to understand the pipeline controversy well because it roused so much transatlantic anger. The Americans may have,

as *The Economist* argued in November 1982, a sensible aim in attempting to persuade their allies to act with greater caution and realism in trade with the USSR. But the issue is "the insensitive means that the Reagan administration chose to pursue that end." The dispute "raised large questions about America's habitual attempts to export its laws to other sovereign nations." Such attempted unilateralism is not, however, an offense invented by the Reagan administration. Canada has long protested U.S. efforts to apply its bans on trade with China or Cuba to subsidiaries in Canada and is happy to find the West Europeans, not to mention the Australians and New Zealanders, now taking measures to block this effort.

More than just the protection of selfish interests makes countries reluctant to try economic sanctions. They have rarely, for one reason or another, produced the desired results. Moreover, every country has on its conscience a record of some weaseling. The allies cannot claim to be holier than the United States, but they are no less holy. Hypocrisy, or at least inconsistency by all, exacerbated the bitter conflict over extraterritoriality. The West Europeans insist on the sanctity of their contracts, and Reagan tells American wheat farmers that the United States always honors its contracts to sell wheat, even to the Soviets. A willingness all around to acknowledge sin and failure and to renounce charges in infidelity and self–interest against others might open the way for consensus on trade with the Soviets-as it might on the content of the General Agreement on Tariffs and Trade (GATT).

A Loose Coordination

NATO did provide an opportunity for diffusing confrontations over Poland, in spite of the efforts of spokesmen and commentators. Although former Secretary of State Alexander Haig, Jr. showed sensitivity, the media in general did their best to undermine NATO's attempts to reach a compromise by making the Brussels meeting on the subject look like an American attempt to force others to follow the U.S. lead. Some even drew comparisons between U.S. actions and Soviet behavior in the Warsaw Pact.

To some extent NATO did help ease the Reagan administration to a posture toward Poland closer to that of the alliance's other members. As for the allies, Canada's case may be typical of their behavior. Canadian leaders initially adopted positions as far from Washington's as those of any West European. The false question of whether or not Canada should support its protector distorted the vigorous debate in Canada about the issue. Canadians should have concentrated instead on finding the wisest course in a common cause. But the nature of the debate placed the Canadian government in an awkward position for rational debate and decision. Under the circumstances, the principle that Soviet misbehavior offends all the allies and not just the United States seems hard to maintain. Both NATO's heedless supporters and its heedless critics must share responsibility for this distorted image of NATO as an association of the dominating United States and its dominated satellites.

The Brussels meeting did provide Canada with the right framework for moving closer to the position of the activists. The prime minister said he had shifted position because Canada owed something to the views of its allies and because the perspective of the West Europeans, who after all live closer to the seat of the trouble, had impressed him. Canadian and American accounts of the meeting revealed a significant difference of opinion. Canadian commentators stressed the amount of agreement reached. Americans judged the results in terms of the extent to which the allies had accepted a NATO policy prescribed by Washington.

Furthermore, crude unity may not always be desirable. Superstitions about NATO unity have plagued the alliance. NATO members must possess the last-ditch will to stand together and must credibly reaffirm that will

from time to time. The futile insistence on unity toward an entire agenda that includes many large and small issues, however, only aggravates the divisions that sap alliance solidarity and steadfastness at the core. For decades the smaller NATO allies have worked quietly but often effectively behind the scenes at the U.N. and elsewhere to give the West a more supple role and image, resisting the pressure of some major ally to be loyal in a rash cause. Looking back at issues such as relations with Beijing, decolonization in Africa, or the Arab-Israeli confrontations, the West possessed a clear advantage because it did not act as a monolith, did not isolate itself as a bloc from revolutionary forces in the world, and did not unanimously reject any prospect of détente. As Windsor points out, West German diplomacy has helped toward Turkey and Nicaragua, French and Belgian toward Zaire, and British toward Oman. "But the usefulness of such actions depended precisely upon the fact that they were *not* coordinated. Were Europe as a whole to try to hammer out a common position towards developments in the rest of the world, it would probably stop the clocks in every crisis. . . . A loose co-ordination probably not only serves European interest better but also the interests of the United States and the Alliance." The allies cannot fulfill this role, however, if they look like Yankee pawns.

The question of whether and if so how NATO should extend its activities outside its original defensive perimeter presents stubborn problems. The Soviet challenge in the Middle East, Africa, and elsewhere raises issues for the whole Western world, not just the United States. Americans understandably think the alliance should pitch in. But how it can do so remains unclear. Contributing troops to a Rapid Deployment Force run by the Pentagon in accordance with U.S. policies and the whims of the Senate is politically inconceivable. Canada and other lesser powers joined NATO so that they could comfortably pool their forces in a multilateral team under combined control. Extending NATO's zone of responsibility seems the logical answer, but that course presents too many obstacles.

The difficulties the United States faced in convincing other countries to contribute to the international peace-keeping force in the Sinai foreshadowed the kinds of problems likely to arise. The problems of putting together a real fighting force would be infinitely greater. As the allies recognized in Korea, command in war must rest in the hands of a strong military power. If the United States did not still have to provide the essential military forces—and it will have to for some time to come in most areas—Washington could more easily share the policy making. Americans, who have no historical experience of being a lesser ally, find the problems of NATO's smaller members in the face of these challenges difficult to understand. Proposals simultaneously as logical and impossible as the multilateral nuclear force of the 1960s may appear again. Any sound formula will be hard to find. Meanwhile, all sides must make a gigantic effort to understand the attitude of the United States, which thinks it bears too much of the burden, and that of other countries asked to sacrifice not just their identities but also their right to decide where and when their citizens should fight and die.

An Encouraging Trend

Before the cynics and utopians have torn NATO apart, all must seek to make more sensitive and effective use of available alliance structures and return to first principles. NATO does not require new mechanisms of consultation or more specific pledges. The allies improved procedures after the disarray over Afghanistan. Over the following year intense consultations on the subject produced the first contingency planning. The allies initiated special restricted ministerial sessions and opened contacts with countries outside NATO. Unfortunately, however, they

failed to devise explicit plans to handle the imposition of martial law in Poland. This omission did not invalidate the exercise; it spurred the special ministerial meeting to reach decisions more effectively. A remarkable degree of consensus was achieved that disintegrated not so much over immediate measures as over a long-term strategy toward the Soviet Union.

The informal meeting of NATO foreign ministers in October 1982 at a secluded resort north of Montreal may presage an encouraging trend. Other such meetings have taken place, but this one occurred at a time when differences over missiles, trade, and other problems in the rest of the world had become especially acute. Consultations in Brussels have grown too stately. Political leaders need to engage in candid exchanges without formal briefs or press briefings. West German Foreign Minister Hans-Dietrich Genscher proposed informal encounters several years ago, and Trudeau gave the idea strong support. The details of the discussions in October have wisely remained confidential, but since then movement toward compromise on the natural gas pipeline among other things has occurred.

It is even more difficult to achieve agreement when governments change, when new people come to power with misapprehensions about the views of other countries and a firm determination to impose their will. Reagan is not the only leader who has needed time to adjust to the recalcitrant facts of international life. Nevertheless, bringing a new American administration to terms is especially important. The change in U.S. position toward the Siberian pipeline may indicate that the new zealots have developed a disposition to compromise. Perhaps they have also found they can achieve allied support more easily when they temper their policies. The wide acceptance of U.S. leadership in the 1982 Lebanese crisis has been impressive. The time may be ripe for an agreement that consultations should precede all actions affecting the alliance and insure coordination of the political, economic, and military dimensions of contingency plans.

The economic aspect of Western defense—Article 2—grows more critical as international relations become more stringent. More than the cost of equipment is involved. The economic health, perhaps even survival, of the partners is at issue. Nothing is more critical for NATO strength than access to energy resources. Questions like credits or technology transfers as well as economic sanctions have been forced on to the NATO agenda, but the allies continue to grope for effective means of economic coordination. Article 2 paid lip service to the importance of economic factors in holding the allies together, but NATO has neither the mandate nor the competence to define broad economic policies. There would be no point in trying to supersede the established economic organs such as the OECD, which has a different membership and cannot engage in strategic planning. Because allied economic interests and predicaments differ more than the need for defense, it is unwise to hope for easy agreement. NATO is not the place to coordinate grand economic strategies for GATT or the North-South dialogue. NATO can, however, serve as a forum to thrash out conflicting views on the economic relations with the Soviet Union.

Opinion has lately been converging over the issues of credits and technology transfers, at least to the extent that all recognize the importance of caution and coordination. The purpose of NATO is not to wage economic warfare. But specific sanctions in certain cases or a policy of rewards and punishments should not be ruled out. A majority of members view indiscriminate economic pressure as inconsistent with the search for reciprocal and mutually profitable relations between East and West. If the representatives in Brussels took a serious look at sanctions and reviewed the record, they might escape the generalities that provoke irritation. It would be useful if the allies recognized NATO as the forum for considering the implications for collective defense of de-

velopments in trade and technology, foreign investment, and banking. All these economic and security questions have arisen over crises in Afghanistan and Poland and to some extent the Falkland Islands. The same questions could again become a bitterly divisive issue in the Middle East.

The West needs to grapple with threats outside NATO even though it is tempting to wait for situations to arise rather than plan in advance. The authors of the recent report on Western security suggest a principal countries approach—those countries especially concerned in an issue or area and able and willing to play a direct role should shoulder the responsibility. They consider it unwise to expect enough consensus in NATO to add regional threats to the regular agenda. Although membership in each proposed group would vary, it would normally include the United States, West Germany, Great Britain, France, and Japan.

Canadians have responded that the "formalization and institutionalization of this approach would be destructive of the fundamental principle that the Alliance is an organization of equal members." The British and French, jealous of their uncertain power, have always desired a central directorate. In the Canadian view this proposal "would further the already discouraging tendency towards division of members into an inner and an outer group." The authors conclude that there "can be no quick fix for the management of the global problems of the alliance." The North Atlantic Council has the experience for long-range planning. Smaller members must develop their own capabilities for political and strategic analysis. "This would raise the self-confidence of their governments and go far to dispel the suspicion that the views of the United States always dominate." The Canadian authors recognize that in certain circumstances members will feel compelled to move forces from the NATO front. The situation is likely to be most serious if and when the United States does so. Other countries' willingness to make up for these deficiencies in NATO would probably be the most logical and acceptable policy, although no one should underestimate the difficulties of implementing such plans.

A little more humility on all sides would help. Americans must acknowledge their own inconsistencies and try harder to think like an ally. The West Europeans should demonstrate greater understanding of the special responsibilities of a superpower. Canada, meanwhile, could resume a more imaginative and constructive role. As the Canadian review has said: "What has passed for Canadian policy has been nothing more than cautious, sometimes qualified, often tacit, acquiescence in multilateral decisions." It might be wise now to raise a louder and less orthodox voice, to stimulate fresh thoughts, and to help restore the sense of community in NATO. Up to a point it is the vocation of lesser powers to act responsibly irresponsible. They can help to open those ideologically closed circuits that rightly worry Hughes. Greater willingness to sacrifice would, of course, have to accompany the louder words.

The moral, political, and strategic superiority of NATO over the Warsaw Pact lies in its pursuit of harmony rather than unity. NATO celebrates the freedom of its sovereign members without indulging—other than rhetorically—in the illusion that it is a partnership of equals. Preserving equilibrium in such circumstances requires constant vigilance and ability to adapt. It is not a problem to be solved. Helmut Schmidt, explaining to *The New York Times* that the Polish crises was not a crises of the alliance at all, added: "The cry of crises in the alliance I have been hearing for 25 years now, at least. This is a routine type of difficulty, and a routine type of controversy within the alliance." The record does not look at all bad. It would surely be healthier for citizens of the alliance to celebrate that record confidently than to portray NATO so stridently as a lost cause. Giving the allies a stronger feeling that the alliance is their cause would effectively strengthen their resolve.

NATO faces at the moment conflicting attitudes on détente among all its members—not just between Western Europe and the United States—that threaten its basic solidarity. Whether the danger is greater than internal conflicts of the past cannot be calculated. The alliance always has been and always will be in danger of breaking up. Recognitition of that fact is essential to holding NATO together.

NOTES

[1]Karl Kaiser, Winston Lord, Thierry de Monthrial, and others, "Western Security: What has Changed? What Should be Done?" *(New York: Council on Foreign Relations; London: Royal Institute for International Affairs,* 1981).
[2]Philip Windsor, "Germany and the Western Alliance: Lessons from the 1980 Crisis." *Adelphi Paper 170 (London: International Institute for Strategic Studies,* 1981).
[3]Thomas I. Hughes, "Up From Reaganism," *Foreign Policy* 44 (Fall 1981), p. 21.

24. The ANZUS Relationship

Paul D. Wolfowitz

Recently confirmed as Ambassador to Indonesia, Paul Wolfowitz gave this address while assistant secretary for East Asian and Pacific Affairs, to the Conference on The American Effect on Australian Defense at the Australian Studies Center of Pennsylvania State University, University Park, Pennsylvania, June 24, 1984. It has been somewhat overtaken by events in 1986.

ANZUS [Security Treaty Between Australia, New Zealand and the United States of America] is an alliance of democratic nations committed to peace. These two facts about the alliance—our commitment to democratic freedom and our commitment to peace—are so fundamental to ANZUS that they would be worth noting at the outset even were they nothing more than very broad statements of purpose. But so far from being mere shopworn generalities, these two facts have great practical significance for the basic role and function of our alliance—and even for its day–to–day management—significance which is often not sufficiently appreciated.

It is because our nations are democracies that the commitments we make to one another are of great practical consequence and also why they are so reliable. For our three nations, vulnerable as we are to the infirmities that are alleged to afflict democracies in the conduct of their affairs, our alliance commitments are important in bringing a fundamental continuity into our relations. But it is also because these commitments represent the commitments of whole nations to one another—not the mere whim of arbitrary rulers—that it is possible to rely on them. There is no task more fundamental to alliance management than the constant nurturing of public support.

Our collective commitment to preserving peace is no less profound in its practical im-

Excerpted from *Current Policy* Series No. 592, Bureau of Public Affairs, Department of State, June 24, 1984, pp. 1–5.

plications for our alliance. It is perhaps to be expected that so much of the discussion of ANZUS concerns questions about what would happen and how the various parties would respond in the event of war. The treaty itself, of course, contains important commitments of mutual assistance in the event of armed attack. Yet it is no depreciation of the importance of those commitments to say that the foremost goal of the alliance is to prevent those commitments from ever having to be called upon. The operation of the alliance in peacetime is every bit as vital as its operation in time of war—indeed, even more so. Particularly in a nuclear age, the task of preserving peace is fundamental to alliance management.

The Determination of National Interest in a Democracy

The old aphorism that nations have no permanent friends, only permanent interests, is still a popular one, but it contains as much concealed falsehood as apparent truth. Viewing the flux and perfidy of 19th–century alliances, it was certainly plausible—and perhaps even somewhat comforting—to believe that geography, historic rivalries, and economic interests provide the constants in a nation's decisions, while policies and alliances form and founder around these fixed goals. A nation, so this view goes, may be obsessed by a particular threat, must have particular ports or trading opportunities—or, conversely, may have no interest in a distant land—and should form its alliances in whatsoever way will promote these ends.

The notion of permanent interests, impermanent friends, left a great deal to be desired as a model for the conduct of international relations, even in the 19th century. And in a nuclear age it is a very dangerous basis for democratic nations to conduct their affairs.

Among its other weaknesses, the notion of permanent interests leads to the dangerous fallacies of permanent disinterest and predictability. These can all too often be used to excuse neglect, a seductive choice for peace–loving democracies that sometimes fail to recognize the aggressive designs of others.

Why, so the argument goes, must a nation spend valuable resources to defend against distant challenges? Why maintain forces without a visible threat? If grand political and military goals are constant, there is no need to reassess defenses and alliances will naturally tend themselves. If decisions are always logical, the need to prepare for unexpected contingencies is quite small.

But we know from long, historical experience that alliances are hard to put together and to keep, that illogical and unpredictable decisions are all too common, and that circumstances can change radically, often without a shot being fired. The fall of the Shah of Iran, the Sino–Soviet split, the attempt to place Soviet missiles in Cuba, even a coup in the small island of Grenada, created new strategic interests and shifted political and military thinking abruptly. Uncertain or ambiguous political commitments, even where interests seemed otherwise clear, led to bloodshed in 1914, in 1939, in 1950, and even in 1982.

I believe that countries, and in particular democracies like the United States and Australia and New Zealand, do have permanent interests. But they are not only or principally the geo–strategic interests on which past debate has centered. Our nations' permanent interests are as much or more in justice and the rule of law, in democracy and freedom, and in peace.

In pursuit of these goals, we have permanent "friends" as well: continuity, reliability, and strong alliances with other nations that share the same values. Surely nations that defend freedom and the rule of law have a sound foundation for the elements of such permanent friendship. But these foundations will only be maintained through consistency, responsible policies, and a commitment to cooperation. The burden of maintaining such cooperation and policies in the first half of this century was too heavy to avoid world conflagration. We must avoid such missteps in the nuclear era. . . .

Managing ANZUS

Once there is the will to take alliances seriously, the problems of managing an alliance come into full play. ANZUS, like NATO, provides the elements for peace. Alliance management is the art that puts meaning into the framework that the treaty provides.

Successful alliance management depends on our success in meeting five critical challenges.

First, as an alliance of democracies, ANZUS inherits the challenges democracies face in running a coherent foreign policy. Policies that do not sustain public support will fail. Needed policies that lack public support can go unrealized. In short, alliance management requires an open and informed public debate led by citizens mindful of the great, not just the immediately visible, threats the future holds.

Second, an effective alliance among three vital democracies requires extensive, ongoing contacts at all levels of government and society. The need for coordinated political and military activities requires close official ties and strong institutionalized consultative processes. But they also require lively, informal public commentary and personal interchanges (including conferences like this one). Together these assure a constant flow of information and views on potential problems, as well as a full awareness of each other's concerns, interests, capabilities, and objectives. Only through such exchanges can alliance managers reach decisions that serve a common purpose.

Such exchanges cannot be turned on and off as crises arise and recede. To be effective, they must continue at all levels over time and reflect the high degree of mutual confidence derived from experience and personal contact.

Fortunately, the management of the AN-ZUS alliance in all three capitals provides precisely that kind of consultative relationship. At the so–called working levels, there are literally daily contacts between both civilian and military officials, including a throughly institutionalized sharing of intelligence and related assessments. At a higher level, there are frequent major meetings of senior officials to exchange views on issues of immediate concern to the alliance.

Most importantly, there is the ongoing dialogue—through meetings, correspondence, and communications—between ministers in the three capitals. The annual AN-ZUS Council meeting provides a vital element that links political leaders and symbolizes the significance of the relationship.

On the military side, even without a pattern of integrated commands and military forces as in NATO Europe, ANZUS alliance managers over the years have built up a pattern of close defense cooperation which assures that ANZUS forces can operate together quickly and effectively, if that is ever necessary. Key elements of this cooperation are joint exercises between our forces, especially our navies.

The third challenge of alliance management is to meet the need for continuity and long–term consistency of policy. President Reagan came into office committed to demonstrating that the United States is a reliable ally and partner. Accordingly, while he has brought strong views of his own to the definition of new policy areas, he has shown great respect for commitments made by previous administrations. That element of con-

tinuity between administrations is essential to effective management of alliances between democracies.

I could cite examples as far afield as the Middle East, Central America, and southern Africa to make my point, but let me stick for now to some of more direct concern to AN-ZUS. In the area of arms control, President Reagan maintained the U.S. commitment to both tracks of the 1979 NATO decision, while offering his new and imaginative proposal on the "zero option" for the arms control track. He announced that the United States would observe the limits of the unratified SALT II [strategic arms limitation talks] Treaty while seeking to negotiate a better substitute for it. With respect to China policy, the President has made very clear his determination to maintain the framework provided by previous U.S. commitments in this area, at the same time that he has worked to put that critically important relationship on a more realistic and stable basis. The views and concerns of our NATO and ANZUS allies were, and are, important in shaping U.S. arms control policy. And I can say from direct personal involvement that ANZUS views were of great importance at critical junctures in the development of this Administration's China policy.

Fourth, there is a need to accept the mutual burdens as well as the mutual benefits of alliance. It is in the nature of alliances that the precise levels of the burdens and benefits will shift over time. Concerns that another partner is getting a "free ride" plague every alliance in some form. Indeed, alliances can be endangered as much as strengthened by too fervent an effort to make all burdens precisely equal at any given moment to the benefits received. What is important to a healthy alliance is that the burdens be shouldered by all parties as needed and when needed, and that the benefits be shared as well.

Article II of the ANZUS treaty binds the partners "separately and jointly by means of continuous and effective self–help and mutual aid" to "maintain and develop their individual and collective capacity to resist armed attack." Because the ANZUS democracies, as the NATO allies, are dedicated to preserving the peace, not fighting a war, there is a tendency in all our countries to resent spending resources for defense that seems unnecessary at the time. Yet, when the danger becomes evident, it may be too late or seem too provocative to begin to rearm. There, once again, a well–informed public is essential.

Domestic political pressures and miscalculations in Argentina led to a wholly unexpected war in the Falklands—a war for which Britain was just barely prepared. British naval planners, prior to the Falklands, assumed that their forces would be used relatively close to home, that they would never have to engage without allies, that land–based air support would always be available, and that landings against hostile forces would not be needed. These comfortable assumptions lowered Britain's defense spending. But an unpredicatable world made them predictably dangerous.

The United States, for its part, is in the midst of a substantial effort to increase its conventional forces. We have done so not to provoke, but to defend; not to escalate, but to provide the means by which problems can be contained. By strengthening our conventional deterrent we help to increase our options and reduce the risks of nuclear war. In this defense effort, too, we have kept our allies closely informed.

The United States attaches critical importance to the opportunity to use Australian and New Zealand ports that provide ready access to the South Pacific and Indian Oceans. We view Australia's and New Zealand's willingness to allow us use of their ports[1] as part of their contribution to ANZUS. We also value efforts to assure standardization or interoperability of equipment and weapons systems, share intelligence, exchange personnel, and consult on problems. The maintenance of U.S. presence in the region, and the demonstration of our ability to operate effectively with our treaty partners, are tangible physical evidence of our treaty commitments. All of the ANZUS nations share in this effort and all benefit from it.

Another and critical element of defense cooperation is that involving the joint facilities in Australia. Although the subject of bilateral agreements between Canberra and Washington, they clearly are within the spirit of the provisions of the ANZUS treaty. Indeed, such is noted in the agreements.

There is, of course, considerable public speculation about the use of these facilities, including gross distortions or misunderstandings of related U.S. defense strategy. The simple truth, as clearly and forcefully enunciated by Prime Minister Hawke on June 6 in Parliament in Canberra, is that these facilities contribute to arms control, effective deterrence, mutual security, and to stability in global strategic relationships. Verification, early warning, and the ability to control our nuclear forces and communicate with them are critical to both stable deterrence and to arms control. In addition, this capability could be critical in preventing some bizarre accident from turning into an unintended catastrophe. For all of these reasons, the facilities are an important, even essential, part of the West's critical and deeply felt commitment to maintain world peace—perhaps the greatest single challenge of this or any century.

Fifth, as alliance managers in all three capitals have recognized from the outset of ANZUS, our treaty relationship is only part of the many–faceted relations between our countries—commercial, historic, cultural, and personal. They are all important. They all affect the course of the relationship and each other. As we approach problems in any one area, we must be careful to see them in the perspective of the entire relationship. If we do so, we will continue to have a strong reservoir of good will and self–interest from which problems can be solved. At the same time, we will recognize that each element of the relationship is part of the whole and that each is important and worthy of our best effort for consultation, compromise, and deference to the interest of all.

For alliance managers the essential task, whether in Washington, Canberra, or Wellington, is to maximize cooperation to mutual advantage when we are on common ground and to contain differences—legitimate though they may be—through the kinds of compromises necessary in an effective working partnership. By so doing, we can assure that competition in commerce and differences in other areas do not threaten cooperation linked to our most fundamental shared interest—mutual national survival.

NOTES

[1]New Zealand refused use of its ports for U.S. nuclear-powered ships in the summer of 1986; as a result, the formal alliance was at least temporarily suspended.

---

25. A New Piece in an Old Puzzle

Charles W. Kegley, Jr. and Gregory A. Raymond

Professor Charles Kegley has served as chairman of the Department of Government and International Relations at the University of South Carolina; Dr. Gregory Raymond teaches political science at Boise State University in Idaho.

Leaders who forge them are heralded as statesmen; those who breach them are branded as traitors. Because they may increase a state's military strength, their supporters call them indispensable; but because they may tie a state to an unreliable partner, their opponents call them entangling. They are alternately praised for war's prevention and blamed for war's occurrence. Much like the sirens Parthenope, Leucosia, and Ligeia in Greek mythology, they are both desired and feared.

The phenomena these statements de-

Excerpted from "Alliance Norms and War: A New Piece in an Old Puzzle," *International Studies Quarterly* 26, no. 4, (December 1982), copyright © 1982, The International Studies Association. (Footnotes have been deleted.)

scribe are, of course, interstate alliances. For centuries their impact on world affairs has been vigorously debated. Some scholars suggest that alliances increase tension, others assert that they help stabilize the international system, and still others maintain that they "neither limit nor expand conflicts any more than they cause or prevent them." Unfortunately, though the literature generated by this debate is voluminous, the evidence it contains on the systematic effects of alliance aggregation is largely impressionistic. As Burgess and Moore have put it, few studies meet the "scientific standards of explicitness, visibility, and repeatability."

Needless to say, without reproducible evidence any analysis of alliance effects is, at best, what Einstein called a *Gedankenexperi-*

ment or, at worst, simply an exercise in naive speculation. In either case, the absence of empirical findings to support these arguments prevents one from knowing with any degree of confidence whether alliances and war are related, and if so, whether that relationship is positive, negative, or curvilinear. As a result of this need to corroborate theoretical insights with empirical evidence, Singer and Small brought the scientific method to bear on the possible connection between alliances and war. Yet, rather than resolving the long-standing debate over the alliance/war relationship, their research actually aroused further controversy by revealing that alliance aggregation and the onset of war were positively related in the twentieth century but negatively related in the nineteenth. Once again, as in so many instances in the past, awareness of the extent of our ignorance increased with the growth of scientific knowledge.

The search for solutions to puzzles has been portrayed as the driving force behind scientific research. Clearly the Singer and Small discovery was puzzling, and thus it inspired several replication studies based on different data sets, measurement techniques, and statistical tests. However, despite this additional research, the relationship between alliances and war still remains a puzzle, for the results of these replications have not converged on a single set of conclusions. Hence it is not surprising that a recent review of the empirical work done in the wake of the Singer and Small study has lamented: "Not only do we face an uncharted sea, as yet no one has succeeded in building a very convincing or watertight ship."

To solve a puzzle, we must possess clues to make an inference about the whole based on what we know from an often incomplete and seemingly disjointed collection of parts. In effect, this obliges us to think like detectives and, as Zinnes points out, "Thinking like detectives makes us look for the not necessarily obvious or even visible operating principles." Given that the alliance/war relationship is a puzzle for which we lack enough

clues, where should we now search? Operating as detectives, can a new piece to this old puzzle be uncovered, one heretofore overlooked? We contend that for too long the cultural attributes of the international system have been neglected in the search for clues, primarily because they are not as obvious or visible as the system's structural attributes. Among the many cultural attributes that could be a missing piece in the alliance/war puzzle, the degree to which international norms support binding commitments is the one most frequently referred to in the traditional literature on alliances. Therefore, this study proposes to determine empirically whether changes in those norms that pertain to the sanctity of alliance commitments have been associated with changes in the amount of war.

A Strategy of Inquiry

Embedded in our call for research on the cultural attributes of the international system is a conviction that the results will not so much compete with the findings of previous studies as they will combine with them to produce a more adequate, multicausal explanation of the alliance/war relationship. Nearly all of the existing system-level studies of this relationship focus on properties of alliances that are the most amenable to observation and measurement. The number of alliances within the international system, the number of poles around which they are clustered, as well as the tightness and discreteness of the clusters, are examples of these relatively concrete properties. Underlying these emphases is an assumption that the structural configurations produced by alliance bonds affect the degree of uncertainty within the international system, and, in turn, the likelihood that war will occur.

There are, of course, different views on which type of alliance configuration is most conducive to preserving peace. According to one school of thought, rigid bipolar structures that contain a large proportion of the system's members help prevent war by clarifying the positions of potential friends and foes. With uncertainty thus reduced, wars are less likely to result from miscalculation or erroneous perceptions. Conversely, a second school of thought contends that highly fluid multipolar structures help prevent war by increasing uncertainty. The cross-cutting ties, overlapping interests, and competing loyalties inherent in this kind of structure make it unclear how much external opposition belligerents would face in the event of hostilities, and thus lead to greater caution whenever war seems imminent.

As these two divergent views demonstrate, our picture of how the pieces in this puzzle fit together is "blurred and sketchy." Conceivably this is because there may be an element of truth in each school of thought. That is to say, the relationship between alliance flexibility and war may not simply be positive or negative as the above views respectively imply. Instead, based on Wallace's research, there is some evidence that the relationship may actually be curvilinear. Thus, if one looks only at data that show when the system initially moves away from a low level of polarization, the relationship would appear to be negative. Alternatively, if one looks only at data that show the latter phases of movement toward a highly polarized system, the relationship would appear to be positive. Like a parabola, the relationship reverses direction beyond a certain point, therein suggesting that very loose and very rigid alliance structures are both war prone. We submit that while this finding helps clarify how the pieces we already have fit together, it is also necessary to determine if an important piece is still missing from the puzzle, namely, whether the degree to which international norms support binding alliance commitments also affects systematic uncertainty and, ultimately, the amount of war.

This assertion assumes that foreign policy decisions are not only influenced by decision maker perceptions of the current international situation; they are also influenced by expectations about the future. When, for instance, a decision maker calculates the expected utility of escalating a serious dispute, he or she attempts to forecast the possible reactions of other states in addition to assessing the relative strength and cost-tolerance of their opponent. Not surprisingly, then, the *casus foederis* of alliances (the circumstances that precipitate and justify their formation) can be traced to the desire of decision makers to reduce uncertainties about the behavior of others. In principle, alliances limit their range of behavior, thereby making the reactions of other states more predictable. To perform this function successfully in practice, allies must be willing to abide by their commitments even at the expense of immediate gain. Uppermost in the minds of decision makers contemplating an alliance is a concern about the trustworthiness of a potential ally in fulfilling the promises to which it professes to agree. Indeed, formal treaties would not be required if these concerns were not present.

Whether allies can be counted on to comply with the treaty obligations they swear to execute is thus critical in estimating the potential impact of alliances. It is important to know, for example, if a commitment is viewed as an irrevocable pledge, similar to the *Nibelungentreue* given by Kaiser Wilhelm II to Austria-Hungary on July 5, 1914. Unless treaty commitments are regarded as binding by the signatories to them, most of the behavioral consequences of formal alliances will lie dormant. Treaties will be, in Lenin's famous words, "Like piecrust, made to be broken." The amount of alliances in the international system, the number of parties to them, the distribution of capabilities they produce—none of these structural properties will matter in a cultural context where decision makers feel free to disregard their commitments *ad libitum*. Formal alliances in such an environment will be merely symbolic; they will be bonds that fail to bind. On the other hand, if treaty commitments are recognized as binding by members of the international system, the capacity of alliances to affect state behavior will be substantial. Therefore, norms governing the flexibility of alliance commitments appear to be critical in explaining the nature of the relationship between alliance aggregation and the onset of war.

Even though the importance of the psychocultural underpinnings of alliance dynamics has been recognized for some time, various methodological obstacles have prevented researchers from analyzing them in a rigorous, empirical fashion. Undoubtedly the most troublesome of these obstacles is that the decision calculus of those leaders choosing to fulfill their commitments has not been open for public inspection, nor, for that matter, have the motives of those who have chosen to disregard their treaty obligations. While we can infer their intentions from biographical material and from the justifications they give for their actions, we are largely precluded from observing how deep (and often unconsciously held) feelings about loyalty, honor, and the like prevail on their preference schedules. If we cannot directly observe the psychomilieu of decision makers, how can we measure the degree of commitment attached to alliance agreements?

Perhaps the most advantageous approach to transcending this methodological obstacle is to shift from the national to a systemic level of analysis. This prevents us from ascertaining the extent to which individual decision makers feel bound by the alliance agreements they make, but it facilitates the study of change in the psychocultural environment of nations, a perspective that has long been advocated but seldom pursued. Moreover, this level of analysis is warranted in an investigation of the relationship between alliance aggregation and war because we are dealing with macrolevel processes best measured with macroindicators.

According to Singer, the international system may be described in terms of three sets of attributes: physical, structural, and cultural. Among other things, the cultural attributes of the system include the distribution of attitudes and opinions among the system's members. International norms are

an expression of those opinions that are generally held throughout the system about specific kinds of state behavior. That is to say, they define the "cultural climate" within which the interaction of the members of the political system takes place. At any given point in time, this rudimentary political culture places greater or less stress on flexibility (as opposed to commitment) in its definition of what constitutes an appropriate conception of alliance obligations. In emphasizing one norm rather than the other, the cultural climate will either facilitate rapid alliance formation and swift realignments, or instead, foster permanence by prescribing faithful adherence to treaty guarantees. Should a long-term trend take hold toward the acceptance of one norm over the other, the international system can be said to have manifested one of many possibilities in its capacity for macroadaptation and transformation.

If the cultural attributes of the international system can serve as a key point of reference for analyzing the behavioral processes that occur within it, how might change in these attributes be detected? The approach taken here involves monitoring changes in the content of the international legal order, since international law is a medium through which prevailing opinions about acceptable forms of behavior are communicated to members of the state system. Furthermore, because alliance "tends to sustain international law . . . and in turn derives support from it," and because "treaties are employed for formal expression of alliance," an examination of changes in treaty law over time should provide reproducible evidence about changes in those international norms pertaining to the sanctity of alliance agreements.

. . . Traditionally, studies of alliance dynamics have conceptualized flexibility in terms of the ability of a given state to form new alliances with any other state in the international system, even its ideological enemies. Alliance formation, in other words, is depicted as a stochastic process; any combination of states is as probable at the upper boundary of flexibility as any other combination. Deviations from this degree of flexibility are often explained by referring to the personal idiosyncrasies of particular statespersons, their domestic political constraints, or simply bureaucratic inertia . . . flexibility can be thought of in another sense. Besides investigating the degree of flexibility that occurs within different structural configurations, we also need to look at the flexibility afforded states by international norms to break existing alliance treaties. We contend that the extent to which treaty obligations are considered binding by prevailing norms affects war by either dampening or intensifying the amount of uncertainty within the international system. Of course, this conclusion must be regarded as tentative until sustaining evidence can be accumulated. But our demonstration that norms regarding the nature of treaty commitments have historically been associated with the amount of war begun exerts pressure for modifying the way research on the alliance/war relationship should be approached in future studies.

One such modification would be to ask if some types of alliance commitments are more likely to be fulfilled than other types. The commitment in an alliance agreement may range from a detailed list of military forces that will be furnished by each party under specified contingencies, to a guarantee of neutrality if any alliance members are attacked to the broader requirement consultation in the event of a military conflict (e.g., the *Dreikaiserbund*). It would be useful if future research could ascertain whether the impact of international norms varies according to the type of treaty obligation.

Another avenue would be to determine what factors lead to changes in those norms that pertain to treaty obligations. Beres has posited that the reliability of alliances is a function of the structural attributes of the international system. In this connection, it would be profitable to see whether the distribution of capabilities within the system at t influences both the degree of alliance flexibility and the openness of contractual norms at $t + 1$.

To sum up, then, . . . international norms constitute a missing piece in the puzzling relationship between alliance aggregation and the onset of war; we now need to begin working on how this new piece fits together with those already in our possession. Our ultimate goal in this endeavor is a multi-causal model, one that organizes future research by outlining how, under a variety of circumstances, various macroindicators can be combined to provide a more adequate explanation of macrolevel phenomena.

chapter 9

FORCE: THE ULTIMATE OPTION

No other human activity is so continuously or universally bound up with chance. . . . Absolute, so-called mathematical factors never find a firm basis in military calculations. From the very start there is an interplay of possibilities, probabilities, good luck and bad that weaves its way throughout the length and breadth of the tapestry. In the whole range of human activities, war most closely resembles a game of cards.

Karl Von Clausewitz

From *On War*, reprinted by permission. Copyright © 1975 by J. M. Dent and Sons Ltd.

One of the mockeries of the modern age is that peace itself seems to rest upon the mutual fear inspired by the magnitude of nuclear destructiveness. The nature of the entire concept of threat takes on new meaning. States have arrived at such a deadlock in their search for security that peace seems to depend upon the degree to which the superpowers can maintain the so-called balance of terror. On the other hand, the possibility that massive destructive weapons may soon be in the hands of many can only add to the insecurity and instability of the entire international system. The threat may now lie in the system itself more than in the actions of a state's immediate neighbors, as before. Although, in a sense, apprehension of what others can do has always been a basis for restraint in international behavior, this is a dubious foundation upon which humanity should rest its hopes for continued peace and stability. The system is highly volatile; there are no guarantees against the kinds of miscalculations, destructive impulses, or even accidents which could lead to an explosion as Chernobyl and 3 Mile Island reminded us in a relatively minor way. The task of leadership is, in the words of McGeorge Bundy, President Kennedy's chief adviser on national-security policy, "to cap the volcano." Kennedy himself said "The genie is out of the bottle."

As the magnitude of the security problem grows and the military claims upon the lives, resources, and direction of society continue to mount, there is the latent danger of the transformation of the nation into a garrison state. There is a subtler aspect to the problem, the risk that military considerations will take precedence over political considerations in the conduct of foreign policy itself. Indications are that, after the Challenger disaster, this may happen to the American space program.

Until the twentieth century, war was viewed as a more or less normal aspect of the working of the state system. Not only was there a legacy of martial valor alive in many countries but there were also deeper reasons for finding war acceptable. All social life is marked by tension and conflict among competing groups, but within the state they are kept under control by government. In the absence of any outside authority to guarantee each nation's security or adjudicate their conflicts, however, war and the threat of war were the accepted means of doing so. War was so accepted a part of international relations that rules by which a state was justified in going to war and by which war should be conducted were codified in that part of international law known as the Law of War. In other words, war was not seen as an aberration but as an inherent feature of a system which lacked any alternative means for regulating conflict among its members. International law was not supposed to stop it, just to make it less horrible.

There were and are as many causes of war as there are types of social and political dissatisfaction and disorder. One study on the causes of war is featured in this chapter, written by the distinguished British military authority, Michael Howard. Another lists the following as the "proximate causes of war":

1) power asymmetry—an unfavorable tilt in the distribution of power;

2) nationalism, separatism, and irredentism—the desire of a people to throw off foreign rule or to annex nationals living under foreign rule;

3) social Darwinism—the belief that societies, like biological species, evolve and advance through competition resulting in survival of the fittest;

4) communications failure—misunderstanding and hostility due to stereotypical images and mutual misperception of intentions;

5) arms races;

6) the exploitation of a foreign war to achieve unity at home;

7) instinctual aggression—the psychological predisposition of people toward aggression;

8) economic and scientific stimulation—new economic and scientific innovations stimulate expansionist tendencies;

9) military-industrial complexes—groups within a society, principally the military, the defense industry, and their political allies, acquire a vested interest in maintaining a state of conflict;

10) relative deprivation—to achieve greater benefits or to relieve the frustration of denial, groups may turn to aggression and political violence;

11) overpopulation;

12) conflict-resolution—war as a device for challenging and changing unacceptable or incompatible conditions between two or more states.[1]

It is the nature of the international system, however, and the threat of war itself that are the greatest causes of war. In the second selection in this chapter, Robert Jervis points to the drive for security that finds expression in arms races and misperceptions of the other side's motives in arming as the paramount cause of great wars. In their systematic study, *Theory and Research on the Causes of war*, Dean Pruitt and Richard Snyder note but disagree with one idea that war is inevitable, though then concede that a "world in which all conflict was avoided would probably be unhealthy, since conflict has a number of positive functions."[2]

As one devastating war succeeded another in the twentieth century, scholars turned increasing attention to the reasons wars were fought whose costs in death and destruction exceeded any possible gain that victory might bring. First and foremost, political leaders were regarded as prisoners of the logic of the system itself. On the eve of World War I, each side, responding to passion and fear, had built up two enormous military blocs. Each feared that an unfavorable tilt in the balance of power would be disastrous, so that when the Austrian Empire appeared threatened with disintegration, Germany felt it had no alternative but to accept the price of going to Austria's defense. France, in turn, felt obliged to support Russia, and while Britain had ties to France, it was the German violation of Belgium's neutrality that provided Britain with the *casus belli*.

Closer analysis, however, reveals that the political and military leaders on both sides had succumbed to a fatalistic acceptance of war. On each side stereotypically hostile images and mutual misperceptions of each other's intentions were allowed to prevail until it was too late to draw back. One study of World War I concludes that the war occurred because each side perceived the cost of diplomatic defeat to be greater, at least in the immediate sense, than the cost of going to war. After all, the cost of the war would only be known once the fighting began, whereas the cost of a diplomatic setback would be felt immediately. This motive appears to have been an important consideration in President Johnson's decision to move massively into the Vietnam War. However pessimistic he and some of his advisers may have been about the outcome, Johnson feared the immediate public reaction that would follow if the United States withdrew its support for Saigon and South Vietnam fell to the Communists. Had Johnson realized that the war would last eight years and involve 2 million casualties, including 45,000 American dead and 300,000 wounded, would he have made the same decision?

In an important study, *Every War Must End*,[3] Fred Ikle demonstrates how prone most leaders, especially military ones, are to overrate their own forces

---

[1]Steven J. Rosen and Walter S. Jones, *The Logic of International Relations* (Cambridge, Mass: Winthrop, 1977), pp. 283–312.

[2]Dean Pruitt and Richard Snyder, *Theory and Research on the Causes of War* (Englewood Cliffs, N.J.:, Prentice-Hall, Inc. 1969), p. 4.

[3](New York: Columbia University Press, 1971).

and underestimate the enemy's. Despite the enormous advances in intelligence gathering, wars are often begun and conducted in ignorance of the enemy's potentiality and determination. An exceptional example of this can be seen in the totally expected resistance by Iran when attacked by Iraq, shortly after the revolution against the Shah. Many years later the objectives have not been achieved and indeed without massive help from friends, Iraq could lose. Military leaders are often ignorant of the political dimensions of modern war and make predictions as if war was not the most unpredictable of all enterprises; "History is the victim of an increasing disposition of military educators . . . to treat war as a science. . . . The focus is on tactics, strategy, logistics, the marshaling of hardware, and the organization of ever unfolding technology. This rationalization or 'scientification' of warfare breeds a disconcerting hubris in its practitioners because it deemphasizes, if it does not altogether deny, the role of what Frederick the Great called 'His Sacred Majesty Chance' . . . no plan of operation can look beyond the first meeting with the enemy, because it cannot govern the independent will of the opposing commander."[4]

The great German theoretician of war, von Clausewitz, argued that war should be conducted for political ends and not just to impose military defeat upon the enemy. But as Ikle points out in his study (and he is not alone), most modern wars (including the Vietnam War), once begun, are fought on both sides to achieve victory. Once a war begins, the military always attempt to dictate the terms on which it will be conducted. Analyzing the Franco-Prussian War of 1871, Fritz Stern writes: "To Bismarck, war was an instrument of policy, and peace-keeping his own prerogative; to Molke [the military commander] any political interference in strategy was a threat to his proper realm of responsibility. Their conflict embittered headquarters and led Molke to withhold vital information from Bismarck . . ."[5]

The same disagreements occurred in World War I and to some extent in all subsequent wars. It was General Douglas MacArthur who attempted to undermine the civilian conduct of the Korean War by declaring, to popular acclaim, that "there is no substitute for victory." It was Winston Churchill who said of the British high command's lies about British casualties in World War I that "they had one set of figures with which to deceive the public, one set with which to deceive the Cabinet and one set with which to deceive themselves." The American military consistently misrepresented and underrated the enemy's capability in Vietnam in order to justify continuing the war long after the impossibility of victory had been clearly demonstrated. All too often it becomes impossible to end a war until one side or the other has been totally destroyed, and this because neither side is willing to negotiate an end to the war. The Iran-Iraq conflict may be an example of this tendency.

Unfortunately, if war is an unavoidable condition of the nation-state system, it has become increasingly murderous and destructive. Since the dawn of the twentieth century, technology has been revolutionizing the relationship of war

[4]Jeffrey Record, "The Fortunes of War," *Harpers* (April 1980), p. 19.

[5]Fritz Stein, *Gold and Iron: Bismarck, Bleichroder and the Building of the German Empire* (London: Allen and Unwin, 1977), p. 145.

to foreign policy and human values. First it was the machine gun and the submarine that produced the horrible war of attrition on the western front in 1914 and at sea throughout the war; then air power and tank warfare destroyed much of Europe, Russia, and Japan in World War II. Now, nuclear weapons and missiles have undercut the traditional relationship of war to foreign policy and human values. Traditionally, a nation expected to use its full military might in a war. Today, the suicidal consequences of a resort to nuclear weapons by either side has raised the question of whether war between nuclear powers is even thinkable.

By the 1930s, leaders were forced to consider the damage that would be done to civilian populations by aerial bombing. It was British Prime Minister Stanley Baldwin who in a moment of despair remarked that "the bombers will always get through," and it was this fear of the annihilative effects of bombing that in part, at least, influenced the policy of appeasement. The advent of weapons capable of causing a thousand times more destruction than all the damage done in World War II has completely transformed the relationship of weapons to international relations. Today, theorists and politicians alike must develop nuclear strategy as much with an eye to avoiding the danger of nuclear war as they previously did with an eye to making the most effective use of their weaponry. According to two authorities,

> Military preparations are no longer made only against the day when the system breaks down and fails to keep the peace; military measures are thought to be constitutive of what is meant by peace, and are important guarantors, if not the sole guarantors, of the system of international relations. . . . Contemporary nuclear strategy is seen as bearing, among other things, the heavier burden of enabling the participants . . . to live together in relative peace.[6]

As Klaus Knorr observes below "the nuclear balance of terror, which is assumed to be safely stable, has inhibited any large-scale use of force between powerful states, whose leaders, as rational actors, are completely self-deterred." Nevertheless, while nuclear weapons may make resort to war unthinkable except as an act of complete national desperation, their deterrent function prompts each side to maintain an enormous arsenal of such weapons, and so long as such arsenals exist, their use cannot be ruled out. In fact, military authorities in both the Soviet Union and the United States have quite clearly stated that under certain circumstances of crisis or war, a resort to nuclear weapons cannot be ruled out. Still, it does seem that fear of a nuclear holocaust has acted as a restraint upon the two superpowers.

Nevertheless, the nuclear deadlock only seems to have displaced each side's preoccupation with security and with the utility and the threat of war away from the nuclear terrain, to attention to the possibilities of subnuclear war. Both superpowers have resorted to the use of force in the postwar era: the United States in Korea, Vietnam and Grenada and the Soviet Union in Hungary, Czech-

---

[6]Barrie Paskins and Michael Dockrill, cited in the second edition of this book, from *The Ethics of War* (1979), p. 194.

oslovakia, Ethiopia, and Afghanistan. Second, neither side has renounced the exploitation of the threat of force for political ends.

> While each of the contestants may possess force sufficient to produce damage the other would regard as unacceptable, they may be unequal in demonstrating resolve to use the force at their disposal. Superior technique in "brinksmanship" or "crisis management" may establish the greater willingness of one side to go to war rather than back down, and so bring a diplomatic victory in its train, as was demonstrated by the United States in the Cuban missile crisis of 1962.[7]

The continuing resort of the two superpowers to the threat of force in the conduct of their relations means that war is an ever-present possibility. It is as if, constrained from the actual employment of nuclear weapons, they have resorted to a process of bargaining, with threats of force as a substitute for actually fighting each other. The objective of such a strategy—called "coercive diplomacy"—is to bend the opponent's will without actually getting into a war. As Paul Lauren has pointed out, the purpose of this strategy of brinksmanship is "to persuade an opponent that his interests would be served best by changing the direction of his behavior;" its success depends upon convincing one's opponent that one has the will and ability to inflict damage upon something the opponent values more then the object in dispute, "and thereby to take the kind of action desired by the coercing state."[8]

While the balance of terror seems to have reduced the incidence of war among the advanced industrial states (Communist and Western), there has been a great upsurge in the number and types of war being fought in Africa. Asia, and the Middle East. Knorr observes in this chapter that "military conflicts have occurred mostly in the Third World, mainly between Third World countries, and this shift is paralleled by the fact that the proportion of world military spending, manpower, and weapons imports outside the capitalist states has sharply increased." The increased frequency of war in the Third World is in part due to: the absence of consensus among many of the new states as to where their borders really are; the unresolved presence of white rule in southern Africa; national xenophobia; and the eagerness with which the Western powers and Soviet Union alike have been willing to supply them with arms and even help them fight these wars. Here again, there is always a danger that one or both superpowers will become bogged down in a war such as the United States did in Vietnam or the U.S.S.R. in Afghanistan, or come into direct conflict as they almost have on occasion in the Middle East.

To return to the dilemma of nuclear weapons: As yet no one has been able to devise a formula which would permit the superpowers to limit the nuclear threat. While nuclear weapons seem essential both as deterrents and symbols, it is not clear what, if any, positive strategic advantage is gained by having such weapons in one's arsenal. How can their possession be translated into concrete

---

[7]Klaus Knorr, *On the Uses of Military Power in the Nuclear Age* (Princeton, N.J.: Princeton University Press, 1966), p. 77.

[8]Paul Lauren, "Theories of Bargaining with Threats of Force: Deterrence and Coercive Diplomacy," in *Diplomacy: New Approaches in History* (New York: The Free Press, 1979), pp. 192–96.

political advantage when their use would be mutually suicidal? Weapons of such massive destructive capacity ought to carry with them the greatest inhibitions from their employment. But this is not the direction in which strategy is headed. Both sides are anticipating the possibility of a limited nuclear war in their current strategic thinking.

In order to reduce the danger of nuclear war, each side adopted what is called a "second-strike" strategy. The second-strike strategy was enunciated in 1962 by Secretary of Defense Robert McNamara. By installing American missiles in underground silos where they could not be destroyed, Washington was in a position to inform the Kremlin that it renounced any resort to a preemptive, or first-strike, attack on Russia. Instead, it would henceforth rely upon the threat from America's invulnerable nuclear retaliatory force to deter the Soviet Union from a resort to war. It was hoped that the Kremlin, knowing that the United States would not attack first, would be persuaded to adopt a similar strategy and thereby minimize the uncertainty and instability that characterized a situation in which each felt it had to strike the first blow if it were to have any hope of surviving.

In the ensuing years, both superpowers have tacitly or actively shaped their deterrence strategy around the concept of the second strike. Each has hardened its missile sites to render them less vulnerable. Among the Strategic Arms Limitation agreements reached at Moscow in June 1972 there was an agreement to abandon the construction of anti-ballistic-missile (ABM) defenses on the principle that any attempt to reduce one's vulnerability to the opponent's second strike would weaken the stability of deterrence. Until recently, each side's missiles were targeted on population centers (called a "countervalue" strategy), rather than on each other's rockets (called a "counterforce" strategy). In effect, each held the other's population hostage against a surprise attack. This has been the paradox of nuclear deterrence: security and stability have rested upon each side knowing that the other could *not* "knock out" its retaliatory capability in the form of land-based ICBMs, bombers, and, more potently, in the form of missiles fired from submarines 200 to 2000 miles off each other's coast. In the last several years, however, uncertainties have arisen due to technological advances in the throw weight, megatonnage, and accuracy of Soviet rockets, the accuracy and warhead numbers of American missiles, and a shift on both sides toward targeting on each other's missiles (counterforce). An entirely new development is the research program announced by the President of the United States known as the "Strategic Defense Initiative", (S.D.I.), sometimes misleadingly referred to as "Star Wars."

There are, therefore, a number of reasons why war, including major wars fought with nuclear weapons, may still be possible. One side or the other may miscalculate the effects of an aggressive action, convincing itself that it can get away with achieving its goals through the threat of force. Or one side may believe that the other is about to launch a military action and that it must strike first; this is the strategy of preemption. It was effectively applied against three Arab states by Israel in 1967, and even more spectacularly in the unilateral strike by Israeli aircraft against an Iraqi nuclear reactor near Baghdad in 1984. In addition, wars may break out, not because of miscalculation arrived at by deliberation (however faulty), but simply by accident, unlikely as this may seem. Or one side may achieve a genuine technological breakthrough in weapons, delivery systems, or defense capabilities, which might drastically shift the existing balance and make war once again appear to be a rational policy choice. Just as America's monopoly on nuclear weapons gave way to duopoly, and just as America and Russia have since been joined by Great Britain, France, and China as nuclear powers, so other states are thought now to be capable of joining the nuclear club, despite the efforts of statemen to prevent it. Local, limited conflicts may grow in area and scope (such as in the Middle East) until they embrace powers with nuclear capabilities. One can easily imagine that nuclear weapons may not be used at the outset of a war, but it stretches the imagination to assume that a country would prefer losing a war or its very existence to using its full arsenal. In such a situation, publics and leaders alike become locked into a face-saving effort to deny reality and therefore reject the political terms for ending the war until it is too late. So we see that although war may be an unavoidable concomitant of the nation-state system, even limited wars are often begun and carried on in ways that have no reasonable relationship to the national interest or to the maintenance of a stable world order.

DISCUSSION QUESTIONS

1. Is war an inherent feature of the logic of international relations? What are some of the causes for wars listed by Rosen and Jones in the introduction to this section? How do these compare with Howard's views?

2. Is the decision to go to war always well thought out by the decision-makers? What evidence does Jervis give that (quite apart from the fact that wars often begin over emotional issues,) the leaders themselves are often caught up on nonrational processes and judgments which, had they been able to act more dispassionately, might have led them to decide against war?

3. What does von Clausewitz mean when he says that wars should only be entered into and fought for carefully calculated political objectives, and not simply to achieve victory at whatever cost? Von Clausewitz wanted decision-makers to realize how unpredictable the outcome of war can be. Does the record of war in the twentieth century up to and including the Vietnam War indicate that people and governments are capable of such wisdom?

4. Do you think anything has occurred in the world military situation in the decade since Knorr wrote his article to change his interpretation?

5. States have always employed their military forces as a means of threatening or coercing the other side. What does Howard mean when he writes that in "international politics, the appetite often comes in eating"?

6. What does Jervis mean by the "spiral" of insecurity? Give some historical as well as contemporary examples.

7. Do you agree with Snyder and Pruitt that conflict serves certain positive purposes in society? Does that mean that war is inevitable?

26. Perception and Misperception: The Spiral of International Insecurity

Robert Jervis

Dr. Robert Jervis, professor of International Relations at Columbia, is the author of *The Logic of Images: International Relations* (1970) and other works.

The lack of a sovereign in international politics permits wars to occur and makes security expensive. More far-reaching complications are created by the fact that most means of self-protection simultaneously menace others. Rousseau made the basic point well:

> It is quite true that it would be much better for all men to remain always at peace. But so long as there is no security for this, everyone, having no guarantee that he can avoid war, is anxious to begin it at the moment which suits his own interest and so forestall a neighbour, who would not fail to forestall the attack in his turn at any moment favourable to himself, so that many wars, even offensive wars, are rather in the nature of unjust precautions for the protection of the assailant's own possessions than a device for seizing those of others. However salutary it may be in theory to obey the dictates of public spirit, it is certain that, politically and even morally, those dictates are liable to prove fatal to the man who persists in observing them with all the world when no one thinks of observing them towards him.

In extreme cases, states that seek security may believe that the best, if not the only, route to that goal is to attack and expand. Thus the tsars believed that "that which stops growing begins to rot", the Japanese deci-

Excerpted from Robert Jervis, *Perception and Misperception in International Politics* (Princeton, N.J.: Princeton University Press, 1976), pp. 83–92. Copyright © 1976. Reprinted by permission of Princeton University Press. (Footnotes have been removed).

sion-makers before World War II concluded that the alternative to increasing their dominance in Asia was to sacrifice their "very existence", and some scholars have argued that German expansionism before World War I was rooted in a desire to cope with the insecurity produced by being surrounded by powerful neighbors. After World War I France held a somewhat milder version of this belief. Although she knew that the war had left her the strongest state on the Continent, she felt that she had to increase her power still further to provide protection against Germany, whose recovery from wartime destruction might some day lead her to try to reverse the verdict of 1918. This view is especially likely to develop if the state believes that others have also concluded that both the desire for protection and the desire for increased values point to the same policy of expansionism.

The drive for security will also produce aggressive actions if the state either requires a very high sense of security or feels menaced by the very presence of other strong states. Thus Leites argues that "the Politburo . . . believes that its very life . . . remains acutely threatened as long as major enemies exist. Their utter defeat is a sheer necessity of survival." This view can be rooted in experience as well as ideology. In May 1944 Kennan wrote: "Behind Russia's stubborn expansion lies only the age-old sense of insecurity of a sedentary people reared on an exposed plain in the neighborhood of fierce nomadic peoples."

Even in less extreme situations, arms procured to defend can usually be used to attack. Economic and political preparedness designed to hold what one has is apt to create the potential for taking territory from others. What one state regards as insurance, the adversary will see as encirclement. This is especially true of the great powers. Any state that has interests throughout the world cannot avoid possessing the power to menace others. For example, as Admiral Mahan noted before World War I, if Britain was to have a navy sufficient to safeguard her trading routes, she inevitably would also have the ability to cut Germany off from the sea. Thus even in the absence of any specific conflicts of interest between Britain and Germany, the former's security required that the latter be denied a significant aspect of great power status.

When states seek the ability to defend themselves, they get too much and too little—too much because they gain the ability to carry out aggression; too little because others, being menaced, will increase their own arms and so reduce the first state's security. Unless the requirements for offense and defense differ in kind or amount, a status quo power will desire a military posture that resembles that of an aggressor. For this reason others cannot infer from its military forces and preparations whether the state is aggressive. States therefore tend to assume the worst. The other's intentions must be considered to be co-extensive with his capabilities. What he can do to harm the state, he will do (or will do if he gets the chance). So to be safe, the state should buy as many weapons as it can afford.

But since both sides obey the same imperatives, attempts to increase one's security by standing firm, and accumulating more arms will be self-defeating. . . .

These unintended and undesired consequences of actions meant to be defensive constitute the 'security dilemma' that Herbert Butterfield sees as that "absolute predicament" that "lies in the very geometry of human conflict. . . . [H]ere is the basic pattern for all narratives of human conflict,

whatever other patterns may be superimposed upon it later." From this perspective, the central theme of international relations is not evil but tragedy. States often share a common interest, but the structure of the situation prevents them from bringing about the mutually desired situation. This view contrasts with the school of realism represented by Hans Morgenthau and Reinhold Niebuhr, which sees the drive for power as a product of man's instinctive will to dominate others. As John Herz puts it, "It is a mistake to draw from the universal phenomenon of competition for power the conclusion that there is actually such a thing as an innate 'power instinct'. Basically it is the mere instinct of self-preservation which, in the vicious circle [of the security dilemma], leads to competition for ever more power."

Arms races are only the most obvious manifestation of this spiral. The competition for colonies at the end of the nineteenth century was fueled by the security dilemma. Even if all states preferred the status quo to a division of the unclaimed areas, each also preferred expansion to running the risk of being excluded. The desire for security may also lead states to weaken potential rivals, a move that can create the menace it was designed to ward off. For example, because French statesmen feared what they thought to be the inevitable German attempt to regain the position she lost in World War I, they concluded that Germany had to be kept weak. The effect of such an unyielding policy, however, was to make the Germans less willing to accept their new position and therefore to decrease France's long-run security. Finally, the security dilemma can not only create conflicts and tensions but also provide the dynamics triggering war. If technology and strategy are such that each side believes that the state that strikes first will have a decisive advantage, even a state that is fully satisfied with the status quo may start a war out of fear that the alternative to doing so is not peace, but an attack by its adversary. And, of course, if each side knows that the other side is aware of the advantages of striking first, even mild crises are likely to end in war. This was one of the immediate causes of World War I, and contemporary military experts have devoted much thought and money to avoiding the recurrence of such destabilizing incentives. . . .

Psychological Dynamics

The argument sketched so far rests on the implications of anarchy, not on the limitations of rationality imposed by the way people reach decisions in a complex world. Lewis Richardson's path-breaking treatment of arms races describes "what people would do if they did not stop to think." Richardson argues that this is not an unrealistic perspective. The common analogy between international politics and chess is misleading because "the acts of a leader are in part controlled by the great instinctive and traditional tendencies which are formulated in my description. It is somewhat as if the chessmen were connected by horizontal springs to heavy weights beyond the chessboard."

Contemporary spiral theorists argue that psychological pressures explain why arms and tensions cycles proceed as if people were not thinking. Once a person developes an image of the other—especially a hostile image of the other—ambiguous and even discrepant information will be assimilated to that image. . . . If they think that a state is hostile, behavior that others might see as neutral or friendly will be ignored, distorted, or seen as attempted duplicity. This cognitive rigidity reinforces the consequences of international anarchy.

Although we noted earlier that it is usually hard to draw inferences about a state's intentions from its military posture, decision-makers in fact often draw such inferences when they are unwarranted. They frequently assume, partly for reasons to be discussed shortly, that the arms of others indicate aggressive intentions. So an increase in the other's military forces makes the state doubly insecure—first, because the other has an increased capability to do harm, and, second, because this behavior is taken to show that the other is not only a potential threat but is actively contemplating hostile actions.

But the state does not apply this reasoning to its own behavior. A peaceful state knows that it will use its arms only to protect itself, not to harm others. It further assumes that others are not fully aware of this. As John Foster Dulles put it: "Khrushchev does not need to be convinced of our good intentions. He knows we are not aggressors and do not threaten the security of the Soviet Union." Similarly, in arguing that "England seeks no quarrels, and will never give Germany cause for legitimate offence," Crowe assumed not only that Britain was benevolent but that this was readily apparent to others. To take an earlier case, skirmishing between France and England in North America developed into the Seven Years' War partly because each side incorrectly thought the other knew that its aims were sharply limited. Because the state believes that its adversary understands that the state is arming because it sees the adversary as aggressive, the state does not think that strengthening its arms can be harmful. If the other is aggressive, it will be disappointed because the state's strengthened position means that it is less vulnerable. Provided that the state is already fairly strong, however, there is no danger that the other will be provoked into attacking. If the other is not aggressive, it will not react to the state's effort to protect itself. This means that the state need not exercise restraint in policies designed to increase its security. To procure weapons in excess of the minimum required for defense may be wasteful, but will not cause unwarranted alarm by convincing the other that the state is planning aggression.

Because statesmen believe that others will interpret their behavior as they intend it and will share their view of their own state's policy, they are led astray in two reinforcing ways. First, their understanding of the impact of their own state's policy is often inadequate—i.e. differs from the views of disinterested observers—and, second, they fail to realize that other states' perceptions are also skewed. Although actors are aware of the difficulty of making their threats and warnings credible, they rarely believe that others will misinterpret their behavior that is meant to be more compatible with the other's interests. Because we cannot easily establish an objective analysis of the state's policy, these two effects are difficult to disentangle. But for many purposes this does not matter because both pressures push in the same direction and increase the differences between the way the state views its behavior and the perceptions of others.

The degree to which a state can fail to see that its own policy is harming others is illustrated by the note that the British foreign secretary sent to the Soviet government in March 1918 trying to persuade it to welcome a Japanese army that would fight the Germans: "The British Government have clearly and constantly repeated that they have no wish to take any part in Russia's domestic affairs, but that the prosecution of the war is the only point with which they are concerned." When reading Bruce Lockhart's reply that the Bolsheviks did not accept this view, Balfour noted in the margin of the dispatch: "I have constantly impressed on Mr. Lockhart that it is *not* our desire to interfere in Russian affairs. He appears to be very unsuccessful in conveying this view to the Bolshevik Government." The start of World War I witnessed a manifestation of the same phenomenon when the tsar ordered mobilization of the Baltic fleet without any consideration of the threat this would pose even to a Germany that wanted to remain at peace. . . .

The same inability to see the implications of its specific actions limits the state's appreciation of the degree to which its position and general power make it a potential menace. As Klaus Epstein points out in describing the background to World War I, "Wilhelmine Germany—because of its size, population, geographical location, economic dynamism, cocky militarism, and autocracy under a neurotic Kaiser—was feared by all

other Powers as a threat to the European equilibrium; this was an objective fact which Germans should have recognized." Indeed even had Germany changed her behavior, she still would have been the object of constant suspicion and apprehension by virtue of being the strongest power in Europe. And before we attribute this insensitivity to the German national character, we should note that United States statesmen in the postwar era have displayed a similar inability to see that their country's huge power, even if used for others' good, represents a standing threat to much of the rest of the world. Instead the United States, like most other nations, has believed that others will see that the desire for security underlies its actions.

The psychological dynamics do not, however, stop here. If the state believes that others know that it is not a threat, it will conclude that they will arm or pursue hostile policies only if they are aggressive. For if they sought only security they would welcome, or at least not object to, the state's policy. Thus an American senator who advocated intervening in Russia in the summer of 1918 declared that if the Russians resisted this move it would prove that "Russia is already Germanized". This inference structure is revealed in an exchange about NATO between Tom Connally, the chairman of the Senate Foreign Relations Committee, and Secretary of State Acheson [during a Senate hearing]:

> Now, Mr. Secretary, you brought out rather clearly . . . that this treaty is not aimed at any nation particularly. It is aimed only at any nation or any country that contemplates or undertakes armed aggression against the members of the signatory powers. Is that true?
>
> SECRETARY ACHESON.   That is correct, Senator Connally. It is not aimed at any country; it is aimed solely at armed aggression.
>
> THE CHAIRMAN.   In other words, unless a nation other than the signatories contemplates, meditates or makes plans looking toward, aggression or armed attack on another nation, it has no cause to fear this treaty.

SECRETARY ACHESON. That is correct, Senator Connally, and it seems to me that any nation which claims that this treaty is directed against it should be reminded of the Biblical admonition that 'the guilty flee when no man pursueth.'

THE CHAIRMAN. That is a very apt illustration. What I had in mind was, when a State or Nation passes a criminal act, for instance, against burglary, nobody but those who are burglars or getting ready to be burglars need have any fear of the Burglary Act. Is that not true?

SECRETARY ACHESON. Very truly.

THE CHAIRMAN. And so it is with one who might meditate and get ready and arm himself to commit a murder. If he is not going to indulge in that kind of enterprise, the law on murder would not have any effect on him, would it?

SECRETARY ACHESON. The only effect it would have would be for his protection, perhaps, by deterring someone else. He wouldn't worry about the imposition of the penalties on himself, but he might feel that the statute added to his protection.

. . . When the state believes that the other knows that it is not threatening the other's legitimate interests, disputes are likely to produce antagonism out of all proportion to the intrinsic importance of the issue at stake. Because the state does not think that there is any obvious reason why the other should oppose it, it will draw inferences of unprovoked hostility from even minor conflicts. . . . If, on the other hand, each side recognizes that its policies threaten some of the other's values, it will not interpret the other's reaction as indicating aggressive intent or total hostility and so will be better able to keep their conflict limited.

The perceptions and reactions of the other side are apt to deepen the misunderstanding and the conflict. For the other, like the state, will assume that its adversary knows that it is not a threat. So, like the state, it will do more than increase its arms—it will regard the state's explanation of its behavior as mak-

ing no sense and will see the state as dangerous and hostile. When the Soviets consolidated their hold over Czechoslovakia in 1948, they knew this harmed Western values and expected some reaction. But the formation of NATO and the explanation given for this move were very alarming. Since the Russians assumed that the United States saw the situation the same way they did, the only conclusion they could draw was that the United States was even more dangerous than they had thought. As George Kennan put the Soviet analysis in a cable to Washington:

> It seemed implausible to the Soviet leaders, knowing as they did the nature of their own approach to the military problem, and assuming that the Western powers must have known it too, that defensive considerations alone could have impelled the Western governments to give the relative emphasis they actually gave to a program irrelevant in many respects to the outcome of the political struggle in Western Europe (on which Moscow was staking everything) and only partially justified, as Moscow saw it, as a response to actual Soviet intentions. . . . The Kremlin leaders were attempting in every possible way to weaken and destroy the structure of the non-Communist world. In the course of this endeavor they were up to many things which gave plenty of cause for complaint on the part of Western statesmen. They would not have been surprised if these things had been made the touchstone of Western reaction. But why, they might ask, were they being accused precisely of the one thing they had *not* done, which was to plan, as yet, to conduct as overt and unprovoked invasion of Western Europe? Why was the imputation to them of this intention being put forward as the rationale for Western rearmament? Did this not imply some ulterior purpose . . . ?

The Russians may have been even more alarmed if, as Nathan Leites has argued, they thought that we behaved according to the sensible proverb of "whoever says A, says Z" and had knowingly assigned Czechoslovakia to the Russian sphere of influence during the wartime negotiations. "How could, they must ask themselves, the elevation of an already dominant Czechoslovak Communist Party to full power in 1948 change the policies of Washington which had agreed to the presence of the Soviet Army in Czechoslovakia in 1945? Washington, after all, could hardly imagine that Moscow would indefinitely tolerate the presence of enemies . . . within its domain!" The American protests over the takeover must then be hypocrisy, and the claim that this even was alarming and called for Western rearmament could only be a cover for plans of aggression. . . .

The explication of these psychological dynamics adds to our understanding of international conflict, but incurs a cost. The benefit is in seeing how the basic security dilemma becomes overlaid by reinforcing misunderstandings as each side comes to believe that not only is the other a potential menace, as it must be in a setting of anarchy, but that the other's behavior has shown that it is an active enemy. The inability to recognize that one's own actions could be seen as menacing and the concomitant belief that the other's hostility can only be explained by its aggressiveness help explain how conflicts can easily expand beyond that which an analysis of the objective situation would indicate is necessary. But the cost of these insights is the slighting of the role of the system in inducing conflict and a tendency to assume that the desire for security, rather than expansion, is the prime goal of most states. . . .

Both the advantages and pitfalls of this elaboration of the security dilemma are revealed in Kenneth Boulding's distinction between

two very different kinds of incompatibility. . . . The first might be called 'real' incompatibility, where we have two images of the future in which realization of one would prevent the realization of the other. . . . The other form of incompatibility might be called 'illusory' incompatibility, in which there exists a condition of compatibility which would satisfy the 'real' interests of the two parties but in which the dynamics of the situation or illusions of the parties create a situation of perverse dynamics and misunderstandings, with increasing hostility simply as a result of the reactions of the parties to each other, not as a result of any basic differences of interest.

This distinction can be very useful but it takes attention away from the vital kind of system-induced incompatibility that cannot be easily classified as either real or illusory. If both sides primarily desire security, then the two images of the future do not clash, and any incompatibility must, according to one reading of the definition, be illusory. But the heart of the security dilemma argument is that an increase in one state's security can make others less secure not because of misperception or imagined hostility, but because of the anarchic context of international relations.

Under some circumstances, several states can simultaneously increase their security. But often this is not the case. For a variety of reasons, many of which have been discussed earlier, nations' security requirements can clash. While an understanding of the security dilemma and psychological dynamics will dampen some arms-hostility spirals, it will not change the fact that some policies aimed at security will threaten others. To call the incompatibility that results from such policies 'illusory' is to misunderstand the nature of the problem and to encourage the illusion that if the states only saw themselves and others more objectively they could attain their common interest.

27. On the Use of Military Force in the Contemporary World

Klaus Knorr

The author is Professor Emeritus of Public and International Affairs at the Woodrow Wilson School, Princeton University, and chairman of the Board of Editors of *World Politics*.

. . . In *On the Uses of Military Power in the Nuclear Age,* I argued that some traditionally important goals for going to war had lost appeal, that the anticipated costs of doing so had markedly risen, and that the expected utility of using military forces internationally had therefore probably declined, in the sense that governments and elites found their useful employment more restricted than was previously the case.

The following were the principal points. The desire for territorial conquest has been the most powerful motive for using force throughout recorded history. Economic and security considerations are among the major concerns that have propelled governments to conquer or defend territory. Prior to the Industrial Revolution, an expansion of territorial possessions meant more control over manpower and resources, sources of supply, markets and outlets for investment. In recent decades, elites have gradually learned, in large part as a result of modern economics and education, that the prime sources of national wealth are ultimately domestic (i.e., savings and investments, technological progress and the upgrading of human resources). They also came to believe that international trade and investment do not require territorial control so long as there is an international economic order that fosters such intercourse. Historical experience has

Excerpted from Klaus Knorr, "On the International Uses of Military Force in the Contemporary World," in *Orbis: A Journal of World Affairs* 21, no. 1 (Spring 1977), by permission of the publisher. Copyright 1977 by the Foreign Policy Research Institute, Philadelphia. (All footnotes have been deleted.)

confirmed these expectations. Several countries became highly developed and wealthy while remaining strictly confined to a small home base (e.g., Switzerland and Sweden), and West Germany and Japan became rich after they lost territories in World War II.

Until not long ago, expansion of territory and territorial control also appealed on grounds of security. Territorial expansion meant more population, more assured access to raw materials and food, which could not be cut off in times of war, and more space that an enemy had to cross in order to reach the local centers of power. These strategic values have also tended to diminish. Manpower is a military asset only to the extent that it is loyal and skillful, and sophisticated technological capacity has become a base of military strength more important than sheer numbers of people. Dependence on foreign supplies that can be cut off in wartime is a serious vulnerability only if war is protracted. The expectation of prolonged warfare, however, has decreased in recent decades because the most powerful modern technology has lent to offensive weapons a vast superiority over defensive arms. Moreover, the development of nuclear missiles has greatly lowered the protective value of territory and distance from prospective enemies.

Four factors have been operating on the cost side. First, memories of the stupendous destructiveness of World Wars I and II, the watching of recent televised conflicts (e.g., Vietnam and Lebanon), and profound anxieties about a possible nuclear holocaust have sensitized an increasing number of people to the costliness of war, and this sensitivity has become particularly important in societies that are no longer governed by traditional warlike elites. Second, nuclear weapons technology has rendered the most destructive arms useless for anything but deterrence between states encapsulated in a balance of terror. In fact, the fear that lesser conflicts between them might escalate to the level of strategic nuclear exchanges gives nuclear powers a strong incentive to refrain from employing conventional forces against one another. Third, the global spread of nationalism, and of the capacity for political and military mobilization, and the export of modern arms to the less-developed parts of the world have made these unattractive targets for intervention or conquest by great powers. The opportunity for cheap colonial aggrandizement and overseas military intervention that the great powers enjoyed from the fifteenth century to the beginning of the twentieth has disappeared. Fourth, while roughly until the end of the nineteenth century aggressive war was generally regarded as natural, legitimate and inevitable, recent decades have witnessed a growing normative revolution; as a result, at least the aggressive use of military force is increasingly held to be illegitimate—a rule imbedded in the charter of the United Nations. The normative costs of resorting to military aggression have thus risen palpably.

Although these developments seemed to this author (in 1965) to point at least tentatively to a diminishing utility of the international use of armed force, he noted (though in retrospect not emphatically enough) two significant qualifications. For one, even if the appeal to use force in behalf of certain economic and security objectives has become deflated, this does not, of course, exhaust the reasons for which governments may resort to arms. Ideological goals, especially, ethnic unification (or liberation) and world order objectives may suggest worthwhile gains. Changes on the cost side appeared to be more conclusive. Even here, however, it was doubtful that military force for purposes of deterrence and defense had lost utility.

The ability to threaten nuclear reprisal was felt to be highly useful as an instrument of deterrence. The enhanced capacity of less-developed countries to resist military attack by great powers had high utility to the former. In addition, normative changes had engendered no normative costs in regard to defense against aggression. The other qualification—about which more will be said below—noted that the various changes in expected utility were not evenly distributed over the world. They had much more of a hold in some societies, especially the capitalist-democratic countries, than in others.

This theme of the declining value of military forces has been pushed a great deal further in more recent writings. For the sake of economy, I will briefly sum up these opinions and propositions without attributing them to individual authors.

This new school of thought asserts that international relationships have recently been experiencing, and are still undergoing, a revolutionary transformation in the following terms. First, the nuclear balance of terror, which is assumed to be safely stable, has inhibited any large-scale use of force between powerful states, whose leaders, as rational actors, are completely self-deterred. Second, societies everywhere are now preoccupied with the solution of economic and social problems on which national welfare depends. The fading of serious questions of military security has facilitated this emphasis on domestic priorities over the previous stress on defense budgets and military service. Third, rapidly growing international interdependence, particularly economic, has been accompanied by the vigorous growth of transnational forces and organizations, including multinational business corporations, which in turn have undermined the primacy of governmental interstate behavior in favor of that of private actors and have greatly reduced the significance of state boundaries. Indeed, as many see it, the classic nation-state, in which military sovereignty reposed, is being increasingly hemmed in and dominated by these forces and is probably on the way out. Fourth, contemporary and international affairs are more and more devoted to problems—economic, environmental and normative—that generate negotiations in which military power is irrelevant, which are more subject to international economic power, and which in any case increasingly require management by authorities and institutions that transcend national boundaries.

The world, according to this concept, is being shaped by forces and visions that are creating new forms of "international life," in relation to which the realities and teachings of the past are largely, if not wholly, irrelevant. The extent to which the members of this new school assert the presence of novel realities or express a vision of the future is often unclear. They apparently believe they are addressing themselves to an international reality that is in the process of swift and irresistible change and that is evidently escaping from the grim shackles of the premodern world.

If these are the arguments alleging that the utility of force is declining, what do we find if we turn to the actual behavior of governments in military matters? Taking the period from 1964 to 1975, and excluding civil wars in which no country intervened directly with troops, we find the following major armed conflicts erupting: (1) the war in Indochina (already under way since 1962); (2) the Six-Day War between Israel and Arab states (June 1967); (3) the invasion of Czechoslovakia by troops from the Soviet Union, Poland, Hungary, Bulgaria and East Germany (1968); (4) repeated armed clashes between Soviet and Chinese troops (1969); (5) the war between India and Pakistan after Indian forces intervened in the civil war in East Pakistan (1971); (6) the Yom Kippur War between Israel and Arab countries (1973); (7) the landing of Turkish troops on Cyprus to intervene in a local civil war (1974); and (8) Soviet-Cuban and South African interventions in Angola's civil war (1975). . . .

. . . Military forces are, of course, also used to threaten other countries. The period from 1964 to 1975 was studded with military threats. Some were dramatic, such as the military alert on which American forces were placed during the Yom Kippur War in order to deter the Soviet Union from intervening militarily. Many were minor, such as when Spain, in February 1975, dispatched gunboats to its North African enclaves of Ceuta and Melilla in response to the assertion of territorial claims by Morocco.

Another body of evidence worth examining is the range of defense efforts maintained by states during the period. While domestic concerns may be an important—and in some instances the dominant—factor in determining the scale of these costly efforts, few will dispute that their chief purpose was to provide for international deterrence and defense, if not aggressive action. . . .

The frequency of armed conflict in recent years, the rise in global military expenditures and manpower, and the expansion of the international trade in arms does not appear prima facie to support any thesis asserting a secular diminution in the use of force or in the expected utility of military capabilities. If there is a pronounced trend, it expresses a remarkable international shift. Military conflicts have occurred mostly in the Third World, mainly between Third World countries, and this shift is paralleled by the fact that the proportion of world military spending, manpower and weapons imports outside the developed capitalist states has sharply increased.

All this is incontrovertible. Nevertheless, it is arguable that most government behavior in these respects is lagging behind changes in underlying realities. Whether it is or is not we cannot know. But we can subject to critical analysis the components of the theses asserting a decline in the utility of force. To what extent is it true or plausible that the costs of employing force have been rising relative to the gains that may be expected from its use?

The evidence concerning the range and imputed value of expected gains is naturally very poor because motivations are involved. It does seem, though, that the notion of economic gain as a justification for the aggressive use of force is far less in evidence, at least superficially, than it was for millennia prior to World War II. . . .

It would nevertheless be imprudent to disregard or unduly belittle economic motives that might fuel military conflict in the future. Severe shortages of food and raw materials, combined with the attempt of states controlling scarce supplies to exploit such control for economic and political purposes, may well serve to preserve some potential—even if a lesser one relative to other issues—for dangerous conflict. Current moves to extend territorial control over the sea are indicative of this prospect.

The use of force to seize or control territory for reasons of military security, also a traditionally important motive, likewise seems to have lost attraction. Yet it has not disappeared altogether. The 1968 Israeli conquest (or at any rate, retention) of the Sinai as a glacis vis-à-vis Egypt and (in 1973) of the Golan Heights, vis-à-vis Syria, come to mind. Since it is doubtful that the Soviet divisions now stationed in Czechoslovakia are required to assure Soviet domination over that country, it is conceivable that their deployment on the Czech-German boundary was an objective of the Soviet invasion from the beginning. But perhaps it was a mere afterthought. Finally, while the United States and the Soviet Union, rivals in the exercise of worldwide naval power, secure overseas bases and support facilities by diplomacy and contract, or by the invitation or consent of allies, it is possible that their activities to support friendly countries and to help overthrow hostile regimes, at times by direct intervention, has had the retention of such facilities, or their denial to the rival power, as a significant objective.

However, the fading importance of some objectives does not mean that there are not other goals that may justify the use of military force. Several other traditional objectives of this kind have lost little, if any, of their urgency or legitimacy, either internationally or domestically. Deterrence of, and defense against, attacks on political or territorial integrity as well as the rescue of citizens facing organized violence abroad fall into this category. Nor is there any lack of grounds on which to justify force for the purpose of revising the status quo. Aside from the Arab-Israeli conflict, which is in some ways unique, the recent military conflicts listed above suggest the contemporary importance of three major issues capable of generating the decision to go to war. One involves disputes over established boundaries that are regarded as unjust by one side or the other. A second, sometimes overlapping with the first, is the protection or liberation of ethnically related peoples; that is, ethnic unification or national reunification. The third issue, apparently the one most productive of international conflict in the world today, is intervention in civil strife, either to support or help combat incumbent regimes. The precise objective or combination of objectives no doubt varies from case to case, but ideological commitments and the desire to maintain or extend spheres of influence, or reduce the interest of a rival power, evidently play an important part. Anyhow, contemporary governments do not seem to lack incentives to consider force or to be militarily prepared for executing that option.

Turning to the cost side, the deterrent effect of the nuclear balance of terror has figured as a major reason for speculations about the declining utility of military force. The risk of a nuclear war that would destroy both sides, it is argued, keeps each side from using lesser military force against the other. So long as the balance of terror prevails, the aggressive use of military force is undoubtedly curbed. But if deterrent power is needed for this purpose, that power has extremely high utility as an insurance of self-protection. Moreover, because strategic nuclear reprisal against lesser military attacks, including attacks against allies, is suicidal under these conditions, and because its threat therefore has low credibility, the maintenance of adequate conventional forces for defense also has a great deal of utility. The effective balance of both types of forces accounts for the military stability in Europe in recent decades—provided, of course, that deterrence was needed to stifle the emergence of aggressive designs. The claim that nuclear technology has engendered a decline in the utility of military force can only refer to one thing: namely, fear that a serious conflict might increase the risk of escalation to the strategic nuclear level has restrained adventurism. This consequence, however, will endure only so long as the nuclear balance of terror and that of associated defense capabilities remain solid. The future is by no means certain in this regard. New technological choices or an unreciprocated decay of the will to retaliate or to provide sufficient capabilities for deterrence and defence could upset this balance.

States without nuclear weapons are apparently little, if at all, restrained in their behavior toward states possessing nuclear arms. (The behavior of North Vietnam and North Korea toward the United States is illustrative.) This is so because a powerful moral stigma has become attached to the use of nuclear weapons, especially against a nonnuclear opponent. The magnitude of the expected moral and political costs constrains their use and reduces their utility in these relationships. The fact that states possessing nuclear weapons are thus inhibited from bringing their most effective military technology into play against the vast majority of countries is greatly to the advantage of the latter. It tends to increase the utility of *their* military forces against the nuclear superpowers, thereby making the distribution of military deterrence and defensive power less unequal than it would otherwise be. . . .

Heightened awareness of war's destructiveness, claimed to have greatly increased in recent decades, should lead to greater reluctance to use military power. Indeed, numerous surveys in highly developed countries provide evidence that confirms this awareness of the costs of using military force. The historical experience of World Wars I and II has apparently lost little impact in Europe and Japan. Such sensitivity is also a function of the development of higher ed-

ucation and communications systems in these societies. Sophisticated news media, in particular television, have reinforced this awareness by the rich display of violence and destruction in more recent conflicts (e.g., Vietnam), and more widespread education has enabled more and more people to appreciate the effects of nuclear war. Freedom of speech and press in these democratic countries facilitates the diffusion of this sensitivity to the physical and psychic costs of warfare, and democratic constitutions permit the awareness to become politically influential.

However, there is far less evidence that this sensitivity is equally developed in other parts of the world, specifically in the communist societies and the LDCs. Of course, restricted access to opinions and attitudes in these countries obstructs the assembly of relevant evidence one way or the other. Such evidence is sparse. But it would not be surprising if this awareness were more thinly spread in those societies where some of the conditions that seem to account for its development in the capitalist-democratic nations are absent or nearly so: namely, a strong sensitivity to the destructiveness of war, broad-based higher education, a huge volume of news production and dissemination under conditions of freedom of speech and press, and lively media competition. . . .

The frequency of recent armed conflict in the Third World does not encourage the view that the new norm has attracted more than a shallow adherence. This is not surprising. After all, the prohibition of aggressive warfare in the UN Charter was a Western, particularly an American, idea, and it was lodged in the charter at a time when relatively few Third World states were present—at a time when decolonization had only begun. Given their historical experience, countries in the Third World are primarily anxious about aggression by great powers.

Thus, it is not difficult to be skeptical about the profound systemic transformations that, as a number of writers have proposed, governments will increasingly be compelled to adapt to, and that tend to make war less feasible and relevant. We have already dealt with the consequences believed (with inadequate justification) to stem from the evolution of nuclear arms. The thesis that contemporary societies are primarily preoccupied with solving domestic political, economic and social problems seems to be true by and large. How much of a systemic change this sense of priorities represents is problematical. Moreover, the thesis often associated with this finding—that the forementioned preoccupation has generally caused societies to turn "inward"—is implausible. The economies of the highly developed capitalist countries are far too dependent on one another to encourage this sort of isolationism, and the vast majority of the LDCs seek the solution of their economic problems predominantly through the establishment of a new world economic order. While these are not problems that commend the use of military force as a solution, the historical record does not suggest that other pressing issues cannot come to dominate the agenda and the international behavior of states. In the past, certainly, societies have not rarely been content to devote themselves for considerable periods of time primarily to domestic problems, only to be seized by, or have forced on them, international issues that claimed priority. There are a number of countries whose structure of priorities is largely shaped by international considerations that do not rule out the use of force. . . .

One can only conclude, unhappily and disappointingly, that the global picture is far from clear so far as the utility of military force is concerned. The components of this picture do not encourage the prediction that the use and usefulness of military force are definitely on the decline. What look like considerable changes in parameters are too ambiguous and have been with us for too short a time to permit confident answers to the questions we have raised. The changes on the cost side (actual, probable, possible?) certainly do not establish the disutility of force, and they could not do so even if we accepted the changes as substantial and if their impact were uniform throughout the world. Rational actors, to be sure, will not resort to force unless they expect gains to exceed costs. But aside from the circumstance that deviations from rationality are not unknown among political leaders, there is a powerful subjective element and a great deal of unavoidable guesswork in estimates of costs and gains. All we can argue is this: if cost-increasing factors persist and become less unevenly distributed, then war will become a less likely choice of action statistically speaking. This would be an important change, but such a downgrading effect would be acting only marginally on a historically high level of readiness to consider military options when vital, or seemingly vital, values are at stake. Even if the costs of using force rose substantially, rational actors would be willing to meet them when expected gains have exceeding appeal. The recent behavior of governments in regard to military conflict, both engaging in it and preparing for it, is in line with this judgment.

28. The Causes of Wars

Michael Howard

Michael Howard, who wrote this article as a Fellow at the Woodrow Wilson International Center at the Smithsonian Institution in Washington, holds the Regius Chair of Modern History at Oxford University, England.

No one can describe the topic that I have chosen to discuss as a neglected and understudied one. How much ink has been spilled about it, how many library shelves have been filled with works on the subject, since the days of Thucydides! How many scholars from how many specialties have applied their expertise to this intractable problem! Mathematicians, meterologists, sociologists, anthropologists, geographers, physicists, political scientists, philosophers, theologians, and lawyers are only the most obvious of the categories that come to mind when one surveys the ranks of those who have sought some formula for perpetual peace, or who have at least hoped to reduce the complexities of international conflict to some orderly structure, to develop a theory that will enable us to explain, to understand, and to control a phenomenon which, if we fail to abolish it, might well abolish us.

Yet it is not a problem that has aroused a great deal of interest in the historical profession. The causes of specific wars, yes: These provide unending material for analysis and interpretation, usually fueled by plenty of documents and starkly conflicting prejudices on the part of the scholars themselves.

But the phenomenon of war as a continuing activity within human society is one that as a profession we take very much for granted. The alternation of war and peace has been the very stuff of the past. War has been

Reprinted by permission of the author from *The Wilson Quarterly*, (Summer 1981), pp 90–103. Copyright © 1981, Michael Howard.

throughout history a normal way of conducting disputes between political groups. Few of us, probably, would go along with those sociobiologists who claim that this has been so because man is "innately aggressive." The calculations of advantage and risk, sometimes careful, sometimes crude, that statesmen make before committing their countries to war are linked very remotely, if at all, to the displays of tribal "machismo" that we witness today in football crowds. Since the use or threat of physical force is the most elementary way of asserting power and controlling one's environment, the fact that men have frequently had recourse to it does not cause the historian a great deal of surprise. Force, or the threat of it, may not settle arguments, but it does play a considerable part in determining the structure of the world in which we live.

I mentioned the multiplicity of books that have been written about the causes of war since the time of Thucydides. In fact, I think we would find that the vast majority of them have been written since 1914, and that the degree of intellectual concern about the causes of war to which we have become accustomed has existed only since the First World War. In view of the damage which that war did to the social and political structure of Europe, this is understandable enough. But there has been a tendency to argue that because that war caused such great and lasting damage, because it destroyed three great empires and nearly beggared a fourth, it must have arisen from causes of peculiar complexity and profundity, from the neuroses of nations, from the widening class struggle, from a crisis in industrial society. I have argued this myself, taking issue with Mr. A. J. P. Taylor, who maintained that because the war had such profound consequences, it did not necessarily have equally profound causes. But now I wonder whether on this, as on so many other matters, I was not wrong and he was not right.

It is true, and it is important to bear in mind in examining the problems of that period, that before 1914 war was almost universally considered an acceptable, perhaps an inevitable and for many people a desirable, way of settling international differences, and that the war generally foreseen was expected to be, if not exactly brisk and cheerful, then certainly brief; no longer, certainly, than the war of 1870 between France and Prussia that was consciously or unconsciously taken by that generation as a model. Had it not been so generally felt that war was an acceptable and tolerable way of solving international dispute, statesmen and soldiers would no doubt have approached the crisis of 1914 in a very different fashion.

But there was nothing new about this attitude to war. Statesmen had always been able to assume that war would be acceptable at least to those sections of their populations whose opinion mattered to them, and in this respect the decision to go to war in 1914— for continental statesmen at least—in no way differed from those taken by their predecessors of earlier generations. The causes of the Great War are thus in essence no more complex or profound than those of any previous European war, or indeed than those described by Thucydides as underlying the Peloponnesian War: "What made war inevitable was the growth of Athenian power and the fear this caused in Sparta." In Central Europe, there was the German fear that the disintegration of the Habsburg Empire would result in an enormous enhancement of Russian power—power already becoming formidable as French-financed industries and railways put Russian manpower at the service of her military machine. In Western Europe, there was the traditional British fear that Germany might establish a hegemony over Europe which, even more than that of Napoleon, would place at risk the security of Britain and her own possessions, a fear fueled by the knowledge that there was within Germany a widespread determination to achieve a world status comparable with her latent power. Considerations of this kind had caused wars in Europe often enough before. Was there really anything different about 1914?

Ever since the 18th century, war had been blamed by intellectuals upon the stupidity or the self-interest of governing elites (as it is now blamed upon "military-industrial complexes"), with the implicit or explicit assumption that if the control of state affairs were in the hands of sensible men—businessmen, as Richard Cobden thought, the workers, as Jean Jaurès thought—then wars would be no more.

By the 20th century, the growth of the social and biological sciences was producing alternative explanations. As Quincy Wright expressed it in his massive *A Study of War* (1942), "Scientific investigators . . . tended to attribute war to immaturities in social knowledge and control, as one might attribute epidemics to insufficient medical knowledge or to inadequate public health services." The Social Darwinian acceptance of the inevitability of struggle, indeed of its desirability if mankind was to progress, the view, expressed by the elder Moltke but very widely shared at the turn of the century, that perpetual peace was a dream and not even a beautiful dream, did not survive the Great War in those countries where the bourgeois-liberal culture was dominant, Britain and the United States. The failure of these nations to appreciate that such bellicist views, or variants of them, were still widespread in other areas of the world, those dominated by Fascism and by Marxism-Leninism, was to cause embarrassing misunderstandings, and possibly still does.

For liberal intellectuals, war was self-evidently a pathological aberration from the norm, at best a ghastly mistake, at worst a crime. Those who initiated wars must in their view have been criminal, or sick, or the victims of forces beyond their power to control. Those who were so accused disclaimed responsibility for the events of 1914, throwing it on others or saying the whole thing was a terrible mistake for which no one was to blame. None of them, with their societies in ruins around them and tens of millions dead, were prepared to say courageously: "We only acted as statesmen always have in the past. In the circumstances then prevailing, war seemed to us to be the best way of protecting or forwarding the national interests for which we were responsible. There was an element of risk, certainly, but the risk might have been greater had we postponed the issue. Our real guilt does not lie in the fact that we started the war. It lies in our mistaken belief that we could win it."

The trouble is that if we are to regard war as pathological and abnormal, then all conflict must be similarly regarded; for war is only a particular kind of conflict between a particular category of social groups: sovereign states. It is, as Clausewitz put it, "a clash between major interests that is resolved by bloodshed—that is the only way in which it differs from other conflicts." If one had no sovereign states, one would have no wars, as Rousseau rightly pointed out—but, as Hobbes equally rightly pointed out, we would probably have no peace either. As states acquire a monopoly of violence, war becomes the only remaining form of conflict that may legitimately be settled by physical force. The mechanism of legitimization of authority and of social control that makes it possible for a state to moderate or eliminate conflicts within its borders or at very least to ensure that these are not conducted by competitive violence—the mechanism to the study of which historians have quite properly devoted so much attention—makes possible the conduct of armed conflict with other states, and on

occasion—if the state is to survive—makes it necessary.

These conflicts rise from conflicting claims, or interests, or ideologies, or perceptions; and these perceptions may indeed be fueled by social or psychological drives that we do not fully understand and that one day we may learn rather better how to control. But the problem is the control of social conflict *as such*, not simply of war. However inchoate or disreputable the motives for war may be, its initiation is almost by definition a deliberate and carefully considered act and its conduct, at least at the more advanced levels of social development, a matter of very precise central control. If history shows any record of "accidental" wars, I have yet to find them. Certainly statesmen have sometimes been surprised by the nature of the war they have unleashed, and it is reasonable to assume that in at least 50 percent of the cases they got a result they did not expect. But that is not the same as a war begun by mistake and continued with no political purpose.

Statesmen in fact go to war to achieve very specific ends, and the reasons for which states have fought one another have been categorized and recategorized innumerable times. Vattel, the Swiss lawyer, divided them into the necessary, the customary, the rational, and the capricious. Jomini, the Swiss strategist, identified ideological, economic, and popular wars, wars to defend the balance of power, wars to assist allies, wars to assert or to defend rights. Quincy Wright, the American political scientist, divided them into the idealistic, the psychological, the political, and the juridical. Bernard Brodie in our own times has refused to discriminate: "Any theory of the causes of war in general or any war in particular that is not inherently eclectic and comprehensive," he stated, ". . . is bound for that very reason to be wrong." Another contemporary analyst, Geoffrey Blainey, is on the contrary unashamedly reductionist. All war aims, he wrote, "are simply varieties of power. The vanity of nationalism, the will to spread an ideology, the protection of kinsmen in an adjacent land, the desire for more territory . . . all these represent power in different wrappings. The conflicting aims of rival nations are always conflicts of power."

In principle, I am sure that Bernard Brodie was right: No single explanation for conflict between states, any more than for conflict between any other social groups, is likely to stand up to critical examination. But Blainey is right as well. Quincy Wright provided us with a useful indicator when he suggested that "while animal war is a function of instinct and primitive war of the mores, civilized war is primarily a function of state politics."

Medievalists will perhaps bridle at the application of the term "primitive" to the sophisticated and subtle societies of the Middle Ages, for whom war was also a "function of the mores," a way of life that often demanded only the most banal of justifications. As a way of life, it persisted in Europe well into the 17th century, if no later. For Louis XIV and his court war was, in the early years at least, little more than a seasonal variation on hunting. But by the 18th century, the mood had changed. For Frederick the Great, war was to be pre-eminently a function of *Staatspolitik*, and so it has remained ever since. And although statesmen can be as emotional or as prejudiced in their judgments as any other group of human beings, it is very seldom that their attitudes, their perceptions, and their decisions are not related, however remotely, to the fundamental issues of *power*, that capacity to control their environment on which the independent existence of their states and often the cultural values of their societies depend.

And here perhaps we do find a factor that sets interstate conflict somewhat apart from other forms of social rivalry. States may fight—indeed as often as not they do fight—not over any specific issue such as might otherwise have been resolved by peaceful means, but in order to acquire, to enhance, or to preserve their capacity to function as independent actors in the international system at all. "The stakes of war," as Raymond Aron has reminded us, "are the existence, the creation, or the elimination of States." It is a somber analysis, but one which the historical record very amply bears out.

It is here that those analysts who come to the study of war from the disciplines of the natural sciences, particularly the biological sciences, tend, it seems to me, to go astray. The conflicts between states which have usually led to war have normally arisen, not from any irrational and emotive drives, but from almost a superabundance of analytic rationality. Sophisticated communities (one hesitates to apply to them Quincy Wright's word, "civilized") do not react simply to immediate threats. Their intelligence (and I use the term in its double sense) enables them to assess the implications that any event taking place anywhere in the world, however remote, may have for their own capacity, immediately to exert influence, ultimately perhaps to survive. In the later Middle Ages and the early Modern period, every child born to every prince anywhere in Europe was registered on the delicate seismographs that monitored the shifts in dynastic power. Every marriage was a diplomatic triumph or disaster. Every stillbirth, as Henry VIII knew, could presage political catastrophe.

Today, the key events may be different. The pattern remains the same. A malfunction in the political mechanism of some remote African community, a coup d'état in a minuscule Caribbean republic, an insurrection deep in the hinterland of Southeast Asia, an assassination in some emirate in the Middle East—all these will be subjected to the kind of anxious examination and calculation that was devoted a hundred years ago to the news of comparable events in the Balkans: an insurrection in Philippopoli, a coup d'état in Constantinople, an assassination in Belgrade. To whose advantage will this ultimately redound, asked the worried diplomats, ours or *theirs*? Little enough in itself, perhaps, but will it not precipitate or strengthen a trend, set in motion a tide whose melancholy withdrawing roar will strip us of our friends and influence and leave us isolated in a world dominated by adversaries deeply hostile to us and all that we stand for?

There have certainly been occasions when states have gone to war in a mood of ideological fervor like the French republican armies in 1792; or of swaggering aggression like the Americans against Spain in 1898 or the British against the Boers a year later; or to make more money, as did the British in the War of Jenkins' Ear in 1739; or in a generous desire to help peoples of similar creed or race, as perhaps the Russians did in helping the Bulgarians fight the Turks in 1877 and the British dominions certainly did in 1914 and 1939. But, in general, men have fought during the past two hundred years neither because they are aggressive nor because they are acquisitive animals, but because they are reasoning ones: because they discern, or believe that they can discern, dangers before they become immediate, the possibility of threats before they are made.

But be this as it may, in 1914 many of the German people, and in 1939 nearly all of the British, felt justified in going to war, not over any specific issue that could have been settled by negotiation, but *to maintain their power,* and to do so while it was still possible, before they found themselves so isolated, so impotent, that they had no power left to maintain and had to accept a subordinate position within an international system dominated by their adversaries. "What made war inevitable was the growth of Athenian power and the fear this caused in Sparta." Or, to quote another grimly apt passage from Thucydides:

The Athenians made their Empire more and more strong . . . [until] finally the point was reached when Athenian strength attained a peak plain for all to see and the Athenians began to encroach upon Sparta's allies. It was at this point that Sparta felt the position to be no longer tolerable and decided by starting the present war to employ all energies in attacking

and if possible destroying the power of Athens.

You can vary the names of the actors, but the model remains a valid one for the purposes of our analysis. I am rather afraid that it still does.

Something that has changed since the time of Thucydides, however, is the nature of the power that appears so threatening. From the time of Thucydides until that of Louis XIV, there was basically only one source of political and military power—control of territory, with all the resources in wealth and manpower that this provided. This control might come through conquest, or through alliance, or through marriage, or through purchase, but the power of princes could be very exactly computed in terms of the extent of their territories and the number of men they could put under arms.

In 17th-century Europe, this began to change. Extent of territory remained important, but no less important was the effectiveness with which the resources of that territory could be exploited. Initially there were the bureaucratic and fiscal mechanisms that transformed loose bonds of territorial authority into highly structured centralized states whose armed forces, though not necessarily large, were permanent, disciplined, and paid.

Then came the political transformations of the revolutionary era that made available to these state systems the entire manpower of their country, or at least as much of it as the administrators were able to handle. And finally came the revolution in transport, the railways of the 19th century that turned the revolutionary ideal of the "Nation in Arms" into a reality. By the early 20th century, military power—on the continent of Europe, at least—was seen as a simple combination of military manpower and railways. The quality of armaments was of secondary importance, and political intentions were virtually excluded from account. The growth of power was measured in terms of growth of populations and of communications; of the number of men who could be put under arms and transported to the battlefield to make their weight felt in the initial and presumably decisive battles. It was the mutual perception of threat in those terms that turned Europe before 1914 into an armed camp, and it was their calculations within this framework that reduced German staff officers increasingly to despair and launched their leaders on their catastrophic gamble in 1914, which started the First World War.

But already the development of weapons technology had introduced yet another element into the international power calculus, one that has in our own age become dominant. It was only in the course of the 19th century that technology began to produce weapons systems—initially in the form of naval vessels—that could be seen as likely in themselves to prove decisive, through their qualitative and quantitative superiority, in the event of conflict. But as war became increasingly a matter of competing technologies rather than competing armies, so there developed that escalatory process known as the "arms race." As a title, the phrase, like so many coined by journalists to catch the eye, is misleading.

"Arms races" are in fact continuing and open-ended attempts to match power for power. They are as much means of achieving stable or, if possible, favorable power balances as were the dynastic marriage policies of Valois and Habsburg. To suggest that they in themselves are causes of war implies a naive if not totally mistaken view of the relationship between the two phenomena. The causes of war remain rooted, as much as they were in the preindustrial age, in perceptions by statesmen of the growth of hostile power and the fears for the restriction, if not the extinction, of their own. The threat, or rather the fear, has not changed, whether it comes from aggregations of territory or from dreadnoughts, from the numbers of men under arms or from missile systems. The means that states employ to sustain or to extend their power may have been transformed, but their objectives and preoccupations remain the same.

"Arms races" can no more be isolated than wars themselves from the political circumstances that give rise to them, and like wars they will take as many different forms as political circumstances dictate. They may be no more than a process of competitive modernization, of maintaining a status quo that commands general support but in which no participant wishes, whether from reasons of pride or of prudence, to fall behind in keeping his armory up to date. If there are no political causes for fear or rivalry, this process need not in itself be a destabilizing factor in international relations. But arms races may, on the other hand, be the result of a quite deliberate assertion of an intention to *change* the status quo, as was, for example, the German naval challenge to Britain at the beginning of this century.

This challenge was an explicit attempt by Admiral Alfred von Tirpitz and his associates to destroy the hegemonic position at sea which Britain saw as essential to her security, and, not inconceivably, to replace it with one of their own. As British and indeed German diplomats repeatedly explained to the German government, it was not the German naval program in itself that gave rise to so much alarm in Britain. It was the intention that lay behind it. If the status quo was to be maintained, the German challenge had to be met.

The naval race could quite easily have been ended on one of two conditions. Either the Germans could have abandoned their challenge, as had the French in the previous century, and acquiesced in British naval supremacy; or the British could have yielded as gracefully as they did, a decade or so later, to the United States and abandoned a status they no longer had the capacity, or the will, to maintain. As it was, they saw the German challenge as one to which they could and should respond, and their power position as one which they were prepared, if necessary, to use force to preserve. The British naval program was thus, like that of the Germans, a signal of political intent; and that intent, that refusal to acquiesce in a fundamental transformation of the power balance, was indeed a major element among the causes of the war. The naval competition provided a very accurate indication and measurement of political rivalries and tensions, but it did not cause them; nor could it have been abated unless the rivalries themselves had been abandoned.

It was the general perception of the growth of German power that was awakened by the naval challenge, and the fear that a German hegemony on the Continent would be the first step to a challenge to her own hegemony on the oceans, that led Britain to involve herself in the continental conflict in 1914 on the side of France and Russia. "What made war inevitable was the growth of *Spartan* power," to reword Thucydides, "and the fear which this caused in *Athens.*" In the Great War that followed, Germany was defeated, but survived with none of her latent power destroyed. A "false hegemony" of Britain and France was established in Europe that could last only so long as Germany did not again mobilize her resources to challenge it. German rearmament in the 1930s did not of itself mean that Hitler wanted war (though one has to ignore his entire philosophy if one is to believe that he did not); but it did mean that he was determined, with a great deal of popular support, to obtain a free hand on the international scene.

With that free hand, he intended to establish German power on an irreversible basis; this was the message conveyed by his armament program. The armament program that the British reluctantly adopted in reply was intended to show that, rather than submit to the hegemonic aspirations they feared from such a revival of German power, they would fight to preserve their own freedom of action. Once again to recast Thucydides:

Finally the point was reached when German strength attained a peak plain for all to see, and the Germans began to encroach upon Britain's allies. It was at this point that Britain felt the position to be no longer tolerable and decided by starting this present war to employ all her energies in attacking and if possible destroying the power of Germany.

What the Second World War established was not a new British hegemony, but a Soviet hegemony over the Euro-Asian land mass from the Elbe to Vladivostok; and that was seen, at least from Moscow, as an American hegemony over the rest of the world; one freely accepted in Western Europe as a preferable alternative to being absorbed by the rival hegemony. Rival armaments were developed to define and preserve the new territorial boundaries, and the present arms competition began. But in considering the present situation, historical experience suggests that we must ask the fundamental question: *What kind of competition is it?* Is it one between powers that accept the status quo, are satisfied with the existing power relationship, and are concerned simply to modernize their armaments in order to preserve it? Or does it reflect an underlying instability in the system?

My own perception, I am afraid, is that it is the latter. There was a period for a decade after the war when the Soviet Union was probably a status quo power but the West was not; that is, the Russians were not seriously concerned to challenge the American global hegemony, but the West did not accept that of the Russians in Eastern Europe. Then there was a decade of relative mutual acceptance between 1955 and 1965; and it was no accident that this was the heyday of disarmament/arms-control negotiations. But thereafter, the Soviet Union has shown itself increasingly unwilling to accept the Western global hegemony, if only because many other people in the world have been unwilling to do so either. Reaction against Western dominance brought the Soviet Union some allies and many opportunities in the Third World, and she has developed naval power to be able to assist the former and exploit the latter. She has aspired in fact to global power status, as did Germany before 1914; and if the West complains, as did Britain about Germany, that the Russians do not *need* a navy for defense purposes, the Soviet Union can retort, as did Germany, that she needs it to make clear to the world the status to which she aspires; that is, so that she can operate on the world scene by virtue of her own power and not by permission of anyone else. Like Germany, she is determined to be treated as an equal, and armed strength has appeared the only way to achieve that status.

The trouble is that what is seen by one party as the breaking of an alien hegemony and the establishment of equal status will be seen by the incumbent powers as a striving for the establishment of an alternate hegemony, and they are not necessarily wrong. In international politics, the appetite often comes with eating; and there really may be no way to check an aspiring rival except by the mobilization of stronger military power. An arms race then becomes almost a necessary surrogate for war, a test of national will and strength; and arms control becomes possible only when the underlying power balance has been mutually agreed.

We would be blind, therefore, if we did not recognize that the causes which have produced war in the past are operating in our own day as powerfully as at any time in history. It is by no means impossible that a thousand years hence a historian will write— if any historians survive, and there are any records for them to write history from— "What made war inevitable was the growth of Soviet power and the fear which this caused in the United States."

But times *have* changed since Thucydides. They have changed even since 1914. These were, as we have seen, bellicist societies in which war was a normal, acceptable, even a desirable way of settling differences. The question that arises today is how widely and evenly spread is that intense revulsion against war that at present characterizes our own society? For if war is indeed now *universally*

seen as being unacceptable as an instrument of policy, then all analogies drawn from the past are misleading, and although power struggles may continue, they will be diverted into other channels. But if that revulsion is not evenly spread, societies which continue to see armed force as an acceptable means for attaining their political ends are likely to establish a dominance over those which do not. Indeed, they will not necessarily have to fight for it.

My second and concluding point is this: Whatever may be the underlying causes of international conflict, even if we accept the role of atavistic militarism or of military-industrial complexes or of sociobiological drives or of domestic tensions in fueling it, wars begin with conscious and reasoned decisions based on the calculation, made by *both* parties, that they can achieve more by going to war than by remaining at peace.

Even in the most bellicist of societies this kind of calculation has to be made and it has never even for them been an easy one. When the decision to go to war involves the likelihood, if not the certainty, that the conflict will take the form of an exchange of nuclear weapons from which one's own territory cannot be immune, then even for the most bellicist of leaders, even for those most insulated from the pressures of public opinion, the calculation that they have more to gain from going to war than be remaining at peace and pursuing their policies by other means will, to put it mildly, not be self-evident. The odds against such a course benefiting their state or themselves or their cause will be greater, and more *evidently* greater, than in any situation that history has ever had to record. Society may have accepted killing as a legitimate instrument of state policy, but not, as yet, suicide. For that reason I find it hard to believe that the abolition of nuclear weapons, even if it were possible, would be an unmixed blessing. Nothing that makes it easier for statesmen to regard war as a feasible instrument of state policy, one from which they stand to gain rather than lose, is likely to contribute to a lasting peace.

chapter 10

ENDS AND MEANS IN FOREIGN POLICY

The idea persists that American public figures can divorce their words from their deeds. In fact, however, such a divorce is difficult in politics and impossible in diplomacy, where precision in language has a special place and importance.

The immoderate words of the early Reagan Adminstration have had a profound effect on actual events and have damaged important U. S. foreign policy interests. In Europe, the casual manner in which some administration officials treated the prospect of a nuclear exchange with the Soviet Union drove discussions of nuclear strategy out of the think tanks and government offices and into the streets. No doubt previous treatment of this vital question had been held in too closed a circle, but street demonstrations are not the best way for a nation or an alliance to determine strategic choices.

From "Lost Opportunities," by Charles William Maynes.
Foreign Affairs, (1986), 64, no. 3. 415

The concept of power traditionally figures large in the analysis of international politics because sovereignty puts a premium upon each state being able to defend its own security and maintain the wealth and well-being of its citizens. The popular notion of power is that of *military* power—of soldiers, ships, guns, nuclear rockets—and there is something to this because only the largest and richest countries can afford to maintain powerful military forces. Nothing illustrates this point more than the fact that since 1945, the world has been dominated by the two superpowers—Russia and America—each of continental scope, each with large, skilled populations, and each in command of a gigantic industrial and scientific base. The foreign policy of every country is conditioned by the state of the nuclear balance of power; no other countries but Russia and America have the power to conduct an independent policy on a world scale. Only a superpower could contemplate anything like "Star Wars."[1]

[1]See Michael Mandelbaum, "Is SDI Technically Feasible?", *Foreign Affairs*, 64, no. 3, (1986), especially section 8, pp 451–454.

Nevertheless, national power or capability is also the product of a state's *will* and *determination* to acquire and employ enormous military forces. National purpose and national will make a critical difference in the relative power of states. The Soviet Union ended World War II with 20 million dead and with much of its economy and many of the cities of European Russia in ruins. Still, by virtue of the ruthless will and determination of the Soviet regime and the capacity for stoic endurance on the part of the Russian people, the Soviet Union not only recovered largely by its own efforts but also acquired the military and nuclear trappings of a superpower. As Howe and Sewell bring out in their selection on "lifeboat ethics," there is a great deal more to power than military might.

Although Communist China has a large territory, an enormous population, and an effective totalitarian regime, it is far from achieving superpower status. Nevertheless, China would be a tough nut to crack militarily because of the spirit of Chinese nationalism and the Chinese capacity to fight with primitive means. Japan and the countries of Western Europe probably have the industrial capacity to increase their military and nuclear power, but for a variety of reasons they lack the will to do so, one reason being that no matter how powerful they became they would still not attain the status of a nuclear superpower. Hence they remain dependent upon the United States for their security while contributing what they can to the overall balance. The fate of the Shah's regime in Iran is a good example of why power cannot be measured or thought of exclusively in terms of military power. The Shah had a standing military force of more than 400,000 troops equipped with the most modern weapons that money could buy. Iran was viewed by Washington as a pillar of strength in the Persian Gulf, yet the Shah's regime fell in less than a year—not from an outside enemy, but from a popular revolution. National power is also dependent upon the morale, loyalty, and support of a people. Nothing has more strikingly demonstrated this then the replacement of Ferdinand Marcos by Corazon Aquino in the Philipines.

Hence, national power, to be effective, must be skillfully exercised or it can become counterproductive. The United States skillfully exercised its national power when it provided Europe with Marshall Plan aid, when it formed the North Atlantic Treaty Organization (NATO) to defend Western Europe and when it sought to identify America's strategy and interests with the movements for independence in the Third World. It did not employ its power skillfully when it sought to defend South Vietnam under impossible circumstances. It not only inflicted a defeat upon itself but it also brought the conduct of American leadership into disrepute. Those who argued that America must not appear to lose the war, lest it lose credibility, actually weakened the basis of America's national power both at home and abroad.

National power is also dependent upon the availability of essential natural resources from overseas (such as oil), upon the security of strategic waterways upon which a state's access to natural resources may ultimately depend and, to some extent, upon the support of one's allies and the availability of bases essential to the projection of national power.

So we see that national power or capability encompasses much more than just military power. National power has its foundations in territorial grandeur and economic wealth; in the morale and dedication of a people to its country and government (even if it is a totalitarian regime); in the level of a country's science and technology; in the effectiveness of its political system; and in the wisdom and skill of its leaders and statecraft. And as Howe and Sewell bring out, it also depends upon taking other peoples' welfare into account.

This brings us to a crucial aspect of power analysis all too often ignored by those who focus on the simple components of power. Power is only effective when it succeeds in accomplishing its purpose. To give a striking example, Soviet and American nuclear weapons are only successful as long as they deter the outbreak of a nuclear war. Once nuclear weapons are used, it will hardly be said that they were an effective form of military power, even if one side "wins."

The success of effectiveness of power depends on its relevance to the political objectives in view. These political objectives will vary enormously, depending on whether we are seeking to deter nuclear war, defend an ally, stabilize a volatile region of the world (such as the Persian Gulf), or give a regime threatened with internal subversion the means with which to defend itself. Strategic and political situations vary enormously in their essential nature, and the efficacy of power resides in a government's ability to apply the appropriate technique. Hence, the understanding of power requires a profound appreciation of the normative context in which it is to be applied. For this reason, the analysis of national power requires a more sophisticated approach than just the mere adumbration of the physical components of national power. As Secretary of State George Shultz recently observed,

> Clearly, nations must be able to protect themselves when faced with an obvious threat. But what about those gray areas that lie somewhere between all-out war and blissful harmony? How do we protect the peace without being willing to resort to the ultimate sanction of military power against those who seek to destroy the peace?
>
> Americans have sometimes tended to think that power and diplomacy are two distinct alternatives. This reflects a fundamental misunderstanding. The truth is, power and diplomacy must always go together, or we will accomplish very little in this world. Power must always be guided by purpose. At the same time, the hard reality is that diplomacy not backed by strength will always be ineffectual at best, dangerous at worst.[2]

It is imperative that we examine what is meant by power or capability and how it relates to the effects that it is supposed to produce, and what it is our leaders really mean when they speak of *power*. Since their intent in having power at their disposal is to influence other countries to act according to their wishes, we might think of *power* in terms of *influence* or *control*. If we do that, we see that influence or control may be exerted by a variety of techniques besides military power. It may be exerted by persuasion, bribes, economic exchange, or agreements not to threaten each other.[3]

[2]From an address at Yeshiva University, December 8, 1984, "The Ethics of Power," Department of State *Current Policy*, No. 642, p. 2

[3]See Charles William Maynes, "Logic, Bribes and Threats," *Foreign Policy*, No. 60, (Fall 1985), especially pp. 111–112.

If we broaden our definition of power to incorporate the notion of influence or control over the actions of other governments, we immediately see that power means more than just military capabilities, important though those may be. It depends on many other components: resources, technology, morale, the effectiveness of the political system, and the wisdom and judgment of the leadership. The successful assertion of military power, as of all forms of power, also depends on knowing whether it is appropriate to the type of influence one is seeking to exert. The situations in which one state seeks to influence another vary enormously, as does its intent or objective. There is a marked difference between the type of military power needed to dissuade the Soviet Union from risking nuclear war and that which is required to prevent revolution in a Third World country. Each situation presents a different *policy contingency framework*, to use the term that one author employs, and the form of power that may succeed in one situation will not necessarily succeed in another.

The *fungibility* or effectiveness of political power resources also depends on the specification of the *scope and domain* in which the power is to be exercised. Not all forms of power are equally useful in all situations. One country may be weak in one situation or in one resource but strong in another. There are severe penalties for applying the wrong type of power to situations in which it is inappropriate. The United States tried for eight years to bomb and terrorize North Vietnam into withdrawing its support for the war in South Vietnam. Apart from the fact that it miscalculated the efficacy of the military means it employed, the United States government failed to understand, and woefully underestimated, the motivation and determination of Hanoi to unify Vietnam at any price. In other words, the effective utilization of power, especially of military power, depends upon its appropriateness to the domain and contingency to which it is being applied. In an even broader sense, Llewelyn Howell, rejecting the "Number One" complex, has asserted that America "has not been able to use its number one position in any significant way."[4]

The assertion of influence involves a relationship of interdependence. To employ power successfully one must first determine one's intent and how it will be *perceived by* the adversary or target of one's influence. For example, if Washington's intent is to enhance the prospects of peace as well as one's security, it is more likely to achieve those objectives by striving to reach agreement with the Russians on arms limitations than by striving for nuclear superiority. National power or capability is neither finite nor infinite. There are many competing claims upon a national economy: claims of trade, education, welfare, and claims of the productive force itself for better wages and living conditions. No state exists in a national-security vacuum—it must meet the economic challenge and competition of other states, as well as the demands of Third World people for help with their economic problems.

A country can overextend itself or confront political and strategic challenges on so many fronts that the cost of meeting its commitments exceeds its national

---

[4]Llewellyn D. Howell, "American Power or American Ego: Why Number One?" *Diplomatic Pouch*, 21, no. 2 (1985), 3. Published by the School of International Services, The American University.

power. This is essentially what happened to Britain between World Wars I and II, and in the aftermath of World War II. Even in 1914, the British Empire was overextended, and the aim of the British government was to preserve Britain's position in the world rather than add to her burden. By the 1930s, it was quite clear that Britain's forces were inadequate for the military and diplomatic tasks which confronted her. "The plain fact which cannot be obscured," Sir Thomas Inskip, the British minister for defense coordination, wrote in 1938, "is that it is beyond the resources of this country to make proper provision in peace for the defense of the British Empire against three major powers in three different theatres of war." This as much as anything explains the policy of appeasement. Unable to mobilize national power adequate to meet the brutal challenge of three renaissant military powers, Britain sought to make concessions in the hope of reducing their aggressive appetites. It was not the technique that was wrong so much as the vain hope that Germany might be appeased. But Hitler had no wish to play by the traditional rules of the game; as one authority has written, his demands could not be "brokered" in exchange for peace. The enormous industrial and economic power that America possessed at the end of World War II relative to the rest of the world largely enabled the United States to determine the terms of global system for almost fifteen years (1945 to 1960). But as the Soviet Union caught up with the United States militarily, and as America's allies and economic rivals caught up with United States technology and industry, it has been harder for the United States to support the burdens of global leadership (or hegemony) with the same almost effortless ease. The cost of the Vietnam War was about twenty times that of the Korean War fifteen years earlier, and elsewhere in the Third World the forces of nationalism and the availability of modern weapons (many supplied by the United States) make the threat of intervention much less convincing (or appealing) and potentially much more costly. As a state's power declines relative to its commitments, it has two options: either it must increase its national power capabilities or it must reduce its commitments. This is what former President Nixon meant by advocating a "low profile." If the United States spends unnecessarily on additional military power, it is likely to weaken the economic and political basis of its strength; it must strike an ever more careful balance between its strategic needs and its national power capabilities. The ethical dimension must also be taken into account. How is one to judge the relationship of ethics to the conduct of international relations? It is to this question that Kenneth Thompson addresses himself in this chapter. The logic of the state system puts a premium upon each state pursuing its own self-interest to the point that its regard for the interests of others is purely expedient. War and other evil actions have for so long and so often been characteristic of governments in their conduct that international politics have become synonymous with "power politics" or *Realpolitik,* the German term for the idea that international politics is a realm divorced from ethical values or moral constraints. By contrast, idealists and liberals believe that wars are caused precisely by the operation of "power politics," which in turn reflect the prejudices and interests of ruling classes or militarists; and that if the later could be changed or superseded by world government, war could be eliminated. Moral values cannot be ignored.

In another selection that follows, Michael Howard, a distinguished British military historian, sets forth a conception of international politics that does not preclude a role for ethical values and moral judgments. In the first place, he argues, the state is not an end in itself; it exists as a means by which its citizens may enjoy a better life. Therefore, it is utterly wrong to accord a quasi-automatic legitimacy to governments to do whatever advances their state's security and self-interest if those actions are likely to cause war and suffering for untold millions of people, including their own citizens. Secondly, starting with the aphorism of the early nineteenth-century Prussian strategist, von Clausewitz, that "war is nothing but the continuation of policy by other means," Howard argues that just as war would be meaningless unless it was conducted for some worthwhile political objective like security, so state policy or the objectives of states would be meaningless unless "determined and judged according to the needs of the international community" of which each state is a part. To put this precept into practice requires a constant balancing between ethical imperatives and strategic considerations. By recognizing the legitimacy of both spheres, the world leader acknowledges the need for a judgment between the potentially conflicting claims of the two spheres: the ethical and the strategic.

The most important key to resolving the conflict resides in the recognition that "political action needs to take constant account of both dimensions"—the strategic and the ethical. Humankind wants a better life; not all people all of the time want to wield more power over their neighbors. Only a handful of regimes are ever ruled by "mad tyrants" for whom war and domination are exclusive goals. (Admittedly conflicts over religion and other absolutes are not easily resolved when they enter into inter-state politics, but they have not been the only cause of war.) According to the late Arnold Wolfers, even the pursuit of security should be viewed as a matter of "more" or "less" and not as a condition to be remedied by absolute superiority. Therefore effective political action for most leaders most of the time ought to consist of reconciling one's state's interests with those of other states rather than imposing one's will upon them. To reconcile the ethical and the strategic requires the statesman or stateswoman to be in touch with the human forces that constitute the taproot of actions by other governments, and to accommodate *as well as to check* governments hostile to one's own interests.

A purely strategic or power-political view will be as inadequate to this task as would be a purely idealistic one. Just as the pursuit of an ethical objective at the expense of political considerations can cause one to ignore "the tedious and murky problems of how to attain it," so an obsessive emphasis upon power (and inferentially upon the emotional cliché of maintaining one's status as number one) can lead those in the national security apparatus to a similar sort of tunnel vision; namely, they become blinded to the fact that they are serving neither their own people nor that of the international community by making strategic imperatives—security, domination of markets, etc.—the exclusive measure of national policy. Nor can they ignore the dimensions of ethics, as Kenneth Thompson makes clear in his comprehensive treatment of several different approaches to this vital component of policy.

DISCUSSION QUESTIONS

1. Why must national power be understood as more than just economic and military power? What is the place of national purpose or will?

2. What is meant by the term "lifeboat ethics"? How does it relate to the more philosophical approaches taken by Thompson and Howard?

3. How does "interdependence" affect the ability of a state to behave (exert its power) independently of other states? What do Howe and Sewall say about this?

4. Explain what Michael Howard means by the "vertical and horizontal coordinates." What about the diagonal?

5. According to Howard, how can ethical values be reconciled with the strategic dimension of power politics? In what ways does Thompson relate human nature and diplomacy?

6. Referring to Professor Khadduri's article on Islam in chapter 4, what similarities do you see compared with Thompson's basic Christian viewpoint on ends and means in foreign policy? What differences?

7. Howard wrote, "That all sounds very fine as a theory. In practice, unfortunately, it settles very little." To what was he referring?

29. The Moral Dimension of Diplomacy

Kenneth W. Thompson

Dr. Kenneth Thompson, Director of the Miller Center for Public Affairs at the University of Virginia, has for many years addressed himself to the interrelationships between politics and ethics.

William Graham Summer wrote: "The amount of superstition is not much changed, but it now attaches to politics, not to religion." In ancient societies, men called on the gods to rid their world of evil, conflict and suffering. If war persisted, they asked the gods to reward their side with victory. What men in their frailty could not accomplish, the gods in their mercy would provide. They would protect the weak and reward virtue. If men could not defend justice in the social order, the gods would assure that justice was done. From ancient tribal deities to the gods who presided over the knights of the round table, their task ultimately was to smooth out the troubled path along which heroic men had to walk.

An opposing view of morality is rooted in classical traditions and certain historic versions of the Judaeo-Christian faith. Moralists, nationalists and religiously oriented people are tempted to make a success story out of their faith. Yet no one, and least of all authentic religious leaders, can guarantee prosperity and success, even though spokesmen of some early religious movements in the colonies and thirteen states sought to demonstrate that outer signs of well-being pointed in the direction of inner virtue. Attacking this viewpoint, Reinhold Niebuhr wrote of two men, one who tithed from his youth and gained great wealth. That man explained his success as deriving from a lifelong observance of religious practices. The

Reprinted by permission of the publisher. *The Review of Politics*, 46, 3, (July 1984). Copyright © 1984, University of Notre Dame, pp. 367–387.

other man, Adam Denger, who employed the young Niebuhr in his grocery store in Lincoln, Illinois, generously extended credit to miners who had lost their jobs. However, the miners left Lincoln without paying their debts and their benefactor suffered bankruptcy. In her biography of Niebuhr, June Bingham writes: "Mr. Denger kept believing that God would protect him if he did what was right. But God let Adam Denger go bankrupt and his young assistant grew up to preach against sentimentality and reliance on special providence."[1] Niebuhr chose as his text the biblical passage: "For He makes his sun to rise on the evil and the good alike and sends rain on the just and the unjust." According to Niebuhr, it is a corruption of religion to hold out the promise that the good man or the virtuous nation will always triumph or that evil empires will be destroyed. Religious people too often are found lobbying in the courts of the Almighty proclaiming their goodness and offering their piety as proof that they deserve special favors. A more profound understanding of man and God would emphasize the tragic element in history. The unending process in diplomacy of balancing the forces of harmony and disharmony is at war with the notion that those who are good and virtuous are destined through some form of divine intervention to inherit prosperity and success.

A more contemporary version of the intrusion of false and superstitious notions about ethics and diplomacy is what Louis J. Halle has called "Pharisaism." He asserts that the posturing of those who claim to be more virtuous than their fellowmen is not true morality. In the parable of the pharisee and the publican (Luke 18:10–14), those who make ostentatious display of their morality, striking moralistic poses and pointing to the iniquity of others, are condemned for their false morality. Politicians and diplomats who are overwhelmingly concerned with the morality of others ought as a rule to be mistrusted. By their attitudes, they would have others believe they have achieved so complete a level of morality they are qualified to judge others. They depend not on the gods for their morality but on their own supposed moral perfection.

Another version of morality is that of Manichaeism which portrays the world in radical terms of absolute good and evil or right and wrong. Americans are predisposed to a form of Manichaeism by early childhood distinctions between good guys and bad guys or cops and robbers. The false logic of Manichaeism lies at the heart of every crusading ideology and of civilization's long record, ever since the wars of religion, of unspeakable brutalities of one people against another. In the end, Manichaeism becomes a negative morality based on punishment and retribution. According to the mythology of Manichaeism, a particular group or class is seen as a Satanic evil. For the Germans the Jews, for the allies the Germans and Japanese, for the bourgeoisie the communists and for the communists the bourgeoisie are the one evil force in the world. Once that evil has been rooted out and eradicated, peace and harmony will prevail. Not by accident, Khomeini depicts the United States as the Great Satan in what is but the most recent form of Manichaeism. Those who belong to groups who for others personify evil may in the name of morality be chastised or destroyed in order that justice be done.

A final version of morality identifies the good with the changing and the novel and evil with past practices. Since the end of the Napoleonic Wars, ever larger groups of Western leaders have denounced diplomacy and international politics as an unhappy stage in the progress of mankind that was bound to disappear once the particular historical circumstances that gave rise to it had been transformed. European diplomacy was an archaism that history would eliminate when reason and morality prevailed. For some writers, a particular social evil caused the corruption of international society: colonies for Jeremy Bentham, trade barriers for Cobden and Proudhon, capitalism for Marx and the absence of self-determination and self-government for liberals. For others, foreign relations themselves were the evil. It was Richard Cobden who declared: "At some future election, we may probably see the test 'no foreign politics' applied to those who offer to become the representatives of free constituencies."[2] Following World War I, the Nye Committee in 1934–36 on behalf of the United States Senate investigated the role of certain financial and industrial interests suspected of having been responsible for the entry of the United States into that war. Not the requirements of the national interest but certain self-seeking groups who profited from the war had plotted the nation's involvement. A small band of manufacturers of war materiel and international bankers had lured us into war. According to the devil theory of war, a handful of munition makers were responsible. If the nation could rid itself of their conspiratorial and nefarious influence, peace would prevail.

In a similar vein, others saw in European diplomacy and power politics the cause of all conflict. In 1943, Secretary of State Cordell Hull on returning from the Moscow Conference, which prepared the way for the creation of the United Nations, proclaimed that the new international organization would lead to the end of world power politics which had ravaged European society. Earlier President Woodrow Wilson, prematurely as history was to record, prophesied that the common interests of mankind were replacing national interests. In 1946, British Minister of State Philip Noel-Baker rose in the House of Commons to say that his government was "determined to use the institutions of the United Nations to kill power politics, in order that, by the methods of democracy, the will of the people shall prevail."[3]

The underlying premise of all these views is the conviction that a certain group or particular social and international order are the evil forces which alone explain the immorality of diplomacy and politics. Along the pathway to a moral international order these evil forces will disappear. Once they are rooted out, an ethical international system will emerge and conflict will come to an end.

Human Nature and Diplomacy

Opposed to the essentially utopian views of the several versions of morality and diplomacy discussed above is a fundamentally different conception of human nature and diplomacy. According to this perspective, human nature has not changed since the days of classical antiquity. Man is good and evil; his virtues and vices persist no less in a technologically advanced than a primitive society. Politics and diplomacy bring out the harshest side of man's nature though sometimes also the best. In ancient Greece, Thucydides whom Hobbes described as "the most Politick Historiographer that ever lived" wrote in the Melian dialogue of the clash between morality and power. Melos had remained neutral during the war between Sparta and Athens but the Athenians, during a long truce, confronted Melos with an expeditionary force and called on it to join the Athenian alliance or be exterminated. When the Melians resisted, Thucydides records the ensuing dialogue. The Athenians explain that justice depends upon the power to compel; the strong do what they have the power to do and the weak accept what they must. Even the gods will not help because they behave toward one another and toward men as the Athenians plan to behave toward Melos. The Athenians conclude: "It is a general and necessary law of nature to rule wherever one

can. This is not a law we made ourselves, nor were we the first to act on it when it was made. We found it already in existence, and we shall leave it to exist forever among those who come after us." Melos resists and is destroyed.

Frederick the Great in his *Origin of the Bismarck Policy* or *The Hohenzollern Doctrine and Maxims*, written for his successor to the throne, summarizes his opinions on religion, morals, politics and diplomacy by saying: "We monarchs take what we can, when we can, and we are never in the wrong, except when compelled to give up what we had taken."[4] Of religion, Frederick wrote: "Religion is absolutely necessary in a State government. . . . [But] there is nothing which tyrannizes over the mind and heart so much as religion, because it agrees neither with our passions, nor with the high political views which a monarch should entertain. . . . When he is about to conclude a treaty with some foreign power, if he only remembers that he is a Christian, all is lost: he will always suffer himself to be duped or imposed upon."[5] Frederick defended the right of religious sects to pray and seek salvation as they wished but found they were destined never to agree. Of justice, Frederick declared: "We owe justice to our subjects as they owe us respect . . . but it is necessary to take care that we are not brought under subjection by justice itself."[6] For Frederick: "Justice is the image of God. Who can therefore attain to so high a perfection."[7] "Behold all the countries in the world, and examine if justice is administered exactly in the same manner."[8] What troubled Frederick most was that if the trends he observed continued, onetenth of his kingdom's subjects in the next century would be engaged in the administration of justice with "that sure and steady way of proceeding which lawyers have . . . [and] that clever manner of preserving their advantages under the appearances of the strictest equity and justice."[9]

On statesmanship and diplomacy, Frederick reduced all moral and political practice to three principles and practices: "The first is to maintain your power, and, according to circumstances, to increase and extend it. The second is to form alliances only for your own advantage and the third is to command fear and respect even in the most disastrous times."[10] Harsh as his maxims seem, Frederick formulated them into a doctrine of reason of state. He warned against displaying pretensions with vanity but insisted that every ruler must have "two or three eloquent men" and leave justification for his actions to them. Only when Prussia has become more powerful will she be able to assume an air of "constancy and good faith, which, at most, is fit only for the greatest powers and for petty sovereigns."[11] Of diplomats, Frederick sought "those who have the gift of expressing themselves in ambiguous terms and susceptible of a double meaning."[12] He went on to say it would not be improper for a sovereign to have political locksmiths to pick locks or open doors nor physicians to dispose of troublesome people who might be in the way. With regard to embassies, Frederick preferred envoys rather than ambassadors for it was difficult to find men of wealth and noble birth and "by adopting this system, you will save enormous sums of money every year, and, nevertheless, your affairs will be transacted all the same."[13] Yet there were cases in which embassies must be on a scale of magnificence, as when rulers sought a political or matrimonial alliance. But such instances were exceptional. Above all, neighbors must believe "that you are a dangerous monarch, who knows no other principle than that which leads to glory."[14]

It is tempting in the modern age to dismiss the insights of Thucydides and Frederick the Great and writers like Hobbes who spoke of a state of nature involving a "war of every man against every man" or the acute analysis of politics by Machiavelli in which might makes right. Yet diplomacy in the last two decades of the twentieth century goes on under the shadow of war. It is worthwhile recalling the political thought of the Founding Fathers. Because of man's nature and the need to remedy "the defect of better mo-

tives," the Founders turned to constitutionalism as providing a system of checks and balances. They wrote of the interplay of opposite and rival interests as a means of equilibrium and constitutional order. Because they understood the human traits of which earlier men had written, they displayed a mistrust of political power, not only that of other states but within their borders. As John Adams put it:

> Power always thinks it has a great soul and vast views beyond the comprehension of the weak and that it is doing God's service when it is violating all His laws. Our passions, ambitions, love and resentment, etc., possess so much metaphysical subtlety and so much overpowering eloquence that they insinuate themselves into the understanding and the conscience and convert both to their party.

Adams was not alone in his concern about power. His intellectual adversary during much of the period, Jefferson, could write in 1798: "Confidence in the men of our choice . . . is . . . the parent of despotism: free government is founded in jealousy and not in confidence; it is jealousy and not confidence which prescribes limited constitutions to bind down those whom we are obliged to trust with power. . . . In questions of power then let no more be heard of confidence in man, but bind him down from mischief by the claims of the Constitution." The exercise of power and the imposing of the will of an individual or group on others was "of all known causes the greatest promoter of corruption." However the Enlightenment may have shaped the thought of early Americans, their views of power reflected a sturdy realization of the hazards and reality of power. Their view of human nature was not far removed from Pascal who explained: "Man is neither angel nor brute, and the unfortunate thing is that he who would act the angel acts the brute." Whatever one's conclusions about ethics and diplomacy ultimately may be, it is important to recognize the limitations which the more sordid and selfish aspects of human nature place on the conduct of diplomacy, including diplomacy in the nuclear age.

The Nature of Diplomacy and Morality

The most cynical of all views of diplomacy is that attributed, whether rightly or not, to Sir Henry Wotton who allegedly identified "an ambassador as an honest man who is sent abroad to lie for the good of his country." The three elements which such a definition embraces are: a concept of the role of lying in diplomacy, an implication that privately the ambassador is an honest man but publicly he is something else, and an acceptance of the inevitability of the "official lie." The conventional response of moralists is to dismiss any reference to deceit in diplomacy yet moralists run the risk of moving to an opposite extreme. As Sir Harold Nicolson wrote: "The worst kind of diplomatists are missionaries, fanatics and lawyers; the best kind are the reasonable and humane skeptics. Thus it is not religion which has been the main formative influence in diplomatic theory; it is common sense."[15] Truth-telling in diplomacy is limited by the fact that diplomacy is not a system of moral philosophy. It is the application, as Sir Ernest Satow wrote, of intelligence and tact "to the conduct of official relations between independent states."[16] Honesty in diplomacy, said an experienced diplomat, doesn't mean telling everything you know.

It is self-evident that differences exist between eighteenth- or nineteenth- and twentieth-century diplomacy. The former involved relationships between monarchs and rulers who belonged to an aristocratic elite. Twentieth-century diplomats are envoys of the people. Broadly speaking, the former were professionals while the latter are amateurs in statecraft. Yet with all the differences, diplomacy everywhere brings into play common characteristics. In describing what was needed of the twentieth-century diplo-mat, Nicolson called for "a man of experience, integrity and intelligence, a man, above all who is not swayed by emotion or prejudice, who is profoundly modest in all his dealings, who is guided only by a sense of public duty, and who understands the perils of cleverness and the virtues of reason, moderation, discretion and tact." Having said all this, Nicolson coyly added: "Mere clerks are not expected to exhibit all these difficult tasks at once."[17]

The crux of the matter is that foreign policy is conducted by sovereign governments. As a function of governmental responsibility, foreign policy must serve the purposes of governments generally; "its primary purpose must be to preserve the union" (Lincoln), informed by the national interest and the dictates of national security. On this point, two well-known American authorities on diplomacy differ in emphasis while agreeing in their conclusions.

The champion of political realism, Hans J. Morgenthau, repeatedly argued that the conduct of foreign policy is not devoid of moral significance. Political actors come under moral judgement and witness to the values of their societies. However, the contemporary environment of international politics is marked both by moral improvement and retrogression. There have been advances in man's respect for human life since the fifteenth and sixteenth centuries when, for example, the Republic of Venice carried on its rolls an official poisoner whose employment depended on his success in disposing of the leaders of rival states. Compare this with the sweeping moral indignation Winston S. Churchill expressed when Stalin at Tcheran proposed, half mockingly but not wholly in jest, that killing 50,000 officers would put an end to the threat of German aggression. Or contrast it with the public reaction in the United States to disclosures concerning possible plans for political assassinations by the CIA. Yet the contemporary international scene witnesses to the decline of international morality, indicating that moral restraints are weakening if not disappearing, as in distinctions in wartime between combatants and noncombatants. According to the Hague Conventions of 1899 and 1907, only soldiers ready to fight were considered combatants and objects of war, but by World War II this distinction had effectively been obliterated in the saturation bombings and harsh treatment of prisoners of war by both sides. The international environment was marked by a decline in international morality brought about in part by the technology of warfare and in part by a diminution of standards concerning the sanctity of human life.

Thus in war as in peace the world has seen moral improvement in some spheres but a decline in others resulting from the fact that universal moral principles which are omnipresent are filtered through circumstances of time and place and through national concepts and cultural practices determining their application. In peace, there remains an enormous gap between, say, American respect for the elemental principle of respect for human life (our refusal to take human life except in extraordinary circumstances—capital punishment, abortion, euthanasia and other carefully defined and delimited exceptions) and practices in other civilizations which have been far more extravagant in imperiling human life for political and ideological purposes (Stalin and the Kulaks, Hitler and the Jews and the punishment of thieves in Saudi Arabia by cutting off their hands). The relations of universal principles to time and circumstances and to the necessities and norms of different nations and civilizations have been controlling. Particular moral imperatives are obeyed by particular nations at particular times and not by others, and this is the overarching characteristic of today's international environment.

George F. Kennan, brilliant American diplomatist and writer, goes further than Morgenthau in writing:

> The governing of human beings is not a moral exercise. It is a practical function made necessary, regrettably, by the need for order in social relationships and for a collective discipline to control the behavior of that large majority of mankind who are too weak and selfish to control their own behavior.

Ambassador Kennan declares further that "government, particularly democratic government, is an agent and not a principal." No more than any other agent (for example, the corporation or the church, especially since the Protestant Reformation) can it substitute itself for the conscience of the principal. In a particularly strongly worded statement applying this thought to the American government as agent of the American people, Kennan asserts:

> The government could undertake to express and to implement the moral impulses of so great a mass of people only if there were a high degree of consensus among them on such questions as: what is good and what is bad? and to what extent is it the duty of American society to make moral judgments on behalf of others and to improve them from the standpoint of those judgments? Such consensus would be difficult to achieve even if we were dealing with a highly homogeneous population, with firm and unanimously-accepted concepts of an ethical nature as well as of the duties and powers of the state. In the case of a polyglot assemblage of people such as our own, it would be quite impossible. If our government should set out to pursue moral purposes in foreign policy, on what would it base itself? Whose outlooks, philosophy, religious concepts would it choose to express? Imbedded in our population are hundreds of different traditions, beliefs, assumptions and reactions in this field. Are we to assume that it, the government, knows what is right and wrong, has imparted this knowledge to the people at large, and obtained their mandate to proceed to bring about the triumph of what is right, on a worldwide scale?

Opposed to the views of the two diplomatic writers is a large and respected body of thought resulting from international law writings. The former American Judge on the International Court of Justice, Philip Jessup, singles out five criteria as essential to an ethical and therefore a successful foreign policy: "sincerity, loyalty, legality, humanitarianism" and what he has called "proper objectives." By sincerity he means the same as honesty or an absence of deceit, vital as he sees it, especially in peacetime. A government suffers from the label that it is not to be trusted. Jessup acknowledges there may be imperatives which lead to deceit of a government's own citizenry but these must find justification if at all under "proper objectives." Louis J. Halle who belongs to the first group of diplomatic writers offers a dissenting commentary on Jessup's opinion, saying:

> From 1955 to 1960 . . . the United States regularly sent its U-2 spy planes over the Soviet Union at high altitudes to locate military installations and report on military activities. Presumably, such planes would have been able to detect any preparations for a surprise attack on the United States in time to give warning. . . . A Soviet system of espionage operating inside the United States was alert to detect any preparations for a surprise attack on the Soviet Union. This mutual espionage contributed to the preservation of the peace, because the observations of the spies on either side, showing that the other was not preparing a surprise attack, enabled each to remain calm and restrained. If such observations had not been available, each side might have been the victim of panic-making rumors that would have impelled it to feel that its survival depended on striking before the other was able to realize some rumored intention of doing so itself.

Halle goes on:

> However, in 1960 when an American U-2, illegally violating another country's air space, was shot down in the middle of the Soviet Union, many idealists in the West were shocked to learn that such espionage by the United

States had been going on, for they regarded it as both immoral and incompatible with the advancement of the cause of peace.

Peace is more secure today, and the prospects of arms control are better, to the extent that the Soviet Union and the United States, through their espionage (in which satellites have replaced spy planes), can each be sure of what armaments the other possesses.[18]

There are significant differences between diplomatic analysts and international lawyers, therefore, on truth-telling. The former are more inclined to say that while there is a universal moral code of truth-telling, there are differing social contexts in which it is applied. In personal and national affairs, men operate within an integrated society where lying is seldom necessary. Mayor Daley's creed for Chicago politics was that a politician's last resource is his word and that lying is not good politics ("if you must lie, it is better not to say anything"). International affairs differ and the difference is one between conditions of civilization and conditions of nature, where because of the half-anarchic character of international society "one man is to another as a wolf." However, for the second group of writers, the international lawyers, truth-telling is an aspect of sincerity plus loyalty plus legality. Law's basic norm—*Pacta sunt servanda*—is a part not only of our own moral creed but of the Koran and most religious teachings. Pragmatism and morality came together in the Hague and the Geneva conventions on the treatment of civilians and prisoners evolving from the pragmatic test of reciprocity.

Morality, Democracy and the International System

A nation, particularly a democratic nation and most particularly the United States, tends to view its actions as taking place within a moral framework. On one hand, it sees itself as subject to certain limitations and judgments; on the other, it looks to national goals and historic traditions as the explanation and moral justification for its course of action. Seldom if ever is foreign policy defended by arguing solely for the maintenance or increase of national power or of national survival. Americans and most other people speak rather of standing for moral purposes beyond the state: democracy or communism, freedom or equality, order or justice and historical inevitability. Whatever cynics may say, foreign policy tends to be articulated in moral terms, even in most authoritarian regimes, whether those terms be social justice, economic equality, the overthrow of colonialism, national liberation or putting an end to an unjust status quo.

To know that men and nations espouse goals and values that transcend national defense or survival is a first step or approach but not a solution to the moral problem. In fact, it is more a claim than an approach; it may bespeak what George F. Kennan and Hans J. Morgenthau have called moralism as distinguished from morality. Moralism is the tendency to make one moral value supreme and to apply it indiscriminately without regard to time and place; morality by comparison is the endless quest for what is right amidst the complexity of competing and sometimes conflicting, sometimes compatible moral ends. Paul Freund of the Harvard Law School based his 1976 Thomas Jefferson Memorial Lecture of the National Endowment for the Humanities on Lord Acton's aphorism "when you perceive a truth, look for a balancing truth." According to Freund, we suffer in Western civilization from the decline of the ancient art of moral reasoning, the essence of which is weighing and balancing not only good and evil but competing "goods."

Freedom and order, liberty and justice, economic growth and social equality, national interest and the well-being of mankind are each in themselves worthy moral ends. How much simpler moral choice would be if the leader could select one value as his guiding principle and look upon the rest as secondary or instrumental. In every human community, however, the choice between right and wrong is endlessly fraught with complexity and grounded in deep moral pathos. There is an inescapably tragic character to moral choice. Within the family, men all too often may be driven to choose between family interests and professional responsibilities. Loyalty to spouse and children may conflict with caring for the needs of aging parents. Within the nation, freedom of speech and assembly may clash with the requirements of security and order. The Supreme Court has declared that freedom of speech does not involve the right to cry fire in a crowded theatre. The right to a fair trial may collide with the right to know and the freedom of the press. Freedom of scientific inquiry apparently does not justify the right of a graduate student to produce a nuclear bomb in his kitchen. Even within the most developed democracy every political and constitutional principle coexists and is related to every other principle, and each is at most a partial expression of morality; for as Reinhold Niebuhr wrote:

> Democracy cannot exist if there is no recognition of the fragmentary character of all systems of values which are allowed to exist within its frame.

On the international scene, the recognition of "the fragmentary character of all systems of values" is more difficult. Nations, and especially the superpowers, see themselves as the repositories of values and ideas that are good for all mankind. National self-determination which postulated the right of every nationality group to organize itself within a nation-state has been supplanted by crusading nationalism with its unique and exclusive mission for the world. Whereas the nation-state was the end point of political development for eighteenth- and nineteenth-century nationalism, it is the beginning of communism and democracy. If the aim is to extend the benefits of systems of values and beliefs to people everywhere, it is difficult if not impossible to accept their fragmentary character. It is this reality which characterizes the international system today.

Practical Morality and Diplomacy

The prevailing approach to the ethical dimension of diplomacy is one which has placed stress on morality pure and simple. Oftentimes defenders of this approach have been driven to take positions their critics describe as moralism and legalism. Those who question whether morality exists for diplomacy ask whether there exist more proximate moral positions that can be discussed under the heading practical morality.

One such approach is that of workability as opposed to the proclamation of abstract moral principles. The objective of foreign policy should be the reduction of human suffering and promotion of social welfare and not the unqualified triumph of abstract principles. Moral appeals to the generality of mankind often constitute not morality but Pharisaism.

Workability is also the test of certain diplomatic historians, notable among them the cold war historian, Norman Graebner of the University of Virginia. History suggests that whenever the United States has introduced towering humanitarian objectives as the main guide to policy it has added to rather than diminished human suffering and subsequently abandoned unworkable policies. In the 1950's, Secretary Dulles's liberation foreign policy offered by the Republicans as a more dynamic alternative to the postwar policy of containment inspired Hungarian freedom fighters to revolt only to discover that American national interest and the facts of geography and power precluded American intervention.

The question is whether proclaiming moral principles may sometimes not do more harm than good. Workability leads diplomatists to measure possible consequences. The issue is not settled by saying the United States must

give the world a vision of hope. The question raised by practical morality is where will that vision lead and will the overall effects be better or worse than what has gone before.

If the first issue is workability, the second is the nature of the international society. The diplomatic school sees the world of American foreign policy as subject to many of the same rules and constraints known at the founding of the republic. To the question posed by the historian Carl Becker at the end of World War II, *How New Will the Better World Be?*, they answer it is neither wholly new nor necessarily better. Why? Because of the nature of man, of international politics and the persistence of the nation-state system. In discussions at Virginia, Hans Morgenthau stated:

> the purpose of foreign policy is not to bring enlightment or happiness to the rest of the world but to take care of the life, liberty and happiness of the American people.

International lawyers are more inclined to argue the existence of a new and better world, the birth of an embryonic world community. The Charter of the United Nations and the Declaration and some nineteen Covenants of Human Rights are said to embody core principles of human rights and fundamental freedoms foreshadowed in the American Declaration of Independence. Judge Philip C. Jessup quoted Secretary of State Elihu Root writing in 1906 to the American ambassador in St. Petersburg regarding a protest concerning the persecution of Jews in Russia:

> I think it may do some good, though I do not feel sure of it. I do not know how it will be received. It may merely give offense. I am sure that to go further would do harm. I am sure also that to publish here the fact that such a dispatch has been sent would do harm, and serious harm to the unfortunate people whom we desire to help. Any possible good effect must be looked for in absolutely confidential

communication to the Russian Government. The publication that any communication has been made would inevitably tend to prevent the Russian government from acting, to increase the anti-Jewish feelings and to make further massacres more probable.

But then Jessup added that the situation today may differ "since human rights have become the subject of international agreements."[19]

Each of the great political traditions has its own conception of human values in society and the good life. For the Christian belief in God and serving one's fellowman is uppermost. For the disciple of classical political thought, the search for virtue in society is the highest calling. For modern political thinkers, the establishment of the best social and constitutional arrangements within existing societies is the foremost objective. The Christian and the classical traditions depend on certain objective values and standards within society and the political process. The values of the two older traditions are ultimately transcendent while those of modern political thought are immanent. Contemporary exceptions include those political theories for which the earlier traditions have residual importance, such as those of the Founding Fathers of the American constitutional and political system.

The prospects of all three political traditions have been diminished by certain forces at work within the present-day nation-state. Christian thought from its beginnings assumed that man necessarily and inevitably lived in two worlds, the city of man and the city of God. The former was the temporary realm of contingencies, imperfection, and sin; the latter was the enduring realm of certainty, perfection and the good. The one was realizable here and now, the other in eternity. The social and political order was structured to reflect, partially at least, the reality of the two worlds. The Christian vision provided for both a horizontal and vertical dimension in human life, with men reaching out to one another in the social order and

seeking to know God in the spiritual order. Government was the custodian of the social and political order and citizens were enjoined to give to Caesar what was Caesar's. The Church was the custodian of the spiritual order and believers were enjoined to serve God with what was God's.

The rise of the modern nation-state and the breakdown of the Corpus Christianum diminished, if it did not destroy, the vision of the two cities. The authority of the one universal church was undermined by the Reformation and the Renaissance. The religion of the prince within emerging political societies determined the religion of the people. Religion and patriotism tended to reinforce one another whereas earlier they had constituted checks and balances on one another. If the universal Catholic church was in part responsible for the union of the two because of its tendency to equate and make itself coextensive with the city of God, the embryonic nation-state was also responsible by becoming the repository of individual and group morality in order to assure political cohesion. Whereas the Church had taught believers the commandment "Thou shalt not kill," princes and rulers taught "Thou shalt kill to preserve the nation-state."

Moreover, other forces were at work weakening the hold of the Christian tradition. The Christian tradition in its historical formulation presupposed a world of sheep and shepherds. The modern era has witnessed the growth of ever more complex societies in which the individual to whom Christianity ministered was further and further removed from primary human relations with his fellowmen. The great society supplanted the good Samaritan. Furthermore, Christianity itself became more and more fragmented. In America a destructive Civil War found Northern and Southern soldiers praying to the same God and justifying their acts from the same Scriptures. During the conflict President Abraham Lincoln wrote that "each party claims to act in accordance with the will of God. Both *may* be, and one *must* be wrong. God can not be *for*, and *against* the same thing at the same time." In recent days Martin Luther King and Jerry Falwell invoked the same Scriptures to defend actions affecting millions of people in diametrically opposite ways. Maintaining a universal Christian tradition is complicated by the rise of sovereign nation-states. Who would deny that the nation provides its citizenry with concepts of political philosophy, standards of political morality, and goals of political action?

If the Christian tradition has been challenged by the circumstances surrounding the modern nation-state, the classical tradition has also been threatened. Modernity has brought about a shift from discussions of the good man and the good state to discourses on political power and political tactics. Classical political philosophy was not unaware of the realities of good and evil in human nature. The Platonic dialogues are filled with examples of cynical and selfish men overriding reason and virtue in their political attitudes and conduct. Yet for the philosopher, contemplating the overall human drama, reason was superior to the irrational and virtue was the standard by which cynicism and selfishness were judged. Man approached his true and best nature in participating in the social and political order. He realized himself as a social and political animal. Classicists also maintained that human fulfillment was attainable within the polity, a small-sized political community marked by face-to-face political discourse. By contrast, few citizens in large nation-states have little if any contact with rulers.

The history of modern times throws a shadow over the classicists' argument for reason and virtue. Wise students of political history such as Reinhold Niebuhr, Herbert Butterfield, and Hans J. Morgenthau have traced the influence of the irrational in politics. The German people, whose culture matched any in Europe, followed a fanatical leader, Hitler, who stirred popular emotions with slogans depicting the Germans as radically superior. Legislative assemblies, in-

tended for prudent deliberation, become the scene of chauvinist and bellicose debate. National self-determination, which had promised satisfaction and peace to the world's people, was Hitler's rallying cry for the annexation of the Sudetenland. Reason proved defective in anticipating the consequences of thousands of apparently reasonable acts. Unintended and unforeseen consequences of reasonable historical acts outweigh the expected or intended results. The Protestant Reformation rested on the right of each individual to read and interpret the Bible, but by strengthening nationalism caused a weakening of individualism. The French Revolution, which promised liberty, equality, and fraternity, led to the submergence of liberty and equality in the Napoleonic Empire.

If Christian and classical thought are criticized for too much opposition to modernity and too great a faith in historical political values, modern political thought links modernity with progress. Whereas the older traditions stand partly in opposition to present trends, modern political theory tends to sanctify them. It glorifies the state and, more particularly, certain branches of government which it favors one after the other as the cycle turns. Transposed to the international scene, modern thought manifests an exaggerated confidence in institutions as instruments for transforming international politics. The rise and fall of popular enthusiasm for each of these institutions in turn has thrown into question the judgment of modern thought. It has also led some contemporary thinkers to reopen the question of the relevance of Christian and classical thought to present-day problems.

Not only has the rise of the nation-state profoundly affected the relation of the great political traditions to politics but so have the changing patterns of international politics and diplomacy. Historically, the Christian and classical political traditions assumed a consensus on values within the Christian and classical world. Four developments have altered the political world within which any of the historic traditions must operate. First, a worldwide system of political ideologies and conflicting religious faiths has replaced the Christian Europe of which historians like Christopher Dawson wrote in tracing the formation of Western Christendom. Universal Christendom has lost out to a pluralistic international system of competing nation-states and cultures. Second, the political faiths which inspired men took on the characteristics of the terrestial world rather than the adornments of the heavenly city. To the extent the latter existed at all it was as this-worldy utopias. Carl Becker wrote about the heavenly city of the eighteenth-century philosophers; Marx and Lenin elaborated a creed that identified the end of history with the Marxist classless society. Salvation was achievable here and now and its standards were not outside but within history. The direct application to international problems of the Christian tradition was undermined by the breakdown of a consensus on values and the disappearance of faith in effective objective moral principles outside history.

Two other developments coincided with and reinforced the above-mentioned changes. They profoundly affected the relevance of the classical tradition. One of these was a consequence of the vast increase in the size of viable political units. The movement from city-states to nation-states culminated in the postwar emergence of the superpowers. That good men would create good regimes became a more difficult proposition to sustain. Good and bad men alike seized power in large collective states claiming that only they were capable of solving the momentous social problems of great masses of people. Events that good men had prophesied were rationally impossible, such as global depressions, world wars, and totalitarianism, followed one another in rapid succession. Mass populations responded to programs defenders argued served all the people. If Americans had any doubt concerning the far-reaching effects of this third development, they had only to compare the deliberative processes of leaders addressing the New England town meeting with Mussolini or Hitler haranguing the German and Italian people with the claim, "forty million Italians (Germans) can't be wrong." In short, the concept of popular sovereignty replaced that of personal virtue.

A fourth development was the radical transformation of political communication. Classical political thought had maintained that personal and collective morality were indivisible. In the modern era not only totalitarian rulers but democratic leaders determined what was moral and the right interests of states. While certain moral principles applicable to individuals survived in the eighteenth-century idea of raison d'etat, contemporary rulers maintained that whatever their personal moral standards on war or slavery, criteria of national unity and preserving the state took precedence. Thus both Christian and classical thought lost their force in the face of far-reaching historical changes.

Modern political thought appeared to offer an alternative to the decline of the ancient traditions. Especially liberalism held out the promise to the great mass of the people of human improvement through universal public education. Today's pressing problems would yield to the workings of free enlightened society. Individuals, ever more transformed by reason and science, would throw off aggressive human traits and archaic political ideas and institutions that had led throughout history to conflict and war. Individual man pursuing his selfish interests would be guided nationally and internationally as if by a hidden hand to act for the common good. Nationally, the process would operate in free-market economies guaranteed to serve the general welfare. ("What is good for General Motors is good for America," a cabinet member in the Eisenhower administration proclaimed.) Internationally, national self-determination promised a peaceful world. Its architects little dreamed that Hitler would invoke a Wilsonian principle to justify his expansionist policies. Then national and international economic stagnation in the 1930s led millions of people to turn to new and more dynamic collectivist solutions. Scientific efficiency also made possible the holocaust.

Not only did the four developments sound the death knell for the meaningfulness and coherence of the three great political traditions; another factor sped the disintegration of the international political order. The values which had introduced a limited degree of stability within single political communities proved ineffective on the international stage. The standards that had assured relative peace within nations proved ineffectual or largely irrelevant in international affairs. What was disallowed or dealt with as an exception to the normal processes of national societies was accepted as inevitable in international society. While civil war represented the breakdown of the political order within nations, war was accepted as the continuation of diplomacy by other means in relations among nation-states.

The problem, as Reinhold Niebuhr discussed it in a succession of treatises on foreign policy, was that in international politics no single moral principle existed for ordering all other moral principles. In international politics, rough-and-ready norms such as "damage limitation" became the overarching principles rather than such benign standards as the quest for the good society or for communities aimed at human self-fulfillment. In the end modern political thought which had promised a new and better world became an even more tragic victim to the bludgeonings of history than Christian or classical thought.

For all these reasons the culmination of history on the international stage has witnessed not the heavenly city but the nuclear age. The end of warfare which liberal political thinkers had predicted yielded to the specter of warfare as universal human destruction. Yet hope has had a rebirth alongside impending disaster. Ironically, human advancement and progress have led not to the refutation of ancient political truths but

to their rediscovery. Prudence has once more become the master virtue in international politics at a moment in time when its absence becomes a threat to human existence. But political prudence was an idea that Aristotle set forth as a guide for political practice as distinct from political contemplation. From Aristotle and Augustine through Edmund Burke to Niebuhr and John Courtney Murray, prudence as an operative political principle was not the rigid formulation or precise definition of what was right or wrong but a method of practical reason in the search for righteousness and justice under a given set of circumstances. Practical morality involves the reconciliation of what is morally desirable and politically possible. It offers few absolutes but many practical possibilities. Prudence, then, is the cardinal precept in the ancient tradition of moral reasoning which some contemporaries would revive. It recognizes with Holmes the need for moral man in an immoral world to find his way through "a maze of conflicting moral principles" no one of which reigns supreme. It undertakes to transform abstract reason into political reason. In a word, it aims to rediscover the ethical dimensions of diplomacy as philosophers and statesmen have searched for and discovered them throughout the ages.

NOTES

[1] June Bingham, *Courage to Change: An Introduction to the Life and Thought of Reinhold Niebuhr* (New York: Scribner's, 1961), p. 62.

[2] Quoted in A. C. F. Beales, *A Short History of English Liberalism*, p. 195.

[3] *House of Commons Debates*, Fifth Series, 1946, Vol. 419, 1262.

[4] Frederick the Great, *Origin of the Bismarck Policy*, European Pamphlets, 12 (Boston: Crosby, Damrell, 1870), p. 6.

[5] *Ibid.*, p. 12.

[6] *Ibid.*, p. 21.

[7] *Ibid.*, p. 22.

[8] *Ibid.*, p. 22.

[9] *Ibid.*, p. 23.

[10] *Ibid.*, p. 43.

[11] *Ibid.*, p. 48.

[12]*Ibid.*, p. 48–49.
[13]*Ibid.*, p. 50.
[14]*Ibid.*, p. 51.
[15]Sir Harold Nicolson, *Diplomacy* (London: Oxford University Press, 1939), p. 50.
[16]*Ibid.*, p. 45–46.
[17]*Ibid.*, p. 76.

[18]Quotations from Morgenthau, Kennan, Halle and Jessup are taken from unpublished papers written for a conference on "Morality and Foreign Policy" held in Charlottesville, Virginia, in June 1977, and jointly sponsored by the Department of State and the University of Virginia.
[19]*Ibid.*

30. Ethics and Power in International Politics

Michael Howard

Michael Howard, holds the Regius Chair of Modern History at Oxford University, where he has been a Fellow of All Souls College since 1968.

The assumption that the exercise of coercive power is in itself fundamentally immoral, and that involvement in power relationships automatically vitiates ethical behaviour, is natural enough. How can good ends be served by evil means? How can one get peace by preparing for war? How can all the mechanisms of military power—the disciplining of soldiers, the development of weapons, the training to kill, the posing of threats, to say nothing of the awful actuality of warfare, shocking enough in the pre-nuclear age, inconceivable today—how can such activities conceivably contribute to ethical goals? Is not the whole 'power system' alien to and irreconcilable with any ethical objectives except those of the barbarian—and in adopting it even to fight barbarians, is one not becoming a barbarian oneself? To adopt the methods

The text of the 3rd Martin Wight Lecture, reprinted with the permission of The Royal Institute of International Affairs from *International Affairs*, 53, no. 3 (July 1977), pp. 364–76 (Some footnotes have been removed; those remaining have been renumbered.) Copyright © 1977.

of coercive power—and economic can be as debasing as military power—is *in itself* considered to be unethical, to debase the cause which those methods are intended to serve.

Are ethics and power in fact such poles apart? Most of us in practice do not consider that they are, and within our own experience we can normally reconcile them without too much difficulty. But this may simply be the result of our own moral obtuseness and intellectual laziness. To provide a satisfactory conceptual synthesis is not so easy. The long debate over *raison d'état*, which Sir Herbert Butterfield took as the subject of the first Martin Wight Memorial Lecture, has never been properly concluded. The tradition that led through Plato and Machiavelli to Hegel, by which all contradictions were resolved in service to a state which was itself the highest value since it made possible all other values, disastrously popular as it became in Germany, has never been acceptable to Anglo-Saxon Liberals—although the Marxist variant which for 'State' would substitute 'Revolution' succeeded in attracting some of them in the 1930s. But perhaps a clue to a more satisfactory formula can be found in the work of another German thinker, albeit one who is seldom regarded as an authority on ethical questions: Karl von Clausewitz.

Clausewitz did not indeed deal with ethical questions as such. He did not fundamentally question the crude Machiavellianism of eighteenth-century politics: the Grotian Law of Nations he dismissed as 'certain self-imposed, imperceptible limitations hardly worth mentioning, known as international law and custom.' But on the relationship between war and politics he did, as we know, have interesting and original things to say; and these may provide useful guidance in any consideration of the relationship between power and ethics.

Clausewitz's theory was teleological. In warfare, every engagement was planned to serve a tactical purpose. These tactical purposes were determined by the requirements of strategy. The requirements of strategy were determined by the object of the war; and the object of the war was determined by State policy, the State being the highest embodiment of the values and the interests of the community. Thus the objectives of State policy ultimately dominated and determined military means the whole way down the hierarchy of strategy and tactics. War was not an independent entity with a value-system of its own.

For Clausewitz State policy was the ultimate mover and justification, the criterion by which all other actions were to be judged—which in itself would make his doctrine as it stands unacceptable to the liberal. But what if one introduces one further, and ultimate, step in the hierarchy, to which State policy itself should be subordinated—the ethical goal? The State itself then becomes not an end but the means to an end. It has a dual role. It exists primarily to enable its own citizens to realise their ethical values; but it exists also to make possible an *international* community of mankind, whose values and interests are ultimately determinant, not only of State policy as such, but of all the means,

military and otherwise, that are used to implement State policy.

Such a pattern goes beyond that 'Grotian' concept of international relations of which Hedley Bull spoke in the second Martin Wight Lecture last year;[1] for although in the Grotian formulation States are governed by a 'Law of Nations' which is based partly on a reflection of the divine order and partly on prudential considerations of self-preservation, they need no justification for their policy beyond the requirements of their own existence. They accept a law of nations as man accepts the laws of a just society: because his own needs dictate that he should do so. But in the Clausewitzian formulation, as we have elaborated it, State policy would be determined by and judged according to the needs of the international community. In the same way as war, if it were not directed by State policy, would be a 'senseless thing without an object,' so State interests and State policy would make no sense and have no justification if they were not shaped in accordance with the overriding needs of mankind. As military power is subordinated to and guided by State policy, so State power should be subordinated to and guided by ethical norms. The relationship would then become one, not of irreconcilable opposition between mutually exclusive poles, but of hierarchical subordination of means to ends.

That all sounds very fine as a theory. In practice, unfortunately, it settles very little. Having stated his own theory, Clausewitz identified the fundamental problem about its application. The military means should always by definition be subordinated to the political object, true: but the military had its own requirements. It had to work according to its own necessities. Only the military specialist could determine whether the goals set by policy were attainable, and if so what the requirements were for attaining them. Military affairs had, as Clausewitz put it, their own grammar, even if they were subordinated to political logic; and the grammar was intricate and ineluctable. Armed forces require bases, and those bases may only be available in countries with which one would, for ethical reasons, prefer not to be allied. National industry, on which military capacity is based, may require access to raw materials available only from countries which are equally politically embarrassing. The successful conduct of the most just and defensive of wars may demand alliance with States whose price is the support of war aims which flatly contradict all one's own normative values—as did those of Italy in the Treaty of London in 1915, that last and most notorious example of power politics and secret diplomacy. Yet rather than yield to Italian demands on Slav territory, would it have been *morally* preferable to have waived the Italian alliance, leaving the Central Powers with their hands free to deal with Russia, and thus prolonging the war if not risking outright defeat?

One can multiply examples endlessly; let me concentrate simply on one. In 1935 there occurred a superb opportunity for Britain to shape its policy in the service of an ethical objective: the implementation of its obligations under the Covenant of the League of Nations by imposing penal sanctions upon Italy in order to deter or punish its aggression against Abyssinia. Not only was the crime unambiguous; the criminal was highly vulnerable. Public opinion, in the 'Peace Ballot,' had recently expressed itself in favour of mandatory sanctions, even at the risk of war. The case might have been deliberately created to test the effectiveness of that new system of collective security and the rule of law which had been brought into being since 1918 to replace the old chaotic system of power politics. It would have been a perfect example of the use of coercive means to attain political ends.

We can now see that there were many reasons why the British government flinched from the test; but certainly not the least was the compromising and unanimous opposition of those experts in military grammar, the Chiefs of Staff. Within the power structure which it was their duty to operate there were two far more serious threats, not simply

to the rule of law in international politics, but to the security of Britain and its Empire: the growing power of Nazi Germany and the increasingly open aggression of Japan. To risk even successful war against Italy would have been to enfeeble the already pathetically weak fleet available to deter Japanese attack in the Far East, and to antagonize a potential ally whose help was, in the eyes of France if not of Britain, indispensable in containing the German threat. The military grammar appeared unanswerable; it was to be that, rather than the ethical imperatives of collective security, which determined State policy.

In retrospect one can say that even in their own terms the military grammarians may have got it wrong. Faced with the real prospect of war Mussolini might very easily have retreated; his catastrophic humiliation would probably have imposed a high degree of caution both on Germany and Japan; a pattern of peace-keeping would have been successfully established. But the arguments of the grammarians could not simply be overridden. The ethical imperative could not be, in Clausewitz's words, 'a despotic lawgiver.' In the last resort the statesmen were, as ever, faced with a balance of imponderables, with problems to which there were no clear-cut ethical solutions.

To say, therefore, that State policy should be subordinated to the ethical imperative as strategic considerations should be subordinated to State policy does not get us very far. The world of power remains stubbornly autonomous; the suzerainty of ethics may be of quite Merovingian ineffectiveness. Moreover such a formulation can lend itself to the crudest of casuistical justification of all coercive means in terms of the ethical end—of police torture of political dissidents in order to preserve a stable and orderly society, of the Soviet invasion of Czechoslovakia in 1968 in order to preserve the stability of Eastern Europe, of the 'destabilisation' of Chile to maintain the stability of the Western hemisphere, of the secret bombing of Cambodia to maintain the independence of South Vietnam. Because such actions may be dictated by the grammar of coercive power, they cannot—any more than can terroristic destruction of life and property or intimidatory guerrilla massacres—be *justified*, i.e. made in themselves ethical, by an ethical object. The dimensions of power and of ethics remain stubbornly different.

Indeed, so long as we think of power and ethics in terms of *dimensions*, we may not go too far wrong. Dimensions do not contradict one another, nor can they be subordinated to one another. They are mutually complementary. Political activity takes place in a two-dimensional field—a field which can be defined by the two coordinates of ethics and power. The ethical co-ordinate (which we may appropriately conceive as vertical) indicates the purposes which should govern political action: the achievement of a harmonious society of mankind in which conflicts can be peacefully resolved and a community of cultures peacefully co-exist within which every individual can find fulfillment. The horizontal co-ordinate measures the capacity of each actor to impose his will on his environment, whether by economic, military or psychological pressures. Movement along this co-ordinate, the increase or decrease in coercive capability, has *as such* no dimension of morality, any more than does any elevation of moral standards necessarily involve an increase in one's power to implement them.

Effective political action needs to take constant account of both dimensions. To concern oneself with ethical values to the total exclusion of any practical activity in the dimension of power is to abdicate responsibility for shaping the course of affairs. To accumulate coercive power without concern for its ethical ends is the course of the gangster, of St. Augustine's robber bands. Indeed it could be argued that each of these uni-dimensional courses is self-defeating; that the co-ordinates, if indefinitely prolonged, become circular. Obsession with ethical values with no concern for their implementation is ultimately unethical in its lack of *practical* concern for the course taken by society; con-

cern for coercive capability without the legitimization of moral acceptance leads ultimately to impotence, and disaster at the hands of an indignant and alienated world. Thus political action, whether in the international or any other sphere of activity, needs to be *diagonal*. Ethical goals should become more ambitious as political capability increases. The political actor, be he statesman or soldier, needs to grow in moral awareness and responsibility as he grows in power. The moralist must accept that his teaching will not reach beyond the page on which it is written or the lectern from which it is expounded without a massive amount of complex activity by men of affairs operating on the plane of their own expertise. The more ambitious and wide-ranging the ethical goals, the greater the power-mechanisms required to achieve them.

In pursuing his diagonal course the statesman is like a pilot reading a compass bearing from which he must not diverge in either direction if he is to achieve his goal. Too rigorous a concern for moral absolutes may reduce or destroy his capacity for effective action. Yet to ignore such norms entirely may gain him short-term advantages at the cost of ultimately reducing his capacity to operate effectively in a world made up, not of robber bands, but of States functioning as moral as well as military entities, whose authority is as dependent on moral acceptability as on coercive capability. He may have to commit or authorise acts which, as a private citizen, he would deeply deplore. No one involved, for example, in the repatriation of Soviet troops from British-occupied Europe to Russia immediately after the Second World War could have felt anything other than distress bordering on misery at the need for such action. But in the political dimension the object of maintaining friendly relations with the Soviet Union in order to achieve yet wider ethical objectives—the peaceful settlement of Europe and of the world as a whole—had to be regarded as mandatory. To call attention to the ethical problems created by such actions is appropriate and necessary; but they cannot be condemned on such grounds unless account is taken of the political dimension as well.

Acton was being less than fair to the world of politics when he declared that power tends to corrupt. What does tend to happen, as I suggested earlier, is that the grammar of power, so intricate, so compelling, becomes for those who operate it a universe in itself— as indeed for the moralist and the reformer, the ethical objective can become an exclusive obsession which makes him disdain the tedious and murky problem of how to attain it. Yet perhaps there is a kind of gravitational force against which statesmen have consciously to fight, which keeps their activities always closer to the horizontal co-ordinate of power than to the vertical one of ethics, which constantly weighs down their efforts to maintain the diagonal. Overloaded political decision-makers and members of huge bureaucracies have enough to contend with in day-to-day management of affairs without constantly searching their consciences as to the ethical implications of their actions. That makes it all the more important that their ethical perceptions should be internalised and operate automatically and continuously. Government departments seldom carry a chaplain on the establishment to provide an ethical input into policy-making.

The appropriate response of the political moralist to the world of power must therefore be not to condemn but to enlighten, to understand, and to acknowledge and accept that the Children of Darkness have a painfully-learned wisdom in their own generation which is deserving of genuine respect. As Niebuhr put it, 'Politics will, to the end of history, be an area where conscience and power meet, where the ethical and coercive factors of human life will interpenetrate and work out their tentative and uneasy compromises'.[2] As a thinker whose ideas were deeply rooted in ethical values, Martin Wight knew that even he could make no serious contribution to the study of international politics without first attaining a full understanding of the coercive factors operating within it. But he never ceased to look beyond these 'uneasy compromises' to the ultimate goal of full and final reconciliation.

NOTES

[1]Reprinted in *British Journal of International Studies*, 2, no. 2 (July 1976), pp. 101–116.

[2]Reinhold Niebuhr, *Moral Man and Immoral Society: A Study in Ethics and Politics* (New York: Scribner's, 1949; first published 1932), p. 4.

31.   Let's Sink the Lifeboat Ethics

James W. Howe and John W. Sewell

James W. Howe is President of The National Alliance for the Mentally Ill and John W. Sewell is President of the Overseas Development Council in Washington, D.C.

. . . each rich nation can be seen as a lifeboat full of comparatively rich people. In the ocean outside each lifeboat swim the poor of the world, who would like to get in, or at least share some of the wealth.

Garrett Hardin, "The Case Against Helping the Poor" (*Psychology Today*, September 1974)

. . . the moment of truth will come the morning when the President must make a choice whether to save India or to save Latin America. . . .

William and Paul Paddock, *Famine 1975!* (1967)

. . . American intellectual circles have spawned a new series of challenges to the morality and efficacy of responding to the needs of the poor countries. One of the surprising aspects of these arguments—one which has given considerable satisfaction to the devoted opponents of such aid and even raised eyebrows among the usually uninvolved—is the fact that these challenges have been spawned *within* the development community, by some who have spent a lifetime advocating help for the poor countries. Unlike earlier challenges which pointed out that much of American aid was used for overt political and military purposes, these new challenges hold that the provision of assistance is in and of itself immoral. Appearing under the rubric of "lifeboat ethics" and advocating the practice of "triage," these challenges take two distinct forms. The first

maintains that some of the poorest countries are beyond saving, that nothing the rich countries do, no matter how generous or wise, can rescue them. Therefore, wasting resources on these countries deprives others that can better utilize them. The second revives Thomas Malthus's predictions of two centuries ago and holds that any help to the developing countries inexorably leads to higher birth rates. By so doing, any amount of aid merely postpones the inevitable famine, which, when it comes, will be even more disastrous because so many more will die. From this perspective aid is immoral because, if it continues, the sum total of deaths and, therefore, of human suffering, will increase.

It is ironic that these challenges have arisen precisely at the time when the developing countries are becoming increasingly important to the United States, just when the rich countries are facing a growing challenge from the developing countries to their dominant position in the international economic system. The most obvious examples of this shift are the actions of the oil-producing countries, which have both raised prices and used their dominance of the world's energy supply to increase their political power. But in many other arenas the developing countries are beginning to press for more equitable access to the world's wealth and for a greater voice in the governance of international economic institutions. The dramatic cohesion of the OPEC countries has tended to obscure a more basic long-term development—a major change in psychology on the part of *all* developing countries. These previously powerless countries will no longer tolerate being taken for granted and are demanding a voice in decisions that directly affect their future. As a result the Americans will find that, whether they like it or not, they are going to have to pay increasing attention to these countries. And most of the low-income countries have as the primary goal their own economic and social development. Thus, American foreign policy is going to have to consider what role should be given to development cooperation in our increasingly interdependent world.

The first group of challengers hold that some countries can never create viable economies and that any resources provided them, whether through aid or other means, are wasted. In fact, if we assist these countries, other countries that have a better chance of survival and that can better utilize scarce resources will be jeopardized. Some who hold this viewpoint invoke the battlefield medical principle of "triage," whereby the wounded are divided into three groups: those who will survive with little or no treatment, those who will die even if treated, and those who are likely to live only if they receive intensive care. In this situation it makes sense to concentrate the available resources on the last group, because doing so will insure that the maximum number survive. Other critics in this group use the analogy of the "lifeboat"—they claim that the rich countries can be likened to survivors in a lifeboat of limited capacity surrounded by others in the water waiting to be saved. If too many of those in the water are rescued, the boat will be swamped and all will perish.

Implicit in the argument of those who advocated "lifeboat ethics" are three premises. The first is that certain nations can never be saved; second, that the world's resources are not adequate and can never be adequate to meet the needs of all; and third, that if sacrificed, certain nations will disappear and will no longer cause other countries problems. Strikingly enough, experience since World War II bears out none of these premises. The developing countries as a whole managed to maintain an average economic growth rate of about 6 percent per year in the decade of the 1960s, a record never equalled by any of the industrialized nations during comparable periods of their development. While there are problems with equating development and economic growth, particularly as it neglects the questions of the distribution of the benefits of growth within countries, the record does not indicate that any nations are beyond being saved. Indeed, it is useful to recall that in 1945 Europe, Japan, China, and virtually *all* of the underdeveloped areas of Asia, Africa, and Latin America were either devastated by war or economically stagnant. Today only 42 of 135 nations that are members of the United Nations are in comparably serious condition. Another score of countries are making measurable progress but are still in a somewhat precarious condition. All other countries are either making self–sustaining progress toward solving their problems or have the financial resources to do so. From another perspective, the population in countries that received aid or were stagnating economically twenty-five years ago constituted perhaps 90 percent of the world's people. Today such countries make up less than half the population, and the "Fourth World" of the poorest countries in greatest need of outside help constitutes only about 25 percent of the world's population.

Many of those who advocate a form of international "triage" use India as their best example of a very poor prospect for development. But in the mid-1960s, when India suffered a large food deficit, its government undertook a massive program designed to increase agricultural production. By 1971 India had essentially closed its food deficit and was able to provide food aid for refugees from war-torn Bangladesh. The reversal of this positive trend in food production in the past two years was the result of adverse weather in 1972 and 1974, a shortage of fertilizer during 1974, and a shortage of fuel to operate irrigation pumps in the same year, most of it paid for with hard cash. (India this year has spent nearly $1 billion on food imports, most of it from the United States.) Barring these three unusual circumstances, India today could be producing all the cereals required to meet the current demands of its people. Thus there is reason to doubt that even those countries considered to be the "worst cases" are beyond saving.

The second premise of those who pose this challenge is based largely on the analysis of the Club of Rome, which holds that the earth's supply of resources is finite and that we will begin shortly to see real shortages. These estimates, particularly those concerning vital raw materials, are much in dispute. But even in the case most cited—the earth's capacity to produce more food—the future is not at all bleak. The opportunity to increase the production of food, particularly in the developing countries, is great. But the Food and Agriculture Organization of the United Nations estimates that unless agricultural production in the developing countries is increased, their grain deficit by 1985 could total nearly 85 million tons, a little more than half the total amount of grain traded in the world last year. However, If the proper measures are taken to increase production—particularly in the developing countries—that deficit could be as low as 10 to 15 million tons of grain. Clearly it is feasible to increase global food production levels if we go about it the right way.

Even if the ceiling on the world food production actually had been reached, there still would be much that could be done to alleviate hunger by some modicum of redistribution. Currently each person in North America consumes each year nearly one ton of grain, mainly indirectly in the form of milk, meat, and eggs. In contrast, individuals in developing countries on the average consume less than four hundred pounds of grain a year, mostly in direct form. Thus it takes more than five times as many agricultural resources to feed an average American as it does to feed the average Indian, Nigerian, or Colombian. And the disproportionate consumption of energy and raw materials by the developed countries follows an even more exaggerated pattern.

Apart from the flaws of the first two assumptions underlying the "lifeboat" and "triage" analyses, these arguments have a still more serious weakness. Their proponents assume that nations—like persons drowning or bleeding to death—simply "die" and therefore cease to be "problems" for the rest of the world. Abandoning such countries does not get rid of them; it merely postpones the time when the problems must be dealt with. National boundaries are inadequate to quarantine permanently the tensions that build up when whole nations begin to disintegrate. Moreover, to solve them at that stage is often more costly than if they had been dealt with earlier. (The dissolution of East and West Pakistan is a recent example of such cost.)

Finally, the proponents of the "lifeboat" analogy do not accurately describe the current global crisis. The rich are clearly not in possession of a secure lifeboat they *alone* command. Instead, the rich and poor "share" the same lifeboat—although the rich, despite their lesser numbers, take up much more space in the boat than the poor and command a far greater share of the supplies necessary for survival. Confronted with the fact that there is a hole in the boat and that the boat is slowly sinking, the rich seem quite sanguine; since the hole is not in their side, they insist, its existence is not their responsibility. Actually, all the evidence of recent history supports a rather different version of the lifeboat analogy, one virtually identical with the "spaceship earth" analogy, in that it recognizes and emphasizes the interdependence of all nations and peoples.

The second set of recent challenges is to the wisdom of helping the poor countries, and is similar to that originally propounded by Malthus many generations ago. The advocates of this view hold that supporting the development of the poor countries by providing food and medicine prevents people from dying, causing populations to continue to grow until they are finally held in check by starvation and disease. These neo-Malthusians feel there would be less human suffering if the rich countries did not directly provide food or medicine, thereby allowing the restraints on population growth to come into play earlier when population levels are lower. Like those who propound the triage and lifeboat arguments, these critics assume the countries being assisted will never be able to lower their birth rates, and consequently that they must "inevitably" experience a massive famine and a consequential increase in death rates at some point in the future. But this central premise ignores a crucial fact—there is no clear evidence that birth rates cannot be brought down in the developing countries, and there are already clear indications that outside support can help to bring down birth rates if it is used to support certain innovative domestic policies.

There is now a growing consensus, underlined by the U.S. World Population Conference held in Bucharest in the summer of 1974, that the problem of population growth cannot be addressed by the provision of contraceptive techniques alone. Rather, the root of the population problem lies in the factors that motivate parents to have large families; its solution depends on changing the reasons for wanting many children.

At least three factors underlie the urge for large families in the developing countries. In many of these countries the worth, as well as the social acceptability, of an individual is still closely linked to the number of children the parents produce. A second factor is that in many societies children are economically *useful* to parents, not only as laborers but also as providers of old-age security. And finally, for many people living at the survival margin—especially if they are women, barred by varying traditions from

participation in other personally satisfying activities—a large family continues to be a major emotional counterweight to the tedium of a bleak struggle to keep alive. . . .

The final irony is that the debate in the United States over the efficacy and morality of providing aid comes precisely at the moment when the challenge from the developing countries encompasses a much broader set of issues. The demands put forth by the developing countries under the heading of the "New International Economic Order" range far beyond aid to cover issues of trade, commodity policy, investment, technology transfer, and decision-making in international organizations. Aid per se is becoming less important than other resource transfers, and Americans may find themselves in the position of arguing about a particular type of response to the needs of the developing countries.

In sum, Americans have already demonstrated that they can affect governmental policy. Private leaders and indeed the public in general have an obligation to reject proposals that nations be written off as unsalvageable and to make clear their response to the argument of the neo-Malthusians. The real choice and challenge before governments and the public in both rich and poor countries is whether or not they will address themselves to the basic causes of uncontrolled population growth. And in this effort development progress—and outside help— have an important role to play.

What will be the response of the U.S. Government and the American people to this historic challenge? It may well be that now is the time for Americans to make it good politics for their leaders to be good statesmen.

chapter 11

HUNGER

Barring a holocaust brought on by man or nature, the world's population today is the smallest it will ever be again. How did it reach a population of four billion? For the first 99 percent of man's existence, surprisingly slowly. For the last 1 percent of his history, in a great rush. . . .

It took mankind more than a million years to reach a population of one billion. But the second billion required only 120 years; the third billion 32 years; and the fourth billion 15 years. If one postulates that the human race began with a single pair of parents, the population has had to double only 31 times to reach is present huge total.

Robert S. McNamara, 1977
president of the World Bank until 1981

The Lord must love the poor; he made so many of them.

Abraham Lincoln

Why a chapter on hunger in a text on international relations? The answer is reasonably simple. There are now more than 4 billion people living on the planet earth, two-thirds of them living under conditions of desperate poverty. The total number is likely to increase to 6 billion by the end of the century. It is not a matter of feeling guilty or idealistic to be concerned about this problem. Overpopulation is a source of extreme pressure on many Third World societies, producing domestic unrest and repression; to some extent, poverty and the upheaval connected with overpopulation are causing not only the violation of human rights but also the breakdown of society itself. Ted Robert Gurr, James Davies, Eric Wolf, and host of other students of violence in Third World countries have noted that peasant fatalism and the sheer time and effort required to stay alive are the only things keeping poverty from taking an explosive form, But how long will this continue while the population piles up in great shanty towns around the principal cities of the developing world? "The bleak statistics which describe living conditions in the least developed countries," according to a recent major American foundation report, "reveal the persistence of human suffering on a vast and unacceptable scale . . . . " More than one billion people live in absolute poverty, "beneath any reasonable definition of human decency," as defined by The World Bank.[1]

While understanding the basic link between food and politics may be "reasonably simple," however, the implications are far from simple. In a brilliant essay, part of which is reprinted in the sixth edition of this book, Donald Puchala and Raymond Hopkins spell out the nature of some of these increasingly serious complexities. World society cannot be insulated against the consequences of overpopulation and hunger. Many Third World countries presently exist under conditions of extreme instability or some form of dictatorship. They are increasingly manifesting their dissatisfaction with the present distribution of the world's wealth through anti-Western criticism in the United Nations. More fundamentally, it is difficult to maintain normal economic and political relations with states which are under such intense pressure. Note particularly the final paragraph of professor Byron Norton's article in this chapter.

The effects of overpopulation are being directly felt. Millions of Mexicans and Caribbean people enter the United States and England legally or illegally each year in an effort to escape their fate. The sending back of upwards of 1 million Italian laborers who had been working in Switzerland, France, and Germany accounts for some of the extreme unrest Italy experienced a few years ago. The magnitude of the population increases in a number of countries such as Brazil, Mexico, Egypt, India, and Indonesia, is likely to reach a critical mass that may have explosive military or political consequences. At the same time, rulers in underdeveloped countries may still recall elections which displaced the late Indira Gandhi from power; enforced population control was one of the issues.

Does all this portend some twenty-first or twenty-second–century doomsday on our crowded planet? Perhaps not. From another, more optimistic perspective, the economist P. T. Bauer has argued that population growth reflects a fall in mortality and therefore an improvement in the position of Third World people:

> Acceleration of growth of population in underdeveloped countries does not by itself provide a valid argument for aid. It is debatable to what extent people would reduce the number of their children if they had access to more sophisticated methods of preventing conception. But even now there is no reason why they cannot reduce the number of children they have, and they will certainly do so if they value higher living standards for themselves and their children.[2]

Bauer believes that all the babies born to Third World mothers are really wanted; that the mother and father sit down and weigh the satisfaction of seeing another child at the mother's breast against the economic and nutritional consequences

---

[1]Cited in "A Case for Attention," *The Rockefeller Foundation in The Developing World,* New York: The Rockefeller Foundation, (1986), p. 3.

[2]P.T. Bauer, *Dissent on Development* (Cambridge, Mass.: Harvard University Press, 1976), p. 123.

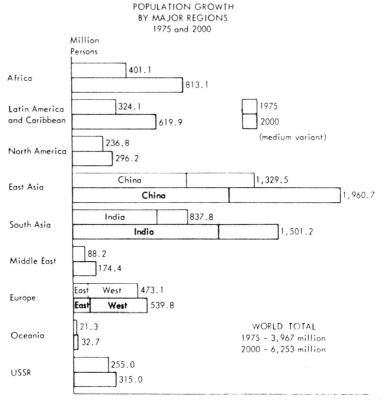

POPULATION GROWTH
BY MAJOR REGIONS
1975 and 2000

Million
Persons

Africa — 401.1 / 813.1

Latin America
and Caribbean — 324.1 / 619.9

1975 / 2000 (medium variant)

North America — 236.8 / 296.2

East Asia — China 1,329.5 / China 1,960.7

South Asia — India 837.8 / India 1,501.2

Middle East — 88.2 / 174.4

Europe — East West 473.1 / East West 539.8

Oceania — 21.3 / 32.7

WORLD TOTAL
1975 – 3,967 million
2000 – 6,253 million

USSR — 255.0 / 315.0

SOURCE From The Department of State Bulletin Reprint, 11/3/1977. U.N. Population Division

for themselves and the child. On the basis of this and other arguments, economists like Bauer dismiss the population problem as not being our responsibility, whereas some highly-respected diplomats such as George Kennan have argued that even though the United States did not create the problem, it still has to deal with it.[3]

One would think that when a problem is as self-evident as global hunger, governments should have no trouble in knowing what to do. But the problem of financing and delivering food to the needy on a global scale is extremely complex. The selection by David Korn indicates some of the obstacles that must be overcome, using Ethiopia as a particularly poignant example of how ideology can undermine both relief and justice.

Agricultural exports are a principal source of American export earnings. Hence, the U.S. must balance off the financial costs of supplying food against the maintenance of a remunerative American agricultural economy. The lack of an international organization with enforcement powers leaves the allocation of food to the play of competing global demands, even though the UN World

[3]See his excerpt in *The Theory and Practice of International Relations*, 6th ed., pp. 273–274.

Food Council, under the remarkable leadership of Maurice Williams, performs an essential advisory function. A greater dedication of national governments to do more to strengthen their own agriculture and reduce population growth is also needed. As we have seen, two experts closely connected with the actual problem—John Sewell and James Howe—have urged that the world not adopt "lifeboat ethics" ("lifeboat ethics" derives from the dilemma which occurs when there is not enough room in a lifeboat to save everyone so some are simply left to drown). This is the argument of the "triage," or "lifeboat," school, which argues that since there is not sufficient room for everyone, the hopelessly impoverished third of the world will just have to be written off.

The fact that foreign aid has been used to finance the existing elites and to preserve the status quo has permitted certain Third World leaders to avoid coming to grips with the problems of agriculture and overpopulation. More stress is needed, according to such distinguished and hardheaded economists as Gunnar Myrdal and Jagdish Bhagwati, on an approach that involves a very broad agreement on objectives and moral values as between or amongst the donor and recipient nations to assure that assistance programs will really deal with the needs of people, including the need for birth-control techniques. This was, in fact, the approach utilized in many international conferences held under the auspices of the Rockefeller Foundation at its famous Center at Bellagio in Italy.

Of course, such an approach would require the government decision-makers in both the donor and recipient countries, and not just earnest conferee-representatives, to put the solution of these problems ahead of their *immediate* self-interest. While more thoughtful national figures may have the wisdom to counsel their current leaders to follow such a course for their *ultimate* self-interest, short-term political, economic, and even military or strategic considerations tend to carry the day. Here theory and practice are badly out of phase.

Besides the unrelenting attacks which LDCs[4] have mounted in the United Nations and elsewhere against great disparities in wealth, there is a real danger that the well-being of the industrial democracies cannot be separated from the need to overcome poverty in the overpopulated, less-developed parts of the world. Meanwhile, the desperation of the situation facing some countries leads to repression, the destruction of human values, and deepening resentment against much of the economically advanced world. On the other hand, a most powerful argument against a greater sharing of wealth between rich and poor nations is that there is no guarantee that people, as individuals, would really benefit much from such a redistribution. The case for redistribution is often made on the grounds that the world is becoming more interdependent, and therefore extremes of wealth must be reduced.

But all too often the Third World leaders who demand a greater sharing of the wealth in the name of their impoverished people are precisely those who maintain the most extreme form of inequality *within* their own societies. One of

---

[4]*Less Developed Countries*; the effort to find an acceptable general term which is appropriate while not being offensive has been going on ever since Westerners were persuaded to stop using the expression "backward nations," some representatives of which bitterly asked who could be more backward than Nazi Germany. Other terms in vogue have been "emergent" or "developing" countries, neither of which unfortunately apply to some of them.

the great ironies of political rhetoric in international forums today is that, far from being apostles of a new and more integrated international system, often they may turn out to be the most ardent exponents of the supremacy of what only a few years ago was regarded as the outmoded principle of national sovereignty. In place of any assurance that redistribution of wealth would go to their own hungry populations, there is much evidence that it would continue to flow to the rich and to strengthening the military and repressive power of some of their own governments. As Korn points out, many of their demands now being heard for equality are not in the name of some new and more humanistic world order, but in the interest of reinforcement of nothing more than their own national sovereignty. In other words, the goal or ideal of sharing is less to advance to some higher form of world order than to retain the existing state-centric order while solidifying their country's position within it.

Robert Tucker has observed, "There is no way of insuring internal equity without setting political conditions for the recipient government that will almost certainly prove unacceptable because these conditions touch the nerve root of its domestic order [meaning the power and privileges of the rich]. In doing so [such conditions] must also strike at the equality of state doctrine."[5] In other words, just as there is presently no way to achieve reforms that touch at the existing patron-client relationship without a revolution, there is no way that the ruling elites could be made to abandon their wealth and privileges in return for a fairer distribution of wealth. However "good" the intentions of those who want to share a greater portion of "Northern" wealth to help impoverished masses in less fortunate areas of the planet, "the rights of the 'needy' will, in practice, remain first and foremost the rights of states and not of individuals."[6]

Throughout this book, we have tried to balance the insights of the theoretical writer with the experience of the practitioner. The discussion of what Sewell and Howe call "this historic challenge" is a sobering one. Yet it remains true that "governments have considerable capacity," as Robert McNamara has written, "to help create a generalized atmosphere of social consensus in an antinatalist direction. Allocations of [foreign aid] and central government funds for community improvements . . . can be conditioned on evidence of [reform] and new-style family norms."[7] One can be permitted to wonder: If the same zeal, effort, and money that is spent on armaments or putting men on the moon had been devoted to overcoming hunger, would the problem still be as acute as it is?

DISCUSSION QUESTIONS

1. What conditions are characteristic of Third World countries that they all share together? Can you think of any which are not plagued with hunger and poverty? What does the Hunger Project study show? What is "IMR"?

[5]"Inequality among Nations and the Future of the International Order," *The Colorado College Studies,* no. 14 (May 1977), p. 25.
[6]Ibid., pp. 25–26.
[7]"Population and International Security," *International Security* (Fall 1977), p. 127.

2. What generalizations about hunger as a world problem can be derived from Korn's analysis of the Ethiopian crisis?

3. Is there an international solution to hunger, or must each country handle its own people the best way it can? Does Norton's conceptual approach help, or is it too theoretical? What does he mean by "locally stable but globally unstable" ecosystems?

4. Which do you think represents the more hopeful approach to the problems set forth in this chapter: fewer babies or more food production? In what specific ways can either be brought about?

5. Do you regard The Hunger Project's conclusions as overly optimistic? Why or why not?

6. In your opinion, what clear responsibility do the developed states have toward overcoming hunger elsewhere, a). in their own interest? b). in other countries' interest? and c). in humane terms? Do you give the same reply in all three perspectives?

32. Ending Hunger

The Hunger Project (1985)

Established in 1977, The Hunger Project's purpose is to generate a global context of individual will, commitment, and responsibility for ending world hunger in this century. As of July 1, 1985, more than 3.5 million persons in over 150 countries had publicly declared their commitment to this by enrolling themselves in The Hunger Project. The book from which this selection is taken is the work of several authors from a number of countries, who shared their ideas and edited one another's work in its production.

Given that we live in a kind of "media age," what we pay attention to often depends on what is prominent in the media at the moment.

An apartment-house fire, an airplane crash, a murder in our city—these are the items of interest that make up our daily news diet. As discrete events, relevant largely only to the current moment, they come and go in our lives with little real impact. They speak to no enduring concern.

And then there are the really important matters of our time, underlying issues that rarely make it to the news because there are no "events"—in the news sense—connected with them. To our personal and planetary loss, these issues do not often emerge from the background to enter our daily concerns.

We do not see, therefore, how their existence—not as events, but as processes—tangibly affects and shapes life for us on the planet. We rarely make any connection between what we call "our lives" and these underlying processes.

The persistence of world hunger is one of those issues that permeates the background of life. With the exception of the occasional news-making event—typically, a famine in which the human disaster is so acute that it cannot be ignored—hunger lives as a process, a persistence, a chronic con-

Excerpted from *Ending Hunger: An Idea Whose Time Has Come* (New York: Praeger Publishers, 1985), pp 2, 3, 384, 386, 388, 390, 391, 393. Copyright © 1985 by The Hunger Project. (Footnotes have been deleted.)

dition. People die day in, day out; and because this is the norm, it is not "news."

For those of us who are adequately fed and for whom food is a commonplace of daily life, hunger—if it is thought of at all—is something "out there"; something tragic, horrible, awful; something we wish did not exist. It is not, however, something we keep front and center as one of our primary and fundamental concerns.

Imagine our concern—and the attention of the world's media—were an earthquake to strike San Francisco, killing 35,000 people in a single day.

Imagine our concern were a virus to descend on London, killing 18 children a minute without stop, week after week after week.

Imagine our concern were nuclear weapons to explode in the capitals of the world's major industrial countries, killing 13 million people and maiming and injuring a billion more in the surrounding countryside.

These are precisely the figures of human devastation resulting from hunger: 1 billion of us chronically undernourished; 13–18 million of us dead a year; 35,000 of us a day; 24 of us (18 of whom are children) a minute. Yet because we view hunger in the background of life, this terrible toll does not enter our headlines, nor, for most of us, our concerns.

For most of us. But not for all.

Today, even as you read, an unprecedented outpouring of public sentiment, concern, and commitment is gathering. Quietly and without fanfare, individuals throughout the planet are declaring their personal commitment to a world without hunger. One by one by one, as *individuals,* not as a part of a movement, men and women in North and South America, Europe, Asia, Africa, and elsewhere are looking into their lives and their world, and choosing to include hunger as one of their life concerns and personal commitments.

They do so on their own, without direction from government, without prodding from the media, without any particular encouragement from their leaders.

They come from every country, worship in every faith, speak in every language. They live in the world's richest countries and in the poorest; some work on the cutting edge of computer technology, and others farm their tribal lands with the same methods as did their grandfather's grandfathers.

What unites them all is their common stand, a commitment, a declaration for the end of the persistence of hunger and starvation by the end of this century. Out of their stand, they are taking a leadership role in the emergence of a worldwide, grass-roots commitment that is unique to our time.

This growing expression of commitment goes largely unreported and unnoticed in the media age. No matter. These are the people the late Buckminster Fuller called "little individuals," men and women who may be unknown to history but who nonetheless are boldly determined to direct the world in which they live.

Looking out at their world, they ask themselves the question, "What will I do to cause the end of hunger?" Their answers, multiplied a millionfold, arrived at newly and authentically each day, are literally speeding up the process of history by ensuring that the end of hunger is an act of creation rather than an event that occurs through the inevitable passage of time.

This book is a product of the demand on the part of thousands upon thousands of these individuals for potent, powerful, accessible information about world hunger, its

persistence, and its end. They are not experts; they have not studied the issues of development, food production, and population growth in depth. Yet they know that in order to increase their own ability to create the end of hunger, they need to be aware of the essential information and the important thinking taking place on these issues.

They are demanding a new kind of information—information that empowers their stand and enables them to be more effective in expressing their commitment; information that is accessible, comprehensive, and up to date; information that makes available both facts and points of view, and distinguishes between the two; information for people who have a job to do in the world and want the tools to get that job done. . . .

As our examination of the five major issues surrounding hunger has demonstrated, there is no scarcity of thinking, approaches, and perspectives on the problem of the persistence of hunger.

Throughout the world, these varying points of view have generated a wealth of policies, projects, and experiments for eradicating hunger. Some have failed spectacularly; others have succeeded, producing results that have literally made the difference between life and death for tens of millions of people. All this has given the world community an expertise and a depth of knowledge and experience that have substantially advanced our progress toward the eradication of hunger from the planet.

"Progress" is a word that is not yet used comfortably in describing a problem as immense as the persistence of hunger and starvation. Only recently did the world's experts begin to agree on the extent of this problem. The notion of measuring the extent of hunger is also very recent; and measuring its elimination is so new as to be almost startling.

Yet in this century—quietly, and virtually without acknowledgement—many countries of the world have shown remarkable success in ending hunger. Since 1900, seventy-five countries have ended hunger within their borders as a basic, society-wide issue. Forty-one of them have accomplished this feat since 1960.

Today, more than half the world's population lives in countries that no longer suffer from the persistence of hunger. What does it mean to say that hunger has ended as a basic issue in the lives of a people? How is this achievement indicated in concrete and measurable terms?

There are many ways to measure the existence of hunger in the world. One of the most widely accepted standards of measurement—used by numerous international agencies, including UNICEF and WHO [World Health Organization]—is the infant mortality rate (IMR). (As pointed out earlier, three out of every four who die of hunger are children.) The IMR measures the number of infants per thousand who are born live who die before their first birthday. Hunger exists as a chronic, persistent, society-wide condition when the IMR of a nation is greater than 50—that is, when more than 50 children per thousand die in the first year of their lives.

All available data indicate that when the IMR goes down, the overall death rate among other age groups goes down as well. Thus, a society's changes or improvements that are reflected in a reduction of infant deaths are simultaneously reflected in a reduction of child and adult deaths.

The IMR can range widely from country to country. For example, in Japan and Sweden, where hunger has ended as a basic issue in the lives of the people, the IMR is 7; in Burkina Faso (Upper Volta), where hunger is widespread, the IMR is 210. That is, of every 1,000 babies born alive, 210 will die before their first birthday.

India, whose population is equal to one-third of the population in all societies where hunger persists as a basic issue, has an IMR of 122. While high, this is an improvement over 1960, when the IMR stood at around 157. Many other nations have registered substantial drops in infant mortality in recent years. . . .

When a country has brought its IMR to a level of 50 or below, hunger as a basic, society-wide issue can be said to have ended. This is not to say that no one goes hungry in countries with low IMRs. Pockets of hunger exist in the United States, for example, where the IMR is 11. Still, as an issue affecting the lives of the vast majority of the people—that is, as a persistent, chronic condition—hunger has ended in countries that have an IMR of 50 or below.

The seventy-five countries that have brought their IMR below 50 are, for the most part, countries that the world considers "developed." They are found in North America, Europe, and part of Asia and Latin America. No country on the continent of Africa has yet achieved an IMR of 50 or below.

In 1900, no country in the world had an IMR of 50 or below. For the first countries that ended hunger—nine of them reached this point by 1940—the process was a slow one. It required pioneering medical, educational, and developmental activities. Now, however, the process seems to be accelerating.

Hunger is ending in various climates, under a variety of political ideologies and economic systems, and using a wide range of agricultural techniques. While more the seventy-five countries in which hunger has ended have a relatively high income level, there are important exceptions—such as Sri Lanka and China, both of which have per capita GNPs of around U.S. $300.

All these countries brought their IMRs to 50 or below using various nutrition-improving measures along with basic preventive-health measures (such as immunization programs and clean-water supplies). Additional successful measures have included: increasing basic education and literacy; redistributing wealth, land, and power; promoting industrial development; increasing agricultural production; and improving food-distribution, -storage, and -delivery systems. . . .

It is both important and heartening to note that there is no single prescribed way to achieve the end of the persistence of hunger in a society. Some countries focused on land reform, while others emphasized food subsidies, collectivized agriculture, or privately owned "family farms." For every country that saw a particular action as crucial to ending hunger, there is a country that ended hunger without it. . . .

Where Hunger Has Already Been Ended

Three Asian countries—Taiwan, China, and Sri Lanka—provide fitting testimony to the plurality of contemporary models for ending hunger.

Taiwan

A successful land-reform plan, supported with financial aid from the United States after World War II, was a key element in ending hunger in Taiwan. Before land reform, peasants paid more than 50 percent of their crops in rent to landlords—70 percent, in more fertile areas. Once land ownership was transferred to the peasants, they no longer had to pay this sum.

To compensate the former landlords, the government set up a ten-year pay schedule, during which time the peasants gave certain percentages of their income to the government. The government then used this money to pay the landlords for their land. Records show that even while they were paying these fees, a typical peasant family's income had increased by 81 percent between 1949 and 1952.

Once the peasants had a stake in their land, some surplus income with which to make improvements in irrigation, and other needed inputs, rice production began to increase. Between 1948 and 1952, the increase was 47 percent.

As production grew and the country's wealth increased, employment rose, construction of new houses increased, and schools were built. The IMR declined from around 155 in the 1930s to 9.1 today. Health care,

education, and family planning all improved, and birth rates declined substantially—from 42.1 per 1,000 in 1954 to 26 per 1,000 in the early 1970s. As this developmental process took hold, industrial capacity increased. Taiwan also opened up new markets, especially with Western countries.

China

While one approach was bringing hunger to an end in Taiwan, a very different program was ending hunger in China. Even during the three decades of revolution (1920–1949), Mao Tse-tung and the Chinese Communist Party emphasized measures designed to eliminate hunger.

During the World War II, China's communists instituted a variety of programs in the areas they controlled. They carried out land reform, set up grain-rationing systems, and extended agricultural credit to peasants. The Chinese formed compulsory primary schools, and formally legislated equality for women.

In the initial years after the 1949 revolution, the Chinese confiscated land from the landowners and gave it to the peasants for their individual plots. However, after a few years, China's farms were collectivized, and their productivity improved considerably.

Along with collectivization, the Chinese government launched many other projects that contributed to the end of hunger. These included:

Simple health care, in the form of "barefoot doctors";

Massive literacy campaigns;

Organization of peasants so that they could set up flood-control projects;

Eradication of major diseases, such as cholera and smallpox;

Establishment of small factories in the countryside, and emphasis on local self-sufficiency; and

Family planning.

In 1950, just after the revolution, the IMR was at least 125. Today it is 44. China has created an economic and social miracle that, in the 1930s, was thought unimaginable People are being fed; full employment exists; the country has a remarkable health-care system for a nation that still has a per capita income of just $304. Literacy is widespread, abject poverty is almost unknown. *And this was done for a population of over one billion people.*

Sri Lanka

Sri Lanka is a third country that has ended hunger as a basic issue. It is a success story of development. Sri Lanka, which gained its independence in 1948, had an IMR of 141 in 1946; by 1983, the IMR was 37. This remarkable drop in IMR occurred despite the fact that the country has remained very poor—its per capita income is just $302, or about $25 month.

Sri Lanka's democratic government has committed itself to meeting the basic needs of its people, and has instituted a program to achieve adequate nutrition through a food-subsidy program. Each person receives one to two pounds of rice per week at no charge.

To achieve food self-sufficiency, Sri Lanka successfully introduced a land-reform policy to provide landless laborers with land for subsistence farming. In addition, between 1953 and 1972 Sri Lanka increased its actively farmed land by 15 percent through irrigation—that is, by almost an additional 5 million acres.

Sri Lanka also improved its health-care system. Of Sri Lanka's expectant mothers, 98 percent receive prenatal care, compared with 10 to 15 percent in India. There is 1 hospital bed for approximately every 350 people, compared with 1 for every 1,500 in India and 1 for every 8,000 in Bangladesh. The life expectancy of sixty-six years is six years above the Asian average.

More than 80 percent of Sri Lanka's population is literate; 71 percent of the women can read and write (a fact that is particularly unusual for a developing country). More-over, Sri Lanka is home to one of the most remarkable self-help movements in the world, Sarvodaya Shramadana, which has made the development process an integral part of Sri Lankan village life.

Ending World Hunger: The Opportunity

The achievement of Taiwan, China, Sri Lanka, and the seventy-two other countries that have ended hunger as a basic issue points the way and provides a foundation for the end of hunger everywhere.

Not long ago, the question was not "Is the world progressing toward ending hunger?" but "Can hunger be ended at all?" Today, there is wide recognition that humanity can, in fact, end hunger. There is a growing consensus among experts that we already have the necessary resources, technology, and know-how to end hunger on our planet in this century.

In 1977, the National Academy of Sciences issued the *World Food and Nutrition Study,* on which 1,500 scientists had consulted. The study concludes:

> *If there is the political will in this country and abroad . . . it should be possible to overcome the worst aspects of widespread hunger and malnutrition within one generation.*

In 1980, the Presidential Commission on World Hunger—a panel of twenty Americans, including scientists, business people, and nutritionists—issued a report. It found that:

> *Each major cause of hunger could be averted or overcome if the human community were to act co-operatively and decisively. Conversely, the persistence of hunger reflects a lack of sufficient political will to eliminate its causes. . . .*
>
> *If decisions and actions well within the capability of nations and people working together were implemented it would be possible to eliminate the worst aspects of hunger and malnutrition by the year 2000.*

In 1980 the Brandt Commission, composed of representatives of seventeen rich and poor countries, issued a report of its two-year study. The study concludes:

> *Mankind has never before had such ample technical and financial resources for coping with hunger and poverty. The immense task can be tackled if the necessary collective will is mobilized. What is necessary can be done, and must be done.*

UNICEF's 1980 *State of the World's Children* report states that, by the year 2000, the number of infant deaths in low-income countries could be reduced to 50 or fewer per 1,000 live births:

> *Although idealistic in the context of past experience, [this goal is] realistic in the sense that the principal obstacle standing in the way of [its] realisation is the will and the commitment to achieve [it].*

The Food and Agriculture Organization (FAO), the largest organization in the world dealing with global food issues, has undertaken a thorough examination of "what needs to be done to achieve the entirely feasible result of abolishing widespread hunger during the two decades ahead." FAO reports that its study, *Agriculture: Toward 2000,*

> *leads to the conclusion that hunger could be abolished. The requirements for doing so are demanding but they are feasible. . . . It is not the purpose of this report to propose another target but rather to point out what needs to be done to achieve the entirely feasible result of abolishing widespread hunger during the two decades ahead.*

These prestigious studies mark a turning point in the global fight to eradicate hunger. They are a recognition of the fact that for the first time in history the world now possesses the agricultural, technological, and financial resources to eradicate the persistence of hunger forever. . . .

The end of the persistence of hunger by the end of this century is now achievable. We have the resources to end it; we have proven solutions for ending it; we have test cases for the end of hunger in those countries that have already ended it. Hunger, given the facts and figures about it, turns out to be one of those fundamental problems that we have proven we can resolve. The end of hunger is now a possibility, but it is not a promise. It is not something that will happen inevitably, regardless of what we do or don't do. Hunger *can* end—but that is not the same as saying it *will* end.

Recent progress notwithstanding, we cannot wait for the end of hunger. If we simply kept on doing what we have done in the past, hunger would still persist in the year 2000. Merely redoubling our existing efforts, or quickening our pace, or intensifying already existing programs will not fulfill the need and the opportunity before us.

We now have the opportunity to see what is missing in the global effort to end hunger. Our world possesses sufficient resources, technology, and proven solutions to achieve the end of the persistence of hunger and starvation by the end of the century. What is missing is the commitment.

Those of us who are interested in the end of hunger, committed to the end of hunger, or working to create the end of hunger now have the opportunity to bring forth this new kind of commitment—a commitment to actually ensure that what can be done shall be done.

This breakthrough in our individual and global commitment can produce the gathering force throughout the planet that every major study has identified as the missing ingredient.

This breakthrough in our individual and global commitment can make the idea of ending hunger by the year 2000 an idea whose time has come.

33. Agricultural and Food Policy: The Conceptual Issues

Bryan G. Norton

Bryan G. Norton, who teaches philosophy and environmental studies at New College of the University of South Florida, wrote this paper while a Gilbert White Fellow at Resources for the Future.

With human population projected to be over one-and-one-half times its 1975 level by the end of this century, and with three-quarters of the population of less developed countries currently undernourished to some degree, it is considered desirable to triple or quadruple food supplies by the end of this century. But the unquestionably high-priority goal of reducing hunger and malnutrition has produced policies that have come under increasing attack by environmentalists who are concerned that haphazard and poorly planned agricultural development will irreversibly damage the world ecosystem. In particular, environmentalists project that, unless the rate of human alteration of natural systems, especially the tropical moist forests, is decreased, there will be a cataclysmic reduction in the worldwide biotic diversity. Nobody knows the full ecological, climatic, economic, and aesthetic consequences of such a simplification of the world ecosystem, but noted scientists claim that this is the most serious environmental problem facing mankind. Indeed, E. O. Wilson of Harvard University says that the projected loss of genetic and species diversity through the destruction of natural habitats "is the folly our descendants are least likely to forgive us."

In the context of this growing alarm, more and more scientists and policymakers advocate the protection (to some degree and in some manner) of the tropical forests. But the relevant concept of protection is not clear. First, it is often not explicit what is meant by "protection." For example, while terms "conservation" and "preservation" are often substituted for each other, these terms have diverging connotations, as the former implies deferred or wise use and the latter implies exclusion from use. Second, the proper object of concern is often not clear. One hears pleas to protect genetic diversity, species, ecological diversity, ecological systems, and, more generally, the productivity of natural forests. These alternative pleas can express quite different, even conflicting, goals.

My remarks will be divided into three sections. First, I will discuss the difference between what I will call the "conservationist" and "preservationist" attitudes toward environmental protection (I use this last term neutrally to comprehend both of the prior ones and as opposed to what might be called the developmental attitude). I will show how the controversy between conservation and preservation can be illuminated by relating it to several competing concepts in ecology and population biology. Second, I will place the controversy in the broader social context of attempts to protect the biological diversity of tropical ecosystems. Third, I will state several conclusions which I believe to be entailed, or at least suggested, by the considerations of the first two sections.

I. Scientific Concepts and Protection Ideals

Many environmental protectionists have felt an intuitive link between their concerns and environmental stability, as is witnessed by the almost incurable desire to appeal to the diversity-stability hypothesis as a cornerstone of our environmental ethic. The core of this intuition is the belief that a system is healthy only if it is in some sense "stable."

Efforts to link environmental protection with scientific concepts have ended in confusion, largely because the concept of stability as it is used in systematic ecology and population biology is multiply ambiguous. A complete survey of such concepts would require more space than is available here, but for my purposes, it is useful to isolate three families of stability concepts:

(1) One group of meanings clusters around the idea of *constancy* and lack of change. The emphasis, here, is on the absence of any reaction to disturbances which occur. Consequently, concepts in this family concentrate on characteristics of systems which allow them to resist change in the face of natural changes from within the system or external disturbances which might alter it.

(2) A second family of meanings (which I will refer to as "resilience" concepts) emphasize abilities of a system to return to a normal state after a disturbance. These concepts are very popular with mathematically oriented population biologists . . . .

Resilient systems are ones which, in the face of disturbances, have mechanisms whereby the various elements re-establish an equilibrium subsequent to a disturbance. This family of concepts, unlike the first, recognizes that systems change through time, but the concept of stability here embodied still emphasizes systematic equilibrium through time. Changes within the system are seen as mechanisms of re-establishing the stable equilibrium.

(3) A system can also be considered stable if it is internally predictable. The central idea of this concept is that a system is stable even through profound changes in structure and function, provided those changes result from predictable, expected patterns, given that future internal states of the system are determined mainly by its present states. For example, if a pine forest ecosystem naturally passes into a mixed hardwood forest in the absence of a major disturbance, this system can be considered stable in the same sense that its alterations are predictable on the basis of causes inherent in the system.

Of these families of stability concepts, the first two emphasized the static features of ecosystems. Of the first, this is obvious. But the same is true of the second family, as resiliency measures emphasized the return to stable points. While resilience concepts recognize that natural systems are characterized by fluctuations and dynamic interactions, stability is nevertheless measured according to the likelihood of repetitions of certain states of the system. While fluctuations are considered normal, they are seen as temporary deviations from a norm that is static through time. The third concept, that of predictability, emphasizes change over time provided that the temporal changes occurring are a natural result of structural features of the system and of systematic interrelationships between functioning elements.

The hypothesis of the present section is that conservationists tend, either consciously or unconsciously, to interpret the health/stability of a system on the model of either (1) or (2) or a combination thereof, while preservationists interpret health/stability in terms of (3). This point requires careful explanation.

Since a conservationist is concerned with *wise use* of a productive system, he/she is mainly interested in one or a small number of products. The concern is to maintain or increase the output of that product. Major structural changes in the system such as a progression to a more mature stage of succession is more likely to decrease than increase production of a particular output, because as the system becomes more diverse, the energy inputs will be distributed more widely. If, as is unlikely, the system would be more productive of the desired element or elements if it were allowed to change, the conservationist will let it change and, at whatever point the desired outputs are maximized, the goal of the conservationist will be to stabilize it there. Consequently, it is natural for the conservationist to measure health/stability using the concepts of a constancy and resilience.

It is natural because this tendency originates in the goals and objectives of the conservationist, who is concerned, first, for human well-being. Humans, while comparative generalists in feeding strategies, find only a few natural products useful for their purposes. Consequently, human needs will dictate a narrow conception of natural productivity—a system will be judged productive only if it generates large amounts of humanly useful products. At the same time, because humans are rational inventors of new techniques and products, not to mention being fickle in taste, it is difficult to project human demand for products beyond a generation or so. I refer here to what economists call the phenomenon of "substitutability". Consequently, the concern for constancy of production of specific outputs is coupled with a tendency to show greatest concern for short and medium-term productivity (at least with respect to specific products).

Given their concern for fulfilling specific human needs and the consequent restriction of concern to a short and medium-range time frame, it is not surprising that conservationists find the concepts of constancy and resilience useful. Further, it is not surprising that, when productive systems begin to change (whether because of natural forces such as succession or artificial forces such as pollution), they propose further management of the system. The goal of such management is to maintain constancy or at least resilience of the system, so that it will continue to produce the desired products.

Preservationists, on the other hand, view natural systems as autonomous, highly integrated and dynamic. Further, they doubt that the knowledge and ability of humans is sufficient to manage a system totally and see each intentional modification of a system by human manipulation as yet another chance for things to go wrong. That is, every management initiative demands more such initiatives. Their concentration on the system as autonomous focuses attention away from particular products of human interest. Consequently, preservationists conceive stability/health in terms of long-term predictability of such systems. They do so because of two separate but related commitments. First, they tend *not* to measure health in terms of short- and medium-run human goals. Secondly, they doubt the ability of humans to manage systems for the long run, regardless of the goals chosen.

As tempting as it is to dichotomize conservationists and preservationists according to concern for humans as opposed to concern for nature, such a categorization would represent a serious oversimplification for two reasons. First, the essential dichotomy at issue here is not between allowing and excluding human use, but between pervasive management permitted by advanced technologies and activities that are ecologically integrated into ecosystem functioning. Indigenous tribes have lived in tropical forests for centuries and their activities are an integral part of the functioning system. When I refer to management, I refer to conversion of the forests which alters the essential mechanisms of the tropical forest system.

Second, the preservationists' rejection of the whole complex of ideas including concern for single products, "health" measured in terms of resilience, management for productivity, and a concern for the relatively short run, can be explained, alternatively, by reference *either* to his rejection of the anthropocentric nature of that complex *or* by reference to an overwhelming doubt that such intense management can be maintained through indefinite time. That is, while a rejection of the tendency to use nature for human purposes could motivate a preservationist (and undoubtedly does motivate some of them), there is an independent idea which is sufficient to provide the same motivation. That is the belief that (at least some) ecosystems are too complex to be managed by human interference and that critical forms of human interference, demand further interference and, in the end, human management leads to human destruction. If the timeframe is long enough, the argument goes, humans will suffer as much as nature from ill-advised tampering. Preservationists advocate a hands-off attitude with respect to at least some systems because they believe it is impossible to manage them. The system and its internal dynamic is too complex and an attempt to measure its health/stability in terms of constancy, resilience, or continued production of a single resource is to ignore the ongoing dynamic of natural systems. But this rejection need not belie an anti-human attitude. Rather it could result from a concern for human existence and quality of life in the long run. On this view, the preservationist would be seen as arguing that humans have a right to use nature, but they do so wisely when they allow at least some ecosystems to exist autonomously. Human beings should adapt their use of nature to the changing products of the ecosystems, rather than managing ecosystems for the production of currently preferred products.

To summarize this section, then, it has been argued that concern for health and stability of ecosystems can be understood according to two complexes of ideas and concepts, which could be encapsulated under the terms "conservationist" and "preservationist", respectively. These two complexes involve importantly different attitudes toward environmental protection, and these have operational analogues in the literature of ecology and population biology. But the difference between the two complexes cannot be reduced to a simple dichotomy of "humanists" versus "nature-lovers" or anthropocentrists versus believers in intrinsic value for nature. The preservationist attitude can be fully sustained on a humanistic basis as long as that basis is coupled with a concern for the very long run and with scep-

ticism about human abilities to manage ecosystems properly over long periods of time.

One more caveat is in order here. The labels "conservationist" and "preservationist" mark no sharp dichotomy. No protectionist always fits one mold or the other, since there will be considerable variation according to the particular resource under discussion. Indeed, preservationists may find it necessary to advocate wise, and perhaps even intense, use of already altered systems in order to lessen pressure to place complex, undisturbed systems under management for greater production. The two labels are most useful in characterizing two ends of an important spectrum in protectionist attitudes. That spectrum introduces less confusion, however, if it is thought of as ranging most basically over areas and/or systems rather than people. There is a preservationist and a conservationist attitude toward various systems. People are judged members of the categories of preservationist and conservationist, derivatively, according to the likelihood that they will advocate the policies associated with those attitudes respectively over a wide range of cases.

II. The Social Context

The contrasts expressed in the preceding section by the conservationist attitudes represents neither a purely scientific nor a purely philosophical dispute. Rather, when those two attitudes clash over a particular land use decision, the resulting disagreement exemplifies a public policy issue. But in the larger social context, the spectrum of protectionist attitudes whether conservationist or preservationist, represented only one end of a spectrum which includes nonprotectionist, developmentally oriented positions. However, the above discussion is helpful in understanding the broader spectrum.

And that broader spectrum is fully exemplified in public policy positions regarding land use in the moist tropics. Advocates range across the spectrum of attitudes toward tropical forests, stretching from a radically developmental to a radically preservationist attitude. The first of these attitudes is exemplified by Sol M. Linowitz:

> ... The process of development in Latin America is agonizingly long and arduous. It must start from the ground up; and the ground itself must first be cleared of jungle, the trail cut through the mountains, and civilization itself introduced before new farms can be laid out and made productive ... The Amazon River, unlike the Mississippi, flows through vast tracks [sic] of what are still sodden, malaria ridden, impenetrable jungle wastelands, its water patrolled by alligators and man-eating snakes.

Radical preservationists, by contrast, insist that tropical forests, either because of their intrinsic value, or because of their services to humans, such as moderation of hydrological cycles, climate control, etc., should be left inviolate. They fear that the forests, even if partially managed for human purposes, will lose their integrity as ongoing and productive systems.

The radically developmental position is unrealistic. Conversion of tropical forests to agricultural and other exploitative uses has obvious short-term attractions for tropical countries facing rising population, economic stagnation, political instability, and demands for land reform and increasing agricultural production. Offering uncleared land to landless peasants can seem a solution to all these problems, especially given that those peasants often experience good agricultural yields in the first years of production. Economic analysis can make this disastrous scenario seem attractive, provided the time frame over which benefits and costs are calculated is sufficiently short and provided the calculations emphasize commercial and monetary values. In a context where a growing population of undernourished poor creates political instability, policymakers in less developed countries may find even short-term solutions attractive.

Here, however, the central facts about the nature of tropical moist forest ecosystems are crucial. The lush vegetation which constitutes tropical forests contains virtually all the nutrients available in the system, since few such nutrients are stored in the soils. Consequently, cleared forest land is not susceptible to the sustained agriculture typical of temperate zones, but encourages shifting, slash-and-burn agriculture. Such agriculture can support only small numbers of farmers because the proportion of fallow land (where the forest is building nutrients) to tilled land (where farmers are using nutrients) must be very high. But the logic of this situation allows, in the short run, the clearing of larger proportions of land and temporary increases in food production, because cleared lands will remain productive for several years as the nutrients from burned vegetation are used and simultaneously leached out by the tropical sun. Only later do the disastrous consequences—burnt-out soils, erosion, siltation of rivers and reservoirs, and even climatic changes—appear. If the proportion of cleared to uncleared land becomes too great to allow effective reencroachment of the forest into abandoned farmlands, the soil will never recover. It will not only be itself useless for crop production, but will no longer be capable of moderating hydrological cycles, it will continue to erode, plugging rivers and reservoirs and creating drought on other, previously productive land. Therefore, slash-and-burn agriculture can be sustained only as long as cleared areas are relatively small and the fallow periods are sufficiently long. The levels of use consistent with these rules governing shifting agriculture permit subsistence farming for only relatively small numbers of individuals. In actuality, the pressures that lead to such agriculture are inexorable. Eventually the rules are broken, and the downward spiral of decreased productivity and increased erosion begins. Thus the radically exploitative attitude ultimately proves self-defeating, because it is unjustified in the face of scientific evidence about how tropical forest functioning bears upon agricultural potential. The human benefits of deforestation, while tangible, are short-lived. Even a computation of purely human benefits of clearing forests, if placed in a time frame of reasonable length, suggests caution.

But the radical preservationist position is unrealistic in another way. Given the social conditions of rapidly increasing human populations, wide-spread malnourishment, and inequitable land tenure policies obtaining in most tropical, developing countries, radical protectionism could be implemented only by ignoring broader human and social problems. From a public policy point of view, the protection of ongoing processes of nature must be seen as one policy goal among others. Central among these is the goal of increasing agricultural productivity in the face of overwhelming population growth in less developed countries. The need for increased food supplies is and must remain a goal of highest priority. Any concept of protection that ignores these pressures will prove unworkable on both humanitarian and political grounds. However important are the insights embodied in radical preservationism, this movement will remain isolated from mainstream policy discussions unless it takes into account human needs and demands. In particular, radical preservationism can justifiably be accused of elitism if it defends the forests in such a manner as to perpetuate the gaps in standards of living between rich and poor nations. It is necessary, then, to embed discussions of forest protection in realistic assessments of how to deal with expanding human demands for food. What is needed is a conception of forest protection that is strong enough to embody the objective of protecting tropical forest functioning over the long run, but flexible enough not to rule out all productive use of forests. At the same time, it is important that such a concept be scientifically respectable and be connected with operationally measurable indices so that it can serve the clear statement of public policy goals concerning

protection while allowing measurement of progress toward those goals.

Thoughtful analysts now reject both the radically developmental and the radically preservationist attitudes. Two more moderate, though quite distinct, intermediate positions have emerged. Of these, the moderately developmental position is well exemplified by Mustafa K. Tolba, the Executive Director of the United Nations Environmental Program, who has said:

> . . . Forestry, as a development activity, is not competitive with other economic sectors such as agriculture. Rather, it is in complementary accord with other sectors. Through their watershed services, for example, tropical forests promote regular supplies of irrigation water. Forestry thus supports agriculture, and the ancient antagonism between foresters and agriculturalists in many tropical lands is not graphically recognized as a false dichotomy.

While recognizing the negative consequences of widespread deforestation, Tolba still speaks of the forests as a human resource and advocates their exploitation. He wants exploitative activities to be limited by the management wisdom of trained forest managers. This position incorporates the concepts and attitudes of the conservationist approach.

In distinction from Tolba's approach, moderate preservationists recognize the demands placed upon forests by expanding human populations without thereby adopting the moderately developmental, or conservationist-management, approach wholesale. Rather, they reason that some use must and will be made of forests and that some areas are going to be intensively managed. They join with conservationists in counseling that these areas be chosen only after careful study of their potential for sustained use. But they maintain their concern for long-term protection of the forests' creative capacities. Consequently, while acknowledging human demands, they advocate the setting aside of large preserves from which modern, technological human society is to be entirely excluded.

While these two moderate positions are far more compatible than the two extreme positions discarded earlier, and while proponents of these positions are capable of congenial dialogue and practical compromise, important practical and conceptual differences remain. Practically, for example, moderate developers find widespread management for human use a reasonable option, as long as that management takes account of the best scientific guidance about the capability of forests to survive in a (perhaps somewhat altered, but) relatively intact state. Moderate preservationists, on the other hand, advocate a patchwork environment in which managed areas are interspersed with inviolate preserves. Conceptually, the difference between these two groups are those originally identified in the conservationist/preservationist dichotomy.

Moderate developers exemplify the conservationist attitude showing concern for production of useful human products and wise use of land, allowing sustained use and avoiding erosion, etc. But, to the extent that this attitude concentrates on stable production of useful products over a few human generations, it ignores the long-term value of the autogenic tropical forest ecosystems which have been for aeons the most creative sources of biological diversity on the planet. The conversion of all of the forests to more intense human use, whether that involves monocultural plantings of wheat and corn or forest monocultures such as rubber plantations, will destroy the existing biological diversity of the tropics and, even worse, will undermine the possibility of future evolutionary creativity. Preservationists need not appeal to intrinsic value of such diversity (even though they may do so). There exist more than adequate reasons couched in terms of purely human, if long-term, benefits.

Insofar as the conservationists have a natural tendency to link ecosystem health to constancy and resilience while preservationists link it to predictability, it is worth examining the comparative advantages of those concepts. A comparison gives far more comfort to the preservationist position. Constancy hardly ever occurs in nature. Even when a system appears constant, it is usually because compensatory changes return the system to equilibrium. While resilience is more applicable than constancy, . . . it too is of questionable applicability to ecosystems. Ecosystems and their structural characteristics are normaly resilient, provided perturbations do not exceed a certain threshold. But if that threshold is exceeded in severity, then the system may collapse or a new equilibrium may be established. Ecologists express this point by saying that ecological systems are "locally stable" but "globally unstable." Consequently, an empirical case can be made that constancy and resilience have, at best, limited applicability to natural ecosystems.

A second difficulty, which is more general but no doubt underlies the first, is that constancy and resilience ignore the dynamic aspects of ecological systems. Systems change through ecological time as a result of successional development. They also change through evolutionary time as a result of natural selection. Insofar as conservationists are limited to measuring health of ecosystems with essentially static concepts, their position is weaker than that of preservationists, theoretically.

This general point gains strength as one moves from a general level to specific applications to tropical forests. As the most diverse and complexly interrelated systems in the world, the tropical forests are extremely fragile (i.e., non-resilient). Evidence now suggests that, as the elements of a system become more complexly inter-related, they become more stable (resilient) locally, but more unstable (nonresilient) globally. That is, complex systems with highly specialized dependency relationships among species seem to be more susceptible to total collapse than are less complex systems. Thus, resilience in the face of small disturbances may be purchased at the cost of decreases in the range of disturbances which can be endured without a major shift in the system's organization. This explains why, as is noted as a virtual commonplace, the tropical forests have proved extraordinarily fragile in the face of human disturbance.

For these empirical reasons, I believe the preservationists' position must be taken very seriously. As noted above, the conflict between conservationists and preservationists is not a purely scientific one and cannot be resolved by empirical means alone. It is, nevertheless, an important point in the preservationists' favor that the full range of empirical data is better comprehended using their concept of predictability than it is by the conservationists' favored indicator of resilience. There seems to be excellent evidence for believing that there are dynamic features of fragile ecosystems, especially tropical ones, which are not fully protected by management intiatives designed to maintain constancy or resilience.

III. Some Tentative Conclusions about Protecting Tropical Forests

(1) Radical developmental positions ignore well-known scientific facts about the results of conversion of most tropical forests for monocultural agriculture. They cannot be justified, in most cases, even if the benefits to humans are computed over unacceptably short time frames—time frames suitable to, perhaps, hit-and-run investors or to shaky governments hoping to reduce social pressures to stay in power for a few more years, but unsuitable to any realistic evaluation of societal needs viewed over a generation or more.

(2) Conservation-minded and more moderate developmental positions are more easily defended as benefiting human populations over a period of a few generations. Productive use of forests which make use of scientific knowledge and management techniques can provide benefits to expanding populations for the indefinite, if relatively short-term, future. For example, silviculture exploiting fast-growing non-indigenous trees for lumber and pulp, food-producing plantation crops, etc. can avoid the disastrous results of erosion while providing significant benefits for human populations.

(3) The conservationist attitude exemplified in (2), however, does not address the legitimate concerns of preservationists. And the concerns of preservationists should not be dismissed as based upon an anti-human nature-fetish of rich elitists. Replacing natural systems with more productive managed systems (no matter how conservation-minded that management is), does not protect the biological diversity of the tropical forests. And that biological diversity is a long-term human resource, and should be protected for purely human reasons.

(4) Preservationists often do speak as if they place intrinsic value upon natural systems—value which is independent of human interests. Without attempting to settle the difficult ethical and metaphysical issues embodied in such claims, it is possible to suggest as an hypothesis that it is often useful to think of nature as if it has intrinsic value. The result of such hypothetical thinking is to emphasize that natural systems are dynamic They change in ecological time, measured in decades and centuries, by passing through successional stages and they change in evolutionary time, measured in millennia. While time frames of this magnitude often exceed human abilities to plan and utilize products, there can be no doubt that humans of the future will benefit if those dynamic and creative processes are allowed to continue. If those benefits are inconceivable in terms humans use to compute benefits and to plan accordingly, it is useful to look at nature's ongoing dynamic integrity as a thing of intrinsic value. If large tracts of tropical forests are left untouched, future genera-

tions will thank us, regardless of whether we were able to conceive, in detail, the benefits they will derive.

(5) With human population, especially in tropical nations, still growing out of control, it is unrealistic to hope that a majority of the tropical forests will remain in a pristine state. However justifiable this position is from a biological, ecological, and evolutionary viewpoint, it must be recognized that national priorities and land use decisions are made in a context of competing goals and objectives. It is unthinkable that the goal of feeding growing human populations should not be a very high priority. However, the present generation has obligations not only to feed current populations, but also not to destroy the ecological and evolutionary creativity of ecosystems. The most reasonable compromise seems to be to strive for a "patchwork" environment.

This recommendation has the advantage of protecting diversity of human populations by providing areas where indigenous tribes can continue their lifestyles which are integrated into ecosystem functioning. Thus, policies encouraging patchy environments preserve traditional alternatives to modern cultures which require radical conversion and intense, eventually destructive, use of forest land. Again, it is seen that concern for preservationist goals is not exclusive of concern for human needs. Rather, it is a concern for protecting the continued functioning of ecosystems, which benefits human cultures integrated into these systems, as well as future generations which will benefit from the preservation of biological diversity.

(6) A patchwork environment can be achieved by isolating some very large preserves, building buffers around them in order to keep them inviolate from human encroachment. These areas should be chosen for their representativeness, for their current diversity, and for their future creativity. Some areas will be exploited at an intermediate level of intensity, in tree plantations, etc. Yet others will be used in the most productive, intense way possible. But even in

the latter areas, great effort should be taken to retain islands of natural diversity such as woodlots, roadwide verges, and fence hedges. It is important to recognize that the strategy here proposed is at best a compromise between two very important human ideals. As such it is not a "solution," but a balancing of priorities in a situation where unfortunate population pressures have and will preclude optimal solutions.

(7) The patchy environment of which I speak will, undoubtedly, be composed of patches within patches. For example, huge areas of the Amazon basin might be considered a preserve, even though some smaller areas within it may be used more intensely. These would represent small patches of intensely productive lands within a large patch of comparatively undisturbed ecosystems. Likewise, huge farm areas will, hopefully, contain a patchwork of less disturbed areas. Because such a plan may represent the only rational means of preserving the biological diversity of the planet, because population pressures will vary greatly across political boundaries, and above all because some areas of the world are clearly more susceptible to sustained, intense food production than others, the optimal solution will have to be international in nature. If the choices as to what to use and what to preserve are to be made rationally, some nations will have a larger percentage in preserves than do others.

(8) Since (7) is true, the responsibilities for protecting preserves cannot be left entirely to individual nations. Some nations may be on the most rational plan less "productive" in the short run in order that they can protect the biological diversity and creativity which is a common heritage of mankind. Such a plan could only work if developed nations accept the protection of biological diversity as a service of commercial value. It is hopeless, as well as irresponsible to attempt to impose upon less developed nations the costs and responsibilities for protecting the biological diversity of the earth, while claiming that diversity is a common heritage of hu-

mankind. If it is the common heritage of humankind, then the costs and responsibilities for protecting it must be shared so that nations within whose boundaries the richest collections of such diversity exist, are not penalized with lower standards of living in

order to protect that diversity. I am aware of the controversial issues of international sovereignty which are implied by this conclusion, but to discuss them would go far beyond my current topic.

34. The Politics of Famine[1]

David A. Korn

A career officer in the U.S. Foreign Service, David A. Korn headed the American Embassy in Addis Ababa, Ethiopia from mid-1982 to mid-1985 and then became a Visiting Fellow at The Royal Institute of International Affairs (Chatham House) in London.

It cannot be said never before to have happened, but it is hardly commonplace: a country massively armed by the Soviet Union and massively supplied with food by the west. It might be supposed that the government of that country must be a master of the acrobatics of international politics or, if not that, at least a model of non-alignment. But the country is Ethiopia and, while western food shipments piles up on the docks of its ports by the tens of thousands of tons, its government reaffirms its dedication to Marxism-Leninism and to alliance with the Soviet Union.

When in the autumn of 1984 western nations launched their very large relief effort, in response to the drought that struck Ethiopia that year and the famine that ensued, they did not require from the Ethiopian government assurances of political counterpart. Some in fact, gave just the opposite assurance: namely, that their very substantial hu-

manitarian assistance would be extended with absolutely no political strings attached. Yet it was natural for the west to hope, if not to expect, that its Herculean effort to save the lives of millions of starving Ethiopians would be appreciated and would prompt the Ethiopian government to take a second look at its international position. Surely it would see that, when it came to basic matters of survival, the west had a lot more to offer than the east. Moscow could give arms to prosecute endless civil wars, but it could provide neither food in time of emergency nor an economic model that would assure the production by Ethiopia of enough food to feed its burgeoning population, even in normal times. Would the 1984 drought and famine not make the government of Mengistu Haile Marian understand, after seven years of striving to copy the Soviet model, that the time for at least modest changes had come?

These hopes have been disappointed. There has been no improvement in Ethiopia's relations with the west and no alteration in its ties with the east: instead, the Ethiopian government has sought to quieten any fears

Printed from *The World Today*, January 1986, 42, No. 1, under the title "Ethiopia: Dilemma for the West." Copyright © 1986 The Royal Institute of International Affairs, London, pp. 4–7.

Moscow might have that the food sent by the west could be a threat to their relationship. And it has stubbornly reaffirmed agricultural policies that have left it helpless in the face of drought. To understand why there has been no improvement in ties between Ethiopia and the west, one needs to look back over the course of events in Ethiopia during 1984 and early 1985.

The Nature of the Famine

Despite all that has been written about it, the Ethiopian famine remains widely misunderstood. Some, in particular the Ethiopian government and its apologists, attribute it almost exclusively to drought and soil exhaustion; others, almost entirely to bad agricultural policies. In fact, it was the product of an explosive mix of the two. Poor rainfall in the north-central areas of Ethiopia, in Eritrea, Tigre, northern Wollo and eastern Gondar, induced the beginnings of a crisis during late 1982 and 1983. But in 1984 a searing drought hit these areas and most of the rest of highland Ethiopia. Normally, after a dry season following the end of the heavy summer rains, the rains come again to highland Ethiopia early in the year, in late January or February and intermittently for several months. Those rains make possible a harvest of grain in May that accounts for between 5 and 15 per cent of the year's crop. Just as important, they provide fodder for animals and soften the soil for planting in the early summer. There was no rain in highland Ethiopia (except for a few scattered showers of no use to agriculture) between mid-October of 1983 and May of 1984. The spring crop was wiped out, and early summer planting was made unusually difficult. The summer rains were lighter than normal and ended in mid-September, a month earlier than usual. When this happened, Ethiopia had no reserve to fall back on. Governmental policies favoured state farms and collectives, though both have given disappointing results. The mass of Ethio-

pia's peasantry continues to farm privately, though without governmental assistance unless it consents to move towards collectivisation. Prices are set so low that the peasantry has little incentive to produce more than what it needs for its own subsistence.[2]

A prudent and concerned government would have needed nothing more than to rise from bed each morning and look at the sky to realise, by the summer of 1984, that Ethiopia was in trouble. Foreign relief workers began to send back to their headquarters in Addis Ababa reports of the devastation done by the drought, and of the growing numbers of starving peasants seeking shelter in the towns along the main road running through Wollo and Tigre. These reports were picked up by western embassies and transmitted to home capitals. But in the absence of attention to the issue by the government of Ethiopia, the party most directly concerned, neither western governments nor the western press were immediately aroused.[3]

The Government's Response

During the summer of 1984, the Ethiopian government was preoccupied to the exclusion of all else with preparations for the formation of the Workers Party of Ethiopia (WPE), by its own definition a 'vanguard Marxist-Leninist party', and the celebration of the tenth anniversary of the 1974 revolution, both in early September. Throughout the summer of 1984, consequently, not a word was spoken publicly by top Ethiopian officials or in the media (all government-owned and directed) about massive famine or unusual drought. Later, after the international media had exposed the extent of the crisis, the Ethiopian government and its Relief and Rehabilitation Commission (RRC) began to rewrite history, claiming that they had not ignored the drought and famine but had simply underestimated its extent, and that when they did sound the alarm western donors were derelict in responding.

This is a cynical distortion of the record. While thousands, perhaps tens of thousands, starved to death, the Ethiopian regime busied itself during the critical weeks of July, August and early September 1984 with the beautification of Addis Ababa for the thousands of guests to come from the Soviet bloc and western communist parties for the founding congress of the WPE and the celebration of the tenth anniversary of the revolution. Triumphal arches were erected and adorned with slogans, enormous posters of Mengistu put up, pavements repaired and streets patched and painted with traffic lines, stars with hammer and sickle hoisted on top of buildings and archways, and fencing put up to hide slums. An ultra-modern convention hall with a seating capacity of 3,500 was constructed by a Finnish firm, with all materials but rock siding imported from Finland and cash paid by the Ethiopian government on the dot. At a minimum, even taking into account the use of 'volunteer' labour, all this must have cost tens of millions of dollars, possibly much more.

In the five-hour speech that he delivered in the new convention hall on 6 September, Chairman Mengistu made no mention of the crisis facing Ethiopia. There were a few brief passages on the general problem of drought, deforestation and soil degradation, but not a word, in a document that ran to 150 printed pages, to raise an alarm against the terrible drought and famine that by that time had unmistakably struck the country. By the time it took cognisance of the situation at the end of September—after western television had brought it to world attention—4m or 5m people were estimated to be at risk of starvation; the figure was later to rise to between 7m and 9m. This tardiness in recognising the crisis and acting to deal with it naturally recalls the dereliction of Haile Selassie's government in similar circumstances in 1972 and 1973. It is a subject of much embarrassment to a regime that claims to justify its existence through service to the people.

The World Acts

Only against this background can the political setting be understood: an Ethiopian government reluctantly obliged to give tardy acknowledgments to the reality of a crisis that had many of the implications of policy failure; and western governments eager to show, to Ethiopia, to the world and to their own public, proof of their humanitarian zeal. Foreign relief programmes were launched on a large scale in October and November.[4]

Food donations were to come mainly from the United States and western Europe, in practically equal amounts. By mid-summer of 1985, these two had pledged approximately 900,000 tons of food aid, to be given either through private voluntary or international organisations or directly to the Ethiopian government's Relief and Rehabilitation Commission (RRC); and many other tens of thousands of food, medicines and supplies came from private western European or American donations. India proudly sent 50,000 tons of wheat, proof of the success of its 'green revolution'. China offered a few thousand tons of corn, and Saudi Arabia flew in food and medicine worth over $10m. But for the most part, it was a western effort. The Soviet Union had made its yearly donation of 10,000 tons of rice in June, before the extent of the crisis could be known.[5] The Soviet Union made no further donation of food during 1984 or up to the first half of 1985, though other east bloc governments sent small shipments of food. (The Bulgarians gave a ton of feta cheese. To the delight of Addis Ababa's large diplomatic and international community, the RRC sold it to local retailers. Since good European cheese was almost impossible to get in Addis Ababa, it was snapped up and garnished foreign tables for several weeks.) Late in 1984, the Soviet Union sent 20 Antonov transport aircraft, two dozen helicopters and 300 trucks, together with crews to operate and maintain them. In the spring of 1985 it added a fully staffed military field hospital. On this assistance it placed the value of $110m. Whatever the accuracy of the figure, senior RRC officials repeatedly acknowledged in private that 90 percent of the assistance received by Ethiopia for the famine came from the west. In public, however, the Soviet Union and its satellites were hailed as Ethiopia's saviours.

Early in October 1984, two senior American figures, Ambassador Vernon Walters and Assistant Secretary of State Chester Crocker met in New York on the margins of the General Assembly, Ethiopia's Foreign Minister, Goshu Wolde. They told their Ethiopian colleague that the United States was ready to launch a very substantial programme for famine relief in Ethiopia. Before doing so, the United States wanted assurance that the Ethiopian government would cooperate in the distribution of food to starving people in all parts of Ethiopia, in other words that no one would be precluded from getting relief assistance for political reasons. Goshu gave this assurance unhesitatingly. AID Administrator Peter McPherson raised this same issue with the RRC Commissioner, Dawit Wolde Giorgis, at the beginning of November in Washington. The memorandum of understanding that they signed, which called for an immediate American donation of 50,000 tons of commodities to the RRC, included a specific pledge by Dawit that food would be conveyed to needy people in all parts of Ethiopia.

The West and Ethiopia at Odds

Implementation proved another matter. A substantial part of the area hit by the drought was in the hands of Eritrean and Tigrean insurgents. Ethiopian government administration did not reach into these areas and the Ethiopian government had no independent means of delivering food there. Estimates of the population of these areas ran from 2.5m to 3.5m. There were only two effective ways of reaching these people: by trucking food through Ethiopian army lines into rebel-held territory through a 'food truce' on both sides; or by bringing it into northern

Ethiopia from Sudan. The former could be done only with Ethiopian government cooperation; the latter raised no such requirement but was sure to meet strong Ethiopian objections. American and UN officials repeatedly asked the Ethiopian authorities to agree to the transport by the UN or some other neutral body of relief supplies across Ethiopian territory into rebel-held territories. Ethiopian government officials rejected these proposals out of hand and denied that there was any part of Ethiopia that escaped the control of the government; in a heated moment of candour, the acting Ethiopian Foreign Minister declared that 'food is an element in our strategy' against the insurgents. When the United States turned to delivering food to northern Ethiopia through Sudan, the Ethiopian government accused it of deliberately aiding the insurgents and alleged that it was also providing arms to the rebels. These charges were formally and vigorously denied by Washington.

These problems provoked heated disputes between the American and Ethiopian governments. But, more fundamentally, it soon became evident that the Ethiopian government and the west had quite different concepts of how to deal with the crisis. The American and western European governments considered the delivery of food to starving people to be the first priority: before all else, lives had to be saved. The Ethiopian government's priorities lay elsewhere. For it, the drought and famine presented the opportunity, long awaited, to launch a large-scale resettlement of population from the north-central areas of the country, which (not by coincidence) were areas of insurgency as well as of drought and famine, to more fertile and better watered lands in the west and south-west. This was Mengistu's pet project, and on his order the entire machinery of the Ethiopian government was immediately mobilised in support of it. He did not visit famine relief camps in Wollo and Tigre until December 1984. But in the second half of October, shortly after his government acknowledged the existence of the crisis, he set off on a tour of western and south-western provinces to identify resettlement sites.

There are plausible arguments for resettlement. Much of the land in northern Wollo and Tigre has been rendered barren and infertile from centuries of overuse. There is unused fertile land available in the southwest, though not so much as the government claims. But what the Ethiopian leader proposed was a massive transfer of population from north-central to western and southwestern Ethiopia. Early announcements spoke of moving between 1.5m and 2.5m people in the first year of a programme begun in mid-November of 1984. Later this was scaled back to about 500–700,000. But even that number was far more than could be resettled with any semblance of order or proper preparation. The foreign assistance agencies of the United States and other western countries had much experience in resettlement. They recognised that it could be a valuable tool in the proper circumstances, but it had to be done with careful preparation and heavy investment in infrastructure, both of which were lacking in this case. Moreover, it was known that the Ethiopian government intended to collectivise all those resettled. In some instances, plots were to be made available for private farming for the first year, but this was only an interim measure to permit the settlers to get on their feet.

Finally, the United States and other western governments feared that such a massive transfer could be carried out only through coercion. Unfortunately, this assumption proved only too correct. Ethiopian authorities repeatedly protested that the programme was wholly voluntary. These assurances lost all credibility in the face of the stream of eye-witness reports that began to come in from western relief workers in the field soon after resettlement began. They told of round-ups at gun point; of people being told that to qualify for distribution of relief food they would have to volunteer for resettlement; of families being separated; of children and the elderly being left behind while the able-bodied young were taken; of people being crowded into open trucks and driven for days without shelter from the fierce sun or adequate food or water to destinations where neither shelter nor food awaited them; and of many deaths en route and upon arrival.

The United States is barred by its own laws from extending development assistance to Ethiopia, owing to the Ethiopian government's failure to make any serious move to compensate American citizens for properties nationalised 10 years ago, in 1975. But even if this prohibition had not existed, the United States would not have agreed to support the resettlement programme. Other western governments did not face legal impediments, but they, too, refrained from assisting the Ethiopian government's programme, albeit in some cases with misgivings. There was something to be said for the programme; people could more easily be made self-sufficient on fertile land than on land exhausted by overuse. But the too-evident political motivation of the Ethiopian government, its plan to use the famine to promote its programme of mass collectivisation—when earlier experiments in Ethiopia with collectivised resettlement had clearly failed—together with stoutly denied but entirely credible reports of massive coercion, made it impossible for any western government to offer its backing. Even the neutrals among the European donors shied away from support of the resettlement programme.

Out of this fundamental disagreement between western governments and Ethiopia over goals and methods grew a crude division of labour. The west did famine relief while the Ethiopian government, with some help from the Soviet bloc, did resettlement. If this sounds logical in theory, it proved to be highly unsatisfactory in practice so far as famine relief was concerned. Practically the only contribution the Ethiopian government made to famine relief was through payment of the salaries for those RRC employees detailed to the famine relief programme, together with the provision of some equipment. Because the Ethiopian regime devoted almost all of its resources to resettlement, it had very little to offer for famine relief. Trucks, always in short supply in Ethiopia, were allocated in support of resettlement. There were never enough to clear the ports of the 100,000 or so tons of grain that began arriving monthly from January on. Predictably, much grain was lost to spoilage through exposure on the docks and while awaiting transport to inland warehouses; early in May a surprise downpour in Assab ruined some 13,000 tons of western-donated grain. And the resources allocated by the government were not sufficient to assure a steady supply of food to the relief feeding centres. In October 1984, Makelle, the administrative capital of Tigre and a centre to which tens of thousands of starving peasants were making an arduous trek in the hope of finding food, was faced with the prospect of exhaustion of its stocks. When frantic western efforts to get the Ethiopian government to mount an emergency airlift or overland convoy brought no adequate response, the United States, Britain, Italy and the Federal Republic of Germany sent in heavy transport aircraft to do the job. The American and British aircraft carried the main burden of resupplying Makelle until mid-summer of 1985.[6] Almost every emergency feeding centre was, at one time or another (and often chronically) short of commodities needed to feed the thousands upon thousands of destitute that waited miserably at their gates. This meant that during the critical first half of 1985 it was impossible to get food to most of those in need. Of a population of 7m believed in danger of starvation early in 1985, relief was reaching only between 2.5m and 3m—and not all of these were getting full rations. Later in the year UN estimates, regarded by many as generous, put the number of those being reached at over half the affected population.

These shortcomings caused much friction between the western donors and the Ethiopian government, but tensions rose to an even higher pitch at the end of April 1985 when local authorities suddenly closed the camp at Ibnet and expelled a population of destitute peasants estimated by western relief workers at 60,000 (the UN gave a substantially lower estimate of 35,000). These people were sent away without food, which for many of them meant almost certain death. In the uproar that followed, Mengistu disavowed the local authorities—though only after his RRC Commissioner denounced the story as a lie and his Foreign Ministry issued a vitriolic statement accusing the west of having fabricated it—and people were allowed to return to Ibnet. Some weeks thereafter, the Ethiopian government proceeded again to close Ibnet, this time in a more orderly fashion. It announced that all relief centres would be closed and explained that this was necessary in order to get farmers back to their land in time to take advantage of the 1985 spring rains—lands that the Ethiopian authorities, in their rush to justify resettlement, had declared too depleted to support cultivation.

Sticking to Old Allies

Under the impact of the famine, the Ethiopian government opened the country's doors to western visitors to an extent unmatched in recent years. In late 1984 and early 1985, western journalists and parliamentary delegations swarmed through Addis Ababa airport along with representatives of charitable organisations and platoons of new relief workers. The Ethiopian media took on a more serious and subdued tone. Apart from an occasional sally against 'imperialism', criticism of the west practically ceased by mid-November of 1984. Western embassies hoped that this heralded the turning of a new page in relations with Ethiopia, but found no confirmation of that in their day-to-day dealings with the government. The Ethiopian media went to great lengths to emphasise the importance of the country's ties with the Soviet bloc. The most meagre Soviet bloc donation was given lavish publicity, while western—

particularly American—grants usually got only occasional and grudging notice. Mengistu visited Havana, Moscow and eastern European capitals in December 1984 and was in Moscow again in March 1985 for the funeral of Konstantin Chernenko, the Soviet party leader. In a televised speech—a rare event—early in February, the Ethiopian head of state made it clear that the drought and famine would have no effect on his government's 'socialist' orientation. As if to underscore the point, he announced stringent austerity measures. Obligatory contribution of one month's salary was followed by strict petrol rationing, a total ban on Sunday driving, and the requirement that all senior government personnel discard their European business dress and don cotton khaki or blue North Korean-style uniforms (later this was extended to all government personnel salaried above $240 per month). In a further step, smacking of 'cultural revolution', tighter ideological controls were slapped on Addis Ababa university. The university and other institutions of higher learning were closed at the end of May, one month before the end of courses, so that students and academic staff could be sent to remote areas to help clear land and build shelters for resettlement. A proposal for Ethiopia to join the east bloc's Council for Mutual Economic Assistance (CMEA) was circulated within the Ethiopian government but evidently was shelved out of fear that such a step would cause a cut-off of western development assistance, if not of humanitarian assistance. Urgent recommendations by the World Bank and the European Community for changes in agricultural policies to give more incentive to the private sector were rejected out of hand by the political leadership after having found a sympathetic hearing among technical experts in the Ministry of Agriculture.

The famine proved a test of Mengistu's steadfastness in his alliance with the Soviet Union. He passed it with high marks. After the September 1984 WPE founding congress, Mengistu assumed the title of General Secretary, in emulation of Soviet leaders.

Early in 1985, civilian Marxist-Leninist ideologues for the first time emerged in top place among his advisers. Mengistu's relations with the Soviet leaders have not always been easy. When the spirit moved him, he has not hesitated to show them that he is not one to take orders. He sent home two Soviet Ambassadors, one in 1978 and the other in 1981. But each row has been quickly patched up and he has shown Moscow consistent loyalty. The Soviet Union may be niggardly in economic aid, and unable to provide food, but it has been and continues to be lavish in supplying arms. Some Ethiopians and an even greater number of westerners continue to hope that Mengistu's embrace of communism domestically and the Soviet alliance internationally is nothing more than a sly act aimed at assuring a steady flow of weaponry. To believe this one has to ignore a substantial body of public evidence that testifies to the contrary.

Mengistu's experience with the Soviet Union and the west during the crisis of the autumn of 1984 and 1985 must have confirmed him in his political preferences. The west pestered him about feeding starving people in the rebel-held areas, complained about lack of Ethiopian government support for emergency relief programmes and criticised the resettlement programme. The Soviet Union and its eastern European and Cuban followers did not importune him on any of these issues; they expressed no humanitarian concerns about people on the rebel side, ran no programmes for the hungry on the government side and did not protest the use of coercion in resettlement. In fact, Soviet aircraft carried thousands of peasants from Tigre and Wollo for resettlement in the south west and west, and their trucks and field hospitals were immediately and unquestioningly despatched in support of resettlement. If they could not offer more, they were at least very compliant.

The west closes a year of massive food donations facing a dilemma in its relations with Ethiopia more acute than before. In 1984, in their eagerness to respond to pressures from their own public to rescue tens of thousands in Ethiopia from starvation, western governments could ignore the likelihood that their assistance would not only save lives but help a regime inimical to their interests and cruelly oppressive of the Ethiopian people. In 1984, western governments could hope for at least some modest changes in Ethiopian policies. At the time, most were not fully aware of the extent to which the Ethiopian regime's agricultural policies had contributed to the catastrophe. Now they find that although the 1985 rains were good and the crop considerably better than in 1984, Ethiopia remains heavily dependent on western food donations to prevent mass starvation.

Despite its many ecological problems, Ethiopia is considered by almost all agricultural experts to have great potential for food production; with the right policies it could become self-sufficient and even an exporter. As a result of bad policies, it finds itself with a large annual deficit, even in the best of rainfall years. Some international organisation experts in Ethiopia, speaking privately, estimate this deficit to be 400,000 tons a year and growing. Yet the Ethiopian regime so far has rejected proposals for change. As Mengistu put it in his September 1985 Revolution Day speech:

> '. . . if it is proved that a specific package of foreign aid or loan is incongruous with the country's path of development, welcoming such aid is tantamount to restoring dependence or neo-colonialism which we had overthrown with a great struggle and sacrifice.'

The dilemma for the west could hardly be more unpleasant: to stop food shipments and allow tens of thousands of innocent Ethiopians to die, or to continue them and thereby enable the Ethiopian government to pursue policies that cause starvation and that seem almost certain to make it evermore dependent on the west for handouts, all the while remaining Moscow's best ally in Africa.

NOTES

[1] The author wishes to state that the views expressed in this article are his own and not necessarily those of the United States government.

[2] For a more thorough review of the subject of Ethiopian government's agricultural policies and problems, see Theodore M. Vestal, "Ethiopia's Famine: A Many-dimensioned Crisis," *The World Today*, July 1985.

[3] At the beginning of September 1984, the American Embassy in Addis Ababa briefed visiting reporters of two major American papers on the magnitude of the drought and famine. They refused to take seriously what they were told.

[4] They had been operating in Ethiopia for many years; during its 1984 fiscal year (from 1 October 1983 to 30 September 1984) the United States committed $222m for humanitarian assistance.

[5] Because rice is not a food known to or appreciated by the peasant populations of the Ethiopian highlands, the RRC protests when western donors propose it. The annual Soviet donation, believed to come from in-kind payment by India for arms debts, is accepted gratefully and given much publicity.

[6] The Ethiopian air force did, reluctantly and after much delay, carry out some 20 flights to deliver relief grain to Makelle in late October after the United States agreed to pay fuel and maintenance costs. But it was very clear that the Ethiopian air force could not be counted on to accept this mission, even with American financing, for more than a very short time.

chapter 12

HUMAN DIGNITY AND OPPORTUNITY

Is it a new country
In another world of reality
Than Day's?
Or did I live there
Before Day was?

I awoke
To an ordinary morning with gray light
Reflected from the street,
But still remembered
The dark-blue night
Above the tree line,
The open moor in moonlight,
The crest in shadow.
Remembered other dreams
Of the same mountain country:
Twice I stood on its summits,
I stayed by its remotest lake,
And followed the river
Towards its source.
The seasons have changed
And the light
And the weather
And the hour.
But it is the same land.
And I begin to know the map
And to get my bearings.

Dag Hammarskjöld,
Markings, translated by Leif Sjoberg and W.H. Auden (New York: Alfred A. Knopf,
1968), p. 222 (This is the last entry in his diary before Hammarskjöld was killed in an
air crash in the pursuit of peace in the Congo as Secretary-General of the United
Nations.)

An earlier edition of this reader concluded by noting that, while phenomena like widespread terrorism may be new, many of the problems the world faces today are similar to those that brought on World Wars I and II. The first war was brought on by an obsessive and escalating rivalry between two blocs of states, and as a prelude to the second war a world-wide depression spawned the rise of Fascism and Nazism. At that time we noted that traditional theories of international politics assume the notion of a normative world culture which successfully mobilized counterforce against the threat to the balance of power. Theory also assumes that competitive actors pursuing their self-interest are likely to shun or minimize war as a rational course of action. At the time we prepared the fifth edition (1978) the Soviet Union and the United States were in the process of negotiating SALT II and there still seemed some hope that détente might continue to prevail. Since then Iran has revolted, Afghanistan has been invaded, SALT II has been shelved, terrorism has increased, each superpower has had to resort to force to meet challenges to its power—the Soviet Union in Poland, and United States in the Caribbean—and a new and more deadly round has begun in the nuclear arms race. The economic situation worldwide has worsened giving rise to unemployment and protectionism among the advanced industrial countries and to desperation and violence among the poorer nations of the Third World. Some of the newly industrialized countries (NICs) are experiencing severe difficulties in meeting their obligations as debtors to banks and international lending institutions. Against this background of pervasive insecurity, terrorism, economic anarchy, and revolution one must ask again: Is the international order breaking down and is the world confronted with a new era of cold war and barbarism? Can human dignity prevail? As Dr. ul Haq argues, is there now a "poverty curtain" just as serious as the "iron curtain" of 40 years ago?

In the superpower sphere the parallels to August 1914 are disturbing. The attitudes and behavior which led the Triple Entente and Triple Alliance to war in August 1914 are present in an acute form in the mid-1980s. The rise of the Soviet Union as a global challenger has provoked the same mix of fear and provocation that marked the British and French response to Imperial Germany after 1898. The same febrile anxiety that marked the German fear that the collapse of the polyglot Austrian empire would undermine German security characterizes the concern with which Moscow and Washington view challenges within their respective spheres of influence. The present crisis is worsened by the fact that Moscow, as part of its bid for global power, seems determined to exploit, from ideological as well as power motives, the fragility and instability of order in the Third World. The Reagan Administration's predisposition to subordinate diplomacy to an all-out military build-up suggests parallels to earlier European obsessions with encirclement. "In seeking to rest its bid for expanded political influence on a substantial military build-up, Moscow, like Imperial Germany, has pursued its goals in a manner which has offered little reassurance about its ultimate aims and provoked the worst fears in the capitals of the opposing alliance."[1] Finally each side seems embarked on a nuclear weapons

---

[1] William D. Jackson, unpublished paper, "The Missiles of August" 1981, a "throwback" reference to the famous Barbara Tuchman term, "The Guns of August" (1914).

program aimed at improving its war-fighting capabilities. The heightened accuracy and destructive power of the latest generation of nuclear weapons cannot help but diminish confidence in the invulnerability and hence deterrent effects of the existing nuclear balance. There are a number of advocates on the American side, and presumably on the Soviet side as well, who believe that a nuclear war is winnable, especially if their side strikes first! This too has its common parallel in the arguments of the military high commands on the eve of World War I that only if they mobilized and struck first could they reap the advantage of surprise. Under such conditions of armed hostility and insecurity, time is working against peace. Terrorism is both a source and a result of this insecurity, but as Wall in his contribution points out, it is not as new as people are inclined to believe. From the perspective of theory and practice, a British authority has recently observed that the fight against terrorism necessitates action that is both practical and symbolic. At the moment we are failing at both levels.[2] Meanwhile, however, both the U.S. Senate and the European community have called for concerted international measures against this perceived threat.

The threat of a nuclear confrontation between the two superpowers develops against a background of deepening, world-wide anarchy. Americans view with trepidation, if not contempt, the decay and fanaticism that prevails in vast reaches of the globe, seldom appreciating the human despair and tragedy that lie behind events such as the rise of a Khomeini or the installation of a marxist regime in Nicaragua. The brave hopes with which Third World governments began their independence a generation ago have been cruelly deceived by obstacles both domestic and external to their economic development. But the causes and consequences of anarchy in the Third World are not limited to the Third World. Scholars are increasingly aware that the world economic system tends to keep the poor, poor and the rich, rich. One does not need to adopt a marxist interpretation to recognize that with the exception of scarce minerals, the poor countries need the products of the industrially advanced states more than the latter need the products of developing societies. That and the limited interest multinationals have in investing in anything but the most profitable sectors of Third World economies limits and distorts their development. The presence of western goods in shops for the rich deepens the sense of injustice and bitterness among the masses, who often cling to their traditional ways and religion and see in material wealth a form of sin and evil.

Despite the increase of terrorism on the world stage, most theories of international relations assume that the state actor is capable of maintaining an effective domestic order and acting externally so as to preserve sovereignty and to protect its citizens abroad. The maintenance of equilibrium and of the presumed self-regulating nature of the state system depends absolutely upon the assumption that each state is capable of maintaining an effective domestic order; further, its ability to function rationally in the external realm depends absolutely upon the maintenance of this domestic order. The world economic system, working largely independently of the state political system (except in so far as

---

[2]Michael Yardley, "What we must do to curb terrorists," The Times (London), September 10, 1986. p. 12.

each state vies to gain maximum economic power for its own society), may actually undermine the conditions of order essential to the smooth functioning of the state system. The newer states are prone to incoherence, foreign penetration, and revolution. This throws a tremendous burden on the international political system and particularly upon the United States, which as the status-quo power, has the greatest responsibility for maintaining global order. In the face of this challenge the United States and (whether they know it or not) the American people have been moved or driven to support those regimes, however repressive, that promise order and to oppose those movements, however just, that threaten revolution. The Philippines may prove to have been the great exception. The fact that the Soviet Union, a totalitarian state, is in a position to preserve its own empire by brute force while exploiting disorder and revolution outside, has seemed to justify and require the United States to intervene as it has in Iran, Guatemala, Chile and Grenada, to say nothing of Nicaragua. The danger is in failing to recognize that such disorder is unavoidable, and that to oppose it everywhere may well be counterproductive, as was shown in Vietnam. This does not mean that the lesson of Vietnam is that *all* interventions are wrong and must be avoided. It means that great prudence must be exercised, and intervention for the sake of demonstrating U.S. will and power may be counterproductive as almost occurred in the Philippines.

It is in this context that the issue of human rights enters the picture. In a world so vulnerable to repression and barbarism, one would think that the protection of human rights should figure at the head of every country's foreign policy agenda. That an emphasis on human rights may constitute an implicit challenge to the legitimacy of many regimes is understandable; but that terror, torture, and murder are necessary to their survival is quite another matter. The invocation of human rights by any government toward another ought always to be prudent and restrained. In his laudable effort to define what terrorism is and is not, Charles Maeckling has made a contribution to understanding this disturbing phenomenon. Strategic and geopolitical issues had more to do with the failure of détente than human rights, and the withdrawal of U.S. support for Argentinean or Guatemalan barbarism can hardly be said to have undermined American security.

In the case of the Soviet Union, both Presidents Carter's and Reagan's emphasis on human rights counted very little compared to the other issues of friction. In the case of the Shah, had he heeded human rights in time he might well have saved his throne. At worst, emphasis on human rights exposes American policy to charges of inconsistency—continuing to provide arms and support to a regime (for example, Nicaragua's Somoza) in the face of human rights violations. Now the successor regime (the Sandanistas) is being accused of its own violations. Nevertheless, the relationship of human rights to international relations is a complex subject and deserves to be treated as such, and Professor Jacobson deals with this phenomenon in an especially wise and sensitive way.

There are at least two aspects of human dignity that need to be clarified. First, every state that belongs to the United Nations and has signed the Declaration on Human Rights undertook to respect human rights, political as well as personal. Yet many of these do not share the Western tradition from which these rights have emerged. The notion of the individual as a self-directing person or as a citizen endowed with civil rights is unknown to many non-Western cultures. "Questions whether a given human grouping has a demonstrable will and capacity to approximate the model of the democratic nation-state; whether its traditional life-style favors the principle of individuation; or whether its customary norms of law and administration allow for the liberty of speech or religion" are questions that must be examined by anyone making human rights as we know them in the West an objective of international politics.[3] It follows that different cultures have brought about different evaluations of the individual's status in society, and different conceptions of right and justice. How can one respect differing cultures and at the same time attempt to reform them in the image of American culture—especially when the material and psychological prerequisites of democracy are nonexistent?

It would not do to dismiss violations of human rights by African, Latin-American, and Communist governments simply on the grounds that their societies do not place the same emphasis upon the individual as does Western culture. Latin America is, after all, part of Western civilization, and several countries (Argentina, Uruguay, Chile, even Brazil) had achieved a high level of democratic rule before the recent violations of legality and torture began and now seem to be returning to it. The Soviet Union is an example of a society in which Marxism-Leninism rejects both in theory and practice the proposition that the individual has rights apart from the society. The situation is somewhat different when it comes to economic and social rights, if only because the Soviet Union is ideologically committed to raising the material standards of the people (not that this justifies ignoring the lack of political rights or the suppression of dissent within the Soviet Union).

A second dilemma with which the issue of human dignity confronts international relations is the inhibition that sovereignty places upon intervention by an outside power into the domestic affairs of another country. In an influential article written before his nomination by President Reagan to head the Human Rights office in the State Department, Ernest Lefever argued against making human rights a goal of foreign policy, on the following grounds: "There is and should be a profound moral constraint on efforts designed to alter domestic practices, institutions, and policies within our states." To do so is to set ourselves up as the judge of other societies which may not share the same values as we do, and "to confuse domestic and foreign policy." Exponents of the human rights campaign "do not take seriously the distinctions in authority and responsibility that flow from the concept of sovereignty." A government must limit its foreign policy to maintaining its own interest in its relations with other countries without trying to change their domestic behavior; in Lefever's words, "we cannot export human rights or respect for the rule of law."[4] In a strongly worded rejoinder, David McLellan argued, after the Senate refused to confirm Dr. Lefever, that "support for human rights . . . is one area where the observation of

[3]Ernest W. Lefever, "The Trivialization of Human Rights," *Policy Review* (Winter 1978), reproduced in the fifth edition of this book, pp. 353–363.
[4]Ibid.

moral principle would do far less damage to and far more good for American national interest than is commonly understood."[5]

There are powerful arguments against letting foreign policy become involved with human rights. For example, it was immediately apparent when President Carter espoused human rights as a goal of American foreign policy that the Soviet Union, among other countries, regarded it as an attempt to interfere in its domestic affairs. The Soviet Union has a certain advantage in these matters, in that it can justify repression of dissent and political rights in the name of higher form of society—communism. At the same time, Communists exploit the freedom of expression and assembly that exists within a democracy as a justifiable part of the class struggle for power—a struggle which, once the communists win, supposedly comes to an end. On the other hand, it can be seen that the Soviet hostility to human rights campaigns is an expression of the Kremlin's insecurity and fear that opposition might well get out of hand and put the legitimacy of the regime itself in doubt.

It became apparent very early in the Reagan Administration that while human dignity as a value in international relations had not been abandoned, the form of American concern had shifted to opposition to terrorism and away from the ways in which other countries treated their own people, which is one reason we have devoted four selections to this topic in this edition. As will be seen, the fourth leads logically to consideration of another fundamental world issue. The fourth selection, by a high World Bank official from the Third World, incisively relates economic realities to human dignity and justice.

DISCUSSION QUESTIONS

1. What is new and what is not new about terrorism? Do you regard retaliation as effective? or necessary whether it is effective or not?

2. Do you agree with McLellan or with Lefever on making human rights a goal of American foreign policy?

3. What are the dilemmas that arise when human rights are made an objective of policy by one government toward others?

4. How does Harold Jacobson relate justice to the strengthening of international order? Does Mahbub ul Haq take a different view?

5. Have the problems described by Irwin Wall been alleviated or intensified by military actions by Israel, South Africa, and the United States against terrorist bases in other countries?

[5]David S. McLellan, "Human Rights: a Rejoinder," *The Theory and Practice of International Relations,* 6th ed. (Englewood Cliffs: Prentice-Hall, Inc., 1983), p. 388.

35. What Terrorism Is and Isn't

Charles Maechling Jr.

Charles Maechling Jr., a senior associate at the Carnegie Endowment for International Peace, has recently been a Visiting Fellow at Clare Hall and Wolfson College, Cambridge University, England.

Bombings and kidnappings in Lebanon and gunfire from the Libyan embassy in London have put terrorism back at the top of the international political agenda. At the summit meeting in London, Western heads of government issued a guarded statement of condemnation. President Reagan has asked 26 Federal departments and agencies for new counterterrorist options and has sent Congress a legislative package aimed at strengthening antiterrorist provisions in the Federal criminal code.

All told, the latest spate of high-level attention may plug a few loopholes but is not likely significantly to diminish the threat. For one thing, the security infrastructure to fight terrorism is in place and operational in most civilized countries. There is hardly a terrorist crime imaginable that is not well covered in the statute books. The real obstacle to effective containment of terrorism is the growth of its international dimension and its politicization by government leaders and the media through a broadening of the definition to encompass virtually all political violence.

Properly speaking, terrorism is the sustained clandestine use of force to achieve a political purpose. But all political violence is not necessarily terrorism. The term is totally inappropriate to suicide attacks on military personnel in a war zone, as in the case of the Marine bunker in Beirut. Even political assassination may or may not be a terrorist act, depending on the degree of commitment to a program of terror behind it. If extended to every variation of insurgency,

armed rebellion and civil warfare, terrorism as a concept loses meaning and becomes a propaganda tool to stigmatize an enemy.

This confusion in terminology does damage in several ways. Failure to discriminate between the deliberate killing of civilians by terrorists and government death squads in order to intimidate a population, and resistance groups' clandestine paramilitary warfare against official and military targets, adds up to the (fallacious) maxim that one man's terrorist is another's freedom-fighter.

By any definition, the Palestine Liberation Organization, Provisional Irish Republican Army and Libyan "hit squads" are terrorists, but one can hardly apply the term to the Polish and French resistance movements of World War II. For the Indian Government to attach this label to Sikh extremists, and for the press to blindly parrot it, is a disservice to public understanding.

The confusion also spills over to remedies. For example, the legislation proposed by President Reagan is off-target. Two of the bills would implement earlier treaties on aircraft hijacking and hostage-taking. Another, much-publicized measure aimed at penalizing American citizens and residents who engage in "training, supporting or inducing" terrorist activities is almost certainly unconstitutional.

Designed to rectify gaps in the law that hampered the prosecution of Edwin Wilson, a former Central Intelligence Agency operative, for furnishing equipment and services to Libya, this bill strikes at a statistically insignificant group while potentially penalizing a wide range of legally permissible activities. In authorizing the Secretary of State to embargo supplies and services to countries and organizations that support terrorism, it could make shipments of food, computers, books and medical supplies a criminal offense. Logically applied, the prohibition would encompass not only obvious targets like Libya but also the contras of Nicaragua and, of course, Saudi Arabia and other Arab states that support the Palestine Liberation Organization. The bill's most objectionable feature is a grant of authority to the Secretary to make determinations unchallengeable in the courts.

What is needed is not more indiscriminate application of the label "terrorist" and superfluous legislation but international cooperation in tracking terrorist conspiracies and blocking the movement of terrorists across frontiers.

The first requirement is better, more up-to-date intelligence through collaboration between national police forces. The second is tighter controls at airports and border-crossing points. In line with Prime Minister Margaret Thatcher's proposal at the summit conference, the third should be an end to immunity for diplomats and embassy installations that depart from bona fide diplomacy, and an international boycott of official personnel implicated in terrorist activities. None of these goals can be achieved without international agreement based on a much sharper definition of what constitutes terrorism.

Reaching a consensus will not be easy. But a start might exclude the predictable attacks common to civil war and anarchy since the beginning of history and concentrate on conspiratorial attempts to export violence to stable, law-abiding communities. Even ideological adversaries should be able to agree that bombings, shootings and other outrages that put the lives of ordinary men, women and children at risk are common crimes that deserve the full measure of international retribution.

---

36. Terrorism and International Relations

Irwin Wall

Irwin Wall, an associate professor of history at the University of California, is a specialist in recent Europe and modern French history.

. . . Terrorism appears to be the scourge of our civilization, and prophets of impending doom regularly warn that it is a symptom of a crisis of global proportions. The specter of terrorists going nuclear worries intelligence analysts and provides the theme for sensationalist novels.

For a romantic revolutionary left, terrorism has become to the 1970s and early 1980s what guerrilla warfare was to the 1960s, a

Reprinted *At UCR* (December 1981), by permission of the University of California Press. Copyright 1981.

formula for successful revolutionary change. For a harried and fearful political establishment in virtually all countries, terrorism is a constant nightmare and a frightful occupational hazard that threatens to deter the most competent from a political career. How serious is the phenomenon?

In total dimensions it is less serious than either the media or the terrorists would have us believe. There are many more murders per inhabitant every year in Los Angeles than in either Belfast or Londonderry despite the reputation of the latter cities as virtual war zones. Between 1968 and 1975 transnational terrorist acts claimed the lives of 974 persons worldwide and wounded another 2,714, less than one-tenth the slaughter perpetrated in a single year on our nation's highways. Aerial highjacking, once thought likely to paralyze international transportation, declined precipitously after 1972–73 and is now only a minor nuisance. Terrorist attacks which were once feared to be in the making against the vital and vulnerable communications and power centers of our technological society have not thus far materialized. It is true that Americans and residents of Atlantic Community nations account for most terrorist victims, and it appears hard to overestimate the importance of the elimination from the world scene of an Anwar Sadat. Still, a glance at the history of terrorism can help to put it further in perspective.

Terrorism: Old Concept

The most commonplace observation to be made about terrorism is that it is not new. The concept of tyrannicide—rightful murder of a wicked prince—is almost as old as recorded history. Modern use of the term, it bears remarking, stems from the use of violence by the French Revolutionary government in 1793–94 to suppress internal rebellion. Government-sponsored terrorism, when practiced by Nazi Germany or Stalinist Russia, dwarfed anything ever contemplated by anti-regime terrorists, and continues to outdo the would-be terrorist revolutionaries of today. The infamous death squads apparently sponsored by the present governments of Guatemala and Argentina simply do not give rise to the sensationalist headlines regularly garnered by anti-regime terrorists, whose exploits, it must be admitted, are much more daring.

The first classic anti-regime terrorist conspiracy in modern history successfully assassinated Tsar Alexander II of Russia in 1881 after 14 unsuccessful attempts. Although the hoped-for revolution did not occur, the Russian revolutionaries articulated virtually all the aims still adhered to by modern anti-regime terrorists. They sought publicity, or "propaganda by the deed," that is, the mobilization of popular revolutionary energies by dramatic example. They tried to intimidate and harass authorities in the hope the regime would lose the will to struggle on. They deliberately invited repression by their provocation in the hope of polarizing society between supporters and opponents of the regime. Later their Balkan followers used terrorism to affect interstate relations in the hope of blocking a particular diplomatic outcome not to their liking. With lesser frequency Russian terrorists also tried to free prisoners and secure ransoms.

The terror was not confined to Russia. Anarchist attempts were made on the lives of virtually all the crowned heads of Europe before World War I, and presidents of the American and French republics were murdered along with the King of Italy, the Empress of Austria, and many highly-placed politicians from Spain to Russia. Yugoslav terrorists murdered the heir to the Austrian throne, Franz Ferdinand, on June 28, 1914, thus unleashing the First World War.

But Austria used the assassination as a pretext to go to war against Serbia, and Germany had more in mind than catching terrorists in offering Austria full support against Serbia's protectors, Tsarist Russia and her French and English allies. Contrary to the beliefs of those who equate terrorism with Marxism or Communism, Marx and Engels disapproved of the terrorist outrages of their day and Lenin soundly condemned anti-regime terrorism as "infantile leftism." Once in power, however, the Bolsheviks took quite another line.

Weapon for Independence

As all this might indicate, terrorism is a form of political violence normally carried out for rational ends. Terrorism forms part of a continuum of violent collective behavior extending through guerrilla wars, coups d'état, insurrections, revolutions, and civil wars. In the twentieth century, terrorism has been most successful in anti-colonial struggles of national liberation, in which occupying powers are likely to lose their will in the face of harassment by the local population. Terrorists played a crucial role in winning Irish independence from Britain in 1920, Algerian independence from France in 1954, and ironically, Israeli independence from England in 1948. The Palestinians have taken at least part of their example from close to home.

Terrorism can be a part of international conflict as well, as the bombing of Hiroshima and Dresden should remind us; these acts were aimed not so much at their victims as at the living, and the Japanese were in fact frightened into surrender. Ironically, the adjective one most often hears in characterizations of terrorism is "senseless." Worldwide, it is almost never that, despite the American experience with lone psychotic assassins.

In isolation from the broader violent conflicts of which it normally is a part, terrorism is rather a sign of weakness on the part of revolutionaries who, in the absence of a mass movement, seek to accomplish dramatic change through isolated violent acts. Waves of terrorism have most often occurred after the failure of a mass movement to fulfill aspirations for change. The Russian revolutionaries turned to terrorism after they failed to arouse the peasantry by means of propaganda and organization. The Italian Red Brigades, German Baader-Meinhof group, and American Weathermen likewise seem to be composed of frustrated remnants of mass movements for change in the 1960s which failed to accomplish their humanistic but utopian goals.

Is terrorism a cause for concern? Obviously. Its greatest danger may be that by overreacting to it, we will abandon our own cherished freedoms. Communist regimes are virtually untroubled by terrorism, but we would not wish to emulate the causes of their success.

Is terrorism preventable? Certainly to a degree, although perpetrators will continue to try their tactics and occasionally succeed.

Does terrorism represent the greatest danger facing us? Hardly. All forms of violence have been made more dangerous by modern technology, conventional warfare most of all. The danger of international conflict and the arms race, the threat of nuclear holocaust unleased by governments, not terrorists, must remain our most fundamental concerns.

---

37. The Global System and the Realization of Human Dignity and Justice

Harold K. Jacobson

Director of the Institute of Social Research at the University of Michigan, Harold Jacobson is also Professor of Political Science and a member of the U.S. National Commission for UNESCO.

. . . A historic consensus has been formed in the years since World War II on the meaning of human dignity and justice, and thus on the overarching goals of international and national public policy and on the broad out-

Excerpted from Professor Jacobson's Presidential Address at the annual meeting of the International Studies Association, published in the *International Studies Quarterly*, 26, no. 3, (September 1982), 320–324. Reprinted by permission, the International Studies Association.

lines of world order. The process has been uneven and gradual. Progress has often been painfully slow. Controversies have been sharp, and there have frequently been contradictory trends. At any given moment and with respect to particular issues, the picture could appear bleak. A broader assessment, however, must be positive. The consensus to which I refer has been expressed in rhetoric at public international fora and in resolutions and conventions that have been adopted in these fora. Unfortunately, the practice of states has not always been guided by the normative standards embodied in the consensus. My point, however, is that broad agreement on goals has been achieved, not that the goals themselves have been realized.

What does the consensus include? First, it embraces the goals of peace and material plenty on which the study of international relations has traditionally been based. Although we seldom mention it, until the twentieth century, war was regarded as a normal and justifiable action of states. Only in the 1970s, when the People's Republic of China and the two Germanys entered the United Nations, were all major states in the global system formally committed through their adherence to the Charter of the United Nations to settle their disputes by peaceful means and to refrain from the threat or use of force (Article 2, paragraphs 3 and 4). Thanks to the near universality of the United Nations, virtually all states in the system have now accepted this obligation. Only since 1945 has war been illegal, and only since the 1970s have all major states been formally committed to this doctrine.

The commitment to achieve material plenty is also embodied in the UN Charter (Articles 55 and 56), and it has been reaffirmed in countless decisions of the UN and other international institutions. Like agreeing that war should be illegal, it was also a far-reaching and significant step for states to accept the obligation to promote "higher standards of living, full employment, and conditions of economic and social progress and development" (Article 55, subparagraph a).

The UN Charter in addition contains an obligation for member states to promote:

> universal respect for, and observance of, human rights and fundamental freedom for all without distinction as to race, sex, language, or religions [Article 55, subparagraph c].

Since human rights and fundamental freedoms were not defined, it could be argued that the only actionable normative standard that states accepted in adhering to the charter was the rule of nondiscrimination. However, through subsequent decisions in the United Nations and other international institutions, detailed meaning has been given to the broad phrase "human rights and fundamental freedoms." This development has not received sufficient attention by students of international relations.

The Universal Declaration of Human Rights, adopted by the UN General Assembly on 10 December 1948, was a historic step in forging the consensus on how individuals should be treated by their governments and by one another; in other words, in defining the conditions of human dignity and justice. None of the states that were members of the United Nations at that time voted against its adoption, and since then no state has explicitly rejected as undesirable the norms that are embodied in it. What is more impressive is the number of states that have accepted legally binding obligations by ratifying or adhering to formal conventions that include the same concepts that were specified in the Universal Declaration. The European Convention on Human Rights (which entered into force in 1953), the International Covenants on Civil and Political Rights and on Economic and Social Rights (which entered into force in 1976), and the American Convention on Human Rights (which entered into force in 1978) are the conventions containing the broadest sets of obligations. Beyond these, there are many conventions in force dealing with specific issues of human dignity and justice. By mid–1981, more than 65 states representing all geographic regions and all varieties of political, economic, and social systems had ratified or adhered to the two UN human rights covenants. There are also many other documents of somewhat less legal force, such as the Final Act of the 1975 Helsinki Conference on Security and Co-operation in Europe, that restate the basic concepts embodied in the Universal Declaration.

No matter what their practices, governments throughout the world have accepted the norms embodied in the many international declarations and conventions that have been adopted by international institutions as a legitimate definition of the conditions of human dignity and justice. About half of the sovereign states that comprise the global system, including within their borders more than half the world's population, have explicitly formally agreed, by signing or ratifying the relevant conventions, to be judged by the standards that have been set forth. By according these standards legitimacy in international fora, the remaining states have implicitly accepted them as appropriate criteria for judgment. We too should accept them. I have yet to see a persuasive argument that the standards set forth in the Universal Declaration of Human Rights should not ultimately be applied comprehensively and universally. Are there some individuals for whom slavery is permissible or who can legitimately be subjected to torture? Are political systems that do not provide for the participation of their citizenry appropriate? The answer to these questions, or to others of a similar character, must be no. This is the answer given resoundingly and repeatedly by those speaking and acting on behalf of governments in international institutions.

What are the notions of human dignity and justice, expressed in the declarations and conventions, that embody the existing international consensus? The consensus definition of human dignity and justice includes peace and plenty, or less flamboyantly, the right to security of person, and access to and the provision of basic human needs, including food, clothing, housing, education, and medical care. It includes the right to constitute a political community based on a sense of shared identity; in other words, national self-determination. The norm of human equality is a basic element in the consensus definition of human dignity and justice. Indeed, as its specific mention in the UN Charter foreshadowed, this norm has come to be stressed in the United Nations above all others, except for avoiding catastrophic war. The other elements of the consensus include the full range of civil rights that have typically been invoked to limit possibilities for the arbitrary exercise of governmental authority and power. They also include the essential ingredients of political democracy or polyarchy: freedom of opinion and expression, freedom of assembly, freedom to belong to associations, and the right to choose one's representatives in government through means of "periodic and genuine elections which shall be by universal and equal suffrage and shall be held by secret vote" (Universal Declaration of Human Rights, Article 21, paragraph 3). It would be possible to elaborate the consensus definition of human dignity and justice in much greater detail. Herbert C. Kelman (1977), in his ISA presidential address some years ago, translated the international consensus from legal to social scientific expression. My main point here is to demonstrate that the consensus exists and to indicate that the concepts are comprehensive and universal.

38. The Inequities of the Old Economic Order

Mahbub ul Haq

At the World Bank in Washington, Mahbub ul Haq has served as director of policy planning and program review. He is from Pakistan.

The Third World is not merely a catch-word today. It is just becoming a political and economic force. A new trade union of the poor nations is emerging. It is united by its poverty—and by its heritage of common suffering. In fact, a "poverty curtain" has descended right across the face of our world, dividing it materially and philosophically into two different worlds, two separate planets, two unequal humanities—one embarrassingly rich and the other desperately poor. The struggle to lift this curtain of poverty and unequal relationships is certainly the most formidable challenge of our time. And it is likely to cover many decades and consume many generations.

Most of the required changes lie right within the control of the Third World—whether in the restructuring of domestic political power, or in the fashioning of new development styles and strategies, or in the search for new areas of collective self–reliance. But a part of this struggle is at the international level—the need to change the past patterns of hopeless dependency to new concepts of equality, partnership, and interdependence. These pages are addressed to this struggle at the international level, though I must make quite clear my own conviction that fundamental reforms in the international order will be meaningless, and almost impossible to achieve, without corresponding reforms in the national orders.

In the pages on the international economic order that follow, I intend to review the workings of the existing world economic order and analyze the concrete basis of the accusation by the poor nations that the present international institutions systematically discriminate against their interests.

Let me also make clear that I am speaking not as an official of the World Bank or as a Pakistani or as an individual. I venture to speak as a citizen from the Third World, in utter frankness and candor, sharing the aspirations and the belief in the common cause that unite all of us in the Third World. Let me turn now to an analysis of the prevailing world economic order from the vantage point of the Third World.

The vastly unequal relationship between the rich and poor nations is fast becoming the central issue of our time. The poor nations are beginning to question the basic premises of an international order that leads to ever widening disparities between the rich and poor countries and to a persistent denial of equality of opportunity to many poor nations. They are, in fact, arguing that in the international order—just as much as within national orders—all distribution of benefits, credit, services, and decision making gets warped in favor of a privileged minority and that this situation cannot be changed except through fundamental institutional reforms.

Reprinted from Mahbub ul Haq, *The Third World and the International Economic Order,* Development Paper no. 22 (Washington, D.C.: Overseas Development Council, 1976), pp. 1–11. Published by Random House, Inc., New York. Reprinted by permission.

When this is pointed out to the rich nations, they dismiss it casually as empty rhetoric of the poor nations. Their standard answer is that the international market mechanism works, even though not too perfectly, and that the poor nations are always out to wring concessions from the rich nations in the name of past exploitation. They believe that the poor nations are demanding a massive redistribution of income and wealth which is simply not in the cards. Their general attitude seems to be that the poor nations must earn their economic development, much the same way as the rich nations had to over the last two centuries, through patient hard work and gradual capital formation, and that there are no shortcuts to this process and no rhetorical substitutes. The rich, however, are "generous" enough to offer some help to the poor nations to accelerate their economic development if the poor are only willing to behave themselves.

In reviewing this controversy, we must face up to the blunt question: Does the present world order systematically discriminate against the interest of the Third World, as the poor nations contend? Or is the demand for a new order mere empty rhetoric against imagined grievances, as the rich nations allege?

There is sufficient concrete evidence to show that the poor nations cannot get an equitable deal from the present international economic structures—much the same way as the poorest sections of the society within a country and for much the same reasons. Once there are major disparities in income distribution within a country, the market mechanism ceases to function either efficiently or equitably, since it is weighted heavily in favor of the purchasing power in the hands of the rich. Those who have the money can make the market bend to their own will. When we start from a position of gross inequalities, the so-called market mechanism mocks poverty, or simply ignores it, since the poor hardly have any purchasing power to influence market decisions. This is even more true at the international

level since there is no world government and none of the usual mechanisms existing within countries that create pressures for redistribution of income and wealth.

But this is not a time to make a general case all over again. The Third World has done it many times over. Rather, it is time for our universities and our research institutions to do some serious work in documenting specific instances of inequities in the world order. In undertaking such a serious analysis, I believe that two "staple diets" we have used so often in the past should be played down. First, we cannot keep the rich nations feeling either guilty or uncomfortable by simply pointing out that three quarters of the world income, investment, and services are in the hands of one quarter of its population. The rich nations are increasingly turning around and saying: "So what? We worked for it and so should you." World income disparities, per se, are not an issue. We also must demonstrate that the prevailing disparities are creating major hurdles for the poor nations to execute their own development and are denying them equality of opportunity. Second, the Third World has often used the argument of instability of commodity prices and worsening terms of trade. This has been overdone and is probably not the heart of the problem. If low earnings are stabilized, they still remain low. It may give our policymakers a little peace of mind but it does not solve anything fundamental. Surely the argument must be that international structures deny us a fair price.

Kinds of Inequality

Ultimately, the reasons for unequal relationships must be sought in international structures and mechanisms which put the Third World at a considerable disadvantage and which cry out for thoroughgoing institutional reforms. Let me explore some of these areas.

There is a tremendous *imbalance* today *in the distribution of international reserves.* The poor nations, with 70 per cent of the world population, received less than 4 per cent of the international reserves of $131 billion during 1970–1974, simply because the rich nations controlled the creation and distribution of international reserves through the expansion of their own national reserve currencies (mainly dollars and sterling) and through their decisive control over the International Monetary Fund (IMF). For all practical purposes, the United States has been the central banker of the world in the post-Second World War period, and it could easily finance its balance-of-payments deficits by the simple device of expanding its own currency. In other words, the richest nation in the world has had an unlimited access to international credit facilities, since it could create such credit through its own decisions. This has been less true of other developed countries, though Britain and Germany have enjoyed some of this privilege at various times. This certainly has not been true of the developing countries, which could neither create international credit through their own deficit-financing operations nor obtain an easy access to this credit because of the absence of any genuine international currency and because of their limited quotas in the International Monetary Fund. The heart of any economic system is its credit structure. This is controlled entirely by the rich nations at the international level. The poor nations merely stand at the periphery of monetary decisions. This is nothing unusual. As in any normal national banking system, the poor get very little credit unless a concerned government chooses to intervene on their behalf.

The distribution of value added to the products traded between the developing and the developed countries is heavily weighted in favor of the latter. The developing countries, unlike the developed, receive only a small fraction of the final price that the consumers in the international market are paying for their produce, simply because many of them are too poor or too weak to exercise any meaningful control over the processing, shipping, and marketing of their primary exports. A rough estimate indicates that final consumers pay over $200 billion (excluding taxes) for the major primary exports (excluding oil) of the developing countries (in a more processed, packaged, and advertised form), but these countries receive only $30 billion, with the middle men and the international service sector—mostly in the hands of the rich nations—enjoying the difference. On the other hand, the rich nations have the resources and the necessary bargaining power to control the various phases of their production, export, and distribution—often including their own subsidiaries to handle even internal distribution within importing countries. In fact, if the poor nations were able to exercise the same degree of control over the processing and distribution of their exports as the rich nations presently do and if they were to get back a similar proportion of the final consumer price, their export earnings from their primary commodities would be closer to $150 billion. Again, there is a parallel here between national and international orders: within national orders as well, the poor receive only a fraction of the rewards for their labor and lose out to the organized, entrenched middle men unless the national governments intervene.

The protective wall erected by the developed countries prevents the developing world from receiving its due share of the global wealth. The rich nations are making it increasingly impossible for the "free" international market mechanism to work. In the classical framework of Adam Smith, the cornerstone of the free market mechanism is the free movement of labor and capital as well as of goods and services so that rewards to factors of production are equalized all over the world. Yet immigration laws in almost all rich nations make any large-scale movement of unskilled labor in a worldwide search for economic opportunities impossible (except for a limited "brain drain" of skilled labor). Not much capital has crossed international boundaries, both because of poor nations' sensitivities and because of the rich nations' own needs. And additional barriers have gone up against the free movement of goods and services—e.g., over $20 billion in farm subsidies alone in the rich nations to protect the agriculture and progressively higher tariffs and quotas against the simple consumer-goods exports of the developing countries, such as textiles and leather goods. The rich, in other words, are drawing a protective wall around their lifestyles, telling the poor nations that they can compete neither with their labor nor with their goods but paying handsome tributes at the same time to the "free" workings of the international market mechanism. Unfortunately, while the rich can show such discrimination, the poor cannot—by the very fact of their poverty. They need their current foreign exchange earnings desperately, just in order to survive and to carry on a minimum development effort, and they can hardly afford to put up discriminatory restrictions against the capital–goods imports and technology of the Western world. There is again a parallel here between national and international orders. Within national orders as well, the poor generally have very little choice but to sell their services to the rich at considerable disadvantage just in order to earn the means of their survival.

Another area in which the unequal bargaining power of the poor and the rich nations shows up quite dramatically is the *relationship between multinational corporations and the developing countries*. Most of the contracts, leases, and concessions that the multinational corporations have negotiated in the past with the developing countries reflect a fairly inequitable sharing of benefits. In many cases, the host government is getting only a fraction of the benefits from the exploitation of its own natural resources by the multinational corporations. For instance, Mauritania gets about 15 per cent of the profits that the multinational corporations make from extracting and exporting the iron ore deposits in the country. Similarly, in Liberia, the foreign investors export an amount equivalent to nearly one fourth of the total GNP of the country in profit remittances.

Such examples are numerous. In fact, it would be useful to tabulate all the concessions, contracts, and leases which have been negotiated between the multinational corporations and the developing countries and to present to the world an idea of what is the present sharing of benefits between host governments and multinational corporations in case after case. Such a factual background not only would illustrate the concrete and specific fashion in which the poor nations get discriminated against in the present world order but also could be a very useful prelude to the necessary reforms.

The poor nations have only a *pro forma participation in the economic decision making of the world*. Their advice is hardly solicited when the big ten industrialized nations get together to make key decisions on the world's economic future; their voting strength in the Bretton Woods institutions (the World Bank and International Monetary Fund) is less than one third of the total; and their numerical majority in the U.N. General Assembly has provided no real influence so far on international economic decisions. In fact, it may well be an indicator of the sense of accommodation that the rich nations are willing to show that they have started protesting against the "tyranny of the majority" at a time when the majority resolutions of the poor nations carry no effective force and when the Third World countries are not even being allowed to sit as equals around the bargaining tables of the world.

To take an example from the world of ideas, these *unequal relationships pervade the intellectual world and the mass media as well*. The developing countries have often been subjected to concepts of development and value systems that were largely fashioned abroad. While economic development is the primary concern of the developing countries, so far it has been written about and discussed largely by outsiders. The mass media, which greatly shape world opinion, are primarily under the control of the rich nations. The Nobel Prize, which is presumably given for excellence of thought, is given to very few in the Third World, even in non-technical fields such as literature. Is it because our societies are not only poor in income but also poor in thought? Or is it because our thought is being judged by standards totally alien to our spirit and we have no organized forums for either the projection or the dissemination of our thinking? The answer is quite obvious. There is no international structure, including intellectual endeavor, which is not influenced by the inequality between rich and poor nations.

There is much other evidence of instances in which unequal economic relationships have led to a denial of economic opportunities to the poorer nations, but the basic point already has been made: in the international order, just as much as within national orders, initial poverty itself becomes the most formidable handicap in the way of redressal of such poverty unless there is a fundamental change in the existing power structures.

In this context, a net bilateral transfer of about $8 billion of official development assistance to the poor nations every year is neither adequate nor to the point: the quantitative "loss" implicit in the just-quoted examples of maldistribution of international credit, inadequate sharing of benefits from the export of their natural resources, and artificial restrictions on the movement of their goods and services (not to speak of labor) would easily amount to $50–$100 billion a year. More pertinent, the poor nations are seeking greater equality of opportunity, not charity from the uncertain generosity of the rich.

Equality of Opportunity

The demand for a new international economic order must be seen in its proper historical perspective. On one level of reasoning, it is a natural evolution of the philosophy already accepted at the national level: governments must actively intervene on behalf of the poorest segments of their populations ("the bottom 40 per cent"), which will otherwise be bypassed by economic development. In a fast-shrinking planet, it was inevitable that this "new" philosophy would not stop at national borders; and, since there is no world government, the poor nations are bringing this concern to its closest substitute, the United Nations.

On yet another level, the search for a new economic order is a natural second stage in the liberation of the developing countries. The first stage was marked by movements of political liberation from the 1940s to the 1960s; the second stage constitutes a struggle for not only political but also economic equality, since the former is unattainable and meaningless without the latter. The demand for a new international economic order must be seen, therefore, as part of an historical process, which neither can be achieved by the poor nations in one single negotiation nor will go away quietly by the simple indifference of the rich nations (or by their misinterpreting it as the faint rumblings of "British socialism," as Mr. Moynihan, former U.S. Ambassador to the United Nations, has argued). In fact, the movement for greater equality of economic opportunity is likely to dominate the next few decades—as much within nations as among them.

At the same time, the developing countries must recognize the intimate link between the reform of the national and international orders. If national economic orders in the poor nations remain unresponsive to the needs of their own poor and if their development strategies continue to benefit only a privileged few, much of the argument for a fundamental reform in the international order will disappear because any benefits flowing from such a reform would go only to a privileged minority in these countries. Moreover, when the international and national orders are dominated by privileged minorities, the possibilities of a tacit collusion between their natural interests are quite unlimited. The developing countries have to learn, therefore, that reforms in their own national orders are often the critical bargaining chip they need in pressing for similar reforms at the international level. . . .

The solution . . . is not piecemeal international reforms—via selective trade "concessions" or somewhat larger foreign assistance—since these achieve exactly the same purpose and provide as temporary a relief as limited social security payments to the poor within a national system. The long-term solution is to change the institutional system in such a way as to improve the access of the poor to economic opportunities and to increase their long-term productivity, not their temporary income.

The basic principles for such a change can be easily established and follow logically from the above analysis of institutional imbalances. For instance, any long-term negotiating package should make provision for:

(1) revamping of the present international credit system by phasing out national reserve currencies and replacing them with an international currency;

(2) gradual dismantling of restrictions in the rich nations on the movement of goods and services as well as labor from the poor nations;

(3) enabling the developing countries to obtain more benefit from the exploitation of their own natural resources through greater control over various stages of primary production, processing, and distribution of their commodities;

(4) introduction of an element of automaticity in international resource transfers by linking them to some form of international taxation or royalties or reserve creation;

(5) negotiation of agreed principles between the principal creditors and debtors for an orderly settlement of past external debts;

(6) renegotiation of all past leases and contracts given by the developing countries to the multinational corporations under a new code of ethics to be established and enforced within the United Nations framework; and

(7) restructuring of the United Nations to give it greater operational powers for economic decisions and a significant increase in the voting strength of the poor nations within the World Bank and the International Monetary Fund.

These ideas will be further developed in my specific proposals for the establishment of a new international economic order.

A New World Order?

The debate on the establishment of a new international economic order has only recently begun. The battle lines are still being drawn; the battle plans of the rich and the poor nations are hardly clear at present. Our world may well be poised uneasily between a grand new global partnership or a disorderly confrontation. Unfortunately, there are very few examples in history of the rich surrendering their power willingly or peacefully. Whenever and wherever the rich have made any accommodation, they have done so because it had become inevitable, since the poor had gotten organized and would have taken away power in any case. The basic question today, therefore, is not whether the poor nations are in a grossly unfavorable position in the present world order. They are, and they will continue to be, unless they can negotiate a new world order. The basic question really is whether they have the necessary bargaining power to arrange any fundamental changes in the present political, economic, and social balance of power in the world.

Let me conclude with three main observations.

1. Tremendous responsibility rests on our universities, our research institutions, and our intellectual forums in the Third World. It is for them to work out carefully concrete instances of systematic discrimination built into the existing economic order—whether the inadequate return from raw material exports, or inequitable sharing of gains from multinationals, or unequal distribution of world liquidity. This should be done in a spirit of serious, objective analysis so that there is concrete documentation available to our negotiators to press this point in international forums. There is no excuse for our not producing sufficient studies on this sub-

ject. If we do not attempt these exercises, the rich nations have no built-in incentive to carry them out. And, in the last analysis, facts are far more powerful ammunition than words can ever be.

2. We must keep stressing, as often as we can, that the basic struggle is for equality of opportunity, not equality of income. We are not chasing the income levels of the rich nations. We do not wish to imitate their lifestyles. We are only suggesting that our societies must have a decent chance to develop, on an equal basis, without systematic discrimination against us, according to our own value systems, and in line with our own cultural traditions. We are not asking for a few more crumbs from the table of the rich. We are asking for a fair chance to make it on our own.

3. Let us make quite clear in our future negotiations that what is at stake here is not a few marginal adjustments in the international system: it is its complete overhaul. We are not foolish enough to think that this can happen overnight. We are willing to wait. And we are willing to proceed step by step. But we are not willing to settle for some inadequate, piecemeal concessions in the name of a step-by-step approach. The advice of Prime Minister Burnham of Guyana at the time of the Commonwealth Heads of Government meeting in May 1975 is pertinent:

There is another danger that needs to be guarded against if we are all serious in our commitment to programmes of positive action which will give life to a new international economic order. It is the danger of deceiving ourselves that we can somehow achieve fundamental change by marginal adjustments and devices of a piecemeal and reformist nature. This is not to say that there is no value in particular approaches. It is to emphasize that we will not make real progress unless we evolve an integrated programme designed to fulfill not merely the aspirations of the developing world but the necessities for survival of the global community.

chapter 13

THE NEW HAVE-NOTS AND THE DEBT CRISIS

". . . . No Man is an island, entire of itself; every man is a piece of the continent, a part of the main."

John Donne

Two distinct debt crises face the international political economy today: 1) the U.S. federal deficit and its international impact and 2) the debts owed to international lenders by developing countries. In this chapter, we are concerned with the latter because to be "developing" is to be in debt.

Before World War II, there was much talk of the "haves *vs* the have-nots," a euphemism for the demands of the aggressive axis powers against the democratic, more passive, and relatively self-satisfied states. Today, the North-South "dialogue" is often called a "confrontation" between the poor two-thirds of the world generally located along or south of the equator, and the economically developed states of the temperate zone, chiefly the United States, Europe, and Japan, but also including Australia and New Zealand. The setting for all this was succintly described in the now-famous "Brandt Commission Report,"[1] and has also been described as the "West-South" or as in Gasparini's contribution in this chapter, "East-South" relationship.

The "South" is not a uniform bloc. The less-developed countries (LDCs) vary greatly in relative wealth, in ethnic composition and political history, and in their capacity both culturally and socially to move toward modernization and development. What they have in common, in addition to nonalignment, is a pervasive poverty and a shared goal of catching up with the developed world.

To achieve some idea of the discrepancy between the developed and less developed, it is pertinent to point out that "all countries of Latin America, Africa, the Middle East, and Asia together produce less than a third of what the United

---

[1]Reproduced in part in the sixth edition of this book, pp. 320–324.

States produces alone."[2] And the gap between the affluent and most of the deprived nations is widening, not narrowing; it is indeed the case that, in international relations, "the rich get richer while the poor get poorer." The new have–nots increased their productivity between 1966 and 1986, but their rate of population growth exceeded their rate of economic growth, and they have been sliding back ever since the 1973 oil embargo. The higher prices from that embargo hurt them much more than the rich Western powers against which they were primarily levied. The more successful are now being referred to as the "NICs" (newly-industrialized countries).

As hope of economic development has dwindled, many Third World countries have increasingly begun to insist that the disparity of wealth and development between North and South is the root cause of their poverty and that the system must be changed. One of their arguments is that because they are too weak and dependent upon foreign capital to protect themselves, they are being exploited. They further assert that their export trade is at the mercy of fluctuating demand for the products in the industrial countries. Changes in consumption patterns or a recession in the United States and Europe may mean a catastrophic fall in prices for their raw materials. In addition to that, the terms of trade for the exchange of industrial goods for raw materials is to them unfair. The price fluctuation and unit value of primary commodities do not average out over time to a rate of increase comparable to the incessant inflation of industrial goods.

Because the advanced industrial countries are not as dependent upon raw materials as the Third World is dependent on finished goods, the latter pays more and receives less. Billions are "taken" from the poor and "given" to the rich through the impersonal mechanism of freely negotiated international trade pricing. Spokesmen for the poorer states argue that the multinationals do not contribute as much as they should to development, developing only those sectors which prove most profitable to the companies and therefore fail to add to the overall fulfillment of the country's most basic and long-term needs. As we have seen, they are unable, however hard they may try, to sell enough to the developed world to pay off their debts. The "debt crisis" is a major world issue, and, as Del Canto and Bolin bring out in their contribution in this chapter, it goes well beyond mere "debt management."

One of the most critical problems facing not only these countries but the United States as well is that of borrowing and repayment. For years, public loans from the United States, Europe, and the World Bank (financed directly by the same governments) have helped the countries of the Third World to meet their investment needs and to cover their foreign debts. Early in the 1980s, nearly 30 percent of all external debts owed by non-oil-producing Third World countries were financed by the World Bank and UN loan agencies, compared to less than 10 percent at the end of the 1960s (their decade of emergence as independent states in many regions, particularly Africa). In the meantime, private banks such as Chase Manhattan and Citibank of New York began loaning and investing heavily in emerging countries—especially in Brazil, Peru, South Korea, the Phil-

[2]Steven Rosen and Walter Jones, *The Logic of International Relations,* 2nd ed. (Cambridge, Mass: Winthrop, 1977), p. 128.

ippines, Indonesia, Argentina, and Mexico.[3] The prosperity of such banking institutions threatened to become dependent on the capacity of these countries to repay the loans. Many of these loans and investment were not only made at a time when it seemed likely that impressive profits could be made from the boom that was occurring in certain of these countries, but they were not made as part of any comprehensive sensible program of development. All the selections in this chapter allude to this in one way or another.

The increase in oil prices and the worldwide recession of 1974 and 1975 cut demand for imports from developing countries and revealed the precarious basis of much of their financing practices. Many were now obliged to spend 30 to 40 percent of their export earnings just to repay their enormous debt overload. This meant that much less money became available to spend on imports, including imports necessary for their development which thus became virtually impossible. The role of the private banks, too, has changed dramatically. They find themselves financing balance-of-payments deficits on an unprecedented scale—a new function quite different from their original task of supplying credit to private investors. As a condition for their help, they, together with the World Bank and International Monetary Fund, insist that the debtor governments must cut back on welfare and reform programs and impose lower wages and harsher working conditions on the poor people who make up their populations. "Anti-IMF" riots are not uncommon as a result.

In order to respond to a new and disturbing set of circumstances, the non-aligned countries banded together in what they call "G77" or the Group of 77 (actually it numbers over 100). Collectively, they demand a moratorium on debt repayments and new international economic order (NIEO) that would mandate the transfer of technology and investment capital free of charge; mandate lower tariffs and a minimum price for their goods (a price that would automatically rise as the price of manufactured goods rose); and that would exert greater control over the multinationals. As might be expected, the developed countries have so far found these terms unacceptable, and it is unlikely that they will do so. The cacophony of harsh criticism crescendoes in the halls of the United Nations, though little change has actually taken place.

The fact of the matter is that in the international political economy there are likely to be less, not more, resources available to help resolve these issues in the years to come. Not only are the advanced states bumping up against the limits of their energy and mineral resources but their own economies themselves may be in deep trouble. Comfortable promises of the 1960s have given way to an uneasy restrictiveness in the 1980s. One authority has described the process in this way:

> Whereas in the past foreign aid programs were largely profitable to the developed nations, the combination of defense spending, aid commitments to loan programs, failures of recipient nations to repay loans, higher costs for raw materials, and competition for markets, make them less so for the future. Multinational corporations are increasingly earning and retaining their profits outside the developed nations,

---

[3]Concerning which *The Economist* used the term "its debt throes" in mid-1986, reminding its readers that Mexico "officially opened the international debt crisis in 1982." In "Mexican Impasse," 299, no. 7450, (June 14, 1986), 19.

and inflation makes it difficult to cater even to domestic priorities without deficit spending imbalances. Fuel imports are shifting capital into hands of oil exporting nations . . . . [Europe and America] do not have regular balance-of-payments surpluses . . . as a result of all these forces, their currencies become less stable. In the face of this, heavy imports and expenditures to maintain markets and supply bases abroad may seem less attractive to them than in the past.[4]

In other words, economic stringencies facing the "have" nations may drive them toward protectionism and toward less aid and investment in the South. Developed countries will hardly be in a position to do more when their own economies flounder. Instead of greater interdependence and integration of Third World economies with the world capitalist system, they may be thrown back even more upon their own resources. This could weaken the present orientation of the capitalist sector of those economies which are heavily dependent for their markets and capital upon the developed states. The Secretariat of General Agreement on Tariffs and Trade (GATT) recently warned that a further trend toward restrictions "would cripple efforts to deal with such pressing problems as servicing debts, creating jobs, and promoting economic growth."[5]

To weather the storm, they would have to turn inward and try to achieve a viable social and political system based upon self–help and slow rates of economic growth (as in China and Cuba) rather than upon the rapid industrialization to which their leaders aspire. For a time, America began to make its compromise with the forces of nationalism in Panama, in southern Africa, and in the Middle East. Reducing its efforts to prop up by overt and covert intervention its control and influence over the status quo, the Carter Administration, (by espousing black majority rule and human rights), tried to get in front of a situation which it could no longer control by economic and military means. The explicit reversal of this posture from the very outset of the Reagan Administration served only to aggravate the predicament and later gave way to a partial return to acceptance of black demands in southern Africa under what was termed a "policy of constructive engagement," now increasingly criticized in Congress and the media.

Economic interdependence will continue to develop between North and South. Gasparini discusses in his article in this chapter "East-South" ties, and a recent Rockefeller Foundation report puts new stress upon "South-South" exchanges. Third World demands are not likely to disappear. It seems more likely than ever that people will have to depend upon self-help efforts within their own national boundaries if anarchy is to be avoided. Meanwhile, the task of diplomacy is to prevent the North-South dialogue from degenerating even more deeply into a true confrontation, as has occurred in the East–West relationship with which we shall deal in the following chapter. In a very real sense, the United States constitutes the hinge or perhaps even the fulcrum between these two gigantic axes of world politics. In a most penetrating analysis of the so–called Ottawa Summit some years ago, Hobart Rowen made the following comments, which demonstrate what was at the time the American concept of priorities between North-South and East-West relationships:

[4]Robert E. Gamer, *The Developing Nations* (Boston: Allyn & Bacon, 1976), pp. 336–37.
[5]Quoted in *The Times* (London). September 8, 1986, p. 17.

The sharp division between the market-oriented Reagan Administration and most of its partners was also evident on North-South and East-West issues.

Despite lip service to global negotiations with the Third World, desired by all the others at Ottawa, the Americans watered down the language to almost meaningless phrases because they remain suspicious that global negotiations are a device fostered by the left-wingers to redistribute the world's wealth.[6]

The political implications of these axial relationships can be healthy as well as unhealthy as far as the world body politic is concerned, but in the words of a leading Washington newspaper editorial on Haiti, "The social conditions that support the development of democracy—more education, better health services, a rising standard of living generally—can be accomplished only over time."[7] While unwilling to accept the premises of the "New International Economic Order," the U.S. stresses its commitment to international development through free enterprise, to mutual cooperation in solving the problems of the hemisphere rather than one of defensive confrontation.

Someone has observed that "world affairs is a great teacher," and even though the United States may appear to the outside world (particularly in those many countries of left and right which do not need to bother with genuine elections) to go through a new planning process every four or eight years, learning *does* take place, even on North-South issues. The question is whether it will take place in time, and whether the North will truly comprehend, in Stephen Krasner's words in this chapter, "what the Third World wants and why."

DISCUSSION QUESTIONS

1. What is the "debt crisis"? How do Bolin and Del Canto see this as more than a management problem? Who suffers more, the "NICs" or the "LDCs"?

2. In light of the newer expression, "The North-South Dialogue (or Confrontation)" should we still speak of a "Third World" when so many changes and differences exist among the many dozens of countries which make up such a world?

3. As we saw in Chapter Six, spokespersons for the state employ the term "national interest" as if its meaning were self-evident. How do the interests (or values) of the countries of the "North" differ from those of the "South"?

4. Why is it imperative that the United States and its allies not approach developing countries simply as pawns or allies in the East-West struggle? Explain why approaching them in such a way may be imprudent, misleading and self-defeating, particularly in terms of Krasner's approach.

5. What developments continue to unite the "South" in its opposition to the advanced capitalist states of the "North"? How does Gasparini bring the "East" into this equation? Explain what a "COC" is.

6. Is Krasner's "fundamental regime change" the same as what Mahbub ul Haq was arguing for in the preceding chapter? What is a "regime"?

[6]"The Ottawa Summit: Reagan Against the World," *Washington Post*, July 26, 1981, pp. F2–3.

[7]"Haitian Democracy in Danger," *The Washington Post*, June 16, 1986, p. A10.

39.   What the Third World Wants and Why

Stephen D. Krasner

A frequent writer on problems of the developing countries, Stephen D. Krasner is a professor in the department of political science, University of California at Los Angeles.

Developing countries have pursued many objectives in the international system. Some objectives have been purely pragmatic, designed to enhance immediate economic well-being. However, the most publicized aspects of North-South relations, global bargaining over the restructuring of international regimes, cannot be understood in strictly economic or instrumental terms. By basically changing principles, norms, rules, and procedures that affect the movement of goods and factors in the world economy, the Third World can enhance not only its economic well-being but also its political control. The emphasis the South has given to fundamental regime change is a manifestation of four basic factors: the international weakness of virtually all developing countries; the domestic weakness of virtually all developing countries; the systemic opportunities offered by the international institutions which were created by a hegemonic power now in decline; and the pervasive acceptance of a belief system embodying a dependency orientation.

At the international level all states are accorded formal equality as sovereigns: The underlying power capabilities of states establish no presumptive differentiation with regard to certain basic rights, especially sole legitimate authority within a given geographic area. At the same time, the present international system is characterized by an unprecedented differentiation in underlying power capabilities between large and small states. Never have states with such wildly variant national power resources coexisted as formal equals. Very weak states can rarely hope to influence international behavior solely through the utilization of their national power capabilities. For them, regime restructuring is an attractive foreign policy strategy, because it offers a level of control over states with much larger resources that could never be accomplished through normal statecraft grounded in dyadic interactions.

The rigidity and weakness of domestic, economic, and political structures in developing countries is a second factor that has made basic regime change important for the Third World. With the exception of a small number of countries, the economies of the Third World are dominated by agricultural and primary sectors with low levels of factor mobility. Vulnerability is high because it is difficult to adjust to external changes. Political systems are also weak; the state cannot manipulate those resources that might lessen the impact of pressures emanating from the international environment. International regimes can limit external vacillations or automatically provide resources to compensate for deleterious systemic changes.

The third element accounting for the prominence of a basic regime change strategy is the set of opportunities offered by the character of post-World War II international organizations. These organizations have offered opportunities that made Third World programs more feasible and effective. The Third World has been able to turn institutions against their creators. Such develop-

Reprinted from Stephen D. Krasner, "Transforming International Regimes: What the Third World Wants and Why," *International Studies Quarterly*, 25, no. 1, (March 1981), 119–148, 161–173. Reprinted by permission of the International Studies Association. (Footnotes have been deleted.)

ments are likely to afflict any set of regimes created by a hegemonic power. This power establishes institutions to legitimate its preferred norms and principles, but legitimation can only be effective if the institutions are given independence and autonomy. This autonomy can then be used by weak states to turn the institutions to purposes and principles disdained by the hegemonic power.

Affecting both domestic incentives and international opportunities in the Third World's quest for a new international economic order has been a belief system associated with theories of dependency. This intellectual orientation has been a critical factor, accounting not only for some of the Third World's success, but also for its extraordinary unity on questions associated with regime transformation. Even economically successful developing countries with flexible domestic structures and conservative political regimes have not broken with the Group of 77. In an atmosphere pervaded by *dependencia* perspectives, such a break could undermine a regime's position with domestic elements. No Third World state openly endorses the norms and principles of international liberalism, even if some of them adopt its rules and procedures. The ideological hegemony enjoyed by the United States at the conclusion of World War II has totally collapsed, and the alternative world view presented by dependency analyses has forged the South into a unified bloc on questions related to fundamental regime change.

The emphasis in this essay on weakness, vulnerability, and the quest for control is not meant to imply that LDCs are uninterested in purely economic objectives. Third World states have pursued a wide variety of goals. These include economic growth, international political equality, influence in international decision-making arenas, autonomy and independence, the preservation of territorial integrity from external invasion or internal fragmentation, the dissemination of new world views at the global level, and the maintenance of regime stability. They have used a wide variety of tactics to promote these

objectives, including commodity organizations, regional coalitions, universal coalitions, alliances with major powers, local wars to manipulate major powers, irregular violence, bilateral economic arrangements, regulation of multinational corporations, nationalization of foreign holdings, foreign exchange manipulation, and international loans.

This essay does not review all aspects of Third World behavior. It concentrates on an area where political objectives associated with control have been highly salient—Third World efforts to enhance power through the transformation and construction of international regimes. By building or altering international institutions, rules, principles, and norms, weaker countries can both ameliorate the vulnerability imposed by their lack of national material-power capabilities and their weak domestic political structures, and increase resource flows.

Third World political behavior, like all political behavior, can be divided into two categories: relational power behavior which accepts existing regimes, and meta-power behavior which attempts to alter regimes. Relational power refers to the ability to change outcomes or affect the behavior of others in the course of explicit political decision-making processes. Meta-power is the capacity to structure the environment within which decisions are made. This structuring can involve the manipulation of institutional arrangements, norms, and values. Relational power behavior accepts the existing rules of the game; meta-power behavior attempts to alter those rules. . .

Most studies of international politics have implicitly emphasized relational power because they deal with war and the use of force. In this arena, meta-power considerations are of limited import because institutional restraints, norms, and rules are weak. Discussions of just war doctrines are prescriptive, not descriptive. Especially with regard to the reasons for which wars are begun, as opposed to the way in which they are conducted, regimes have had little effect. Rules related to tacit mutual restraints have developed during some wars, but they have been inchoate and weak. War outcomes are determined by the relative national material capabilities for the actors involved: what resources are nominally under the jurisdiction of the state, and how well the state is able to mobilize and efficiently deploy these resources.

In issue areas other than the use of force, however, regimes have been more salient. Agreement on norms and rules can prevent suboptimal outcomes that would otherwise occur when individual rationality does not maximize collective utility. These situations are associated, for instance, with free riders or, to cite a second example, with prisoners' dilemma. High levels of economic activity are impossible without predictable patterns of behavior. Such patterns will evolve into habits, usage, and conventions with some normative connotations. Wars involve relational power strategies based on national power capabilities; nonbelligerent issue areas are susceptible to meta-power strategies designed to alter regimes.

Third World states are interested in employing both relational power and meta-power. Proposals for regime change, voiced by the less developed countries, reflect an effort to exercise meta-power. The objective of these proposals, of which the program associated with the New International Economic Orders (NIEO) is the most recent and salient, is to transform the basic institutional structures, norms, principles, and rules that condition the international movement of goods, services, capital, labor, and technology. Such transformation is particularly attractive because the ability of Third World states to accomplish their objective solely through the exercise of relational power is limited by the exiguity of their national material-power capabilities. These alone could not resolve the vulnerability problems of poorer states.

Most Third World proposals for regime change have been made in international organizations. Debates within these organizations have been concerned with institutional structures, norms, and rules, not just the transfer of resources. However, the NIEO and other proposals for regime change have been but one of many kinds of interaction between the North and the South. With regard to actual resource movements, the most important settings have been national and bilateral, not universal. In such settings, developing states have usually sought to use relational power to enhance specific economic interests. They have not tried to alter regimes. (Oil and some other raw materials, as well as some national regulation of multinational corporations, are the major exceptions to this generalization.)

When, for instance, a developing country borrows on the Euro-dollar market, it attempts to get the best possible terms. It does not, however, challenge the ability of private financial institutions to base their decisions on maximizing private economic returns. When a state negotiates a stand-by agreement with the International Monetary Fund (IMF), it attempts to use relational power to adjust the terms and conditions of the arrangement. It does not, however, challenge the authority of the IMF to sign an accord that specifies targets for economic policies. The modal form of interaction between industrialized and developing areas has involved the transfer of resources and the exercise of relational power, and has taken place in bilateral arenas . . .

Some examples of relational power and meta-power policies in national and bilateral (as opposed to multilateral) settings are shown in the following table. Multilateral settings are further broken down into North-South arrangements and South-South arrangements. The entries in this table are examples. However, their frequency is meant to be in proportion to actual conditions. The upper left and lower right cells are the ones in which most activity takes place.

Behavior that falls within one of the cells is not incompatible with behavior that falls within another. In recent years the Group of 77 has pressed for generalized debt relief (at least for the least-developed states) at universal international forums such as UNCTAD and the United Nations General Assembly, while down-playing this issue at multilateral financial institutions such as the World Bank and the IMF, where weighted voting prevails. Algeria pursued "pragmatic" policies with respect to liquefied natural gas exports while Boumedienne acted as the leader of the Non-Aligned Movement. The pursuit of different goals in different forums is not inconsistent or incoherent. It does not reflect disagreement between politically oriented foreign affairs officials who do not understand economics and finance ministry officials who recognize the "realities" of global interdependence. Rather, the variety of Third World strategies manifests a variety of objectives.

This essay is concerned with only one aspect of Third World behavior—the lower right-hand cell of Table 1. Developing countries have sought to alter regimes in a variety of issue areas. They have attempted to create new institutional structures or to change patterns of influence, particularly voting allocations, in existing structures. They have sought to establish new international norms.

And they have tried to change rules. Many of these quests have been successful.

Third World demands for regime restructuring cannot be seen in any simple way as a reflection of economic failure. During the postwar period the overall rate of growth of developing areas has been faster than that of industrialized countries. Trade patterns have become more diverse with regard to partners and commodities. Indicators of social well-being, including life expectancy, infant mortality, and literacy, have dramatically increased in many areas. The economic performance of the South during the postwar period has been better than that of industrialized countries during the nineteenth century.

However, the South continues to suffer from an enormous gap in power capabilities at the international level and from social rigidity and political weakness at the domestic level. Creating new regimes that reflect Southern preferences is one way to deal with these structural weaknesses.

There have always been small states in the modern international system. Before the industrial revolution, however, there was little variation in levels of economic development.

Table 1

Negotiating Forum		Behavior type	
		Relational Power Behavior	Meta–Power Behavior
National and Bilateral		IMF stand–bys Euro–dollar loans Tax treaties Bilateral aid Orderly marketing agreements	Some regulation of MNCs Control of oil production
Multilateral	South–South		OPEC Andean Pact Collective self-reliance
	North–South Multi-fibre agreement		New Articles of Agreement for GATT Generalized systems of preferences Commodity agreements Aspects of Lome convention Integrated program for commodities 0.7% aid target

With regard to per capita income, the richest country was only about twice as well off as the poorest at the beginning of the nineteenth century. Now, the richest countries are 80 to 100 times better off than the poorest. The combination of small size and underdevelopment has left many Third World states in an unprecedentedly weak position....

There is little prospect for fundamental change in the foreseeable future. In a study for the United Nations, Leontief has estimated aggregate and per capita income in the year 2000 for different areas of the world, under different assumptions. To meet his optimistic target for LDCs growth, Leontief argues that "two general conditions are necessary: first, far-reaching internal changes of social, political and institutional character in the developing countries, and second, significant changes in the world economic order. Accelerated development leading to a substantial reduction of the income gap between the developing and the developed countries can only be achieved through a combination of both these conditions." Even if these conditions were met, the gap in power capabilities as indicated by GNP between the North and the South would still be enormous. Leontief estimates that the share of global aggregate output accounted for by the less developed countries would rise to only 22% in the year 2000.

Thus, if attention is focused on the GNP gap between the North and South, the situation of Third World countries is bleak. Few can hope to challenge even medium to small size industrialized countries in the area of aggregate economic activity. Even with rapid rates of economic growth, the absolute gap is now so large that it cannot be closed in the foreseeable future.

Using GNP figures as a measure of power capability has the advantages of easy comparability and accessibility; however, it also has the disadvantage of obscuring potential variations in power capabilities across different issue areas. Yet, even at a disaggregated level, there is little evidence that Third World countries can act effectively by utilizing only their national material resources. In the area of raw materials cartelization efforts have failed—with the exception of oil—although coffee exporting states have had sporadic success in pushing up prices by buying in London and New York, and copper producers in withholding stock from the market. The fundamental problem for the exporters of primary commodities is that there is a high temptation to cheat on any cartel scheme, because the marginal rewards of additional revenues for Third World governments strapped for resources are very high. With regard to trade in manufactures, Third World exporters depend far more on Northern markets than industrialized countries do on manufactured goods from the South. Northern countries have import competing industries capable of producing the same products, while the South does not have alternative markets. With regard to bank lending, large Third World debtors, especially Mexico and Brazil, have secured some leverage through the consequences of default. While this has given them continued access to credit markets, it has not enabled them to alter the basic nature of credit relations or to keep interest rates down. Smaller debtors carrying heavy burdens are rolling over their old debt but having difficulty securing new loans.

There are two major exceptions to these comments about Third World national power capabilities in specific-issue areas. The first is OPEC, where the combination of excess financial resources and inelastic demand has enabled Third World countries to raise prices eightfold in nominal terms over the last seven years. The second is national control of multinational corporations. Many developing countries have excluded MNCs from certain sectors, nationalized or unilaterally altered the concessions of petroleum and hard mineral corporations, and limited the ownership share of foreign nationals either generally or in specific industries. Control over access to their territory has been an important source of leverage for LDCs. Host-country nationals have also learned about market access and technology, which has given them more bargaining power. However, the pressure that can be exercised by host countries is limited by the ability of firms to relocate in more hospitable countries.

Aside from oil and domestic regulation of MNCs, few Third World states have any ability to alter their international environment solely through the use of national material–power capabilities. Their small size and limited resources, even in specific–issue areas, is the first condition that has led them to attempt the fundamental alteration of international regimes. Conventional statecraft based upon national material attributes is unlikely to reduce vulnerabilities. A meta-political strategy designed to alter rules, norms, and institutions offers an attractive alternative, if only by default.

The second condition that has driven Third World states to attempt a transformation of international regimes is the weakness of their own domestic societies and political systems. The international weakness of most developing states, as indicated by their small aggregate output in comparison with that of industrialized states, suggests that they cannot directly influence the international system. It also suggests that they will be subject to external forces that they cannot change. Small states are usually more heavily involved in the world economy. In 1973, trade (exports plus imports) was equal to 37% of GNP for developing countries, 29% for industrialized countries. In the same year, 48 out of 87 LDCs had trade proportions greater than 50%.

Although small states, as a rule, are more heavily involved in the world economy, state size does not determine internal capacity to modulate the pressures emanating from an uncertain international environment. A small, adaptable state could adjust to many regime structures. Such a state could accept its lack of influence at the international level but remain confident of its ability to deal with environmental disturbances over a wide range of international rules, norms, and institutions.

The ability to cope with environmental disturbances is a function of the mobility, flexibility, and diversity of a country's resources. A country with highly mobile, flexible, and diverse factors can absorb external shocks. It can adjust its pattern of production, imports, and exports to maximize its economic returns under different environmental conditions. Adjustments might be directed by the state or the private sector. The first alternative requires a strong political system, one in which the state is capable of resisting pressures from domestic groups, formulating a coherent strategy, and changing social and economic structures. The second alternative requires a well-developed private market with high levels of communication and information.

At early stages of development, countries lack the capability to absorb and adjust to external shocks. This incapacity is produced by rigidities inherent in traditional structures. In an elegant analysis concerned with problems of national dependence, Jowitt elaborates five characteristics of a traditional or status society. First, a status society is based upon exclusive corporate groups, which lock individuals within a rigid structure. Second, social action is determined by personal rather than impersonal norms. Different individuals are treated in different ways because of ascriptive characteristics. Third, the division of labor in the society is based on assignment to specific ascriptive groups. An individual's economic activity is permanently established by his group membership. Fourth, the ontology of the society stresses the concrete and discrete. General principles that can be applied to a wide range of situations are eschewed. Fifth, the world is seen composed of "concrete and discrete elements—that is, indivisible units—economic, social, cultural, and political resources are seen as being finite and immobile rather than expanding and flexible." By contrast, modern societies are market rather than status-based. Interactions are governed by impersonal norms of action. The individual and the nuclear family, rather than the corporate group, are the building blocks of the society.

Modern societies are less vulnerable to external changes because their factors are more mobile. Better-trained workers can perform a wider variety of tasks. More-developed capital markets can more readily reallocate investment resources. It is easier for an industrial worker to move from one factory to another than for a peasant to shift from one crop to another, much less move from agrarian to industrial employment. In his seminal study of the power aspects of international trade, Hirschman argues that "the inherent advantage with respect to all these aspects of the mobility of resources lies overwhelmingly with the great manufacturing and trading countries as opposed to countries in which agriculture or mining predominates."

The transition from traditional to modern society is taking place in the Third World, but it is a slow and difficult process. It is not unidirectional or irreversible, as events in Iran and Cambodia demonstrate. Most developing countries are still in what Chenery has called the early phase of the transition from a traditional to a modern economy which occurs at per capita income levels from $200 to $600 (in 1976 dollars). In this phase, societies are vulnerable to external shock. Most employment is still in agriculture. Cross-national data indicate that, on average, industrial output does not exceed agricultural output until per capita incomes of $800 are reached, and that industrial employment does not exceed agricultural employment until per capita income is $1600. . . .

The rigidity of the social and economic structure in developing countries is reflected in the political system. Most central political institutions in the Third World are weak. The state is often treated as but one more compartmentalized unit. Its ability to extract resources from the society is limited. Efforts to combine diverse social and material units are likely to be frustrated by the compartmentalized nature of the society. Economic activity that takes place outside the market cannot be effectively tapped by the government. Often the state is unable to resist pressure from powerful society groups. Low levels of skill and education make it difficult to formulate effective economic policies. . . .

Tax structures offer the opportunity to illustrate differences between the political capabilities of industrialized and developing countries. Tax collection is generally a good indicator of the ability of the state to extract resources from its own society. Developing countries collect a smaller proportion of their GNPs than industrialized states and rely more heavily upon trade taxes; the level of state revenue is, therefore, more subject to international economic vicissitudes.

Third World countries are poor and their governments cannot tax much of what there is. In 1973 total government revenue was equal to 33.5% of GDP for industrialized countries and 19.9% for developing countries. Mali was able to collect only 1.5% of its GDP, Nepal only 5.6%. The lowest figure for industrialized countries was 21.6% for Japan; the highest 51.7% for Sweden. . . .

Government revenues are but one indicator of the impact of the world economy on particular states. The experience of the developing countries in the 1974–1975 recession does, however, suggest a source for their concern about trade vacillations that has been largely ignored. One of the persistent complaints of Third World countries has been that they suffer from substantial trade fluctuation. While the vacillations in trade experienced by developing countries have declined, they are still much larger than those affecting industrialized countries. The Third World has argued that these vacillations inhibit their economic growth. However, no empirical substantiation has been found for this claim. . . .

While vacillations in trade may not be related to economic growth, they are related to the state's ability to extract revenue. Political leaders can be more sensitive to threats to their command over resources that can be used for immediate political purposes than they are to threats to the long-term economic growth prospects of their countries. Third World disaffection with the trading regime may be rooted in the weak domestic political structures of LDCs which necessitate reliance on trade taxes.

There is one major exception to these generalizations about weak political and rigid social structures in Third World countries. The newly industrializing countries, or NICs, have been able to adjust effectively to the international environment. Singapore, Hong Kong, Taiwan, South Korea, and Brazil have adopted aggressive export-oriented strategies. In Hong Kong the private market has acted effectively in a laissez–faire situation. In the other NICs the government has been more active. In Korea and Brazil for instance, the state explicitly decided to promote export-oriented growth and move away from protectionism in the early 1960s. Despite domestic pressure, both were able to maintain lower effective exchange rates, a precondition for international export competitiveness. Through the 1970s, the NICs were able to adjust to restrictions imposed by industrialized nations by developing new product lines and diversifying their exports . . .

The NICs are one of the two groups of dramatic success stories with regard to economic growth, or at least transfers, in the postwar period. The other is oil-exporting states. If purely economic considerations are used to explain the behavior of developing countries, the difference in foreign policy orientations of countries in these two groups is difficult to understand. Both the NICs and the OPEC countries have dramatically benefited from the present system. While none of the NICs have taken a leading role in the South's efforts to restructure international regime, a number of OPEC countries have been at the forefront of the Third World movement. Algeria and Venezuela have taken leading roles in the Group of 77. Iraq, Libya, and now Iran are hardly devotees of the existing global order.

While the NICs and OPEC countries are comparable with regard to income growth and export earnings, their vulnerabilities to changes in the international economy are dramatically different. The NICs are moving toward flexible economic structures and strong political systems capable of adjusting to shifts in the external environment. The OPEC countries now enjoy enormous bargaining power as a result of the inelastic demand for petroleum and the low opportunity costs of controlling supplies for the surplus OPEC states. However, few OPEC countries would be able to adjust to alterations in bargaining power. Their domestic factors are immobile. Their political structures are weak. The international radicalism of some OPEC countries is not compatible with a conventional orientation which explains the disaffection of developing countries as a manifestation of their lack of economic success.

Domestic structural weakness, a manifestation of traditional social norms, and political underdevelopment, together become a second factor that makes international regime transformation attractive for almost all Third World countries. The external environment is inherently threatening even in the absence of any direct effort by more powerful states to exercise leverage. International regimes controlled by developing countries can mitigate the exposure of developing areas to systematically generated changes. They offer some control in a situation where the lack of domestic adjustment capacity precludes effective cushioning against external shocks.

Demands for regime restructuring have occupied a dominant place in North-South relations, not simply because this approach could compensate for the international and domestic weakness of Third World states, but because the postwar system offered developing countries a setting in which to pursue this strategy: The prominence given to meta-political goals has been a function of opportunities as well as needs. The postwar liberal regime, especially the importance that it accorded to international organizations, provided the Third World with forums in which to press their demands . . .

In the postwar period, the Third World has made international organizations a centerpiece of its demands for regime change. The South has succeeded in dominating the agendas of all major multifunctional universal organizations. The North has been compelled to respond rather than initiate. Convening an international conference places an issue on the agendas of Northern states. Position papers have to be prepared. Voting positions must be determined.

Debates and resolutions presented at international forums have altered norms, rules, and procedures in a variety of ways favored by developing countries. Various resolutions have endorsed 0.7% of GNP as a target for concessionary capital transfers from the North to the South. While this norm is more honored in the breach, it is still held up as a goal that has been accepted by the North as well as the South. The percentage of concessional aid transferred by multilateral institutions has increased from 6% in 1962 to 27% in 1977. . . . In the immediate postwar period there was no accepted international norm for the level of aid, and policies were unilaterally set by donors.

In the area of trade, developing countries have used GATT to legitimate concessional treatment. During the 1960s, the industrialized countries agreed to institute a generalized system of preferences that would eliminate tariffs on some products from developing countries. The nontariff barrier codes and revisions to the GATT Articles of Agreement negotiated during the Tokyo Round provide for special and differential treatment for developing countries, although more symmetrical behavior is expected as countries reach higher stages of development. These changes are a fundamental break with the two central norms of the postwar trading order: nondiscrimination and reciprocity. The South has enshrined new principles emphasizing development and equity, not just secured exceptions from the old liberal rules.

Southern pressure exercised at international forums has secured acceptance of the principle that major parts of the global commons are the common heritage of mankind.

Developing countries have made claims on radio frequencies and outer space, even though they do not now have the technical capability to utilize them. Mining activity in the deep seabed will be controlled by an international authority and revenues from the exploitation of manganese nodules will be taxed to provide assistance to the South. Some developing countries have called for the internationalization of Antarctica, although their ability to press this claim has been impeded by the lack of a suitable international forum. The common heritage of mankind is radically different from the prevailing principles before the 1960s, which recognized the right of a state to claim unutilized areas that it could occupy or develop.

Even in the area of monetary affairs, that bastion of postwar conservatism, the South has had some success, at least within the regime's formal institutional manager, the IMF. While LDCs did not get an aid link with SDRs, they did get an allocation based on quotas. The industrialized nations had originally wanted virtually to exclude developing countries. The partial use of IMF gold sales to establish a Trust Fund (which makes loans to developing countries with few conditions at concessional interest rates) is a form of international taxation for aid. The Fund has begun to liberalize its conditions for stand-by agreements. In an international environment, in which the scope and growth of Fund activities will depend in part on continuing willingness of developing countries to use its resources, the organization has moved to change its rules and procedures if not its basic principles.

In general the institutional structure has become more responsive to the South. By using its voting majority in the General Assembly, the South has been able to create new institutions, especially UNCTAD and UNIDO, which represent its interests. Even in established forums, where votes are not equally divided, the South has changed voting power and decision-making procedures. Mutual veto voting arrangements for major decisions now prevail in all international financial institutions, including the Fund. In the Inter-American Development Bank, the largest of the regional lending institutions, and in the United Nations Development Program, the Third World has a majority of votes. In the newest international financial institution, the International Fund for Agricultural Development, votes are equally divided between OPEC countries, non-oil developing countries, and industrialized countries.

Thus, in a variety of issue areas the South has been able to alter principles, norms, rules, and procedures. It is difficult to imagine similar success in the absence of institutional structures that provided automatic access for developing countries. By taking advantage of the autonomy that the hegemonic power, the United States, was compelled to confer on international organizations during the period of regime formation at the conclusion of World War II, Third World countries have been able to alter regime characteristics during the period of American hegemonic decline. The relationship between underlying national power capabilities and regime characteristics has become increasingly incongruent.

While vulnerabilities that arise from domestic and international weakness provide the impetus for Third World demands—and international organizations the opportunity to realize them—the form and unity of these goals have been shaped by the pervasive acceptance of dependency orientations. Most developing countries have explicitly accepted arguments that attribute their underdevelopment to the workings of the international economic system rather than the indigenous characteristics of their own societies. The belief system has been endorsed, not only by individual states, but by international organizations close to the Third World, such as UNCTAD and the UNDP, as well as by important groups with claims to speak for the North as well as the South. Individual states may reject dependency prescriptions in practice but even the most

conservative lack a belief system to offer in its stead.

The dependency orientation serves important functions for Third World states both internationally and domestically. At the international level, dependency arguments have provided a unifying rationale for disparate Southern demands. Calls for special and differential treatment are justified by the contention that the South has been treated unjustly in the past. Existing norms and rules are rejected as inherently exploitative. A coherent intellectual orientation has been particularly important because of the strategy of using international organizations to promote meta-political goals. In such arenas the ability to define issues and control the agenda is critical. Such initiatives are facilitated by a widely shared and internally consistent analytic framework.

Dependency perspectives are also linked to domestic political conditions in Third World countries. Given the limitations on effective state action, foreign policy is an attractive way to build support. Prominence in universal coalitions can enhance a Third World leader's domestic position. Castigating the North can rally bureaucratic, military, and popular elements. The structure of international organizations affords Third World statesmen an opportunity to play on the world stage, a platform which they could not mount if they had to rely solely on the domestic power capabilities of their countries. Even if their activity is perceived as a minor walk-on part by more powerful countries, an effective leader may transform it into a major role for domestic political consumption.

Third World leaders who follow such a course must find ideological arguments that resonate with their domestic populations. The most accessible themes reject existing international regimes. For most countries in Asia and Africa, if not Latin America, the central historical event is decolonization. Anticolonialism and nationalism are widely accepted values endorsed by virtually all groups in the Third World. Dependency arguments are widely diffused. A Third World leader who opts for enhancing support through international behavior will reject existing rules, norms, and institutions. The most vigorous support for Third World demands for regime transformation has come from countries where such policies contributed to domestic political legitimacy. External policy has helped to define the internal character of the regime for its own constituency. . . .

The countries of the Third World have not simply sought higher levels of resource transfer. They have wanted to restructure international regimes. In some cases they have succeeded. The New International Economic Order is the successor of SUNFED, and the First and Second Development Decades. It will be followed by other programs with different names but the same import—control, not just wealth. The NIEO, and its antecedents and probable successors, cannot be understood through analogies to reform efforts within national polities such as the labor union, consumer, welfare, and civil

rights movements in the United States. These were movements based upon shared norms; the South rejects the liberal norms of the American-created postwar system. They were movements content to share power within existing structures; the South wants effective control over new structures.

The demands of the South are a function of the profound international and domestic weakness of most Third World states. These demands may temporarily abate but they will not disappear. Since most states of the South cannot hope to garner the national resource capabilities needed to assert effective control in the international system, they will continue to press for international institutions and norms that can offer them some control over the international environment. In the pursuit of this goal, they will enjoy some success by taking advantage of institutional structures that were created by the powerful to serve their own purposes. In this and other ways, the power of hegemonic states is dissipated by the very structures they have created.

---

40. LDC Debt: Beyond Crisis Management

William H. Bolin and Jorge Del Canto

William H. Bolin is Vice Chairman of the Bank of America NT&SA. He has been involved in lending operations to less-developed countries over the greater part of his career, especially in Latin America. Jorge Del Canto, Director of the Western Hemisphere Department of the International Monetary Fund for 21 years, is currently a consultant on monetary affairs.

. . . This article focuses on the longer-term aspects of the problem. Its thesis is simple.

Excerpted from *Foreign Affairs*, 61, No. 5, Summer 1983, 1099–1112. Reprinted by permission. Copyright © 1983 The Council on Foreign Relations, Inc. (Footnotes have been deleted.)

It is that the real problem regarding LDC debt, in the long or even medium term, is the source of future credit for their imports of capital goods. In the absence of increased public money, new mechanisms are needed to assure access to private funds. There is an urgent need for a system which would have practical political appeal, and we believe that such a system should seek to mobilize support from the export sectors of the industrial countries through joint financing by the national export credit organizations, private commercial banks, and the World Bank.

In exploring the need for such a system, and its possibilities and potential difficulties, we shall briefly look first at the present situation and the measures now underway, then at the needs of the LDCs and the potential sources of future credit, and finally at what a joint financing mechanism might look like. Its aim would be to tap private funds on a new basis that would effectively meet the needs of the LDC, especially for imports of capital goods, and thus contribute greatly to their resumed growth and to the welfare of both industrialized and developing countries.

II

The use of private bank funds by the more advanced LDCs has been going on since World War II and began to be an important component of their external financing in the late 1960s. Such credit has been intrinsic to their rapid economic growth and their demand for exports from the industrialized world. Over these years various countries have encountered and have overcome numerous liquidity problems—some of them very alarming. However, the sudden rush of Mexican capital out of that neighboring country immensely dramatized the speed with which prolonged recession, combined with unrealistic economic policies, could produce difficulties even for a country with an excellent payment record. Those events in Mexico, followed by the experiences of several other major borrowers, understandably have attracted widespread attention. All eyes have been focused on the commercial banks' portfolios of debt and the accumulation of current maturities.

One aspect of concentrated attention on maturing debt has been rapid effective co-operation among commercial banks, governments, the International Monetary Fund (IMF) and the borrowing countries themselves to confront the problem. Their cash advances and rescheduling arrangements have prevented a collapse of confidence in the world financial system. The arrangements have required greater discipline and more rapid adjustment by borrowers. They also have allowed the borrowing countries to continue importation from the industrialized world, although at a lower rate.

All of the parties to those arrangements have recognized that we have been passing through the longest period of recession since World War II, with its drastic impact on commodity prices, volume of trade, and interest rates. Both borrowers and lenders had expected continuing inflation. All of them realize, also, that credit to developing countries is indispensable for world economic recovery and growth.

Outside that circle of direct participants there has been considerable creative thought aimed at the rescue of LDC borrowers and their lenders from the problems of the present portfolio. The tendency of these analyses has been to take a "snapshot" of today's problem and devise a sweeping "now" solution. In fact, the present situation needs to be viewed as one frame in a moving scenario that began decades ago and will extend even farther into the future.

The principal LDC borrowers from private banks are the semi-developed countries which, by their nature, must be continuous and growing importers of capital and credit. No nation has yet moved from "underdeveloped" to "industrialized" without steadily increasing flows of credit, even when following enlightened policies to stimulate local capital formation and attract foreign direct investment. To be "developing" is to be in debt. Semi-developed countries are structural capital importers whose productivity in the use of capital is high. The more natural and human resources such a country has, the more it needs to borrow to make use of them.

Each year since World War II, these countries have produced and exported more and more raw materials as the industrial world's supplies have fallen short of demand. In the process, the developing countries have diversified their exports and trade flows. Each year they have purchased more and more capital goods and materials manufactured in the developed world, coming to account for between 25 percent and 40 percent of the export-oriented employment of the United States, Canada, Europe and Japan. U.S. trade with LDCs has grown the most of all. . . .

III

In this moving panorama, the present portfolio is not where we most need to focus regarding *new* mechanisms. Proposals such as asset recycling or discount of private bank loans to LDCs are not pointed at the real problem. The fundamental question is where the new money will come from in the future.

Loan portfolios of major commercial banks have been built up over years of complex client relationships and involve a great variety of public and private borrowers in each country. Apart from the transfer risk—the lack of availability of dollars—these loans represent a wide array of commercial credit risk. They are being rescheduled case by case in the only way that is practical or feasible. One by one, the countries are concluding arrangements in which the IMF and commercial banks are advancing new funds, and banks are extending all or part of loan maturities falling due in the . . . period of greatest stress. In each case, the rescheduled loans and new advances are arranged in response to programs of the borrowing governments worked out with the IMF to adapt exchange rate policies to present realities, hold down current expenditures, increase revenues, and expand domestic savings, so as to meet future payments of principal and interest.

The probability of success in managing the present portfolios through the recession in this way is high. The basic reason is that the fundamental productivity of the principal borrowers continues intact. Many developing countries—like industrial nations—have structural problems in their economies. Some have invested in uneconomic import substitution, and some have allowed agricultural development to lag behind industry. However, we are not dealing with economic machines that have broken down. Ninety percent of LDC debt to U.S. banks is owed by 15 countries. The basic economic sectors, although under strain, are functioning productively in all of them.

These countries all have distinct strengths and weaknesses. The refinancing of their debts therefore has to be tailored very specifically.

The rescheduling as such, of course, does not solve all of the problems of LDC debt. The time borrowed by stretching out maturities must be followed by continuous application of sound policies with due attention to structural weaknesses. There must also be a background of reasonable economic growth in the industrialized countries.

The money borrowed has been used mainly to buy or create something. Local and foreign funds gathered since World War II by the semi-developed countries have been employed primarily to increase production. Much of that new production is only now coming on stream and will add steadily to future repayment capacity. Internally generated savings for LDCs accounted for roughly 18 percent of their GDP in early 1960 and increased to over 25 percent of GDP by 1980. As a group, developing countries have devoted a greater proportion of their cash flows to the investment sector than have industrialized countries. Real domestic investment among LDCs increased by 8.1 percent annually over the past 20 years compared to about 4.4 percent for industrialized economies. Until the recession, debt grew at essentially the same pace as production and exports. When debt of the 15 major borrowing nations is compared to their growing economies and international trade, it may be questioned whether many countries in fact overborrowed up to the period of the recession. Furthermore, the main increase in debt took place in a decade of high world inflation and frequently negative interest rates. The same capital goods imported today would require even more debt.

The current problem is not the ability to produce. The problem is that assets were acquired with debt having maturity schedules based on expected income which has not come on stream as planned, primarily due to a sudden change of the industrialized world from inflationary boom to deflationary recession. In some countries the problem has been made worse by incorrect fiscal, monetary, and foreign exchange policies, with resulting disintegration of public confidence and discouragement of exports. The countries are not helpless before present events. They can change unrealistic policies, and most of them are doing so rapidly. It is increasingly recognized by the economic authorities of the countries that realistic policies work for their own eventual political benefit, as well as improving credit-worthiness.

The process of rearranging the debt maturities of a basically productive borrower to allow time for policy changes to improve cash flow is not "postponing the problem." This is a standard solution used every day by banks in both domestic and international lending, for large and small borrowers. The very creation of the IMF was an expression of worldwide judgment that such liquidity problems do indeed exist from time to time—and have solutions to which the government concerned can contribute significantly by better economic management.

This patient case-by-case approach, negotiated by the people with the most intimate knowledge of the practical possibilities and political complexities, is indeed working. Banks have no illusions about these reschedulings. Further adjustments may well have to be made later in some of the programs. The rescheduling arrangements af-

ter all are based on government commitments to policies, the results of which cannot be projected precisely in numbers. Also, expectations of exports may evolve differently, IMF-guided reschedulings are usually designed to be at the very outer edge of the country's economic and political capacity. If they later need adjustment to changed conditions—and the productive machine is still operating adequately with the sound policies—such "re-reschedulings" are not significantly different from the original exercises. Neither are they intrinsically less sound than "new" credits made to the countries five years from now—or the ones made and repaid five years before the present recession. In respect to transfer risk, it is the amount of service on principal and interest of total outstanding debt in relation to total foreign exchange earnings that matters—not the specific loan to which repayments pertain. Overall, the countries by their nature will build debt until they themselves become capital exporters. With all its resources, it took the United States well over a century to become a source of surplus savings for the capital-short parts of the world.

IV

Sweeping solutions which would remove the present portfolio from the hands of the original lenders certainly cannot be relied upon to produce new lending from the banks so "assisted." How many boards of directors would be responsive to programs of new loans for borrowers whose existing loans—and potentially, future loans—were subject to arbitrary judgments requiring write-off? Neither lenders nor borrowers are seeking such a one-way ride to nowhere in order to handle the present portfolio.

Governments of the industrialized countries will need to continue their important role. The U.S. Federal Reserve and the Bank for International Settlements (BIS) have been acting very decisively in the present difficulties and should continue to do so as needed. Central banks of the industrialized countries need to organize better all aspects of the international safety net, to meet unpredictable emergencies. They should continue to give quick, effective assistance to any specific banks suffering from faltering public confidence, as they do in situations of purely domestic origin.

However, the political realities in the United States and other countries constrain the direct role of governments in meeting the long-term credit needs of LDCs. There is not a very clear public memory of the late 1920s and early 1930s, when shrinking trade combined with financial crisis led to a major depression. Accordingly, there has been little public discussion of the really central problem. What, in fact, will be the source of new financing for LDCs to import capital goods in the future?

V

A quick survey of the practical possibilities for increased flows of funds from the existing channels is not encouraging.

The present austerity programs of these borrowers certainly will reduce demand for new credit drastically for the next few years. Beyond that, it can be hoped that lower fiscal deficits and more realistic domestic interest rates and tax policies will improve internal savings and capital formation. One wonders how much more the countries can be expected to accomplish in this respect, bearing in mind how high their savings and investment rates have been compared with the rest of the world. Middle income LDC domestic savings reached the equivalent of 24.5 percent of GDP in 1980. Let's assume very optimistically an improvement to 25.5 percent in that rate by the 15 principal LDC borrowers, which would produce $11 billion per year. These domestic currency funds would partially substitute for foreign currency borrowings.

We need to note that the semi-developed or "newly industrialized" countries, which are the large borrowers from private banks, by definition are building more capital-intensive economies. They have growing needs for machinery and equipment, technology, infrastructure, and public utilities for a rapidly urbanizing society. This element can be expected to utilize a large part of the improved domestic savings.

More realistic policies regarding foreign direct investment can assist to an important degree (and bring improved technology and management). However, in the wake of prolonged inflation and lagging domestic investment in the United States and much of Western Europe, foreign investment will come to the LDCs only very selectively and with expectations of relatively high returns. . . .

The World Bank and the regional development banks would be the most logical sources of increased credit. Their long-term money is the kind best suited to a world of slower economic growth and numerous long-term structural adjustments. It is in the very best interest of the industrialized nations to increase substantially the funding of the World Bank and most of its regional counterparts. Unfortunately, the public of the United States is very far from an adequate recognition of the implications of continued LDC growth for its well-being. Few voters understand what it means to them, in terms of employment opportunities, that 40 percent of U.S. exports go to LDCs. Still fewer understand that exports to LDCs will continue only if there are future flows of credit to the importing nations.

In terms of net new flows to all LDCs, in 1981 the World Bank added $3.8 billion, other multilateral agencies $5.1 billion and bilateral flows $10.7 billion. An optimistic view of member government support for the World Bank . . . would put increased World Bank net lending at $5 billion more per year. One can add $6 billion for the regional institutions and $14 billion for bilateral credits and aid, based on straight-line projections [since 1973]. This adds up to $25 billion per year in new flows of credit or grants. However, in recent years a large share of all such loans and grants have gone to countries other than the 15 nations which are the largest borrowers from the private commercial banks. Those large semi-developed borrowers, which have been the cause of recent concern, are not likely to receive more than $7 billion per year from all official institutions without significant changes in lending policies by these organizations.

Latest estimates of the net borrowing of the 15 largest borrowers, reflected in national development plans and current adjustment programs (and taking into account their maximum efforts to increase domestic savings), show their requirements to be in the neighborhood of $50 billion per annum. How will the need compare with resources? After deducting $10 billion of direct investment and $7 billion from public funds (World Bank, bilateral aid, etc.) this probably leaves a minimum gap of $33 billion annually.

VI

Such a gap between economic need and the funds from aid programs and multilateral development banks grew throughout all of the 1970s. It was filled by the commercial banks' lending of Eurodollars. Such private lending to LDCs increased at an annual rate of 32.5 percent from 1972 through 1981 in current dollar terms, averaging $29 billion per year. In 1972, according to World Bank estimates, financial-market outstanding credit to LDCs amounted to only $36.7 billion. The total rose to $273.4 billion by late 1981. This latter amount accounted for an estimated 60 percent of total LDC outstanding foreign debt in that year.

It appears probable that the principal private banks in international lending—some 60 multinational private institutions and a few hundred regional and secondary banks—will indeed continue lending to LDCs. This is not because they are permanent captives of the borrowers, any more than they have been captives of Chrysler Corporation or New York City. It is because the semi-developed countries represent the most dynamic part of the world economy; they have become indispensable sources of raw materials, and vital markets, for the industrialized countries. There will continue to be demands for credit generated by the banks' corporate clients, who rely increasingly on the developing world for their prosperity. In an atmosphere of even modest world growth, loans to the governments of rationally managed industrializing nations should compare reasonably with other credit opportunities.

However, the rate of increase of such lending is likely to be less than in the 1970s. Banks may be discouraged by their governments from continuing their participation. Continual dramatization of the problems of LDCs might affect confidence of investors and thus indirectly reduce the capacity of the banks. Barring these potential impediments, the major banks will remain in the business because they will find it to be sound. However, it would be unrealistic to expect that they will continue to fill a steadily increasing portion of the requirements, as in the past.

Let us assume that the major private banks do increase their lending at a rate equal to the rate of increase of their capital funds. Ninety-four percent of all bank lending to LDCs is conducted by the largest 60 banks. If capital funds of these banks grow in the next five years at a rate equal to expected inflation, this would supply $28 billion of new credit each year to the 15 major borrowers. Assume, for the sake of simplicity, that the small regional U.S. banks and the secondary banks of Europe, Japan and the Middle East on average maintain their present absolute levels of outstanding credit. Add the $28 billion of commercial bank contributions to the previously mentioned sources to give total new available funds of $45 billion annually. Subtract that total from the estimated requirements of $50 billion and there is still a shortfall of $5 billion per year.

Net IMF financing has increased rapidly from $1.2 billion in 1980 to $5.6 billion in 1981 and $6.3 billion in 1982; it is further expected to increase to $13.5 billion in 1983. However, it is not included in the flows estimated above, because such financing is strictly to provide temporary relief to tight liquidity positions, eliminate payments arrears or build up minimum reserves and not for development financing.

These are all estimates, of course, and in general they reflect an optimistic view of the amounts that will be in fact available from various sources of finance. All are based on expectations of moderate economic growth in the industrialized countries. They assume no new major obstacles to restrict international trade expansion or restraints imposed by regulatory authorities that reduce commercial bank lending. However one adds it up, there is still an unfilled need of significant magnitude.

VII

It would appear that one of three things must happen. If nothing new is done, the developing countries will meet their debt servicing obligations. However, they will lag further in their growth and become a brake holding back the prosperity of the rest of the world.

Alternatively, existing multilateral and government financial institutions can be strengthened with public funds to expand their activities and return their contribution to its previous relative importance.

The final possibility is that new mechanisms or channels of finance may be created to utilize private savings. This paper examines briefly some potential mechanisms to meet further future LDC financing needs, primarily with private monies, using taxpayers' funds on a small enough scale to be politically feasible in the next few years.

Each of the two principal sources of LDC credit today—multilateral institutions and the private banks—have some strengths and some limitations regarding LDC lending. The private banks have flexible, quick, efficient access to the largest pool of internationally mo-

bile funds in the world today—the Eurodollar market. As the product of years of inflation, most of the money is available only with the interest rate fixed every few months. The total amount and ownership of such floating-rate funds shift continuously, but there is a core amount which is quite stable as to its availability—at a price—and the private banks know how to obtain it, wherever it may be, on the best possible terms.

Lending to the 15 major LDC borrowers represents only about 10–15 percent of the assets of major banks. Their other activities as depositories of short-term funds and as domestic lenders place definite limits on the proportion of banks' portfolios that can be committed to LDC loans at long term. Also, while commercial banks have a superior capacity to evaluate medium-term lending for productive enterprises, they have less capacity to analyze the final shape of a country's development program, long-term public policies or overall natural resources.

The World Bank group has these latter capabilities. (So do various regions and government institutions in varying degrees.) The World Bank also has the strength of substantial stable fixed-rate funds, from its capital and from its long-term bonds. These funds are indispensable for loans of 15 years or more. Because of legal and policy restrictions, the World Bank currently does not mobilize floating-rate funds in a major way out of the Eurodollar markets—the only international private source of money available on the scale needed.

New solutions should attempt to make use of the strengths of each of the principal lenders. Ideally, World Bank long-term money should be conserved for the long-term maturities. Lending capacity of the private banks should be used primarily for the shorter-term financing to match their liquidity considerations and their best expertise.

One idea which has been under discussion for the past two years has been to increase the leverage of the World Bank. World Bank lending presently is restricted to funds from its own capital, paid in by the member governments, plus proceeds of its medium- and long-term bonds placed in capital markets. These are issued to the extent of unpaid but callable capital. Under this system the World Bank borrows and lends an amount roughly equal to its paid-in and callable capital—a gearing of one to one.

There have been proposals to increase this gearing in the World Bank itself. This is a very useful approach and should be studied actively. It may have the disadvantage of impact on one of the Bank's principal strengths—its ability to place its long-term bonds in the market on nearly the same terms as the U.S. government.

A variation of this idea would be to form a subsidiary of the World Bank which would be more highly leveraged and would borrow directly from the Eurodollar market to raise floating-rate funds, with which to carry the early maturities of long-term programs. This would also seem to be worthy of study and presumably has been receiving it. In the end, most bond specialists would expect some impact on terms of the World Bank's long-term borrowing under any such solution. It would be a trade-off, but probably a good one. In any event, there appears to be resistance to the concept and it has not moved forward so far.

Another theoretical avenue for using private Eurodollar funds on a larger scale without drawing commercial banks beyond prudent levels would be a scheme of guarantees or insurance against country risk. Several versions of this idea have been under discussion for some time. Expanded public "country risk" insurance is worthy of analysis—as is the possibility of government co-operation and support for private insurance and reinsurance schemes.

VIII

In general, such proposals so far have lacked political appeal, because of the level of understanding in the United States and else-where about the general public good to be derived from them.

The question arises, therefore, as to what sectors of the major industrial countries would be most likely to understand and support a program for increased lending to LDCs. It seems probable that these would be the exporters of capital goods. Stagnation in the semi-developed countries spells sharply reduced imports of machinery, equipment and technology from manufacturers in the United States, Canada, Europe and Japan. Recent drastic reductions in Mexican imports have brought this point home in the United States.

In each of the industrialized countries there is an entity (such as the U.S. Export-Import Bank) specifically created to maintain and increase exports by various credit techniques. Is it possible to imagine a new organization closely allied with the World Bank, but legally separate from it, which would be backed by the export credit entities of the principal industrialized countries? Such a new organization could be leveraged more highly than the World Bank. It could also be housed with the World Bank and, for a fee, have access to its analyses and loan judgments, as well as its accounting and other support services. The world doesn't need another public or private bureaucracy to increase loan activity—just a different balance sheet. Even the board of directors of the new entity could be made up of the same individuals who represent those countries on the World Bank Board of Governors—or they could be the Executive Directors from those countries.

What would such an "Export Development Fund" do? It would make loans beyond the optimum maturities for private banks (seven to eight years) and less than the 15-year or longer maturities that make best use of World Bank monies. The new organization would obtain its loanable funds by placing its own floating-rate 8-to-14 year notes with investors in the Eurodollar market. Initially, such notes might be taken up by the private commercial banks participating in the early maturity loans.

Such direct obligations of a multinational entity owned by public authorities of major industrialized countries, holding a diversified portfolio of World Bank-approved loans, clearly would represent a different level of risk than individual loans to specific countries. Over time, a secondary market might be created for such obligations so as to provide them with some degree of liquidity. Initially, it may be necessary for the export credit organizations or some multilateral institution to stand ready to repurchase the notes under specific circumstances, until the new loan portfolio is built up and a "track record" established.

New lending to LDCs for imports of capital goods would combine the forces of the various institutions. In a given large project or program, up to 20-year financing would be arranged, with commercial banks taking the early (one-to-seven year) maturities, the World Bank taking the later (15–20 year) maturities, and the new entity carrying those in the middle. All of the loans would have been evaluated by the World Bank and the private banks. Loans to a given borrower would be linked together by cross-default clauses, or would simply constitute separate "tranches" of one loan.

Apart from adding more private money to the total supply, such a scheme would also provide, on average, longer-term credit. This will be important in a future of basic economic adjustments and slower average growth. The concentration of private bank financing on the earlier maturities of long-term loans will make it possible for commercial banks to keep short-term trade credit growing with trade.

Obviously, a formidable series of obstacles would stand in the way of such a program, but there might be a shorter list of roadblocks for this device compared with others. The central political appeal is that the new financing would be related to the exports of the industrial countries in a visible manner.

Many aspects obviously need study. Would each national export credit organization be able to take a broad cooperative view of the interests of its exporters and modify charters or policies to invest in a joint effort? Could these organizations promote financing which would not be directly and immediately linked dollar-for-dollar to exports from their own countries? Would the World Bank be able to carry out the role described without diluting its present effectiveness?

Could a market be created for the new floating-rate notes and how? There is a market of uncertain size now for medium-term floating-rate notes of major corporations in the Eurodollar market.

Could notes of the new entity be placed at rates which, when reloaned, would not exceed the cost of the only available alternative—private bank floating-rate loans? Do the various export credit organizations have the legal capacity to invest (by equity shares or by subordinated debt or by "callable" obligations) in such an organization? Could they acquire that authority where it doesn't exist?

There can be a question as to whether the borrowing countries could soundly take on longer floating-rate obligations, in view of the difficulty of predicting cash flows far into the future. They are currently doing so, in general, for loans of ten years. One approach to this problem would be to have the World Bank absorb some interest costs when rates rise above certain ranges, being repaid when they fall below, with any final difference added to or subtracted from its own long-term fixed-rate loan, at the end of the financing. This concept is embodied in a recently announced program for expanding co-financing between the World Bank and commercial banks.

Answers to these questions should be pursued. The present comments are intended primarily as catalysts to begin discussion and to focus thinking beyond the present "crisis management." Clearly, something new is needed soon to provide the continued growth of credit to LDCs which will be vital over the years ahead to promote world trade and sustain world recovery.

41. East-South Economic Relations

Emilio Gasparini

A member of the Economic Directorate of the North Atlantic Treaty Organization, Emilio Gasparini frequently writes on aspects of the international political economy.

Although some economic and military aid from the USSR to North Korea was recorded in the early 1950s, it is customary to set the economic debut of Warsaw Pact countries on the developing world scene in 1954, when Moscow extended a $6 million loan to Afghanistan, followed in 1955 by a $250 million military agreement with Egypt. Since then, East-South exchanges have grown into a business which in 1983 had a $40 billion commercial turnover, and global strategic, political and military implications. The purpose of this article is to offer a mainly quantitative assessment of recent developments in economic activities by the Warsaw Pact—USSR and East Europe—in the Communist Developing Countries (CDCs), which include Cambodia, Cuba, Laos, Mongolia, North Korea and Vietnam, and non-communist Less Developed Countries (LDCs)—all other developing countries outside Europe.

Overview

For the sake of brevity, several specialized topics, such as joint ventures, co-operation agreements, training schemes, and educational programmes are not dealt with here, and the focus of attention will be economic aid and arms supplies. Since 1976, intra-CMEA[1] pricing procedures have included

Excerpted by permission, *NATO Review*, 33, no. 2 (April 1985), Copyright © 1985, The Atlantic Council of the United States. (Most footnotes have been deleted; those remaining have been renumbered.)

another assistance element—technically not definable as aid—accruing to the three developing members—Cuba, Mongolia and Vietnam: trade subsidies, mainly in the form of low prices for Soviet oil, and, for Cuba, high prices for its sugar. In 1983 these benefits represented about 50% of "concessional disbursements," which comprise the sum of aid and subsidies.

The quantitative evidence shows that: (i) trade subsidies, all accorded to CDCs and depending on CMEA pricing procedures, represent about one-half total Communist gross disbursements; and (ii) unlike Chinese and Western aid, Soviet bloc economic assistance concentrates on a relatively few countries: Cuba, Vietnam, Mongolia, Afghanistan and Cambodia took up 88% of the bloc's gross disbursements in 1983—a year which represented the rule, not the exception. Cuba alone accounted for over 58% of gross disbursements and over 99% of trade subsidies from the USSR, the corresponding percentages for East Europe being 51% and 100%. Among the LDCs, Afghanistan absorbed 50% of Soviet and 20% of East European gross disbursements.

A high level of concentration also appears to be one of the main features of Soviet bloc weapons deliveries to the developing world.

Although the decision to sell weapons is a political one, the specifications, the volume and the prices of the weapons traded by the bloc is also determined on economic grounds. Raising convertible currencies is one of the bloc's priorities, and this explains the concentration of deliveries on three Middle

Eastern, usually solvent countries: Syria, Iraq and Libya. Also in 1983 they were the top clients ($3.685 million, or 55% of the total), each one of them receiving more weapons than all CDCs taken together (much as in 1982). When Algeria is added, 59% of the bloc's deliveries go to four Arab countries. The Middle Eastern situation presents therefore not only political opportunities but is also an economic asset for the Soviet bloc.

The CDCs are comparatively poor customers and receive unimpressive amounts of Soviet weapons, although at times their armed forces have to be restocked to keep the local regimes in power (e.g. Vietnam was delivered $1,500 million in 1979). Finally, the appearance of Nicaragua on the clients list since 1980 is to be noted more for its political significance than for the unlikely economic benefits for the Soviet bloc.

The USSR and the LDCs

In the 1980s, Soviet economic programmes in non-communist developing countries (LDCs) reflect decisions to maximise political and economic returns with limited aid resources. Key elements of the Soviet programme for the 1980s include:

(1) Support for Marxist client states, such as Afghanistan and Ethiopia, whose economies are experiencing particular difficulties. This group receives large amounts of grant aid and long-term credits for a variety of uses not usually financed by Moscow—commodities and fuel, technical services, and project studies.

(2) Credits on easy terms to a few favoured countries, such as India, where Moscow is attempting to protect or project its political and economic influence.

(3) A growing use of trade credits to promote equipment sales to earn hard currency and to increase the Soviet presence in Third World economies.

New Soviet project aid commitments in 1983, at over $1,150 million, were at their highest level since the late 1970s. Nearly three-quarters of these commitments were granted to Afghanistan and the three Indian sub-continent countries.

Ethiopia and Nicaragua were the two other notable recipients in 1983. As far as deliveries are concerned, a moderate growth was recorded in project and commodity aid, half of which was funnelled to Afghanistan. . . . this provoked a degree of change in the pattern of regional deliveries compared to previous years.

Despite considerable increases in the 1980s, Soviet bloc trade probably does not account for more than 8% of LDCs' turnover. However, this percentage conceals a more complex strategic, economic and political reality, because at least 40% of Soviet exports consist of arms. For a number of LDCs, the USSR is a vital and sometimes sole arms supplier, making these countries dependent on Moscow for both arms and the necessary follow-on support. By contrast, exports under aid agreements ($656 million in 1983) continue to represent only about 4 to 6% of Soviet exports to LDCs. Disbursements of development aid and trade credits together accounted for about 30% of Soviet equipment exports in 1983. Yet, some deliveries on favourable terms are merely a means to sell machinery and equipment which would not otherwise be competitive. The LDCs offer Moscow its only major outlet for civilian machinery and equipment outside the Soviet bloc.

East Europe and the LDCs

Total East European agreements recovered strongly from the very low level of 1982 to reach $371 million in 1983. Bulgaria was the largest donor with its credit of $140 million to Nicaragua; Rumania and Czechoslovakia provided almost all the remainder.

The level of East European project and commodity aid deliveries, at just under $100 million in 1983, is the lowest for more than a decade and reflects the pressure on these countries to reduce their aid commitments and switch increasingly to non-concessional credits. There were particularly sharp falls in the level of East European activity in both the Middle East and Latin America.

From an economic point of view, LDCs represent suppliers of raw materials in exchange for somewhat outdated, but comparatively cheap, East European manufactured goods. The usual positive balance for the East also provides badly needed convertible currency. Sales of technical services also add to the benefits derived for Eastern Europe, and so do the limited ($641 million in 1983) but not negligible deliveries of weapons.

The Warsaw Pact and the CDCs

After a dramatic increase at the turn of the 1970s, Soviet gross disbursements to Communist Developing Countries slightly diminished in 1983. Gross disbursements to Cuba (about 68% of the CDCs total) fell from $4.1 billion in 1982 to $3.8 billion in 1983. The oil subsidy fell dramatically as the Cubans continued to make serious efforts to reduce their overall oil consumption and the CMEA average oil price continued to rise, while OPEC prices fell. In contrast, the Soviet sugar premium rose by nearly $0.5 billion in 1983 to $3.1 billion although total Soviet sugar imports fell from the high 1982 level. There were again some hard currency sugar purchases, but they were only minimal compared with 1982. Also the Russians continued to pay a premium price for their imports of Cuban nickel.

After Cuba, Vietnam remains the next major recipient of Soviet aid. . . .

Warsaw Pact Arms Supplies to Developing Countries

Arms deliveries from the Soviet bloc as a whole, and from the Soviet Union in particular, to the developing world in 1983 reached $6,668 million. This value marks a 3.1% decrease with respect to 1982 ($6.883 million).

In 1983 substantial arms sale agreements were concluded with an increase of almost 50% over 1982 ($12,067 million compared to $8,254 million). Such levels underscore the great stake the Soviet bloc has in the export of weapons for the future, particularly in the crisis areas of the Middle East. However, the spectacular leap of sales is mostly due to an agreement with India worth about $5 billion and another with Libya worth $4 billion.

Moscow's earnings from its military exports are the largest and most dynamic element in the trade with LDCs. The economic importance of arms exports from the Soviet bloc, over and above the political implications, has been increasing, the main aim being to procure hard currency. In 1980 and 1981 minimum estimates of the hard cash obtained from weapons by the USSR were $2.5 billion; in 1982 it increased to at least $3 billion; in 1983 it may have fallen to a minimum of $2 billion, due to payment difficulties experienced by the Middle East customers, which are usually the main and most solvent buyers. In addition, the USSR accepted at least $3.7 billion worth of oil in 1982 and 1983 in payment for military equipment (much of this oil was resold for hard currency). The trend toward relatively larger oil-for-arms barters is accelerating, as well as the concession of longer credit terms.

Warsaw Pact Military Personnel in LDCs

Advisory services and training, important components of Soviet bloc military assistance programmes, have continued to expand sharply. Much of the growth derives from increased transfers of advanced weapons although security and intelligence support have also become important. Through personnel assistance, Moscow hopes to expand its influence in LDCs, a goal most East European countries feel obliged to support to varying degrees. In recent years, hard currently earnings from these programmes have provided an additional incentive.

Achievements and Prospects

Since the mid-1950s, Soviet and East European policies towards the developing world have undergone several changes, the most important of which has been a shift in emphasis from economic to military deals. This change became clear in the late 1960s, and by the 1970s net economic aid to the non-communist developing countries averaged only about $350 million, reaching a peak in 1980 of $592 million. On the other hand, weapons deliveries to these LDCs averaged $2.6 billion in the 1970s, and twice as much, $5.2 billion, between 1980–83. This emphasis on weapons deliveries is due in part to the fact that the LDCs draw on Soviet economic credits at a low rate because most Soviet goods are inferior in quality, and therefore LCDs prefer Western equipment with the exception of arms where the Soviets, tending to specialise in this sector, have a comparative advantage. In addition, trade between the Soviet Union and the LCDs lacks economic complementarity (except for arms), because both of them import goods and machinery and export raw materials (90% of Soviet exports to non-socialist countries). By contrast, the Communist Developing Countries have always received much more economic aid (let alone subsidies) than weapons.

Aware of its comparative economic weakness, Moscow has advised developing countries, even those which rank as close friends, to look for economic assistance from the West. Nevertheless, Soviet economic activities do represent a challenge for three reasons in particular: firstly, the amount of military assistance and hardware is totally out of proportion to economic aid; secondly, the Soviets have a comparatively large personnel presence, both economic and military, which provides Moscow with an additional instrument of penetration; and, thirdly, they behave in a very opportunistic way, thus when prospects appear to be fruitful, the Soviets and Cubans can move very quickly, as was seen in Chile (1972), Angola (1975), Ethiopia (1977), Nicaragua (1981) and Grenada (1982).

Moscow's opportunism, however, is tempered by objective resource constraints—cumbersome commitments vis–à–vis Communist Developing Countries, and the country's limited economic situation. Thus the USSR will continue to be selective in aid, affording priority to its three privileged clients—Cuba, Mongolia and Vietnam.

Finally, it is noteworthy that as a result of these military and economic activities, the LDCs currently owe the Soviet Union approximately $20 billion, 75% of which is due on the military account. This debt will potentially generate future income for the USSR either in the form of guaranteed deliveries of commodities or in cash. LDC debt problems, however, are likely to prevent many of these countries from meeting scheduled payments, and it would arouse considerable resentment and hostility if Moscow insisted on punctual repayment or some sort of non-economic compensation.

NOTES

[1] The Council for Mutual Economic Assistance (CMEA) is the economic grouping of the socialist countries and comprises the USSR, Bulgaria, Czechoslovakia, German Democratic Republic, Hungary, Poland, Rumania, Cuba, Mongolia and Vietnam.

chapter 14

CONFRONTATION AND THE NONALIGNED

There are at the present time two great nations in the world, which started at different points, but seem to tend towards the same end. I allude to the Russians and the Americans. . . . All other nations seem to have nearly reached their natural limits, and they have only to maintain their power; but these are still in the act of growth. All the others have stopped, or continue to advance with extreme difficulty; these alone are proceeding with ease and celerity along a path to which no limit can be perceived. . . . Their starting point is different and their courses are not the same; yet each of them seems marked out by the will of Heaven to sway the destinies of half the globe.

Alexis de Tocqueville, *Democracy in America* (1835)

As we have seen, the basis of North–South tension is primarily economic. Another axis of world politics, East-West, is military, or strategic with much of the world determined to "stay out" or remain "nonaligned" with either side in the Soviet-American confrontation.

The framework of Soviet-American accommodation that Kissinger and Nixon tried to establish was based on the assumption that by recognizing each other's vital political, economic, and strategic interests, the two superpowers could end the cold-war era of conflict and confrontation. Unfortunately, Kissinger could not get the Kremlin to abandon entirely is competitive activities. Secretary of State Cyrus Vance and President Carter continued the uphill struggle to salvage détente, only to have their policies swept away by the Soviet invasion of Afghanistan. The United States has never been able to establish the degree of linkage or Soviet accommodation to American interests that Washington feels is essential to our security and to global stability. As for the Reagan administration, the era of détente is dead. Confrontation is once again center stage for the major actors, be it over an arena such as outer space or a journalist like Nicholas Daniloff.

Détente (a French word simply meaning "relaxation of tension") had been introduced early in the 1970s to denote the gradual easing of the old Soviet-American cold-war relationship toward a more relaxed and less hostile relationship. Its development rested upon two changes in the world situation. First and foremost, Kissinger managed to reorient United States foreign policy away from an ideological obsession with anticommunism toward a more pragmatic and realistic assessment of the actual nature of the American national interest. Détente represented a greater willingness to define American foreign policy in terms of the balance of power, in terms of strategic rather than ideological goals and objectives. Containment would continue to be the basis of United States foreign policy, but Washington would be more willing to negotiate issues such as strategic arms limitation than before, and Moscow, acting in its own long-term interest, would also become willing to do so. This is basically Professor Gaddis's argument in the article utilized in this chapter.

On the Soviet side, détente was adopted as a response to the equalizing of the strategic balance between the two superpowers that had come about because of the American defeat in Vietnam and the Soviet achievement of nuclear parity. The politburo under Leonid Brezhnev responded to the Nixon Administration's offer of détente partly because it fit in with the Soviet doctrine that there is nothing theoretically incompatible between the attempt to maintain peace with the capitalist superpower and at the same time practically to advance Soviet political interests. Détente was also welcome in Moscow as a means to offset the strategic pressures caused by the U.S. normalization of relations with China. Unfortunately, in their zeal, Nixon and Kissinger failed to take account of these Soviet exceptions and failed to educate the American people to the limited nature of the new relationship until it had become discredited. It was also fervently welcomed by the nonaligned states desperately anxious to avoid the consequences of a new World War. China meanwhile gradually committed itself to the nonaligned bloc and in 1985 declared itself the leader of the Third World, although it did not take part in the eighth summit the following year in Africa.

Meanwhile, the Third World had assiduously been cultivating among its members it own new strategic concept. Rather than becoming pawns (either in a cold war or in a détente) of either the First or Second Worlds it would remain protected under a neutral umbrella called "nonalignment." It has now been in existence for over 30 years. The Afro-Asian conference which convened in Bandung, Indonesia, in 1955 and the Belgrade, Yugoslavia conference six years later were two landmarks in the new states' efforts to define their relation with the rest of the world and indeed with each other.

Perhaps the high point of détente came in June 1972, when Nixon and Brezhnev signed agreements limiting nuclear weapons systems (SALT I), and in the following year when each side signed an agreement to avoid engaging in conflicts that might involve confrontation and nuclear war. Its low point came when Carter withdrew the SALT II treaty from the U.S. Senate for fear it would be defeated in the wake of Afghanistan. In its place, the Reagan Administration speaks of linking all outstanding issues and tension points between the two countries and responding to new crises, not at times and in places of Russia's choosing, but of Washington's. For example, a response to an intervention in a neighboring country would probably not take place there but in an entirely different part of the world, or even on an entirely different kind of an issue, such as trade. Nonaligned states fear this will draw them into the struggle against their will and in spite of their policy.

While the element of tactical surprise might be new, this shift of emphasis probably represents no real change in the relationship from the Soviet viewpoint. The old "two-track" conceptualization of peaceful coexistence, "that is, peaceful diplomacy and a policy of getting along with the capitalist West combined with a dialectical militance in the areas of ideology and class struggle, with material support for revolutionary movements,"[1] is still in place. Brezhnev underscored this dialectical fusion of opposites for the twenty-fifth Soviet Party Congress in 1976 in these words:

> We will come forward wherever our consciences and our convictions may lead us. . . . Détente in no way replaces, nor can it replace, the laws of class struggle. . . . Détente creates favorable conditions for the broadest dissemination of the ideology of Socialism. . . . The ideological battle between the two systems (capitalist and socialist) becomes more intense.

In this debate, he succeeded in convincing his skeptical colleagues that the Soviet Union could exploit détente to avoid the dangers of unrestrained conflicts which might result in nuclear war, while maintaining its ideological vigilance and quest for an eventual socialist "victory." Gorbachov follows in a similar path.

In line with their ideological formulations and with their spirit of opportunism, the men of the Kremlin always drew a sharp distinction between détente 1) as a basis for reducing the chances of nuclear conflict and acquiring Western investment and technology, and 2) as a means of harmonizing American and Soviet values and interests to whatever extent might be feasible. However, it was always axiomatic that the Soviet Union need not and must not deny itself the possibility of globally asserting itself wherever the political situation, as in Africa, the Middle East or, as James Wolfe makes clear in his short article below, Central America offers an opportunity for Soviet intervention. Whether the Kremlin can blend its paramount search for security against nuclear war with the risky and provocative support for revolution and defeat of the capitalist order is dubious. Nor has the United States in turn viewed détente as marking the cessation of its struggle for security and stability any more than it meant an end to the long-standing if sometimes overshadowed, American strategy of containment. In Europe, in the Far East, the United States still maintains a structure of alliances and is determined to enhance its military (particularly naval) power in order to limit the risk of Soviet expansion. One of the most unconventional expressions of the Reagan administration's conception of the internal dimension of this doctrine took the form of Vice President George Bush's going to Paris, after Mitterand chose his cabinet, to object to the new French premier's inclusion of a few Communists. The Quai d'Orsay was as offended as the White House would have been if a foreign government had objected to any of its cabinet appointments or if any of the nonaligned governments had been subjected to such pressure.

[1]Louis L. Ortmayer, "The Several Faces of Détente," *Book Forum* III, November 4, 1978, 483.

One of the great obstacles to nuclear-arms control is that each side continues to upgrade and develop new weapons faster than they can be controlled. Weapons engineers on both sides are engaged in a relentless search for ever newer and more sophisticated weapons, so that each side accuses the other of seeking a numerical and qualitative advantage such that it could strike first and destroy the other's retaliatory capability. The nonaligned neither want nor are able to compete on this level. The second obstacle to reaching an arms-control agreement follows from this. For the decade between 1962 and 1972, deterrence was thought to rest upon the possession by each side of an invulnerable nuclear retaliatory capacity. By this is meant that whoever attacked first could not hope to knock out all of the enemy's missiles deployed in underground silos, on submarines, or in the bomb bays of B-52s kept on constant airborne alert. Each side, knowing that the other retained sufficient undamaged missiles to destroy the other several times over, would hesitate to risk an attack. To nonaligned states, this is a slender seed upon which to rest the future of the planet. In the words of George Liska, "nonalignment reflects the peculiar conditions of a world in which Communism is rising and Western colonial empires have virtually disappeared in fact if not in memory." But those memories persist, and as Professor Onuf brings out his new essay, produce part of what he terms the "paradox of Nonalignment." The Third World has, by its own choice, been left out of the process of deciding great issues like arms control and nuclear disarmament, but realize that their people have just as much at stake as have those of two mighty protagonists and their respective aligned associates in Europe and elsewhere. Instead of détente becoming a world-wide basis for a well-crafted and publicly supported policy for the long-term management of our competitive relationship with the Soviet Union, it became what Robert Kaices of the *Washington Post* called "a political pinball bounced off countless independent points of power and interest in American society." Ironically, détente was used by Nixon and Kissinger to win the 1972 presidential election and then by Ronald Reagan to win the 1980 election for exactly the opposite reason. It has been used by optimists, farmers, and manufacturers to justify the sale of grain and machine tools to the Soviets, and by right-wingers and militants to condemn Carter and Vance as naïve dupes. As Gaddis points out, in his article a more realistic view would have recognized that détente did not end the era of Soviet-American competition, but might have provided a basis for influencing Soviet foreign policy toward caution and moderation had its leverage been used more intelligently and consistently in that direction. Nonaligned powers might well have been brought into this process.

The collapse of détente has not altered the essential stake that both superpowers have in limiting their conflict so as to avoid the ultimate folly of a nuclear war. It is probably wrong to believe that American leverage can be achieved by restoring American military superiority or by reverting to unilateral acts of coercion designed to scare the Russians off. The need is both to recognize and negotiate with the Kremlin as a global equal while insisting that such a relationship cannot be on terms that undermine the ability of the United States to maintain a secure and stable international order.

Perhaps the greatest dilemma that confronts international relations is the security dilemma—the difficulty (perhaps impossibility) two adversaries have in developing confidence that the other does not intend to attack it or undermine its power position. This dilemma is clearly at the heart of Soviet-American relations which is in "a position of unstable equilibrium," as Jonathan Alford has phrased it.[2] Everything in the relations between the two superpowers—ideology, strategy, and advances in weapons technology—predisposes toward an unstable balance in which neither can feel confident that a gain or advance by the other will not lead to a fatal defeat for itself. However much confidence each side's deterrent posture and armaments ought to give it, the very competition and insecurity that is built into the fabric of international relations promotes distrust and rancor. It is for this reason that nonalignment, as Nicholas Onuf puts it, has always been both a movement and a principle. This may be one reason Third World countries are so prone to condemn American Cold War moves while readily accepting American assistance.

DISCUSSION QUESTIONS:

1. Show the connection between Third World nonalignment and the confrontation between the First and Second Worlds.

2. How did the American idea of détente differ from the Soviet idea or concept of "peaceful existence"? Why does Pell feel we should return to détente? Why is his opinion important?

3. Why does the constant upgrading and development of new weapons make it difficult to control or cap the arms race through agreements like SALT I and II?

4. What would you judge Soviet intentions vis-á-vis the United States to be? Having read the article by Gaddis, how do you think we can best deal with the Soviet Union and reduce the risk of a nuclear war?

5. In light of Onuf's analysis of nonalignment, do you see any prospect that the tripartite division of the world into East, West, and neutral can be replaced by a more universal concept, such as originally intended in the United Nations system?

6. Do you feel that the Third World states could be more influential in taming Russo-American confrontation if they became *less* nonaligned? Or would this merely produce two more massive alliance systems?

[2]In an article on "The East-West Balance" reproduced in the 6th edition of this book (1983), pp. 356–364.

42. The New Challenge in Superpower Relations

Claiborne Pell

The only U.S. Senator to have first served as a Foreign Service Officer, Sen. Claiborne Pell is ranking Democratic member of the Senate Foreign Relations Committee.

. . . . Just how closely we now verge on catastrophe is beyond our power to know. But we can envisage, as a group of eminent scientists recently did, how devastating an unrestrained war would be. And we know also that in preparing for such war—which we do on the theory that extensive preparations will deter it—we spend prodigiously of human and material resources which could otherwise be allocated to eradicating human misery and elevating human society. I have never felt it a foolish exercise to contemplate, as President Eisenhower did in his farewell address, the extraordinary good we might accomplish if we were ever able to reallocate modern military budgets into constructive endeavor. To do so, of course, would require fundamental change in U.S.–Soviet relations.

In considering how such fundamental change might be accomplished, we must recognize precisely what we are talking about. We are not talking simply about U.S.–Soviet diplomacy, though that is an ingredient. Our scope must be wider, for what we are really examining is the interaction between two huge and profoundly different societies, each shaped by its own culture and governed by its own political system. What transpires in the relationship between these two great nations must necessarily occur within the limits of what those two cultures and political systems make possible. In short, to reflect clearly

Remarks by Senator Claiborne Pell in the annual Griffith Lecture of the Graduate Council of the School of International Service, the American University, April 19, 1985. Reprinted with the permission of Senator Claiborne Pell.

on U.S.–Soviet relations, we must be keenly aware of the domestic foundations on both sides, for it is on those foundations that the relationship—for better or worse—must stand.

The American Side

Let us focus first on the American side—and begin by looking back some 13 years to 1972, which represents a prominent landmark in the superpower relationship. Leonid Brezhnev was President of the Soviet Union and Richard Nixon was President of the United States. And the two men came together that year to sign a series of agreements that were intended, in broad terms, to end the state of cold war that had characterized East-West relations since the end of World War II.

The operative concept of that moment was "detente"—a lessening of tensions. And the guiding theory, from the American perspective, was to engage the Soviet Union—through an elaborate network of political, economic, and arms agreements—in a relationship that would temper the adversarial nature of East-West relations through activities serving a common interest. The centerpiece of this arrangement was nuclear arms control in the form of the SALT I agreements: the ABM Treaty banning most defensive systems and the Interim Agreement placing limits on offensive nuclear systems. Other accords signed that year provided for expanded trade and increased cultural, scientific, and educational exchanges.

Reflect on how fundamental a change this

moment seemed to represent—not just in American *policy* but, even more importantly, in American *politics*. Before and during his Vice Presidency in the Eisenhower-Dulles years, Richard Nixon had built a political career warning of the danger of the Communist menace both at home and abroad. His stewardship of the detente policy in 1972 thus appeared to signify a virtual revolution in our politics such that American politicans would no longer have to live in fear of being attacked from the right with charges of being "soft on Communism." Our ultimate "Cold Warrior" had gone to Moscow to make peace, and he appeared to be putting an end to what a distinguished historian, Richard Hofstadter, once described as "the paranoid style in American politics."

Yet, as it turned out, the appearance of fundamental change in American politics and in U.S.-Soviet relations was misleading. For almost immediately, the detente policy began to unravel, principally because of a loss of domestic support. In part, this decline may be traced both to Vietnam and to Watergate, which by early 1973 had begun to undermine the legitimacy of the Nixon presidency and his ability to guide the new course in East-West relations he had charted.

The essence of the problem was a still-unresolved issue in American politics: how the United States should conduct its affairs with a Soviet state that remains rigidly authoritarian at home, repressive in its hold on Eastern Europe, opportunistic and sometimes adventurist in the Third World, and increasingly powerful in its military build-up of conventional and nuclear forces. Richard Nixon had temporarily quieted this debate. But he had not ended it; and with the decline of his presidency the debate resurfaced full force.

Critics of detente argued that to conduct arms control with the Soviet Union was a dangerous sham—that public opinion in the United States and Western Europe would be lulled into a false sense of security and that the Soviets would cheat at every opportunity. They contended too that trading with the Soviet Union was simply a way of fulfilling the old Leninist prophecy that American capitalists would eventually sell the rope with which they themselves would be hanged—in other words, that trading with the Soviets was a foolish subsidy to our enemy.

Supporters of detente bore the burden of making the more complicated argument that detente was not a policy of friendship; it was a policy of securing our own interests through arrangements with the Soviet Union that benefited both sides. East-West relations, they argued—and I was among them—is not a "zero-sum" game in which one side's benefit has to be the other side's loss. . . .

The Soviet Side

But what, meanwhile, of the Soviet side? How have Soviet officials viewed events over the past 13 years?

When Presidents Brezhnev and Nixon met in 1972 to sign the SALT I agreements, that moment undoubtedly represented to the Soviets a landmark in their policy, just as it seemed to be in ours. They had, after years of striving, finally achieved an arsenal of nuclear weapons and delivery systems comparable to our own. And the Nixon-Brezhnev accords were giving substance to the idea that they were now equal players on the world stage.

It seems clear that, under Mr. Brezhnev's leadership, the Soviets invested an immense amount of emotional energy in the concept of the new age of detente. But what they were unwilling to invest was the measure of moderation in their own behavior necessary to overcome American doubts about the wisdom of detente. Instead, the Kremlin played directly into the hands of America's detente critics by pursuing their nuclear build-up, by underwriting Cuban intervention in southern Africa, and by continuing their repression of Soviet and East-European dissidents.

From the Kremlin's perspective, American complaints about the lack of Soviet "moderation" were hypocritical. The United States, Soviet officials argued, was steadily modernizing *its* capabilities and searching for ways to strengthen *its* hand in the geopolitical competition; why should the Soviets be expected to behave differently? And Soviet domestic affairs were, they stated impatiently, *their* business. Nonetheless, detente depended upon American public support and by the mid-1970's, as that support faded, the Soviets could do little but watch with growing resentment as detente faded too.

Meanwhile, beginning in 1977 when Brezhnev fell seriously ill, the Soviets entered what became an agonizing eight-year succession crisis. After lingering in office for five more years, Brezhnev was succeeded by two elderly men from his own entourage and generation—Andropov then Chernenko—both of whom entered office with terminal illnesses. Throughout this period Soviet policy was essentially unchanged: cautious but opportunistic abroad, and repressive at home. In East-West relations, with the death of detente confirmed by the election of Ronald Reagan, the Soviets turned to a new game—of striving to split the Atlantic Alliance politically by playing to West-European fears of nuclear war. But in the absence of a vigorous and credible Soviet leader to make the Soviet case, such efforts failed to achieve the desired effect.

. . . accession to the Soviet leadership by Mikhail Gorbachev has, however, changed the equation of recent years. The Soviet Union now has a young and apparently dynamic leader. And the question we face is how U.S.–Soviet relations—and the competition for international opinion—will be affected.

Mr. Gorbachev and his wife have been likened to President and Mrs. Kennedy. But we should not be misled by that analogy. What it signifies is that the Soviet government may now have a much more persuasive and appealing spokesman for Soviet policy, who could prove to be a serious adversary for President Reagan in the court of world opinion. But what it does not signify—what it *could not* signify—is a dramatic or fundamental change in the nature of the Soviet Union.

Mr. Gorbachev has risen to the top of a system which will remain in place, subject only to the most gradual and evolutionary change. It is a system built on a myth—the myth of infallible leadership. And Mr. Gorbachev would tamper with that myth only at his political peril. In the realm of foreign affairs, infallible leadership means that the Kremlin never errs, that only foreigners make mistakes, and that threats to the security of the Soviet Union come only from malign foreign actions—along with those few unpatriotic Soviet citizens who dissent from the Kremlin's wisdom.

Soviet ideology and all that goes with it—the ingrained paranoia and the institutionalized repression—is unfortunately a fact of life which Mr. Gorbachev's accession has not changed. Over time, he may be able to temper the rigidity of Soviet life and Soviet behavior in foreign policy. But it may also turn out that his leadership serves only to reinforce the existing Soviet system, with all its liabilities.

What Is to Be Done

We cannot know which of these courses the Soviet future will take. But what we can do is play our own role with shrewdness and some wisdom. There was, I think, a soundness and validity to the precepts of the detente policy of the early 1970s. And it is to those precepts that we should return.

The Soviet Union will not soon change. But there *are* ways for the United States and the Soviet Union to engage in constructive, businesslike arrangements. The record proves it. Eisenhower and Khrushchev arranged the Austrian State Treaty of 1955, which provided for the withdrawal of Soviet troops. Kennedy and Khrushchev negotiated the Limited Test Ban Treaty of 1963. Willy Brandt undertook a successful policy of Ostpolitik, which eased tensions in Berlin and Central Europe. Nixon achieved constructive agreement with Brezhnev on a variety of subjects. And Ford and Carter negotiated useful U.S.-Soviet arms control agreements, which unfortunately were never ratified by the Senate because of detente's declining popularity.

Our first priority, of course, must be the control of nuclear arms. But we should not lose sight of the fact that the danger from nuclear arms arises not from the technology but from the animosity and mutual ignorance of the two superpowers who possess it. We should therefore be attuned to every opportunity to break down the barriers of isolation, to bring the Soviet leadership and Soviet citizens to the West as often as possible, and likewise to have American officials and citizens visit Russia. Mutual knowledge does not guarantee deep friendship, but the process of striving for better relations—over all the obstacles that exist—can at least temper the mutual alienation that now endangers both sides.

Many years ago, Winston Churchill said "it is better to jaw-jaw than to war-war." He was right then; and he remains right today. We need to be strong but we need also to be wise. That is the perennial challenge of American foreign policy. And it is the challenge we face anew today as we begin to shape our relationship with the new generation of Soviet leadership.

---

43. The U.S. and Revolution in Nicaragua

James H. Wolfe

Dr. Wolfe, International Affairs Editor of USA Today, *is professor of political science, University of Southern Mississippi, Hattiesburg.*

DECOLONIZATION, independence, and internal strife characterize the stages of development through which many emergent states have passed. Revolutionary turmoil historically has provided the impetus for political change, and the U.S. is not an exception. Both the War of Independence and the Civil War were armed struggles against an old order. Other nations have had parallel experience. The struggle for power between the center and the periphery frequently leads to internal warfare, as does the political assertion of class interests. Against the background of this historical awareness, why does the U.S. invariably encounter difficulty in adjusting to revolutionary regimes? In the contemporary world, the case of Nicaragua stands out.

During July, 1979, anti-government forces overthrew the dictatorship of Anastasio Somoza, whose family had ruled Nicaragua for two generations. The fighting was short and decisive, leaving the dictator to withdraw into an obscure exile. A transitional period of moderate rule followed, but within two years, the Sandinista movement had firmly secured all levels of power. In 1982, orchestrated elections resulted in the formation of a collective leadership, the principal figures of which are Pres. Daniel Ortega and Minister of the Interior Tomas Borge. Dissident fac-

Reprinted from *USA TODAY*, 114, no. 2488 (January, 1986), 9. Copyright © 1986 by Society for the Advancement of Education.

tions under the umbrella label of "contras" continue to wage a guerrilla war in the remote border regions of the country, but their military potential remains unclear. Initially supported by the U.S., the guerrillas faced a setback in May, 1984, when Congress voted to halt military—as opposed to humanitarian—assistance. A year later, both Democrats and Republicans on Capital Hill reversed themselves in the aftermath of Ortega's mission to Moscow, and they reinstated military aid.

During 1985, Pres. Reagan exercised his authority under the export Administration Act to impose an embargo on U.S. trade with Nicaragua. This action merely accelerated the decline in commercial relations between the two countries. In the past five years, the volume of trade has declined from $410,000,000 to $168,000,000. The resort to economic pressure to effect a change in policy is, however, questionable in both an international legal and political sense. The impact of the embargo, for example, has resulted in a diversification of the Nicaraguan economy, and therefore reduced its dependence on the outside world. Improvisation and austerity programs have proven to be effective defenses against external pressure.

Internally, the embargo gave the Sandinista regime an opportunity to tighten its control under the slogan of national unity in the face of foreign intervention. Critics of the government must now face the charge of sedition. Externally, other countries have moved quickly to develop new markets and to solidify the links between themselves and the Sandinistas. Since 1979, Brazil, Bulgaria, Cuba, East Germany, France, Libya, Mexico, Spain, and the Soviet Union have provided an estimated $1,700,000,000 in assistance to counterbalance the loss of credits from the World Bank and the phasing out of programs by the Agency for International Development.

Of particular interest is the role of multinational corporations. Exxon has a refinery in Nicaragua, which continues to function on the basis of spare parts imported from Mexico. Nevertheless, the embargo has had

its effect. Among those hardest hit are producers in the private agricultural sector. Approximately 80% of meat production remains in private hands, and this commodity constitutes the second largest export to the U.S. Private farmers in need of replacement parts for American-manufactured equipment face a dilemma. Meanwhile, the Japanese have again demonstrated their alertness to new trade opportunities.

A series of military events in neighboring Honduras provides a background to the embargo. Following Ortega's April, 1985, visit to Eastern Europe, reports circulated in Washington of a possible interventionist act. Borge responded in that his security forces were ready to react with vengeance against those Nicaraguans sympathetic to the interventionists. Similarly, Minister of Defense Humberto Ortega warned that thousands in Central America would take up arms in defense of the revolution. Meanwhile, U.S. military experts disagree sharply in their estimates of the force required to overcome organized resistance—a month and 60,000 men represent a minimum. Others suggest the possibility of a much longer war involving a substantially greater military commitment. European governments would probably dissociate themselves from this operation, with the result that the political gains would not approach the military costs of the operation.

The difficulty in charting U.S. policy is that it resembles a pendular movement. Years of neglect were followed by intense involvement, which may give way to disengagement born of frustration. An apparent instability to cope with the processes of political change and the need to revise policies accordingly have led successive administrations to opt for decisive action, rather than pursuing a policy of watchful waiting combined with humanitarian aid. Despite such provocations as Sandinista assistance to guerrillas in El Salvador, an excessive response to revolutionary acts may result in terror, and thereby strengthen the possibility of extremists in a society whose stability should be the goal of U.S. Policy.

44.   The Paradox of Nonalignment

Nicholas G. Onuf

Author of *Law and the Global Community* and other works. N. G. Onuf is Professor of International Relations at the American University School of International Service in Washington, D.C. and also teaches at Columbia University and Johns Hopkins University.

Throughout its history, nonalignment has been represented two ways, as a policy born of principle and as a movement. Characteristically the policy and the movement are assumed to be related—the policy informs the movement, giving it coherence, while the movement is the vehicle for the policy's expression. Ordinary usage separates policy and movement for conceptual purposes and links them for descriptive ones. If the exact nature of the connection remains unexamined, it is because no one finds it problematic. Yet the words themselves suggest otherwise.

Policies are typically produced by governments or other institutions which have among their tasks the translation of principles into programs of action. Policies guide this translation. The circumstances in which they do so are normally highly structured; fixed roles and routines prevail. Such settings allow for the production of policies responsive to changing demands in principle and adjusted to the changing modalities of implementation. Indeed it is somewhat misleading to speak of a policy process when structural considerations are so clearly paramount.

The association of policy with rules and roles, institutions and organizations, of high specificity and permanence, for which governments are indeed paradigms, connotes a Classical view of politics. Contractarian theories of obligation and order, rights as procedural guarantees, separation and balanc-

This essay is printed, in part, for the first time in this edition.

ing of power and responsibility—all of these are features of politics in a Classical mode, revived from Greco-Roman civic practices and rationalized in the Enlightenment. By discriminating between public and private realms, restricting most people's participation in public life to occasional formal acts like voting, and ultimately equating politics with government, the Classical view stabilizes, then constrains and finally suppresses politics. This is but one of many paradoxes. The ascendancy of the state is at once politics at its most distilled, the very essence of politics, and the denial of politics in favor of principles, policies and programs.

Rousseau, the French Revolution and the rise of national consciousness—all reactions to rationalism and the confinement of politics to the state—confronted Classicism with an alternative, Romantic sensibility, which finds expression in the language of process, change and growth. It depends on organic metaphors, while the Classical mind prefers mechanical ones. Romantics like motion, but not in the Newtonian sense of motion governed by firm, invariant laws and always predictable. They see it as movement, spontaneous and unpredictable.

We are all familiar with the importance and vitality of Romanticism in the artistic and literary culture of the Nineteenth Century, and its persistence into our own day. From its beginning the arena for Romantic politics has been the struggle against foreign domination. The Greek independence movement over a century and a half ago became the paradigmatic instance. An authentically national movement triumphed with attention and help from Romantic intellectuals. Ever since, struggles for independence have been, necessarily and appropriately, deeply Romantic. Intellectuals, many of them literary figures, learned Romantic politics in imperial centers, found themselves alienated and radicalized, and returned home. They practiced their politics and became vectors of disaffection. Movements emerged. . . .

Decolonization is one of the great Romantic triumphs of human history, as inevitable as it was unexpected in its scope and intensity. Liberation leaders personified the romance of the struggle. They gave meaning to sacrifice, turned rage from within to without, instilled pride. They emboldened the oppressed. When these leaders met in Bandung, they were already legends. Merely for them to be together was a legendary event. Their self-consciousness and solidarity made Bandung a creative act. If Bandung were a legendary act of creation, what issued was a global movement, melded from a series of local struggles. Until then, only those combatting what was underway had given it global meaning, reacting to it as dangerous and highly contagious disease, every outbreak of which was to be isolated and duly suppressed. To deny the psychological effects of being diseased and isolated, to reject them as conditions imposed by others' language and behavior; to assert instead the moral sickness of the standing order; to find strength in numbers, to see one cause, to affirm the vitality of one great movement—this is the legacy of Bandung.

What gives content to the movement is the world into which it is born. The world was, and remains, obdurately Classical. At first blush, this may seem a grossly inappropriate characterization. After all, two huge, dynamic countries, each with a Romantic sense of destiny and an extreme, even irrational hostility toward the other, stood ready to do apocalyptic battle. Yet if we look beyond the heat and baleful light of this situation, we find something quite different.

In the first place, nothing changes. The two powers remain inalterably opposed, unwilling to risk the costs either of winning or losing. In the second place, they have no great reason to countenance such risks and costs. In most respects, they like the world the way it is. Bipolarity freezes the global situation to their advantage, allowing them a tacitly coordinated policy of divide and rule roughly in proportion to their respective capabilities. In the third place, though this situation may be relatively easy to diagnose today, it has forty years of being in place. At the time of Bandung, it worked no differently, but it was considerably better disguised as the passionate rhetoric and skittish behavior of the participants. The Cold War has always been a spectacle the proportions of which obscure the fact that there has never been anything political about it. Politics could be inferred from the static situation in which the spectacle was presented, but could not be seen in its staging. In the best Classical manner, politics is in the hands of those few individuals whose positions enable them to speak to and for large passive audiences—the "publics," East and West—while they privatize power and distribute privilege for their benefactors and themselves, their cohorts in friendly or dependent countries, and even their publics as a reward for pliancy.

If this is a proper picture of the world at the time of Bandung, nonalignment is the only conceivable policy for members of the new movement to adopt. It is, after all, a world of no real movement. Any sign of movement is a threat to this static reality and therefore liable to suppression. Nonalignment as a policy coopts a Classical strategem, which is to contain any new movement. By containing themselves, weak, new countries avoid provoking either of the Classically oriented great powers into acting. Lacking excuses for more aggressive policies, these adversaries are content to view each other as contained, and act accordingly by not acting against anyone.

Nonalignment as self-containment resembles the rationale for protecting an infant industry in a world of competition. The infant movement, merely to survive, must erect barriers against others' opportunistic activities. As long as these barriers hold, the movement need not face a harsh world, but then it is prevented from fulfilling its Romantic presumption that it must grow, not merely survive, so as to be able to change the world into which it has come. This is the greatest paradox of nonalignment. The nonaligned movement is Romantic in origin and ambition. The policy of nonalignment is a Classical response to threat, alien to the movement it must protect. Were the movement stronger, it could use the Romantic policy of engagement to advantage. For a brief interval, a decade ago, oil seemed to provide the needed strength and engagement ensued. The decade since is a painful reminder that the movement is indeed too weak to forego the protection of self-containment.

As we all know, some infant industries fail to grow. Instead they become a privileged beneficiary of a system rigged to keep anybody's share of benefits from changing. The problem for the nonaligned movement is identical. By protecting itself, does not the movement succumb to the presumption that nothing changes, that its modest perch on the fringe of the status quo is the best that ever can be hoped for, and that containment, since it is generalized for the world, is not only tolerable but, as the passage of time reveals, even appropriate? Movements with no movement have died, their skeletons remaining as fixtures in the standing order.

A paradox need not eventuate in paralysis. Indeed the paradox presents itself as a problem for the movement, but problems can have solutions. The problem for the nonaligned movement is to create a sense of movement, and thus of vitality and the promise of a future, notwithstanding the static consequences of the standing order. Nor can this be merely a matter of illusion. Proclaiming that one is ready to spring into action at a moment's notice does not prevent sclerosis—any stance hardens if it is maintained too long. There must be movement to keep up the sense of movement.

One possibility is to find sheltered spots in which to move. The most obvious, propitious location is the United Nations, an arena within which, after all, nonaligned countries have real advantages. Movement here takes the form of parliamentary maneuvre, fostered by the need to draft resolutions and form winning coalitions for their passage in the General Assembly. That this maneuvering is repeated with infinite minor variation year after year, and that it affords the opportunity for engagement on safe terms, makes it an appealing strategy for the nonaligned. In effect the United Nations is a playground for the youthful members of the movement to learn their political skills and test their strength. Yet the paradoxes of the depoliticization of public places and the perpetuation of infancy operate here. Either nonaligned countries restrain themselves, in which case their behavior becomes part of the public spectacle devoid of meaning; or they behave rambunctiously enough to make the keepers of the standing order close down the facility. Faced with these choices, the nonaligned become dutiful children even on their own ground.

This not to say that some important testing and learning does not take place in the United Nations. To the extent the nonaligned movement operates as if it were a parliamentary party, it has made the most of its possibilities. A party is of course a special kind of movement, one that accepts the requirement of internal discipline for successful achievement of objectives, and defines those objectives by reference to the parliamentary situation. Put in this way, any such learning is of doubtful value. The long-term cost of internal discipline is institutionalization of the movement, typically in the form of a leadership apparatus. Such an apparatus represents consolidation of control and the opportunity to sell out to the standing order.

The cost of defining objectives by reference to the parliamentary situation is a more subtle one. It assumes that important resources and opportunities for control reside in that setting. Clearly this is not the case with the United Nations. Or it posits the existence of a similar situation outside the organization, in some larger arena of world politics, in which the skills and strengths of a party can be used to good effect. It would seem though that this kind of learning is not transferable, because the larger world is not run on parliamentary premises, not even by the remotest analogy. That the United Nations was made in liberal-constitutional self-image of the United States does not mean that the United States trusts that model in hands other than its own. Even less does its partner-antagonist on the world scene, the Soviet Union.

To harness the movement's energy for parliamentary purposes is probably a good way to use the protected circumstances offered by the United Nations to sustain the movement in the short run. But time is the enemy of this policy: time springs the traps of depoliticized spectacle and permanent infancy, or proves the policy's irrelevance to the larger world of Classical order and control. The worst outcome is a party in which institutionalization compensates for lack of a plausible program and place to pursue it.

The alternative to movement in a hostile, highly structured world, or in its protected but irrelevant margins, is movement within the movement. It is gratifying to note that the movement has indeed taken substantial advantage of this important possibility. The motive force for internal movement is the periodic summit. The availability of fast, convenient transportation and the possibility of focusing attention on themselves induce leaders to expend increasing shares of their time and attention on these periodic peer meetings. Yet the parade of summits is a phenomenon of contemporary international relations to which scholars have devoted remarkably little attention. It would be wrong, however, to dismiss these occasions because nothing of consequence is decided at them. From the point of view of the standing order, their most striking and successfully exploited feature is their apparent frivolity, which masks the private preserve of politics in the name of politics for public consumption.

Misdirection is not the only possible function of periodic summits. They foster a cycle of work and preparation, just as do five-year economic plans, regular elections and annual budgets. This cycle of activity imposes itself as much on a highly organized bureaucracy as it does on a movement, but with a particular benefit for the latter. It fosters discipline and a sense of direction in the absence of organizational routines. So long as pressure to centralize preparatory activity is resisted, the summit cycle can substitute for a permanent bureaucracy, leaving the movement mobile but not drifting. Furthermore, summitry supplies participants and audiences both with a succession of psychologically important states of mind: initiation, endeavor, accomplishment, relief and reflection. To put the matter metaphorically, summitry involves a phase of engagement and commitment comparable to moving uphill, a phase of triumph and catharsis at the top, and a phase of return and disengagement.

The very language of summitry invokes a meaningful and satisfying kind of activity—people like to climb mountains and gain significant therapeutic value from doing so. To argue the irrationality of making a strenuous effort to go up mountains for the fleeting opportunity of being at the top and the illusion of seeing all (the way up, the way down, the ways not taken), only to have to come down, misses the point. People do it for the sake of having done so, for the moment at the top, for the changes in their feelings. They do so on grounds that are deeply Romantic; they disavow any Classical requirement of proportionality in justifying their behavior. To the extent that summitry reaffirms the Romantic core of the nonaligned movement and provides a sense of movement which is neither pointless or Classically proportioned, it serves the movement well.

Summits have points—that is the point. . . .

Indeed a review of the Final Acts of each Summit from Belgrade in 1961 to New Delhi in 1983 shows just such shifts which, along with the steadily growing number of topics subject to discussion, prompt a genuine sense of movement. Certainly all those who are steeped in the movement's history—including especially the nonaligned leadership—must appreciate the pattern of shifting emphases over the years and respond to them as real and meaningful movement.

If we use the Final Communique of the Bandung Conference as a baseline, we find an emphasis on economic development through North-South cooperation and on cultural cooperation among nonaligned countries. The connection between economic cooperation for development and nonalignment in principle, though ambiguous and possibly contradictory, is left undeveloped. While cultural cooperation draws from and supports the solidarity of the nonaligned world, it is given no "political" purpose, such as to promote self-reliance. To the extent the Classical order makes politics impossible or illusory, any attempt on the part of the nonaligned to articulate and effectuate a policy like self-reliance, which we do find twenty years later, must be devoid of political meaning. Nevertheless we are obliged to speak of politics in such a policy context for lack of another term any less paradoxical in its implications.

Although nonalignment was the principle animating the conferees at Bandung, it was not yet recognizable as a policy. The Declaration of the Belgrade Summit voiced an important change in these terms. Now the emphasis was on decolonization and the identification of a series of problem areas. Nonalignment thus acquired two distinct policy orientations. One linked nonalignment with decolonization, so as to provide nonalignment with the raw material of its existence, namely, new nonaligned countries. That the Soviet Union was able to identify itself with the revolutionary struggle against colonialism had the effect of pulling the policy of nonalignment away from the impartial position implied in principle. That the United States and its allies represented a greater threat to the principle by virtue of their superior power, globally deployed, and colonially imposed cultural affinities, made this policy "deviation" necessary from the nonaligned point of view.

The second policy orientation acquired at Belgrade was to articulate the substance of nonalignment by reference to such specific trouble spots as Algeria, the Congo and Guantanamo. The formulation of grievances is of course the obvious way to make policies out of principle, especially when colonialism is the common grievance. To the extent that these particular trouble spots disappear, policies would seem to be successful and movement achieved. Other problem areas like apartheid, Palestine or the German question are harder to frame as matters of decolonization and imply policies less easily reconciled with the principle of nonalignment. The Belgrade conferees also declared their concern for the latter sort of problems, understandably enough, even though movement on them could hardly have been expected. . . .

The latest in this series of Summits was held in New Delhi. 1983 was a year of severe tension and sense of crisis. Quite appropriately, the New Delhi Political and Economic Declarations drew attention to global crises of arms escalation, debt and depression, assigned responsibility to the aligned, and exhorted them to act on these crises. At best exhortation is a weak policy but perhaps the only one available in times as desperate as these. The detailed coverage of specific problems and issues, by now a fully developed catalogue in Summit declarations, failed to disguise the lack of any coherent policy orientation, either politically or economically, and the corresponding lack of direction the nonaligned movement currently displays. . . .

45. The Future of Détente

John Lewis Gaddis

A leading exponent of the idea that historians should comment upon current affairs, John Lewis Gaddis is Distinguished Professor of History at Ohio University.

One of the occupational hazards of being a historian is that one tends to take on, with age, a certain air of resigned pessimism. This comes, I think, from our professional posture of constantly facing backwards: it is not cheering to have to focus one's attention on the disasters, defalcations, and miscalculations that make up human history. We are given, as a result, to such plaintive statements as: "Ah, yes, I knew it wouldn't work out," or "I saw it coming all along," or, most often, "Too bad they didn't listen to me."

Such, I am afraid, is the tone we historians have taken in looking at the last decade or so of Soviet-American relations. Détente, we now tell each other, was not an end to cold war tensions but rather a temporary relaxation that depended upon the unlikely intersection of unconnected phenomena. There had to be, we argue, approximate parity in the strategic arms race, a downplaying of ideological differences, a mutual willingness to refrain from challenging the interests of rivals, an ability to reward restraint when it occurred and to provide inducements to its further development, and the existence of strong, decisive and intelligent leadership at the top in both Washington and Moscow, capable of overriding all of the obstacles likely to be thrown in the path of détente by garbled communications,

Excerpted from "The Rise, Fall and Future of Détente," *Foreign Affairs*, 62, no. 1, (Winter 1983–4), 354–377. Reprinted by permission. Copyright © 1954 by the Council on Foreign Relations, Inc. (Footnotes have been deleted.)

sullen bureaucracies, or outraged constituencies. To have found all of these things in place at the same time, we maintain, was about as likely as some rare astronomical conjunction of the stars and planets, or perhaps a balanced budget.

As a result, we have tended to see the revival of the cold war as an entirely predictable development rooted in deep and immutable historical forces. Those of us who hedged our bets about the durability of détente can now comfortably pat each other on the back, exchanging statements like: "We were right all along," or "Too bad they don't listen to historians," or "Isn't pessimism fun?"

But if historians are ever going to provide much in the way of usable guidance to policymakers—which is to say, if we are not going to leave the field wide open to the political scientists—then we are going to have to address not only questions of what went wrong, but of what might have been done differently. Were there things that could have been done to avoid the collapse of détente? Might these provide a basis for reconstituting it—perhaps in a more durable form—at some point in the future?

. . . the failure of détente grew in large part out of its never having been fully implemented: that significant components of that strategy—components critical to its success—were never really put into effect. Let me illustrate this point by discussing three areas: linkage, the military balance, and human rights.

(1) Linkage

The objective here was to try to change Soviet behavior through a process of positive and negative reinforcement: Russian actions consistent with our interests would be rewarded; those of which we disapproved would in some way be punished. But this implied a clear and consistent view of what American interests were, and of the extent to which Soviet behavior either enhanced or undercut them. That clear vision, in turn, implied central control over the linkage process: one could not divide authority and still expect coherent strategy.

But division of authority is precisely what occurred. The late Senator Henry Jackson and his congressional colleagues torpedoed the 1972 Soviet-American trade agreement by requiring increased rates of Jewish emigration before credits and most-favored nation treatment would be provided—this despite the fact that the agreement itself had been intended as a reward for Soviet cooperation on Berlin, SALT, the Middle East and Vietnam. Later on, others outside the Administration took it upon themselves to decide where in the Third World the Russians should have shown restraint in return for the favors we had provided them, or to what extent they should have cut back on military expenditures, or what internal changes they would have to make in order for the negotiating process to continue.

Now it is probable that the Administration overestimated from the beginning what linkage could accomplish. The Russians made it quite clear that they would feel free to continue competition in Third World areas; moreover, as Kissinger later acknowledged at least with respect to Vietnam, the Administration may have exaggerated its degree of control in such areas in the first place. Still, a final assessment on the principle of linkage cannot be made because the Administration was never allowed to define precisely what was to be linked to what, or to deliver the rewards it had promised in return for cooperative behavior.

(2) The Military Balance

Détente was, as we have seen, an approach to containment based on the perception of diminishing military means, these having declined as a result of the Vietnam War. The idea had been to attempt to constrain the Russians without further constraining ourselves. In the field of strategic weapons, Nixon and Kissinger accomplished their objectives with remarkable success: they managed to convince the Russians that they needed a SALT agreement more than we did, despite the fact that the agreement actually negotiated limited weapons programs only Moscow was likely to pursue. What is not often recognized about SALT I is that Nixon and Kissinger had intended to couple it with a military buildup of their own in areas not restricted by the agreement—notably, the B1 bomber, the Trident submarine, and the MX and cruise missiles.

But again, this could not be done without congressional approval, and once more the problem of divided authority came into play. Senator Jackson again imposed his priorities on the negotiating process, this time with a demand for across-the-board numerical equivalence in strategic weapons systems, despite the fact that the military had never sought, and Congress would never have authorized, building programs to reach those equivalencies. Vietnam had brought anti-military sentiment on Capitol Hill to an unprecedented intensity; there grew out of this a corrosive skepticism toward all government pronouncements on defense needs—including its warnings, now known to have been conservative, on the extent of the post-SALT Soviet military buildup. As a result, strategic modernization programs that Nixon, Kissinger, and Secretary of Defense Melvin Laird had intended to accompany the SALT I agreement were seriously delayed; more seriously, in order to get even these scaled-back appropriations through Congress, the Administration had to make significant cutbacks in conventional forces as well.

The consequence of this is something still

not fully appreciated to this day: that the Nixon and Ford administrations presided over the most dramatic reallocation of resources from defense to domestic purposes in modern American history. Defense spending as a percentage of total national budget had dropped from 44 percent at the time Richard Nixon took office in 1969 to 24 percent by the time Gerald Ford left it in 1977. Defense spending as a percentage of gross national product went from 8.7 percent in 1969 to 5.2 percent in 1977. To be sure, some reduction in military spending would have occurred in any event as the Vietnam War came to an end. But reductions on this scale clearly exceeded what the two administrations wanted, or what, in retrospect, can be considered to have been wise, in view of what we now know of Soviet military spending during the same period. If, in the case of linkage, the carrots Washington had intended to use to make détente work had been held back, now, in the military field, so too had been the sticks.

(3) Human Rights

One of the grounds upon which the strategy of détente was most criticized was that it ignored the moral dimension of foreign policy. The United States could not expect to have its views prevail in the world, the argument ran, if those views were at variance with the deepest and most fundamental principles for which the nation was supposed to stand. Only by abandoning strategies based solely on considerations of power could the United States achieve the respect it needed both at home and abroad if its policies were to succeed. . . .

[Nevertheless] *containment** will no doubt remain the central focus of our strategy in world affairs for some years to come. The Soviet Union shows no signs of contenting itself with the existing distribution of power in the world; experience certainly should have

*Italics provided, Editor.

taught us by now that our capacity to moderate Moscow's ambitions by any means other than some fairly crude combination of sticks and carrots is severely limited. Still, there are a few things we might learn from our experience with containment to this point; things any future administration might do well to keep in mind as it seeks to devise strategies for dealing with the Russians.

(1) One is precisely how little we have learned from the past. We have shifted back and forth between the polarities of limited means and unlimited interests—between the risks of discrimination and the excesses that flow from its absence—having to learn each time the problems with each approach, oblivious, for the most part, to the possibility that we might do better with less dramatic swings of the geopolitical pendulum. Has the time not come to attempt to build into our policy-formulation process some sense of what has gone before, and at least of what elementary conclusions might be derived from it? There are various ways in which this might be accomplished: one might establish a permanent nonpartisan staff for the National Security Council, the only key policymaking body in this field that does not now have one; one might draw in a more formal and systematic capacity than is now done upon the expertise of retired presidents, national security advisors, secretaries of state and other experienced "elder" statesmen; one might even take the drastic step of encouraging high officials actually to read history themselves from time to time. The point would be to get away from our amnesiac habit of periodically re-inventing the wheel; after all, the general shape of that device is reasonably well understood and may not need to be rethought with each revolution.

(2) A second and related priority should be to insulate our long-term external concerns from our short-term internal preoccupations: no single deficiency in our approach to strategy and diplomacy causes us more grief than its subordination to the volatile and irresponsible whims of domestic politics. As a historian, and therefore some-

thing of a skeptic about the possibilities of human perfection, I cannot be very optimistic about achieving this. Indeed, the trend, in recent years, has been in just the other direction, toward the more frequent and more flagrant intrusion of politics into national security issues, and toward longer and longer periods of time required to repair the damage. No other great nation in the history of the world has fallen into the curious habit of re-thinking its foreign policy at quadrennial intervals to meet the anticipated desires of a particular small and snowy northern province, or one chiefly noted for the production of corn and pigs. A compression and rationalization of our presidential selection procedures would help remove these temptations; so too would a return to the tradition of bipartisan consultation on controversial foreign policy questions, a direction in which the Reagan Administration quite wisely is moving. What is really needed, though, is a change in our standards of political decorum: if we could get to the stage at which it would be as unacceptable to play politics with critical issues of foreign and national security policy as it has now become to joke about women and minorities from public platforms, then we would be well along the way toward solving this problem. But not until then.

(3) At the same time, there should be a greater and more deliberate effort made to relate national security policy to the national economy. We should never again succumb to the illusion that means are infinite, and that therefore the ends of strategy can be formulated quite independently of them. Means in fact will always be limited in some way; the art of strategy consists largely of adjusting desirable ends to fit available means. The Vietnam experience ought to have taught us that no nation can sustain a defense policy that wrecks its economy or deranges its polity; we need to recapture Eisenhower's insight that there is no more critical foundation for national strength than the national consensus that underlies it.

(4) We could also learn to be more precise about just what it is we are out to contain. Is the adversary the Soviet Union? Is it the world communist movement? Is it the great variety of non-communist Marxist movements that exist throughout the world? Surely in an era in which we rely upon the world's most populous communist state to help contain the world's most powerful communist state, in an era when some of our best friends are socialists, there can be little doubt about the answer to this question. And yet, as our current policy in Central America and the Caribbean shows, we persist in lumping together the Soviet Union, international communism, and non-communist Marxism in the most careless and imprecise manner— to what end? It is a fundamental principle of strategy that one should never take on any more enemies than necessary at any given point. But we seem to do it all the time.

(5) It follows from this that we could also make greater use than we do of our friends. Most other nations heartily endorse our goal of a world safe for diversity; few, given the choice, would align themselves with the quite different goals of the Russians. Nationalism, in short, works for us rather than against us. And yet, we seem to go out of our way, at times, to alienate those who would cooperate in the task of containment. The blank check we have extended to the Israelis over the years—however useful in producing occasional grudging concessions on their part— has nonetheless impaired our ability to make common cause with the other nations of the Middle East whose interests we largely share: that the Russians have been able to take so little advantage of this situation is more a testimony to their ineptitude than to our wisdom. Our support for Taiwan for years prevented any exploitation of the Sino-Soviet split, and to this day retains the potential for weakening our very important relationship with mainland China. Our attitude toward white minority regimes in southern Africa has not always been best calculated to win us influence in the rest of that continent, most of whose leaders emphatically share our desire to keep the Russians out. Recently we

even went out of our way to alienate some of our closest European allies by imposing a set of sanctions on the Soviet Union that no one thought would work, while at the same time, and for the sake of a domestic constituency, withholding another more potent set of sanctions (on grain) that might have. Containment would function more efficiently if others shared some of the burden of containing. And yet, we sometimes seem to make that difficult.

(6) Another trick that would make containment work better would be to take advantage, to a greater extent than we have, of the Russians' chronic tendency to generate resistance to themselves. This is one reason why Moscow has not been able to exploit the opportunities we have handed them in the Middle East and Africa; it is why they have such difficulty consolidating opportunities they have taken advantage of themselves, as in Afghanistan. It is a cliché, by now, to describe the Soviet Union as the last great imperial power; what is not a cliché, but rather one of the more reliable "lessons" to be drawn from the admittedly imprecise discipline of history, is that imperial powers ultimately wind up containing themselves through the resistance they themselves provoke. Nothing could be clearer than that this is happening to the Russians today, and yet we seem not to take it much into account in framing our policies. We should.

(7) It would also help if we would cool the rhetoric. The current Administration is hardly the first to engage in verbal overkill, but the frequency and vividness of its excesses in this regard surely set some kind of record. The President has informed us that Jesus—not Kennan—was the original architect of containment. The Vice President has recently criticized not only Soviet but Tsarist Russia for arrested cultural development, pointing out (with some historic license) that country took no part in the Renaissance, the Reformation or the Englightenment; this would appear to be the diplomatic equivalent of saying: "Yeah, and so's your old man!" These are childish, but not innocent, pleasures. They demean those who engage in them, and therefore dignify the intended target. They obscure the message: how many people will recall Ambassador Charles Lichenstein's eloquent and amply deserved condemnation of the Korean airliner atrocity once he had coupled it with his offer to stand on the docks, waving goodbye to the United Nations? That the Russians themselves have long been masters of the art of invective is no reason to try to emulate them; this is one competition in which we can safely allow their preeminence.

(8) Finally, and in this connection, we should keep in mind the ultimate objectives of containment. That strategy was and still should be the means to a larger end, not an end in itself. It should lead to something; otherwise, like any strategy formulated without reference to policy, it is meaningless. There is a tendency in this country to let means become ends, to become so preoccupied with processes that one loses sight of the goal those processes were supposed to produce. We have been guilty of that to some extent with containment; we have missed in the past and are probably today still missing opportunities to manage, control, and possibly resolve many of our disagreements with the Russians, apparently out of fear that such contacts might weaken the public's resolve to support containment. But that is getting things backward. The original idea of containment was ultimately to facilitate, not impede, the attainment of a less dangerous international order. It would not be a bad idea—from the point of view of everybody's interests—to get back to that concept.

epilogue

THE STATE OF THE FIELD

Editor's note:

It seems appropriate in place of the usual Introductory Text and Discussion Questions, to open the finale of this edition with some not-so-blank verse, which, while penned a quarter-century ago, still captures the contradictions in rhetoric and power in today's world. Burt Marshall is one of the most respected foreign affairs analysts in Washington, having written The Limits of Foreign Policy (1954) and other books, served on the policy planning staff of the U.S. Department of State and taught as a professor at the School of Advanced International Studies of The Johns Hopkins University.

46. Observations on the State of the World

Jeopardy multiplies. Concord is near.
The balance of terror means freedom from fear.
War is outdated. Convergence will bring
An end to all rancor. Détente is the thing.

Détente is a trap. To be candid and terse,
The Western Alliance is doomed to disperse.
The Communist purpose, adroitly concealed,
Is to pick up the pieces and conquer the field.

The issues dividing the Communist realm
As Peking and Moscow contend for the helm
Will succor mankind from a nuclear brink.
The Reds aren't red—only pleasantly pink.

Hail to peace, and a pox on the nuclear curse!
A protracted Cold War would surely grow worse.
Détente is our hope, the Alliance our shield.
So don't give an inch. Come to terms. Never yield.

Keep vigil globally. Stay in our yard.
Mend our defenses, and lower our guard.
Upright in leadership, prone to defer—
Equally vow to contest and concur.

Giving the back of our hand to our friends.
Proffer the foeman the palm of amends.
Tough on antagonists, kind to allies—
Strengthen connections while weakening ties.

Umbrellas in hand and our banners aloft—
True to a creed unrelenting and soft—
Cleave to mobility. Follow the trend
Flexibly fixed toward a nebulous end.

Pledges evaporate. Treaties abort.
Mutable statemanship summons support
For structures of comity vaunted to last.
The redesigned future will mimic the past.

Charles Burton Marshall, 1962.

Printed by permission of the author, Charles Burton
Marshall, 1986.

47. The Study of "I.R.": How It Developed

William C. Olson and Nicholas G. Onuf

N. G. Onuf is Professor of International Relations at the School of International Service and has also taught at Columbia and Johns Hopkins universities; William C. Olson is a Visiting Fellow at the Royal Institute of International Affairs in London and has served as director of the Rockefeller Foundation Study Center at Villa Serbelloni in Italy. He has just completed seven years as Dean of the School of International Service of the American University in Washington, D.C.

> Yet the fact remains that Mr. [Woodrow] Wilson (because of the rude precisions of the Jusserand Memorandum) and Mr. Lloyd George (in view of his amazing predilection for the unexpected) both rejected, and indeed resented, any written formulation of what, or how, or when, they were supposed to discuss. The effects of this disinclination on their part were deplorable in the extreme.
>
> Harold Nicolson *Peacemaking 1919* (Boston, Houghton Mifflin Co.: 1933) p. 103

The late Sir Harold's devastating conclusion contains a lesson obviously less related to the respective British and American nationalities of the two statesmen than to his enlightened despair about preparation for the intelligent discussion of international affairs after the First World War. If half the motivation for developing a new kind of study was the preservation of peace (which has not been achieved), surely the other half arose from recognition of the need for a different approach to the organization and understanding of knowledge about the relations of states (which has been achieved). At a time when the future of humanity seemed to depend upon mastery of the subject, the ways in which international rela-

Excerpted by permission from "The Growth of a Discipline: Reviewed" pp. 1–18 in *International Relations: British and American Perspectives* (Oxford: Basil Blackwell Inc., 1985) edited by Steve Smith. Copyright © British International Studies Association, 1985.

tions had hitherto been analyzed proved inadequate. A new discipline was born because it had to be. . . .

What are teachers of International Relations now trying to accomplish? Are they working to advance the field through their students, or aiming for something quite contradictory to that incremental intellectual process, satisfying the state by producing civil servants and diplomats to pursue its national objectives? Or have they yet another purpose: serving the cause of peace or other cosmopolitan values? These are all very different aims, and they cannot be made one merely be asserting that the intention is to produce diplomats as well as scholars, and enlarged awareness in everyone. . . .

What indeed is a discipline? Though some regard it as unimportant, this question continues to be a matter for considerable debate. Here, the distinction must be made between 'discipline' in the formal sense, implying a subject with particular characteristics that distinguish it from others, and the more informal interpretation that suggests the systematic study of subject-matter, with or without the 'credentials' of separateness. One can go back to Machiavelli for an attempt to be systematic in the way one looks at social phenomena (indeed, Georg Schwarzenberger of the University of London once characterized him as 'the founder' of the science of international relations) but if one seeks to delineate the features of this discipline which are distinct—fundamentally distinct—from those of other social science subjects, it is not only difficult to do so but controversial as well.

Harry Howe Ransom has suggested what some of these distinguishing points *ought to be:* first of all, a distinct subject-matter; secondly, agreed-upon abstractions or models; thirdly, concepts uniquely adapted to the analysis of international behavior; fourthly, a specialized vocabulary, with precise definitions; fifthly, standardized analytical methods allowing re-testing or replication of initial analysis; and finally, a central system for cataloguing, evaluating and communicating research and its results. One might usefully take these criteria and examine how far specialist work in International Relations and the other social sciences meet these requirements. Such a dual test might reveal a set of characteristics shared by all social sciences, with distinctions between particular subjects being less significant than is commonly thought. It may be true that criticisms made of International Relations as a discipline can to some degree be levelled at other disciplines as well. International Relations might therefore more profitably be regarded as an 'inter-discipline.' This would concede that, while such study may not qualify as a separate subject, it does reflect an increasingly coherent orientation which integrates the contributions of the other social sciences in a special way.

Definitions of International Relations may provide more clues to growth than debates about the term 'discipline,' especially if one examines representative definitions, in their briefest and most fundamental forms, over the period since International Relations began to emerge as a separate subject sixty-five years ago. At the outset, a book appeared which presented a novel organization of existing knowledge, *Diplomacy and the Study of International Relations* (1919), by D. P. Heatley, lecturer in history at Edinburgh. Admitting that 'history does not give much encouragement to the promulgators of schemes of Perpetual Peace,' Heatley divided his book into sections on diplomatic history, international law and ethics, but made no attempt to define the term 'international relations.' In 1922, however, James Bryce provided the simple statement in the opening pages of his *International Relations* that he was dealing with 'the relations of States and peoples to one another.' By 1944 Grayson Kirk and Walter Sharp declared that their purpose in preparing *Contemporary International Politics* was to 'explore and examine those fundamental forces which in the authors' view are most responsible for the motivation of foreign policy, schematically considered.' Ten years later, Hans J. Morgenthau and Kenneth W. Thompson, in the book *Principles and Problems of International Politics*, argued that the 'core of international relations is international politics, and . . . the subject matter of international politics is struggle for power among sovereign nations.' In *Contemporary Theory in International Relations* (1960), Stanley Hoffmann asserted that 'the discipline of international relations is concerned with the factors and the activities which affect the external policies and power of the basic units into which the world is divided.' More recently, in writing of International Relations as a science, John Burton described its concern 'with observation and analysis, and with theorizing in order to explain and predict the operations and processes of relations between states, and of the world system as a whole.'

The differences and similarities between these definitions, which span a period of over forty years, are equally striking. One crucial distinction lies in references to the rationale for the study; whereas the earliest cite peace as the purpose, the latest seek rigorous procedures to achieve understanding. This is a profound change not because scholars today are less devoted to peace than their counterparts were fifty years ago, quite the contrary, but their devotion to peace is separate from their devotion to scholarship and now takes a different form. Whereas then there was hope of permanent and universal peace in a new order of international organization and law, there is now an acceptance of the likelihood of continued tension and uncertainty which a number of distinctive disciplined perspectives can perhaps comprehend but not change.

Does all this mean that despite its possible failure to gain recognition, International Relations has developed a certain orthodoxy? As early as the 1960s, Burton thought this was implicit in the discipline's preoccupation with state power and interest. In his attempt to evolve a general theory, he started with an inclusive definition of the discipline's subject matter. In keeping with this orientation, most writers today would agree with P. A. Reynolds's distinction between International Relations (which studies all 'boundary-crossing transactions of whatever nature among whatever units'), international politics (embracing 'behaviour of, and interactions among states'), and international studies (which contains 'both of these, but also all studies that would illuminate or have a bearing on them'). Evidently we have built a mansion with many rooms and expansive grounds.

Major Phases

Five overlapping phases of development seem to suggest themselves. The first was the historical phase, during which students endeavoured to explain how the present had been formed from the past. This was combined with a legalistic approach, which saw states increasingly implicated in a complex set of rules of their own devising. The First World War demonstrated the political as well as disciplinary limitations of historical and legalistic methods, not only for an understanding of international relations but also for their improvement. As C. K. Webster said in his inaugural lecture as Wilson Professor in the University College of Wales:

This is the first Chair of International Politics founded in this country, and though in other countries there are professors whose duties are akin to mine, there is no general acceptance of the principles of the study. Indeed, even if such principles had existed before the Great War, that event has so sapped the foundations of International order, and changed so remorselessly our conceptions of International Relations, that a recasting of our ideas would be necessary. But of course no ordered and scientific body of knowledge did exist in 1914. Perhaps, if it had, the catastrophe might have been averted; for its mere existence would have been proof that men were thinking about very different things than actually were occupying their attention.

The second phase was of organization, in which an emerging discipline had as its foundation the ordering of the world through the new international institutions resulting from the peace settlement at Versailles. This approach, in the face of the challenge to the League system by expansive dictatorships, gave way to a third phase, based on the analysis of great power interplay. During this exciting and disastrous period, military strategy, often within the context of the pseudo-science of geopolitics, came to fascinate many students of International Relations. After a brief return to another institutional phase, as the United Nations rose like a phoenix out of the ashes of the Second World War, a fourth phase developed, overshadowed by the cold war and colored by controversies over the place of ideology in the study of world politics. As the bipolar nature of this second post-war era appeared to dominate world politics, so did the language of 'realism'—of state power and interest—dominate public policy and scholarly discourse.

The mid-to-late 1950s marked a new phase of sanitized realism. The basic assumptions of realism—the autonomy of state actors, maximizing behavior in the name of national interest, necessary competition for scare values, concern for stability in a conflict-prone system—were not only unchallenged at this time, they were hidden from view amid claims that International Relations *could* have the value neutrality appropriate to the positivist frame then and (to a somewhat lesser degree) still prevalent in the social sciences. Value neutrality could obtain, that is, if the underlying concepts of International Relations could be rendered in a purely abstract form, if these abstractions were assembled into generalizations possessing the explanatory and predictive characteristics of powerful theories in natural science, and if suitable tests employing quantitative methods could be derived from the logical entailments of posited theoretical relationships. Apparently a discipline could only exist if it was based on science in the strictest sense of the term. To the extent that the first post-war generation of scholars weaned on Morgenthau (at least in the US) endorsed assumptions proper to realism, there was indeed a consensus that International Relations could aspire to standing as a discipline in its own right, as defined by science.

The realist 'paradigm,' as we have come now to call such consensual but largely unspoken agreements on theories giving meaning to day-to-day scholarly activities, assured those involved that their world of discourse was 'real' and important; that theoretical, empirical and policy-relevant work was justified under an informal division of labor; that cumulative knowledge, theoretically and procedurally grounded, spelled progress in the Enlightenment tradition that underlies all scientific and technological endeavor since the 'scientific revolution' of the sixteenth and

seventeenth centuries. Needless to say, the power of this view, which made International Relations a discipline as well as a vocation, exercised its greatest influence in the United States. Rapid expansion of the universities, the success of the German ideal of doctoral training and research so much reinforced by emigré professors like Morgenthau, and the willingness of US elites to accept, even to relish, the responsibilities of being the world's greatest power and promoter or peace and prosperity (an enduring dimension of the national psyche)—all these factors contributed to the rapid growth of International Relations and to its institutionalization during the 1950s and 1960s.

One fissure in the US consensus on a science-based, power-oriented International Relations was immediately observed; J. David Singer defined it as 'the level-of-analysis problem.' Macro-level, systemic thought, much influenced by sociology, and the micro-level behavioural work, influenced in its turn by psychology, might be defended as necessary and complementary aspects of a normal science paradigm, just as theory and experimental science constitute any discipline in the positivist mould. In practice, the quest for an underpinning theory on the one hand and the dogged pursuit of testable propositions on the other played on temperamental differences among individual scholars, emphasized methodological pluralism, highlighted the substantively fissiparous character of International Relations, and sorted scholars into seemingly hostile camps arranged on two sides of a great divide: systemic theory versus behavioural science.

The aridity of conceptual development for its own sake, the inflated nature of high theory claims, and epistemological challenges to the organic imagery of most systems-level thinking, condemned theory to an earlier eclipse than science. There are today few theorists working in the paradigmatic tradition, Kenneth Waltz and Robert Gilpin serving as lonely examples. Procedurally based science has fared better, if only because it can respond to criticism with plausible efforts to rectify procedural inadequacies. As to charges that it is nothing more than trivial, mindless empiricism, the safe reply is always that the shape of cumulative knowledge can only be seen retrospectively.

The deeper flaw in the realist/science paradigm was not discovered so readily. The realist position on power and interest, and the scientific value of detachment were called into question by the war in Vietnam. Yet revisionist historians and insurgent sociologists came to this realization first. International Relations, with its comparatively conservative frame of reference established by political science, only slowly responded to disquiet over the US role in the war, and then in a variety of ways.

Some scholars challenged the normative implications of realism, and called for a misnamed 'post-behavioral' phase that would restore concern for peace and world order to its central position. Peace research in the US tended to be much influenced by social psychology and its interest in frustration, aggression, misperception and cognitive distortion. Many European peace researchers, steeped in Marxism, were openly hostile to positivist science. Their willingness to brand America an imperial power alienated some US scholars even though they too had reservations about realism, struck others as rhetorical and inconsistent with the scholarly need for careful expression, and seeped into the consciousness of yet others, strengthening their incipient radical views. World order studies were rooted in a progressive legal-institutional tradition that most students of International Relations thought naive and unlikely to achieve its stated task of devising a plausible strategy for moving from the allegedly moribund 'war system' to a world order that optimized liberal and humane values. The diverse threads of these radical schools lacked a conceptual loom of the same scope and power as realism, and they were not brought together, even loosely, until the last few years.

Other scholars challenged the substantive assumptions of realism head-on. The importance of actors (multinational corporations, terrorists, religious faiths, ethnic groups, etc.) other than states was asserted. These assertions opened up the field of International Relations but cost the discipline its definition. The realist preoccupation with power, defined for all intents and purposes in military terms, was also challenged. A multiplicity of issue areas, with distinctive instruments of power and inhibitions on their use, replaced the homogeneous picture given by realism. Once this alternative view was acknowledged, it was easy to attack realism for underestimating the interdependence of states which had so many cross-cutting interests and constraints on the free use of their power in all arenas.

Arguably, these challenges to realism constituted a revival of the Anglo-American liberal tradition of functionalist and legal-institutionalist thought, cleansed of excessive faith in universal institutions like the League, and adapted to the complex, bureaucratically defined features of contemporary international life. In Britain, there was a corresponding revival of interest in David Mitrany's work and admiration of John Burton's 'cobweb' imagery of world societal relations. Transnational, interdependence and issue area arguments do seem to have a coherence lacking in peace research. They appeal to the many 'moderate' scholars in the US and Britain by supporting detente and accommodation of North-South issues. The resuscitation of this tradition of thought, so prominent a hundred years ago, has been strengthened by the rediscovery that international economics are extremely significant politically.

The most notable development of the last decade has been the institutionalization of a new field of International Relations called international political economy, which combines attention to economic matters, acknowledgement of non-state actors, interdependence and issue areas. It also involves the claim that a better version of realism is now possible—one that sees states like the

US using its great power in specific issue areas such as international finance through the emplacement of the Bretton Woods system to sustain its position; and sees that the shift in power, as a function of world capitalist developments, away from the US since, say, 1965 or 1970, has resulted in significant changes in the capacity of the American government to manage the international financial 'regime' (as evidenced by the abandonment of the gold standard in 1971). In the US Robert Keohane and Stephen Krasner are especially identified with this highly sophisticated neo-realism; in Britain Susan Strange is pre-eminent. Pulling in the other direction, away from any affiliation with realism, is the Marxist version of international political economy, from which liberal scholars increasingly draw their insights. Thus dependency theory, theories of imperialism and assessments of the crises and contradictions of late capitalism have intruded into the discourse defining international political economy as a field of International Relations.

If Anglo-American liberalism shows signs of merging with a revised realism, we must not conclude that this spells a new era of disciplinary consensus. On the contrary, the consolidation of this subject of international political economy as a coherent field parallels the redefinition of the old realism as national security studies. The nuclear peril, detente's deterioration, the conservative tide of opinion in the Anglo-American world resulting in the Reagan and Thatcher governments, the willingness of defence and intelligence agencies to contract out studies of national defence problems, the striking if perverse intellectual power of much strategic and deterrence thinking all contribute to realism recapturing its geopolitical origins in the Second World War and insure its relevance for those inclined towards a relatively conservative world view.

We are seeing perhaps the permanent bifurcation of International Relations into two sub-fields, reflecting the antinomy of the main intellectual traditions in the subject: Anglo-American liberalism, with its attachment to rationalism-instrumentalism and functionalism but without necessarily endowing these theories with ameliorative consequences; and Continental reason of state, reinforced by a sense of implacable conflict in a world ever more capable of inflicting harm. If the fifth phase was the erosion of the discipline's substantive and epistemological harmony between realism and science, then the next phase, perhaps already under way, will be the evolution of these two vital and growing fields—international political economy and national security studies—as disciplines in their own right, distinguished on substantive, ideological and (as they progress) procedural and institutional grounds.

Changing Elements

International Relations therefore can hardly be said to have developed by a series of logical steps, with each advance leading systematically to still greater discoveries and insights in orderly progression. Rather, it has been subject to fundamental re-examination as changes in world politics and trends in allied disciplines have invalidated approaches which has earlier seemed both useful and intellectually legitimate. Yet one can identify, in reviewing landmarks in the literature, a fairly high degree of consensus during the discipline's period of rapid growth concerning what the most respected scholars have set forth as the principal elements for study. So whereas 1919 marked a fumbling for ways of comprehending and controlling the relations of contending power centres, and 1969 the high point, the last fifteen years betray uncertainty and slippage, for good and sufficient reasons. Twenty years ago, F. H. Hinsley thought that the study of International Relations was 'still in the state in which biology was before Darwin.' Today, the vice-chancellor of Cambridge might say, 'before Linnaeus.'

Careful study of world politics certainly began before the end of the First World War, as Stephen H. Bailey pointed out in 1938 in his discussion on the origins of International Relations. But, though one could point to diplomatic history, or to international law, or even to the beginnings of political science, nothing which could be remotely described as a distinct subject in international relations existed. Perhaps we are not all historians because of the reluctance of diplomatic historians, like many other practitioners in that field, to deal with contemporary problems. The demands of the discipline of history in terms of evidence could simply not be met by those dealing with contemporary affairs who were unwilling to wait fifty years for archives to become available. In law, there were certain underlying assumptions which limited the application of legal methodology to the development of International Relations. Anglo-American international lawyers of that period tended to rely upon a case-study approach, and only some tentatively and reluctantly were prepared to move from precedent to prediction. Political science was at that time emerging as a discipline on the Western shores of the Atlantic, a process which to this day is incomplete in the United Kingdom and only recently undertaken on the continent. . . .

In terms of the new literature, strategic studies began to take the place of the study of international institutions, even before the outbreak of the war. Partly because of and partly as a corrective to Haushofer's work, geopolitics was the fad of the day. In the midst of the war, Harold and Margaret Sprout produced an important reappraisal entitled *Foundations of National Power* (1945), based on a syllabus utilized in the training of young naval officers. Before his untimely death, Nicholas Spykman won respect and esteem for geostrategic perspectives, developing one of the most effective team-research enterprises ever to appear, in the form of the Yale Institute of International Studies. Despite the fact that immediately after the defeat of the Axis Powers there was to be a renewal of the emphasis upon international peace and understanding, analysis of the make-up of na-

tional power had already become a central feature of International Relations.

It was as natural for a rebirth of idealist internationalism to occur at the end of the war as it had been for strategic and power analysis to flower during that war. But the period of enthusiasm for and almost exclusive concentration upon the United Nations and UNESCO's humanistic programme to treat conflict as a problem of misunderstanding or mental pathology was a very brief one. The disappearance of the improving thrust of the earlier post-war phase marked the fact that the world had fundamentally changed. Just as one must never forget the atmosphere of 1919 in understanding how and why the discipline started up in the way it did, so one must never lose sight of the fact that the tensions of the cold war prevented a lasting return to the optimism of the 1920s by practitioners and scholars alike. This cold war phase was influenced for a time by an ideologically laden geopolitics, which lingered on in the preoccupation with protracted conflict. More important was the shift by leading scholars away from broad analyses of the balance of power to a more restricted focus on national policies and decision-making. Frederick Sherwood Dunn and his co-workers at the Yale Institute of International Studies led the way, joined by such diverse institutions as Morgenthau's Center for the Study of American Foreign and Military Policy at Chicago, and a post-war Air Force offshoot, the Rand Corporation, on the west coast. Later, the (now International) Institute of Strategic Studies in London became one of the most prestigious manifestations of this approach.

The next stage of development reflects the generalizing aspirations of theory. Theoretical positions put forward so strikingly in what George Liska called 'the heroic decade' (1955–1965) now seem untenable and even pretentious as *theory*. Their lasting value has been in conceptual and taxonomic clarification: steps necessary to bring International Relations level with the study of biology as it stood between Linnaeus and

Darwin. The organic imagery of systems thinking makes the comparison with biology more apt than Morton A. Kaplan's grandiose claim that International Relations, after the pattern of positivist science, was awaiting its Galileo. Would-be Galileos, with significant support from the US government and the assistance of modern computing, began large research programmes involving the gathering and analysis of vast amounts of quantitative data. Science depends on reliable measurement; the science of International Relations would create its own measured reality. However such an ambition could not succeed to the extent needed to convince the sceptics, and those toiling to create the conditions of science became increasingly isolated from the rest of the International Relations community.

The largest research programmes (Charles McClelland's World Events Interactions Survey, at the University of Southern California, J. David Singer's Correlates of War Project, at the University of Michigan, and Rudolph Rummel's Dimensionality of Nations Project) employed a substantial number of graduate students as research assistants. The quantitative skills and commitment to International Relations as a science acquired by students working on all such programs had lasting effect. Many of these individuals now occupy faculty positions throughout America and, to lesser extent, Britain. They may be the greatest long-term legacy of the era of research programs, which came to an end with the playing out of the Vietnam war and government support for such research. A scientific orientation is now an institutionalized part of the discipline. In the US it is strongest in the public universities in the east. (Curiously, this pattern is to be found in the social sciences as a whole.) But the fact that professors in the old, influential private universities of the east are called on for policy advice in Washington aggravates this tendency. A similar phenomenon can be observed in Britain, where interest in International Relations as a science is stronger in the 'redbricks,' while Oxford and Cambridge cling to their traditional commitment to international history and international law.

The most recent phase represents a return by *some* academics to the universalist and normative preoccupations of the discipline's founders. The emergence in the last decade of peace and world order studies on a scale sufficient to warrant academic institutionalization—journals, degree courses and the rest—may well make these the proper successor to International Relations as a claimant-discipline, truer to International Relation's original aspirations and orientation than either of the barely coexisting and increasingly self-contained International Relations fields of international political economy and national security studies.

Diverging Ideals

Obviously, these overlapping phases of growth, stressing in turn history and law, institutions, strategy, national policy, conceptual development and science, and now renewed ideological considerations, acknowledgement of the subject-matter's complexity, and concomitant field differentiation within the discipline, are distinct neither in time nor in scope. None of them has fully disappeared (nor should have done), nor is any of them predominant. Each is simply suggested as one of the 'growing points' of the subject over a period of years since 1919.

To consider those decades in a different way, several ideals may be said to have motivated professional analysts in the discipline. They were neither necessarily consistent nor simultaneous in time with one another. The first of these was the ideal of purpose, which characterized the approach of many people on both sides of the Atlantic, an ideal of world statecraft which saw analysis as the servant of peace and international understanding. In some ways, the second ideal, the ideal of discipline, was contradictory to this, because it insisted on looking at the world as it was rather than as it should be. In a sense, this contradiction was divisive.

In another sense, however, the disciplined attitude helped to develop a consensus among scholars, at least during the subject's expansive period, concerning the character and scope of the subject-matter. Closely tied to this second ideal was a third, that of political realism, based on the insistence that the study of international relations involved the analysis of power and the national interest. Along with this, one sees the beginnings of the important new ideal of science, in the nineteenth-century sense of a systematic undertaking. This was quite different from, but led to, what was to emerge twenty years later in the methodologies of positivist science. These were to be adapted for an understanding of international relations not only from other social sciences, but from natural science as well. A fifth ideal (though some have regarded it as a curse) is that of eclecticism, the widespread willingness and even demand to utilize the wide range of the social sciences, the humanities, distinguished journalism, and even sophisticated novels) such as Harold Nicolson's *Public Faces* of 1933) in seeking an understanding of the forces at work in world politics.

Perhaps one reason for the delay in accepting International Relations as a discipline lies in what has been recognized from the beginning, that the subject impinges upon and draws from so many other subjects, each with its own disciplinary characteristics. We have always been experts in the art of borrowing, something which is both a strength and a weakness. In one of the earliest treatments, *An Introduction to the Study of International Relations* (1916), several British authors representing different disciplines— history, law, economics, and philosophy— endeavoured to apply their insights to the subject. Six years later Bryce observed that International Relations was a vast discipline covering every branch of the principal human sciences—ethics, economics, law and politics. Quincy Wright's survey in the *The Study of International Relations* (1955) counted more than a dozen contributing fields of practical and theoretical analysis. More re-

cently, other fields such as comparative politics and area studies, and public goods, social choice and game theory have entered the scene. The approaches and methods of the behaviorial sciences have been particularly influential in the analysis of the determinants and dynamics of state relations. Yet sociologists and psychologists themselves have only occasionally occupied a significant place in the study of International Relations.

This may not always be so, however. The extraordinary interest among younger, post-Vietnam students of International Relations in the sociologist Immanuel Wallerstein's 'world-systems' concept, which is greatly influenced by neo-Marxist studies of imperialism and dependency, poses the possibility of an institutionalized branch of sociology (sometimes called macrosociology) parallel to International Relations in political science. The central position of Marx in the development of sociology as a self-conscious discipline matches the place of Machiavelli in political science, and helps to explain the parallel evolution of radical and conservative International Relations traditions in sociology and political science respectively. Even with regard to power, a central concept in the study of International Relations by political scientists, sociologists have made frequent and significant contributions.

Ecology may be a different case. As early as the late 1960s scholars like Robert C. North drew attention to world problems that transcended national boundaries, such as the population explosion, environmental degradation and racism. Many of these concerns were crystallized in the popular as well as the academic consciousness by the publication of the Club of Rome's first report, *Limits to Growth* in 1972. The uncomfortable forecast of the collapse of civilization in the West within a matter of decades, if nothing were done to curb its exponential industrial growth, caused a sensation. Repudiation of the report by economists, who often hold a redemptive view of technological innovation, and scepticism by political scientists (including International Relations specialists), who felt the report was politically naive and who tend to be equilibrium-minded, like economists, in their conceptual concerns, has resulted in a focus of activity dominated by systems engineers and computer modellers called global modelling. Without purporting to replace International Relations, global modellers attempt to reconceptualize the planetary situation (as do sociologists) even more broadly than students of International Relations, by including all circuits of human activity and social arrangements of import to the dynamics of global capitalism.

Another field—national security studies—which has different (and mixed) disciplinary anchors and empirical referents, and yet is parallel to International Relations, thrives in the current climate of concern over nuclear weapons. Physicists, engineers, meteorologists, physicians and theologians are all lending their expertise in a virtual explosion of reports on the nuclear situation. The fusion of disciplinary perspectives in the heat of passionate concern tells us how quickly distinctive fields can emerge under propitious circumstances. The report of the Harvard Nuclear Study Group (1983) also suggests that academic respectability has already been conferred on these efforts and, inasmuch as two of the group's members are prominent International Relations specialists, that a *rapprochement* with International Relations is welcome.

A further point of high-level interdisciplinary attention has been the worsening material conditions for large populations in the non-industrial world, with the crisis in North-South relations both contributing to the precipitated by this situation. The role of economists in discussions about international development tends to overshadow that of International Relations specialists trained as political scientists. Nevertheless, the propensity for interdisciplinary teams of agronomists, hydrologists, demographers and so on to use highly visible political figures like Willy Brandt (the Brandt Commission) makes their work part of the International Relations tradition, by being interdisciplinary and

by locating themselves, however, imperfectly, in a tradition of public discourse which has always been a frame of reference of International Relations: consider the place of Thucydides and Machiavelli in our sense of what International Relations is about. It remains for International Relations professionals to 'recapture' in a disciplinary sense, subject-matter of such importance that it has 'escaped' into the realm of public debate where all people of professional standing, and high reputation, feel equally competent to engage. This is not to suggest that International Relations specialists should suppress such debate on the grounds of superior knowledge, but that they should guarantee its value to public policy by pointing out the limitations of arguments voiced from a professionally narrow or less well-informed perspective.

One may well conclude from these recent trends outside International Relations that professionals from other disciplines, by virtue of their sometimes innocent concerns, are demarcating the frontiers of the discipline for those of us within it. Our reception of these endeavours, wary or indifferent, contributes to problems of 'boundary maintenance,' to borrow a systems concept. Is International Relations narrowing as a result? A different interpretation is possible—one that admits to increasing disciplinary interdependence. Frontiers are no longer set by fiat. In Clifford Geertz's words, this is a time of 'blurred genres' in social thought. Supporting this view is the pattern of interdisciplinary interests now emerging among younger International Relations scholars like Richard K. Ashley, David Earle Bohn, Friedrich V. Kratochwil, John Ruggie and Roger D. Spegele. They are exploring interpretive sociology, hermeneutics, linguistic theory, literary criticism, the study of discursive practices, and aspects of modern philosophy. These tendencies are not easily discriminated, for they represent a wave of interest among social scientists in several disciplines in what is indeed an interdisciplinary movement in the humanities much influenced by

Continental thought. If, as it appears, our access to the humanities is no longer mediated by the discipline of history, then we are likely to be affected by modernist sensibilities in art and literature far more than in the past. Post-positivist inclinations will gain substance and support.

A sixth ideal is suggested by the new, interdisciplinary movement within post-positivism: the ideal of a cosmopolitan discipline in which adepts from many cultures enrich the discourse of International Relations with all the worlds' ways of seeing and knowing. This ideal is no doubt implicit in the global aspirations of the International Studies Association, but an international membership indicates the successful diffusion of the Anglo-American cognitive style and professional stance rather than the absorption of alien modes of thought. As teachers, we find many talented students with non-Western backgrounds deeply resentful of a discipline they see as smug and parochial in its attitudes to the world. If coherence within International Relations is finally a product of Anglo-American nurturing, disciplinary and cosmopolitan ideals may never be reconciled. . . .

---

48. Joining Theory and Reality

Michael Banks

A founding member of the Centre for the Analysis of Conflict (CAC), Michael Banks is a Lecturer in International Relations at the London School of Economics and Political Science.

Everyone who studies international relations (IR) must confront the problem of trying to understand the world society as a whole. To do this is to theorize. All discussion of world affairs rests upon assumptions about which things are the ones that really matter. This applies to everything in IR: from the causes of war to human rights; from Paraguayan foreign policy to nuclear weapon deployment in Europe; from economic sanctions to the reform of the UN. The importance of prior assumptions is self-evident if the topic itself is theoretical, like conflict resolution or decision-making. But it is not so obvious in the case of statements that seem at first to be explicitly factual, such as a reference to terrorism in Ireland or to the rise of a market economy in China. Upon reflection, it becomes clear that terrorism is extremely hard to define, and that a market economy depends on a whole series of conditions including mobility of labour, freedom of information, and entrepreneurial class and so on. Terrorism, therefore, can only be properly identified in the context of a theory of social stability and change; and a market economy only within a theory that deals with politics and culture, not just economics.

It follows that it is wrong to think of 'theory' as something that is opposed to

Excerpted from Margot Light and A. J. R. Groom, eds., "The Inter-Paradigm Debate," *International Relations: A Handbook of Current Theory*, (Boulder: Lynne Rienner Publishers, Inc., 1985), pp. 7–13. Copyright © 1985, Margot Light and A. J. R. Groom. Reprinted by permission.

'reality.' The two cannot be separated. Every statement that is intended to describe or explain anything that happens in the world society is a theoretical statement. It is naive and superficial to try to discuss IR solely on the basis of 'the facts.' This is because whatever facts are selected—any at all—are literally abstract. They are chosen from a much bigger menu of available facts, because they are important. The question is: why are they important? And the answer to that is: because they fit a concept, the concept fits a theory and the theory fits an underlying view of the world. In the same way, each 'island' of theory in the literature of IR (about deterrence, say, or political integration) is itself part of a more general mental map which shows how the world society is structured and which aspects of it are the most significant. This chapter is concerned with these general schemes of thought.

Of course, everyone who begins the study of IR is already equipped with an image of the world's geography, climate, politics, economy and culture. But this impression is rarely as coherent and rigorous as social science requires, which means that the serious student of IR needs to consider afresh the problem of how to picture world society as a whole. To do this is not easy. There are more than four billion people, living in more than 170 states, and spread across five continents. Fortunately for the IR theorist, modest generalization is immediately possible in that everyone shares a single ecosystem, has similar needs and hopes, and is subject to the interdependent effects of global industry and trade. But in other ways they are very different: in nationality, ethnicity, language, culture, social system, ideology, and especially levels of wealth and forms of political organization. Together, all these similarities and contrasts make for a highly complex world society. The problem for the theorist is to simplify the complexity without distorting it. That task, in turn, requires attention to the procedures of theory-building.

Theory-building

Theory consists of both analysis and synthesis. To analyse is to unravel, to separate the strands, or to take to pieces. To synthesize is to reassemble, to piece together the parts in such a way as to compose a whole that makes sense. General theory in IR, then, consists of dividing the human race into sections, noting the significant properties of each, examining the relationships between them, and describing the patterns formed by the relationships. Interesting problems arise at every stage. Some of these are methodological. How should we set about observing things, defining them, measuring them and comparing them? Others are theoretical, because theory consists of forming ideas or concepts to describe aspects of the world, classifying them, and considering the various ways in which they interact. How many sections of world society are there? How should they be subdivided? What properties of each section are we interested in? Which relationships matter, and for what purposes? In short what are the appropriate units of analysis, what are the significant links between them, and what are the right levels on which to conduct the analysis? And there are further theoretical questions even beyond these, because all theories of society are, at root, ideological. Theories simultaneously express the political values of the theorist, and also help to shape the world which is being analysed. Human beings, . . . need to be acutely critical of their own assumptions.

The State of the Discipline

None of these questions has ever had definite answers in the study of IR—and that is just as it should be. If any discipline is to remain alive and well, then its general theory must be constantly undergoing challenge and modification. This is because progress in knowledge consists of asking new questions, hopefully getting better answers, and checking the answers (again, a matter of method) for accuracy, simplicity, consistency and normative implications. The field cannot offer unquestioned 'truths' about the structure and processes of the world society. But it can offer a reasonably coherent general explanation, however tentative, which shows how the specific research areas (such as arms control or economic development) fit together into an overall scheme.

Today, the field contains not one but three such general explanations: realism, pluralism and structuralism. Strictly, they should be called 'paradigms,' but they are also more casually termed perspectives, approaches, world views, frameworks or general theories. The debate about their respective merits occupies centre stage in the discipline, although much of the literature about it tends to be very confused. There are two main reasons for the confusion. First, there are more analysts than synthesizers. Most scholars do not conduct research on general theory at all, but instead on smaller-scale problems which produce 'islands' of theory. . . . Second, old and new approaches are intermingled. The current literature has inevitably grown out of the past, and much of it either describes old debates or mixes contemporary issues with the earlier ones.

In historical terms, there are two main groups of writings about IR theory: works published before, and after, the First World War. The earlier group forms the classical heritage of IR. It contains studies of political theory, law, history and diplomacy produced over several centuries before the shock of the Great War created a professional discipline for the study of world politics. Much of this literature is of superb quality and continuing relevance. . . . It has also inspired a body of more recent scholarship which seeks to draw upon the classical insights. Valuable contributions include Wight on comparative state systems, Beitz on justice, Nardin on law, Donelan on reason of state, Walzer on the morality of war, and Mayall on international community.

The second historical category is that created by teaching and research as IR became established in universities after 1918. During its growth, first in the West and later worldwide, the academic discipline has developed through three stages. These are usually known as the traditional, behavioural and post-behavioural periods. . . .

Within each of the periods since 1918, there has been a 'great debate' about general theory, which means that the inter-paradigm debate of the 1980s is the third in the succession. Realism-idealism came first, running right through the traditional period from 1918 to 1950 and reaching an intellectual peak with Carr's masterly critique of idealism in 1939. Before Carr, idealist or liberal views dominated the field, fuelled by the horrors of the Great War. After Carr (and after appeasement had failed to prevent the Second World War), the realist school not only took charge but produced an all-pervasive general theory of power politics, elegantly censured by Hoffmann.

Then, in the 1950s, the first debate was pushed aside. Behaviouralism erupted, and its crusade for empiricism and scientific procedures provoked a confrontation with traditionalists which lasted through the 1960s. At its onset in 1955, the state of the discipline was majestically surveyed by Wright. The sharp exchanges, sometimes called 'revoluntionary,' were fully analysed in Knorr & Rosenau, and the eventual successes and failures were vividly narrated in the autobiographical essays commissioned by Rosenau. Like idealism before it, behaviouralism never challenged the underlying realist paradigm; it focussed on research methods, as idealism had focussed on values and policy prescriptions. Both left the crucial state-centric assumptions of realism in command.

From about 1970 onward, the post-behavioural phase developed into a triangular 'inter-paradigm' debate which did focus on the assumption of a state-centric world. By 1980 realism was pitted against structuralism and pluralism. Awareness of just how deep were the new divisions came hesitantly at first, beginning with discussion of the importance of Kuhn's 'paradigm' philosophy for the field, and then accelerating. The pattern is well recorded in a series of articles on 'how many paradigms are there?' A representative sample would begin with Phillips and Lijphart in 1974, and follow via Inkeles in 1975, Sullivan and Banks in 1978, Rosenau in 1979, and Pettman in 1981, to the most searching piece to date: Alker & Biersteker in 1984. Their survey analyses IR syllabuses in leading US universities, deplores the extreme parochialism thus revealed, and identifies a wider global discipline which is split between traditional-realist, liberal-behavioural and radical-dialectical approaches. . . .

---

49. The Responsibilities of Competence in the Global Village

J. David Singer

Professor of Political Science at the University of Michigan, J. David Singer served as President of the International Studies Association in 1985–86. The following is excerpted from his Presidential address on taking office in Washington, D.C. in March 1985.

Much is at stake, our talents are many, yet so little has been done. Worse yet, so little has been attempted. World affairs specialists in most countries lead a rather priviledged existence, largely insolated from danger, oppression, poverty and boredom. To be sure, most of us earn these privileges, working diligently and even creatively at our tasks as teachers, researchers, and writers, but perhaps we define these tasks too narrowly.

Many of us, too often, are fine organization men and women, but is our constituency that limited? Is our responsibility that circumscribed? At the risk of furthering my reputation as a modern Don Quixote, let me suggest that those are *not* windmills out there. They are, rather, towers of indifference, ignorance and incompetence, and if we have not helped to erect them, we have done much

too little to bring them down. Until we do, the global village remains in great jeopardy. Since most of us believe that our efforts—whether in the academic, governmental, journalistic or commerical vineyards—do and should have some impact on the human condition beyond our immediate circles, I address here the question of what these efforts might be. But it would be naive to assume that we also share identical priorities, loyalties and policy preferences; thus, in offering one man's reflections on our proper professional roles, a frank statement of his normative-theoretical point of departure is in order.

I begin with the premise that beyond our individual, professional and national self-interests we do need to give higher priority to the welfare of the entire human race, including those global citizens yet to be born. This requires that we demand higher standards of competence and compassion from our governments, parties and associations before lending our support. This also requires us to attend more carefully to the legitimate interests of other groupings, and perhaps most important, to recognize that 'the national interest' may often be contrary to the very real and human interests of those diverse groups that make up our own society. Another normative premise needs to be made clear: too many of us, eager to be of service to the state—especially service that is well rewarded—are willing to suppress our own professional judgments so as to avoid being denied that privilege. Sometimes, we even go so far as to acquiesce in the dubious proposition that our decisionmakers know more than we. *None* of us knows enough about the dynamics of world affairs, but surely those of use who devote our professional lives to the subject need not be too quick to defer to provincial political elites recently come to their nation's capital. Nor need we be unduly impressed with the functionary who assures us that if *we* had access to *his* top-secret information, we would readily endorse his views; those of us who have worked with classified information in most governments know that it rarely changes the overall picture and often serves purposes other than those that are claimed.

Before leaving this topic, a less conventional but equally important assumption needs to be articulated: many propositions about world affairs that we regard as purely normative—and thus beyond the reach of logic or evidence—can be translated to some extent into *empirical* propositions. For example, some of us may believe that it is immoral for a government to lie or mislead another in international negotiations, or to threaten force against their civilian population, while others would assert that the national interest represents a higher morality, demanding leaders who have the stomach to lie or murder. While I know of no systematic research on the empirical efficacy of dishonesty to date, one could imagine a study designed to put the proposition to the test. Similarly, the efficacy of the threat of force (without discriminating between civilian populations and

other targets) has already received some scholarly attention, and the research problem is far from insoluble, unless of course we accept the foolish fatalism of the post-behavioural syndrome which too often eschews systematic empirical research entirely.

The Priorities: Poverty and War

It is one thing to assert that knowledge can make a difference, and that our responsibilities extend beyond ourselves and our own nations, and quite another to identify those responsibilities and then go on to suggest some sort of priority among them. Let me attempt that, but in a very restricted fashion. As I see it, the human race has an extraordinary array of problems, some physical and some emotional, some more menacing than others, some closer in time, and many of them falling quite unequally upon different regions, races, genders, classes and political groupings. In the short run, two of these problems seem overwhelmingly critical, and though I focus on them here, this is not to suggest that all others are insignificant.

Simply put, these are the global security problem and the global development problem, and merely by so labelling them we emphasize their interdependence. We must put an end to war and we must put an end to poverty and starvation. Some of us believe that we cannot solve the development problem until we solve the security problem, and vice versa, and all too often one's view depends on which of them is most immediately threatening. Those who experience (or, more precisely, speak for those who experience) the tragedies of poverty, whether in the Third and Fourth Worlds or in the First and Second Worlds, tend to give highest priority to the development problem. And those for whom an adequately high material quality of life is no longer a concern tend to give higher priority to the security problem. As the immediate threat of death or disablement from grinding poverty begins to recede, one can begin to attend to the threat of death and disablement from war, civil or international.

But there may be more to the question than the immediate situation of the observer. Many analysts accept the proposition that poverty is major 'cause' of domestic and international conflict, much of which ultimately escalates to war. And while one can make a plausible argument as to why this *should* be so, the empirical evidence reveals a *negative* correlation between the poverty levels of nations (aggregated as well as per capita) and their war-proneness. Even if we look at civil war, there tends to be a curvilinear relationship, with very few cases occurring in the extremely poor or extremely rich societies; the very poor are too weak, physically as well as politically, nor do they have the incentive for violent change that typically requires both the hope based upon a small taste of economic progress and the aggressiveness based on a frustration of that hope. The rich, of course, have even fewer incentives.

If poverty seldom leads to war, it follows that its elimination or amelioration will have little effect on the incidence of war: we may want to give development the highest priority for normative or ideological reasons, but not because we expect it to reduce the incidence of international war.

Recognizing the possibility that, as a white male, middle class and middle aged, well-fed and healthy, in a relatively prosperous society, my concern for the poor and starving might not be as strong as it should be, let me nevertheless summarize the counter-arguments. A useful point of departure is an itemization of the ways in which the search for security among the industrial powers inhibits and corrupts the search for development among the pre-industrial societies. The most obvious, of course, is the deflection into military preparedness of funds that might have gone into development assistance programs. While there is no assurance that the annual world military spending (nearly 600 billion dollars in the 1980s) that could meet the essential food and health needs of the

developing countries for two decades would indeed go to that purpose, it is clear that the funds that do go to the military cannot go to development.

But military preparedness programs mobilize more than money; they mobilize the minds of their citizens in a way that is destructive both at home and abroad. As the financial resources of a major power go to the military sector over a long period of time, two important consequences develop. One is the incremental shift in political power away from those who might be fairly cosmopolitan, farsighted and humane, and toward those who seldom give high priority to such considerations. The policies of the nation become increasingly militarized, and with that shift, the resources that *could* have gone to economic development assistance go instead to military buildups, arms transfers and other military assistance programs.

The second consequence of this mobilization is an ethical and emotional one. Governments, however centralized, cannot milk the public economically, intrude into their political freedom, conscript their sons, and poison their environment with weapons tests, unless there is a sufficiently widespread and strong belief among mass publics and elites in the legitimacy of these depradations. That requires a propaganda and socialization program of some magnitude and duration, and the more successful that program, the more xenophobic the public and the opinionmakers will become; with these cognitive and affective trends, we should not be surprised to find two attendant shifts. One is the obvious shift toward greater belief in the importance of military force as an instrument of national security; for even in the most autocratic of societies, cognitive dissonance is uncommon. The other is an increasing indifference to those whom Franz Fanon called 'the wretched of the earth.' Persuaded of the threat to the nation from enemies at home and abroad, and acquiescing in the threat or use of mass murder as a legitimate instrument of national survival, there is little room for concern, altruism or generosity, not to mention far-sighted self-interest. (For the present, I am ignoring the effects of military preparedness programs on the domestic scene and on the moral integration of the citizens and their society.)

Another dysfunctional linkage between the major power rivalry and economic development is found in their struggle for influence in the underdeveloped regions, and while less obvious, the effects of these rivalries may be equally pernicious. First, there is the eagerness to put and to keep friendly regimes in power, and it seems that—along with economic and military aid—no ploy is beneath these powers: from bribery and subversion to assassination and insurgency, all are used by the leaders of the 'free world' and the 'socialist camp' to depose less-than-friendly regimes. And to maintain these staunch supporters of democracy and/or socialism, no amount of terrorism, torture, repression and intimidation seems excessive. Without suggesting that these instruments of political influence are entirely the creation of Washington and Moscow, Paris and Prague, the initiative, the training and the resources typically originate north of the equater. That it is easy to find indigenous elites and counter-elites to carry out these unsavory deeds should come as no surprise. How many political leaders and their opponents in the Third World have come to power or to opposition without outside support? And even when the struggle for power in the developing countries is not violent, brutal and evil, it is heavily burdened by East-West rivalry. This is not to say that essentially domestic issues are of no consequence in Third World local politics, but that the superpower rivalry is so pervasive that the money, the men and the methods can usually be traced back to the Soviets, the Americans or their allies.

This corruption of the political process in the southern hemisphere's under-developed nations has, in turn, a disquieting effect on their economies and their foreign policies. Given the ubiquitousness of the fluctuating standoff between East-leaning and West-leaning regimes in most regions, the high incidence of rivalry, conflict and war in these areas is virtually foreordained; all too often, these are proxy wars between regimes and armies that are financed, trained, equipped and sometimes even led by the superpower rivals. Such externally stimulated conflict not only leads to death, devastation, brutality, flight and famine, and to a steady drain on the financial resources of the regional economies, but to the incurring of high opportunity costs as well. External funds that might have gone to development go to the military. Occasional surpluses in the balance of payments that might have gone to investment in agricultural infrastructure often go to pay for training military personnel in overseas war colleges and military academies. In addition, military expenditures typically (not always) inhibit economic growth, generate inflationary pressures, enhance the rate of debt accumulation, exercise an upward push on interest rates, mortgage the nation's economic future, and encourage more attention to short-run considerations.

Then there is the competition for human resources; Third World economies need a fairly larger cadre of trained public administrators, foreign ministry personnel, commercial managers, industrial technicians, mining engineers, harbor pilots, agricultural specialists and health-care professionals, to name but a few. But if the educational facilities are limited, offshore training expensive, and armed forces' salaries (not to mention related personal and political perquisites) high, it should come as no surprise that there will be insufficient talent for development purposes. Further, because the resources are greater, the recruiting incentives less idealistic, and the role of the military often more of a domestic constabulary than a national defense force, one typically finds rather higher levels of corruption in the military than in other sectors of developing societies, and the larger the military the more pervasive its corrupting influence.

Closely related is the problem of negotiating equitable terms of trade or reasonable roles for their nationals in the multinational corporations resident in their countries. Addiction to military 'preparedness' and dependence on the supplier are hardly conducive to a strong bargaining stance.

There are other ways, more political, in which the militarization of these nations, through cold-war incentives and blandishments, turns out to hamper development. One is the increasing boldness of major power interference in the domestic political process: those who pay the piper *expect* to call the tune, and in order to ingratiate themselves with donor nations, local parties and factions are inclined to put domestic issues into the terms of their patrons to the north, often distorting and submerging bona fide issues in a sea of ideological rhetoric. One extension of this pressure, of course, is in the foreign policy realm. Rather than address the very real security and economic interests of their nations vis-à-vis regional neighbors, eagerness for funds and equipment along with dependence on the donors for spare parts and technical support, all too frequently makes these regimes inclined to do their master's bidding.

This arraignment should suffice. As long as the East-West rivalry continues, the possibilities for highly symbiotic relations between local elites and one or another of the major powers are extraordinary. And to the extent that these possibilities are exploited, misallocation of material, demographic and psychic resources will be endemic, and the processes of economic, social and political development will be stultified. Short-run considerations will overwhelm those of long-run health and welfare. . . .

What We Think We Know and Need to Know

. . . While we have a moderately solid basis for doubting the efficacy of sustained military buildup as an instrument of national security, we have considerably less evidence on the relative efficacy of *alternative* instruments or substitute strategies. This is not merely a scholarly misfortune, nor can we write it off as the inevitable by-product of a relatively new discipline. It is a bona fide failure—one among many—of our profession, with ominous human consequences. This is not to say that systematic historical and empirical research could readily show us the most adaptive paths to national security, or that governments will jump eagerly to put into practice the results of high-quality research. The path from knowledge to practice is a long one, strewn with many obstacles, cognitive, emotional, ethical, epistemological and tactical; but *without* relevant knowledge, the likelihood of adaptive national security policies in the nations of the world is menacingly close to zero.

Why should this be so? I begin with the premise that all political decisionmaking is a form of collective and incremental behavior. It involves individuals who, despite a sharing of some basic ideological tendencies and perhaps even some relatively similar experiences and social origins, nevertheless have diverse interests and often incompatible priorities. The participants, while ostensibly employed to identify, choose and carry out policies that are supposed to enhance the security of the nation and maximize the interests of the society as a whole, tend to be equally if not more concerned with the maximization of their factional, bureaucratic and individual interests.

Then there is the above-noted inadequacy in our knowledge base; the amount, quality, and relevance of our research to date is far from adequate. And even if this were not the sad case, would that knowledge be adequately understood and applied? Not if our foreign policy elites are recruited from among those who are pre-scientific or, worse yet, anti-scientific in their outlook, incapable of evaluating conflicting evidence and comparing incompatible analyses. While we would hardly seek finance ministry officials from the ranks of shopkeepers or health ministry staff from among those who write advertising copy for patent medicines, we do almost as poorly when we recruit for ministries of defense and foreign affairs. If we have yet to provide for the training of enough scientifically oriented practitioners, it should not surprise us to find so few in positions of policy influence. But that merely pushes the problem back one step; we have so few fully prepared decisionmakers because we have too few universities that provide a sufficiently rigorous education, and too few professors sufficiently prepared to properly staff our universities.

How do we break out of this vicious circle? There are several ways of going about this, but let me emphasize that neither the problem nor its possible solutions have gone unnoticed in the past—merely list some recommendations made to the US National Academy of Sciences panel on the state of the social sciences in 1967. We might provide for: (a) traditionally trained scholars to 'tool up' on their own through postdoctoral or retaining grants; (b) undergraduate and graduate students to train at those institutes and universities around the world at which the more systematic and rigorous preparation is offered; and (c) expansion of the curriculum at the more traditional schools to include more teaching in the social science mode. There are, of course, other possibilities by which to increase the competence of the teachers, researchers and practitioners (as well as journalists) in the world affairs field. When, and if, such a program were instituted—perhaps via a UN diplomatic academy—we could expect a gradual improvement in teaching and research, followed in due course by improvement in the formulation and execution of policy. With such a development, the case for going with the extra-rational considerations of self and faction—because there is no way to tell which policies would produce the best outcome for the nation as a whole—would be seriously weakened. The practitioners, their critics, and the journalists will not only have more solid knowledge available, but will also be more able to evaluate and apply that knowledge.

In principle, this may sound interesting,

but precisely what do we think we already know, what do we not yet know, and what is it that we need to know? First, let us distinguish between knowledge and belief, noting that we often confuse the two; many of us *believe* certain generalizations to be empirically true, but since these beliefs vary widely from nation to nation, class to class, faction to faction, time to time, and even from page to page in the writings of the same analyst, beliefs would be better treated as hunches or hypotheses, to be examined against the relevant evidence. Second, let us recognize that even systematically generated knowledge is often tentative and far from final. In all scientific disciplines, there may be a strong consensus that a certain proposition or theoretical model is indeed correct and yet have it overturned by subsequent research. This is less true of empirical generalizations than of explanations and theories, but it does happen, and we need therefore to be somewhat tentative in accepting research findings—and, more specifically, explanatory inferences from them—as if they were eternal verities.

Third, we might want to distinguish among existential, correlational and explanatory knowledge. Students of historical cases often absorb large bodies of existential knowledge, but seldom do so in a self-aware and comparative fashion such that a set of *data* might emerge. Rather, they tend to focus on one or a few cases in a non-operational manner, generating bits of existential knowledge, rather than a coherent set of data, not to mention correlational or explanatory knowledge. Existential knowledge of a scientifically useful sort is, then, a series or string of observations produced by the same classificatory criteria, and correlational knowledge is a succinct, precise and operational statement of the extent to which two or more bodies of existential knowledge go together across some population of cases. Whereas the existence of existential and correlational knowledge is relatively objective and unambiguous, explanatory knowledge tends to be more subjective or, in the philosophy of science vernacular, intersubjective. That is, any one of us might look at a theoretical model and at the correlational knowledge and deductive reasoning that allegedly support the model, and then conclude that the goodness-of-fit between the model and the evidence is sufficiently compelling. But unless a reasonable fraction of the specialists concur, it is difficult to say that explanatory knowledge has been provided. . . .

While some of us have labored in that theoretical vineyard, in the empirical one, or in both, we seem to have a long way to go to bring evidence and our models into powerful juxtaposition. In several of my own papers one finds the crude outlines of such a model built around the cybernetic concepts of self-correcting and self-amplifying feedback while attending to the intimate links among the individual, subnational, and extra-national actors in world politics, but its convergence with the historical evidence remains all too fragile. Having said this, however, let me underline the implications of the phrase above: models that are so vague, ahistorical and preoperational as to defy empirical disconfirmation just will not suffice. We can no longer afford the luxury of that unproductive division of labor in which too many of us sit in our armchairs and conjure up elegant but irrelevant 'theories,' and others laboriously generate correlational knowledge that recognizes no theoretical parent.

An Excess of Tolerance

There should be little ambiguity about the line of reasoning followed here. The human condition is, on balance, morally unacceptable. Too many of our fellows continue to die prematurely from war, terrorism, assassination, poverty, starvation, disease, and even more of them suffer untold misery, pain and degradation en route to the grave. Nor is this unsavory state of affairs restricted to the people of the Third and Fourth Worlds. In the First and Second Worlds, we not only have intolerable levels of violence and mis-

ery, but, equally sad, a degree of incompetence, corruption and indifference that no civilized society need accept, and whose continuation is an affront to any self-respecting human group. Moreover, we in the North have brought the entire family of man all too close to the brink of extermination by our acquiescence, if not active participation, in this costly, immoral and destructive struggle to the death between the military leviathans and their supine allies.

Despite the lateness of the hour and the monumental grief that has already been inflicted, there may still be time. But the little time that remains will not be used effectively if we continue business as usual. We have in this Association, and in the ranks of other professions, the talent, the numbers and, yes, the potential clout to turn the world around. We represent, if I may use the cliché, humanity's last, best hope: political elites, counter-elites, researchers, teachers and publicists—a good fraction of the taste-makers and opinionmakers—and a small but critical fraction of the decisionmakers as well. Yet we remain impotent while the wheel of destiny moves us ever closer the brink of unmitigated disaster.

Despite the good fortune of our intellect, education, institutional support, relative autonomy and vista of opportunity, we seem to be caught up in a social trap of ominous proportions. As scholars, too many of us have overinterpreted the doctrine of tolerance. In our reluctance to impose our own standards (a commendable characteristic if not carried to excess) we accept research that is conceptually imprecise, methods far inferior to those available, empirical premises (implicit as well as explicit) that fly in the face of existing evidence, and ideological predispositions so shortsighted and self-centered as to discredit all but the most parochial. As teachers, we again are much too tolerant: rather than encourage and reinforce those students who are most concerned, motivated, autonomous and gifted, we often enfeeble them in our tolerance of intellectual sloth and ethical indifference. And in the name of objectivity and our repugnance for indoctrination, we typically help to legitimize the assertions of our tribal shamans and the policies of those who have climbed to power over the bodies of their less ruthless countrymen.

As journalists, we are again guilty of inordinate tolerance: we accept and repeat, as objective news, statements that all too often fail even the mildest standards of accuracy and logic, honesty and even-handedness. For reasons outlined below, we eschew the role of a countervailing force, enter into immoderately symbiotic relations with our sponsors and our sources, and often convert what could be an honourable profession into another arm of the entertainment industry or a transmission belt of the ruling elites. In the West, this tendency has gone so far that we now refer to the exception as 'investigative journalism!'

One might well point out that what passes for tolerance in intellectual circles is really little more than a fig leaf behind which we conceal acquiescence in the dominant views of our particular time, place and social niche, and *in*tolerance of alternative views. Too many of us seem bent on authenticating Karl Mannheim's dictum that an objective and rigorous social science is impossible because none of us can rise above and detach ourselves from the blinders of class, culture and nationality.

Let me conclude, then, by urging a reconsideration and a redefinition of the various roles taken on by international studies specialists. Much needs to be done if our research, teaching and practice is to be turned to the benefit of the global village. Our responsibilities in scientific, pedagogical, journalistic and policy analysis terms are great, and the need is apparent. But there are obligations of competence in *ethical* terms as well, and these may be even more difficult to meet. Leaving aside the inadequate knowledge base and the ambiguity of the evidence as to which policies are most likely to produce which consequences, we must recognize that the problems of human survival are not purely scientific. They are to

an appreciable extent ethical as well. In the face of limited, contradictory and inconclusive evidence, we cannot afford to remain immobile and acquiescent; an integrated human being acts, and must act, day by day, on the basis of inadequate evidence; political passivity while waiting for all the evidence is hardly the mark of a mature scholar-citizen.

Worse yet, these empirical and theoretical inadequacies often serve as camouflage for less savory explanations. To put it indelicately, too many of us find all too many temptations to 'go with the flow' in our nation's policies. For the *academic*, East or West, North or South, challenging the conventional wisdom can be costly. At the least, we can suffer loss of credibility in the eyes of the establishment, exclusion from professional groups, conferences, committees, and diminished financial support for our research, our travel, and our students' stipends. At the most, we pay an even higher price for dissidence: underemployment, unemployment, expulsion and even incarceration. When we conform, we and our professional allies, however mediocre, tend to be recognized, rewarded, reinforced and lionized. Even greater rewards typically go to those with that supreme skill of deviating just enough from the party line to appear innovative and original, but not far enough to appear subversive or naive.

For the *journalist* in many societies, the incentives and constraints can be equally awesome. The reporter and columnist 'who goes along, gets along.'. . . The reporter with too many assignments who finds it easier to write up his or her story on the basis of a governmental press release will receive a friendly welcome at that agency, and those whose columns rest on interviews with key officials but not with readily located critics often find themselves invited to voyages on aircraft carriers or luncheon at the Foreign Office. Conversely, how often are the national security 'naysayers' in the media invited to select briefings and not-for-attribution 'backgrounders?'

Moving from academic and media circles

to those directly involved in the *policy* process, the incentives and constraints are even more formidable and the temptations more excruciating. Whether serving full-time in a governmental agency or as a temporary or part-time consultant, we have little difficulty discovering the main configurations of the establishment line, but the decision to deviate in other than a minor and tactical fashion is particularly painful. To do so is to court professional disaster; and if one is not actually dismissed, the same treatment is always meted out in the universities, research institutes, and the media: isolation, ridicule, suspicion, and all the instruments of coercive conformity. Nor is it only the incentive of advancement and survival in one's career. There is also the more noble motivation of serving one's nation and perhaps of acquiring sufficient seniority and credibility to help deflect the regime away from a course that seems pregnant with disaster and into more adaptive channels. As a consultant, I have been often astonished to hear a colleague agree with an official position that he or she has previously questioned or rejected. On discussing the matter in private, the explanation has all too often been the familiar strain of credibility-enhancement: 'If I go against the consensus now, who will listen to me later?'

While admitting the strength of that temptation, we ought not to overlook the counter-arguments. First, such calculated acquiescence strengthens the clout and legitimacy of the dominant line. Second, it helps to delegitimize and reduce the credibility of the colleague who *does* take an honest stand, whether sound or not in terms of the policy problem. Third, such going along could make the difference between choosing a more adaptive policy or getting one's nation into serious trouble, and given the frequency with which the conventional view—reinforced by the vagaries of domestic politics, group dynamics and bureaucratic gamesmanship—turns out to be ill-founded, it is dangerously wrong.

In sum, there are many reasons, some of them all too persuasive, why international studies specialists fail in their responsibilities. Nevertheless, we have as a profession done so much damage, brought humanity so much grief, and helped us drift so much closer to the abyss of World War III that it is now time to take a fresh look at our past performances and our current responsibilities. We have it in our power to go along with the post-1945 polices and thus accelerate the momentum toward disaster, or to step back, pull up our socks, shoulder our intellectual and ethical obligations, and perhaps slow down and reverse these ominous trends.